Newman and his Age

Newman and his Age

SHERIDAN GILLEY

Christian Classics
Westminster, Maryland

First published in 1990 by
Darton, Longman and Todd Ltd
89 Lillie Road, London SW6 1UD

First American edition published in 1991 by
Christian Classics, Inc., 77 West Main St., P.O. Box 30,
Westminster, Maryland 21158

Library of Congress Catalog Card Number: 91–73301

ISBN 0–87061–186–0

Phototypeset by Input Typesetting Ltd, London
Printed and bound in Great Britain by
Courier International Ltd, East Kilbride, Scotland

MATRI MEAE
ET
CARLO BORROMEO
GRATIAS

Contents

Contents

Preface

Newman was once distressed by a lady who called him a saint. 'Saints are not literary men', he wrote in rebuke, 'they do not love the classics, they do not write Tales.' Nor do they write biographies, which take their toll of those who must live with the enthusiasms and obsessions of the biographer. In the many ups and downs which composing a work like this entails, I owe a debt to the students who have helped me to sustain my fascination with Newman by studying his life and works with me at Durham. More especially I must thank Robert Forsythe, Nicholas Humphries and Fr Carl Turner, who first urged me to teach a course on Newman, and two of my research students, the brilliant Stephen Thomas and my saintly Elizabeth Varley, whose monographs about the rhetorical basis of Newman's heresiology and about William Van Mildert, the last Prince-Bishop of Durham, are to be published by Cambridge University Press. I have also to thank Dr Eamon Duffy and Dr Peter Toon for their comments on parts of the text, the staff of Darton, Longman and Todd for their expert assistance in producing it and, for much patient typing of inky manuscripts, Andrea Marshall, Stephen Holland and my dear wife Meg. Life with Newman is the nearest she will come to living with a saint – even one who only wished 'to black the saints' shoes – if St Philip uses blacking in heaven'.[1]

'An Autobiography in Miniature'

John Newman wrote this just before he was going up to Greek on Tuesday, June 10th, 1812, when it only wanted 3 days to his going home, thinking of the time (at home) when looking at this he shall recollect when he did it.

At school now back again.

And now at Alton where he never expected to be, being lately come for the Vacation from Oxford where he dared not hope to be – how quick time passes and how ignorant are we of futurity. April 8th 1819 Thursday.

And now at Oxford but with far different feelings – let the date speak – Friday February 16th 1821 –

And now in my rooms at Oriel College, a Tutor, a Parish Priest and Fellow, having suffered much, slowly advancing to what is good and holy, and led on by God's hand blindly, not knowing whither He is taking me. Even so, O Lord. September 7, 1829. Monday morning. ¼ past 10.

And now a Catholic at Maryvale and expecting soon to set out for Rome. May 29, 1846.

And now a Priest and Father of the Oratory, having just received the degree of Doctor from the Holy Father. September 23, 1850.

And now a Cardinal. March 2, 1884.[1]

Introduction

This is the biography of a man and the history of a mind. It is a romance of the intellect and the story of a growth in faith, with a priest and prophet as its hero. Other men have pondered the meaning of their lives, and the significance for the soul of its journey through the world. But few have had Newman's power to describe this theme in words, while insisting that it fell short of words in mystery. Newman's biography is also, therefore, a book about his religion, which with its double dimension of meaning and mystery holds the key, he believed, to the mystery of life itself.

No one was more conscious than Newman that religious truth is a matter of intellectual meaning, of binding dogmas stated by reason at its most refined in the clear light of day. Yet no one was more conscious than Newman that the very words in which dogmas are defined, though hymned by the noblest of composers and even given by God, only show us through a glass darkly the mystery which they profess to reveal. For God himself is a mystery, and the mystery of God is only more opaque than the mystery of human personality, that infinite depth within the soul which lies open to the mystery of God. Thus in Newman's counter-revolution against the rationalist theory of knowledge, religious truth is discovered and transmitted, not merely in reason, but in ways of which mankind is sometimes hardly conscious, in custom, conscience, authority and tradition, and through the heart, the affections and the will, and by the power of love from heart to heart. And so an understanding or incomprehension of dogma and a willingness to receive or reject it occur at a profounder level of personality than reason, in the encounter with the God in others and within the soul.

A life modelled on such beliefs might sound like a windy sermon, with nothing to say to our frail humanity, or like a dance of Platonic categories beyond the limitations of this fallen world. But as Newman's convictions were strained through the oddities and accidents of his personality, through the intensity of his loves and hates, so they cease to echo like a lifeless hagiography and become human. The danger of hagiography, however, is especially clear with Newman, because no one else has ever quite so wonderfully dramatized his own inner and outer lives – as the sensitive spirit and imperial intellect of an imperial nation and university and Church. Again and again, the biographer becomes, despite his own critical unease, a

1

humble scribe, quoting Newman's words to describe his deepest thoughts and feelings: not for nothing was his best known work called an *Apologia pro Vita Sua*, one of the most moving autobiographies in the language.

There can be few individuals who have left the biographer such vast materials to tell one man's story. Both as a Georgian and as a Victorian, Newman had 'an innate passion for hoarding' and, with his relatives, 'kept masses of manuscript debris that most people would have destroyed'.[1] But he also sifted and destroyed much that he considered valueless – in 1874, he burnt the original of the early journals which he had selectively transcribed in 1872–3, so acting as a sort of self-censor. Thus he continually returned to re-edit his past, just as he rewrote his published works, as if to make sure that any biographical monument was in greater part of his own fashioning.

'One never can know what may happen after one's death', he wrote. 'Fidgetty, prying, illnatured persons keep memoranda, which sooner or later see the light.'[2] No one, however, so assiduously wrote such memoranda as Newman. He was, as the great French scholar Henri Bremond, an expert taster of spiritual essences, described him, '*le plus autobiographique des hommes*'.[3] Thus Newman's own preference was for lives which like Arthur Stanley's *Arnold* were primarily composed of letters by and to their subject; 'a man's life lies in his letters', he wrote to his sister Jemima.[4] 'My own notion of writing a life is the notion of Hurrell Froude's', he told Fr Henry Coleridge, 'viz. *to do it by letters* and to bring in as little letterpress of one's own as possible.'[5] He himself generally hated biographers. Yet there was an artlessness about his habits of accumulation and destruction, of conservation and self-correction, which tells more about him than he knew. Bremond calls one of his principal qualities '*autocentrisme*', a sort of reference of all things to the self, which religion could transmute but not destroy. If Newman was a saint, it can only be because he showed his flaws with an unselfconsciousness which was part both of his fidelity to truth and of his ruthlessness with others and himself. It is true to him to quote his own words, sometimes against himself, and to show how his principles and prejudices acquired a complexity and character which belong to him and him alone.

Such an enquiry must, however, range more widely, beyond Newman himself, to describe the passions of the last days of unreformed Oxford and of the death-throes of the European confessional State, and the triumphs and trials of the Catholic Revival, Anglican and Roman. As a theologian and a believer, Newman was at different times the exponent of the two most widely diffused forms of Christianity, Evangelical Protestantism and Roman Catholicism. He was the lifelong enemy of the liberalism now ascendant in Western Europe and North America; and he tried to redefine the faith of the Church of England. These themes require an understanding of the strengths and weaknesses of the English and Oxonian and Christian traditions, and an engagement with the English and European conservative traditions, especially as the latter is embodied in Roman Catholicism. This is, therefore, a critical study which seeks to place Newman's intellectual and spiritual development in its historical setting.[6] It is about Newman, but it is also about his age.

No one in such matters can escape his own convictions, and every biographer of Newman has seen in Newman a mirror of himself. Wilfrid Ward depicted an over-sensitive intellect caught between neo-Ultramontanes and liberal Catholics, as Ward was caught in his own generation between integralists and modernists. Meriol Trevor was more concerned with his humanity than his thought, Ian Ker with his thought than his humanity. Newman himself believed in the interaction of the two. This volume tries to put flesh on Newman's ideas, showing the relation of spirit to intellect, love to reason, mind to heart. But there can never be a definitive biography of Newman, only new Newman biographers. Newman himself is the prince of English autobiographers, and one of the greatest letter writers in the English language, as well as the greatest of English theologians. He is, after Bunyan, at once the most profound and passionate of our religious pilgrims; and that must be the best excuse for retelling his story.

Part One

The Preparation

1

Beginnings

Great men often come in dynasties, but there is little hint of intellectual or spiritual eminence in John Henry Newman's commercial origins. His father's family was of East Anglian peasant ancestry, descended from a poor tailor, William Newman, who had acquired a few acres of land in his village of Swaffham Bulbeck in Cambridgeshire. His son was another William, whose legacy to his grandson John, born in 1734, was solidly practical, a big curtained tester-bed; and it was John who left the village – perhaps taking the bed with him – to seek his fortune in London as a grocer or 'coffee-man' in Leadenhall Street and, through the Worshipful Company of Musicians, to become in 1764 a Freeman of the City of London.[1] The grocer's son, another John, became a clerk and then partner in the private banking house of Harrison, Prickett and Newman that flourished through the years of prosperity of the French wars, and married at Lambeth Parish Church in 1799 Jemima Foudrinier, the daughter of a wealthy London paper manufacturer descended from French Protestant Huguenot refugees from Roman Catholic persecution. Mrs Newman brought her husband business connections as well as a £5000 dowry. By 1812, John Newman was a partner in the bank of Ramsbottom, Newman and Ramsbottom at 72 Lombard St, the other partners being Richard Ramsbottom, a brewer and distiller, MP for Windsor in 1807, and his nephew and more active partner John, MP for the same seat in 1810. John Newman rose fast in a fast expanding world.

John and Jemima were living at 80 Old Broad Street near his bank, around the corner from 'the sign of the Globe',[2] when their eldest son John Henry was born, by the classic definition a true Cockney, on 21 February 1801; and Richard Ramsbottom and an uncle were the child's godfathers when he was baptized on 9 April 1801 at the now vanished ten-sided Wren church of St Benet Fink, which was squashed into an awkward site in the heart of the City of London.

In the following year, the family marked its prosperity by moving to the more salubrious and spacious five-story Bloomsbury address of 17 Southampton Street, now Southampton Place, whose handsome grey brick Georgian facade survives. Light still floods through its great square-paned windows, but of the internal decoration, which included the wallpapers that

7

were among Newman's earliest memories, all that remains from his time are a few cornices and two dainty marble fireplaces, one with fluting and exquisite oval insets carved with grapes and vine leaves, to show the beauty which surrounded him in childhood. Jemima also took the baby to her mother in-law's house in Fulham which boasted a garden breakfast-room with 'two cardracks with a lion on them, and pictures of the prodigal Son, and of somebody giving alms to the poor, and of the Unjust Steward',[3] and with its breakfast things gleaming in the sun, as the little boy saw them on coming down early one morning. John Henry also remembered the loft with apples on the floor and a mangle.[4] His first brother, Charles Robert, destined to be the black sheep of the family, was born in 1802; the eldest sister, Harriett, in 1803; and another brother, Francis William, in 1805.

In 1804, the growing family acquired a country home as well, the already mellowed brick Georgian Grey Court House at Ham beyond Richmond, where Newman recalled a 'large plane, a dozen of *tree*-acacias, with rough barks, as high as the plane – a Spanish ches[t]nut, a larch. A large magnolia, flowering (in June 1 think) went up the House, and the mower's scythe, cutting the lawn, used to sound so sweetly as I lay in a crib, in a front room at top'. The garden ran down to 'the long Ham walk of double elms', and the house faced a road that led down to the river. Along the river road lived the neighbours, the venerable hairy-faced JP Mr Bradley whom Mr Newman called 'the old lion', and Lady Parker with her macaw.[5] In 1805, the young John Henry lay in bed at Ham watching the candles at the windows burn in honour of the victory at Trafalgar. 'I know more about it', he wrote afterwards of Grey Court, 'than any house I have been in since, and could pass an examination in it. It has ever been in my dreams.'[6] Here also he learned to play billiards, a game he never played in later life. The idyll was brief – the family gave the house up in 1807 – but even when still a schoolboy, Newman dreamed about it 'as if it was Paradise'.[7] Newman belonged to the world which discovered the autobiographical vividness of early childhood. It was on his journey to the Peloponnese off Ulysses' Ithaca that he 'thought of Ham and of all the various glimpses, which memory barely retains and which fly from me when I pursue them, of that earliest time of life when one seems almost to realize the remnant of a pre-existent state';[8] as if, following the teaching of Plato and Newman's great contemporary Wordsworth, it is in such childhood visions of heaven that we catch a distant glimmer of our own eternal home.

These intimations of immortality assumed strange forms. 'I used to wish', Newman recalled, 'the Arabian Tales were true: my imagination ran on unknown influences, on magical powers, and talismans . . . I thought life might be a dream, or I an Angel, and all this world a deception, my fellow-angels by a playful device concealing themselves from me, and deceiving me with the semblance of a material world.'[9] The modern sensibility mocks such notions, one wit declaring that Newman's idea that he was an angel 'remains an interesting hypothesis'.[10] It would be truer to say that 'the only mystery about Newman was that he did not give a damn for this world',[11] either for its this-worldly prosperity or its this-worldly happiness. This other-worldly vision was rooted in his own childhood religious experience which gave him the Platonic sense of another world more real than this one. The rumour of his deceiving fellow angels recurs in one of his most widely sung hymns:

> And with the morn those angel faces smile
> Which I have loved long since, and lost awhile.[12]

The angel faces later lost awhile had been glimpsed in the gardens of Grey Court.

These musings may have touched the boy's relations with his much-loved paternal grandmother Elizabeth Newman and his favourite aunt Elizabeth Good Newman ('Betsy'), who together taught him the Bible and catechism. But his gentle dreaming was quite untroubled by the religious terrors of some stricter, darker, Georgian and Victorian childhoods, and must have been quite incomprehensible to his hearty and uncomplicated businessman father, whose idea of pleasure was good food and company, as at the large and simple dinners with cronies at the Beefsteak Club, which met to feast on 'vast beefsteaks sizzling on pewter plates, garnished with baked potatoes, Spanish onions, beetroot and eschalots, followed by a single course of toasted cheese, washed down with porter in pewter tankards, whisky toddy or punch'.[13] John Newman was, however, proud of his forward son, who recited 'The Cat and the Cream Bowl' at his fourth birthday party in Southampton Street and Cowper's 'Faithful Friend' on his sixth at Ham. In a household full of children – his youngest sisters, Jemima and Mary, were born in 1808 and 1809 – he played the eldest son's dominating role. In his sister Harriett's 'clever books', novels based on family memories, he appears reprimanding his brother Charles Robert for wearing gloves: 'It is not respectable, Robert; indeed, it is not respectable';[14] while as 'George' at thirteen, he believes that 'he was clever enough to persuade anybody to do anything he chose',[15] and is heralded by a quotation from Crabbe:

> George was a boy with spirit strong and high
> With handsome face and penetrating eye[16]

– though the authoress might also have referred to the large chin and already prominent hooked nose. His teasing and quizzing of his sisters was a very small beginning of the later master of irony and satire. But the surviving records of kindly banter belong to a childhood secure in its affections and delightful in its setting, no more so than in the children's summer rural retreat with aunt and grandmother at the vine-covered Vine Cottage at

Norwood. Here was a gypsy-haunted landscape of heath, farmland and woodland still unsullied by the vile encroachments of London, a world utterly remote from those other English children who laboured miserably in the mines and factories to make it possible.

Newman's education was also kindly, at least by the savage standards of the time. He was only seven when his proud father mercifully sent him, albeit a little prematurely, not to the brutish beargarden of one of the great public schools, then in their utter anarchy and decadence, but to a private boarding academy run by a clergyman, Dr George Nicholas, in a ramshackle old rectory in Ealing. Newman was entered on 1 May 1808, and at first lingered in the hall, afraid to enter the big room with the other boys – 'O sir! they will say such things! I can't help crying',[17] he protested to the headmaster, who had to drag him firmly in. Dr Nicholas was, however, a kindly man, to whom Newman became greatly attached. The cleric had inherited the school by marrying his predecessor's daughter, and was building up a juvenile clientele which dressed in 'knee-breeches, top-hats, pantaloons, hessians, tail-coats and cravats',[18] and which was to include such distinguished figures as Captain Marryat, Tom Huxley, Sir Henry Lawrence, W. S. Gilbert and Newman's own friend the sculptor Richard Westmacott. Huxley's father was a master at the school, the future King of France, Louis Philippe, was an occasional visitor, and there was a despised French teacher proper, an *émigré* priest, who was 'simply made a butt',[19] Newman's first Catholic clergyman. Outside the classrooms lay the avenue of limes that Newman saw felled in full blossom nearly half a century later, and twelve acres of playing fields, as the youngest brother Francis remembered them, for 'cricket and rounders, and in the winter months football; petty fives against every petty wall; hopping and hop-scotch, patball and trapball, prisoner's base (or bars?), tops of several kind, and multiform games of marbles':[20] games which were still played in glorious Georgian freedom, unsupervized and unorganized by Victorian masters. Newman himself solemnly recorded, however, that 'his school-fellows have left on record that they never, or scarcely ever, saw him taking part in any game'.[21] His own school verses written at the age of fifteen are firmly non-participatory and sedentary:

> Here as we sit, and view the boys at play
> Rejoicing in their sunbright holiday,
> While some at fives attack the patient wall,
> And others glory in the bat and ball,
> Be our employ in philosophic ease
> Calmly to eat the scanty bread and cheese,
> Which black-eyed Johnson of th' untidy cap
> Cuts off for twopence to each hungry chap;

And, to beguile away the ling'ring time,
To choose some subject, gay or grave, for rhyme.[22]

The couplets he quoted in later life were those of the Augustans Cowper and Johnson. He had a special liking for Crabbe. More obviously Romantic was his introspectiveness, which appears in the first entry in the one-page 'Autobiography in Miniature' that he finished in 1884: 'John Newman wrote this just before he was going up to Greek on Tuesday, June 10th, 1812, when it only wanted 3 days to his going home, thinking of the time (at home) when looking at this he shall recollect when he did it'.[23] He preserved until his death this thought about a time when he would think about the time when he thought it.

But like others of his social class, he had to learn to ride and to dance, enjoyed boating and bathing – by which he meant plunge diving rather than swimming – and even, in a mysterious incident to which only one reference survives, tried when he was fourteen 'to go round the Isle of Wight in an open boat *in July* in the midst of a persevering drizzle and a dangerous sea'.[24] His diary entries and letters from the age of nine indicate a healthy interest in greengages and pears, in 'Sugar candy', 'Barley sugar', 'Damson tart', 'Almond cakes', and in 'mince Pies, Turkies, and the other good things of Christmas',[25] as well as in glass eyes for his kite. The angel had a normal earthy side.

There was, however, another path to enchantment. He haunted Dr Nicholas' door with a companion when music was played in the evenings, until the eavesdroppers were themselves overheard and admitted to the performance. At the age of ten, his father gave him a violin, and he even wrote a 'little opera'.[26] It is one of Newman's claims to greatness that he is the finest musician in prose of the nineteenth century, the master of those other Oxonian masters, Arnold and Pater. It was not the least of the services of Dr Nicholas that he should have encouraged the boy's gift for music.

Not that Newman was ever but delighted to go home. 'Sum ire domi in minore tempore quam hebdomadâ. Huzza. Utinam irem domi cras', he wrote, above some doggerel verse about his friend Mr Laurie:

Laurie one day
To his brother did say
'I got a sack
Of the best tabac'.[27]

The Latin of the introduction to the verse is spirited, but hardly more distinguished than the English. His first Latin verse book of the following year opens,

In montem Domini altum quisque ascendere possit,
Cui cor est purum, cui manus innocuae.[28]

Newman had almost no contact with Latin Christianity, but he was in
later life startled to find the verse book prefaced with the drawing of an
upright cross beside beads with another cross suspended, although the firmly
Protestant Anglican churches of his youth were as innocent of crosses as of
rosaries. He had, however, been with his father in the old Bavarian embassy
chapel in Warwick Street to hear some music, and recalled 'a pulpit and a
preacher, and a boy swinging a censer'.[29] Dr Nicholas himself was no great
classical scholar, though the boys acted the comedies of Terence, in which
Newman played Hegio in *Phormio*, Syrus in *Adelphi*, Davus in *Andria* and
Phythias in *Eunuchus*, the last a woman's part and (a mark of the uninhibited
spirit of the later Georgians) handmaid to a courtesan.[30] In the more Puritan
late Victorian time, Newman himself was to expurgate these Latin comedies
for performance by the pupils in the Oratory school in his old age. But he
was never, for all his mastery of Greek and Latin, a classic in the professional
and well-drilled public-school sense. Rather, his excellence lay in the sensitivity and terseness of his powers of composition in the languages he had
to learn, and it was on this ground that, as he proudly recalled, Dr Nicholas
testified that 'no boy had run through the school, from the bottom to the
top, so rapidly as John Newman'.[31]

In 1812, the boy wrote a mock drama, a satire on the Prince Regent, and
a 'dramatic piece' featuring Augustus. In 1815 he created periodicals called
'*the Spy*' and '*the Antispy*', written against each other, and set up a Spy Club
with another periodical called the *Portfolio* which ran to twenty numbers
between November 1815 and May 1816, and which won a contribution from
the American minister John Quincy Adams, whose sons were at Ealing
school. It was followed in 1816 by the forty numbers of the *Beholder*.[32] His
younger brothers were to claim that the Spy Club was marked by three
degrees in the orders of its membership, distinguished by different coloured
ribbons, and with Newman himself as Grand Master, and that its secrecy
attracted 'the *profanum vulgus* of the uninitiated' who 'forced the door open,
swept away the faithful officer on guard, seized the papers, and tore off the
badges':[33] but then Charles and Francis thought that when John Henry
Newman became a Roman Catholic, the club had been a sign of his early
Jesuitical proclivities. It might also be considered an evidence of that power
to win disciples which was to remain with him throughout his life.

The Waverley novels, *Waverley* itself and *Guy Mannering*, which he read in
bed in the light of the early summer mornings,[34] fed his imagination, providing a traditionalist Romantic antidote to the intellectual unsettlement of the
time – Walter Scott was a Christian and a Tory. He also loved another
form of Romantic writing, Robert Southey's fantastic poems on mythological
themes, especially 'Thalaba the Destroyer', a strange Arabian epic thickly

peopled with spirits fair and foul, which Newman was to consider 'the most sublime of English poems . . . I mean *morally* sublime', because of the titanic struggle against evil of its God-directed and predestined adventurer-hero. Newman admired Southey in part because his epics 'generally end, not with a marriage, but with death and future glory',[35] and he learned by heart Southey's 'Kehama', with its theme of a Hindu heaven to be earned by inhuman hecatombs of sacrifice, and with its bloodcurdling climax in the horrors of the Hindu hell.

Newman's curiosity naturally prompted his interest in the contemporary attack upon religion. At fourteen he 'read Paine's Tracts against the Old Testament, and found pleasure in thinking of the objections which were contained in them'; also 'some of Hume's Essays; and perhaps that on Miracles. So at least I gave my Father to understand; but perhaps it was a brag'. There was a similar excitement in 'copying out some French verses, perhaps Voltaire's, in denial of the immortality of the soul', and thinking ' "How dreadful, but how plausible!" '[36] In fact, this early encounter with unbelief, though transient, was of the greatest intellectual importance for Newman's future. It left an abiding impression of the strength of the eighteenth-century rationalist case against Christianity, which even in Newman's revolt against the eighteenth century, was always to make him appear a sceptic to those with more confidence than he in the religious powers of right reason on its own.

This happy, contained and privileged world was perhaps too self-sufficient. Newman's father complained that his children did not care for outside company. But the self-sufficiency was suddenly shaken by economic ruin: like Mr Sedley's business in *Vanity Fair*, John Newman's bank, Ramsbottom, Newman and Ramsbottom, was forced to close its doors in the financial crisis that followed the victory over Napoleon. The blow fell in March 1816, a month after John Henry's fifteenth birthday. Ramsbottom senior first skulked in his house, then did nothing to avert calamity, but John Newman and the junior Ramsbottom managed with difficulty to refund all their depositors within a month, thereby averting the public humiliation of bankruptcy.[37] Newman senior was helped by his former partners to find a new job as manager of a brewery in Jane Austen's quiet provincial town of Alton in Hampshire. Southampton Street was let, the daughters went first to Vine Cottage and, when that had to be surrendered, the family was reunited at Alton in October 1817 in a fine Georgian house. The family correspondence kept a note of cheer, Mrs Newman writing to her son about a concert with the violinist Spagnoletti and the prima donna Madame Fodor-Mainvielle, and about 'the selection from Haydn, Cherubini, Mozart, the Dutchman etc.', the last a family joke-name for 'van' Beethoven.[38] Newman's own letter to his aunt on the exodus from Norwood teases his sister Harriett for her sorrow and reports a public lecture, on Galvanism, from which he preserved his father's caricature of the lecturer.[39]

This heartiness, however, may have been on the surface. For John Newman, now almost fifty, the disgrace was a kind of death; his cheerfulness and self-esteem and the family's sense of economic security were gone for good. The Alton venture was *déclassé* enough in itself. Brewing was, after all, a 'trade', albeit a respectable one, but it was not even for John Newman to be a successful one; and however self-controlled, the household was shattered by the father's failure: perhaps most of all the hitherto indulged mother and her eldest son, though all stood loyally together. When Newman revisited Alton in 1834, the dreadful past returned. 'I consider he did so very much for me at a painful sacrifice to himself', Newman wrote to his mother about his father, ' . . . As we came near [Alton], and I saw Monk's Wood, the Church, and the hollow on the other side of the town, it was as fearful as if I was standing on the grave of some one I knew, and saw him gradually recover life and rise again.'[40] Mrs Newman's reply recalled the Alton interlude as 'a period of such anxiety and fearful augury of greater trials progressively advancing, that I scarcely think I should wish to revisit the place.' As to her husband, she had 'always a nervous dread' lest his children could remember him 'only in pain and sorrow'.[41]

One can, indeed, only speculate from the shame and strain in Newman's later accounts of the matter, of its effect on a sensitive, proud and intelligent young man; it is notable that conversion following a family bankruptcy also befell the great Evangelical Bishop of Liverpool J. C. Ryle, while Newman's fellow Roman convert and cardinal, Henry Edward Manning, was to undergo an Evangelical conversion after the failure of his father's bank, though William Manning's was the greater disaster, as he was formally bankrupted at once, and fell from a far greater height in the banking world. Dr Nicholas was especially indulgent to the Newmans in their difficulties, but John Henry, still at school, fell seriously ill, with sufferings 'keen, terrible . . . with experiences before and after, awful, and known only to God'.[42] The sickness and its attendant lassitude, and its aftermath, religious conversion, made the first great division in his life: they lay like a gulf severing him from the untroubled happiness of childhood, and in his own view, changed him for ever.

2

Conversion

Newman was only one of the numerous great Victorians to have come under the influence of Evangelical Protestantism. His rival Manning, his friends the Wilberforces, his future fellow Oratorian Frederick William Faber, the agnostic George Eliot, the High Churchman Gladstone, all had some training in the school for saints, which by 1820 disputed with the Utilitarian philosophers, the disciples of Jeremy Bentham, the dominion of the English popular mind, and had laid the foundations for the massive expansion of nineteenth-century English religion.

In the thirty years from 1790, the Evangelical advance was manifest in the hugely increased membership of the Methodist Churches founded by John Wesley and George Whitefield. In the same generation, evangelistic and charitable associations had proliferated on every hand for the cure of every moral and social ill, while new missionary societies plotted the conversion of the heathen in the remotest corners of the earth. Within the Established Church of England, the Anglican Evangelical movement had its Jerusalem in Cambridge, where Isaac Milner, President of Queen's College, and Charles Simeon, Vicar of Trinity Church, influenced fifteen generations of students. The movement had its Rome in the leafy south London suburb of Clapham, where the wealthy laity of the 'Clapham Sect' gathered around the ministry of John Venn and excercized an ever expanding influence on the nation's fashionable social and political life. Their figurehead and symbol, William Wilberforce, with a fortune derived from the Baltic trade, was the emancipator of the negro slave, the kindest of fathers and best of friends and the personal embodiment of the national conscience; and Wilberforce and his Clapham associates, the so-called 'Fathers of the Victorians', mediated to countless 'nominal' or lukewarm unconverted Christians the values of the Christian hearth and home, a piety and morality centred on family prayers and the sober and godly disciplines of Sabbatarian religion.[1]

It is not surprising that so broad and deep a current of feeling, touching every aspect of the national life, was marked by division and contradiction, and drew on forces seemingly opposed. Wilberforce had not been reluctant to recall the upper and middle classes to Christianity as a safely conservative and moderately reforming preservative from the apocalyptic terrors of the French Revolution, in a crusade blessed by the dying Edmund Burke.

15

Wesleyan Methodism was Tory on top, often more rebellious below; among the working-class rural 'ranting' Primitive Methodists who came into existence in the first decade of the new century, faith was as often a reflection of radical values as a substitute for them. The stage was set for the Victorian conflict of Liberal Chapel and Tory Church, embodying class resentments and parochial rivalries which the Gospel itself only widened. But Evangelical religion was part of still broader tendencies: as an element in a romantic pride in English nationhood, during and after the Napoleonic wars; as a reinforcement to the discipline of work in the age of the Industrial Revolution; and as a religious sanction to the proprieties of pre-Victorian puritanism. The Protestant component of this nationalism was to be strengthened by No-Popery dislike of renascent Irish Catholicism, missionary Christianity by an alliance with commerce, God and mammon in happy union, moral strictness hand in hand with religionless respectability. These semi-secular reaches of the Evangelical tide touched Newman as they did everyone; yet in his youthful suspicion of radicals and Methodists, his love of the Church Establishment and pride in his Englishness, he was to be like many Anglican Evangelicals, but also at one with his more conservative fellow countrymen. The strain in Evangelicalism proper which affected him most acutely was one at the very heart of the rightly converted man, a fear of those outward worldly signs of Evangelical influence and success which were possible marks of inward Gospel failure. The young Newman, dreaming at Ealing, was deeply bitten by the bug of Evangelical other-worldliness.

That other-worldliness might seem to be a legitimate deduction from the Christian evangel. Christ proclaimed a kingdom not of this world, whose Prince was the Devil and which was one with the flesh and with the original sin in man from his conception. The Evangelical dogmatic corpus was essentially a soteriology offering salvation from sin. Its strength lay in the integration of its dogmas with common religious experience. The repentant sinner, with his conviction of his own sin, was 'justified' – he was regarded by God as just – through his faith in the merits of Christ crucified, his belief that Christ had died especially for him. Faith came with conversion and an assurance of God's forgiveness through the Holy Spirit; and the justified sinner was 'regenerate' – born again in the Spirit, which began his refashioning in holiness, in Christ's image. In Wesley's distinctive view, there was also a possibility of perfection, of complete deliverance from sin: a doctrine indignantly rejected by other Evangelicals, who also disagreed about whether conversion need be instantaneous, or if an assurance of forgiveness was given to all.

The older Wesley kept an open mind on these last matters, but had to argue against Calvinist Antinomians, who taught that the justified and elect had no need to obey the moral law and to perform good works and could not fall away into sin; and more moderate Calvinists, who in their belief that Christ died only for the elect repudiated the Wesleyan 'Arminian' belief in the universal offer of the grace earned on the cross by Christ for everyone. The complexities of Wesley's open and optimistic theology suggest eclecticism if not incoherence; but the eclecticism did a little to blur the great distinctions between the spiritual condition of the convert before and after his conversion, and between him and other men. A similar blurring was produced by the growing convergence of Calvinism and Arminianism among the moderate Evangelicals like Simeon within the Clapham Sect, and by a still wider recognition that conversion was not usually instantaneous. Yet for all Evangelicals, Arminians and Calvinists, Churchmen and Dissenters, the divide still remained between the godly and the run of 'nominal' Christians living in unconverted worldliness.

How, then, was the convert, the real or vital Christian, to show his difference from the worldly in the churches of the unconverted? The monastic solution to the problem was not available to eighteenth-century Protestants, who resolved it either by founding societies which became new sectarian Churches, or by establishing little godly churches within existing Churches, *ecclesiolae in ecclesia*. Methodists and other Dissenters did the first, Evangelicals within the Church of England the second. A right relationship with God also required other 'peculiar', that is distinctive, patterns for the Christian life: sobriety in demeanour and dress, and an eschewal of every worldly enjoyment, from the licentious stage and the casual brutal entertainments of a depraved aristocracy and people to the minor vices of novel reading, tea drinking, and even tobacco. The consequent suspicion of the pleasure principle was epitomized by James Stephen's first and only cigar, which he found 'so delicious that he never smoked again'.[2] All such indulgence obscured the cardinal point that true happiness lay not in this world but another.

Yet God had so loved the world that he sent his only Son to save it; and within the moderately Calvinist Evangelicals of the Clapham Sect there was a more balanced attitude to innocent worldly pleasures as God-given, and a genuine concern for the purely this-worldly happiness of the slave and the poor which made many conservative Evangelicals philanthropists and reformers. The 'ten thousand compassions'[3] of the Evangelical charities and missions represented a hope that the world might be saved, as did the Gospel's advance among the great and good. The Clapham Evangelicals displayed a warm interest in literature and human culture, and a willingness to join in co-operative effort with non-Evangelicals and even non-Christians. The early Evangelical Anglicans of the generation of Wilberforce were not simply 'other-worldly'; rather, they effectively subscribed to a world transforming 'holy worldliness' while still claiming to be religious.

When, then, Newman became an Evangelical, he also became part of a movement of religious values and ideas which had attracted both rich and poor, and which lay at the heart of the mainstream culture of his age. But whatever his later opinion of Evangelicals as 'Peculiars' – the word meant

17

distinctive rather than odd – he never lost his conviction that it was by and through them that he became a practising Christian. The 'human means of this beginning of divine faith'[4] in him was the Revd Walter Mayers, a clergyman who had undergone a conversion in 1814 as the result of an escape from an accident, and whom Dr Nicholas had appointed in the same year as the senior classical master at Ealing. Newman, weakened by illness and domestic calamity, and still lingering at the school after the departure of his contemporaries, was especially receptive to the books which Mayers lent him, 'all of the school of Calvin'.[5] There was a notable English bias in Mayers' list, which was of lasting importance for Newman's intellectual development; he was encouraged to immerse himself in the English Calvinist tradition, rather than in Calvin himself, and in the end he was to weigh Protestantism in the balance and find it wanting by reading its English exponents rather than the theological giants of the continent, like Luther and Calvin himself.

He afterwards precisely dated the period of his conversion from 1 August 1816 until the 21 December,[6] and his most famous account of the matter, written in his *Apologia* nearly half a century after, so mingles the elements of inner religious experience and intellectual conviction that there can be no easy separation of the two. Indeed the essence of the change in Newman lay in their interconnection, as the intellect assented to the dogmas which found their echo in the heart. This was the very model and pattern laid down, as Newman declared, by 'the writer who made a deeper impression on my mind than any other, and to whom (humanly speaking) I almost owe my soul', Thomas Scott, Rector of Aston Sandford in Buckinghamshire, whose spiritual autobiography *The Force of Truth* described his own conversion over a period of three years from Unitarianism to 'a zealous faith in the Holy Trinity'.[7] The dogma of the Trinity was written on Newman's mind at his conversion, as he set out to build it up with proof-texts from Scripture, and with texts in support of that uncompromising early war-song of the Christian faith which he was to come to love, the Athanasian Creed.

Less lasting was the impression he received from another Calvinist writer, William Romaine, of the High Calvinist belief in the doctrine of the final perseverance of the saints to the heaven for which God had intended them. 'I received it at once', wrote Newman, 'and believed that the inward conversion of which I was conscious (and of which I still am more certain than that I have hands and feet) would last into the next life, and that I was elected to eternal glory.'[8] Also imprinted on his mind was the linked teaching of Calvinist predestination, though he thought others 'simply passed over, not predestined to eternal death. I only thought of the mercy to myself'. In other words, he never received the 'detestable doctrine', as he afterwards considered it, of double predestination, of the unrighteous to hell as well as of the saved to heaven. But he also accepted, in their Calvinist form, the tenets of 'heaven and hell, divine favour and divine wrath, of the justified and the unjustified',[9] the dogmas of a 'mere' or common Christianity which he was to retain in their essentials as a High Churchman and Roman Catholic.

It was within this Calvinist context that he absorbed from the eighteenth-century Anglican Bishop Thomas Newton's *Dissertations on the Prophecies* the teaching of a long line of Protestant exegetes 'that the Pope was the Antichrist predicted by Daniel, St Paul, and St John'.[10] Newton was not a Calvinist, but Newman followed him in computing the 1260 years of the reign of Antichrist from the Book of Daniel, and the number of the Beast, 666, from the numerical equivalents to 'Lateinos' in the Greek and Hebrew alphabets, on the principle that Newton's theories, as Newman told his Aunt Elizabeth, were 'extremely ingenious and also *satisfying*; (I mean they account and explain well)'.[11] Thus he dated the Pope's anti-Christian character from his usurpation of the Byzantine temporal power, bringing the end of the world in 1987:

A.D.
727 – the Pope revolted from the Exarch of Ravenna
755 – obtained the Exarchate of himself
767 – the worship of Images was fully established

$$
\begin{array}{c}
\text{A.D.} \\
727 \\
\underline{1260} \\
1987\,[12]
\end{array}
$$

Yet with this went Newman's most un-Protestant conviction and 'deep imagination' 'that it would be the will of God that I should lead a single life',[13] though the original setting of the idea was his Evangelical concern for purity and suspicion of dancing and the theatre, as well as his own distinctive 'feeling of separation from the visible world'.

There is, none the less, a mystery about this commitment to celibacy, which has been common in Catholic cultures, rarer in Protestant ones, though some Protestants have seen it as a good, like Wesley. Newman's own passion for purity was not unconnected with his fastidiousness, neatness and love of cleanliness and cold bathing. He noticed himself that he could hardly claim as a virtue his instinctive dislike of grossness. To the Irish poet Aubrey de Vere, his 'slight form and gracious address might have belonged either to a youthful ascetic of the middle ages or a graceful and high-bred lady of our own days'.[14] Something in his celibacy should also be allowed for setting and culture: Newman attended an all-male school and university, as an Oxford don he was required to be single, and he was bound by vows to be so as a Catholic priest. By the convention of the need to possess a middle-class income, he could not have afforded to marry until he enjoyed

19

a decent living from a parish; and he lived through a period of increasing sexual strictness.

This only partly explains why the great loves of his life were for John Bowden while a student, Hurrell Froude and Frederic Rogers when a don, and Ambrose St John as a Catholic priest. Newman wrote to his closest friends as 'Charissime' or 'Carissime'; but the lack of any overt genital element in his affections makes it grossly inappropriate, despite Geoffrey Faber's suggestion to the contrary,[15] to call them homosexual. It was an age which in its innocence was unafraid of strong expressions of love between individuals of the same sex, and one of the greatest poems of the period, *In Memoriam*, was the celebration of such an affection. Again, with the softening of Augustan decorum in this at least, there was little of that stiff-upper-lip reserve about the public display of tears or other deep feeling which came in towards the end of the nineteenth century. Yet even by the histrionic and expressive standards of the time, no one could have had a more intense emotional life than Newman, so that his complete lack of any overt hint of sexual feeling can only suggest that his adolescent conversion displaced, generalized and transmuted such feelings into those heightened and sharpened sensations of the vividness of his surroundings and of other people which were somehow paradoxically a part of his experience that matter was unreal.

It must be added that except when for a period, under the influence of Hurrell Froude, he sometimes disparaged marriage, there is no evidence in Newman of misogyny. He always treated women as his intellectual equals. His acutest theories were hammered out in letters to his mother and sisters, and to Mrs Catherine Froude, as his deepest griefs and hurts were to be poured out to Emily Bowles.

In any case, Newman's commitment to celibacy was an intrinsic part of his sense that he was henceforth wholly God's. It was this sense of separation from the visible world, in the meeting between God and himself, that gave a unity and coherence to his dogmatic ideas; and in that sense of separation, it might be thought that Newman had not been changed from his boyhood – even his acceptance of the doctrine of final perseverance had, in his own words,

> some influence on my opinions, in the direction of those childish imaginations which I have already mentioned, viz. in isolating me from the objects which surrounded me, in confirming me in my mistrust of the reality of material phenomena, and making me rest in the thought of two and two only absolute and luminously self-evident beings, myself and my Creator . . . [16]

In short, Newman's discovery of God was a rediscovery of the deepest neo-Platonic yearnings of his childhood. By 1821, in thinking over his conversion, he had decided that 'my own feelings, as far as I remember, were so different from any account I have ever read, that I dare not go by what *may* be an individual case'.[17] By 1826, he spoke of having undergone 'a returning to, a renewing of, principles, under the power of the Holy Spirit, which I had *already* felt, and in a measure acted on, when young'.[18] The conversion was not, in Protestant terms, a wholly new beginning, but a reassertion of the sensations of an earlier one. Calvinist Evangelicalism gave these sensations an intellectual sanction; but the experience which it validated was not an Evangelical conversion at all.

This would seem to be supported by Newman's own later testimony: 'in truth', he wrote of himself, 'much as he owed to the evangelical teaching, so it was, he never had been a genuine evangelical':[19] a conclusion also drawn by some Evangelical readers of the *Apologia*, who when they read his account of his conversion, wrote to tell him so. 'Although Newman was deeply influenced by Evangelicalism', adds a modern scholar, following Newman's own afterthoughts, 'his was not an emotional conversion of the Evangelical kind, going through the stages of "conviction of sin, terror, despair, news of the free and full salvation, apprehension of Christ, sense of pardon, assurance of salvation, joy and peace, and so on to final perseverance".'[20] On this understanding of the matter, Newman's experience did not correspond to the classical Evangelical pattern, in which the essential element is the individual believer's overpowering – even instantaneous – sensation of joyous liberation from sin, in the realization that Christ, in pardoning or justifying the sinner, has taken all the burden of his sins upon Himself.

This is, however, too simple a view of the range and variety of the understanding of conversion within the Evangelical world of the 1820s. For the moderate Calvinists of the Clapham Sect like Mayers, there was little subjective stress on intensity of personal feeling. Mayers pragmatically insisted that most conversions were not instantaneous but took time – in Newman's case, nearly five months of reading and prayer. Again, Mayers thought that conversion was usually occasioned by providential adversity: in Newman's case, the financial ruin of his family. Again, it should have unrepeatable consequences – as it confirmed Newman's belief that he was elected to eternal life. And even though the doctrine of final perseverance was apparently fading by the time he was twenty-one, he never lost the once-and-for-all sensation that God had in some way chosen him. When he had been fourteen years a Roman Catholic, he wrote about the event as though he was still an Evangelical – as though the child he had been before his conversion had been a stranger: 'I know perfectly well, and thankfully confess to Thee, O my God, that Thy wonderful grace turned me right round when I was more like a devil than a wicked boy, at the age of fifteen'.[21] Throughout his life, he remained more certain of his conversion than that he had hands and feet. In that, he was changed, changed utterly.

There was then here both continuity and discontinuity. Newman undoubtedly had the Evangelical conviction of sin: 'Heu miser ego!' he recorded, 'peccavi. Aeternam damnationem mereor propter portentosa facinora mea'.[22] He saw his place in hell. Indeed this Evangelical gloom was least Evangelical, as has been suggested, in being unrelieved by the Evangelical joy of the sense of liberation from sin, and was deepened by Mayers' insistence on the need for daily repentance and on the moral character of conversion which must bear fruit in a transformed life. Newman also owed this moral stress to Thomas Scott, for 'what I also admired in Scott', he wrote, 'was his resolute opposition to Antinomianism, and the minutely practical character of his writings. They show him to be a true Englishman, . . . and for years I used almost as proverbs what I considered to be the scope and issue of his doctrine, "Holiness rather than peace", and "Growth the only evidence of life" '.[23]

In short, against the radical Evangelical tendency to put all the stress upon conversion, and to make Christ's work for the saved sinner a denial of the need for moral effort – even in extreme cases of the need to obey the moral law – Newman learned from the Evangelical tradition itself the Catholic doctrine of that other need to grow in holiness after conversion, in a better and higher keeping of the moral law which Christ had come not to abolish but to fulfill. Newman saw no disparity in this matter between, on the one hand, the Calvinism of a treasured present from Mayers, William Beveridge's *Private Thoughts*, which he made the cornerstone of his devotions and on which he modelled his prose, and on the other, the writings of the High Church Non-Juror William Law, who had seen as the aim of Christianity the living of a devout and holy life. It was that goal which carried Newman beyond his Calvinism through a breach in the fabric of his Evangelicalism to the older Catholic Christianity which is nothing less than the imitation of Christ.

But Newman's earliest Christology centred not even so much on the Trinity as on the Atonement, or what he called the doctrine of the Lutheran apprehension of Christ: the faith of the believer not in what he could do himself, but in what Christ had done for him on the cross. So ran the adolescent verses which he preserved, while apologizing for them as doggerel:

> O grant that I may persevere
>   And finally obtain
> A glorious crown, purchased for dear,
>   That ever may remain
> Purchased for dear, for by the Blood,
>   Of Jesus it is given
> Who suffered death, the Just & Good,
>   That we may live in heaven.[24]

Newman also found the Protestant doctrine of justification by faith in Christ alone, that our own works make no contribution to the salvation he has won for us, as the guiding principle of Joseph Milner's Evangelical *History of the Church of Christ*, which divided Christians into good ones who held the doctrine and bad ones who denied it, or between 'real' Christians and 'nominal' ones. Milner was a Lutheran rather than a Calvinist and did not discuss Calvin, but Newman received this distinction in its most ultra-Calvinist form, that there is 'a sharp separation between the elect and the world', 'that the converted and the unconverted can be discriminated by man, that the justified are conscious of their state of justification, and that the regenerate cannot fall away'.[25] It was on this basis that Newman saw the people around him as divided in the starkest, most other-worldly manner between the lost and the saved, just as he saw his own life divided by his conversion. Yet it was Milner, the teacher of this fundamental divide between 'real' and 'nominal' Christians, who gave Newman his vision of history as a conflict between orthodoxy and rationalist unbelief; and it was Milner who delighted Newman and set his thoughts on a wholly different path by quoting, albeit inaccurately and selectively, long extracts from the Fathers of the Church in the early Christian centuries, who were to be Newman's masters, and a music to his soul.

Everyone must begin somewhere, and the profoundest continuity in Newman was not even so much with his childhood as with his Evangelical beginnings, in God's self-revelation towards him which was also his discovery of himself. This enhanced his centredness on the self: but as a French master of the spiritual life, Louis Bouyer, puts it, 'How, then, did it come about that this "self", so adamant in its nature, was suddenly projected into the "self" of that Other and became wholly obedient to Him? That no doubt is the crux, the mysterious element, in this conversion'.[26] Thus Evangelicalism gave Newman's religion its profound individualist sense that the ultimate realities are God and the self, and that all the world is well lost beside them. He already had the profoundest self-consciousness of his own distinctiveness. He acquired by grace, if he did not have by nature, the Evangelical seriousness, the sense of the need to redeem the time, for which an account must be given to eternity; the habit of anxious introspection and the minute self-searchings of the failures of the human heart; and all this in the watchful sense of one who knows himself under the steady gaze of God. The danger of this view was a spiritual egotism which needed correction from a stronger dose of love of neighbour in the communion of the Church and of mankind; but a believer would hold that such convictions lack bedrock if not grounded on the ultimate and supreme love of God alone.

That came to Newman through Protestantism, and it is above all in Newman that one can see that the nineteenth-century Catholic revival had its beginnings in the Protestant tradition. '*Sit anima mea cum Sanctis*', wrote

23

the Victorian High Churchman G. W. E. Russell. 'May my lot be with the Evangelical Saints from whose lips I first learned the doctrine of the Cross.'[27] Newman's Evangelical faith was, moreover, no mushy pietism, but gave a sharper edge to his mind. Calvinism is one of the world's finest systematic theologies, and whatever its alleged spiritual defects, it is a spur to hard precise thought. It is striking how far Newman's chief Evangelical Calvinist mentor Scott anticipates Newman the High Churchman, in his horror of all forms of theological liberalism, of Socinianism, Pelagianism and Arminianism, and in his determination to state the true doctrine of the Church of England. The Calvinist experience of conversion was the beginning of Newman's mature devotional life; the dogmas of Calvinism were the beginning of his intellectual life. Doctrine was the objective correlative to a living experience; but Christianity was about the life of the mind as well as about the life of the heart. Or to choose a metaphor, the building would be buffeted and had hardly begun to rise above ground; but its foundations were secure.

3

Trinity: Triumph and Failure

Newman's conversion won him no sympathy from his father, a conventional Anglican of the easygoing eighteenth-century Latitudinarian type, who disliked references to hell and the so-called cursing psalms. 'I do not pretend to be a religious man', he would say, 'I am a man of the world.'[1] Despite his parlous financial state, he was determined to send his brilliant boy to university, though undecided which one to choose. Newman recalled 'in illustration of the seeming accidents on which our course of life and personal history turn, that, even when the post chaise was at the door, his father was in doubt whether to direct the post boy to make for Hounslow, or for the first stage on the road to Cambridge'.[2] The decision for Oxford was taken by an old family friend, John Mullens, the blind curate of St James's, Piccadilly; and when Mullens failed to find Newman a vacancy in Mullens' old college, Exeter, his Exeter friends directed him to the Vice-Chancellor, Dr Thomas Lee, President of Trinity, who had Newman entered as a commoner at his own college. He matriculated on 14 December 1816, when he was still more than two months short of his sixteenth birthday. Mullens, doubtful of his choice, was reassured by Dr Nicholas' warm approval: 'Trinity? a most gentlemanlike College'.[3]

The first two terms for the degree were suspended by dispensation, and Newman spent them at home in steady reading – covering between mid March and the first of June 'five plays of Sophocles . . . ; Cicero's *De officiis*, *De amicitia*, and *De senectute*; four satires of Juvenal, about twenty selections from Horace, and fourteen chapters from the Gospel of St Matthew in Greek'.[4] Early in June 1817, however, rooms became unexpectedly available in college, and Newman came into residence for a brief three weeks, when 'the Term was far advanced, the Commemoration close at hand, the College Lectures over, and the young men on the point of leaving for the Long Vacation'.[5] It was part of the laxity of the system that this brief sojourn could count as the keeping of a term, when the University was settling down to the prolonged summer break which was then one of the many blessings of academic life.

The greatest blessing was simply Oxford herself. It was in part because Oxford was so lovely that she was so well loved. Even today, the visitor can feel a little of Oxford's loveliness in the years of Newman's residence, when the crumbling golden ashlar of the colleges rose above the dusty or muddy streets and huddle of the little medieval town: before the colleges pulled down the medieval houses to make money, and Lord Nuffield built his motor car factories at Cowley. The green and golden fields went right to the ancient walls, and the traveller looked from afar on the vision splendid of the gleaming city of the dreaming spires:

> And that sweet City with her dreaming spires,
> She needs not June for beauty's heightening.[6]

So wrote Newman's great aesthetic lay disciple, Matthew Arnold. Even to a commentator in 1900, the vision had been still more lovely when Newman was young:

> It was said in those days that the approach to Oxford by the Henley road was the most beautiful in the world. Soon after passing Littlemore you came in sight of, and did not lose again, the sweet city with its dreaming spires, driven along a road now crowded and obscured with dwellings, open then to the cornfields on the right, to uninclosed meadows on the left, with an unbroken view of the long line of towers, rising out of foliage less high and veiling than after sixty more years of growth to-day. At once, without suburban interval, you entered the finest quarter of the town, rolling under Magdalen Tower, and past the Magdalen elms, then in full unmutilated luxuriance, till the exquisite curves of the High Street opened on you, as you drew up at The Angel, or passed on to the Mitre and the Star.[7]

The beauty also reflected power. Oxford was much more than a university: it was still a great national institution, an ecclesiastical corporation with a central place in the nation's life, in part through the network of influence of her graduate clergy in thousands of parishes in southern and midland England, in part because Oxford was the intellectual powerhouse of official English religion and the spiritual capital of the Established Church. The quintessential Oxonian spirit was, moreover, an influence of a peculiar type. Here was a world dedicated in form if not wholly in substance, to the ancient ideals of godliness and good learning. Here the college Fellows were celibates, living a mode of life laid down in the middle ages, under regulations and a discipline never repealed if not always observed. Here were still the echoes, no more, of the fantastic, outdated loyalties of the home of lost causes, to Pope and Pretender, quite dead in the rest of England; and here, where the Gothic arches of chapel and library and dining hall still whispered, in another of Matthew Arnold's phrases, the 'last enchantments of the Middle Age',[8] young men might dream of crystalizing those enchantments into a revival of the Catholic faith.

The fate of a world of ideas trembled on Mr Mullens' choice of university, as Newman would no doubt have given his heart to one place or the other, and might have surrendered it to the Protestant and scientific ethos of Cambridge. Even the all but vanished Oxonian tenderness for Popery was in the nature of an eccentric local tradition rather than an internationalist enthusiasm, and the Oxford Movement was to be rooted, not in a perverse affection for an alien Roman Christianity, but in a love and loyalty for Oxford.

Yet more was needed for such a revival than the atmosphere so congenial to the new romantic mood. The celebrated intellectual mediocrity of the place was part of its charm. The University's reputation in the eighteenth century has been greatly damaged by Gibbon, who described the time he spent at Oxford from 1752 as the most idle and unprofitable of his life, under the tutorship of the lazy 'monks of Magdalen', 'decent easy men, who supinely enjoyed the gifts of the founder'; whose 'dull and deep potations excused the brisk intemperance of Youth', and who in one case 'well remembered that he had a salary to receive, and only forgot that he had a duty to perform'.[9] The University's other famous literary alumnus, Dr Johnson, thought better of his *alma mater*, and in the Age of Reason, Oxford was in a measure out of the intellectual swim in her fidelity to the Church and to tradition. The recent history of the eighteenth-century University gives a more balanced and rounded picture of Oxford than Gibbon's, whose experience was only of one college over fourteen months; but, for all its efforts, it rather damns with faint praise, indicating that at best the teaching and teachers were more often competent than brilliant and that the institution needed reform.[10] It should be added that if Gibbon's opinion has devastated the reputation of the Georgian University, Newman created a mythology for it which marked the nineteenth-century revival of its intellectual life.

The young Newman's Oxford was still as Gibbon remembered it, somewhere between a semi-secular monastery and a gentleman's dining club; but the new examination statute of 1800 revised in 1803 and 1807 had introduced two honours schools, those of Literae Humaniores in classics, and mathematics and physics, and a better instruction in divinity. A thorough grounding in classics, mathematics and divinity comprised Newman's curriculum of undergraduate study; and though the 'Oxford renaissance'[11] dated from the 1820s, with such notable sideproducts as the Oxford Union and the first Oxford–Cambridge boat race, the sleepy atmosphere was already lifting in the second decade of the nineteenth century, as growing numbers of privileged, well-educated and well-fed young men began with a new seriousness to aspire to an epic achievement as sportsmen and statesmen, scholars and saints.

Newman himself found that reform was in the air in the stricter discipline of his new tutor at Trinity, Thomas Short, formerly a schoolmaster at Rugby and a new kind of more efficient university teacher. Thus were also the

27

delights of his first university friend, John William Bowden, with whom he shared a birthday and from whom he was to be inseparable throughout his student career, and the splendid appearance of the collegiate food and drink: 'Fish, flesh and fowl, beautiful salmon, haunches of mutton, lamb etc and fine, very fine (to my taste) strong beer, served up on old pewter plates, and [in] mis-shapen earthenware jugs. Tell Mama', he wrote to his father, 'there are gooseberry, raspberry, and apricot pies. And in all this the joint did not go round, but there was such a profusion that scarcely two ate of the same joint'.[12]

The earnest and fastidious young Evangelical was, however, disgusted by the bibulousness among those undergraduates who 'sat down with the avowed determination of each making himself drunk . . . if any one should ask me what qualifications were necessary for Trinity College, I should say there was only one, – Drink, drink, drink'.[13] Walter Mayers warned him that he would find 'the ridicule of the world among the strongest weapons Satan can employ'.[14] There was consolation for his awkwardness in Mayers' further denial of the rule that 'Ridicule is the test of truth'.[15] Newman fancied himself laughed at for his dress, and as the college emptied, sat uncomfortable and solitary at dinner, with an army of servants around him, eating veal cutlets and peas 'so much to myself that I could hear the noise I made in chewing through the empty hall', until 'one came in, . . . but I had not been introduced to him . . . Consequently we preserved an amicable silence, and conversed with our teeth'.[16] He had come up at an odd time of year, and was therefore not part of any group. The quadrangles were deserted, and he had to accost a tutor 'in top-boots on horseback'[17] to find out who would give him a list for summer reading, which at first seemed neither expected nor prescribed.

His liking for his small community of two tutors, President, Vice-President, Dean and Junior and Senior Bursars, and of sixty or so lively youths, was to be tested when in November 1817, as was not unusual with freshmen, some older students tried to get him drunk at a wine party to which he was summoned with his violin. He expected to accompany flutes: instead, he heard a smothered laugh when announced as 'Mr Newman and his fiddle'. At first, his host would not pass round the second bottle till he had finished his first glass, and Newman refused to play the violin to the company, which he left despite vigorous protests after drinking three glasses in an hour. Eleven days later there was some mild enough ragging: 'Is it gentlemanly conduct to rush into my room', he enquired of his diary, 'and to strut up to the further end of it, and ask me in a laughing tone how I do; and then, . . . to run and bolt the door, and say they are hiding from some one?' Newman refused another 'pressing and pressing' invitation to wine from his visitors, who told him that he read too much and overdid it. There was a hollow of 'Let him alone, come along', and his door was thrown open. 'I said such conduct was not the conduct of gentlemen – and ordered them to leave the room. One then said he would knock me down, if I were not too contemptible a fellow. (He was 6 feet 3 or 4 inches high, and stout in proportion . . .)' But the matter apparently ended happily enough the following day. 'The One has been here just now, and said he was very sorry for his conduct, that a sudden gust of passion had overset him – that I had acted very well, that he had seldom or never seen any one act more firmly. I told him not to think more about it. He shook hands and went.'[18]

Newman was only sixteen, to stand up to six feet four, but there was a priggishness about his virtuous sobriety which may have made him a butt, though this was disarmed by his dignity and sincerity. His Evangelicalism was not directly a target – it might have been considered caddish to attack a man's religion – but he was over-devoted to his books in a place not yet very serious about its learning, and he was marked by his standoffishness. His Beefsteak father, a clubbable man, would surely have handled matters better.

Not, of course, that he was a teetotaller – the word had not yet even been coined. His crockery included 'Two Pair Bottle Stands', 'Two Dozen Wine Glasses' and '6 Goblets',[19] and his college bill for his first full term included six bottles of the 'Best Sherry' and eighteen of the 'Best Port', – a 'shameful take-in' by the college, he considered it, as he had a separate arrangement to buy port and sherry through his father's quondam clerk at the *Star*.[20] Another expense was the deep and dismal mourning which he was required by the Proctors to wear, with the rest of undergraduate Oxford, on the death of Princess Charlotte: 'Black coat, black waistcoat, black trowsers, black gloves; black ribbon, no chain to the watch; no white except the neckcloth and the unplaited frill'.[21] So garbed, he took his first communion in the cedar classical splendour of Trinity Chapel, but the black silk glove 'would not come off when I had to receive the Bread, and I had to tear it off and spoil it in my flurry . . . '[22]

His solitude was filled with hard reading, except in the evenings, when his eyes seemed poorly and he practised his violin. A good deal of the teaching was on an elementary level. He was astonished when the Euclid class started at the Ass's bridge, 'a proposition quite at the beginning', and had to convince his sceptical mathematics tutor that he had read the first five books of Euclid, even if his knowledge was imperfect. The students were given some choice in the selection of the works in which they were examined for the termly Collections, though, as Newman told his mother, 'Every one must take up some Greek, Latin, Mathematics, and Divinity. I have taken the whole of Xenophon's Anabasis – . . . two tracts of Tacitus, the 5th Book of Euclid (the hardest book of Euclid) (tell Harriett and Jemima it is the *ratio of ratios* Book) and the Gospels of Luke and John; this is rather fagging for a month or six weeks . . . I quite forgot Mary's birth-day – ', he added, 'a pretty brother'.[23] He listed off the mathematical work in comic Gilbertian manner, assuring Mrs Newman that he knew 'all about Multiple super-particular, submultiple subsuperparticular, subsuperpartient of the less inequality, sesquialteral, sesquiquintal, supertriquartal and subsuperbitertial . . . Indeed', he added, 'I dream of four magnitudes, being proportionals'.[24] It was a mistake to choose the *Anabasis*, which he already knew, rather than Herodotus, which would have advanced his Greek. But though he was still young for university examinations even at an elementary level, he was to pass the Collections, and establish a relationship of mutual esteem with his tutor Thomas Short.

His first year was to be crowned with glory. In the following term, in 1818, he laboured away for Collections on 'five books of Herodotus, Virgil's Aeneid, Mechanics, and the Pentateuch, Joshua, Judges, and Ruth';[25] and such was his success that he recalled that when at Easter his father came to Oxford to take him home, Thomas Short 'went to meet him [Newman senior] as an old friend, and holding out his hands said, "O, Mr Newman, what have you given us in your Son" '.[26]

The prodigy and the report about him were carried for congratulations to Dr Nicholas at Ealing; and with the encouragement of his father and of Short, who was credited with being responsible for opening up the Trinity exhibitionership to outside competition, Newman was entered for the scholarship in April 1818 against ten other candidates, four Trinity men and six outsiders. Newman was not a good examination candidate, as he was spectacularly to prove, and Mayers' warning against 'the Oxford Logicians' and his own other-worldly suspicions of worldly glory made him resort to prayer as a preservative against the temptations of success: 'Let me not rely too much upon getting this scholarship – let me not be lead [sic] away from Thee by the hopes of it'.[27] The examination was oral and at sight, and was judged by the votes of the college Fellows. It included mathematical exercises, Latin verses, Latin translation, a Latin theme, 'then a chorus of Euripides – then an English theme – then some Plato, then some Lucretius, then some Xenophon, then some Livy'.[28]

The worst of it was awaiting the outcome of the trial. 'I felt the tortures of suspense so much, that I wished and wished I had never attempted it . . . I was not very well. My head ached continually. I tried to keep myself as cool as possible, but I could not help being sanguine'. 'Even he with whom I am most intimate [Bowden] thought my case desperate and betted against me'.[29] Newman's youth was also an obstacle, as the examiners might have thought that he could always try again. He dropped some broad hints to his family that he was trying to win the scholarship, but gave no direct word until he could report success. 'At last I was called to the place where they had been voting' he told his mother: 'the Vice Chancellor said some Latin over me: then made me a speech. The Electors then shook hands with me, and I immediately assumed the Scholar's gown.' Newman had obliquely answered an enquiry from one of the defeated candidates about the winner, but 'On returning with my newly earned gown I met the whole set [of losers] going to their respective homes. I did not know what to do. I held my eyes down'.[30] Privately he ascribed the whole glory to God: 'I prayed . . . and yesterday, out of his infinite loving kindness He gave me the scholarship. O praised be the Lord God of Israel who only doth wondrous things!'[31]

His mother presented him with the collected works of Francis Bacon in honour of his success: no bad gift for the future philosopher. The triumph was crowned in May by passing the far easier Responsions, the preliminary examination for the Oxford degree, for which he was examined by his later friend and foe, Edward Hawkins. Newman did a Euclidian exercise and chose 'the last five books of Herodotus and the odes and epodes of Horace'.[32] His scholarship guaranteed him an annual income of £60 for the next nine years.

'What a happy meeting this!' said Mr Newman on his son's return home.[33] Newman scrupulously kept the account of his generous allowance from his father – £327 between December 1816 and the award of the Trinity scholarship in 1818.[34] His success was the more precious because John Newman's affairs were getting steadily worse: in December 1818, he had to mortgage his personal assets for a loan of £1000 from his old friend Richard Capel, a banker and founder-member of the Stock Exchange, whom he was, humiliatingly, never able to repay.[35] In another way, the scholarship meant for Newman a brief liberation from overmuch striving, and between June 1818 and early 1819 he broadened his interests and enjoyed himself with studies not all directly related to his degree. He devoted the summer of 1818 to the liberal Protestant John Locke, his master in philosophy, who taught him his epistemology and confirmed the subjective element in his thought by deriving ideas from the impressions made on the mind by the senses – which was ultimately to imply for Newman that what is real to us is private and personal to ourselves.

In the summer of 1818, Newman also read the historian Edward Gibbon, and in December, he began to analyse Thucydides in 'that pseudo-Gibbonian style, in which it amused me at this time to compose'.[36] At Christmas, he wrote 'A Winter Eclogue' for his sister Harriett, which was musical as well as Shakespearian in inspiration:

> There is in stillness oft a magic power
> To calm the breast when struggling passions lower . . .
> There is a spirit singing aye in air
> That lifts us high above each earthly care;
> No mortal measure swells that silent sound,
> No mortal minstrel breathes such fragrance round,
> – The angel's hymn or melting harmony
> That guides the rolling bodies thro' the sky . . . [37]

This passage was printed as part of a longer work, when Newman wrote and published, with John Bowden, a poem in two cantos called 'St Bartholomew's Eve',[38] a story based upon the massacre, in which 'the unfortunate union of a Protestant gentleman with a Catholic lady' ends in their 'tragical death' 'through the machinations of a cruel fanatical priest, whose inappropriate name was Clement. Mr Bowden did the historical and picturesque portions, Mr Newman the theological. There were no love scenes, nor could there be, for . . . the parties had been, some time before the action, husband and wife . . .'[39] The poem was a splendid hit at the cruelty and fanaticism of Rome:

> Mid the recesses of that pillar'd wall
> Stood reverend Clement's dark confessional.
> Here Rapine's son with superstition pale
> Oft thro' the grated lattice told his tale;
> Here blood-stain'd Murder faulter'd, tho' secure
> Of absolution for a faith impure – . . .
>
> Mistaken worship! where the priestly plan
> In servile bondage rules degraded man, . . .
> – Where every crime a price appointed brings
> To soothe the churchman's pride, the sinner's stings,
> Where righteous grief and penitence are made
> An holy market and a pious trade![40]

The most zealous anti-Catholic could hardly have said more. Newman must have smiled when, as a cardinal, he marked the lines as of his own composing for Bodley's librarian. The meeting between the lovers, the Catholic lady and the Protestant gentleman, also by Newman, is pure rodomontade:

> And Florence knows – see! see! the quick-drawn breath,
> The cold cheek sick'ning with the hues of death –
> The starting eye – the feeble tott'ring frame –
> The faint wild shriek with which she sounds his name –
> 'Julian!' – 'My wife, my dearest, then again
> I see thee, love! and have not pray'd in vain!'[41]

The poem sold only seventy-six of the two hundred and fifty copies of the first canto; Newman made good the publisher's loss. Again with Bowden, he started a periodical called *The Undergraduate*, which ran under their anonymous editorship to six weekly numbers, and ventured satire on undergraduate drunkenness and the university curriculum – as the editor, in this case Bowden, flies to the moon on the hippogriff once ridden by Ariosto's hero Astolpho to find lost parcels like 'the application of the men of a certain College . . . and the first class list of another', and still smaller items, 'the wit of a Don' and 'the lenity of an Examining Master', together with commodities which 'would prove, at Oxford, an invaluable treasure', such as the 'practical utility of Aristotle' and the 'sense and advantage of Logic'.[42]

This last contempt for logic was one which Newman was to develop rather than outgrow. It was possibly this levity which made his position seem so awful to himself when his name as editor, rather than Bowden's, was made public by students in Magdalen: 'The whole day I was so weak I could hardly walk or speak . . . ', he told his mother. 'What? can any one fag, fag, and be an author? Alas, "the third day has come a frost, a nipping frost".'[43] The periodical was resigned back into the hands of its publisher. It was perhaps chiefly notable for Newman's appeal for a university debating society, to be 'a school for the future senator or lawyer' and, ironically in the light of later events, to exclude nothing 'but the politics of the last 100 years'. 'Oh! for some undaunted spirit to make the circuit of the Colleges, and like the Gothic King [Roderick] of the poem of Southey, to rouse those around him to nobler views and feelings!'[44] The proposal was only four years premature to the creation of the forerunner of the Oxford Union.

This idealism was the fruit of leisure to taste and listen and enjoy. 'Sunday Evening. Bells pealing. The pleasure of hearing them. It leads the mind to a longing after some thing I know not what.'[45] He had eight lessons in drawing, and the Dean of Trinity, the Revd William Morgan Kinsey, took him to the geological lectures given by the new professor the Revd William Buckland, who was creating the new science, and held his audience not only by the brilliant clarity of his discourse, but by stalking the classroom brandishing the thighbone of a hyena or the jawbone of a bear.

None of this interest in the secular, however, could reconcile Newman with the drunkenness of the party for the 1819 Trinity Gaudy, on the Monday after Trinity Sunday, which was at first put off because there were two warring sets within the college and therefore no subscription for the wine. But then the rivals were reconciled, and 'this wicked union' was 'profanely joked upon with allusions to one of the expressions in the Athanasian Creed'. The whole affair was a blasphemy on the Blessed Trinity, the heart of Newman's intellectual convictions, and his powers of dramatizing himself are declared in his letter about it to Mayers. 'I keep quiet, for all have pledged themselves to go – yes, all but one, a poor despised awkward man, of unprepossessing appearance and untidy person, who, I really think, has more proper sense of religion than them all together.'[46]

When Newman's fellow collegians had discovered his feelings, they had sensibly let him go his own way. But his behaviour looked like a rebuke in itself; and as he later acknowledged, he 'had not a grain in his composition of that temper of conviviality so natural to young men, and could not even understand the enjoyment experienced by "a number of lads drinking bad wine, smoking bad cigars, and singing bad songs far into the night" ', so that his disgust with such drunkenness 'was no merit in him'.[47] Perhaps his other-worldly pride as a 'poor despised awkward man' was a deeper sin, however well it exemplified Mayers' repudiation of the notion that 'Ridicule is the test of truth'.

Newman's own temptations were intellectual – as he read Herodotus, Thucydides and Gibbon through the summer of 1819, and rejoiced, despite Gibbons' every fault, in his 'happy choice of expressions, his vigorous compression of ideas, and the life and significance of his every word . . . O who is worthy to succeed our Gibbon! Exoriare aliquis! and may he be a better man!'[48] The aspiration to be a Christian Gibbon was not one which Newman quite fulfilled. The other great historical influence upon him was Scott: after rehearsing the structural weaknesses of *Ivanhoe*, Newman went into raptures to his mother over volume two of the work, with its famous scene of the burning of Front-de-Boeuf's castle. 'I never read any thing that surpassed it . . . O what a poet! . . . O certainly a poet . . . Author of Waverley, thou art a second Shakespeare.'[49] There was a falling off in volume three, but 'I think I never read such a magnificent scene as that between Richard and Friar Tuck'.[50]

His secular ambitions returned. He considered a career in law and, in November 1819, was entered at Lincoln's Inn. In 1820, he attended Professor Edward Nares' history lectures, 'hearing that the names [of those who went] were reported to the Minister'.[51] His literary aspirations led him to write two poems for the Newdigate prize, both failures. His 'red hot Tory' Latin Prologue in heroic metre for Dr Nicholas' school production of Terence's *Andria* was spoken by his younger brother Francis as head boy and exalted the dead George III and his dead son the Duke of Kent;[52] while in June 1820, he was misled by his old school friend Richard Westmacott into writing two comic songs for a London farce starring the comedian John Pritt Harley, a youthful indiscretion which more than fifty years later he feared might 'raise a laugh' against him.[53] The angel might seem to be declining into worldliness.

Yet the mood was a temporary one, as there hovered over his head two thunderclouds, his father and finals, to remind him that this trifling was sin. In November 1819, the brewery failed, the family had to leave Alton, and John Newman declined into the keeper of a London pub and brewhouse. Aunt Betsy and Grandmama, who had shared the house at Alton, were now installed in pretty but damp accommodation in Strand-on-the-Green by Kew Bridge, where Betsy opened a 'Finishing School for Young Ladies' which took in Jemima and Mary as non-paying pupils as well as the daughters of relatives and friends.[54] In writing to Harriett, the irreverent Newman was to compare the contrarieties of his aunt's clientele to a bowl of punch, 'Mrs B. being the rum, Miss B. the water, Mrs J. the lemon and all of you the sugar'.[55] The venture was not a financial success, though it lingered on for seven years.

The decline in his family's fortune worried Newman less than finals. In June 1820, in a letter to his mother, he called the undergraduate's career 'a picture of a whole life, of youth, of manhood, and of old age'.[56] His period of 'manhood', of 'idle' self-indulgence, as he now came to see it, had set in with winning the exhibitionership, but he was working hard again by April 1819 and in November, with Bowden, put his mathematics in order by hiring a tutor, James Ogle, who was later to be Regius Professor of Medicine. By July 1820, he was solitary in Oxford during the long vacation and 'had Trinity College, its garden and library, all to himself; and in his solitude, pleasant as he found it, he became graver and graver',[57] as he laboured at Aristotle and Isaac Newton for an average of twelve hours a day. In term time, his active methods of study with Bowden ought to have succeeded, as they 'filled copybook after copybook with their mathematical problems, made chronologies and abstracts of their histories, quizzed each other on Aristotle's *Ethics* in the manner of a viva voce, and analyzed various plays of Aeschylus in the light of the principles laid down by Aristotle'.[58] The examiners' central interest lay in Aristotle's *Ethics*; and the two scholars gave six autumn weeks of careful study to the work, following this up with practice answers to the questions set on the text in years gone by.

What unnerved Newman as the examination approached was a deepening sense of having failed God by his light-minded ingratitude after his earlier success with the Trinity exhibition, as if he were now once again facing a choice between intellectual and moral excellence, with scholarly triumph as a sign of spiritual failure. Thus he wrote to Francis, 'Let me get no honours, if they are to be the slightest cause of sin to me':[59] this was itself possibly a rationalization of the fear of failure. There was also tension between the harassed father and overworked son, which Francis recalled as a bitter row over the new King George IV's attempt to deny royal honours to his estranged wife Caroline for alleged fornication with her servants. John Newman was a generous-minded man, well aware of George IV's secret marriage to the Catholic Mrs Fitzherbert and loveless neglect of his Queen, and he mistook John Henry's moralistic horror of Caroline for base pandering to authority – or, as Francis described it, misunderstood 'fanaticism for self-seeking'. 'Well, John!' the father exploded, 'I suppose I ought to praise you for knowing how to rise in this world. Go on! Persevere! Always stand up for men in power, and in time you will get promotion.'[60] Francis, though religiously in agreement with his brother, thought his father in this matter '*more Christian*'.

Newman was never a time-server, but he was undoubtedly ambitious, at least for academic honours. Through the months of 1820, his reading ground on, with a burst of enthusiasm to his sister Jemima about the 'sublimity' of Aeschylus and his disgust with 'the dry, stiff, formal, affected, cold, prolix, dignified Sophocles'.[61] He continued to pour out anxious prayer, and to his sisters quoted from Johnson's *Vanity of Human Wishes*:

> Still raise for good the supplicating voice
> But leave to Heav'n the measure, and the *choice*.[62]

But to Mayers he doubted the sincerity of this resignation to the will of God. 'I often find that I am acting the part of a very hypocrite; I am buoyed up with the secret idea, that by thus leaving the event in the hands of God, when I pray, He may be induced, as a reward for so proper a spirit, to grant me my desire. Thus my prayer is a mockery.'[63]

There was, therefore, an underlying fear in Newman that his religion was a sham, and this was mixed up with premonition of failure. Everyone had high expectations of him and that made disappointment more appalling. In fact, the prospects were poor. Trinity had taken no firsts since 1813 and, according to Newman, the students perhaps rather conveniently declared that unless their college had some success in the exam 'we have determined it is useless to read'.[64] Trinity was not yet accustomed to the examination system, and Newman was not well prepared; and though a Trinity don, John Wilson, coached him daily in mathematics from the beginning of the October term without remuneration, he decided to throw over Aristotle's *Rhetoric* and a possible first class in classics in order to retrieve his mathematics, even before disaster fell. Newman was called up for examination a day before he expected, 'lost his head, utterly broke down, and after vain attempts for several days had to retire, only making sure first of his B.A. degree'.[65] 'The examining Masters were kinder than it is possible for me to express . . . ', he wrote. 'When I got into the schools I was so nervous, I could not answer half a dozen questions.'[66] In the upshot, he was awarded no honours in mathematics, and in classics his name appeared 'under the line' which divided the second class degree from what was later to be called a third. He had, effectively, achieved a pass degree and a third.

Newman took his degree on 5 December 1820, and now felt at peace. His scholarship at Trinity had seven years to run and would enable him to seek ordination and await the advent of a fellowship. He had acquired a knowledge of Greek and Latin literature and habits of study and of hard unremitting work which never left him. The range of his reading, and some key examination texts, like Aristotle's *Ethics*, with its teachings that there is a practical moral judgement for everyday life, that moral truth is not as demonstrable as mathematical and that good habit has a part in the development of character, had begun to fill his storehouse of ideas. Yet his own inmost inner life lay elsewhere. 'Well, Newman', declared an acquaintance, 'I would rather have your philosophy, than the high honours to which you have been aspiring.'[67] In passing this remark on to his mother he may sound a little smug, but it was nothing less than the truth.

4

Oriel: Triumph and Tribulation

Newman's love of scholarship seemed to blossom more freely when he was released from the constraints of preparing for his degree. He was soon learning Aeschylus' choruses by heart, with the idea of setting one or two of them to music: 'then', he told Jemima, 'I have to compose a concerto; then to finish the treatise on Astronomy, part of which I took up for my examination'. Then follows an apparently wholly serious list of further reading, showing the range of his interests: 'Hydrostatics'; 'Optics; Euripides; Plato; Aristophanes; Hume; Cicero; Hebrew; Anatomy; Chemistry; Geology; Persian and Arabic; Law'.[1] By May 1821, he had written his 'famous piece of Music' with two movements, and with a piano part for Jemima and Mary, though the melodies had not turned out 'light and airy', as he had told his mother, but 'as all my attempts at melody, very heavy'.[2] He also intended to take down more of Buckland's mineralogy lectures, though in the end he decided that 'the science is so in its infancy, that no regular system is formed'.[3] This was one point of origin of Newman's conviction that the shifting sands of natural science in his own day could not be the foundation of a dogmatic natural theology, a point to be reinforced in 1823 by Buckland's proof of Noah's Deluge from the discovery of the bones of extinct British tigers gnawed by equally extinct hyenas in a cave in the Vale of Pickering. Buckland, an excellent scientist, later changed his mind that this was evidence of the Flood, and Newman did not trust religious scientism again. 'If "the Spirit of God" is gas in 1850', he was to write in that year, 'it may be electromagnetism in 1860.'[4]

His own earliest published incursion into philosophy was a long letter to the Clapham Sect's organ the *Christian Observer*, arguing against human prejudgement of the Christian mysteries, especially by a priori argument; but he was shaken in 1821 by his discovery that it was unlikely that either St Peter or St Paul had spoken of election or final perseverance to the unconverted, the first crack in the armour of his Calvinism.

In July 1821, he had to leave his rooms in college and go into lodgings; he lived from October above Seale's coffee house, from which he supplemented his meagre scholarship income as a private tutor – his first paying pupil brought him a hundred pounds a year. In July, his family had the excitement of George IV's coronation: he and his sisters got up early to see the procession, in which he was chiefly delighted with the crown: the 'green of the emerald, the red of the ruby, the yellow of the topaz are imitable by coloured glass', he told his aunt, ' . . . but the sparkling brightness of the diamond and the soft lustre of the pearl are inimitable'.[5] Queen Caroline failed in her attempt to gatecrash the ceremony in the Abbey, but after her death Newman abjectly repented his uncharity towards her: 'O that I had prayed more earnestly for her life! when she was getting better, I was wicked enough to feel somewhat disappointed. I know not why. Poor Princess!'[6] His critical faculty was alive to the vengeful side of his fierce moralism.

The atmosphere in Southampton Street was still strained. Newman senior worried about the growing distance between Charles and his older and younger brothers, who were united in their loyalty to the Calvinist Mayers: when they told their mother that they intended to receive Communion fortnightly, John Henry wrote that 'she seemed to think I began to be righteous over much, and was verging upon enthusiasm'.[7] John Henry also regretted his constant impatience with the uncompromising Francis, who precipitated a row with his father by refusing to commit the sin of copying an urgent business letter for him on a Sunday. The elder brother's opinion was demanded, and he supported Francis. 'A scene ensued', he recorded, 'more painful than any I have experienced.' There was a reconciliation the following day and, given the great difference in attitude between the sons and their father, John Henry considered 'his forgiveness of us an example of very striking candour, forbearance, and generosity'.[8] John Newman was under awful pressure. On 1 November 1821 he was declared bankrupt, and John Henry offered his mother consolation: 'distress comes from without . . . few families but what are disturbed from within. Many are wasted by death – many distracted by disagreements – many scattered. We have not had to weep over the death of those we love. We are not disunited by internal variance – we are not parted from each other by circumstances we cannot control. We have kind and indulgent parents . . . '.[9] To his aunt Newman wrote that 'the glory of religion is seen in affliction' and 'that God is cutting away all ties which might bind me to the world . . . '[10]

John Henry's need for money was now pressing, and might have been solved by taking up the offer of a tutorship in a wealthy household; but from autumn 1821 he also had to support Francis, who came to Oxford to stay with him at Seale's and prepare for university entrance. On 15 November 1821, Newman decided to try for one of the two vacant fellowships at Oriel. In his novel *Loss and Gain*, he was to recall his feelings about his candidature, in the story of his hero one night ascending to the top of one of Oxford's many towers 'with the purpose of making observations on the stars', and while his friend set the pointers, 'he, earthly-minded youth, had been looking down into the deep, gas-lit, dark-shadowed quadrangles, and wondering if he should ever be Fellow of this or that College . . . '[11]

It was not merely a religious decision, but also an academic one, when on his father's admonition 'to make up my mind what I was to be',[12] he chose on 11 January 1822 to go into the Church, a requirement for becoming a Fellow. John Newman, however, was also worried about John Henry's over-devotion. 'Religion, when carried too far, induces a softness of mind', he counselled his son. ' . . . no one's principles can be established at twenty. Your opinions in two or three years will certainly, *certainly* change . . . Take care, I repeat. You are on dangerous ground . . . Do nothing ultra . . . I know you write for the Christian Observer. My opinion of the Christian Observer is this, that it is a humbug.' His son's letter in the paper had been 'more like the composition of an old man, than of a youth just entering life with energy and aspirations'. John Henry afterwards acknowledged the wisdom of this advice, given from his father's 'general knowledge of the world'.[13]

Yet that knowledge of the world seemed useless in January 1822, when the contents of Southampton Street were sold to pay John Newman's creditors, though a creditors' meeting was proposed by the assignees in May to retrieve Mrs Newman's 'brooches, bangles, ear-rings and so forth'.[14] Newman had neglected his father's warning to remove his chattels to Oxford, and the family bid too low to save his music. He 'was obliged to shuffle' when a puzzled admirer found it at an auctioneer's and returned it to its owner half a century later: 'How can I answer', he rejoined, 'for a boy's negligence fifty years ago'.[15] Such a matter was no business of strangers. It signalled the family's painful decline into ever cheaper lodgings from Kentish Town to Holborn and Covent Garden, and the father's decline towards a premature death.

'I felt much affected, and quite shed tears to think I could no longer call myself a boy',[16] wrote Newman to his mother after his twenty-first birthday. He was also daunted by the prospect of the Oriel fellowship examination. The two successive Provosts of Oriel, John Eveleigh and Edward Copleston, had taken a leading part in securing the new examination statute of 1800, and had placed the college at the forefront of the reform of the Oxford curriculum; and at a time when most Oxford posts were closed to candidates from particular places or institutions and filled by processes of interest, patronage and personal connection, Oriel chose its Fellows, not on the basis even of the honours achieved in the narrowly classical and mathematical curriculum of the schools, but by 'a trial, not of how much men knew, but of *how* they knew . . . '[17]

Thus the entrance exam was a test not so much of knowledge as of quality of mind. As it was put to Newman, an Oriel fellowship was 'great in point of emolument, in point of character it was immortality'.[18] The Fellows of the college included some of the ablest scholars in Oxford: the Provost, Edward Copleston; his successor as Provost, Edward Hawkins; Richard Whately, later Archbishop of Dublin; above all, the most brilliant undergraduate of his generation, John Keble; and 'who indeed', wrote Newman to his mother, 'will not rightly wonder at the audacity of him, who being an Under-the-line himself, presumes to contend with some of the first men in the University, for a seat by the side of names like Keble and Hawkins?'[19]

His parents were alarmed by this evidence of depression or illness. His father may have feared another breakdown and now wanted him to withdraw.[20] 'Your fault is want of self confidence',[21] wrote his mother, while his tutor, Short, though not discouraging, had few hopes for him: on his record, he was possibly the least academically distinguished of the eleven competing candidates, and had spent much of the preceding year improving his knowledge of such unexamined subjects as chemistry, geology, mineralogy and composing music. Visits to the Provost and to the Dean of Oriel, James Tyler, gave him a strange sensation of confidence, but what really stood him in good stead was simply that he had been diligently studying the Latin lectures, *Praelectiones*, by the Oriel Provost Edward Copleston, and had thereby mastered the '*idea* of Latin composition'[22] in writing an essay for the university Latin essay prize on classical polytheism. He did not win the prize, but the exercise taught him to write a flowing Latin of his own, and greatly advanced his long search after a Latin style. It was just such a proficiency that Oriel admired.

The fellowship examination began on 6 April 1822 on Holy Saturday with a translation into Latin of part of a *Spectator* essay on Milton's *Paradise Lost*, and an English essay on a Ciceronian motto, which Newman employed to write about the personal difficulty that had long preoccupied him, of how to find through self-knowledge the Aristotelean mean of self-confidence, between lack of confidence on the one hand and conceit and arrogance on the other. This philosophy, however, then failed him. Easter Sunday was a misery, 'from mortification at having given the Fellows a bad opinion of me by some careless blunders';[23] while 'possessed with the idea that I had all but disgraced myself, and stiff, oh how stiff! with sitting 8 hours on hard benches', he imagined he had an eruption on the spine. On the Monday, he limped through his Latin theme which he put in uncorrected, and answered only five of the twelve mathematical questions, feeling so ill in the middle of the day that he could only pace about in Oriel hall. This was a freedom of movement not permitted by more modern examiners; indeed, he wrote, the 'examination throughout was most kind and considerate, and we were supplied with sandwiches, fruit, cake, jellies, and wine – a blazing fire, and plenty of time'.[24] On Tuesday, he made a recovery and did nine of the ten logic questions in the morning, before beginning the viva voce in the afternoon.

Newman's earlier papers so impressed the electors that unknown to him three of them, William James, Joseph Dornford and Tyler, went round to Trinity to find out more about him; and while Thomas Short as his tutor kept the visit confidential, Short was so excited that he called in Newman, who was on the point of giving the whole wretched business up, and reassured him with kind words and a shared dish of lamb cutlets and fried parsley. Thus fortified, Newman returned on the Wednesday to the viva voce examinations on nine classical texts, only two of which he had seen before, which carried the examination to Thursday evening. On the last two days of the ordeal he found consolation in the motto of serenity and peace of mind set in the glass of Oriel hall – 'Pie repone te' ('Lovingly rest thou') – which was to console him often in the future.[25]

The electors met on Thursday night to choose the two successful candidates, and on Friday morning the Provost's butler was sent round with the news to Newman's lodgings in Seale's, where he was playing his violin. 'This in itself disconcerted the messenger', not accustomed to fiddling Fellows, but the butler's own favoured set form of giving the message was in itself an odd one: ' "he had, he feared, disagreeable news to announce, viz. that Mr Newman was elected Fellow of Oriel, and that his immediate presence was required there" '. Newman thought this 'savoured of impertinent familiarity, merely answered "Very well" and went on fiddling'. He then had to reassure the butler that he had the right rooms and man; but no sooner had the servant left than Newman flung down his instrument and dashed down stairs with all speed to Oriel College, past 'the eloquent faces and eager bows of the tradesmen' now anxious for his custom.[26] At the gate of Oriel, by 'the very tower, which had been the scene of torture', the Fellows waited to welcome him. 'I could bear the presence of Copleston, and many other of the lights of Oriel; but when Keble advanced to take my hand, I quite shrank and could have nearly sunk into the floor, ashamed at so great an honour.'[27] At one o'clock, there was chapel and the two new Fellows were installed, the other one being a blameless future cleric unknown to fame, John Ottley. 'I sat next Keble yesterday at dinner', Newman wrote with awe to Charles, 'and, as I have heard him represented, he is more like an undergraduate than the first man in Oxford – so perfectly unassuming and unaffected in his manner.'[28] They familiarly called him Newman and he was 'abashed to find I must soon learn in turn to call them "Hawkins" "Keble" "Tyler" '.[29] As Oxford understood the matter, he had more than redeemed his disaster in schools. The examination failure had joined the society of the immortals.

It was also tremendous honour for the little college of Trinity. 'I had hardly been in Kinsey's room a minute', wrote Newman to his mother, 'when in rushed Ogle [the mathematics tutor] like one mad. I then proceeded to the President's and in rushed Ogle again. I find that T. rushed to E.'s room, and nearly kicked down the door to communicate the news. E. in turn ran down stairs. Th. heard a noise and my name mentioned, and rushed out also, and in the room opposite found E. W. and Ogle leaping up and down, backwards and forwards. Men rushed in all directions to Trinity to men they knew, to congratulate them of the success of their College.'[30] 'Kinsey is in raptures', Newman reported to Charles, 'and Ogle declares that nothing has given him so great gratification since he came to his present situation, it being uncertain whether he means, since he took his first class, since he became M D, since he undertook the Tutorship of Trinity, or since he married Mrs Ogle.'[31] Some undergraduates complained that they had lost a day's reading by the clamour of the privilege for which Newman had to pay, the ringing of the bells in the three towers of Trinity to proclaim his triumph to all Oxford.

It was a breathless leave-taking. Newman 'ever felt this twelfth of April, 1822, to be the turning point of his life, and of all days most memorable'. 'Trinity had never been unkind to me',[32] he was to recall. But Oriel College was to be the making of him.

Newman owed his election in part to Copleston's contempt for 'the quackery of the Schools'. 'Every election to a fellowship', the Provost later wrote, 'which tends to discourage the narrow and almost the technical routine of public examinations, I consider as an important triumph. You remember Newman himself was an example. He was not even a good classical scholar, yet in mind and powers of composition, and in taste and knowledge, he was decidedly superior to some competitors, who were a class above him in the Schools.'[33] This testimony is a mark of Copleston's own conception of education, 'to *exercise* the mind of the student . . . rather than to pour in knowledge': a principle which Newman was to make the foundation of his *Idea of a University*. Its expression was the Socratic method of Copleston's teaching, a vigorous dialectic with the student which 'taxed the industry of even the most attentive'.[34] Again, it was Copleston who gave the college its philosophical bias towards the study of the ultimate questions of logic and ethics: of logic as the structure of human thought, and of ethics as the mainspring of human action, the fundamentals of all humane studies.

Copleston also gave the college its tone, and the years of his provostship, 1814 to 1828, were the golden age of Oriel, when it made its contribution to the late Georgian 'Oxford renaissance' of scholarly study. It was said of its common room that it 'stank of Logic', and the senior Fellows were collectively known as the 'Noetics', because of their devotion to knowledge. The distinctive atmosphere was symbolized by the circulating teapot which replaced the wine pottle of the other colleges and which caused the standing joke of the undergraduate cry at the gate, 'Well, Porter, does the kettle boil?'[35] This undue sobriety of Oriel was partly responsible for the intellectual sharpness of its debates, which were to be variously described as 'a wholesome intellectual ferment' or 'a morbid intellectual restlessness'.[36]

These were overwhelming surroundings for a shy young man, and at first Newman sat speechless or near stuttering, partly in awe, partly out of his sense of the distinctiveness of his own Calvinist views, partly out of 'a vivid self consciousness, which sometimes inflicted on him days of acute suffering from the recollection of solecisms, whether actual or imagined, which he recognized in his conduct in society'.[37] John Bramston, later Dean of Winchester, was then an undergraduate. Sixty-five years later, Newman reiterated his love to Bramston, who when Newman had scarcely dared look around him 'in the middle of Gentlemen Commoners and recherché wines' had 'sat next to me and took pity on me'.[38] Newman's colleagues, remembering his ill-success in schools, began to doubt their choice – and were alarmed by a 'half malicious' rumour of his violin-playing in public as a member of 'a club of instrumental music', 'a diversion', as Newman somewhat comically recalled it, 'innocent indeed in itself, but scarcely in keeping or in sympathy with an intellectual Common Room'.[39] Someone had to be deputed to draw him out and discover if there was anything in him; the task fell to Richard Whately.

There was no way of being shy with Whately. Recently married, he was only in his mid thirties, nicknamed the 'White Bear', 'some six feet high, and stout – not so much in flesh as in muscle and breadth of bone'.[40] He was a great partygoer who could hold fashionable ladies spellbound for hours, and was celebrated for his appetite, the string of herrings in his room on which he breakfasted, his extravagant dress and his dog Sailor, whom he had trained 'to climb trees in Christ Church meadow and drop from their overhanging branches into the Cherwell'.[41] Less creditably, he liked throwing stones at birds. He sprawled rather than sat and was, wrote Newman, 'free and easy in manners, rough indeed and dogmatic . . . but singularly gracious to undergraduates and young masters, who, if they were worth any thing, were only too happy to be knocked about in argument by such a man'. Indeed, Newman continued, he liked to have 'cubs in hand whom he might lick into shape, and who, he said, like dogs of King Charles's breed, could be held up by one leg without yelling'. Whately's friendship was 'a bright June sun tempered by a March north-easter', his 'sharp, rude, or positive' qualities being offset by 'kindness of heart', 'real gentleness' and a 'generous spirit', especially towards the young.[42]

Whately's first period of influence on Newman lasted only from June until early August in 1822, when he was off with his new wife to his Suffolk rectory. He was not learned or a reader, being concerned about the structure of thought, not its materials; he was writing a textbook on logic, and liked to get through 'the drudgery of composition' by beating out his ideas on the 'anvils' of the people around him. In July, he lent Newman his unpublished 'Analytical Dialogues' to copy out and use as a basis for an article on logic which he had to write for the *Encyclopedia Metropolitana*. Newman had not mastered the subject in his finals, for want of an illuminating text, and Whately's own *Elements of Logic* was to be published four years later, and was to remain a standard student book for many years, by offering an exposition of the subject as the way to the mastery of clear thought. But the book took form in his revisions and corrections of Newman's 'rude essays of a probationer Fellow of twenty one', and pays a warm tribute to Newman's own assistance which Newman himself considered over generous.

43

Whately had discovered that far from making a mistake in its selection, Oriel had appointed in Newman 'the clearest-headed man he knew'.[43] The greater gainer of the two was Newman. As he told its author when the *Elements* appeared, it was Whately who had brought him into the fellowship of his peers and imparted his initial sense of intellectual independence: who, as he recalled to Whately, 'first gave me heart to look about me after my election and taught me to think correctly, and (strange office for an instructor) to rely upon myself'.[44] Whately taught Newman to think, and to think for himself.

Whately's main lesson to Newman was that logic had to be of practical use to life. The young don was also improving his powers of Latin composition on the model of Copleston, and working away at his Greek and Latin authors, Thucydides, Livy and Virgil, in the spirit of the anxious prayer of Psalm 117: 'Prosper Thou the works of my hands upon me, Good Lord, oh prosper Thou my handiwork – '.[45] He had to slave away the summer of 1822 with a paying pupil, 'a little wretch, aged 17';[46] after his departure, Newman wrote to Harriett, 'Liber sum – and I have been humming, whistling, and laughing out loud to myself all day. I can hardly keep from jumping about'.[47] The young man's payment of £90 was the more necessary, as John Henry had now to support Francis in Oxford; having failed to get the lad into Trinity, he had him placed, on 29 November 1822, on the books at Worcester, said to be a cheap college. By the kindness of Tyler, Francis was fed at a reduced rate from the Oriel buttery until he could get college rooms. Newman's diary is full of self-reproaches for his bad temper towards his younger brother, but he assured his mother that Francis was a better mathematician and classicist than he was.[48] 'As to Francis', Newman told his father, 'you will very much distress me, if you think at all of money about him.'[49] Indeed even in his hostile reminiscences of John Henry, Francis acknowledged his elder sibling's generosity. 'I cannot join any of the *panegyrics* on my brother', he wrote, 'yet he was certainly a *high-minded* fanatic in regard to money. My second brother, Charles Robert . . . [would say,] "John ought to have been a Prince; for he always spends money like a Prince". Out of his poverty John spent first on me.'[50]

Newman was earning five guineas a page, then no inconsiderable sum, by writing for the *Encyclopedia Metropolitana*, and by February 1823 he had four pupils, one from Exeter College, 'very docile and very *nice*'. This was a vast improvement on the one pupil of the year before, and he could only marvel at 'the most wonderful and most parental manner in which the Lord has supported Francis and myself . . . '[51] 'How beautiful is the admonition', Newman told his mother, ' "Be careful for nothing . . . " ';[52] though he was to be plagued by want of money, and to have to borrow it and even pray for it, in order to meet Francis' expenses in the coming year. A loan for £60 from Tyler made him 'quite rosy and joyful',[53] while a letter containing £35 produced the ejaculation, 'O gracious Father, how could I for one instant mistrust Thee?'[54]

Newman showed his new fluency in Latin in his oration as Probationer Fellow in Oriel hall: he reread the text fifty-one years later, 'with sad tenderness, as if I loved and pitied the poor boy so ignorant of the future, who then wrote and delivered it before the Provost and Fellows, now almost all dead, but to whom I then looked up with great reverence and loving pride'.[55] Copleston called the discourse 'spirited', firing, or so Newman thought, his vanity; but this received a check when he again failed to win the Latin prize, for an essay on the theme of ancient slavery.

He was convinced of his own good fortune in having got anything at all in the preceding year, in a weaker field of candidates than the one in which, in April 1823, Newman's future ally Edward Bouverie Pusey was elected to a fellowship. This devout and serious young aristocrat, born in 1800, was oppressed by rigid and unbending parents, who refused him leave to marry his beloved Maria Barker. Newman's first view of him captures his unhappiness: 'His light curly head of hair was damp with the cold water which his headaches made necessary for comfort; he walked fast with a young manner of carrying himself, and stood rather bowed, looking up from under his eyebrows, his shoulders rounded, and his bachelor's gown not buttoned at the elbow, but hanging loose over his wrists. His countenance was very sweet, and he spoke little'.[56] In Newman's account, Pusey, oppressed by headache, had torn up his first examination paper in the fellowship competition and withdrawn, only to be forced back to the examination room by his friends; but the examiner, the old-fashioned High Churchman Dr Henry Jenkyns, who later as Canon Professor at Durham won the reputation of being as 'clear as ice, cold as ice, hard as ice', had on this occasion the sense and humanity unusual in examiners to reassemble Pusey's discarded paper from the scraps. Pusey at first worried Newman by a piety which was deep but not Evangelical. 'That Pusey is Thine, O Lord, how can I doubt? . . .' Newman wrote in his journal, 'Yet I fear he is prejudiced against Thy children. Let me never be eager to convert him to a *party* . . . ':[57] an odd sentiment, in the light of their later common history.

Religion was still causing division in the Newman household. Newman's least satisfactory brother, Charles, was indulging the ordinary doubts about Christianity of some of the more sensitive in his generation, like the 'antecedent improbability of eternal punishment' and whether mankind was bad enough to deserve it. An argument between the brothers on these themes took up a walk between Turnham Green and Knightsbridge, Newman insisting that a right understanding of the Scriptures required divine assistance, but that he 'did not confine salvation to one sect – that in any communion whoever sought truth sincerely would not fail of heaven . . .' His temper was not improved by 'a most pelagian discourse' in St Martin-in-the-Fields, denying the essential meaning of Original Sin, and he argued with his father 'with very unbecoming violence', in which mood, character-istically, he blamed himself for letting himself 'degenerate into a contemptu-ous manner' out of pride.[58] Thus on the one hand, he was insisting to Charles that while error in scientific matters was not morally dangerous, a man who erred in religion 'is said to be incapable of true moral excellence, and so exposed to the displeasure of God . . . '[59] On the other hand, on his twenty-third birthday, he found consolation in God for this lack of moral excellence in himself. He was still rather solitary, in spite of his friendship with Pusey, so that Copleston, meeting him on a long walk, uttered with his characteristic courtesy a phrase from Cicero which Newman was to treasure about his seeming double absorption in himself and God: 'Nun-quam minus solus, quàm cùm solus': 'never less alone than when alone'.[60] 'The days and months fly past me', he wrote in his diary, 'and I seem as if I would cling hold of them, and hinder them from escaping. There they lie, entombed in the grave of Time, buried with faults and failings and deeds of all sorts, never to appear till the sounding of the last Trump . . . '[61] The sense that time was short, eternity long, had already laid hands upon him.

5

The Crisis of Evangelicalism

The religious current of the time, however, was changing Newman's view of eternity. In the 1820s Anglican Evangelicalism underwent a major internal crisis in a developing division between, on the one hand, the Clapham Sect moderates, who almost in the spirit of the liberal apostles of progress looked hopefully to the emergence of a Christian culture and a converted world, and, on the other, the more pronouncedly puritan and other-worldly Evangelicals. The latter despised such a reliance on the arm of flesh and, on the basis of their literalist understanding of certain texts in Scripture, espoused a stricter Calvinism, often thought of conversion as necessarily instantaneous, were inclined to decry the need for good works and for obedience to the moral law, considered the Pope to be Antichrist and even expected the imminent return of the Lord to usher the millennium to a darkening and sinful world. The converts to this 'premillennial' view of the Second Advent were to include such leading figures of the Anglican Evangelical party as Edward Bickersteth and the seventh Earl of Shaftesbury. Another well-connected school of premillennial prophets, under the leadership of the great London Presbyterian preacher Edward Irving, in 1830 revived the ancient Pentecostal practice of speaking in tongues and later founded the Catholic Apostolic Church, which adopted a new hierarchy of angels and apostles and a richly Catholic liturgy. Yet another inspired Evangelical visionary, the Church of Ireland clergyman John Nelson Darby, founder of the Plymouth Brethren, taught contempt for human culture, and with Irving laid the foundations of modern fundamentalism. It was Darby whose pure and simple Scripturalism was to win for a time the allegiance of Francis Newman and a number of his Oxford contemporaries. The circles around Irving and Darby in the 1820s included aristocrats and bankers, and represented an old and powerful strand in the Protestant inheritance, but the result of their activity was a 'crisis of Evangelicalism',[1] which helped estrange a number of bright young Evangelicals like Newman from the Protestant tradition altogether and divided the movement at the very moment when it most appeared to be a success.

In a certain sense, Newman was in the other-worldly camp. He held the Pope to be Antichrist, and cared nothing for the this-worldly transforming optimism of Clapham. Without believing in the premillennial Advent, he

47

was fascinated by prophecy, even by the numerology of Daniel and Revelation, and he saw God as the judge of a darkening and sinful world. He was only optimistic in the sense of doubting that human affairs had ever been otherwise. His Calvinism was of the severer type and temper, and took time to outgrow. Even his development of a higher doctrine of baptism and ministry was shared by one strand in radical Evangelicalism, which in the late 1820s found expression in Irving's preaching, and bore its exotic fruit in the formation of the Catholic Apostolic Church.[2] But Newman's conversion had not been instantaneous, he was even over concerned with good works, and he was distinguished from the majority of radical Evangelicals by his moralism, his desire for holiness, his Christian humanist love of culture and of Oxford, and his slowly growing appreciation of the doctrines of Tradition and of Holy Mother Church.

The first sustained attempt to change his religious views was made by the new Regius Professor of Divinity, Charles Lloyd, a sort of ecclesiastical Dr Johnson. In preparing for ordination, Newman and a number of young Fellows, including Pusey, attended Lloyd's lectures, though they were more in the nature of a catechism of the class which had to prepare to reply to Lloyd's questions on the basis of prior reading. The lecturer was at once impatient of Newman's Evangelical views while showing his liking and respect for him. Lloyd perambulated his classroom and 'was free and easy in his ways, and a bluff talker, with a rough lively good natured manner, and a pretended pomposity relieving itself in sudden bursts of laughter, . . . large in person beyond his years, . . . and taking snuff, . . . he would sometimes stop before Mr Newman, . . . fix his eyes on him as if to look him through, with a satirical expression of countenance, and then make a feint to box his ears or kick his shins . . . '[3]

Though 'constrained and awkward' in his presence, Newman found 'nothing offensive or ungracious in all this',[4] and held the lecturer in the same affection as the other pupils, the more so when after only six months in the class Lloyd suggested that he undertake some major work of scholarship. Lloyd also taught that the Prayer Book was adapted from the primitive and medieval missal and breviary, a point to be later elaborated by the *Origines Liturgicae* of another High Churchman, William Palmer. But Lloyd devoted most of his attention to what Newman was always to find the least sympathetic way of recommending religion, by external proofs of it from creation and history, and though Newman always held him in 'affectionate and grateful memory' he left Lloyd's lecture room as he entered it, a Calvinist, and Lloyd did not 'leave a mark upon his mind, as Whately had done'.[5]

His attendance on the lectures almost ceased, when he found his first parochial cure through the good offices of Pusey, the curacy of the parish of St Clement's, Oxford. The Rector, John Gutch, was incapacitated and nearing eighty, and the church needed rebuilding to accommodate a growing population of fifteen hundred souls, and to reclaim them from the dissenting meeting houses and alehouses, into which, as Newman put it, making no distinction between them, the people 'have been driven for want of convenient Sunday worship'.[6] The curacy was not worth more than £50 a year, but the young curate had the energy for other work. After finishing an article on Cicero, work got for him by Whately, for the *Metropolitana* at four in the morning, he took charge of Walter Mayers' pupils by walking the eighteen miles to Mayers' parish of Worton by breakfast. His new priestly task meant much more to him than a career. He was ordained deacon in Christ Church on 13 June 1824, noting the date with an emotional outburst in his diary. 'It is over. I am thine, O Lord; I seem quite dizzy, and cannot altogether believe and understand it. At first, after the hands were laid on me, my heart shuddered within me; the words "for ever" are so terrible . . . At times indeed my heart burnt within me, particularly during the singing of the Veni Creator. Yet, Lord, I ask not for comfort in comparison of sanctification . . . I feel as a man thrown suddenly into deep water.'[7]

'It is over. I am thine, O Lord.' Perhaps any Evangelical might have said and written so, but Newman's own consciousness of his supreme dignity and responsibility as a priest was one source of that higher doctrine of priestly ministry which was to take him where few Evangelicals would go. Again, like Thomas Scott, indeed like many Evangelicals, who disliked the popular stress upon conversion rather than holiness of life, there was nothing un-Evangelical in Newman's reference to sanctification; it was just that his Evangelical doctrine of sanctification was to carry him into a Catholic one.

There was also the influence of Oriel itself, and especially of Edward Hawkins, Vicar of the central Oxford parish of St Mary the Virgin, a dull man to the outside world, and an obsessive hypochondriac; 'on the ground of health he never drank wine, and was accustomed to say that he should not live beyond forty'.[8] He lived to be over ninety. To Newman, however, he was a fanatical precisionist of cool and calculating temper, whose accuracy of utterance and expression left another mark upon his mind. Though there were only twelve years between them, the relationship with Hawkins was 'virtually that of Tutor and pupil'[9] and began after Whately's departure, but deepened in the summer of 1824. Hawkins taught Newman 'to weigh my words, and to be cautious in my statements. He led me to that mode of limiting and clearing my sense in discussion and in controversy, and of distinguishing between cognate ideas, and of obviating mistakes by anticipation, which to my surprise has been since considered, even in quarters friendly to me, to savour of the polemics of Rome'.[10] Thus Newman's mental habit of making sharp and subtle distinctions was in origin Oxonian rather than Papist, and came from Oriel and Hawkins. It was this precision in Oxford men, raised like Newman on Aristotle's logic rather than on the splendid abstractions of Plato, that so annoyed the religious rivals of Samuel Wilberforce and the political opponents of Gladstone, and made Thomas

Huxley, with his very different scientific training, so heartily suspect all three.

Of course, Hawkins had no desire to lead Newman to Rome, but he acted as the primary dissolvent of his Evangelicalism. Thus he moderated the language in Newman's first written sermon, which in the starkest Calvinist manner, 'divided the Christian world into two classes, the one all darkness, the other all light . . . ' But, claimed Hawkins, 'religious and moral excellence is a matter of degree. Men are not either saints or sinners; but they are not so good as they should be, and better than they might be, – more or less converted to God'.[11] This was exactly what Newman found. At one of his earliest death-beds, the dying man made all the right professions; but Newman afterwards discovered that he had been a drunkard, and his wife neglectful. 'I was too gentle', Newman wrote when made aware of his error. ' – Lord, pardon me – .'[12]

There was, then, both good and evil among his parishioners, and that made the Calvinist distinction an unreal one: it was impossible to divide them into sheep and goats on the basis of either their everyday belief or behaviour. Rather, their conduct indicated a complexity in their moral and religious condition to which Evangelicalism did not do justice. By 1825, Newman was on the point of repudiating a central strand in his Calvinism, because of a growing conviction, 'gained by personal experience, that the religion which he had received from John Newton and Thomas Scott would not work in a parish; that it was unreal; that this he had actually found as a fact, as Mr Hawkins had told him beforehand; that Calvinism was not a key to the phenomena of human nature, as they occur in the world'.[13]

Yet all of this required a painful mental adjustment. Newman had to reshape his whole intellectual landscape, and that required hard dogmatic thought. Hawkins particularly criticized one aspect of Newman's sermon for implying a denial of the doctrine of Baptismal Regeneration, which High Churchmen, like Richard Mant in his work of 1812, an *Appeal to the Gospel*, believed was taught in the Church of England's *Book of Common Prayer*, and which declared that a child at his baptism was automatically washed from the stain of original sin and reborn in the spirit to a new state of life.[14] The strictest Evangelicals taught instead that regeneration went with conversion: with an experience, not a rite. There were a number of intermediate doctrines by which moderate Evangelicals strove to give an acceptable meaning to the Prayer Book's words; Mayers taught Newman that while baptism might sometimes confer a full interior regeneration, for others there was only an exterior regeneration admitting the child to the visible Church, inferior to the completeness of spiritual regeneration itself.[15] The Evangelical position implied the sharp distinction between the visible Church of the baptized and the invisible Church of the elect; and Newman's objection to the fuller church teaching was the concrete and practical one, that the mass of baptized Christians showed no evidence of their new regenerate condition.

The gulf between God's chosen and the rest was not a baptismal rite which had been externally applied to all: it was an invisible change in the mind and heart, a conscious new sonship to the Father of lights, bearing fruit in a devout and holy life.

Yet Newman could only consider the argument afresh by looking more deeply into his Calvinist assumptions, when Hawkins had him read *Apostolical Preaching considered in an Examination of St Paul's Epistles*, by a future Archbishop of Canterbury, John Bird Sumner, a spokesman for the moderate Evangelical Churchmanship which the Evangelical radicals were to make more self-conscious. Sumner thought it unprovable that Paul had preached individual election and predestination to the unconverted; so that even if the Apostle had believed in Calvinist doctrines, they were no part of his regular preaching and should not figure in ours. Where Paul speaks of election, it was of groups, not of individuals; indeed the doctrines of individual election and of a special 'efficacious grace' for the elect were immoral and Antinomian in tendency, leading logically to that belief in Final Perseverence which Paul expressly contradicts.[16]

Sumner did not say that all Calvinist doctrine was false – but that even if true, it was uncertainly scriptural, no part of ordinary Apostolic preaching, often unhappy in its moral effects and therefore not for everyday use. Thus Sumner's point was primarily pastoral, which carried weight with the young curate. Sumner did not teach the High Church doctrine of automatic Baptismal Regeneration. Newman saw, however, that he ought on the basis of clearer intellectual alternatives to adopt either Calvinism or Baptismal Regeneration, though for the moment he wished 'to steer clear of both, at least in preaching', and got 'so distressed and low about it' one evening that he even thought 'I must leave the Church'.[17]

By 13 January 1825, however, he wrote, possibly in reference to Lloyd's lectures, that 'the great stand is to be made, *not* against those who connect a spiritual change with baptism, but those who deny a spiritual change altogether',[18] and Sumner's book had the unintended result 'beyond any thing else, in routing out evangelical doctrines from Mr Newman's Creed'.[19] In May 1825, on his ordination as a priest in Christ Church, he reflected on the great distance he had travelled in the past year. 'Then, I thought there were many in the visible Church of Christ, who have never been visited by the Holy Ghost; now, I think there are none but probably, nay almost certainly, have been visited by Him . . . Then, I thought the *onus probandi* lay with those who asserted an individual to be a real Christian; and now I think it lies with those who deny it.' He was still not maintaining that 'the Spirit always or generally accompanies the very act of baptism', but he had concluded that all his parishioners had probably received a visitation of the Spirit and a measure of divine grace, even though they were 'weak and uncertain'[20] in their religious opinions. The turning point had clearly come.

Calvinism, however, had attracted Newman partly because it had an intellectual cutting edge and claimed to satisfy the mind. Now that this clear doctrinal system was in question, he was not prepared to rest in ambiguity and vagueness; he wanted a dogmatic system, a coherent statement of what religion taught. If Calvinism was untrue, perhaps sacramental Christianity was true. The doctrine of baptism was a kind of test case of the two systems. The alternative to regeneration at conversion was regeneration at baptism: and even from the Calvinist viewpoint, the second had its strengths. If God chose his people in baptism, then the gratuity of his choice was enhanced. The infant did not have the power to choose God; in baptism God chose him, baptizing whom he would as electing whom he would. Nor was faith a condition for this choice, which was why the Church could baptize new babies: rather faith was a fruit of election which the baptized in maturer years would be called upon to show. Moreover Calvinism, thought Newman, tended to acknowledge a man's faith only if he manifested it in works which then became a public test of faith. Outward conduct – the conduct of other-worldliness – then became the badge of Christian Churchmanship, rather than a rite whose spiritual consequence was visible to the eye of faith alone.

But on the basis of Baptismal Regeneration, the only test of the Christian is that conferred in baptism, for there is a baptismal grace of liberation from sin and admission to Christ's kingdom in all the baptized, perhaps even in those who show it least. All church members have received the spiritual privileges purchased for them by Christ, which have not wholly been eclipsed by actual sinning. The worst of Christians has this privilege, even though he still has a duty to improve upon it, in a life of Christian faith and holiness. Christians have received a tremendous gift, and though when it lies neglected, it may come to nothing, the giver will never take it away.

Yet the strength of the Evangelical position had been that it demanded a response both in an inner experience and outward works; and there was an obvious objection to the claim that the real spiritual condition of a child was changed by pouring water on his head and uttering a formula. Baptismal Regeneration seemed to separate experience and doctrine: the babe felt nothing and believed nothing in baptism; nor perhaps do some adults. Newman's point was, however, a practical, a moral one: that regeneration properly belonged to a realm of mystery, from which the obvious public testing displaced it. To submit the mystery and complexity of baptism to inspection and human judgement was to deny its spiritual and moral power. Even a non-believer might feel that the rite would more deeply influence mankind if Christians believed that it produced its own effects of itself, rather than by judging it critically against an experience or conduct which had no divine guarantee.

It was, however, possible for an Evangelical to hold that elected children were regenerate in baptism, in virtue of their election and the faith of their sponsors; it was far more difficult for him to assert that *all* baptized children were regenerate. On that basis, the words of the service were a charitable presumption, like the presumption in the burial service that the dead man was in heaven – not an assurance that the rite would have effect. Yet the subject was still a grey area in the 1820s: it was conflict in the following decades between High and Low Churchmen which was to sharpen the Evangelical position into a denial of Baptismal Regeneration altogether. The change in Newman's position did not mean a final severing of his links with Evangelicalism; but it directed him towards a new theological system founded upon a conviction of the tremendous value of the rite of admission to the visible Church.

Again, it was Oriel which set him on this path. One Fellow of the college, the somewhat eccentric and ineffective Revd William James, taught Newman the doctrine of the Apostolic Succession – that the Church enjoys a continuity of life and teaching authority and ministry with the Church of the Apostles. This occurred in 1823, 'in the course of a walk, I think, round Christ Church meadow', and it is not clear that the teaching then took hold: 'I recollect', he wrote in the *Apologia*, 'being somewhat impatient of the subject at the time'.[21] It was Hawkins, however, whose sermon on the related topic of Tradition converted Newman to the belief that the Bible 'was never intended to teach doctrine, but only to prove it'.[22] The Church is to teach, the Bible to prove the Church's teaching, which is essentially contained in the catechisms and creeds; or, in other words, the teaching of Christianity comes from the living Church and the Bible sustains the Church's teaching. Hawkins' exposition fell short of later High Anglican doctrine, but it sowed the seeds of Newman's full-blown development into the belief that Christianity reaches far beyond the individual Bible-reading Christian into the infinitely varied collective experience of Christ's Church. There have always been, of course, Christian solitaries; but this is not the general vocation which the God of Scripture intended for mankind.

6

Evangelical to Liberal

Among the new curate's first death-beds was his father's, in his late fifties, on 29 September 1824:

> That dread event has happened. Is it possible! O my Father, where art Thou? I got to Town Sunday morning. He knew me, tried to put out his hand and said 'God bless you'. Towards the evening of Monday he said his last words. He seemed in great peace of mind. He could, however, only articulate, 'God bless you, thank my God, thank my God['] – and lastly 'my dear.' Dr C. came on Wednesday, and pronounced him dying; he might live 12 hours. Towards evening we joined in prayer, commending his soul to God. Of late he had thought his end approaching. One day on the river, he told my Mother, 'I shall never see another summer'. On Thursday he looked beautiful, such calmness, sweetness, composure, and majesty were in this countenance. Can a man be a materialist who sees a dead body? . . . [1]

Seventeen months later on his birthday, Newman was overwhelmed by his sense of ingratitude to his father, reflecting 'with much bitterness that I might have softened his afflictions much by kind attentions which I neglected. I was cold, stiff, reserved. I know I hurt him much . . . Why could I not have said how much I owed to him, his kindness in sending me to Oxford &c &c . . . It is over, irrevocable. O for a moment to ask his forgiveness . . .'[2]

In this he was no harder on himself than on others. Lloyd told Pusey that while Newman's parishioners liked their new curate, they thought that he 'damned them too much' – not, Newman considered, by dwelling on hell-fire, but 'on the corruption of the heart'.[3] Yet Newman was also capable of tenderness: one of his early death-beds was that of a twenty-two year old woman whom he had assiduously visited, and whose eyes at their last meeting 'looked at me with such a meaning, I felt a thrill I cannot describe – it was like the gate of heaven . . .'[4] He was on good terms with the local Dissenting minister, feeling that he needed an ally against the sheer weight of irreligion, and assured Dissenters that he would be happy to do them any service out of church, while still maintaining that a 'good dissenter is

of course incomparably better than a bad Churchman – but a good Churchman I think better than a good dissenter'.[5]

In October 1824, he became Junior Treasurer of Oriel, and by December
was raising thousands of pounds for the new St Clement's: the subscriptions
included £100 from one of the University's MPs, his future antagonist Sir
Robert Peel, while Pusey gave a stove to the Sunday school which Newman
set up in February 1825. Other, more academic, duties crowded in: in
March, Whately, newly appointed Principal of St Alban Hall, a small and
undistinguished residence for weaker exiles from the colleges, made Newman
his Vice-Principal, and effectively 'Dean, Tutor, and Bursar',[6] as well as
acting Principal in Whately's absence. This left little time for scholarship,
though Newman showed his uneasiness with the radical Evangelical millen-
arian school by denying in a review the Revd Edward Cooper's argument
that Napoleon was Antichrist. Newman was also kept busy with his pastoral
duties at St Clement's, which included an attempt to secure the discharge
from the army of a parishioner who had deserted his wife and ten children.
He drove away the singers at the church by taking down their gallery, a
high-handed clerical act which augured ill for the innumerable such disputes
in the Church of England in the future.

Newman dated from early in 1825 his intimacy with Henry Woodgate, a
kind and lovable young man who was another of Whately's anvils, and who
dined with him fortnightly for some years. In May 1825, he lost his beloved
paternal grandmother Elizabeth Newman, aged ninety-two: 'Thou hast
made her my earliest benefactor', he wrote, 'and how she loved me!'[7] She
had delighted in the wayward humour of the black sheep Charles, and there
was another foretaste of things to come in Newman's correspondence with
Charles, who had announced his conversion to the anti-religious Socialist
views of Robert Owen, who, Charles asserted, 'for practical motives to
action . . . beats St Paul hollow . . .'[8]

It is in his letters to Charles over his apostasy that Newman began his
long debate with unbelief. He concluded that as the 'internal evidence
[of Christianity] depends a great deal on *moral feeling*', so the rejection of
Christianity arises 'from a fault of the *heart*, not of the *intellect* . . . not from
mere error of reasoning, but either from pride or from sensuality.'[9] 'We
survey moral and religious subjects through the glass of previous habits;
and scarcely two persons use a glass of the same magnifying power.' Charles'
error, then, lay in supposing that 'unassisted reason is competent to discover
moral and religious truth', for people differ about religion by temperament
and personality, and when given the ignorance in us of many things 'beyond
the reach of our present reason, . . . it is perhaps *impossible* now to prove to
us' the Christian revelation from God.[10]

It is difficult today to recapture the mental climate, dominated by the
Revd William Paley's *Evidences of Christianity* and *Natural Theology*, in which
the claims of religion were thought to be susceptible of certain external

55

proofs, from the evidences of divine design in creation and of divine providence in history. Newman himself was feeling his way towards a more sophisticated view of religious and philosophical conviction in which a person's character and dispositions have a part in forming his beliefs.

It was, unfortunately, all too clear that whether Charles' opinions were right or wrong, his infidelity was rooted in a mental condition which was twice to lead the family to get an opinion on his sanity. Newman père had doubted Charles' ability to support himself, and in 1825, John Henry, through Bowden, got Charles a job as clerk in the Bank of England. But Charles remained an irritant. 'Why is it you thus persecute me?', burst out Newman to him in 1828, to a demand for an immediate reply to a letter. '. . . It is hard I may not be left alone . . . Years past you have from time to time attacked and insulted me, forcing me into correspondence from which to *you* no good could ensue.'[11]

The irritant was, moreover, a costly one. Charles' Socialist convictions brought him into conflict with the Bank's directors, and he resigned his post in 1832. When Newman was on the continent in 1832–3, Charles got hold of and ran through his inheritance from his mother of £1000, which, as he put it, he might as well have thrown in the gutter. In 1833, as an usher at a school in Herstmonceux in Sussex, he bit a boy and quarrelled with his principal, then lived with a woman not his wife who neglected and exploited him; she left him locked up and pawned his clothes for money in order to get drunk, and he had to be rescued from her squalid clutches by his strong-minded aunt Elizabeth. He had a series of brief jobs as a schoolmaster before spending three years from 1842 in Bonn. Because Charles' Socialism taught him that his character was not his responsibility but simply the result of circumstance, 'just as if he were a cripple or bedridden', noted Newman, so he was resigned to living on his family. This comfortable doctrine left John Henry and Francis with half a life-time's duty of subsidizing the unrepentant prodigal, who none the less inconsistently resented his dependence, and broke out 'into acts of wildness and cruelty, chiefly towards his relations'.[12] Towards the end, Newman paid tribute to his brother's abilities – his knowledge of French and German, his philosophical acumen and his personal qualities, 'upright, sensitively honest, generous, openhanded, and affectionate'. These were, unfortunately, spoiled by 'preposterous pride and want of common sense', an insistence on his equality with his superiors, and a fatal indecision, like Baldassarre in George Eliot's *Romola*, 'whose memory and mind gave way suddenly whenever he had come to the point of reaching to some decisive act'. Charles' own opinion was that 'all the Newmans are mad', only Francis being madder than John Henry. As the only atheist in the family and the least satisfactory of all the Newmans, Charles' 'aimless, profitless, forlorn life'[13] can only have pointed the moral of the pointlessness of existence without religion, and reinforced Newman's developing view that atheism had its origins in some personal defect or moral failure.

Newman found another armoury of arguments against unbelief congenial to his temper in the eighteenth-century Bishop Joseph Butler's *Analogy of Religion*, which had been written against the Deists, and which he began to read in June 1825. From this he took the principle that God's way of telling mankind about himself in natural and revealed religion is complex and mysterious, on the model of his working through Nature. But where Butler's argument along these lines is rather commonsense in character, as befitted his own prosaic personality and that of his century, Newman read him in romantic mood as teaching, like Keble in his poetry, that Creation is a mysterious sacramental manifestation of the Godhead, showing its divine author in the broken and partial manner which was, rationally considered, a characteristic of religion itself. This oddly tied in with Newman's sense of 'the unreality of material phenomena', which were, *sub specie aeternitatis*, no more than the symbols of a reality greater than themselves. The second main point which Newman took from Butler was that 'Probability is the very guide of life'.[14] This was ultimately to suggest to Newman that in so far as religious conviction is reasonable, it results, not from Whately's kind of binding syllogistic logic, but from 'an *assemblage* of concurring and converging probabilities'.[15] But then, the probabilities accumulated in one mind are absent from another: and that was to be a significant part of the final answer to Charles.

There was, however, an intellectual radicalism in Newman's letters to Charles which was perhaps most apparent in his attitude to Scripture, and which never left him. He told his younger brother 'that the New Testament is not Christianity, but the *record* of Christianity', which 'is not overthrown by the detection of spuriousness or faultiness in its own professed books, much less is it by errors, granting such, in the Old Testament'.[16] This was certainly light years from the scriptural literalism of the time. He was, in any case, becoming more liberal himself. In March 1825, he undertook to write articles about the pagan miracle-worker Apollonius of Tyana and about the subject of miracles for the *Metropolitana*, and though he maintained the standard distinction between reliable scriptural and unreliable extra-scriptural miracles, his reading included such sceptical writers as Hume and Conyers Middleton, and of the last he later thought that he 'had imbibed a portion of his spirit'. In 1826, he projected an article, never written, on the Ante-Nicene Church for the *Metropolitana*, but he afterwards declared his language about the Fathers in the encyclopedia 'flippant', even while he considered that the Church of the Fathers had always remained his 'beau ideal'.[17]

This liberalism arose from the eclipse of Newman's Evangelical Calvinism, which left him as open to rationalist arguments as to sacramentalism. 'A cold Arminian doctrine, the first stage of Liberalism was the characteristic aspect, both of the high and dry Anglicans of that day and of the Oriel divines', he recalled of himself. 'There was great reason then to expect that on Newman's leaving the crags and precipices of Luther and Calvin, he would take refuge in the flats of Tillotson and Barrow, Jortin and Paley':[18] that is, with the divines of the liberal and rationalist Latitudinarian tradition, who in his view reduced Christianity to a provable minimum of what Christians must believe.

The influence upon him of one of the 'Oriel divines' of rationalist temper, Whately, was at its height in 1825, but it was in 1826 that Whately gave Newman's thought another turn by publishing anonymously – he never admitted to the authorship – his *Letters on the Church. By an Episcopalian*. This work, he told Newman, would make his blood boil, with its argument 'that Church and State should be independent of each other';[19] that while the Church owed obedience to the State in temporals, the State had no power over it in matters spiritual, as the Church was not the creation or creature of the State, but had its foundation and authority in Christ. 'Let churchmen then, not the *clergy* only, but all members of your Church . . . protest and petition . . . against the profanation of Christ's kingdom, by that *double usurpation*, the interference of the Church in temporals, and of the State in spirituals', wrote Whately; ' . . . we ask of the government only that protection which it is bound to extend to all classes; – as a Church, we ask nothing of it, but TO LET US ALONE!'[20]

This was a call, which in its radical and agitatory rhetoric, anticipates the Oxford Movement itself. The point was certainly foreign to the dominant Erastian temper of Anglican Christianity, in which, whatever the theory of Church–State relations, in practice the State had usually controlled the Church. Just as the so-called liberal Hawkins had taught Newman the value of Tradition, so Whately supplied the second Catholic principle of the Oxford Movement, 'the idea of the Christian Church, as a divine appointment, and as a substantive visible body, independent of the State, and endowed with rights, prerogatives, and powers of its own'.[21]

Yet in 1826, Whately's influence on Newman was otherwise on the wane. In January, Newman decided to accept a tutorship in Oriel after Easter, and that would greatly increase his work load in the college. On 21 February, he resigned both his Vice-Principalship at St Alban Hall and his curacy at St Clement's. His parish clerk afterwards declared 'that Mr Newman's labours in that parish far exceeded any that could be named in other Oxford parishes at that date'.[22] The Fellows of Oriel were up until nearly 2 a.m. on the morning of Friday 31 March to elect two new members, Robert Wilberforce and Richard Hurrell Froude: 'may God be with us', wrote Newman in his diary.[23] Wilberforce, the son of the great Evangelical emancipator of the slaves, was to be one of the leading High Church theologians of his day, before like Newman becoming a Roman Catholic. But the new transforming influence on Newman was Froude's. Even on Froude's election,

Newman described him to his mother as 'one of the acutest and clearest and deepest men in the memory of man'.[24] Whately may have suggested the principle of the Oxford Movement, but it was Froude's attitudes and activities from which the Movement was to come.

The 'bright and beautiful' Richard Hurrell Froude was the sort of figure more likely by his wit and charm to dazzle his contemporaries than posterity, which can only know him through his occasional writings. Born in 1803, the eldest son of Robert Hurrell Froude, Archdeacon of Totnes and Rector of Dartington in Devonshire, Hurrell was the type of right-wing intellectual counter-revolutionary perhaps more common on the continent than in Britain, where conservatives usually like to consider themselves stupid. In the *Apologia* Newman paid tribute to 'the gentleness and tenderness of nature, the playfulness, the free elastic force and graceful versatility of mind, and the patient winning considerateness in discussion, which endeared him to those to whom he opened his heart'.[25] Yet Froude had been left an emotional orphan by the death of his dissatisfied, beautiful and fragile mother, and while he inherited his father's convictions, his early bereavement may have sharpened the streak of cruelty in him which had led him to torment his younger brother James Anthony, the future historian. He came to a kind of happiness through his hero-worship of the sanctity of John Keble, who assuaged but did not abolish those deeper feelings of guilt which may – the evidence is slight – have been rooted in an ambiguous sexuality. On entering Oriel, he set out to practise in secret an amateur Catholic asceticism, sleeping on the floor and denying himself food, which he recorded in the diary that Keble and Newman were to be so ill-advised as to publish to a mocking or hostile world.

Froude's *outré* temperament, the reverse of Newman's in this, also found expression in a love of daredevil escapades and hard physical recreation such as riding, sailing, skating and hunting, in a hatred of shams, and in a ruthless logic and a taste for barbed epigrams, directed especially against progressives, 'march of mind' men, and other proponents of the burgeoning liberalism of the age. His religious attitudes might be considered advanced or reactionary, according to prejudice. His dislike of the Reformers and affection for the most ardent apostles of sacerdotal power in the medieval Church, and even for the Puritan champions of ecclesiastical theocracy, were to make him the father-founder of Anglo-Catholic clericalism, if not of Anglican Ultramontanism; and Newman's summary of Froude's developed position shows the direction of the school which he helped to form. 'He felt scorn of the maxim, "The Bible and the Bible only is the religion of Protestants"; and he gloried in accepting Tradition as a main instrument of religious teaching. He had a high severe idea of the intrinsic excellence of Virginity; and he considered the Blessed Virgin its great Pattern.'[26] These were developments subsequent to his entry into Oriel. His belief in the Real Presence in the Blessed Sacrament, in medieval miracles and in self-mortification and penance were to offer Anglicanism a new ideal of sanctity, and to become an essential part of Newman's view of things as well.

All this as yet lay hidden in the future. At first, Froude was repelled by Newman's vestigial Evangelicalism and incipient liberalism, but Francis Newman had already scented crypto-popery in his brother in a sermon teaching Baptismal Regeneration, and in an incident variously dated but possibly occurring in 1824 when John presented him, to his horror, with a papistical engraving of 'La Madonna col Divoto', showing the Virgin Mary with mendicant supplicants.[27] Yet there is little contemporary evidence of the bitterness of after years, except in John Henry's self-reproaches for ill-treating his sibling, and John was proud of Francis when in May 1826 he took his final examinations. 'I hereby send you a young person from Oxford, to whom I hope you will be kind for my sake', wrote John to his mother. ' . . . You must indulge him in some things poor young gentleman – he has got some odd ideas in his head of his having been lately examined . . . and of a general belief in Oxford that his name will appear in both first classes . . . He can mend shoes, string pianos, cut out skreens [sic], and go on errands . . . I forgot to say that he could sharpen knives. – He is very docile, while kindly treated, and quite harmless. – Do not frighten him . . . '[28] Francis took his double first a week later, and it was as a brother in arms in the fight for God that Newman greeted him on his twenty-first birthday, in verses which also recalled that they had been the twin favourites of their grandmother:

> My brother, we are link'd with chain
>   That time shall ne'er destroy;
> Together we have been in pain,
>   Together now in joy;
> For duly I to share may claim
> The present brightness of thy name . . .
>
> Dear Frank, we both are summon'd now
>   As champions of the Lord; –
> Enroll'd am I, and shortly thou
>   Must buckle on thy sword;
> A high employ, nor lightly given
> To serve as messengers of heaven! . . .
>
> O! may we follow undismay'd
>   Where'er our God shall call!
> And may His Spirit's present aid
>   Uphold us lest we fall!
> Till in the end of days we stand,
> As victors in a deathless land.[29]

There is, however, the suggestion of an opening of a rift between the brothers in a sixty-six quarto page document, 'Remarks on Infant Baptism 1827',[30] with which John tried to convince his sisters against Frank of the truth of Baptismal Regeneration. Here were the hints of those high claims of Newman's priesthood which were to break and sunder and divide them.

This same high view of priesthood carried Newman into a religious understanding of his duty to his pupils. As one of the tutors of his college, Newman was sorely tested, for his 'sacred' view of his tutorial role was revolutionary. 'He began by setting himself fiercely against the Gentlemen-Commoners, young men of birth, wealth or prospects, whom he considered (of course with real exceptions) to be the scandal and the ruin of the place.'[31] One of these young men, later Sir Charles Murray, always considered Newman a coward for not having interrupted the merry party who cut the bell-rope by which he had been summoning the porter to stop their late night singing. Another, James Howard Harris, afterwards the third Earl of Malmesbury, alleged in his old age that Newman's class had advanced his table until he was jammed into a corner.[32] It seems that the last story belongs to another tutor, William James, and was promptly contradicted by another of Newman's pupils and later disciple, Frederic Rogers, Lord Blachford; and the imputation of cowardice is difficult to reconcile with Newman's active campaign against the college rowdies.

But with the studious aiming for honours, 'he cultivated relations, not only of intimacy, but of friendship, and almost of equality, putting off, as much as might be, the martinet manner then in fashion with college tutors, and seeking their society in outdoor exercise, on evenings, and in Vacation'.[33] His main object was to make his pupils devout, and he annoyed Copleston and Tyler by querying the requirement that students receive communion once a term. When Newman complained that an undergraduate champagne breakfast had followed the rite, Tyler did not 'wish to know it,'[34] though to Newman, this was a profanation of the Sacrament. In these matters lay the beginnings of his religious influence on students, for whom he offered a pastoral care which, despite discouragement from the college authorities, widened the office of tutor beyond the formal task of academic instruction.

There was another portent for the future in the strange individual who joined the Oriel common room in October 1826. Joseph Blanco White had been a Canon of Seville Cathedral and had been seduced away to the liberal cause and then to England, before coming via Unitarianism to the Anglican ministry. He had gained an Oxford diploma and a reputation, not least in the most illiberal High Tory and Orange Protestant quarters, by his writings which drew on his reminiscences of Spain, attacking the Roman Catholic Church and providing the argument for the opponents of Catholic Emancipation that, as slaves to priests and the Pope, Roman Catholics were not entitled to full civic equality. He shared Newman's love of the violin, and was to instruct Newman's friends in the use of the Roman Breviary, while warning Newman that the logic of his ideas was leading him Romewards. He was to mourn the decline of so refined a mind as Newman into bigotry, but his own later relapse into Unitarianism was again to prove to Newman the instability of the faith of the Oriel Noetic circle, though it was Whately, whose liberalism was suspect anyway, and who had taken White to Dublin as a tutor to his children, who was to suffer the deeper embarrassment. Where, in this flux of opinions, was a lasting resting place? Newman later thought that he had been 'beginning to prefer intellectual excellence to moral; I was drifting in the direction of the Liberalism of the day. I was rudely awakened from my dream at the end of 1827 by two great blows – illness and bereavement'.[35] But for the moment, he was content to go with the tide.

7

Liberal to High Churchman

'Do you know that Bishop's wigs are made of *cow*hair . . . nay from cow *tail*?'[1] Newman asked his mother. This irreverence was more seriously expressed in his puzzlement over the sense in which Christ was fully God, and in a sermon 'On the Mediatorial Kingdom of Christ' in Oriel chapel in May 1827 he considered the terms of the Athanasian Creed 'unnecessarily scientific', compared with the Nicene Creed. He later recognized that he had been indulging the freedom of languge, afterwards declared heretical, about the Son's subordination as if he was inferior to the Father, which had been common in the early Christian centuries before the Council of Nicaea. The crypto-liberals of Oriel were shocked: though Copleston liked the sermon, Whately 'accused it of Arianism. Hawkins thought it dangerous, and Blanco White thought it systematized more than Scripture does'.[2] It was the high point of Newman's liberalism, and was ironic in so far as, he was rather unfairly later to muse, 'Whately, Hawkins, and Blanco White, were all verging then towards Sabellianism themselves'[3] – Sabellianism and Arianism being for the later Newman touchstones of the heresy of denying fully divine honours to Christ.

Yet there was now a High Church influence on Newman as well, in the person of John Keble. Keble was born in 1792, the son of a country priest, also named John, and never thought of any calling but the ministry. He went up to Oxford in 1807, proved himself the most brilliant student of his generation, took double first class honours in 1810, and was elected a Fellow of Oriel in 1811. He resigned his Oriel tutorship in 1823 to become his father's curate, and it was only in 1836 that he became Vicar of Hursley where he lived for thirty years until his death. He held, however, no high ecclesiastical or academic office beyond his fellowship, except the Oxford professorship of poetry. Otherwise he was buried for forty years as the curate and vicar of country parishes, in a life well-hidden from the world.

Why was such a brilliant student so unrewarded by his Church? The answer lies partly in the controversial character of his religious opinions, but more in his acute sense of his own 'limitations'. These were imposed by his shyness and reserve: a personal reserve which he was to turn into a principle of aesthetic theory, and a dogma in theology. At a simpler level he had no wish to shine. He deliberately made his university teaching dull

– something most academics achieve without effort – lest others should wrongly praise him. He took as a motto the injunction 'Don't be original', and he was ideally placed to transform his tradition because his sole aim was to keep it as it was. His early views were more liberal than they later became; for all his celebrated gentleness with his friends, any boy who failed to raise his cap to Keble in his parish received a stick across his shoulders. But his own young manhood was dominated by his love for his father, and his highest ideal was to perpetuate his father's kind of rural ministry. Thus his loyalty to his Church was too strong to be broken, so that he felt no temptation to join the Church of Rome because of the sins of the Church of England. The Church might apostatize almost everywhere, he thought, but it would still survive whole within his own parish. His father gave him the old-fashioned High Church loyalty to the religious establishment and its parochial system and what went with them, strong Tory politics, and a love for England and King George.

These formidable convictions might have seemed a ruinous legacy. The conventional historiographical view is that in the eighteenth century, High Churchmanship fell on evil days, often declining into pure politics. Many so-called High Churchmen were simply Church-and-King Tories, zealots for the Tory party and the traditional connection between Church and State, 'Erastians' acquiescing in a Babylonian Captivity wherein the Church was state-controlled. Their fiercest passions were hating Methodists and loving tithes; they were untheological, sometimes irreligious. Among the notorious 'two bottle orthodox' Fellows of Oxford, High Churchmanship meant a taste for port and claret. At best, the Church-and-King Tory was a stout-hearted English gentleman, at worst, he was doubtfully a gentleman, let alone a Christian.

Even devout High Churchmen were affected by a rationalism which made them proverbially 'High and Dry' to the point of lifelessness. In their worship, they kept to the letter of the Prayer Book, in their cold repudiation of Dissenting irregularity. Their sermons were cautious and elegant statements of beliefs too ingrained for emotional expression; there was no appeal to the imagination and the senses, and only the most formal poetry. Despite their high doctrine of Church and Sacrament, there was no ritualist nonsense about them. Indeed as High Churchmen most of them were proud to be Protestant, among the strongest anti-papists in England. Their characteristics, therefore, were a strong Protestantism, a pronounced formalism, a rational 'High and Dryness'; and a loyalty to Church, King and Prayer Book which was at root religious, but which sometimes smacked of tribal prejudice.

This was only one side of the picture, and the school was not dead which could claim the loyalty of Dr Johnson, the greatest of all Englishmen. There was an intellectual tradition among the disciples of John Hutchinson, who expounded an anti-Newtonianism and thought that the letters of the Hebrew alphabet contained the key to human knowledge, and there was a pastoral tradition represented by William Jones of Nayland, whose writings impressed the young Newman. Even religious experience was not wholly discounted. Recent scholarship has suggested that Newman and his friends were responsible for the unfair denigration of the sophistication and theological complexity of the older High Churchmanship. Many of the High Churchmen were not mere Erastians, as Anglo-Catholic historiography has tended to claim, but were faithful exponents of the classical English conception of the State and civil magistrate as the guarantors of the rights of the Church, and of the ideal of sacral monarchy and of the Establishment itself as the means to a religious end, the preservation and sanctification of a Christian nation and people.[4]

But the old tradition after 1790 could seem unintelligently conservative and the very reverse of 'Romantic', appearing at its most defensive in its hatred of emotional excess and enthusiasm in religion, that 'pretending to extraordinary revelations and gifts of the Holy Ghost' which Bishop Joseph Butler told John Wesley was 'a very horrid thing'.[5] The Evangelical appeal to an immediate experience of God, of a bloody Christ dying for human sin, was regarded as a kind of madness revolting every canon of Augustan good taste as well as the Churchman's insistence on settled ministry and Church order. Evangelical enthusiasm was also lower class and vulgar. The devout Anglican, like William Jones of Nayland, was a gentleman of breeding and culture; his fastidiousness was a badge of social caste, a mark of refinement and good manners. He knew that he belonged to polite society, in this world and in another.

These qualities were strengthened after 1790, in the face of an outpouring of 'enthusiasm' quite horrifying to High Churchmen. They were stunned by the raw energy of the secular apocalyptic of the French Revolution, and by the destruction of the aristocracy, King and Church in France, which they could only ascribe to Satan. Even in England, democratic radicals, allegedly French spies and sympathizers, appealed by wild oratory to the lower passions of the lower orders; but other signs of the times were as unsettling. There was the sinister spread of Evangelical enthusiasm within the Church Establishment itself; there was the mushroom growth outside it of Methodism and Evangelical Dissent; there were the stirrings of popish enthusiasm in Ireland. Even in literature, there was the dissolution of form and rule in the Romantic revival. After all, Southey, Coleridge and Wordsworth had begun their public careers as Unitarians and sympathizers with revolutionary France, and though Wordsworth outgrew his flirtation with Gallic radicalism and with the young French lady who had borne him a child, and though all three of these 'Lake Poets' had become defenders of the Church of England in middle age, the conservative suspicion of Romanticism was confirmed by the atheism of Shelley and the profligacy of Byron.

Shelley was a notorious atheist, a virulent anticlerical, a red-hot republican. The

> Anarchs and priests, who feed on gold and blood
> Till with the stain their inmost souls are dyed,[6]

had every reason to dislike him. High Churchmen were, therefore, suspicious of the new appeal to imaginative experience: such experience was dangerous and destructive. Perhaps Shelley as an aristocrat could do what he liked in the old eighteenth-century manner; but the cost was paid by Mrs Shelley, as also by Lady Byron. The outburst against Byron was part of a growing if spasmodic reaction, like Bowdler's Shakespeare, against everything 'Romantic' that threatened religion and the family. Such notions were as unsettling as the expression of raw emotion in the new democratic politics, the mass conversions achieved by Primitive Methodist hedge preachers and the resistance to authority preached by the Catholic Association in Ireland. This seething mass of unrests and discontents could only heighten the High Churchman's emotional reserve, his insistence upon formal control.

In 1827, however, Keble won national fame by publishing a book of Romantic religious verse, *The Christian Year*, one poem for each Sunday, red letter saint's day and service of the Anglican *Book of Common Prayer*. Some of these verses have become familiar to everyone as hymns – 'New every morning is the love' and 'Bless'd are the pure in heart' are the best known – and in the nineteenth century the habit grew up in devoutly High Anglican households of reading Keble's verses before the morning service. Keble's achievement, however, was to show that there was a devotional depth in the Prayer Book which was in harmony with the deeps of contemporary Romantic experience. By adapting the Wordsworthian model, he invested the book with the fascinations of the Romantic mood. To use a word which he and Newman were to give its currency in modern English, *The Christian Year* subtly changed the Anglican *ethos*, the atmosphere in which Anglicans said their prayers. Newman was to consider that Keble 'woke up in the hearts of thousands a new music, the music of a school, long unknown in England'.[7] More simply, he restored the Prayer Book to its central place in the mainstream culture of the age.

Yet even Keble's poetry was not innocent of a polemical or controversial intent. In the preface to *The Christian Year*, he declared that while the Church of England sets a 'sober standard of feeling in matters of practical religion', 'in times of much leisure and unbounded curiosity, when excitement of every kind is sought after with a morbid eagerness, this part of the merit of our Liturgy is likely to be lost . . . ' This is a repudiation of the 'excitement' and 'morbid eagerness' of the revolutionary atheism of France and Shelley, and of the extra-liturgical preaching of the Evangelicals, whom the new High Churchmen were especially to despise and dislike for the public display of pious emotions which were beneath the notice of a gentleman. To these excitements, to be considered both vulgar and immoral, Keble opposed the Prayer Book's '*soothing* tendency', and as Professor of Poetry at Oxford, he was to enunciate in his *Lectures on Poetry* a total aesthetic in which the Prayer Book had an essential place.

In this, Keble trod a strait and narrow path. On the one hand, he wanted to arouse the devotional senses in worship. But he felt that such feelings are the profounder, indeed the more intense, if strictly controlled within a set of old liturgical forms. Emotion in both religion and politics is dangerous and anarchic, a threat to Church and State; it requires the discipline of an established and accepted sound form of words, and against the wild excesses of Dissenting and radical enthusiasm, against the preaching of the village ranters and the oratory of the democratic and trade union politicians, it was this control over the emotions that the forms of the Prayer Book were fitted to supply.

All this was to seep into Newman's soul, but it took time to become explicit in his theology. At first glance, he found Keble's 'hymns' 'quite exquisite . . . I was afraid they would have been heavy';[8] but his growth into High Churchmanship was greatly hastened by sudden calamity. There was no hint of such disaster in the summer of 1827, as he prepared himself to act as an examiner in the schools, but the exercise was almost as hard on the examiner as the examinee, and by July he was reading hard eight hours a day: Hebrew grammar, 'all five volumes of Mitford's *Greece* and nearly two of Niebuhr's *Rome*', as well as 'some Homer and the *Clouds* of Aristophanes twice over, all of the *Fasti Hellenici*, twenty-seven "items" from the Greek orators plus eight speeches of Demosthenes, "F. Clinton on the Population of Greece" and "on Demosthenes" '.[9] He also had to coach two students, Robert Wilberforce's younger brother Henry, 'small and timid, shrinking from notice, with a bright face and intelligent eyes',[10] and his own future bugbear and persecutor, the notorious 'Golly', Charles Portales Golightly. In August, Newman, his pupils, his mother and Mary moved to Hampstead, where for six weeks he took duty for the Revd Edward Marsh, but the Evangelical fatalist Marsh's house turned out to be 'so full of bad vermin that we were obliged to leave it. When I wrote to him about it (he was a most meek, gentle, amiable man) he wrote me word that it was one of the trials of this life, and so must be borne'. 'I was eagerly, but not very logically, High Church',[11] Newman recalled, and he won the favour of one old-fashioned High Churchman, Dr Christopher Wordsworth of Trinity College, Cambridge, uncle of the poet, by quoting in a sermon the sixteenth-century founding-father of Anglican theology, Richard Hooker. A reference in a charity sermon to the canons of 1603 produced the reaction that it was charity to listen. The laity would resent such clerical pretensions to authority in the Church of England.

In September 1827, Newman and Robert Wilberforce stayed at the home of his clergyman-friend 'Ricks', the Revd Samuel Rickards, at Ulcombe in Kent, where his host's children took delight in sitting in Newman's lap in a great armchair, 'pulling off and then putting on his glasses'.[12] There he wrote 'Snapdragon. A Riddle', in Mrs Rickards' flower book, comparing the scentless flower on the wall of Trinity with his own hidden celibate and academic life:

> Nature's vast and varied field
> Braver flowers than me will yield,
> Bold in form and rich in hue,
> Children of a purer dew;
> Smiling lips and winning eyes
> Meet for earthly paradise . . .
>
> May it be! then well might I
> In College cloister live and die.[13]

Robert Wilberforce later took Newman to see his father, the great emancipator, at his home at Highwood. But even the Ulcombe visit had been a time of hard study, and though Newman was then suffering from 'low fever', his confidence in himself as an examiner should have been secure.

In fact, he had again read too hard and overtaxed himself. He was then disturbed in October by the long-threatened collapse of his aunt Elizabeth's private establishment at Strand-on-the-Green, and he and Francis had to bail her out, Newman taking the precaution of cutting the banknotes for her in two and sending down the bundles of numbered halves by separate stage coaches. 'My dreams', he wrote, 'were full of the Schools and of examinations.' On the 23 November 1827, when in the schools, Newman heard that Copleston had been promoted to the see of Llandaff, so that there would be the upheaval of the election of a new Provost in Oriel. I 'dreamed of it that night', he wrote, 'and (I believe) the next – drooped during the Saturday . . . and on Sunday felt the blood collect in my head; on Monday [I] found my memory and mind gone, when examining a candidate for the first class . . . and was obliged to leave the Schools in the middle of the day.' He was 'leached' on his temples, and took advice from his new doctor, Macaulay's cousin George Babington, whom he met at the Wilberforce home at Highwood. He had no pain, but 'a twisting of the brain, of the eyes. I felt my head inside was made up of parts. I could write verses pretty well, but I could not *count*'.[14] He withdrew from the schools exactly seven years after his own failure in them in 1820. Two of the traumas of his youth, bankruptcy and examination terror, had returned to haunt him, and that, combined with the excitement over the forthcoming contest in college, had completed his collapse.

Much worse then followed, the sudden illness and death on 5 January

1828 of Newman's favourite sister Mary in her nineteenth year. As she was dying, she repeated some of Keble's verses which she had learned by heart. A young lady of Huguenot descent, Maria Giberne, Walter Mayers' sister-in-law, was staying with the Newmans when Mary died and thought that at the funeral John Henry 'seemed like a walking corpse . . . '[15] The following month, Walter Mayers also died, in early middle age, and Newman had to give his consolation to his friend's young widow and preach at his funeral: 'this world is but a shadow and a dream – ', he told her, 'we think we see things and we see them not – they do not exist, they die on all sides, things dearest and pleasantest and most beloved. But in heaven we shall all meet and it will be *no* dream . . . '[16]

Death, and the unreality of the world, and thoughts of his sister, haunted him as he rode through the Oxford countryside, his head ringing with lines of Keble's which he could hardly imagine not his own: 'Chanting with a *solemn* voice, mind us of our *better choice*'; but beyond words lay 'those indefinite vague and withal subtle feelings which quite pierce the soul and make it sick. Dear Mary seems embodied in every tree and hid behind every hill. What a veil and curtain this world of sense is! beautiful but still a veil . . .'[17] Even when his health and spirits were restored by November, the haunting continued. 'A solemn voice seems to chant from every thing. I know whose voice it is – it is her dear voice.'[18] He wrote 'Consolations on Bereavement' in her memory:

> Death came and went – : that so thy image might
>   Our yearning hearts possess,
> Associate with all pleasant thoughts and bright,
>   With youth and loveliness;
>   Sorrow can claim,
> Mary, nor lot nor part in thy soft soothing name.
>
> Joy of sad hearts, and light of downcast eyes!
>   Dearest, thou art enshrined
> In all thy fragrance in our memories;
>   For we must ever find
>   Bare thought of thee
> Freshen this weary life, while weary life shall be.[19]

Illness and bereavement had recalled him from dreams of intellectual pride and excellence to religious seriousness, reminding him that time and this world are fleeting. He did not know it yet, but his brief flirtation with liberalism was over.

The beginnings of Newman's repudiation of liberalism lay in his estrangement from his beloved Noetic mentor Hawkins, in the closely knit society of Oriel. But first, Newman supported Hawkins against Keble in the election for the new Provost; 'I knew Hawkins and he had taken me up, while Keble had fought shy of me', he recalled.[20] Keble was repelled both by Newman's Evangelicalism and liberalism, and it was from Hawkins, not Keble, that Newman expected the introduction of sterner disciplinary measures in the college. To a colleague, he defended his vote for Hawkins: 'we are not electing an Angel, but a Provost. If we were electing an Angel, I should, of course vote for Keble . . . '[21]

Yet it was 'at the very moment' that Hawkins became Provost that Newman became aware of 'his own congeniality of mind with Keble',[22] an awareness to which he was much assisted by Froude. 'Do you know', Froude was to ask, 'the story of the murderer who had done one good thing in his life? . . . I should say that I had brought Keble and Newman to understand each other.'[23] This in turn was the product of Newman's deeper understanding of Froude, and it was Froude's authority that Newman invoked to Blanco White in March 1828, for his own argument 'for lowering the intellectual powers into hand-maids of our moral nature', on the ground that intellect and opinion were secondary to some more fundamental disposition of personality. 'Each mind pursues its own course and is actuated in that course by tenthousand indescribable incommunicable feelings and imaginings. It would be comparatively easy to enumerate the various external impulses which determine the capricious motions of a floating feather or web, . . . so mysterious are the paths of thought.'[24] The tatters of liberalism and Evangelicalism still hung around Newman for Froude, who told Robert Wilberforce in September 1828 that Newman was 'a fellow that I like more, the more I think of him; only I would give a few odd pence if he were not a heretic'.[25] They had not yet found their common cause.

All ran smoothly with Newman's relations with Hawkins for a year. On 14 March, Newman's old teacher Lloyd, now Bishop of Oxford, instituted him as Hawkins' successor as Vicar of the parish of St Mary the Virgin. 'It was to me like the feeling of spring weather after winter;' Newman recalled, 'and . . . I came out of my shell.'[26] The church, for all its splendour, which includes the baroque barley sugar columns at the entrance below the statue of the crowned Virgin and Child from the time of Laud, had the distinction of housing the university sermon, but the bulk of the normal congregation were the tradesmen and servants dependent upon the colleges. The new incumbent was soon busy catechizing the children, but it took time for the fame of his sermons to gather an elite audience from the wider world of Oxford.

In that world, Pusey was taking life at a rush: within the year he was ordained and married to Maria Barker, had published his influential defence of German theology – 'sadly deformed with Germanisms',[27] Newman told Harriett – and had achieved the position which he was to hold until his death as a Canon of Christ Church and Regius Professor of Hebrew. John Bowden also married, into the formerly Catholic Swinburne family of Northumberland. Newman was honoured by his appointment from the Bishop of London, William Howley, as a Whitehall preacher, he thought through the kindness of Lloyd. He also welcomed the promotion to the bishopric of Chester of the Evangelical John Bird Sumner, whose work had so influenced his abandonment of Calvinism. Howley and Sumner were to be the next two Archbishops of Canterbury. In the flourishing, expanding, powerful Anglican culture of the period, the doors seemed open to limitless preferment, despite the thunderclouds now gathering around the peculiar possessions and privileges of the ancient Church of England.

Her salvation was to be found in another time and place. In 1827, Pusey brought back for Newman from Germany a collection of the writings of the Fathers – 'huge fellows they are, but very cheap – *one* folio costs a shilling!',[28] Newman told his mother; and in the summer of 1828 he 'set about to read them chronologically, beginning with St Ignatius and St Justin'.[29] In August, he stayed at Fairford with the Kebles for the first time – '*the first symptom of our growing intimacy*'[30] – and saw the poetry of *The Christian Year* written on their faces. He suffered agonies in December with toothache, which he treated by steaming his head 'doctore injubente with camomile flowers';[31] but he could rejoice to Rickards in February 1829 over the reforms which, under Hawkins as Provost, had been made in the college:

> first the diminishing [of] the Gentlemen Commoners, from 20 to 8 or 9 – [he exaggerated] Then the dismissal of the Incurables – Then the rejecting unprepared Candidates for admission . . . Then the giving chance vacancies to well recommended and picked men. – Then the introduction of paper work into the Collection-examination. – Then the refusing testimonials to unworthy applicants. – Then the revival of a Chapel Sermon at the Sacrament – then the announcement of a prize for Greek Composition . . .

But, continued Newman, the best change was the most recent, agreed with Froude's support and Wilberforce's approval, 'a radical alteration . . . of the lecture system', in which the 'bad men are thrown into large classes', while the 'better sort' were assigned to small ones, 'principally with their own Tutors quite familiarly and chattingly'. Newman acknowledged that Hawkins had not 'taken the initiative in these innovations – but has always approved, sometimes kept abreast with us – and at Collections has slain the bad men manfully', so that the students declared that 'the Provost was as bad as a Tutor' and would no longer retaliate the tutors' blows upon them. Newman discounted Wilberforce's 'way of railing against the Provost', but it seems that Newman himself did not quite yet realize how deeply Hawkins disapproved of the whole business.[32]

Hawkins distrusted the special attention that the tutors were giving to the especially bright pupils; some of these, like Henry Wilberforce, Samuel

Francis Wood, brother of the first Viscount Halifax, and Frederic Rogers, in later life Lord Blachford, became Newman's disciples and friends. Wood and Rogers came up in 1827, as Newman was coming out of his shell with a vengeance. He was ceasing to be a follower in the society of his seniors and was becoming a leader among his juniors. The election to the Oriel fellowships in April 1829 brought in two of his supporters, J. F. Christie, and his own pupil and future brother-in-law, the good gossip Tom Mozley, who was so entertainingly to libel the Oxford Movement in his highly readable and inaccurate reminiscences. Tom's younger brother James, a gifted theologian who also formed a particular attachment to Newman, came up in 1830. Newman had, therefore, a band of kindred spirits in the college among the undergraduates and junior Fellows; and among those junior Fellows there was now unrest that having been a 'Tribune of the people' when a mere Fellow himself, Hawkins was now abandoning the cause of reform, 'assuming state and pomp', separating himself from his colleagues and identifying himself with other Heads of Houses on the Hebdomadal Board, and 'courting the society and countenance of men of rank and name, whether in the world, or in the state, or the Church'.[33]

It was the classic case of poacher turned gamekeeper; and it came to an issue over Catholic Emancipation, the demand by Roman Catholics to hold public office under the Crown, especially in the British Parliament. Newman apparently signed the Oxford Convocation petition for Emancipation in 1828, with the liberal minority in the University, but he declined to do so in 1829, just as the measure was made inevitable by the Irish tumults attending the election of the Irish Catholic liberator, Daniel O'Connell, as MP for County Clare. The Home Secretary, Sir Robert Peel, had been opposed to Emancipation in the interests of the Church Establishment; he now changed his mind, resigned as MP for the University of Oxford, and sought re-election. Newman was not even now opposed to Emancipation in principle. 'The clamours of the Catholics are but the accidental development of the jealousy Ireland must feel towards a country which has stolen her Parliament and independence. It is not a religious question . . . Enlighten the Irish, Protestantize them – Macte tua virtute [strengthen your strength] – it is right – but you only make them more formidable opponents.' He regarded Emancipation as inevitable, and did not think that the Church would be hurt by it, even though the measure was 'the *symptom* of a systematic hatred to our Church borne by Romanists, Sectarians, Liberals and Infidels. If it were not for the Revolution which one would think must attend it, I should say the Church must fall. But we depend on no human support'. Indeed he thought that under such a threat, the Church would gain, the country lose. It was his first public controversy, and he still had the self-mocking humour to be amused by the 'glorious enunciations I have excathedrized'[34] at the end of this letter to Rickards about it all.

His objection in the matter was chiefly to Peel, as the representative of the University, and therefore of the Church, suddenly changing his mind about Emancipation on grounds not religious: 'It is not pro dignitate nostrâ, to have a Rat [for] our member'.[35] His argument was hardly coherent, as he had himself declared the issue not a religious one, so that Peel had presumably the right to make up his mind on the secular demands upon him as a politician and statesman. Yet the matter *was*, for Newman, religious in the sense that it marked 'the incroachments of philosophism and indifferentism on the Church',[36] as the State ceased to recognize the one true religion, a change symbolized for Newman by the fire with which the madman Jonathan Martin had just burnt down the choir of York Minster. Newman's fierceness was that of a young man who with his friends has found a cause: he half humourously asked Rickards to have a poster 'printed in letters of gold on Satin', in support of Peel's Church Evangelical opponent, Sir Robert Inglis:

Ye lovers of our Constitution as it is, vote for the patriotic Sir R. I. – Ye high Churchmen, vote for the Anti-catholic Sir R. I. – Ye Evangelicals, vote for Sir R, a decided man. – Ye Ch Ch men, vote for your own House-man – (Ye Wikhamists for a Wikhamist) – Ye Tories, for a country-gentleman. – Ye lovers of political integrity and straightforwardness, vote against Mr Peel. –

'Do rouse Lord Winchelsea [sic], and play the man!', concluded Newman to Rickards, whose patron, the arch-Protestant Earl of Winchilsea, was to challenge Wellington to a duel over the Emancipation issue. 'Rouse all the bigotry of Kent, do.'[37] When Peel lost, Newman exulted to his mother on the 'glorious Victory . . . We have proved the independence of the Church and of Oxford'.[38] To his sister Jemima, he invoked the Oxford *ethos*: 'Oxford has never turned with the turn of fortune. Mistaken we may have been, but never inconstant. We kept to the Stuarts in misfortune. Better be bigoted than time-serving'.[39]

Newman's behaviour shocked the Noetics, not least Blanco White, who in earlier years had opposed Emancipation on the ground that Catholics were illiberal themselves, but now supported it on the liberal principle of civil equality in religion. Whately took the 'humourous revenge' on Newman, as the latter recalled it, of assembling a party of the University's Anglican archreactionaries among the 'two bottle orthodox', 'a set of the least intellectual men in Oxford' and those 'most fond of port; . . . placed me between Provost This and Provost That, and then asked me if I was proud of my friends'.[40] Whately saw that the decisive break between Newman and the generation of his teachers had come.

But the most affected of the Noetics was Hawkins, who without consulting the Fellows of his college, went off to a political meeting in London to pledge his support for Peel, and on finding his common room colleagues against him 'contemptuously to their face called the great Tory movement "their cabal" '.[41] The political dispute merged, however, into an academic one. The tutors had not asked for Hawkins' opinion of their scheme of dividing the students into two categories, good and bad, for public and private lectures, which they had communicated to Joseph Dornford, then Dean: it seems that in spite of Newman's assertion to the contrary, they had feared the Provost's veto if asked. Hawkins, however, authoritatively voiced his disapproval in the Easter term of 1829, and more formally at a college meeting of 2 November. He claimed to value the tutors' services, but his view was the sensible one that the pre-existing arrangements had been satisfactory, and that it was wrong to assign students exclusively to different tutors who might differ markedly in abilities and opinion from one another; and he had strong views on his responsibility as Provost for the care of all students, bad and good.

Newman thought that Hawkins disliked Froude and Wilberforce as tutors, and that his sense of dignity was offended by Froude's familiar and slangy ways with his pupils. Newman argued against him that the tutorship was a university office accountable to the Vice-Chancellor, and that the Provost could easily discover by his examination of the students if the scheme was a successful one. He also thought that his relations with his pupils were primarily pastoral, and a necessary implication of his obligations as a priest: and that 'unless he could make his educational engagements a fulfilment of his ordination vow, he could have no part in them'.[42]

But Hawkins had no idea of the depth of this conviction, and 'adopted a superior tone, implied that overwork made Mr Newman look at things unhealthily, and was for ever inquiring "how he felt today?", so that it became a joke among the Tutors . . . '[43] The matter came to a head in April 1830. The former Provost, Copleston, supported Hawkins on the ground that the new arrangements meant the adoption of the very system of tutorial cramming for examinations which Oriel had always avoided. On 5 May, Newman agreed to retire from his tutorship on the understanding that the tutors other than the senior tutor should be henceforth called assistant tutors in the university calendar, to show their dependent position. This was unacceptable to Hawkins, who in mid June indicated that he would retire Newman, Froude and Wilberforce from their tutorships by not assigning them further pupils as their present ones finished their courses. He was to break their strike by appointing other tutors in their place, among them Newman's future foe Renn Dickson Hampden. Newman never lost his love of Hawkins, but henceforth, until his submission to Rome, their relations were, he remarked, in 'a state of constant bickerings – of coldness, dryness, and donnishness on his part, and of provoking insubordination and petulance on mine'.[44]

The incident was important because it cemented his friendship with his ally Froude, and enabled him to get on with his reading of the Fathers. 'I am so hungry for Irenaeus and Cyprian – I long for the Vacation', he told Harriett in June 1829;[45] and Froude encouraged him in his heightening churchmanship, as in his dislike of Henry Hart Milman's *History of the Jews*, which by its irreverent tone – it called Abraham a sheik, and Moses a fakir – rather than by its actual content seemed to mark to Newman the incursion of a new kind of liberalism into the Church. So he told Froude that while willing to omit parts of the Athanasian Creed, 'to lose the damnatory clauses and to curtail it even would be to flatter the vain conceit of the age'.[46] In 1829, he thought the Church needed something like the 'R Catholic friars' to defend it in its peril,[47] and on Lady Day 1830 he introduced saint's day services into St Mary's. He was horrified by the 1830 July Revolution in France: 'They seem the most wicked nation on earth – ', he told Jemima, 'and King Charles and his ministers are a set of poltroons for not staying to be shot or guillotined'.[48] Here was a red hot Tory indeed.

'The tendency of the age is towards *liberalism*', he concluded, ' – i.e. a thinking established notions worth nothing – in this system of opinions a disregard of religion is included . . . *moral* truth is not acceptable to man's heart; it must be enforced by authority . . . ' Given the decay of trust in religious authority, the suspension of miracles and of the 'learning and talent' on the side of faith, and the spiritual ban on relying on 'the patronage of the great', what was required was that system of Church government *'actually established by the Apostles'*, which was 'the *legitimate* enforcement of Christian truth. The liberals know this – and are in every possible manner trying to break it up . . . '[49] If the essential characteristic of a High Churchman is belief in the authority of the Church, then Newman was now a High Churchman, pure and simple. He had also found the foe of the High Church principle, liberalism, with its view of faith as mere sentiment or opinion.

Yet in Newman's mind, Evangelicalism itself, with its ties to Dissent and unease with Church authority, and its espousal of the Protestant idea of the right of private judgement, was unwittingly acting as a channel for the liberal tide, and in 1830 he moved to sever his chief remaining links with the Evangelical school. In the row over Catholic Emancipation, however, he had acted with the stronger anti-Catholic Evangelicals, and in March 1829 he became one of the secretaries of the Oxford branch of the Church Missionary Society. The society was the greatest voluntary institution of Anglican Evangelicalism, but its Oxford branch was under radical Evangelical influence, part of this stemming from Newman's brother Francis. The strictly Calvinist principal secretary, John Hill, opposed Newman's request to disassociate the Oxford branch from sermons preached on its behalf by two of the Oxford radicals, Henry Bulteel and Richard Waldo Sibthorp. They well illustrated the odd directions of the ecclesiastical wind. In 1831, Bulteel 'abjured the church as anti-Christian before a congregation of a thousand assembled in his garden',[50] veered towards the tongues and healings of the Irvingites, and then set up a Strict Baptist chapel in Oxford behind St Ebbe's. The still more adventurous Sibthorp was to precede Newman into the Roman Catholic Church, return to Anglicanism, and then go back to Rome again – though he had the Prayer Book service at his grave.

Against such wayward adversaries, contemptuous of all Church order, Newman had printed on 1 February 1830 an anonymous tract, *Suggestions respectfully offered to individual Resident Clergymen of the University, in Behalf of the Church Missionary Society*, 'by a Master of Arts', which he distributed among these resident clergy. In the tract he urged that in the interests of Church order, the Church Missionary Society should be placed more firmly under episcopal and clerical control, in an attack on that principle of lay – and sometimes non-denominational – voluntary association which was at the very heart of the Evangelical enterprise. At a meeting of the society in March 1830, Newman unavailingly suggested a large number of changes – how many was later disputed, but Frank claimed 254 – in the 'cant' Evangelical phraseology in the branch report, but at the subsequent annual meeting Newman was voted out of office as secretary, and a hardline Calvinist replaced him.[51] It is possible that although Francis was not present on the occasion, it was he who made public his brother's authorship of the offending pamphlet and urged his replacement.[52] In June, Newman resigned from the Bible Society,[53] which was even more open to his objections, as it included Dissenting members on its committee. Francis, now completely under J. N. Darby's influence, decided to leave England with a missionary party for Persia led by a Devonshire dentist, Anthony Groves. The ideological estrangement between the brothers was complete.

There were, however, a number of paradoxes here. It might be said that in this series of incidents, Newman was breaking away from the radical Evangelicals, and not the moderates; but his own view of the darkness of the times gave him a considerable sympathy for these 'Propheticals', as he called them, 'a hopeful progeny from the Evangelicals. I wish they would discard some of their notions and they should have my sanction . . . About Calvinism I do not care in the abstract. Persons for me may out calvin Calvin, so that they avoid two practical errors – 1. *judging their neighbours* – and thinking because a Higher Power has (according to their creed) divided the world into two, that they can divide it also. 2. Putting forth Christian motives etc. solely, always, and to all men – which leads ultimately to no men feeling them'.[54]

Newman's absorption of the Evangelical prophetical temper appears in his very rejection of its specific teaching. In his unpublished Advent sermons of 1830, he argued like Edward Irving that the biblical texts to do with prophecy have too many meanings to be absolutely clear, in an implicit rejection of the popular Evangelical view that every symbol had only one meaning and every prophecy only one fulfilment. When the prophets predicted the destruction of Jerusalem, declared Newman, they may refer to the fall of the city at the time of Jeremiah or of the Apostles, or again at the end of the world. Curiosity and idle imagination will soon tire of the contradictions of a subject so obscure. The Old Testament prophets did not date their prophecies, and 'so in the case of the future trials of the Christian Church – they will come suddenly, tho' they are foretold – because being told obscurely, men will not be at the pains to attend the warning'. Rather, insight into prophecy is a matter of moral depth, of holiness of life, and the holy man will see that the world is always wicked, divine judgement is always falling, and the greater judgement of Christ's returning may at any time occur. 'There is nothing new under the Sun – one age succeeds another – and the people of the earth rage and swell, then subside, then collect their force again.' 'They bought, they sold – they married and were given in marriage, till the wrath of God fell upon them . . . The sun rose on Sodom, bright as usual, that very morning of wrath when God rained fire upon it.' There are many disastrous portents of the last age; 'God's vengeance upon the Jews' and on the cities of Babylon, Egypt and the East, whose destruction Scripture likens to the burning of the world at the Second Coming. Another sign of the end is a *'scoffing unbelief'*, a part of the liberal progressivist mentality and self-trust rooted in the false English pride *'in our own greatness as a nation'* and in 'our glorious far-spreading empire on which the sun never sets'. The beloved disciple had foreseen while writing the Book of Revelation the 'mad impiety' of the English liberal mind, with its 'great variety of opinions and parties – an open licence to blaspheme'.[55] In his own way, Newman was still more Evangelical than Frank, and it was as if the very Evangelical energies and passions which led some into Irvingism or the Brethren or the Strict Baptists were also leading to a Catholic revival in England.

Frank's own journey was an ill-fated one. He was in love with Maria Giberne, 'a beautiful, buxom, dark-haired, cow-eyed, foolish Juno' of a woman, who unfortunately gave her love to other women and her deepest devotion to John Henry. 'Bless the Monk!!!! In spite of my ill-will to him!' she wrote, recalling her first meeting with John. 'Oh! Oh! Oh!' Nevertheless, 'Je sentis naître tout de suite une espèce de confiance en cet étrange mortal [sic]'.[56] From Aleppo, Frank begged her to marry him. He was attacked by a mob, nearly died of the plague which killed Mrs Groves at Baghdad, and was more converted by, than converting, the unconvertible Muhammadans.

With Charles hopeless, and Frank often absent, it was John who had the care of his mother and sisters. From a temporary home at Brighton in 1828–9, he moved them first to a cottage at Horspath near Oxford, and then to the pleasant village of Nuneham Courtenay, where they had spent two months in 1828. Newman took long wet and muddy rides out to dine with them in 1829 and 1830, riding back and forwards to Oxford. Harriett and Jemima hoped for the attentions of Henry and Robert Wilberforce, and Mrs Newman did not want to return to Brighton, so in October 1830 John set them up at a much more convenient distance, in his own parish, in a pair of cottages converted into a house called Rose Mount on Rose Hill between Iffley and Littlemore, from where the ladies could make social forays into nearby Oxford. From June 1831, Newman had his own apartment in the house, 'consisting of a hall, staircase, study and bedroom', where he could sleep outside college; from his study window he viewed the spires of Oxford. In 1833, there was another move, briefly to The Cottage, Iffley, and then to a home called Rose Bank. His sisters 'kept house, sewed, painted "coloured landscapes" and read at random' and above all, did good works for the Vicar.[57] In 1834, John Henry defended his mother to Francis from the charge of 'keeping up "the lust of the eye and the pride of life"' by such vanities as employing a servant in livery, and he described the round of the females of the household as one of dedicated Christian charity:

> They are the instruments of temporal good to 200 people at Littlemore – they teach the children, set an example to the Parents, and, even where they cannot do all they wish, they make people better who otherwise would become worse; – and moreover they have friends, . . . through whom they do good to my people in various ways, as in finding the young women places etc etc.
>
> True, they might give up housekeeping, and live in lodgings as somewhat cheaper, but then where would be the kitchen for Littlemore, with broth and messes? where the rice and tapioca from a housekeeper's closet? in a word, they enable me to spend a large sum upon the poor which I could not spend satisfactorily myself. How [he later added] can I manage a parish without women? I suppose my money goes further, than yours in journeying to Persia.[58]

This might stand as a general defence of the unobtrusive middle-class pastoral concern of the women of the nineteenth-century Church of England, beyond the tumult and the shouting of the new High Churchmen like Newman; but that unobtrusive work was given a new urgency by the crisis in the Church.

8

The Crisis of the Church

The idea of recalling the Church of England to a true understanding of herself is one perennially beset with problems. As the creation by a number of traditions, she claims the glory of medieval Roman Catholics and Protestant Reformers, of Puritan and High Church divines, and even of men like Wesley and Newman who have founded or seceded to other communions. The history of the Church of England is like the history of England, a clash and conflict between rival traditions, Erastian and anti-Erastian, Catholic and Protestant, conservative and liberal, sectarian and latitudinarian: and none of these has ever quite lost the fight or been excluded from her. Despite expulsions and secessions of liberal, Protestant and popish-minded clergy, she retains the whole spectrum of English religious opinion, from the crypto-Roman Catholic to the crypto-infidel. Thus the curious insularity of the Church of England has been offset by the self-contradictory complexity of her theologies; despite the claims for Anglican theological method, as defined by Richard Hooker in the sixteenth century, as an amalgam of Scripture, Tradition and reason, the diversity of Anglican theologies defines Anglican theology, and the unity of the Church of England is not susceptible of theological definition. The Church's unity is of a different character: it arises from her self-understanding as a profoundly national institution, with a sense of continuity through fifteen hundred years, and with her own part played in every phase of English history.

This was the Church of England's understanding of herself, as an equal partner of the English State, co-extensive with the English people; as the English State in its spiritual aspect, as the English people at prayer; or as Matthew Arnold described the Church, as the 'most national and natural' of institutions. But the argument was pragmatic; it only held good for as long as the English nation was in communion with the Church of England. This was *de facto* the case in the later sixteenth century apart from the Roman Catholic minority and an inconsiderable number of sectaries; and despite the multitude of new denominations which arose out of the religious ferment of the Interregnum, the non-Anglican proportion of the population was small in the mid and later eighteenth century. It is true that Bishop William Warburton's redefinition of the Church–State relationship of 1736 had to take account of the novel toleration of non-Anglicans, yet his view of the alliance presumed a continuing confessional state, even if this was one in which the Church was effectively state-controlled. An old-fashioned 'hereditary Church-of-Englandism' prevailed in thousands of country parishes, and there was a general acquiescence in the establishmentarian status quo by a population which was Erastian in fact if not in theory, while Trinitarian orthodoxy was the official ideology of State and Church.[1]

Moreover, in the conservative reaction which followed the French Revolution, a more principled High Churchmanship, that of the non-Erastian 'Hackney Phalanx', dominated ecclesiastical appointments and politics – especially during the fifteen-year Tory prime ministership of Lord Liverpool – under the ecclesiastical leadership of a retired wine merchant, Joshua Watson, and the Revd Henry Handley Norris, Rector of South Hackney, so that between 1812 and 1827 'the union of Church and State appeared to be working more in the Church's interests and in accordance with the ideal of Hooker, than at any time since the reign of Charles II'.[2] The State actually voted a million and a half pounds for new Anglican churches in 1818 and 1824, and it was this continuing and even increased state support for the Establishment which made more startling and dramatic the changes soon to follow.

Yet the Church's position had been weakening for more than half a century, as England entered on her imperial century as mistress of the seas and workshop of the world. The challenge induced a crisis of self-identity about the Church's role as the Church of the English. The Industrial Revolution had created the unchurched masses in the cities of the north, leaving the greater part of the parish clergy ministering in the rural south and midlands. These social changes lay behind the massive expansion of Nonconformity after 1790, inspired by religious rationalism and even more by Evangelicalism. In much of Britain, the Church of England became a minority Church, either through the spread of practical indifference or of religious dissent. There was also a Roman Catholic population explosion in Ireland, with an overflow into the industrial towns of mainland Britain; and the Church of England was linked from 1800 with a Protestant Church establishment in Ireland which was a small minority of the Irish people. Meanwhile the growing inequalities of clerical income were exacerbated by the increase in clerical wealth brought about by the changes and chances of the Agricultural and Industrial Revolutions, by soaring coal revenues and improvements in tithe and glebe and rentals from enclosure. These gentrified the clergy, making the Church more than ever attractive as a featherbed and source of outdoor relief for aristocratic unemployables. Nepotism, simony and corruption were rife within the Church. There was a busy commerical traffic in the sale of livings, and episcopal patronage was the foundation of the wealth of many a clerical family. 'At Ely, Bishop Sparke gave so many of the best livings to his family that it was locally said that you could find your way across the Fens on a dark night by the number of little Sparkes along the road . . . when he secured a second canonry for his second son, he was so filled with pious gratitude that, as a thank-offering, he gave a ball at the Palace of Ely to all the county of Cambridge.'[3] Such unselfconsciousness about the abuse of privilege has a certain impressiveness.

This unselfconsciousness did not last. Such men were an obvious target in the 1820s for English Whigs and Radicals who denounced the Church of England as the most expensive and pastorally inefficient in the world, an obvious barrier to the realization of the self-evident Utilitarian good proclaimed by the disciples of Jeremy Bentham of the greatest happiness of the greatest number. Is the Church of England useful to make men happy? What a withering, unanswerable question that was. True, the Church was probably a more decorous institution than the society she served, at a time when professional standards were low; when parliament was a hive of jobbery and rotten boroughs, when the doctor might have bought his degree, and the law was notorious for inefficiency and delay, when the Civil Service was full of well-paid sinecures, and commissions in the army were sold, and when the worst of moral examples were set by the Royal family. From the radical viewpoint, the Georgian Church of England was only the corrupt ecclesiastical arm of a corrupt and venal State and Crown; but she could no longer be considered a truly national institution, if she was perceived to be, as a later phrase had it, the Tory party at prayer.

The outcome in the 1820s was a vicious republican anticlericalism rare in English history. Never, it seemed, did so many Englishmen wish to strangle their King with the entrails of the Archbishop of Canterbury. The writing for the Church Establishment appeared to be on the wall when the repeal of the Test and Corporation Acts in 1828, and Catholic Emancipation in 1829, gave full rights to Dissenters and Roman Catholics to sit in Parliament. In 1830, a new Whig government was elected, with a mandate to reform the Church; and it was allied to non-Episcopalians and non-Protestants in a legislature which was the highest voice in the Episcopalian Protestant Church of England. Where, in this 'crisis of the Church', was the argument for the Church of England now?

From an international perspective, these events in England belong to the slow death of the European confessional State, of the State supported and buttressed by a rich and powerful monopolistic Church. But in the English setting, they took on a special character, and showed up the ambivalence of the conception of the Church of England as a national and temporal institution, which also happened to be the Body and Bride of Christ. The crisis was to give a novel prominence to the alternative claim, that the Church of England was, in the supernatural order, the local embodiment of the Holy Catholic Church. The Church seemed less than a wholeheartedly accepted national institution when, in a letter to his mother, Newman surveyed her enemies in 1829: 'the uneducated or partially educated mass in

81

towns' fed on the popular Deist publications of Richard Carlile; 'Utilitarians, political economists, useful knowledge people – their organs the Westminster Review, the London University'; then 'schismatics, in and out of the Church', the Calvinist Baptists and political indifferentists. Against these, the Church party was 'poor in mental endowments', and depended 'on prejudice and bigotry'.[4]

Newman thereby accepted Whately's estimate of his new High Church friends as unintelligent bigots and had even come to a view which explained this, the theory called Traditionalism by contemporary French Catholic intellectuals like de Bonald and de Lamennais. The fundamental idea was scriptural and patristic, prominent in the Alexandrian Fathers such as Clement: that God had given a general revelation of his truth in what Newman called 'the unsophisticated infancy of notions', which later generations had been unable to prove, but which they continued to revere 'from pious and honest feeling (it may be) or from bigotry or from prejudice'. It required a profoundly moral mind to grasp or understand these truths afresh, like Richard Hooker in the sixteenth century, or Bishop Joseph Butler in the eighteenth: indeed such a grasp demanded a moral insight impossible in rationally clever, superficial men like Froude's *bête noire* the Utilitarian radical Henry Brougham, or, Newman added with a gratuitous insult towards a great English and Oxonian Tory, John Wesley. 'Moral truth is gained by patient study, by calm reflection, silently as the dew falls, unless miraculously given, and, when gained, it is transmitted by faith and by "prejudice". Keble's book [*The Christian Year*] is full of such truths; which any Cambridge man might refute with the greatest ease.'[5] It is notable that Newman should instinctively oppose Keble's Oxonian mind to the liberal, rational, scientific and Protestant temper of Cambridge.

Keble's Romantic moralism also connected creative inspiration not with reason but morality: goodness is the doorway to beauty and truth. The idea appears in the essay on Aristotle's *Poetics* which Newman contributed in January 1829 to Blanco White's short-lived *London Review*, in which he urged that a 'right moral state of heart is the formal and scientific condition of a poetical mind'. Whatever might be said of Byron, Burns was 'of much really sound principle at bottom', his beauties being due 'to the remains of a virtuous and diviner nature within him'. Conversely, 'the poetry of a vicious mind will be inconsistent and debased; that is, so far only poetry as the traces and shadows of holy truth still remain upon it'. The most sceptical of men, like Hume and Gibbon, will also be the least poetical. 'Revealed Religion should be especially poetical', and the Christian with spiritual insight will see the world through the poet's eyes.[6]

But morality and right religious opinion were also inextricably bound up in Newman's mind with the notion of ethos which sprinkles his letters to Froude – the ethic and spirit of a time or place, the latter more precisely called the genius loci, which is more than a merely intellectual summary could ever quite grasp or describe. Newman developed these ideas from Keble, and from Bishop Butler's Rolls Chapel sermons on conscience in one of his most masterful short productions, his university sermon in April 1830 on 'The Influence of Natural and Revealed Religion Respectively'. Against the teaching of orthodox rationalist divines, Newman insisted that natural religion is not the discovery of man's unaided reason in nature. Rather, it arose externally from the general revelation of God to all mankind in the dispensation of paganism, and it is this general revelation which speaks to God's internal witness in the moral conscience in every man. For 'Conscience is the essential principle and sanction of Religion in the mind', and reveals God in the sense of obligation which it arouses towards him. Conscience 'implies a relation between the soul and a something exterior, and that, moreover, superior to itself', a tribunal or judge or lawgiver to whom it realizes that it owes obedience; and as conscience is strengthened by habitual exercise, so it strengthens its awareness of that 'Supreme Power . . . "the blessed and only Potentate, who only hath immortality, dwelling in light unapproachable, whom no man hath seen or can see" '.[7]

Thus a conscience which is exercised and strengthened discriminates more clearly between right and wrong actions, and raises the possibility or prospect of a judgement on those actions in rewards and punishments in a future life: so that it might 'be even questioned whether there be any essential character of Scripture doctrine which is without its place in this moral revelation'. Even the heathen 'are not in danger of perishing, except so far as all are in such danger, whether in heathen or Christian countries, who do not follow the secret voice of conscience, leading them on by faith to their true though unseen good. For the prerogative of Christians consists in the possession, not of exclusive knowledge and spiritual aid, but of gifts high and peculiar'.[8] All men have contact with that original revelation and all have conscience to inform them of the image of God.

Yet while '*attainable*' among the heathen, the knowledge of God was not '*actually attained*', for in religion as in life moral and religious truth is communicated by the power of 'a personal presence', and how, in pagan lands, 'should the beauty of virtue move the heart, while it was an abstraction?'[9] Polytheism shivered the image of the personal God into the degraded anthropomorphisms of the Greco-Roman pantheon, while God himself remained an abstraction even for the greatest Hellenistic philosophers: but then how could they rise to the vision of him, never having seen the personal witnesses to his chosen people, either 'Angel or Prophet, much less the Son of God manifested in the flesh?'[10] Any cause, political or moral, needs the force of a leader, of an individual to embody its teaching and proclaim it to others; and in the Christian dispensation, God revealed himself in and as a person, in the life of Christ, which 'brings together and concentrates truths concerning the chief good and the laws of our being, which wander idle and forlorn over the surface of the moral world . . . ' Thus the natural religion imparted by our intimations in conscience of God as our lawgiver and judge, and of Heaven and Hell, 'failed in practical effect',[11] and revealed religion supplied the deficiency; but general tradition externally and the internal monitor of conscience still lead mankind to seek that complete revelation given in the person of Christ of the personality of God.

This teaching, which has also been called personalism, bore the implication which Newman always, if sometimes uneasily, was to hold, that unbelievers were bad men who had stifled rather than developed from their consciences a knowledge of the good and the image of God. But it also implied that reason has but a 'subordinate place in our nature'.[12] In religion and morals, reason is the instrument of conscience, and there can be no meaningful debate with the atheist who lacks the image of God which conscience reveals within the soul. Newman developed this argument in December 1831 in his sermon on 'The Usurpations of Reason', in a parallel between an infidel and a blind man lecturing on light and colours: 'he might discourse with ease and fluency, till we almost forgot his lamentable deprivation; at length on a sudden, he would lose himself in some inexpressibly great mistake, betrayed in the midst of his career by some treacherous word, which he incautiously explained too fully or dwelt too much upon . . . ' In short, just as reason is the servant of sense experience in the realm of fact, and depends on sensation for a knowledge of its materials, so conscience and revelation supply the matter for sound religious argument: and without them, no meeting of minds is possible. Thus 'it is as absurd to argue men, as to torture them, into believing', for the infidel like the blind man lacks the correct information on which true argument depends.[13]

There is something in this of Whately's logic – the view that reasoning does not give us new information: it is strictly about rightly arguing, once the materials for argument have been supplied. At another level, Newman's view is the old Evangelical exaltation of heart over head. On yet another, it is the teaching of the contemporary Romantic Anglican philosopher and poet, Samuel Taylor Coleridge, in his *Aids to Reflection* of 1825, that the imaginative and intuitive, spiritual and moral, perceptions of the meaning and purpose of things in the Reason go deeper than the superficial rationalist grasp of the Understanding. It also has a touch of Kant's categorical imperative: 'the starry skies above me and the moral law within me'. But this also means that as with sense experience itself, the information which conscience provides must be assumed: 'since the inward law of Conscience brings with it no proof of its truth, and commands attention to it on its own authority, all obedience to it is of the nature of Faith.'[14] Thus ultimately whether imparted by general or particular revelation, pagan or Christian, or by the internal testimony of conscience, religious truth is essentially the gift of authority, as Newman later described it in his developed summary of his master Keble's teaching: 'Conscience is an authority; the Bible is an authority; such is the Church; such is Antiquity; such are the words of the wise;

such are hereditary lessons; such are ethical truths; such are historical memories, such are legal saws and state maxims; such are proverbs; such are sentiments, presages, and prepossessions'. Keble 'even felt a tenderness, I think, in spite of Bacon, for the Idols of the Tribe and the Den, of the Market and the Theatre. What he hated instinctively was heresy, insubordination, resistance to things established, claims of independence, disloyalty, innovation, a critical, censorious spirit'.[15]

Keble showed, therefore, a tenderness towards the Old Religion of the Roman Catholics, hallowed as it was by ancient tradition; and that tenderness was rare among the High Church No-Popery Tories of his time. But he could not accept Catholic Emancipation on modern liberal principles. The difficulty was that traditionalist theory identified theological and political liberalism, though in some of the major movements of the time, in the Belgian rising against Holland in 1830 and the Polish rising against Russia in 1830–1, political liberalism and Catholic orthodoxy were allied. The same was true in the theory of the French Catholic traditionalist Lamennais, though afterwards condemned by Rome. Keble and Newman, like the contemporary Pope Gregory XVI, seemed to align traditionalist attitudes with the defence of entrenched privilege, whereas in England and supremely in Ireland Roman Catholicism and political liberalism were friends. In another paradox, the defence of the established constitution in Church and State implied a connection with some of the least religious forces in English public life, those hard hunting, gambling, drunken Tories whose religion was the establishmentarian principle and nothing more. The traditionalist theory needs, however, to be grasped, for an understanding of what might seem difficult to defend in Newman's behaviour in the years to follow.

Again, in feeling the deadness of the High Church tradition, Newman was less than just to the organizational skills of the Hackney Phalanx, who ran the old High Church charities and propagandist and missionary agencies like the Society for Promoting Christian Knowledge and the Society for the Propagation of the Gospel, and who were promoting church extension and a vast increase in the provision of popular religious education through the National Society. Yet Newman's diagnosis of the Church's ills was surely correct in its demand for an original intellectual and doctrinal response to the attacks upon it. The idea now dawning on Newman's mind was that if the Church of England was only doubtfully the Church of the whole nation, she was still the English Catholic Church.

It was, then, with thoughts of 'the pollution of such men as Lord Brougham', Lord Chancellor in the 'vile Ministry' of the new Whig administration,[16] that Newman, having considered writing a work on the Anglican Thirty-nine Articles, turned his attention to a proposal from Hugh James Rose for a history of the Councils of the Early Church, as part of a Theological Library being edited by Rose and Archdeacon William Rowe Lyall of Colchester. Rose, a stern unbending High and Dry Churchman of the old school, had written an influential work attacked by Pusey, popularizing the thesis that modern German theology was rotten with liberal rationalist heresy. Newman at first supported Pusey; but like Pusey himself, he had largely come round to Rose's point of view, and it is partly Rose's influence which is to be seen in his work on the Arian heresy.

Newman began the book in June 1831, but broke it off to go and stay with the Froudes in Devon in July. He and Hurrell travelled down by the channel steamer, sleeping on the deck, where Froude caught a cold and developed the influenza which Newman blamed for his friend's later fatal illness. Newman himself was overwhelmed by the langour and visual richness of the West Country, by 'the extreme deliciousness of the air and the fragrance of every thing . . . really I think I should dissolve into essence of roses, or be attenuated into an echo, if I lived here', he told his mother. ' . . . The rocks blush into every variety of colour – the trees and fields are emeralds, and the cottages are rubies. A beetle I picked up at Torquay was as green and gold as the stone it lay on, and a squirrel . . . bright brown red. Nay, my very hands and fingers look rosy, like Homer's Aurora, and I have been gazing on them with astonishment.'[17]

The pastoral was brief. The crisis in Church–State relations reached a new intensity in October 1831, when twenty-one of the Anglican bishops joined the majority of peers to reject the first Reform Bill in the Lords. In the aftermath, the bishops and clergy were rabbled and insulted by mobs all over England; in Bristol the Bishop's palace was burnt to the ground, in an echo of a similar incident in Paris, while the guilty twenty-one replaced the Pope in the Guy Fawkes effigies burnt in November. In Derby, the mob smashed the Mozleys' windows. Neither Newman nor Froude was greatly exercised by the secular politics of the matter. 'If it was not for a personal hatred of the Whiggs [sic]', Froude wrote to him, 'I should care comparatively little for the reform bill';[18] but the episode strengthened in Newman his sense of vocation to the Church. He feared an invitation from Whately, appointed by the Whig administration Archbishop of Dublin, to follow his old teacher to Ireland, for 'if times are troublous', he assured Harriett, 'Oxford will want hot headed men, and such I mean to be . . .' The invitation never came. 'He knew me better', Newman concluded afterwards, 'than I knew myself.'[19]

Meanwhile, his work on the Fathers was advanced by a handsome present from his friends and pupils of a further thirty-six volumes of their writings, 'Austin, Athanasius, Cyril Alexandrinus, Epiphanius, Gregory Nyssen, Origen, Basil, Ambrose, and Irenaeus'.[20] He hoped to better the work of his predecessors. 'The standard Divines are magnificent fellows, but then they are Antiquarians or Doctrinists, not Ecclesiastical Historians – Bull, Waterland, Petavius, Baronius and the rest – of the historians I have met with I have a very low opinion – Mosheim, Middleton, Milner, etc – Cave and Tillemont are highly respectable, but biographers.' 'Really I have nothing to wish, as I am', he told Rickards, 'and would willingly compound, according to the epitaph, to live and die a Fellow of Oriel.'[21]

Another piece of the jigsaw fell into place in December 1831 when Keble was elected Professor of Poetry. Newman affirmed his belief in the 'doctrine of the Genius loci'[22] of Oxford, the spirit of the place, the ethos out of which the Oxford Movement was to come. In early 1832, the ostensible immediate cause of the Movement, the Roman Catholic pressure to reform the Protestant Church of Ireland, was also on his mind. Under the influence of the Irish William Palmer of Worcester he decided simply that the Establishment was the ancient Church of Ireland, 'that the Papistical Church is quite recent, being the direct creation of the Roman See during the last two centuries . . . I am truly glad the Orange Spirit is up, and hope those [Whig] vermin will have enough to do with them'.[23]

There were a number of paradoxes here: the future Cardinal looking to support from Orangemen and denouncing the Roman Catholic Church in Ireland, which was the Church of the great majority of her people. Again, the Church Establishment in Ireland was indefensible: with four highly paid archbishops, two more than in England, and eighteen bishops, the Irish Church was an ecclesiastical slum, with a following of only about ten per cent of the Irish population, and a clergy supported by the unwilling tithes of the largely Roman Catholic peasantry. The difficulty was that Roman Catholics had to resort to liberal politicians for the redress of their grievances, and Newman regarded liberalism in both politics and religion as the unclean spirit of the age. He took this to the length of preferring a Churchman's candidature to that of the better qualified Horace Hayman Wilson for the Sanskrit Chair in Oxford, darkly alleging to Samuel Wilberforce, brother to Robert and Henry, that 'Dornford knows for certain that he [Wilson] kept a woman at Calcutta'.[24] Wilson was successful, but even given the intense excitement over the Reform Bill, which was passed in June 1832, amid continuing execration of the Church, Newman's attitude was excessive. As a partisan, he was not always fair.

Yet on another level, he was achieving intellectual maturity. In July 1831, he finished writing his book for Hugh James Rose – only to have it 'plucked', Oxford examinees' language for turned down, by Rose's fellow editor Archdeacon Lyall. Lyall told Rose that the work was 'thoroughly *English*, and in many places strikingly good', but it did not fit into their projected Theological Library, being not a history of the Councils, but of Arianism. Nor was it an introductory textbook, but presupposed a knowledge of the subject in the reader, and worse, wrote Lyall to Newman in November, employed the anti-Protestant and 'Romanist' idea of a secret tradition and invoked the notion from Clement of a general revelation to the pagans.[25] Lyall also objected to Newman's sharp perception that some of the ante-Nicene Fathers had fallen short of later orthodoxy; even granting this was so, conceded Lyall, on the role of grace, the office of the Holy Spirit and of the Trinity and Original Sin, they had wholeheartedly believed in Christ's Atonement and Divinity. Lyall was glad when Newman arranged to have the work published by Rivingtons, and he was right to sense a departure from classical Protestantism, for it was Tradition and the principle of doctrinal development, founded on a clear vision of the complexities and ambiguities of early Christianity, that were to carry Newman on to Rome.

But the work was in no sense a conventional history. Rather, as the product of a love affair between a scholar and his subject, it represented Newman's discovery of the great Church of Alexandria – as he recalled in one of the finest passages in the *Apologia*:

The broad philosophy of Clement and Origen carried me away; the philosophy, not the theological doctrine . . . Some portions of their teaching, magnificent in themselves, came like music to my inward ear, as if the response to ideas, which, with little external to encourage them, I had cherished so long. These were based on the mystical or sacramental principle, and spoke of the various Economies or Dispensations of the Eternal. I understood these passages to mean that the exterior world, physical and historical, was but the manifestation to our senses of realities greater than itself. Nature was a parable: Scripture was an allegory: pagan literature, philosophy, and mythology, properly understood, were but a preparation for the Gospel. The Greek poets and sages were in a certain sense prophets; for 'thoughts beyond their thought to those high bards were given'. There had been a directly divine dispensation granted to the Jews; but there had been in some sense a dispensation carried on in favour of the Gentiles. He who had taken the seed of Jacob for His elect people had not therefore cast the rest of mankind out of His sight. In the fulness of time both Judaism and Paganism had come to nought; the outward framework, which concealed yet suggested the Living Truth, had never been intended to last, and it was dissolving under the beams of the Sun of Justice which shone behind it and through it. The process of change had been slow; it had been done not rashly, but by rule and measure, 'at sundry times and in divers manners', first one disclosure and then another, till the whole evangelical doctrine was brought into full manifestation. And thus room was made for the anticipation of further and deeper disclosures, of truths still under the veil of the letter, and in their season to be revealed. The visible world still remains without its divine interpretation; Holy Church in her sacraments and her hierarchical appointments, will remain, even to the end of the world, after all but a symbol of those heavenly facts which fill eternity. Her mysteries are but the expressions in human language of truths to which the human mind is unequal. It is evident how much there was in all this in correspondence with the thoughts which had attracted me when I was young, and with the doctrine which I have already associated with the Analogy and the Christian Year.[26]

No passage in the book itself rises to the height of this magnificently musical afterthought about it, and it is a young man's book, written with enthusiasm but without the rhetorical grace and effortless flow of Newman's later books, 'the most imperfect work', he called it, 'that was ever composed'.[27] None, however, contains so many of his characteristic ideas. The chief of these was God's economy or the divine accommodation of his revelation to the low level of human moral and spiritual understanding in different ages of the world's history. This had its ecclesiastical counterpart in the idea of reserve: that just as Christ had spoken in parables to the multitude, so in 'fulfilment of our Lord's command, not to give that which is holy to dogs, nor to cast pearls before swine', the ancient Church had withheld its teachings from its catechumens until they were morally and spiritually enlightened to receive them in the fullness of faith. This was christened the '*Disciplina Arcani*' or discipline of the secret by a seventeenth-century Roman Catholic scholar, and was a sanction to the idea of secret tradition so disliked by Lyall. But it harmonized with Newman's High Church principle, derived from Hawkins, that it was for the Church to teach, especially in the creeds, and for the Bible to prove its teaching; and 'the economical method, that is, of accommodation to the feelings and prejudices of the hearer, in leading him to the reception of a novel or unacceptable doctrine',[28] had been not merely the method of St Paul, but of the incarnate God himself.

The book is, however, also an exercise in theological apologetic against the rationalist and liberal enemies of the Church. Anxious to acquit Alexandria of responsibility for its heresiarch-presbyter Arius, Newman derived the heretical tradition from the Judaizing influence on the rival see and school of Antioch, a city notorious for its 'luxuriousness', where 'coldness in faith' was, as ever, 'the sure consequence of relaxation of morals'.[29] Newman also drew a line to Antioch from the third-century Sabellian Paul of Samosata, who thought of Christ as a deified man different only in degree and not in kind from the Prophets. The Sabellian denial of a full divinity to Christ, like the Arian version of the same heresy, became for Newman a kind of litmus test of modern unbelief. To blacken Antioch the more completely, Newman also exculpated the heresies of the Alexandrian Origen, but then, for all his scholarship, Newman was making a polemical point about the orthodoxy and heresies of his own day. 'The religious philosophy of the Alexandrian Fathers recalled the Platonism of the Oxonians ... The Sophists were the Noetics. Paul of Samosata was not unlike Whately. The Arians might be compared to the Protestants. Bending over this far-away past Newman saw in a mirror an idealised picture of his surroundings and reassured himself with the reflection.'[30]

Thus Newman's reaction against a rationalist syllogistic logic among his Noetic teachers occurs in his quotation from the Church Father Epiphanius describing the Anomoean heretics as arguing about the Godhead 'by means of Aristotelic syllogisms and geometrical data'. Arianism itself was 'founded in a syllogism'.[31] 'Then, however, as now, the minds of speculative men were impatient of ignorance, and loth to confess that the laws of truth and falsehood, which their experience of this world furnished, could not at once be applied to measure and determine the facts of another.'[32] More comically, an Arian prelate is described as 'establishing the principle of liberalism at Constantinople'.[33] Such rationalists had no sense of mystery, or of the impossibility of the human mind out of its own devices divining the infinite glory and grandeur of God. These modern parallels are sharpest in Newman's portrait of the neologists of the Eclectic School encouraged by Julian the Apostate. 'Who', concludes Newman in a tremendous rhetorical question, 'does not recognize in this old philosophy the chief features of that recent school of liberalism and false illumination, political and moral, which is now Satan's instrument in deluding the nations, but which is worse and more earthly than it.' The ancient heretical school had preserved at least a religious ceremonial embodying 'substantial truth'; and that had given its disciples 'somewhat of a lofty and serious character, utterly foreign to the cold, scoffing spirit of modern rationalism'.[34]

Newman was arguably at his best, not in his black and white contrasts of Antioch and Alexandria, which are too simple, tendentious and over-drawn, but in his portraits of his hero and *alter ego* Athanasius, Bishop of Alexandria, who had fought for orthodoxy *contra mundum*, and of the men in the middle such as the weak Pope Liberius, orthodox himself but a heretic under pressure, and the orthodox Meletius with his personal tenderness for heretics. It should also be said that in writing out of his current preoccu-pations, theological and political, Newman did no more than any good scholar does, for an ability to see a parallel between past and present makes the difference between a living history and a dead one. This was true of Newman's two masters, Gibbon and Milner, who both moved their contemporaries, but a living history is not a good one if it distorts or neglects its evidence, and on that ground, that he had distorted his evidence, Milner was a bad historian where Gibbon was a great one. Unfortunately, Milner's theological preoccupations led him to his distortions in sorting out the good men from the bad ones, and Newman's scheme, for all his depth of theologi-cal insight, is open to a similar objection. But modern patristic scholarship, which tends to serve a liberal cause, is no different, in its present preoccu-pations, from Newman's. It is perfectly proper, where the evidence permits, to find and revivify the present in the past, for if the past has nothing to say to the present, it is hardly worth studying at all.

What the past had to give the present for Newman was that vision of the early Church which stood in judgement on the Church of England. Even

Bishop Charles James Blomfield of London, accounted a High Churchman, had disgraced himself in Newman's eyes by promoting Evangelicals and by allegedly declaring in an aside 'that belief in the Apostolical succession had gone out with the Non-jurors'.

> With the Establishment thus divided and threatened, thus ignorant of its true strength, I compared that fresh vigorous Power of which I was reading in the first centuries. In her triumphant zeal on behalf of that Primeval Mystery, . . . I recognized the movement of my Spiritual Mother. 'Incessu patuit Dea' [By her stately step she showed herself a Goddess]. The self-conquest of her Ascetics, the patience of her Martyrs, the irresistible determination of her Bishops, the joyous swing of her advance, both exalted and abashed me. I said to myself, 'Look on this picture and on that'; I felt affection for my own Church, but not tenderness; I felt dismay at her prospects, anger and scorn at her do-nothing perplexity. I thought that if Liberalism once got a footing within her, it was sure of the victory in the event. I saw that Reformation principles were powerless to rescue her. As to leaving her, the thought never crossed my imagination; still I ever kept before me that there was something greater than the Established Church, and that that was the Church Catholic and Apostolic, set up from the beginning, of which she was but the local presence and the organ. She was nothing, unless she was this. She must be dealt with strongly, or she would be lost. There was need of a second reformation.[35]

The study of the Fathers has always been a distinctive feature of Anglican theology, but surely no Anglican had ever studied them with the intensity and passion of Newman. Lyall does not seem to have realized that in the manuscript of the *Arians* he was reading a revolutionary tract, nowhere more so than in Newman's conclusion: 'that, should the hand of Satan press us sore, our Athanasius and Basil will be given us in their destined season, to break the bonds of the Oppressor, and let the captives go free'.[36]

Had Lyall but known, there was an even more un-Anglican, Roman, strand in Newman in his views about celibacy. His note to Robert Wilberforce expressing 'sorrow' at the latter's marriage may have been simple regret at the loss of an Oriel Fellow, as celibacy was a condition of a fellowship; and Newman could write movingly to Pusey on the death of his daughter Katherine on the satisfaction of having 'given eternal life and happiness to an immortal spirit'.[37] But he thought that the Church wanted 'expeditos milites – not a whole camp of women at its heels, forbye brats'.[38] This was in the spirit of the incipiently tubercular Froude, who asked Newman (whom he addressed as 'Dulcissime') to accompany him and his father in an attempt to recover his health by wintering in the Mediterranean. In an age when extravagant expressions of friendship were commonplace,

there is a deeper note than affection in the verses in which Newman was to
recall his first intimation that Froude's illness might be mortal:

> And when thine eye surveys,
> With fond adoring gaze,
> And yearning heart, thy friend –
> Love to its grave doth tend.[39]

Newman now leaped at the opportunity of travelling to Italy by sea
'without touching Gallic earth . . . which is an abomination',[40] he said, for
its associations with revolution. The party set out from Falmouth on the
Hermes on 8 December, the departure enlivened by the escape of a duck
from the livestock among the ship's stores: 'I should have liked to have let
him off', Newman wrote to his mother, 'but the poor fool did not know how
to use his fortune'[41] and was recaptured. The mingled tedium and excitement
of the ship's voyage not only spurred Newman to indite long letters to his
mother and sisters, but to continue to pour out poems, 'startling oracles or
newly discovered inscriptions in a strange character',[42] as one of his friends
was to describe them, 'gnomic' in their 'brevity of form and sharpness of
diction', with the 'pervasive awareness of sin and guilt, the honest fear of
death, and the sense of the embattled soul compassed round by trials' which
give them 'an appeal beyond the purely doctrinal'.[43] His muse descended
at Whitchurch, where he was waiting for the mail coach to Falmouth and
was seized by the vision which was to haunt his journey, of a change within
himself;[44] he expressed it in a poem about his guardian angel, a doppelgänger
and symbol of his better self, remoulding his spirit in the image of Christ:

> ARE these the tracks of some unearthly Friend,
> His foot-prints, and his vesture-skirts of light . . . [45]

The change was in part his new sense of vocation to God and his Church,
beyond the sacred ties of family. He wrote 'Wanderings' on board ship off
the Lizard:

> ERE yet I left home's youthful shrine,
> My heart and hope were stored
> Where first I caught the rays divine,
> And drank the Eternal Word.
>
> I went afar; the world unroll'd
> Her many-pictured page;
> I stored the marvels which she told,
> And trusted to her gage.

Her pleasures quaff'd, I sought awhile
   The scenes I prized before;
But parent's praise and sister's smile
   Stirr'd my cold heart no more.

So ever sear, so ever cloy
   Earth's favours as they fade;
Since Adam lost for one fierce joy
   His Eden's sacred shade.[46]

There was to be the 'fierce joy' of another sort in the battle for the Church of God in England. As Newman gazed at his first sight of foreign land, the morning sun shining on the golden coast of Portugal and 'the foam rising like Venus from the sea',[47] and saw above the wave, in the hitherto unexperienced and indescribable clarity of the Lusitanian air, the line of Torres Vedras, made famous in England by Wellington's defence of Lisbon, he transcribed another set of verses for Jemima, on the evils of private judgement:

1

Poor wanderers, you are sore perplexed
To find that path which Christ has blest,
   Tracked by His saintly throng:
Each claims to trust his own weak will,
Blind idol; – so ye languish still
   All wranglers, and all wrong.

2

He saw of old, and felt your need,
Granting you prophets of His creed,
   The throes of fear to swage;
They stored the rich bequest he made,
And sacred hands have safe conveyed
   The charge from age to age.

3

Wanderers, come home! when erring most
The Church aye kept the faith, nor lost
   One grain of holy truth,
She ne'er has erred, as those you trust,
And soon she shall shake off her dust,
   And REIGN as in her youth.[48]

9

Siren Lands

The Mediterranean, and Italy especially, offered liberation to many wealthy and leisured or cultivated Englishmen, seeking an ancient classical culture or a refuge from disgrace or respite from illness, or just a seat under the cypresses and a life-giving sun. Byron fled there, Keats and Shelley died there, the Brownings eloped there, Ruskin found there a new imaginative world. For Newman, his journey was to be a testing and trial, but unlike a later generation of High Churchmen, he set off with no overwhelming interest in the rituals of the Roman Church, and with a stronger interest in the future and foreign chaplaincies of the Church of England.[1] Thus he pondered the coming battle for England, and saw the nation falling under the judgement of God, in the verses on 'England', the 'TYRE of the West', composed at sea:

> He who scann'd Sodom for His righteous men
>   Still spares thee for thy ten;
> But, should vain tongue the Bride of Heaven defy,
>   He will not pass thee by;
> For, as earth's kings welcome their spotless guest,
> So gives He them by turn, to suffer or be blest.[2]

The poem, with its Old Testament hatred for great imperial cities, also has that distaste for 'trade' of aristocrats and academics in all ages. But it was in a spirit of righteous indignation that in Newman's first port of call, the harbour at Algiers lately conquered by the French, he 'would not even look at the tricolour',[3] as he claimed in the *Apologia*, because this was the flag of the Revolution and the international symbol of the liberal cause. While the vessel stocked up with coal in Malta, he spent a 'most wretched Christmas day' in quarantine, a 'Christmas without Christ', as he called it in his verses, deprived of the sacrament and 'of the comfort and order of an Established Church', while he admired the island's windmills from afar and listened to the bells of the churches, 'deep and sonorous . . . in a most painful way':[4]

I hear the tuneful bells around,
    The blessed towers I see;
A stranger on a foreign ground,
    They peal a fast for me.

O Britons! now so brave and high,
    How will ye weep the day
When Christ in judgment passes by,
    And calls the Bride away![5]

The ship bore the party on to Zante and Patras, and even in winter the warm south cast its spell: 'really I never knew before what ecstacy was', Newman wrote to Jemima, 'and the dreamy relaxation after it is most delightful . . . The chain of Parnassus rises before us, shrouded in clouds, which the eye cannot pierce, yet the imagination can. I have landed on the Peloponnese'. Yet though he shared the conventional classical love of the Greek sea, 'the scene of old Homer's song and of the histories of Thucydides',[6] it was the Greek Fathers who, as ever, rose before him:

All thine is Clement's varied page;
And Dionysius, ruler sage
    In days of doubt and pain;
And Origen of eagle eye,
And saintly Basil's purpose high
To smite imperial heresy,
    And cleanse the altar's stain.

For thee the glorious preacher came
With soul of zeal and lips of flame,
    A court's stern-martyr guest;
And thine, O inexhaustive race!
Meek Nazianzen's heaven-taught grace
And royalhearted Athanase,
    With Paul's own mantle blest.[7]

The modern Greeks, though of mixed blood, were almost as interesting – the men's dresses 'most picturesque, consisting of "the snowy camese", spoken of by Byron, then an embroidered waistcoat – a plaited and frilled white petticoat to the shins and a large great coat with the arms hanging down behind, "the shaggy capote". – Their faces and figures were very fine'.[8] The next landing place was the English colony of Corfu, where Newman spent the New Year of 1833 and enjoyed an English dinner in the house of the commissioner Colonel Baker, the connection of a close schoolfriend – the meal, he wrote to his mother, was 'English salmon, sherry, mincepies' and 'a Turkish sweetmeat, soft and insipid, like Otto of roses and honey'.[9] He found the Greek clergy 'of the lower rank, as our methodist . . . very ignorant, but moral in their lives',[10] and saw their liturgy, and thought that there was little objectionable in their service books, though he wondered why Protestants should consider Rome Antichrist, when the Greek Church had the same corruptions. At Malta again, he and the Froudes farewelled the *Hermes* and spent twelve days in quarantine in the Lazaretto. When released, Newman thought longingly of St Mary's and Littlemore, in the midst of 'that most exciting religion which is around me – statues of Madonnas and Saints in the Streets, etc etc. A more poetical but not less jading stimulant than the pouring-forth in a Baptist Chapel'. Such reflections again raised the spectre of the crisis in England: 'all one can say of Whigs, Radicals and the rest is, that they know not what they do'.[11]

After nearly a month in Malta, Newman and the Froudes took the Naples steamship to Messina and Palermo. He was intensely moved by the great lonely temple ruin of Segesta, bound only by the squalor of a shepherd's hut and muddy yard and dogs. But he found a similar contrast everywhere, and wrote to his mother that the 'mixture of grandeur and filth in the towns is indescribable'. Palermo especially was 'the filthiest, yet the noblest city, I have seen', its 'children and youths . . . with features sunk and contracted with perpetual dirt, as if it was their only food', while the offspring of the poor in the inn at Calatafimi, where the party stayed after the mule ride to Segesta, 'slept in holes in the wall' which smelled 'like a wildbeast's cage, almost overpowering us in our room upstairs'.[12]

The steamer took them on from Palermo to Naples, where Newman thought the population 'immersed in the most despicable frivolity and worst profligacy, which is so much connected with religious observances as to give the city the character of a pagan worship'.[13] From there he saw the temples at Paestum, Herculanaeum and Pompeii, and the beautiful cliffs, ravines and waterfalls of Salerno and Amalfi, far eclipsing in beauty the mere fashionable watering hole of Naples itself. From afar he glimpsed through the rain the castle of Salerno, where he later learned that Hildebrand, Pope Gregory VII, had died, the great architect of the power of the medieval papacy, afterwards the subject of a memoir by Newman's friend John Bowden. Newman found the peasantry impressive, and discounted tales of banditry, attributing a fatal attack on an English couple some years earlier to their own bad luck and imprudence. He saw the antiquities in the Naples Museum, where he was told of those 'odious Mosaics etc collected from Pompeii . . . atrocious beyond power of words to stigmatize', suggestive of the thought that the fire from Vesuvius was 'as strictly judicial as that which overwhelmed the cities of the plain',[14] a punishment for sins too dreadful to describe.

This passage, with its apocalyptic references, was written after Newman and the Froudes reached Rome on 2 March 1833, and there his impressions on a superficial level were in marked contrast to those of Naples: 'Every thing here is so bright and clean – and the Sunday kept so decorously'[15] – almost like England. 'And now what [can] I say of Rome', he asked Harriett, 'but that it is of all cities the first, and that all I ever saw are but as dust, even dear Oxford inclusive, compared with its majesty and glory. Is it possible that so serene and lofty a place is the cage of unclean creatures?'[16] The Roman clergy were said to be more moral than the Neapolitan, and though 'the choristers at St Peter's are as irreverent as at St Paul's', there were 'no trumpery [sic] ornaments or absurd inscriptions in the streets, profaning the most sacred subjects'[17] as in Naples.

This was Newman's introduction to the sobriety of Roman religion, and contains the hint of his later break with his future disciple Frederick William Faber, whose taste was more extravagantly Neapolitan. Yet Newman could not rid himself of his notion of Rome as understood by Protestants from the prophetic Books of Daniel and Revelation. 'Here we see the only remnant of the 4 great Enemies of God – Babylon, Persia, and Macedon have left scarce a trace behind them – the last and most terrible beast lies before us . . . in all the visibleness of its plagues.'[18] This refers to the empires described under the images of the ungodly beasts of Daniel and Revelation, one of them, in Revelation, pagan Rome: the problem lay in the relation of pagan to papal Rome, and Newman had the idea that the latter was not identical with the Antichrist, which lurked in the colossal ruins of the ancient city, and infected the Church, and might even ascend the papal throne.

He saw the Pope himself in great state, distributing dowries to white-robed girls in S. Maria-sopra-Minerva, but the ceremony of kissing the papal foot, which he could not endure for its want of apostolic humility, made him think of the union between the Roman Church and 'that enemy of God, who from the beginning sat on her 7 hills, with an enchantress's cup' – the Scarlet Woman of the Book of Revelation – 'as the representative and instrument of the Evil Principle'.[19] To Pusey, Newman still wondered if the numerology of Revelation contained the key to Romish corruption: 'whether the 1260 years of [the Church's] captivity begin with Constantine – it seems a remarkable coincidence that its termination should fall about on the Reformation',[20] itself the source of modern infidelity as well as of so much good. And all this was sadly difficult to reconcile with Newman's more favourable view of Rome: 'There is so much amiableness and gentleness, so much Oxonianism, (so to say) such an amusing and interesting demureness, and such simplicity of look and speech, that I feel for those indeed who are bound with an iron chain . . . '[21] He expressed his puzzlement in lines sent to Harriett which he wrote as he 'walked along the Appian Way over the Pontine Marshes, while the horses were changing':

> How shall I call thee, Light of the wide West,
>   Or heinous error-seat?
> O Mother erst, close following Jesus' feet!

> Do not thy titles glow
> Mid those stern judgement fires, which shall complete
> Crime's weary course and heavenawarded woe?[22]

So much good and bad were mixed together. 'Dead flies cause the precious ointment to stink.'[23] Part of this was English sensibility: 'I have seen a woman in the midst of her prayers spit about – and a priest at the altar in the most sacred part of the service'.[24] But underlying this fastidiousness lay the deeper imaginative stain of the Roman Antichrist. Newman's old Evangelical strain of judgement on Popery was shaken, but was alive and well.

His puzzlement was enhanced by a meeting with the architect of the coming Roman Catholic revival in Victorian England, Dr Nicholas Wiseman, Rector of the English College, born in Spain of an Irish family and educated for the priesthood in England. Wiseman was a flamboyant purple figure, born to be a cardinal, an internationally famous Syriac scholar in his twenties, with an effortless facility in all he did except administration. Even now he was only in his early thirties. As Froude described the meeting, he and Newman went to Wiseman 'to find out whether they would take us in on any terms to which we could twist our consciences, and we found to our dismay that not one step could be gained without swallowing the Council of Trent as a whole . . . that the doctrine of the infallibility of the Church made the acts of each successive Council obligatory for ever . . . '[25] In fact, it was Wiseman's subtle combination of doctrinal intransigence and warm personal goodwill that was to make so many conversions to Roman Catholicism in England. Perhaps Froude was more disappointed in the meeting than Newman, for with his higher abstract admiration of the Roman system, the younger man had been appalled by the moral squalor, as he saw it, of the Italian Church, and called its clergy 'wretched Tridentines'. Wiseman hoped the travellers would return to Rome. Newman replied, in prophecy, 'We have a work to do in England'.[26]

Political events now gave that work a new urgency. A letter from Harriett and Jemima written on 21 February 1833 brought word of 'all the mad schemes of Government, and of the despoiling of the poor Irish Church'.[27] The Irish Church Temporalities Bill, introduced in the Commons on 12 February, proposed to abolish two of the Irish archbishoprics and eight of the bishoprics by uniting them with adjacent dioceses at the next vacancy; and the vague but notorious clause 147 was intended to divert the money elsewhere, perhaps to Roman Catholic education, or even to the payment of the Catholic priesthood. Newman heard about the measure when in Naples: 'well done, my blind Premier', he wrote of the Whig Earl Grey, in a rather mixed metaphor, 'confiscate and rob, till, like Samson, you pull down the political structure on your own head . . . '[28]

The Bill filled his mind, and he 'had fierce thoughts against the Liberals'.[29]

He and Froude christened their poems *Lyra Apostolica* and sent two of them off to Hugh James Rose for publication in the *British Magazine*, founded in 1832 as the organ of resistance to Whig reform of the Church. Newman's verses were to be published underneath the motto chosen by Froude from the Homer lent them by the Prussian minister in Rome, the fanatically anti-Catholic Chevalier Christian Bunsen, 'the words in which Achilles, on returning to the battle, says, "You shall know the difference, now that I am back again" '.[30]

Newman was further annoyed when word came to Froude from Keble of Thomas Arnold's *Principles of Church Reform*. Arnold, a former Fellow of Oriel and now headmaster of Rugby, a post to which he had pipped Newman's former tutor Thomas Short, was not yet the most famous schoolteacher in English history. Once a friend of Keble's in the latter's more liberal youth, he· was called Whately's bottle-washer, and his proposal that Dissenters should be allowed to worship in parish churches outside the normal hours of service was regarded by loyal Churchmen as an ecclesiastical Noah's Ark, containing beasts both clean and unclean. This was the old liberal Latitudinarian idea of a national establishment, including all Trinitarian Protestants and otherwise excluding only Jews, Quakers, Unitarians and Roman Catholics. The idea was marked by that condescension towards Dissenters made more famous by Arnold's son Matthew: Arnold senior did not think that non-Anglican Protestants should be forced to suffer the debasement of taste inbred by worshipping in their ugly conventicles. Newman saw the incipient liberalism of the older Noetics now made explicit in the younger one, and was moved to irony. Surely it was illiberal of Arnold to exclude the Jews, Papists and Quakers? To avoid too many sects in some places for one day, why not force Judaizing Evangelicals to worship on Saturdays? The Catholics could have the Evangelical vacancy, the Jews could also take Saturday, and the Mohammadens Friday. And why not space for Socinians and 'Sandemonians' [sic]?[31]

Arnold was also deeply interested in that very German theology from which Rose had argued that modern heresy had come. In a conversation in Rome with the Revd Anthony Grant, either about a certain view of Scripture or Arnold's opinion that the German liberal historian Niebuhr was a Christian, Newman asked, 'But is *he* [Arnold] a Christian?' The question was passed by Grant a thousand miles back to Arnold, via another well-known liberal, Julius Hare, and was to produce a heavy letter from Arnold to Grant that Newman 'must not be allowed to utter such speeches without being warned of their evil nature and tendency'.[32] Arnold's hostility was to have consequences that Newman was to rue.

In Rome, Newman bought a cameo for Maria Giberne, who had befriended his sisters, and was devoted to him for the rest of her long life. There then followed an adventure, inspired by his fascination with the sheer

99

wild and sometimes slovenly beauty and exoticism of his surroundings, that nearly brought him to an early grave.

'Can there be a greater proof that I am become a liberal, a march-of-mind man, a man of the world', he wrote to Henry Woodgate, ' . . . than my refusing to return home with the Froudes and running down to Sicily instead? . . . you will not be surprised to be told that I habitually desecrate the Sabbath by travelling and visiting; that I visit the theatres, and am glad to accept invitations from the wealthy English adulterers here, who are the attraction of the place.'[33] This playfulness had no good reason but itself. Sicily was, despite its ancient culture, a wild rough place where the English were regarded as great lords but where travellers were sometimes murdered; and Newman had no excuse for returning, except the island's enchantment. The Froudes left him for Cività Vecchia on 9 April, to travel through France and then home, and on his return to Naples Newman climbed Vesuvius with the English chaplain and gathered materials for his journey, 'a set of cooking utensils and tea service – curry powder, spice, pepper, salt, sugar, tea, and ham; cold cream, a straw hat, and a map of Sicily'.[34] He also hired mules and a servant called Gennaro, whom he was soon to describe as 'a treasure – very sharp-witted and ready – an old campaigner, having served thro' the Peninsula – a sailor in his earlier days – and in the Victory at the battle of Trafalgar – domesticated in England since he was 4 years old, yet a perfect Neapolitan in language – he does not read nor write'.[35] Gennaro was to be an even greater treasure than Newman could have known in hiring him, and indeed was to be 'humanly speaking the preserver of my life'.[36]

At first, all went well. Newman set out from Naples in the Yarmouth sailing ship, the *Sarepta*, on 19 April and after a bout of seasickness and a day 'becalmed off Stromboli' reached Messina on the 21st, a Sunday.[37] Having failed to find the English resident, a Mr Morrison, Newman set off for the south on Monday at the head of a cavalcade consisting of his servant, 'two mules, and several muleteers . . . Even the gallant D. [Joseph Dornford, his old Oriel colleague, a rather unclerical cleric as a veteran of the Peninsular Wars] could not', Newman wrote to Harriett, 'have succeeded more fully in uncassocking himself. In addition to grey trousers, I had a straw hat and a flannel jacket – so that my neckcloth was the only black part of me. Nor had I any such exuberance of spirits, which would bear up against the ridiculousness of this exterior. I was setting out on an expedition, which was to be pleasant in memory rather than in present enjoyment'.[38]

From the Roman theatre at Taormina, however, the view 'was a nearer approach to seeing Eden, than anything I had conceived possible. O happy I, it was worth coming all the way, to endure the loneliness and sadness of my progress and the weariness of the voyage to see it. I felt for the first time in my life with my eyes open that I must be better and more religious, if I lived there'. For all the difficulty he had in sleeping for the stings of the fleas – 'you in England have no idea was [what] a Sicilian flea is', Newman told Harriett – even the frogs on the road between Giardini and Giarra were 'the most musical animals I have hitherto met with'. But there was, again, the contrast between the splendour of the landscape and the abject poverty of the people. The so-called inn near Etna 'was the most forlorn place I ever was in – on the ground-floor, one window and no glass – 3 doors with boards gaping to the external air – brick floor in pieces – filthy walls . . . '[39] Newman thoroughly cleansed himself of travel stains at the hotel Corona d'oro in Catania, but his boat from there to Syracuse, a thirty-five foot oar-driven *'speronard'*, with no more covering than an awning, became becalmed, he had nothing to eat and had to sleep on the ground six miles from the city beside 'the only vulgar Italian I have met with', miserably tormented by fleas. At Syracuse, he saw the fount of Arethusa 'and rowed up the Anapus to gather the papyrus', and visited the remains of the temples of Jupiter and Minerva. He was taken by some English companions to the wedding of a judge's son to the daughter of the Russian consul, and 'went in a *traveller's* dress! thinking, goose as I was, to be incognito and merely to *see* – you may fancy we were all lions'.[40]

There was another trying sea voyage back to Catania. The sirocco sprang up, the company slept in the boat in a cove near Syracuse, and reached Agosta at 8 o'clock in the morning. 'Delays of obtaining pratique, passport, etc., etc., kept us till 3 p.m., when we set forth on mules for Catania with the belief that the distance was twenty-two miles. By the time it grew dusk we had gone fourteen miles, and descended to the water's side; when to our dismay we learned we had eighteen miles before us, three rivers to ford or ferry, a deep sand to traverse for half the way, and the danger of being plundered.'[41] Suspiciously the guide lost his way, but then found it after half an hour, and the party reached Catania between eleven and twelve. The next day Newman had a fever, but after rest and recovery he decided to turn inland for Agrigento in the south with its great temples. The weather was exceptionally wet even for this season of rain, and Newman wondered whether travelling on Sunday had 'not brought all this upon me'.[42]

The rain had brought fever to the area, but after the first day's journey, on Wednesday 1 May to Adernò, the second day began in another landscape like Eden, 'hills thrown about on all sides, & covered with green corn, in all variety of shades, relieving [-ed] by the light (raw sienna) stone of the hills . . . sometimes with deep valleys on the side, & many trees, high hills with towns on the top as S. Filippo d'Argyro . . . ' Newman went forty-two miles on the mule in great pain, and 'set out walking, the mules coming after – & fell to tears thinking of dear Mary . . . ' He lay down for an hour at Regalbuto, had to be helped by Gennaro to a wine-shop at S. Filippo, but at Leonforte found the inn, 'a fair one', occupied 'by some Sicilian Duke' and 'was forced to wander about for a lodging for a night'. He found

101

a second-rate hostelry and in the morning tried to get up but fell back 'too ill to do so'.[43]

The duke having departed, Newman moved to 'a comfortable & gaily ornamented room' at the better inn, tried half a rhubarb and ginger pill and sent out Gennaro for camomile, which turned out to be a familiar medicine in the place. Newman considered the tea from the leaves too rough, but one made with the flowers was 'beautiful' and 'most refreshing'. To the best of his recollection, he had bowel and stomach pains, but what he recalled far more vividly was his mental anguish, as he felt that 'God was fighting ag[ain]st me', because of his own 'self will', the very vice he had preached against in Oxford.[44] He now discerned this in his desertion of the Froudes, even in profaning the Sacrament by unworthily receiving it during his battle with Hawkins over the tutorship. 'I bitterly blamed myself, as disrespectful & insulting to the Provost, my superior.' He dictated to himself a letter to be sent to William James, the Fellow of Oriel, 'stating in strong terms my self-reproach; & I was not to preach at St Mary's or any where for a length of time as a penitent unworthy to show himself'. He also imagined that his 'professed principles' were 'mere intellectual deductions from one or two admitted truths' taken second hand from Keble, which he loved rather than possessed. 'Yet still I said to myself "I have not sinned against light".'[45]

Newman's worst misery came on Saturday 4 May, as he counted the number of flowers and stars in the wallpaper and listened to 'the miserable whine of Sicilian beggars' outside the door. 'Who can describe the wretchedness of that low feeble monotonous cry, which went on I cannot say how long.' He was relieved by the harp and clarinet-like music of some passing players, and may even have taken an evening walk. Gennaro was anxious to move on, and they discussed the idea of having a litter made to get him to Palermo. The servant thought his master dying and told him 'a story about a sick officer he had attended on in Spain, who left him all his baggage & then got well'. Newman 'did not see the drift of the story at the time' – that Gennaro would have liked something in his will. It was a small lapse in a service of complete devotion, but while Newman directed the man to write to Froude if he died, he said 'I do not think I shall', and either 'I have not sinned against light' or 'God has still work for me to do' – he thought the last.[46]

At first, he seemed to make a partial recovery. He spent Sunday 5 May eating every half hour, and then went out on an evening mule-ride towards Palermo. He decided that his illness was 'all fancy', and, confusedly, 'that God meets those who go on in *His way*', and that it would be a shame not to see Agrigento; so he set off with Gennaro on Monday morning. He felt weak after half a mile again, demanded chicken from the servant, became very thirsty, and began eating the ripe oranges by the wayside: 'not sweet or tart', he decided to tell his mother and sisters, 'but a fine aromatic bitter'.

His throat seemed to suffocate him, he desperately wanted water, and 'took to eating the leaves of the trees'. After seven miles, he was laid on his blue cloak in a hut or tent, in which a party of poor peasants watched over him with lively interest, and though he could not understand their Sicilian dialect, he imagined that someone had come in to ask them for money for prayers for the souls in purgatory. He then felt fingers on his pulse. It was a passing doctor who prescribed a drink of camomile, lemon and sugar, and urged him to go to the nearby town of Castro Giovanni. Newman heard a passing diligence, which he thought might contain English travellers, and successfully insisted that Gennaro bring one of the party to him. They were German, but one of them spoke English, and Newman gave him a letter of introduction to an Englishman in Palermo, thinking to alert his friends to his condition. He made an affectionate leave-taking of 'the poor people in the tent', and promised to mention their name in England, but was to forget it. Gennaro burst into tears. He held Newman sideways on the mule and together they managed to climb the hill to Castro Giovanni. With some difficulty he found the patient lodgings in a private house. Newman was to remain there three weeks.[47]

Newman was bled. Only four ounces of blood were taken, as he was so weak that his attendant feared to take more. He was also dosed with 'English' Epsom salts, and had rows with Gennaro, who wanted him to drink tea instead of the prescribed lemonade. His illness was diagnosed as a gastric fever, then rife in the neighbourhood. He escaped diarrhoea, but had an 'obstinate costiveness' and pains in the bowels and could not urinate, so that he swelled up. Elsewhere the illness was attended by what the local people called cholera. Newman's illness had dissipated his smattering of Italian, so he corresponded with the doctor in Latin, and, characteristically, kept the letters between them. 'He, I suppose, was no deep Latin scholar, and pretended my Latin was nonsense – but it is very good, particularly considering I was so ill.'[48]

Poor Newman. The doctor gave his patient some of his own sulphur, then castor oil every two hours. Newman thought that the illness had reached a crisis after eleven days, and spent the nights in 'the dreamy confusion of delirium – sitting on a staircase, wanting something, or with some difficulty – very wretched – & something about my Mother & Sisters. – How I dreaded the long nights – lying without sleep, as it seemed, all through the darkness'.[49]

He was oppressed by the heat. He had difficulty getting nurses, but Gennaro slept in his room, and he got some relief from the camomile flowers near his bed. He also had his muleteer sit with him, and apply vinegar 'with his great bullet tips of fingers . . . to my nose in the middle of the night'. He soon, however, discharged the man, who disputed his wages for the rest days with no travelling and even took the case before the local magistrates. The invalid also suffered from the noise of a great fair under his window, and from the daily Mass bell, which he wanted Gennaro to stop. 'The master of the house was very civil – he heard I liked music, & he got some performers to play to me in the next room. It was very beautiful, but too much for me'. The blood in his head seemed to rise in his ears, he suffered 'from a wearisome continual cough' and spitting which his attendants tried to prevent, 'saying it would hurt me', by letting more blood. 'I had piles too, and was obliged to have leeches & burning hot steam – & then a preparation of herbs very cooling. I was given the prescription, but lost it. Mallows, I think, was one ingredient.' His side was sore from too much lying on it, and he began to itch – he later thought 'that it was the return of insects to feed on me', perhaps no bad sign, as they had left him alone in his illness. For all the care and kindness he received, a medical practice, consisting, apart from the herbs which might have helped, of bleeding by incision, sulphur, Epsom Salts, castor oil, vinegar and more blood-letting by leeches, suggests the stamina then required to survive not the illness but the doctor.[50]

But Newman was very grateful to both the doctor and the master of the house, the lawyer Luigi Restivo, and to the one or other presented 'a pocket compass, thermometer, a Virgil, and I *think* some other Latin Book, and perhaps some other things. The doctor took a fancy to something which Gennaro thought was too expensive to part with, or, as I fancy from the event, wished the Master of the House to have'. The servant took it away from the doctor, and carried a complaint to the magistracy, who partly out of curiosity paid Newman a visit, though he did not understand a word they said apart from Gennaro's interpretation. Their talk of the English soldiers quartered at Castro Giovanni during the Napoleonic Wars may have suggested his dreams about armies, one of which scaled Castro Giovanni, while another sailed from Reggio to join yet another at Messina to take a tower. He also thought that he was ill-mannered enough to speak to the Empress of Russia: 'in the case of great people, one should not speak, but be spoken to'.[51]

As he got better, Gennaro gave him an egg baked in wood ashes for breakfast, with tea and cakes. 'How I longed for it! and when I took the tea, I could not help crying out from delight. I used to say "It is life from the dead!" I never had such feelings. All through my illness I had depended on Gennaro so much I could not bear him from the room five minutes. I used always to be crying out for I don't know how long together 'Gen-na-roooooo.' Newman was touched by the scrupulous honesty of the poor people around him, who had him and his possessions completely at their mercy. But he was especially grateful to his servant. 'Gennaro had charge of clothes, money, every thing. I lost nothing. A large sum of money came to me from Palermo in dollars safe. He paid nothing without asking my leave; and though he had coveted all my effects, if I died, yet even then he wished them formally bequeathed to him – and, as it was, when I got to

England, I had lost after all only one common (3/6) shirt in all, & . . . perhaps a pair of stockings or a towel.'[52] Newman corresponded in Latin with Restivo after his return to Oxford, and sent him a Bible, expressing the hope that 'Ecclesias nostras, Siciliensem et Anglicanum, mutua charitatis officia tenerent! . . . Vale, vir Benevolentissime', Newman concluded, 'Fortis sis, et abundes in fide, in veritate, in bonis operibus . . .'[53]

In the aftermath of the illness, Newman's lips peeled, his fingernails darkened, and later he thought that his hands had turned yellow. At first, he leaned on his servant and hobbled on a stick, even after he got to Palermo, a journey of three days. He overcame his 'great compunction about travelling through the Sunday'. 'My joy, however, was too great for me at first. I never saw such a country. The Spring [was] in its greatest luxuriance. All sorts of strange trees – very steep and high hills over which the road went; mountains in the distance – a profusion of aloes along the road – Such bright colouring – all in tune too with my reviving life. I had a great appetite and was always coaxing (as I may call it) Gennaro for cakes.' At Palermo Newman was given beef broth, and that gave him 'something of the ecstatic feelings which the tea had given' him at Castro Giovanni.[54] But his recovery also made him restless. 'Before starting from my inn in the morning of May 26th or 27th, I sat down on my bed, and began to sob violently.' Gennaro asked what ailed him. 'I could only answer him, "I have a work to do in England".'[55]

'I was aching to get home; yet for want of a vessel I was kept at Palermo for three weeks. I began to visit the Churches, and they calmed my impatience, though I did not attend any services.'[56] He wrote:

OH that thy creed were sound!
For thou dost soothe the heart, Thou Church of Rome,
 By thy unwearied watch and varied round
Of service, in thy Saviour's holy home.
 I cannot walk the city's sultry streets,
 But the wide porch invites to still retreats,
Where passion's thirst is calm'd and care's unthankful gloom.

There, on a foreign shore,
The homesick solitary finds a friend:
 Thoughts, prison'd long for lack of speech, outpour
Their tears; and doubts in resignation end.
 I almost fainted from the long delay
 That tangles me within this languid bay,
When comes a foe, my wounds with oil and wine to tend.[57]

The 'oil and wine' of the shrines of the Siren Land offered a deeper comfort to his restless soul.

He said nothing of his illness in his letter to his mother, to whom he wrote homesick 'with much longing',[58] but he did describe it in a congratulatory epistle to his dear friend Frederic Rogers, who, he saw from a local newspaper, which he kissed in delight, had just been elected a Fellow of Oriel. Newman had another supporter, indeed a worshipper, in the other Fellow just elected, Charles Marriott. 'I have *not* been weather-bound or shipless, taken by the Barbary pirates, or seized as a propagandist of Liberalism', he assured Rogers jocularly enough.[59] The memory of the illness returned to him gradually, and the many-layered accounts of what had happened to him well illustrate the problems for a biographer, as they extend from his letters to Rogers and Henry Wilberforce, through reminiscences of 1834, 1835 and 1840, with a last entry in 1874: 'I wonder I have not mentioned how I simply lost my memory as to *how* I came to be ill and in bed – and how strangely by little and little first one fact came back to me, then another, till at length I realized my journey and my illness in continuity'.[60]

Newman's illness was almost certainly typhoid fever, possibly contracted from eating some delicious oysters from a polluted bed in Lake Fusaro, near Naples.[61] In the aftermath of his recovery in England, his hair all fell out, and for a brief time before it had regrown he wore a wig; yet the quickness of his return to health was to be astonishing. The whole episode of the illness had something of the unreality of nightmare. 'What strange dreamy reminiscences of feeling', wrote Newman at one point of his narrative of the event, 'does this attempt at relation raise!'[62] It is in Newman's letter to Henry Wilberforce begun 16 July after the return to England[63] that there first appears the intimation of the role of God in this, the third of the great illnesses of his life, the first being before his conversion and the second in schools before Mary's death. Over a very long lifetime, Newman enjoyed singularly good physical health, which may have made these lapses from it seem the more dramatic: but none of the three illnesses was merely physical and, like any good Evangelical, Newman had to fit them into a pattern of special providences for himself. In the beginning of his account of the Sicilian illness, written in 1834 after the Oxford Movement had begun, the incident achieved its classic significance as the experience of trial before the work that God intended him to do. 'I could almost think the devil saw I am to be a means of usefulness, & tried to destroy me . . . O my God, keep me still from being the sport & victim of Satan. By Thy Mercies in Thy Son's Holy Table which I have this day partaken, be to me a Savior.'[64] He had not sinned against light after all.

He had also to say goodbye to Gennaro, who got drunk in Palermo, and wanted Newman's favourite old blue cloak, which had accompanied him in all his wanderings, as a leaving present. It was 'a little thing for him to set his services at', but Newman could not bear to part with it, though he did give Gennaro £10 above his wages, then no small sum, and a letter of reference. The servant intended returning to his family in Naples, and later found a place with Lord Carrington's family in England. 'What I should have done without him, I cannot think', wrote Newman. 'He nursed me as a child. An English servant never could do what he did', for all that he 'had once been deranged; and was easily overset by liquor'.[65] For all Newman's dislike of the filth, frivolity and superstition of Palermo, he at least had nothing of a quality which disfigured even a great-hearted liberal like Macaulay, the nineteenth-century English gentleman's instinctive sense of superiority to Italians.

'At last', he wrote, 'I got off in an orange boat, bound for Marseilles . . . We were becalmed a whole week in the Straits of Bonifacio',[66] where he wrote what became his most famous hymn, 'The Pillar of the Cloud', the title having reference, in an image which is changed in the poem, to the sign which led Moses and Israel through the wilderness:

> LEAD, Kindly Light, amid the encircling gloom,
>   Lead Thou me on!
> The night is dark, and I am far from home –
>   Lead Thou me on!
> Keep Thou my feet; I do not ask to see
> The distant scene, – one step enough for me.
>
> I was not ever thus, nor pray'd that Thou
>   Shouldst lead me on.
> I loved to choose and see my path; but now
>   Lead Thou me on!
> I loved the garish day, and, spite of fears,
> Pride ruled my will: remember not past years.
>
> So long Thy power hath blest me, sure it still
>   Will lead me on,
> O'er moor and fen, o'er crag and torrent, till
>   The night is gone;
> And with the morn those angel faces smile
> Which I have loved long since, and lost awhile.[67]

The poem owed some of its Victorian popularity to the subliminal lilt of the setting for it composed by the great hymn writer John Bacchus Dykes. Newman was to be irritated by the Evangelical Bishop Edward Bickersteth's attempt to popularize his own unauthorized fourth verse, which made specific reference to Christ. Indeed lacking any dogmatic Christian reference, it could be sung and enjoyed by the non-theist Ethical Societies, and joined that non-denominational legacy of sacred song which is among the most important of the heirlooms of middle-class England. But the verses also summon up another image, of the time and place of their making: of a lonely pilgrim in a summer sea, with the light of battle in his eyes.

Part Two

Anglo-Catholicism

10

The Oxford Movement

Newman disembarked at Marseilles and travelled straight to Lyon. On his arrival, his ankles were so swollen that he had to be lifted from the carriage and supported by his fellow passengers to 'a miserable, dirty inn', yet the best in the town, where he rested for a night and a day. From Lyon, he wrote to his mother that France was 'truly *La Belle France* in all externals. I am enchanted with it':[1] though in the *Apologia*, he claimed when at Paris to have 'kept indoors the whole time, and all that I saw of that beautiful city was what I saw from the Diligence',[2] in a private protest against the great revolutionary sin-city of liberalism. Perhaps the difference between the two impressions lies in the word 'externals': France was all glorious without, corrupt within. He took a steamship from Dieppe to Brighton, and the night mail to London, before returning on 9 July to Oxford, where he found Frank just home from Persia. On 14 July 1833, Newman heard Keble preach a sermon on 'National Apostasy' before the judges of the assize in his own St Mary's church. 'I have ever considered and kept the day, as the start of the religious movement of 1833', he wrote in the *Apologia*.[3] The Oxford Movement had for him begun.

Newman's word on the matter was good enough for his later disciple Richard Church, Dean of St Paul's, one of the finest scholars produced by the Victorian Church of England, and the Anglican Churchman who supremely inherited from Newman his fastidious literary taste and mastery of English prose. From Newman's *Apologia* and Church's classic history, *The Oxford Movement*, the 'myth' of July 14th,[4] of the significance of the sermon, passed into the historiography of the subject, though the great Anglo-Catholic scholar F. L. Cross has argued that the event was hardly noticed by Newman's immediate contemporaries. Pusey may have been present, but passed no judgement on it, and his published copy of the sermon remained uncut until his death. Its reputation is a singular instance of Newman's ability to give a heightened quality to events in a drama in which his was one of the principal roles.

The sermon itself is couched in generalities, but would have delighted a Scottish Covenanter for its Old Testament analogy between the Israelites rebuked by Samuel for wanting a king like the heathen, and an England throwing off its age-old allegiance to Christ and his Church. Keble ascribed this in the present to the 'growing indifference' and 'fashionable liberality' of his own generation, who were guilty of an 'APOSTASY'[5] which would bring the nation under divine judgement in this world or another and which possibly heralded a new persecution of the Church recalling its earliest days. He concluded with a text:

> *Why do the heathen rage, and the people imagine a vain thing? The kings of the earth stand up, and the rulers take counsel together, against the Lord, and against His Anointed. . . .* [6]

Apart, however, for rather vaguely calling for 'INTERCESSION' and 'REMONSTRANCE', Keble had no practical course of action to suggest, but there was more fire in his way of making the contemporary reference specific in the preface to the first edition of the work, dated 22 July, which Newman corrected for the press: 'The Legislature of England and Ireland, (*the members of which are not even bound to profess belief in the Atonement,*) this body has virtually usurped the commission of those whom our Saviour entrusted with *at least one voice* in making ecclesiastical laws, on matters wholly or partly spiritual'. The note to the sentence refers the reader to 'the suppression of certain Irish Sees, *contrary to the suffrage of the Bishops of England and Ireland*', by a legislature which has also declared 'that the Apostolical Church in this realm is henceforth only to stand, in the eye of the State, as *one sect among many* . . .' How, then, could loyal Churchmen remain in communion with the Establishment 'without any taint of those Erastian Principles on which she is now avowedly to be governed? What answer can we make henceforth to the partisans of the Bishop of Rome, when they taunt us with being a mere Parliamentarian Church?' It was for Churchmen to resist the tyranny of such an intrusion into matters spiritual, 'unless we would have our children's children say, "There was once here a glorious Church, but it was betrayed into the hands of Libertines for the real or affected love of a little temporary peace and good order" '.[7]

This onslaught on 'Erastians' and 'Libertines' in the Preface is a good deal more exciting than the sermon; and the modern Oratorian Newman scholar Fr Henry Tristram suggests that the real beginning of the Oxford Movement was Newman's university sermon of 22 January 1832,[8] 'Personal Influence, the Means of Propagating the Truth', with its argument from the example of the Apostles that a 'few highly-endowed men will rescue the world for centuries to come . . . it has happened before now, that comparatively retired posts have been filled by those who have exerted the most extensive influences over the destinies of religion'.[9] Newman was to ponder the character of this personal influence more deeply in the *Apologia*. A movement of spiritual ideas, he thought, required the unity of antecedents: 'a common history, common memories, an intercourse of mind with mind in the past, and a progress and increase in that intercourse in the present'.[10]

The heart of the Oxford Movement was just this, the personal loyalty and affection between Newman, Froude and Keble, and their love and affection for Oxford.

But as Newman recognized, he and Froude were still nobodies; and a good part of the difficulty of the Oxford Movement was to lie in its strained relations with the people whom it needed to make a noise, its influential friends. The first of these were Hugh James Rose and William Palmer of Worcester. Palmer spent long hours in conversation with the solitary tubercular Froude in the summer of 1833. A graduate of Trinity College, Dublin, he was full of the wrongs of the Irish Church, and arranged a meeting at Rose's rectory for 25–29 July at Hadleigh in Suffolk, attended by Froude, Rose, Rose's curate R. C. Trench, later Archbishop of Dublin, and the Revd Arthur Perceval, a royal chaplain and Fellow of All Souls, and cousin to Spencer Perceval, who was the son of the assassinated Prime Minister and a pillar of the Catholic Apostolic Church. Rose was the major figure, and became in the autumn the first Professor of Divinity in the new High Church University of Durham, founded by the local clergy to inhibit any Whig spoliation of their indecently wealthy church. At Hadleigh, the difference showed itself between the new High Churchmen and the old ones, whom Froude was to christen 'Zs', and who, like Rose and Palmer, wanted an orderly movement in the old Hackney manner with formal committees, petitions and protests.

Newman's mature judgement on the Zs lies in his remarks about Palmer. 'He was the only really learned man among us. He understood theology as a science; he was practised in the scholastic mode of controversial writing; and, I believe, was as well acquainted, as he was dissatisfied, with the Catholic schools.' He was to impress the Roman theologians who thought Newman muddle-headed: but then, his cool, dry, analytical orderly Hackney mind was at the remotest pole from Newman's own. Newman was to think him for all his cleverness and learning 'deficient in depth; and besides, coming from a distance, he never had really grown into an Oxford man . . . nor had he any insight into the force of personal influence and congeniality of thought in carrying out a religious theory, – a condition which Froude and I considered essential to any true success in the stand which had to be made against Liberalism. Mr Palmer had a certain connexion, as it may be called, in the Establishment, consisting of high Church dignitaries, Archdeacons, London Rectors, and the like, who belonged to what was commonly called the high-and-dry school. They were far more opposed than even he was to the irresponsible action of individuals. Of course their *beau idéal* in ecclesiastical action was a board of safe, sound, sensible men. Mr Palmer was their organ and representative; and he wished for a Committee, an Association, with rules and meetings, to protect the interests of the Church in its existing peril'.[11]

Palmer, then, was fatally outside the Oxford ethos, and nothing could have been less like a 'safe, sound, sensible' man than Froude. The leaders of the Oxford Movement went their way on the basis of love of Oxford and the brotherhood; the calm, cool, committee-men methods of Hackney were not for them.

'We have every thing against us but our cause', Newman wrote to his former pupil Charles Golightly. 'O that we had some bishops for us. The Clergy are dead . . . We are writing without limit . . .'[12] What a contrast was here with the early Church, as Newman described it in the first four of his 'Letters on the Church of the Fathers' which he sent to Rose for publication in the *British Magazine*. He was now no detached scholar, but was turned conspirator and agitator, and on 11 August he reported to Golightly that he had helped form a society in Oxford for 'rousing the Clergy' to '*assist* the Bishops by our voice', and to get their clerical friends to do likewise, with the ultimate view of presenting an address to the Primate. 'Our main doctrine is the Apostolical Succession and the exclusive privilege of Bishops and Priests to consecrate the Bread and Wine.' The society would 'protest against doing any thing directly to separate Church and State', but it would be necessary 'steadily to contemplate the contingency of such an event' – and 'to make the Church more *popular* than it is – how, is of course a question'.[13]

The willingness to consider, perhaps even to threaten, disestablishment, in the interest of the spiritual authority of the Church, was a throw-back to the Non-Jurors, something which was anathema to Erastian High Churchmen and to the more principled ecclesiastics of Hackney. Even Keble demurred at it and at the anti-Tory notion of making the Church 'more *popular*', an idea suggested by Newman's study in the *British Magazine* of St Ambrose, which was bound up with his ambition to rouse the laity, and which was to be a commonplace of Catholic democracy and of the continental clerical right. At a meeting held on 13 August, the new association's aim was simplified to that of stirring up 'our brethren to consider the state of the Church, and especially to the practical belief and preaching of the Apostolical Succession'.[14] Newman was also keen on maintaining the integrity of the Prayer Book against liberal or 'Socinian' demands for its reform; its role was already taking form as the banner of the Anglo-Catholic Revival. Keble drafted a series of pledges which placed a heavy sacramental emphasis on the teaching that bishops and priests alone had the 'Apostolical commission' to impart the only 'expressly authorized'[15] means of divine grace, through Christ's Body and Blood. In short, the one safe way to salvation for the English lay through the threefold ministry of the bishops, priests and deacons of the Church of England.

In this doctrine, the new Anglo-Catholic heirs of the High Anglican tradition were inheritors of a development which had taken form over three centuries. The Tudor founding father of Anglican divinity, Richard Hooker, had regarded the episcopal order of the Church as a matter of positive, not eternal law, which might be abolished if abused, as it had been abolished by the Protestant reformers on the continent. Church order was, then, part of that 'ecclesiastical polity' which was for the Christian Crown and nation to determine. For many Anglicans before and after him, so for Hooker, the threefold order of bishop, priest and deacon was simply the traditional mode of ministry under which most Christians had lived and which, under providence, the English state and people had reformed and so preserved; and episcopacy did not belong to the eternal essence of Christianity, namely those truths which 'supernaturally appertain' to Christian profession and are 'necessarily required in every particular Christian man'.[16]

Hooker, however, also espoused the apparently contradictory view advanced by the Hispano-Flemish divine, Hadrian à Saravia, not himself in episcopal orders, that 'the Apostles themselves left bishops invested with power above other pastors':[17] an idea reinforced for Hooker by his battle with the radical Puritans who taught that only the Presbyterian form of Church government was sanctioned by Scripture. After Hooker, the Laudian tradition took form against the Puritans around the *de jure divino* theory of the episcopate, that the episcopal order had been directly ordained by Christ. This attachment to episcopacy was confirmed in the 1640s by the blood of the martyrs, Laud himself and Charles I, who were held to have died for it, and the preface to the Ordinal imposed upon the Church by the Act of Uniformity in 1662 was interpreted with a new strictness to confine the Anglican ministry completely to clergy who had been episcopally ordained.

Yet strict episcopalian theory was not for foreign consumption, as it was not applied with any consistency to non-episcopalian Protestants on the continent, whose orders had been recognized even by sacramental High Churchmen like the seventeenth-century John Cosin. Lutherans and Calvinists had Christian Churches, even if second-rate ones; German or Genevan silver was good, though worth less than episcopal gold. Thus in much if by no means all Anglican theological writing, episcopacy was defended as of the *bene esse* of the Church, but as not of the *esse* – for the better of the Church, but not its essence; a matter on which Anglicans, characteristically, felt that they had special cause for self-congratulation.[18] This position was, however, further eroded among High Churchmen by the growing isolation of the High Church party from foreign Protestants in the later eighteenth century. The rule of the Hackney divines of the generation before the Oxford Movement, like Archdeacon Charles Daubeny and William Van Mildert, the last Prince Bishop of Durham, was 'no bishop, no church': 'where we find the order of bishops, priests, and deacons regularly appointed, there we find the church of Christ', wrote Daubeny; 'and without these . . . it is not called a church'.[19] Dissenters were schismatics outside the Church; their fate was a mystery, but like drunkards and adulterers they were beyond the official channels of salvation.

In this, then, Newman was heir to a past position, but it was certainly not the sole or perhaps even the dominant Anglican one, and here, as in other matters, he was to find himself contradicted by the variety and disunity of the Anglican theological tradition.

Newman insisted himself in 1836 that the essence of apostolic order lay in the possession of spiritual hereditary monarchy, rather than in the precise three-fold form, as the form had varied down the centuries. Yet it was the strict three-fold theory that he set out in the most startling language in the first three of his *Tracts for the Times*, of four, four and seven pages respectively, dated 9 September 1833 but in fact circulated from early August. Tract 1, 'Thoughts on the Ministerial Commission. Respectfully addressed to the Clergy', was a veritable trumpet blast, far more so than Keble's sermon: 'Do we not all confess the peril into which the Church is come, yet sit still each in his own retirement, as if mountains and seas cut off brother from brother?' As for the bishops, 'black event as it would be, for the country, yet . . . we could not wish them a more blessed termination of their course, than the spoiling of their goods, and martyrdom'. After this unlikely blood-curdling image of a persecuted apostolic prelacy – perhaps suggested by the mobs of two years before – came the argument: 'Should the Government and country so far forget their GOD as to cast off the Church, to deprive it of its temporal honours and substance, *on what* will you rest . . . ? Hitherto you have been upheld by your birth, your education, your wealth, your connections; should these secular advantages cease, on what must CHRIST'S Ministers depend?' The Dissenting clergy unsupported by the State were 'the *creatures* of the people' – but 'Is it not our very office to *oppose* the world?' The clergy were given the authority to do so by 'OUR APOSTOLICAL DESCENT'.[20]

> We have been born, not of blood, nor of the will of the flesh, nor of the will of man, but of God. The Lord JESUS CHRIST gave His Spirit to His Apostles; they in turn laid their hands on those who should succeed them; and these again on others; and so the sacred gift has been handed down to our present Bishops, who have appointed us as their assistants, and in some sense representatives.[21]

Newman supported the claim with the words of ordination from the Prayer Book, especially the dispensation to the priest to forgive sin: 'Whose sins thou dost forgive, they are forgiven; and whose sins thou dost retain, they are retained'. The exordium of the tract was a blast at the Whigs. 'A notion has gone abroad that they can take away your power . . . They think it lies in the Church property, and they know that they have politically the power to confiscate that property . . . Enlighten them in this manner. Exalt our Holy Fathers, the Bishops as the Representatives of the Apostles, and the Angels of the Churches; and magnify your office . . . CHOOSE YOUR

SIDE. To remain neuter much longer will be itself to take a part. *Choose your side* . . . abstinence is impossible in troublous times. HE THAT IS NOT WITH ME IS AGAINST ME, AND HE THAT GATHERETH NOT WITH ME SCATTERETH ABROAD.'[22]

'It is sometimes said, that the clergy should abstain from politics', Newman wrote in Tract 2, on 'The Catholic Church': Christ's kingdom is not of this world. But the text is fully compatible with 'a zealous and active interference in matters of this world', and 'when the Nation interferes with the rights and possessions of the Church, it can with even less grace complain of the Church interfering with the Nation'. For 'Christ when He ascended, did not leave us orphans, but appointed representatives of Himself to the end of time'.[23] Those representatives were his, and not the State's, and what he had given them, the State had no right to take away.

The third tract, on 'Alterations in the Liturgy', was a response to liberal and Evangelical criticism of the *Book of Common Prayer*. The liberal objection was to references to hell and to the 'imprecatory' or cursing psalms and to the damnatory clauses of the Athanasian Creed. Newman dismissed these cavils as 'savouring of the shallow and detestable liberalism of the day', and stigmatized these liberal cavillers as 'worldly men, with little personal religion, of lax conversation and lax professed principles' – to be identified 'with this great Statesman, or that noble Land-holder, who considers the Church two centuries behind the world'.[24] This was a clear reference to sceptical Whig grandees like Lord Melbourne who according to legend once declared that he supported the Church, not 'as a pillar', but 'as a buttress . . . from the outside', and is supposed to have left an Evangelical sermon, remarking that 'Things have come to a pretty pass when religion is allowed to invade the sphere of private life'.[25] Newman thought that such men of the world really 'dislike the *doctrine* of the Liturgy'. They 'do not like the Anathemas of the Athanasian Creed',[26] and it was the Athanasian Creed, a particular liberal bugbear, which was to become the special symbol of Anglo-Catholic resistance to liturgical change, because it was just such liberals whom the Creed brings before the judgement seat of God.

Evangelicals, on the other hand, worried not only that in the Prayer Book the baptismal service pronounces the child regenerate, but that there is a charitable presumption in the burial service that the dead man or woman is saved. 'Do you pretend you can discriminate the wheat from the tares? Of course not',[27] wrote Newman: yet he himself would have welcomed the restoration of a 'godly discipline' whereby notorious sinners, including dead ones, could be excommunicated and excluded from the services of the Church. The real objection, he thought, was not to the burial service as such, but to the practice of applying it indiscriminately to everyone, which then naturally gave rise to the complaint that it could not possibly describe the notorious sinner in the grave.

A crude Marxist could have an easy time with this: an institution is threatened in its properties and privileges and gets religion, compensating for its temporal losses by reasserting its spiritual authority. It would be truer to say that it is just such a crisis which gives the spiritually minded in such institutions their chance of authority, for Newman had no obvious interest in power or property himself, and was anxious to avoid questions of Church property and secular politics, which he thought smacked of the self-interest of the Erastians or 'Zish'. There were, however, directly ecclesiastico-political reasons for the appeal of his argument to others: the insistence that a Church had to have bishops to be a Church conveniently unchurched Protestant Dissenters who, lacking bishops, had no Churches. Moreover, the mushroom growth of Dissent after 1790 forced the Church of England to reconsider her own sources of spiritual authority, as the other leg of Hooker's argument on her behalf was so much weakened, because she could no longer claim to act out of the consent of the nation as a whole. The Hackney divines had assumed that the Church was unshakably by law established. The Oxford Movement could no longer be sure.

The Tracts, however, also represented an explosion of that aggression in Newman which he recalled in the *Apologia* as a mixture of fierceness and sport. In the *Lyra Apostolica*, he had said that 'before learning to love, we must "learn to hate": though I had explained my words by adding "hatred of sin" '. His Arian history argued for 'no mercy' to heretics – though 'not even when I was fiercest', he wryly recalled in the *Apologia*, 'could I have even cut off a Puritan's ears, and I think the sight of a Spanish *auto-da-fé* would have been the death of me. Again, when one of my friends, of liberal and evangelical opinions, wrote to expostulate with me on the course I was taking, I said that we would ride over him and his, as Othniel prevailed over Chushan-rishathaim, king of Mesopotamia. Again, I would have no dealings with my brother [the heretical Francis Newman], and I put my conduct upon a syllogism. I said, "St Paul bids us avoid those who cause divisions: you cause divisions: therefore I must avoid you" '.[28] He took a delight in agitation, and suggested to Froude the 'innocent Economy' of a letter to *The Times* to get his new Oxford Association publicity, by beginning 'Our bigots are on foot again etc' and 'noticing the inconsistencies of men who were Tories turning Radicals, and who profess Episcopal obedience acting without a Bishop':[29] so early in the Movement had Newman defined a contradiction which Anglo-Catholicism would never overcome.

The Oxford Association was also a problem. Its committee comprised Keble, Palmer, Newman, Froude, Tom Mozley, Arthur Perceval, the squarson Sir George Prevost, the fine preacher Edward Blencowe, who was to die young, Charles Marriott and Keble's brother Tom, with Palmer and Newman as secretaries. But the Association was a brake on the Tracts, as Palmer insisted that none be issued without the committee's approval when there were hostile reactions to their inflammatory style. Newman now feared that his forthcoming work on the Arians would 'offend and hurt men . . . Yet what can one do? Men are made of glass – the sooner we break them and get it over, the better'. He suspended the publication of more Tracts until in late October Palmer changed his mind. He was to change his mind again.[30]

Indeed some of Newman's views were revolutionary. Not only did he toy with the idea of the Church as a popular power; he extolled the patristic exposition of the principle of the community of goods as described in the Acts of the Apostles. It would have been odd if the author of the Anglo-Catholic revival had declared himself a Christian communist. It would have been even odder in the Dean of Oriel, a position to which Newman was elected on 17 October: '(. . . a much more dignified office than at Trinity)', he called it, 'and full of business'.[31] Yet so far from imbibing the Hackney spirit from Palmer, on 21 October 1833 he began a series of letters to the ultra-Evangelical *Record*, seeking allies in a body of radical supernaturalists like himself. He was, therefore, less enthusiastic about Palmer's 'Suggestions for the Formation of an Association of the Church' as a grand national institution. Newman expressed to Palmer his dislike, already voiced against the Evangelicals, of voluntary societies not sanctioned by bishops. He wanted local informal bodies: 'one diocese may be more high Church than another, one may modify the Tracts of another etc . . . I am for no committee, secretaries etc – but merely for certain individuals in every part of the country in correspondence with each other, instructing and encouraging each other . . . '[32] His fundamental fear, however, was of a heavy institution stifling his freedom to develop his radical ideas.

That was the function of the Tracts, of which more appeared in early November. They were posted in bundles to scores of sympathetic clerics and laymen who sometimes distributed them on horseback. They were intended to excite. 'We are in motion from the Isle of Wight to Durham and from Cornwall to Kent', Newman wrote. 'Surely the Church will shortly be delivered from its captivity under wicked men, who are worse than Cushan-rishathaim or the Philistines.'[33] Yet as he said in a memorandum, 'Instructions for Propagandists', 'We have no concern with politics. We have nothing to do with maintaining the temporalities of the Church . . . Beware of any intemperance of language . . . If men are afraid of Apostolical ground, then be cautious of saying much about it . . . *Recollect* that we are *supporting* the Bishops . . . '[34] His difficulty was to separate religion from politics, and to recommend his own kind of radical religion to his conservative clientele without giving offence. Old fashioned Churchmen were Tories. They loved the Church, but that love was bound up with their hatred of Whiggery, and they had no necessary sympathy with the new Oxford theology.

The chief of the 'Zs', however, was a friend. Newman's *Arians*, published on 5 November, was criticized by Hugh James Rose and Bishop John Kaye of Lincoln for its historical view of the *Disciplina Arcani* in the early Church.[35] Yet Rose, himself a man of fire and spirit, endorsed the Tracts, and inspired

Newman's recommendation to Palmer on 24 October of a 'Declaration or Address to the Archbishop' from the clergy 'expressive of our attachment to the Doctrine and Discipline of the Church'. The address, drafted by Froude, passed back and forth between Oxford and Palmer's High and Dry London clergy, and the radical document became a tame one. 'The word "Bishops" at the close has been put in here and taken out there 5 times *sub silentio*',[36] Newman wrote to Froude. Here was evidence, as Newman told Tom Mozley, of the 'great jealousy of the Tracts both among Xs and Zs', the Evangelicals and High and Dry Churchmen.[37] Yet Henry Wilberforce reported a favourable reaction from the Evangelical Bishop Charles Richard Sumner of Winchester. 'O! that he would take us up – I would go to the length of my tether to meet him',[38] wrote Newman; he thought that Evangelicals might have been impressed by his Tract 8, 'The Gospel a Law of Liberty', in which he argued that the Gospel says little by way of specific commands because God wants obedience from the heart.

The Evangelicals had fire in their bellies, and might have seemed more promising recruits than the High and Drys. On 13 November 1833, Newman told Froude and John Bowden, the author of Tract 5, the first by a layman, that Palmer and Henry Handley Norris of Hackney again wanted a simple association and the Tracts stopped altogether.[39] There were now eleven of them, eight by Newman and two by the Kebles, Tom and John, who asserted in Tract 4 that Dissenters were separating themselves from 'THE ONLY CHURCH IN THIS REALM WHICH HAS A RIGHT TO BE QUITE SURE THAT SHE HAS THE LORD'S BODY TO GIVE TO HIS PEOPLE'.[40] The Tracts stated dogma dramatically. They were what Newman called not 'regular troops, but sharpshooters'.[41] The difference between the 'Ys' and 'Zs', the new 'Apostolicals' and old High Churchmen, was already a clear one in tone and method, if as yet in little else.

The idea of provoking was also Froude's, especially against the Zs. 'Do keep writing to Keble and stirring his rage', he admonished Newman: 'he is my fire but . . . I may be his poker.'[42] Newman felt their inadequacy: 'we have scarcely any [Tracts] for the poor', he told Keble, 'and not many for the Clergy, or (again) the middling Classes'.[43] To clerical critics like Samuel Rickards, he compared the Tract writers to men 'climbing a rock, who tear clothes and flesh, and slip now and then, and yet make progress . . . *The Association has nothing to do with the Tracts*', which unlike the Association were the work of Oxford men. 'Willingly would I (if I) be said to write in an irritating and irritated way', he asserted, 'if in that way I *rouse* people . . . '[44] He described to Rose Palmer's address for the Archbishop as 'milk and water', though it would teach the clergy to combine, 'strengthens the Archbishop against his opponents', and brings out the Church 'as a body and power distinct from the State'.[45] Moderate churchmen would rally round an insipid production like the address, where a range of views might separate them from the opinions in the Tracts themselves.

It was, however, the radical Evangelicals wh o first took flight altogether. In early December 1833, the Calvinist editor of the *Record* scented Popery in the Tracts, derided the doctrines of the Apostolic Succession and Real Presence, and then parted from Newman with expressions of esteem and regret. 'So these ganders', he rather complacently concluded, 'have just managed to give us a most flaming advertisement.'[46] But the ultra-Evangelicals would be formidable enemies, and the danger with Newman's own ultra opinions was that he might fall out with nearly every one.

Against this loss, he still had the support of Rose, who thought the Tracts *'not too strong'*[47] and was more than willing to publish in the *British Magazine* what Newman called the *'trash'* of his *Home Thoughts Abroad*. Rose rebuked Palmer for his reservations, though he may have diplomatically 'lost' Newman's letter to the *Magazine* attacking the Bishop of Ferns' argument that the State had the right to reorganize the Church of Ireland; against which Newman urged, in violation of every sound conservative principle, that 'Hooker's view of the union of Church and State' was superseded now that *'the legislature is no longer the representative of the laity of our Church'*.[48]

Newman would have caused even greater horror among old-fashioned High Churchmen had they known how far he took his commitment to celibacy, into emotional difficulties over the marriage of his friends. He and Froude were reported in 1832 to have been upset by the wedding of George Ryder, Newman's former pupil at Oriel and son of the Evangelical Bishop of Gloucester, to Sophia Sargent, the daughter of another Evangelical cleric. Her sister Emily married the future Bishop Samuel Wilberforce and her sister Caroline the future Cardinal Henry Edward Manning. Newman had imparted a reluctant consent to Ryder. 'It is quite absurd to suppose that you are not *at liberty* both to marry and to go into the Church – ', he told him, 'indeed I think that country parsons ought, as a general rule, to be married – and I am sure the generality of men ought, whether parsons or not. The celibate is a high state of life, to which the multitude of men cannot aspire – I do not say that they who adopt it are necessarily better than others, though the noblest ethos is situated in that state.'[49]

Now, however, the extraordinary Sargent girls claimed another ecclesiastical victim, as yet another of the daughters, Mary, won a heart still closer to Newman's affections, that of his former pupil Henry Wilberforce who, according to Frederic Rogers, 'purposes to be gradually weaning himself from Newman's friendship, because he knows (he says) that when he marries he will be cut, in common with Ryder . . . '[50] Henry was frightened to tell Newman, who drafted but did not send a strangled letter of rebuke for not speaking to him more frankly:

My poor dear foolish Henry,

Dear, for auld lang syne – foolish, for being suspicious of me . . . When have I ever questioned the propriety of your marrying . . . ? But you surely are inconsiderate – you ask me to give my heart, when you give yours to another . . . it is a little hard for a friend to separate himself from familiarity with me . . . and then to say, 'Love me as closely, give me your familiar heart as you did, though I have parted with mine.' Be quite sure that I shall be free to love you, far more than you will me – but I cannot, as a prudent man, so forget what is due to my own comfort and independence as not to look to my own resources, make my own mind my wife, and anticipate and provide against that loss of friends which the fashion of the age makes inevitable . . . I have done it towards all my friends, as expecting they will part from me, except to one, who is at Barbadoes. I dare not even towards my sisters indulge affection without restraint . . . You know very little of me, if you think I do not feel at times much the despondence of solitariness – . . . you really have hurt me. You have *made* a *difficulty* in the very beginning of our separation . . . [51]

The '*difficulty*' was in part the fault of Newman's sister Harriett, who had herself admired Henry and wanted to marry him. 'She triumphed in her heart over me, that H W married, *as I knew she did*', wrote Newman. 'He on the other hand fancied that she was the best person to communicate the news to me – He told her to do so – she never did it.'[52] Henry assumed from Newman's silence that he *was* being cut, but he still said nothing about the matter to Newman, who therefore began spreading his incredulity of the report in every direction – only to learn from Rogers that when Henry 'came near, and saw how fierce you looked, his heart failed him . . .'[53] The incident betrayed a hothouse possessiveness in Newman which was not in any overt way sexual, but which was sharpened if not caused by his double ethos of discipleship and priesthood. For all his general licence to parsons to marry, his train of thought and feeling followed Froude into a view of the clergy as a separate caste, a holy brotherhood consecrated to God alone, and set off by their celibacy from other men.

Yet Newman's thought on the matter was more mixed than this. His lines on St Gregory Nazianzen in 'The Married and the Single' acknowledge another side to the argument:

> My sons, be still, nor with your parents strive:
> They coupled in their day, and so ye live.[54]

It is the celibate, however, who has the last word. Yet Newman's feelings had clearly to do with priesthood: he had no such reaction to the marriage of his friend John Bowden, who was scribbling more lay tracts and distributing them in the wilds of Northumberland, 'on the very *frontiers of Episcopacy*'. Bowden was, on Froude's suggestion, also busy with a life of the great medieval reformer Hildebrand, Pope Gregory VII, in defence of the proper spiritual independence of the Church: his 'little ones', Bowden reported, 'have not forgotten "Mr Newman" '.[55]

Bowden also heard from Newman his mixed feelings over the Duke of Wellington's election as Chancellor of the University. Keble and Newman would have preferred Archbishop Howley. On 6 February 1834, a clerical delegation including Keble presented the long-meditated grand address with seven thousand clerical signatures to the Archbishop, who was 'almost affected . . . They say there has not been such a day for the Church for years'.[56] Newman also commended a similar address from Palmer for lay signatures, which had been 'manufactured in London' and 'pushed forward by a Committee of Lawyers and barristers' headed by Joshua Watson and Colonel Clitheroe.[57] It received two hundred and thirty thousand signatures, including the Duke of Wellington's, and on 27 May was presented to the King. The presentations signified the demise of Palmer's Association, as it lost its object, and it was the Tracts which survived.

In early 1834, Newman condensed the seventeenth-century John Cosin's work against Transubstantiation into two tracts. This was good anti-Catholic Church and King stuff, but liberalism seemed more dangerous than Popery. Newman was now to lose out to a liberal, being 'floored'[58] in his attempt to become the Oxford Professor of Moral Philosophy, the post going to another Fellow of Oriel, Renn Dickson Hampden. 'I have met my conqueror and departed',[59] Newman told Henry Wilberforce, quoting Aeschylus' *Agamemnon*. Hampden was also a Noetic, and was a great friend of Whately and of Arnold, and in the Whig attack upon the Church, he would be Newman's foe.

'I was so sure of being elected Moral Philosophy Professor,' wrote Newman, 'that I wished the title inserted in my title page to my Sermons . . . '[60] The sermons are not directly controversial, but have the severe moral tone of one who no longer had the Evangelical doctrines of election and assurance to provide a promise of salvation, and who had not yet come to the more comforting teachings of Rome on indulgences, confession, human merit and the intercession of the saints for the forgiveness of sin.[61] The most penetrating of the sermons is on 'The Religion of the Day', with its analysis of the modern English tendency to make belief a matter of elegant good taste. In the Dark Ages, argued Newman, 'Satan took the darker side of the Gospel; its awful mysteriousness, its fearful glory, its sovereign inflexible justice'. Now, however, the Devil had made of religion the very opposite, by explaining away 'those fearful images of Divine wrath with which the Scriptures abound . . . Every thing is bright and cheerful. Religion is pleasant and easy; benevolence is the chief virtue; intolerance, bigotry, excess of zeal, are the first of sins'. Sin itself is also identified with the grosser vices which offend a fastidious refinement, open profligacy, drunkenness, cursing and swearing while the more subtle vices take their place. Some Christians had co-operated with anti-Christian men to secure by human effort a millennial kingdom which is nothing more than 'the elegance and refinement of mere human civilization', and had so emphasized a reasonable '*Natural Theology*' that the reality of judgement is forgotten. Rather, declared Newman, 'it would be a gain to this country, were it vastly more superstitious, more bigoted, more gloomy, more fierce in its religion'. Such tempers are not desirable in themselves, but they are better than the false security of the sleeping Jonah, and Newman pointed to the text that our God is a consuming fire, whose wrath will avenge the sins of the world. 'The fear of God is the beginning of wisdom; till you see Him to be a consuming fire, and approach Him with reverence and godly fear, as being sinners, you are not even in sight of the strait gate . . . Fear and love must go together; always fear, always love, to your dying day.'[62] Whatever might be thought of the message, it had reality for Newman's hearers. It remained to be seen if it would save the Church.

But as the Church's salvation was also to be found in patristic study, so Newman was anxious not to be superficial and 'take facts and Fathers at secondhand',[63] and in March 1834 he began work on an edition of the fragments of another Alexandrian, the third-century Bishop Dionysius, writing a Latin commentary on the variants in the Greek manuscript. After seventeen months of labour, the work was to fall a victim to his immediate interests in preaching and polemic, and so remains unpublished to this day; but it was this continuing unobtrusive labour of scholarship which through all his other occupations remained his refuge and abiding place, and an inspiration in the coming din of battle of warring ideologies and creeds.

11

The Via Media: An Uncertain Spring

Newman did not only win disciples in Oxford by his academic theology. Rather, he attracted a following, in the best Protestant manner, by his preaching. One of the earliest testimonies to its power was that of William Ewart Gladstone, who went down as early as 1831, and did not think 'that there has been anything like his influence in Oxford, when it was at its height, since Abelard lectured in Paris. I myself, in my undergraduate days, saw just the commencement of it. It was beginning to be the custom to go and hear him on Sunday afternoon at St Mary's'.[1] There is some contemporary evidence of Newman's effect on Gladstone: Newman thought it wrong to ask so young a man to commit himself to the Tracts in October 1833, but numbered him among his followers a month later.[2] Yet Newman's matter and manner of delivery made no bid for popularity. He preached non-controversially on self-denial and the hunger for holiness, and on the majesty and awe-inspiring and all consuming love of God for man. One of his converts simply wrote that he 'rooted in their hearts and minds a personal conviction of the living God'.[3] But his speech was quick and his voice was low, and though it had a strangely musical quality, there was nothing obviously oratorical to attract the hero-worshipper, as he did not either vary his tone or move about or even gesture. Rather, he entered with such an imaginative power into the doubts and temptations of his hearers that they were caught up into a sense of the drama within themselves, even as they were transfixed by his projection of the utter reality of the supernatural world and by the sheer simple directness of his language describing it. Preaching or writing, he was calm and passionless as marble, and might well feel 'like the pane of glass . . . which transmits heat yet is cold'.[4] Yet his very restraint hinted at the fire within, suggesting a spiritual depth the more fascinating for being so artlessly concealed.

These qualities are summed up by Hurrell's younger brother James Anthony, who came up to Oxford in 1835. Newman disliked Evangelical preaching of the Atonement for its want of reserve, and for bandying the most sacred doctrine of Christ's suffering about like a talisman or charm to convert. His own preaching of the Passion was exactly the reverse. As Froude recalled it, Newman paused in his recital:

For a few moments there was a breathless silence. Then, in a low, clear voice, of which the faintest vibration was audible in the farthest corner of St Mary's, he said, 'Now, I bid you recollect that He to whom these things were done was Almighty God'. It was as if an electric stroke had gone through the church, as if every person present understood for the first time the meaning of what he had all his life been saying.[5]

Treat the doctrine in tones of quiet, though it is tremendous; even hide it; then when you unveil it, strike, and strike to the heart.

It was this quality of hidden power, of an heroic self-control over a buried inner fire, that was missed by Matthew Arnold, when he wistfully recalled Newman's preaching in old age. 'No such voices as those which we heard in our youth at Oxford are sounding there now. Oxford has more criticism now, more knowledge, more light; but such voices as those of our youth it has no longer . . . Newman . . . was preaching in St Mary's pulpit every Sunday . . . Who could resist the charm of that spiritual apparition, gliding in the dim afternoon light through the aisles of St Mary's, rising into the pulpit, and then, in the most entrancing of voices, breaking the silence with words and thoughts which were a religious music – subtle, sweet, mournful?'[6] The description suggests Newman's grace, but not his strength. It recognizes the Greek in Newman, but not the Hebrew.

Gladstone came up to Oxford in 1828, Arnold took his degree in 1844; the years between were those of Newman's slowly expanding influence on the undergraduate mind, though there were sets in the University, Protestant or philistine or sporting or immoral, where that influence can hardly have existed. It had, however, a great deal more body than Arnold's spectral apparition. As Arnold noted, Newman 'seemed about to renew what was for us the most national and natural institution in the world, the Church of England'.[7] Institutions are only renewed by combat, and Newman stood uneasily poised between fighting for the old institution and making a new one – or in another of Arnold's phrases, between an old world and one struggling to be born.

For the old world, though seemingly dying, was refusing to die, despite the multitude anxious to see its funeral. The pressure for reform of the Constitution came in good part from Dissenters and Roman Catholics who objected to the privileges of the Established Church. Thus the Anglican monopoly on the performance of legal marriages was a grievance to Roman Catholics, if only to a minority of Dissenters, most of whom had no scruples about undergoing the Anglican ceremony. But Newman saw the Whig aspiration to introduce civil marriage as an opportunity to defy the State and to reassert the spiritual independence of the Church. He thought of a petition entreating Parliament 'not to reduce us to the alternative of disobeying Caesar or God'. If civil marriage were to be introduced, 'Might we not as a quid pro quo . . . demand the right of not being obliged to marry

Dissenters?'[8] He drew up a petition to the Commons asking that the clergy be exempted 'from the necessity, under which the existing state of the Law places them, of solemnizing Holy Matrimony according to the rites of the Church between persons who forsake her Communion, and deny her Sacred Doctrines and her Spiritual Authority, [and insult the persons of her Ministers]':[9] the last clause was omitted from the circulated version in deference to Keble and 'in order to get more subscriptions'.[10] The petition received the 'corrections of Rose, [Benjamin] Harrison, Palmer, Perceval, and Thos Keble'. 'The Kebles (I believe) will not (cry Dissenters' banns) . . . nor Mozley – nor I – ', wrote Newman ' . . . To my mind it is not a point for the Bishop to determine, but of conscience. The Bishop cannot give me a licence to derogate from *his* authority – he has not selfdestructive power – to uphold him *and the Church* is a plain Christian duty. Again I will not call that Holy Matrimony which may be but a licenced concubinage.'[11] This refusal to obey the State might look like a liberal stand against liberalism; in fact, it was behaviour to be repeated wherever nineteenth-century Churchmen were forced into rebellion because they were opposed to a State which was in liberal hands.

Newman could generally expect support on such an issue from the old-fashioned High Churchmen, but their caution made him angry. He was annoyed with Rose, their chief, for not inserting in the *British Magazine* either his own letter or that of the Irish anti-Catholic polemicist Robert McGhee protesting against the Whig suppression of the Irish sees, 'considering that in that suppression, the King's Coronation Oath was violated, that the nation has solemnly countenanced and recognized that violation, that O'Connell and his party . . . broke their solemn oaths too, that . . . the said suppression was done in a most Erastian spirit, . . . that the Irish Church disgracefully acquiesced in it, and the English Church had not protested . . . '[12] Rose retorted that he was grieved with Newman's charge of '*Sudden Conservatism*' and that he had borne with 'the degradation of a connexion with Periodic Literature – and all the revilings which are daily poured upon me'[13] simply out of duty. To Keble, Newman wrote that he had never reckoned Rose 'in his opinions as one of ourselves'. Though a 'man of high and ardent mind, lively perceptions, and ready eloquence', he did not take 'an accurate and firm view of any subject which was clouded by political interests and the influences of friends and superiors'. Rose did not have a '*view*'[14] and was simply not 'ultra' enough for him.

Yet there could be no effective Oxford Movement without allies. Newman was also in conflict with what he considered to be an Evangelical attempt to take over the old High Church propagandist Society for the Promotion of Christian Knowledge, but he tried to make common cause with the Evangelicals and Rose in a movement led by the Regius Professor of Divinity, Edward Burton, to protest against a Whig Bill to admit Dissenters to Oxford, by relieving them of the requirement that they subscribe on matriculation to the Thirty-nine Articles which defined the theology of the Church of England. A 'splendid meeting' of 'Professors, Deans and Tutors'[15] in Burton's rooms on 21 April 1834 inspired an 'Oxford Declaration against the Admission of Dissenters',[16] for which Newman advanced the argument in the Tory *Standard* newspaper that with compulsory chapel and divinity courses and fellowships restricted to Anglicans, 'to admit Dissenters among us would be in fact to repeal our entire *corpus statutorum*',[17] under which the spirit and power of one faith pervaded everything. This, he wrote, might seem absurd to the enlightened, but '*till* the absurdity is brought home to our minds, a stone wall lies across their course, which they cannot surmount. Till they beat us out of our (so to call it) obstinate bigotry, they cannot overawe us. Jolterheaded conscientiousness, stupid prejudice, blind passion, epidemic fanaticism, such inconvenient principles of action have no *fears*. Practical men, men of enlarged views, should understand this'.[18] Rose approved a further petition against university reform drawn up for the undergraduates' parents and guardians, but demurred at some of Newman's activity to Palmer. Newman insisted that he had merely seized his opportunity. 'Here was the power of moving an influential body', he wrote to Rose; ' – "shall I leave it, on the chance of doing something better tomorrow?" '[19]

A further intervention prevented the grant of an honorary degree to Talleyrand as 'an Apostate Bishop',[20] while Newman attended the levees of the Archbishop and the Duke of Wellington for the Duke's induction as Chancellor, 'as the tory nobility deserted Ascot and poured into Oxford to witness a tremendous triumph'[21] for the conservative cause. 'Oh', wrote Newman, 'that the Church had but a manifestation one tenth part as glorious as the Tory one was! tho' much of the highest feeling and principle was mixed with it, and the Bishops and all names and propositions which had any reference to Church welfare [were] rapturously applauded in the Theatre . . . The Duke will gain good (I trust) from being among us . . . and the Undergraduates again will have gained something to burn within them for 20 years to come . . . '[22] The Duke was moved by his reception and became 'noticeably more zealous in defence of the church',[23] but he was not a reliable ally to Newman, as events were to show.

On 30 June 1834, Newman implemented an all but universally neglected aspect of Prayer Book teaching, namely to hold a daily service by saying Morning Prayer in the chancel of St Mary's. 'The whole question of [the neglect of] the Rubrics is a melancholy one', he wrote. 'Things are so bad that one keeps silence.'[24] It was, however, his failure to keep silence that got him into what he called in undergraduate manner a 'scrape' over the issue of the Church's responsibility for marriage. One of his parishioners, a Balliol pastrycook called Jubber, left an unsigned note late on the afternoon of 30 June that he wanted Newman to take his daughter's wedding at 9 a.m. the next morning. Newman did not learn their names until an hour and a half before the service, and then had to face the problem that Miss

Jubber was not baptized, her father being a Baptist and her brother having sought baptism for a secular motive which had made Newman's curate, Keble's gentle poet-disciple Isaac Williams, reluctant to perform the rite. The family occasionally came to church, and Newman had discussed baptism with Jubber and presented him with a volume of his sermons. Newman now refused to marry the girl, the father accused him of superstition, and Newman replied that the daughter was an 'outcast' from the Church – meaning that she was a child of wrath until baptism made her God's.[25] Newman apologized for seeming 'harsh or unkind' to the girl, and the couple decamped to the neighbouring church of St Michael's, where a less knowledgeable or intransigent cleric married them. Mr Jubber took exception to the term 'outcast', and made a fuss about it in the Oxford press; the matter was taken up by *The Times* and reached the House of Commons. The very drunkards made songs on the 'Reverend Ruffian', 'Parson Purblind, alias Paul Pry':

> There's not a rubber
> Where *outcast* Jubber
> Is not thought an injur'd Woman
> There's not a party
> Where young Men Hearty
> Would not horsewhip Mr Newman.[26]

Poor Mr Newman had to explain himself to his Bishop, Richard Bagot, whom he had had no time to consult, and who afterwards indicated not by direct reply but through the Archdeacon that, as Newman wrote, he 'certainly *wished* me to marry the parties, did it occur again',[27] as indeed he was required to do by law. The Bishop, though a High Churchman, was embarrassed by an inconvenient stand on principle in a matter in which the Church's duties and responsibilities were under attack and legislative revision – as the Whigs legalized civil marriage in 1836. Most marriages remained Church ones, and the change was more dramatic in principle than practice.

But it seemed a massive change in principle, and to Tom Mozley, Newman took the high religious line that 'First marriage is more of a religious rite (or sacrament) than burial, yet the rubric commands to withhold burial to the unbaptized. Secondly, in charity to the party unbaptized – whom I had been urging to baptism, and who would think after all that it was but a form. Lastly from the rule of the Primitive Church'.[28] To Bowden, scandalized that Westminster Abbey, dedicated to St Peter, had no service on the Sunday of St Peter's Day, Newman wrote that what had annoyed him in the Jubber affair was that he had been accused of rudeness, which had not been the case: 'As to refusing marriage to unbaptized persons, we must make a stand *somewhere* . . . '[29] His stand would only have inconvenienced the minority of Dissenters who were Baptists and Quakers. 'It was not a question of Dissenter and Churchman – not a question *who* baptized. She [Miss Jubber] was not baptized at Meeting House or Church.'[30] Yet as he told Henry Wilberforce, the incident enabled him to assert two principles, 'that baptism is of importance, and that the Church is above [the] Law'.[31] He wrote to Harriett that he wanted to show that a cleric could defy the law.[32] On the other hand, in so far as the Church was still an establishment and the Church and State were one realm as of old, he insisted to Wilberforce that 'as to the *spirit* of English Law that decidedly is for me . . . I *as a Churchman* do not acknowledge as British subjects those who are not Churchmen'.[33]

None of this was coherent. Newman was in the difficult position of invoking a disestablishmentarian principle against adversaries who were no more consistent than he was, in relieving the Church of its privileges and yet still subjecting it to official state control. As for the Jubbers, Newman heard in 1835 that two of the girls, one of them the lass whom he had declined to marry, were being baptized and confirmed, and in 1836 he himself had the pleasure of baptizing three Jubber children, and yet another in 1838. By taking a theological stand, he had won a pastoral point. Yet at the time, he felt his own isolation, and rebuked Froude for being in Barbados. 'Keble and Pusey, (and Williams) take my part', Newman wrote to Froude, 'else I am solus. Abused beyond measure by high and low – threatened with a pelting, and a prosecution – having anonymous letters – discountenanced by high Church and low Church. It should be you.'[34]

Not that Newman was quite alone. Arthur Perceval's 'Account of Religious Sects at Present Existing in England', Tract 36, snappily divided the erring into three camps, '*Those who reject the Truth*' (Socinians, Jews, Deists and Atheists), '*Those who receive and teach a part but not the whole . . .*' (Presbyterians, Independents, at least ten types of Methodist, Baptists and Quakers) and '*Those who teach more than the Truth*' (Romanists, Swedenborgians, Southcotians and Irvingites). Now these three categories, infidel, Dissenter and Papist, were united to destroy the English branch of the Catholic Church. But Newman's voice was the dominant one in the Tracts: of the fifty published by the end of 1834, he had written seventeen, and a number of others were simply edited collections from the writings of seventeenth and eighteenth-century High Church divines, William Beveridge, John Cosin and Thomas Wilson. Newman's Tract 31, 'The Reformed Church', was an elaborate set of comparisons, in the patristic manner, between the religion of the Old Israel and the New. Tract 33, 'Primitive Episcopacy', tentatively suggested an increase in the number of bishops, essentially for a pastoral purpose, as in the early Church. Tract 34 insisted on the importance of the external observance of the 'Rites and Customs of the Church'. Tracts 38 and 41, *The Via Media*, were written as a dialogue between '*Laicus*' and '*Clericus*' and popularized the Latin phrase of the title, echoing Aristotle's mean, which defined 'the glory of the English Church' as occupying a middle way betwen Popery and Puritanism or popular Protestantism. Older High Churchmen in declaring themselves Protestant, had rejected not Protestantism but radical Puritanism, but Newman thought that modern Protestantism had now departed further from the Catholic faith than the original Reformers had done, so that what was required in England to undo this great historic drift from Catholicism over the centuries was 'a SECOND REFORMATION'.[35]

The principle if not the phrase *Via Media* went back to the sixteenth-century Archbishop Matthew Parker's definition of a 'golden mediocrity' in discipline and doctrine in the Church of England between Rome and Geneva. It had been reiterated in the seventeenth century in George Herbert's praise for Anglican maiden decency against Roman gaudiness and the sluttishness of Dissent. In the generation before the Oxford Movement, the idea was popularized afresh in an influential tract by two Irish High Churchmen, John Jebb, Bishop of Limerick, and the layman Alexander Knox, a disciple of John Wesley.[36] Again, there was nothing wrong, according to High Church tradition, in Newman's combination of militant No-Popery and militant anti-Puritanism. The *Via Media* idea, however, contained more than a hint that the Protestantism and Catholicism of Anglicanism were equally half-baked, and though Newman denied the 'idle calumny' of the elder Pitt's famous remark that the Church of England had 'Calvinistic Articles, and a Popish Liturgy', there was the seed of the dissolvent of his Anglicanism in the judgement 'that the Liturgy, as coming down from the Apostles, is the depository of their complete teaching; while the Articles are polemical, and except as they embody the creeds, are only protests against certain definite errors'.[37] But the Articles were the bulwark of Anglican privilege in Oxford, and it was the Articles, as obvious statements of Protestant doctrine, which were to be the Achilles' heel of the Oxford Movement's attachment to the Prayer Book, and were to assume a new significance as a measure of its gradual departure from the moderate Protestantism of the High Church tradition.

At first that danger seemed remote. Newman's bid was for the great middle ground of old-fashioned moderately High Church and Tory opinion strongest among the country parsons and those clerical Oxford MAs with the right to vote in the University's Convocation. The opportunity to rally them was to be offered by Hampden who, Newman reported to Rose in August 1834, 'has just published a pamphlet which, I fear, destroys our glory',[38] urging that Dissenters be admitted to Oxford by abolishing the need to subscribe to the Thirty-nine Articles. The breach was sharper with another Oriel Noetic, Archbishop Whately, who complained to Newman of a 'most shocking report'[39] from some Oxford undergraduates that the previous spring Newman had kept away from receiving communion with Whately in Oriel chapel. Newman denied the story – he had taken a communion the same day in St Mary's, and did not know of Whately's presence at Oriel until after the service; 'yet, on honest reflection', he wrote to the Archbishop, 'I cannot conceal from myself, that it was generally a relief to me, to see so little of your Grace, . . . I have had great alternations and changes of feeling, – defending, then blaming your policy, next praising your own self and protesting against your measures, according as the affectionate remembrances which I had of you rose against my utter aversion of the secular and unbelieving policy in which I considered the Irish Church to be implicated . . . ' Because of his past gratitude to Whately's kindness, 'had not something from within resisted, I should certainly have adopted views on religious and social duty, which seem to my present judgement to be based in the pride of reason and to tend towards infidelity, and which in your own case nothing but your Grace's high religious temper and the unclouded faith of your mind have been able to withsta.id'.[40]

Whately was hurt by the charge that he had led anyone into ' "the pride of reason", or any other kind of pride', and recited back to Newman his own earlier tribute. 'I for my part', Whately declared, 'could not bring myself to find relief in escaping the society of an old friend . . . '[41] Newman's reply, though courteous, described Whately's liberal opinions as 'so peculiar in themselves, and (if you will let me add) so dangerous'. He claimed to have repudiated when in Naples the very notion that Whately could have acquiesced in the destruction of the Irish sees; he had remembered the Archbishop's lofty opinion of the inherent rights of the Christian Church, 'and I thought you never would allow men of this world so to insult it'. Afterwards, Newman claimed, he had kept silent, 'and I only felt', he wrote, 'what I hinted at when I wrote last, a bitter grief, which prompted me . . . to hide myself from you'.[42] The hardest quarrels are between former friends. Past friendship and present differences made meeting too painful, and in spite of a courteous encounter in 1838, the two never had close relations again.

The war was also heating up with Rome. Newman had now decided that whatever the abuses of medieval religion, 'the Church of Rome apostatized at Trent',[43] because only then, after the medieval era, had she officially taken the medieval abuses into her formal teaching system. But the younger Tractarians were forming friendships and arguing with Roman Catholics on the continent. One of these, the Hebraist Benjamin Harrison, had gone to Paris to study Arabic with Pusey's friend Sylvestre de Sacy, and had got into a newspaper correspondence on theological matters with the Abbé Jean-Nicolas Jager in the columns of the new populist Catholic journal *L'Univers réligieux*, founded by the great patristic editor the Abbé Migne. Jager was especially interested by the theme of what constituted the Rule of Faith, as expounded by Jebb and Knox in their work on the *Via Media*, drawing on the fifth-century St Vincent of Lerins' famous *Commonitorium*;[44] and in September 1834, the flagging Harrison drew Newman into his defence of the Church of England. Newman submerged himself in the old Anglican controversy with Rome, and in a draft letter not sent to Jager wrote self-deprecatingly as 'a nameless individual . . . occupied . . . in humble parochial duties and the classical education of youth', and 'no theologian'.[45]

There is, however, no want of self-assurance in his first response to Jager, translated into French by Harriett or Jemima and partly published in December, partly at the end of January 1835. Newman identified the fundamentals of the Rule of Faith, which were binding on Christians as 'necessary for Church Communion',[46] with the formulae in the creed which had been passed on in Tradition but which were ultimately provable from Scripture. He followed the Anglican Caroline divines like Bishop Joseph Hall in distinguishing the creed from the mass of non-fundamental doctrines also received in Tradition, and from those Roman Catholic additions to the fundamentals, which were based, in Roman theory, on pure Tradition and not Scripture, and which were guaranteed by the Church's infallibility. This Roman theory, Newman argued, could be refuted from Tradition, as it was not in conformity with the argument of St Vincent of Lerins, who had made Tradition secondary and subordinate to Scripture. Thus where the liberal insisted on believing in too little, the Roman Catholic was required to believe in far too much, including some traditions which were edifying but which were not binding on Christians, and others which corrupted or distorted the primitive creeds.

Newman's sharp distinctions, however, cut through a mass of difficult problems which they did little to resolve. One was simply the binding character of the Thirty-nine Articles, which he wanted to use to hedge Oxford against Dissenters, even though these Articles were no part of the primitive creeds. The anomaly of the barrier was clear to the new University Chancellor, Wellington, who put pressure to abolish subscription to the Articles at matriculation on the Hebdomadal Board comprising the Heads of the Oxford colleges. These worthies had followed circumspectly in the wake of the anti-subscription agitation; and Newman's contempt for their want of spirit was boundless. Under chancellerial prompting, they voted by a majority of one on 10 November 1834 to abolish subscription at matriculation and to replace it with a declaration to conform to the discipline and worship of the place. 'Thus', wrote Newman bitterly to Keble, 'in order that our defenders may pass well in the eyes of men of the world, the Truth is to be given up';[47] 'when one accommodates the age, one hurts posterity',[48] he added to Samuel Wilberforce. For the moment the threat faded: the Whigs fell, Wellington took office and the Hebdomadal Board, opportunistic as ever, reversed its vote. Yet to moderates, the measure seemed an intelligent compromise, making unlikely more radical change. Even moderates were insufferables to Newman, men indifferent to his deeper aim, of restoring the dogmatic principle in English religion.

The measure to relax subscription had Provost Hawkins' support, and the division between the junior and senior dons of Oriel was complete when two and a half weeks later Hampden sent a copy of the second edition of his tract on abolishing subscription to Newman, who acknowledged its 'tone of piety' but solemnly informed its author that the principles of the work, more especially those in the postscript, tended 'altogether to make shipwreck of Christian faith'.[49] Hampden had, in fact, got to the root of the difference between them, in the sharpness of his reaction to the identification of 'systems of doctrine – or theological propositions methodically deduced and stated – with the simple religion of Jesus Christ . . . '[50]

Liberal forms of Christianity tend to assume that there is a 'simple religion' of Jesus to be disentangled from the mass of dogmatic statements about him. Newman did not see that Hampden was personally orthodox in believing in the formal theological propositions in the creeds; what he did see, in his fidelity to the dogmatic principle, as Hampden apparently did not, was the implication of Hampden's opposing principle, that if the creeds were secondary and inessential to some less definable fundamental, 'the simple religion of Jesus Christ', then there could be no firm basis for holding to the credal truths in which Hampden claimed to believe. Newman's reaction to Hampden was a kind of obverse to his reply to Jager. To the liberal, Newman insisted that he must believe the creeds. To the Papist, he insisted that nothing but the creeds need be believed. Yet that juxtaposition was also too simple, as Newman himself was to perceive.

This excitement took its toll. Newman spent much of January 1835 at Bowden's house in London to recoup and rest and see a doctor, and met his future rival cardinal, Manning. Among the houses where he left his card was Gladstone's. After Bowden's early death in 1844, and that of Newman's later friend James Robert Hope-Scott, who was in 1852–3 to provide him with a similar recuperative refuge, Newman was to think of himself as a bird of ill omen:[51] his friends had died, not he. Even now, he had to give consolation to Robert Wilberforce, whose wife, Jemima's sometime rival Agnes, had died in childbirth, and to Hurrell, who was suffering from a 'long fit of blue devils' in 'Nigger land', as in his disagreeable racist manner he called Barbados, where the emancipation of the slaves so long fought for by Wilberforce senior was beginning with difficulty to come into effect. Froude 'felt it a kind of duty to sustain in my mind a habitual hostility to the niggers, and to chuckle over the failure of the new system – as if these poor wretches concentrated in themselves all the whiggery dissent cant and abomination that have been ranged on their side . . . Floggings too are just as common and perhaps more severe than they used to be – only they are inflicted by the magistrate instead of the owner . . . '[52]

A further letter from Froude on the emancipation issue more temperately suggested that 'all parties say what they wish and there is no believing a word';[53] it is also difficult to reconcile his remarks with the picture of Froude teaching his black class at Codrington College the mystery of Babbage's machine, the ancestor of the modern computer. But apart from the disagree-able associations of the word 'nigger', Froude was chiefly abusing the Bar-bados blacks because he loathed their Evangelical and liberal champions in England, and it should be added that in these as in Froude's other biting remarks can be seen the odd effects of galloping consumption. Newman was incapable of writing and thinking in such a manner; but he did not suffer from Froude's 'blue devils'.

He was, however, in danger of becoming emotionally and spiritually threadbare from submergence in continuous controversy; even though the joust with Jager was generating more light than heat. Newman thought that the Abbé in his voluminous answer to his first letter was 'so weak that so far it is no fun',[54] which hardly does justice to the Abbé's own fun with the incoherencies of Anglicanism. Where Harrison had allowed six hundred years of purity of faith to the Primitive Church before the popish apostasy, Newman acknowledged only four hundred and fifty. Jager could find nowhere in Scripture or antiquity Newman's distinction between fundamen-tal and non-fundamental articles of faith, and could not understand how Newman could exclude all but one of the Thirty-nine Articles, on the canonical books of Scripture, from the list of fundamental truths, when these same Articles were imposed as if they were fundamental on the Anglican clergy. In the creeds, Jager insisted, Anglicans acknowledge as fundamentals truths sanctioned by Tradition and not Scripture; and as Newman accepted the authority of the first four Councils of the Church, he was inconsistent in rejecting Trent. Jager added that all Protestants receive their faith just as Catholics do, from Tradition, 'from their catechisms, creeds, parents, teachers, and ministers';[55] and that in the Thirty-nine Articles, Anglicans have contradicted the faith of that very antiquity to which Newman was appealing. By March 1835, Jager had published the greater part of two lengthy letters in nine instalments in reply to Newman in *L'Univers*, before moving the controversy to the weekly *Le Moniteur religieux*. Newman began work on a reply in July, and for all his remarks about Jager, 'the most ignorant of men and the most inconsequent of reasoners',[56] his opponent forced him to develop a much more sophisticated understanding of Tradition than he had held before.

Beset on one side by Roman Catholics, Newman had to defend himself against Evangelicals like James Stephen, the colonial under-secretary and belle-lettrist of the Clapham Sect, who told Samuel Wilberforce that he found Newman's sermons 'harsh and repulsive'. Newman, Stephen thought, 'raises a standard of thought and sentiment which elevates him immeasur-ably above the poor Evangelicals whom he despises – in every quality, excepting only that of touching other mens hearts and influencing their conduct. In these respects Charles Simeon is worth a legion of Newmans'.[57] In response to the mischief-making Samuel Wilberforce, who passed these comments on to Newman, Newman satirized the way in which the

'Peculiars' read Scripture according to their own particular scheme, as in denying the value of good works against faith:

> I hope I shall not be light in speech, if I paraphrase a passage of scripture after their manner to illustrate what I mean – 'Let not a widow be taken into the number under three score years old, having been the wife of one man, well reported of good works (not done in her own strength, but through the grace of the Holy Spirit) if she have brought up children (as real spiritual sons of God, having the renewal of which baptism is the outward sign) if she have lodged strangers, if she have washed the saint's feet (not as if the outward work was any thing, unless there is a real change of heart within,) if she have relieved the afflicted, (not trusting to her own doings, however charitable and useful, but renouncing her own righteousness for the pure and perfect etc) . . . [58]

In this manner, the Evangelicals put their jargon and gloss on the mass of Scriptural texts which fail to support them. To Wilberforce and Stephen, Newman wrote that the Evangelical spirit tends to liberalism and Socinianism; and as to the charge that the first volume of his sermons 'induces fear, and depression', Newman granted it. 'It was meant to do so. *We require the "Law's stern* fires." We need a continual Ash-wednesday.'[59] This tone was lightened in the second volume of his sermons, published on 27 March 1835. The exchanges with these sons of Clapham were, however, good tempered, but less affectionate than one with Newman's old Noetic friend now turned Socinian and Unitarian, Blanco White, who was touched by Newman's letter to him though it was 'nothing but a groan, a sigh, from beginning to end'.[60] Against this was the chorus of praise from the old High and Dry school, led by Joshua Watson, for Newman's pamphlet on the need for suffragan bishops to provide better pastoral care for the burgeoning English population. Watson desired 'personal acquaintance with the Author, whom hitherto I have had the pleasure of knowing only by his works and his friendships'.[61]

Blanco, however, was outside the struggle in Oxford which was renewed in March 1835, when the promise of the Whig return to power under Melbourne produced another vote by a majority of one in the Hebdomadal Board to substitute a declaration for subscription at matriculation. The conservatives rallied, establishmentarian and Evangelical, High and Dry and Tractarian, to draw in the outside clerical MAs, who poured into Oxford for Convocation to vote down the proposal by 459 votes to 57, amid scenes of great enthusiasm:

> This vile declaration, we'll never embrace it,
> We'll die ere we yield – die shouting '*Non placet*'.[62]

There was an irony in the victory. It was to shouts of 'Placet' and 'Non placet' that a greater drama unfolded thirty-five years later, at the Vatican Council, when Newman was on the 'liberal' side. Hurrell Froude, back from Barbados, returned to Oxford the day before the Convocation and cried 'Non placet' with the rest in his last vote in any election, before going down to Devon. He was not to live to see his beloved Oxford again.

Yet the controversy exposed a contradiction in Newman. He was not himself satisfied with the Articles: 'tho' I believe them to be entirely Scriptural . . . ', he wrote, 'I think they accidentally countenance a vile Protestantism. I do not tell people this, lest I should encourage a scoffing at authority'.[63] He was compelled to defend the confessional principle with a weapon of which he increasingly disapproved.

The main liberal enemy of that principle in Oxford was now Hampden who, when the anti-subscription bill came before Parliament, 'alone had spoken out openly in favour of a change, and . . . cooperated with the liberal [Lord] Radnor and sceptical [Lord] Holland to enforce change by act of parliament'.[64] Hampden bore the brunt of the attack from a book edited by Newman on the subscription issue, in which Newman himself alleged that Hampden was a Socinian in the postscript. Henry Wilberforce acknowledged to Hampden the authorship of his contribution, in fact largely by Newman, and Hampden exploded to Newman about his disgust with the latter's 'dissimulation, and falsehood, and dark malignity . . . You have been among "the crafty firsts" ', he wrote, ' "who have sent their silly seconds" to fight their mean and cowardly battles by their trumpery publications . . . I charge you with falsehood, because you have sent out to the public what you know to be untrue', out of 'a fanatical persecuting spirit' and a 'proud orthodoxy'.[65] Newman was amused by the hint in Hampden's letter that had they been laymen they might have duelled: 'Is it not well', he wrote, 'that the Long Vacation should come as a cool evening to extinguish these flames?'[66] In fact, Radnor's bill to abolish subscription to the Articles at entry into Oxford was thrown out in July 1835, and Newman's duel with Hampden was not pursued but postponed.

The half century from 1830 saw the most remarkable boom in church building and restoration in English history, and Newman's practical contribution to this revival, after his rebuilding of St Clement's, was his plan for a new chapel for his four hundred and seventy parishioners at Littlemore, Oriel voting £100 and half an acre for the building. 'If you know any rich man furnished with ability, I have no objection to be indebted to him',[67] he wrote to Henry Wilberforce, with whom his relations were still strained after Henry's marriage. The affair was complicated by Newman's refusal to state the grounds of his complaint and by his sense of injury towards Harriett, and there is a verbose and tiresome emotional delicacy about the endeavours to heal the breach between them – Newman drafted one letter four times. In July 1835, their friendship was renewed not to be broken, with

Newman's agreement to be godfather to Henry's first child John William Wilberforce, mingling the emancipator's name with Newman's own.[68] On 21 July, the ailing Mrs Newman laid the foundation stone of the new Littlemore chapel, designed by the resourceful Tom Mozley. In his address, the Vicar recalled Jacob's vision of the ladder of the angels and his pillar at Bethel, and David and Solomon in the building of the Temple and its rebuilding under Ezra. But he took a deeper consolation from the bones of four Christians found buried east–west under the chapel site. 'The dust of His Saints and Servants is beneath our feet . . . Every thing that is new is like grass, withering ere it is grown up; but the Word, and the Church, came of old from the everlasting God, and abide for ever.'[69]

It was in this brooding over the great mystery of the Church that in July, in a letter to Froude, Newman conceived the germ of his answer to Jager, in a distinction between two kinds of Tradition: an Apostolical Tradition, transmitted from bishop to bishop and containing the fundamentals of Christian doctrine necessary to belonging to the Church's communion; and the Prophetical Tradition comprising all that vast body of beliefs which were part of the privilege of Christian believing, but which were less than authoritative and binding.[70] In his reply to Jager, Newman identified the Apostolical Tradition with the Apostles' Creed, pointing out that Athanasius had not even insisted on the homoousios of the Nicene Creed as a condition of Church communion. The Prophetical Tradition was named after the Old Testament Prophets who, like the Doctors of the New Law, Newman saw, in the manner of Calvin, primarily as teachers or expounders; and in that prophetical teaching, Newman had a vision of a vast system of divinity, too large to circumscribe:

> a vast system not to be comprised in a few sentences, not to be embodied in one code or treatise, but consisting of a certain body of truth permeating the Church like an atmosphere, irregular in its shape, from its very profusion and exuberance. That body of Truth is part written, and part unwritten, partly the interpretation, partly the supplement of Scripture; partly preserved in intellectual expressions, partly latent in the spirit and temper of Christians; poured to and fro in closets and upon housetops, in liturgies, in controversial works, in obscure fragments, in sermons. This I call Prophetical Tradition, existing primarily in the bosom of the Church itself, and recorded in such measure as Providence has determined in the writings of eminent men.[71]

Yet the Prophetical Tradition will contain untruth as well as truth. Christians receive it 'with trust and affection', but it is not binding upon them like the Apostles' Creed.

Newman's letter, however, had its inconsistencies. In reply to Jager's allegations about the Protestant right of private judgement, Newman replied

138

that 'We have those documents, namely the three Creeds, the decisions of at least the first four general Councils, our liturgy, the office and the Thirty-Nine Articles'.[72] These formularies, however, go far beyond the Apostles' Creed; and Newman's complaint that Jager had not appreciated his defi-nition of the 'fundamentals' as a condition of Church communion, not as necessary to salvation, seemed to suggest that it was not necessary to salvation to belong to the communion of the Church. Newman retorted that Rome was '*the cruel Church*' in insisting on too much, where the Church of England admittedly insisted on too little.[73]

His defence of the Articles was particularly lame. He reiterated his belief in the Church's 'power to *develop its fundamental Creed* into Articles of *religion*, according to times and circumstances; to develop is not to create. Articles of religion are not essentially fundamental articles, as articles of faith are'.[74] Why, then, if say, the Thirty-nine Articles are not fundamental, should the Church of England make them binding on her ministers? And if there is a developmental power in the Church, why should the Apostolical or Episco-pal Tradition not reach beyond the Apostles' Creed to the longer 'Creed' of Pope Pius IV at Trent? The point was seized on by Froude. 'What is to be the end of expansions?' he exclaimed; 'will not the Romanists say that their whole system is an expansion of "the H.C.C. [Holy Catholic Church] and the Communion of Saints"? Also what are the Nicene and Athanasian Creeds but expansions? Also to which class of tradition [Apostolical or Prophetical] do you refer the Athanasian Creed? for I suppose you will admit that it carries in its form the assertion of its fundamentality. In short – Why treat a subject of great perplexity and deep and general interest on a narrow and insufficient ground which may avail in one or two controversies with the Romanists . . . but which in no way serves to meet the general question . . . ' As to Newman's insistence on referring all essential dogmas to Scripture, 'I cannot see', wrote Froude, 'what we owe to our Protestant predecessors that should make us so very anxious to skrew a sense out of all their dogmata'.[75]

But Newman was not simply writing out of a sense of loyalty to the Protestant formula that the whole faith was contained in Scripture: he thought that this was a patristic formula as well as a Protestant one. So he told Froude that he was drawing in his horns on his theory of the '*disciplina arcani*', which had been 'founded on the hypothesis of Apostolical Traditions co-ordinate with Scripture'.[76] More essentially, he was still working with the old High Church Rule of Faith: one Bible, two Testaments, three creeds, the decrees of the first four General Councils and the faith of the first five centuries of Christianity, the faith of the early Church, pure and primitive and undivided. This was still the static ideal of the old High Anglican theology. But Newman's vast cloudy conception of the Prophetical Tradition was both as the work of the spirit and as the body of the Church's formal teaching, containing the devotional instruction of the liturgy as well as the writings of the theologians. It implied that the Christian faith was a total form of life far more complex than even its highest intellectual articulations, with an infinite capacity for change and growth within itself. And so it was the Prophetical Tradition which loosed him from his moorings, and pushed him out into an unknown sea.

12

The Via Media: Early Summer

Newman's rooms in Oriel 'communicated with what was no better than a large closet, overlighted with an immense bay window over the chapel door'. In this 'prophet's chamber', he said his prayers in the summer of 1835, so that Tom Mozley, returning to college late one night, 'could even distinguish the words'.[1] These were the devotions of a soldier under fire. Newman faced war on three fronts external to the Church, against the Protestant Dissenter, the Papist and the Infidel, and on two internal ones, against Evangelicals and liberals. Some of these enemies coalesced in his mind, as when he fused the Papists and liberals: 'The Romanists', he wrote, 'seem so heartily to take up the cause of such vile persons as O'Connell, Hume etc'[2] – Joseph Hume being a prominent theological liberal as well as a radical in politics. It was the Roman controversy, however, which led to his decision to redefine the Tracts, which in August 1835, he declared 'defunct, or in extremis',[3] though Pusey was to publish his Tract on baptism at his own risk. Pusey's writings on the sacrament were to run to three Tracts, Nos 67, 68 and 69 in the series, published between August and October, 208 pages long, with elaborate tables comparing ancient and modern baptismal liturgies. This work or works marked the transformation of the Tracts from flysheets into learned treatises, distinguished by some of the best scholarship of the age.

But Pusey brought more than erudition. As an aristocrat, a canon of Christ Church and a professor, he was 'one who furnished the Movement with a front to the world . . . he was able to give a name, a form, and a personality, to what was without him a sort of mob . . . '.[4] He was everything that Rose could have been to the Movement in daily contact and loving friendship, had Rose lived in Oxford. Pusey's erudition was as phenomenal as his charities were munificent and his piety was profound, and it was the Movement's need for a solid foundation in devout Christian learning that he was supremely fitted to supply.

This desire for Christian learning inspired Rose's demand on Newman[5] for a new history of the Church based on a translation of the great work by Louis XV's confessor Claude Fleury, to redress the baleful Protestant effect of the eighteenth-century Lutheran church history by Mosheim, and to reshape the existing Protestant pattern of Anglican religious thought. Yet that new pattern was to be antipapist as well as anti-Protestant: as Newman

141

reported to Henry Edward Manning in September 1835, the Tracts were to be put 'on a new footing', with Keble as editor, and with publicity like the advertisement proclaiming 'Popery examined and refuted in the Tracts for the Times for 1836',[6] which he asked Manning to place in his local county newspaper. To Bowden, Newman wrote of this No-Popery plan for the Tracts from Dartington, where Froude lay slowly dying, 'merely kept alive by the prayers of his friends, as the Israelites by Moses uplifted hands'. 'First', Newman wrote, 'we shall have inquirers turning Papists, if we do not draw lines between ourselves and Popery. Next it will do us good, if we show we do differ from the Papists. Thirdly it is availing ourselves of a popular cry – . . . Fourthly, it was [will] be anticipating other parties by giving our own views of Romanism – and fifthly it is a very effectual though unsuspicious way of dealing a back-handed blow at ultra-protestantism.'[7]

The first fruit of this resolve was Newman's Tract 71, rechristened 'On the Mode of Conducting the Controversy with Rome', which 'has overtaken us "like a summer's cloud" ', he wrote, from the long security which Anglicans had enjoyed, in 'that peaceful condition in which the presence of the civil magistrate supersedes the necessity of the struggle for life and ascendancy . . . '[8] The tract, however, was a double-edged production, acknowledging not merely in the Roman system 'the intrinsic majesty and truth which remain in it amid its corruptions', but urging the wrong basis of many popular objections to Rome and the difficulties in the Anglican position. There was no point in denouncing wicked Popes in a Church which could boast Henry VIII and the eighteenth-century Latitudinarian Bishop Benjamin Hoadly; and Newman acknowledged that the Church of England was *'incomplete*, even in its formal doctrine and discipline'. She was, Newman thought, naturally 'exposed to imperfection, . . . at the distance of 1500 to 1800 years from the pure fountains of tradition', and 'surrounded by political influences of a highly malignant character'.[9] Even her Eucharistic liturgy was 'in one or two places . . . in intention defaced by the interpolations of [the Reformer Martin] Bucer', and the Article on Justification was so wrongly interpreted 'as to render almost hopeless the recovery of the true meaning'.[10]

This assault on the fundamentals of Anglican Protestantism left a narrow and insecure base for a No-Popery alliance with other parties in the Church; Newman, in no sense a politician for all his astuteness, was trying to forge a coalition which was to fall to pieces the moment that his allies got wind of his own distinctive views. His old anti-Catholic acquaintance, the Prussian minister in Rome, Chevalier Bunsen, declared that the new High Churchmen were aiming at 'a popery without its authority, protestantism without liberty, and evangelicism without spirituality'.[11] Newman thought this 'fun', and gently mocked two moderate and not unsympathetic Evangelicals whom he met at breakfast at Henry Wilberforce's vicarage, Bishop Sumner of Winchester and his chaplain, the latter 'a specimen of donnishness grafted on spiritual mindedness, i.e. a constrained way of behaving which is redolent with both conceits . . . Perhaps however they looked on me as a great wild beast'.[12] The wider Protestant world certainly ridiculed the new High Churchmen, as Newman gleefully reported to Pusey, 'as half prig, half dandy, perfumed and powdered, and a little corpulent, one-third Protestant, one third Papist, one third Socinian'.[13] Evangelicals might echo Newman's No-Popery cry, but they would take care to choose better company.

This sense of the oddity of Newman's views was shared to a degree by all his family. Charles told his older brother that he was thinking of returning to religion, but not in a way that John Henry would like; while Newman asked Francis if he was 'approaching Charles's? notions', having just heard that Frank had denied 'the personality of the Holy Spirit and the duty of praying to Christ'. Newman saw Frank's development into what became Unitarianism as no more than the logical consequence of imbibing to his peril the 'cursed Protestant principle' of 'selfsufficient inquiry' or private judgement in preference to resting on 'the unanimous witness of the whole Church'.[14] The dogmatic difference between the brothers was now more than ever a personal one, and Newman wrote to Froude of Francis that he 'could have no intercourse with him – my tie to the Church as a Clergyman destroying the claim of relationship . . . ',[15] in mere loyalty to soul-affirming truth. Frank married in December 1835. 'I trust', wrote Newman coldly, 'it may be of service in taking off his thoughts from the extravagances in which he has hitherto indulged.'[16]

Keble also married at the old age of forty-three, 'and told no one . . . which silence . . . ', reported Newman to Froude, 'the said College [Oriel] puts down, I suspect, to a romantic delicacy and tenderness – whereas others emunctioris naris [more keenly scented] think they see in it an opinion that marriage is a very second rate business'.[17] Keble also became Vicar of Hursley and relinquished his fellowship. Newman put the case against clerical matrimony to another bachelor cleric, Simeon Pope:

Were you married and at the head of a fine and flourishing family, I may say an increasing family, with nine altogether, four boys and five girls, and a tenth expected, would you not have troubles? or were they all girls, would you not say, 'girls *are* such an expence, and my girls are not particularly showy or well favoured' – or if they were boys, one would be sent away from school for striking a praepositor, another would dabble in wet and dirt till he got the scarlet fever, and the eldest would run off to Gretna Green with some milliner's apprentice. Or Mrs P. would be for ever on the look out for balls and sights, in spite of your grave admonitions that a Parson's wife should keep at home. Or she would have a tongue and a temper, and make your home twice as doleful as it is now. And then bad times would come – the Clergy would be called on for unlawful concessions – and you would say, 'why really I cannot afford to keep a conscience. Give me a large fat rectory, and I can suffer a little taxing and fining; but what with my four sons (now going on for College) and my five daughters (the youngest turned nine) I cannot stand on punctilios.[18]

Could a bachelor more easily stand out for truth? Ambition is, like heresy, a matter of moral choice, subtly conditioned by the atmosphere around it. Newman probed the ethos of heresy more deeply in Tract 73, 'On the Introduction of Rationalistic Principles into Religion', a dissection of the views of two popular religious writers, the Scots Thomas Erskine of Linlathen and the American Jacob Abbott. Erskine, wrote Newman, treated the doctrines of Christianity as a sanction to man's moral sense: so that the Trinity 'is only influential as it exhibits the moral character of God',[19] in a restatement of the ancient Sabellian heresy that the Persons of the Trinity describe nothing more than God's mode of dealing with mankind. To Newman, Sabellianism embodied the rationalist principle that the Godhead must be completely intelligible to the human mind, on the basis that 'I cannot believe anything which I do not understand'.[20] Thus Christianity, being intelligible, can be proven to be true because it is in harmony with man's moral nature and its needs.

Against this position, Newman argued that Christian Revelation is not easily intelligible. It is a Mystery, addressed to faith and not reason, for it is not 'a revealed *system*' which is rationally coherent in its parts, but 'a number of detached and incomplete truths belonging to a vast system unrevealed', 'like the dim view of a country seen in the twilight, with forms half extricated from the darkness'.[21] Thus God has given us in Christianity only a small and fragmented part of that vast body of truth which lies forever hidden from us; and no systematic theology is possible, for while there is much that reason can do in theology, it can only contemplate disconnected pieces of the divine design, and hope to grow in holiness into a deeper understanding of what God has chosen to reveal. It is, therefore, folly, granted our ignorance, to pick and choose among those parts of Revelation which can be shown to be morally useful. In this, Erskine was like those Evangelicals who made the test of Christian doctrine its meaning in conversion. But the value of a truth divinely given is not to be assessed simply by the pleasant feelings which it gives us, or by its appropriateness to our moral need, or by the judgement of human reason upon it. In all these approaches to religion, man is hopelessly reaching further beyond his grasp than the farthest star.

Newman's treatment of Abbott, a sentimental popularizer, like his discussion of Erskine, did not impugn their personal orthodoxy. Rather, he dwelt on their 'leading idea', their 'habit of thought', which led them into heresies of which they were unaware: the Sabellian reduction of the Trinity to modes of divine action implicit in Erskine, implied the Socinian denial of divinity to Christ in Abbott, for whom Christ was more a human instrument of divine redemption than the fully Incarnate God-man. The same idea was impressed on Newman by a work published by Blanco White after his apostasy, in which the eccentric Spaniard asserted that 'Sabellianism is Unitarianism in disguise'.[22] A heretic might hide his heresy from himself with the Sabellian formula that Christ was God's means of salvation, while implicitly accepting the Unitarian or Socinian denial that Christ was God.

But this idea of unconscious heresy had its problems, and meant that the heretic is not necessarily a morally bad man, whose heresy is a matter of deliberate choice, as Newman usually thought, but is the unreflecting victim of his own logic – and even more, like the parson with expensive sons and daughters, the creature of his *ethos* despite himself. The issue of whether a heretic was culpable for his heresy because he had neglected conscience, the voice of God within the self, was one that Newman never quite resolved. A heretic might, Newman thought, be unaware of his heresy, and his personal faith could be distinguished from his formal opinions: a distinction which Newman was to struggle to observe in his conflict with Hampden which was soon to follow.

There was, however, a temperamental difference between Newman and Hampden, as well as an intellectual one. Hampden was stout, vulgar in his tastes and habits, and utterly lacking in the ascetic and fastidious Newman's grace of manner and charm of utterance; 'he stood before you like a milestone, and brayed at you like a jackass'.[23] But the resumption of hostilities with Hampden was not wholly of Newman's making. 'How long', wrote Hugh James Rose to Newman, 'are such books as Hampden's [*Course of lectures introductory to . . . moral philosophy*] to come forward from Professors and Heads of Houses? How long are they to come forth unreproved?'[24] Hampden's opinions were again a matter of urgent moment when in January 1836, the Regius Professor of Divinity, Edward Burton, died. Pusey and Newman feared that Hampden or some other 'forerunner of Antichrist'[25] would fill the vacant chair, but Newman also felt that the coming crisis was the heaven-sent '*opportunity* of speaking our mind. Poor Keble's spirit was vexed for years, . . . he was eating his heart, unsuccessfully attempting to analyze his own presagings . . . it is as if providence were clearing the space between two armies and forcing men to choose their side . . . The men now rising are of a very different school from the men of 40 or 50 . . . Pie repone te . . . Really we have nothing to fear . . . '[26]

Then, for the moment, a quite different outcome appeared possible. Rose, as Howley's chaplain, told Newman that Pusey, Newman himself and Keble were in first, fourth and fifth places in the list of names recommended for the Divinity chair by the Archbishop to Lord Melbourne. Newman wrote to tell Keble of his outside chance, and urged him not to reject it as coming from a Whig, but to embrace it 'as a soldier at the bidding of his superiors going on any service. This is a King's office – as a loyal subject can you abandon him to Hampden?'[27] But Whately, supported by Copleston, pushed Hampden's candidacy, and on 8 February, 'someone saw at the Post Office . . . a letter addressed to Dr H. by Lord Melbourne, which was forthwith concluded to be an offer of the Professorship, and Dr H. not denying it . . . the report spread quickly thro' the place'.[28] As Hampden accepted the appointment by return post, and the King almost as promptly gave his assent, the matter was quickly concluded; but the public uncertainty over what had been decided played straight into Newman's hands. He, Pusey and the High Church Walter Hook organized a meeting on 10 February in the Corpus Christi common room, which adopted a petition to the King protesting the appointment, which on the following day was despatched to the Archbishop of Canterbury with seventy-six signatures. The two Archbishops protested to the King and Prime Minister, and as the Tory press joined in the clamour, Newman seized the occasion to draw the whole body of conservative church opinion, Evangelical and Erastian and old fashioned High Church, into a crusade for the Tractarian cause.

But for the clamour to have substance Hampden had to be shown to be a heretic: and on 10 February, Newman worked through the night to compose for the printer an anonymous forty-seven page work, *Elucidations of Dr Hampden's Theological Statements*, which was rushed into publication on the 13th. Newman exploited the obscurity of Hampden's language, especially his distinction between the 'facts' of Scripture, which the Professor following Bishop Butler declared to be revealed, and the dogmatic credal statements about those facts which he denied the status of Revelation. Hampden's position is the exact obverse of a more modern Anglican liberalism, which disputes or denies the 'facts' of Scripture – like the Virgin Birth or Empty Tomb – while still claiming to accept the dogmas built upon them. In this, Hampden was more orthodox than Newman thought: Newman believed that Hampden limited divine Revelation in Scripture to 'historical fact', whereas Hampden's understanding of fact included the dogmatic Scriptural 'facts' which Newman thought that he was rejecting.[29] Thus Hampden declared his belief in the Trinity and the Incarnation. He only denied that the credal language about these doctrines had been revealed. Hampden shared Newman's hostility to a theology of logical deduction: hence his rejection of scholasticism. He also agreed with Newman's conception of the inadequacy of language about God to its object. Where they differed was over the status of the dogma of the Nicene and Athanasian Creeds. For Hampden, the Creeds and the traditional theology about them are simply statements in human language conditioned by past circumstance and culture. They conveniently define the terms for living in communion with a Church, and they teach – and even protect – the divinely given facts of Scripture. But there is nothing directly God-given about them, and they can be recast as the times require. Thus religious tests requiring assent to them could be mistaken, and even a Unitarian, who believed in Scripture, might be essentially orthodox in upholding the divinely given facts, for all the formal heresy of his doctrinal denials.

Newman was appalled. He did not claim that the creeds were like Scripture, directly inspired and revealed, but he thought that the language of dogma, though human, has an infinite depth of meaning beneath the letter because it participates in the divine mystery which it inadequately describes. The earthly vessels hold heavenly treasure, and the creeds are the work of the Spirit in the Church, and Hampden's reduction of dogmatic and credal statements to human cultural productions is a liberalism subversive of the heart of the Gospel. In Hampden's defence, it could be argued, as Dean Church did, that 'he did not consciously mean all that he said',[30] and it was cruelty in Newman to take his unorthodox side, and show him what it implied.

This was, however, now a political debate larger than any in Newman's experience. Melbourne's resolve to stick to his guns can only have been reinforced by private assurances that Newman and Pusey 'were disguised Roman Catholics; and that Newman was a violent and ultra bigot who had acquired notoriety by refusing to marry an Oxford girl because she was a Baptist'.[31] The Prime Minister would not let Hampden withdraw: 'Be easy, Doctor', he said. 'I like an easy man'.[32] But the King was moved to insist that Melbourne again consult the Archbishop. The Prime Minister presented the matter to his Cabinet as one affecting the honour of his government, and remained unmoved by further meetings with the King and Archbishop. 'I do not know what to wish – we gain and lose on both alternatives', wrote Newman to Bowden. 'If he [Hampden] is not appointed we have gained a victory . . . And whoever succeeds, will be virtually curbed in any liberalistic propensities by our present proceedings and their success. On the other hand, if H. is appointed, . . . the Ministry will be at open war with the Church – the Archbishop will be roused, and a large number of waverers in this place will be thrown into our hands.'[33] Though William IV protested that Melbourne had not made clear to him how controversial Hampden was, the decision to appoint him was made public on 20 February.

This delay, however, gave the storm ample time to rise higher. In self-defence, the beleaguered Hampden retained his headship of St Mary's Hall and his membership of the Hebdomadal Board, so that when the Board voted on whether he should remain to discuss the issue, he secured by his own vote the majority of one in his favour. According to Newman, he 'turned to the Vice-Chancellor "as head of the present inquisition" and told him he would find as bad things as his in the Sermons of Mr Pusey, Newman, or Hook'.[34] Hampden's charge was of crypto-popery, and the battle was already preparing in which the liberals called the High Churchmen Papists, and the High Churchmen called the liberals infidels.

This was, then, just the opening shot in a long guerilla war. The gathering of dons in the Corpus Christi common room in charge of the anti-Hampden

agitation sent up two 'requisitions' which came before the Hebdomadal
Board on 29 February, to 'extract erroneous theses from Hampden's works
and condemn them by Convocation', and to ask the University hierarchy
'to accept attendance at the lectures of the Margaret professor rather than
the regius professor as a qualification for ordination'. The first proposition
expressed the University's opinion of Hampden's heterodoxy, the second
widened this to a judgement by the Church. Both proposals were lost in
the Board by a heavy majority. 'The heads would not condemn one of their
own number.' The dons in Corpus set up a committee of six 'representing all
shades of conservative opinion', 'an ideal camouflage for the Tractarians',[35]
ranging from Newman and Pusey through the High and Dry men to the
ultra-Calvinist Evangelical John Hill; its renewed measure over the Bishops'
certificates was only defeated in the Hebdomadal Board by Hampden's
casting vote. As Newman stirred up his clerical friends to make public
protests, he caught a rumour of his new-found fame in Melbourne's
expression of puzzlement over how a small College like Oriel had 'produced
so many men of *Neological* opinions. There was Whately and Arnold – and
now again this Dr Hampden – And then in another way Keble and
Newman'. The Prime Minister, who fancied his own theological acumen,
had also sent for the Tracts, 'and', Newman reported, 'Pusey has forwarded
him both volumes. This is a secret – It is curious', he concluded, 'that in
so little a time we have lifted up so loud a cry'.[36]

It was, then, in the heat of the fray, that Newman endured his own long
expected 'widowing', in the news from Archdeacon Froude of Hurrell's
death, at the age of thirty-three, on 28 February 1836. 'I can never have a
greater loss', Newman wrote to Bowden, ' . . . he was to me, and he was
likely to be ever, in the same degree of continual familiarity which I enjoyed
with yourself in our Undergraduate days; so much so that I was from time
to time confusing him with you and only calling him by his right name and
recollecting what belonged to him, what to you, by an act of memory . . . I
never on the whole fell in with so gifted a person – in variety and perfection
of gifts I think he far exceeded even Keble – for myself, I cannot describe
what I owe to him as regards the intellectual principles of religion and
morals . . . every thing was so bright and beautiful about him, that to think
of him must always be a comfort. The sad feeling I have is, that one cannot
retain on one's memory, all one wishes to keep there and that as year passes
after year, the image of him will be fainter and fainter'.[37] Newman planned
the posthumous publication of his friend's papers, and Froude's father asked
Newman to select a volume from his library. Newman discovered the copy
of Bishop Butler bespoken, and made the fateful choice of the Roman
breviary.

Newman's love of Froude was of its time and setting. Dean Church
recalled the Oxford Movement's Oxford as:

a place where every one knew his neighbour, and measured him, and was more or less friendly or repellent; . . . where every fresh statement or every new step taken furnished endless material for speculation or debate, in common rooms or in the afternoon walk . . . feelings were apt to be more keen and intense and personal than in the larger scenes of life . . . the man who attracted confidence and kindled enthusiasm, . . . whose private conversation and life was something ever new in its sympathy and charm, created in those about him not mere admiration, but passionate friendship, or unreserved discipleship. And these feelings passed from individuals into parties; the small factions of a limited area. Men struck blows and loved and hated in those days in Oxford as they hardly did on the wider stage of London politics or general religious controversy.[38]

Church thought the detached and clumsy Hampden an odd figure to encapsulate that High Church hate which was the obverse to the fierceness of their love. The anti-Hampden clamour found vent in clerical meetings and resolutions all over England. The Corpus Christi Committee adopted on 10 March 1836 a report drawn up by Pusey, denouncing 'the *Philosophy of Rationalism*, or the assumption that uncontrolled human reason, in its present degraded form, is the primary Interpreter of God's Word', and a Declaration that Hampden's published works tended to subvert 'the whole fabric and reality of Christian truth'.[39] In March the delicate balance in the Hebdomadal Board was tilted against Hampden, as it voted to lay a statute before the University Convocation to take from him 'the power of appointing Select Preachers and judging of heresy'.[40] Hampden delivered 'a quietly orthodox inaugural lecture',[41] he was assailed in a ponderous attack by Pusey, and though the two University Proctors announced that they would veto the statute, as they had the power to do, four hundred non-residents flooded into Oxford, to shout 'Placet' in Convocation in the Sheldonian Theatre, their anti-Hampden passions inflamed by Thomas Arnold's attack on the High Churchmen in the *Edinburgh Review*, in an essay entitled 'The Oxford Malignants', 'which was timed to the day'.[42]

'Arnold is amiable and winning', Newman wrote three weeks before, comparing him with Hampden, who was '*judging by his writings*', 'the most lucre loving, earthly minded, unlovely person one ever set eyes on'.[43] This was in a private letter: in public, Newman took care, like the Corpus Committee, to cast no imputation on Hampden's personal religion. It was Arnold who carried the language of personal abuse into public discourse, in an assault on the 'few obscure fanatics' among the new High Churchmen like Newman, worthy heirs of Hickes the Nonjuror, who 'found his religion perfectly compatible with falsehood and malignity'. The last word undoubtedly suggested the title of the article, not chosen by Arnold, but perfectly consonant with its content. The Movement's assault on Hampden was, Arnold declared, the outcome of '*moral wickedness*' and of 'mingled fraud, and baseness, and cruelty, of fanatical persecution. And, for such persecution, the plea of conscience is not admissible; it can only be a conscience so blinded by wilful neglect of the highest truth, or so corrupted by the habitual indulgence of evil passions, that it rather aggravates than excuses the guilt of those whom it misleads'.[44] The article betrays the hurt of the wound so casually inflicted by Newman three years before, but its argument, that false opinion arose from a perverted conscience, was rather close to Newman's own.

The violence of Arnold's language hardly helped his cause, and the retirement of the pro-Hampden Proctors and the appointment of new ones left Hampden exposed to the wrath of Convocation, which voted on 5 May to deprive him of the right to appoint Select Preachers, while the excluded anti-Hampden undergraduates shrieked abuse and broke the windows of the Sheldonian, and stormed the locked doors to get admission to the gallery.[45] The penalty on Hampden might seem small enough, but it stalled the tide of reform in the University and stiffened Melbourne's reluctance to appoint liberal bishops or divinity professors: Arnold never got a mitre, and had to be content with the chair of modern history. The incident also marked the peak of Tractarian influence as the rallying point of the Anglican reaction against liberalism: never again would Newman, Pusey and Keble have the archbishops and the bulk of the Church behind them.

Arnold, however, was also declaring his progressive Whig and liberal prejudice against the whole atavistic and reactionary High Church tradition. The ultimate in such atavism to liberals was Popery, and a flurry of Protestant, Whig and radical writers began probing the Oxford Movement for crypto-papist ideas. Their delvings were assisted by Dr Wiseman, hot from Rome and lecturing to large audiences in London; the former Dean of Oriel, James Tyler, reported to Newman that Wiseman was invoking Newman's authority for the importance of oral tradition and the concession that Rome had not apostatized till Trent.[46] It was through this No-Popery cry that Newman's methods were used against him – the liberals crying Popery where Newman had cried heresy, and meting out to Newman his own treatment of Hampden. Indeed in a measure, Hampden rehearsed Newman's sufferings. Newman was to be censured by the Bishops over Tract 90 as Hampden had been censured for his lectures. The country clergy were to brand Newman a Papist as they had branded Hampden an infidel. Pusey was to be inhibited from preaching, as Hampden had been inhibited from appointing preachers; and Convocation was to seek to censure Newman as Hampden had been censured, and like Hampden, Newman was to be rescued by the Proctors' veto. Dean Church's comparison of Oxford with Renaissance Florence might remind the modern reader of stilettos; and the Oxford Movement was to deserve its punishment because it declared the war which from the very outset, all the parties fought with no quarter and no charity.

The Movement's Achilles' heel was, then, its anti-Protestantism, which bred its dissatisfaction with the Church of England as she was, as in Newman's defence to Robert Wilberforce of praying for the dead: 'I sometimes am quite frightened', he wrote, 'at the thought how great a talent our Church is hiding in a napkin'.[47] His anti-Protestantism was grimly humorous. Comparing the Evangelicals around Maria Giberne to Goliaths suddenly encountered '(*don't* tell them all this) by one or two Davids', Newman declared that 'we will show these Midianites what Gideon can do'.[48] One No-Popery enthusiast, an Irish chaplain to Whately, deceived some readers with an attack on the Tracts in the form of an approving pastoral letter from the Pope;[49] while Newman found 'uncommonly amusing' the great Evangelical Edward Bickersteth's 'Bull' against the Tracts, as Rose had called it. 'The screams he utters against Popery', wrote Newman to Rose, 'are just as if he were actually griped and squeezed by it, as a man by a bear, uttering intermittent shrieks – of a boy ducked in a pond by his playmates, half choked by the water and half able to cry out.'[50]

But these attitudes were no laughing matter: the Evangelicals wielded power, and Newman was vulnerable because of the complexity of his new attitude to Rome. In the preface to the third volume of his *Parochial Sermons*, dedicated to Archdeacon Froude, he argued 'that if Popery be a perversion or corruption of the Truth, as we believe, it must, by the mere force of the terms, be like that Truth which it counterfeits'.[51] This was a subtle way of saying when accused of Romanism, that one is not a Romanist, because the corruptions of Rome are like the truth. A similar sharp but subtle distinction between Popery and Catholicism appears in 1836 in Newman's curious debate, 'Home Thoughts Abroad', which he had begun to publish in 1834 in the *British Magazine*. It opens with friends in argument before the spectacular view of Rome from Bunsen's Prussian ministry – a view evoking in a Christian 'the bitterest, the most loving, and the most melancholy thoughts'. One of the disputants is an Anglican papalist who sees no hope save in union with the Holy See: his faith in a 'bigotry' 'as old as the Gospel itself' recalls Froude.[52] The other speaker points to the spread of the Anglican communion into new continents, the existence of the Oriental as well as the Roman Churches, and the greater fidelity of Anglicanism to truth. 'Foundation we have as apostolical as theirs, . . . and doctrine much more apostolical.' Even Scots Presbyterianism is 'a providential phenomenon, . . . unknown to St Austin', embodying the faith of a people.[53] His interlocutor questions the solidity of the High Church tradition. 'What is the ground of Andrewes and Laud, Stillingfleet and the rest, but a theory which has never been realized? . . . a fine-drawn theory, which has never been owned by any body of churchmen . . . The actual English Church has never adopted it . . . she has ranked herself among the Protestants, and the doctrine of the Via Media has slept in libraries . . . Protestantism is embodied in a system; so is Popery: but when a man takes up this Via

Media, . . . he will be judged, and fairly, to be trifling, and bookish, and unfit for the world.'[54]

The answer to such criticism lay for Newman in recognizing the passing of the '*system* of Laud', but the survival of his principle. 'Charles is the King, Laud the prelate, Oxford the sacred city, of this principle; just as Rome is the city of Catholicism, and modern Paris of infidelity.'[55] But local political embodiments of any idea must perish, even Oxford herself. 'The Church alone is eternal; and, being such, it must, by the very law of its nature, survive its friends.'[56] True, the Church of England might now seem to be in captivity, as Daniel in Babylon; but 'We, too, who are in captivity, must *bide our time*'.[57] For God does not need state protection: 'our one tangible object is to restore the connexion, at present broken, between bishops and people . . . we need no Magna-Chartas or Coronation oaths . . . we wish to maintain the faith, and bind men together in love'.[58] The passing of the old Church–State system would mean the reassertion of the old High Church principle in a new form.

> When the day of trial comes, we shall be driven from the established system of the Church, from livings and professorships, fellowships and stalls; we shall (so be it) muster amid dishonour, poverty, and destitution, for higher purposes; we shall bear to be severed from [the] possessions and connexions of this world; . . . we shall educate a certain number, for the purpose of transmitting to posterity our principles . . . we shall . . . attempt to be evangelists in a population almost heathen.[59]

Newman was only to realize this prophecy by becoming a Roman Catholic. The tract still bore witness, however, to his dislike of saint and Mary worship, which were to be the severest doctrinal obstacles, with the Papacy, to his acceptance of Roman Catholicism. It also shows the clarity with which he would foresee the eclipse of the confessional State, and a world in which the High Church principle would have to survive without traditional privilege and government support.

Yet as Newman confessed to Rose, his dislike of the Establishment had meant a substantial shift in his loyalty to the Church of England. 'I do *not* love the "Church of England – ".' he told Rose. He did love 'the old Church of 1200 or 1600 years, the Church of the builders of our Cathedrals, the Church again of Andrews, Laud, Hammond, Ken, and Butler, (so far forth as they as they agree together, and are lights shining in a dark place) . . . I love the Church too as embodying the good characteristics of the English ethos'. But he did not love 'the creature of Henries and Williams', the Church enslaved by the State, which had 'never been one reality, except *as* an Establishment. Viewed *internally*, it is the battle field of two opposite principles; Socinianism and Catholicism – Socinianism fighting for the most part by Puritanism its unconscious ally', in a 'doctrinal licentiousness', 'as bad and more like "a brothel" '. Rome, on the other hand, had retained 'what *we might have kept* – so much that was high, elevating, majestic, affecting, captivating'; so that for all the 'impossible barriers' between Rome and England, 'My heart *is* with Rome, *but not* as Rome, but as, and so far as, she is the faithful retainer of what we have practically thrown aside'.[60] There had been a time when like Froude and Keble, Newman had been 'bigoted' to the Church of England. Newman's understanding of Roman error was not yet in equal balance with his vivid sense of the imperfections of the English Church, but he was no longer blindly prepared to execrate the one and extol the other.

This slow estrangement of Newman from his spiritual mother could not but exacerbate the difficulties in his relations with his mother and sisters. When they came to Oxford to be near him, they were distressed when his business kept them from him. 'And, when they, in their kindness, tried, however delicately and considerately, to overcome what was to them an invisible obstacle, then I got worried; I got worried by their affectionateness.' They 'did not like some of my greatest friends', he wrote, and 'from the first they did not like the distinctive principles of the Oxford Movement; and, the more it developed, the wider did their difference from me in respect to it grow'.[61] This was in spite of the growing intimacy between the sisters and Newman's friends and disciples the Mozleys. Jemima married Tom Mozley's wealthy brother John, who ran the family printing and banking business in Derby, on 28 April 1836. The union was one of which Newman, for once, unambiguously approved, as did his mother, who was perhaps over impressed by the Mozley's pretensions to gentility, their enormous drawing room and twenty beds. But she only held together until the wedding was over, and died three weeks later. 'If you knew', Newman wrote to his Aunt Elizabeth, 'how dreadfully she has suffered in mind, and how little her wanderings left her like herself, you would feel, as we do, that it really is a release.'[62] The death, as always, plunged Newman into his apocalyptic mood. 'It will make me look forward more earnestly for the day', he wrote to Bowden, 'of Christ's coming to end this troublesome world, and bring her back.'[63] He spent a week in 'dreadful dejection', and at the funeral Anne Mozley recalled him 'still kneeling at the altar when all was over, lost in prayer and memory'.[64]

This left only Harriett unprovided for, and Harriett provided for herself by marrying her brother-in-law's brother Tom Mozley, Newman making this way straight for them by getting Tom the Oriel living of Cholderton, 'an exceedingly pretty village . . . rich in chestnuts, elms, limes, and id genus omne',[65] in the windswept waste of Salisbury Plain, where Froude and Keble had planned the parsonage. Until her last months, Mrs Newman disapproved of Tom, and there was a financial impediment to the union: Harriett had little money and the incumbency was worth only £225 a year, but Newman gave her a start with £30 in spare cash and his mother's plate and furniture. He thought that the disparity in age – Tom was three years younger – was offset by Harriett's still youthful appearance, but Newman also wanted six months mourning for their mother before the wedding. Harriett, however, was in a hurry, – she was thirty-three – and invoked the example of their own parents, who had both married within months of parental deaths. 'I never can approve of a fellow like Mozley marrying – ', wrote Newman to Bowden, 'but if it must be, it is a great happiness to find him brought nearer to me by his offence against monastic rule. He is a most affectionate, unselfish, generous person; and there is no one to whom I could with greater comfort entrust a sister.'[66] Samuel Rickards performed the service at the end of September 1836, and in the comparative poverty and isolation of Cholderton, Harriett conceived her stories of the old Newman family life, while her relations with her older brother were marked by a growing coldness. Newman's intimacy with Tom also suffered: 'every one when he marries is a lost man – a clean good for nothing', wrote Newman to J. F. Christie, another High Church friend of Tom's; ' – I should not be, surprised to be told that Mozley would not write another letter all his life'.[67]

Charles and Frank continued to be a trouble, Charles by receiving the sacrament despite his crazed religious notions and some private infidelity too shocking to describe. He arrived to stay overnight with Newman in January 1837, lightly clad in the depth of winter on a walk to London. On his loss of his latest position, Newman told Jemima that 'People think him eccentric, and will always part with him after a half year or two'. Newman was prepared to surrender to Charles his own £1000 inheritance from his mother, but thought 'that he should do penance some while longer'.[68] Frank was partly displeased by a volume which Newman sent him as a present to his wife, and accused Newman and Jemima of wanting to be leaders of a sect. Newman did his best to avoid him because he made divisions.

There had been a dramatic revolution in Newman's private relationships. Within seven months he had lost Froude and his mother, 'my dearest and most intimate friend, and her who more than any one connected me with this earth',[69] as well as his sisters in wedlock and the home which they had tried to make for him. Newman's letters to Jemima remained as rich and warm as ever, but there was little about his three other, ever more remote, surviving siblings, now entering on middle age, to remind him of the happy bustle of Southampton Street, the united swarm of six strong, vital and clever children, and the self-confident father and pretty mother with her brood around her, in her young and happy days.

13

The Via Media: High Summer

Newman's scholarly routine included the daily composition or translation of a Latin sentence. He was an unflagging worker; but a propagandist's work is a weary one, especially when it requires the double labour of popularization and of creating the scholarship to sustain it. His Tract 75, 'On the Roman Breviary as embodying the substance of the devotional services of the Church Catholic', was the offspring of his legacy from Froude, and it attempted to make more widely available the devotional riches which were unknown to Anglicans, as well as the sources of the Prayer Book itself. Newman loved the Breviary for its reliance on the Psalms and for its sobriety and restraint; 'it keeps up attention and rouses the imagination towards the course of the Christian year, without exciting it', he told Henry Wilberforce. It was a pity that women did not know enough Latin and Greek, as 'Latin devotions are majestic and austere – Greek are much more pathetic and animated . . . The great advantage of a dead language is that it keeps one sober'. The Breviary's other virtues included the stress on morning devotion when the mind is 'most fresh. To leave the body of our prayers for night, is like putting off religion to a deathbed'. Again, the Breviary prayers were short and so unwearisome. 'Dear Froude', Newman noted, 'used to say that "long prayers" were peculiar [Evangelical] and came in at the Reformation.'[1] In February 1837, Newman began to hold a weekly tea soirée for undergraduates in term, and at Easter, to hold a weekly communion at St Mary's. By early 1838, he had begun to recite the Breviary hours and to note his regular fasting. In March 1838, he heard his first confession, from an undergraduate. His slow transition to a more Roman ethos had begun.

Yet while he already thought the proper Anglican ethos much nearer to Popery than to Protestantism, nothing was further from his mind than conversion to Rome as in 1836, he delivered a series of lectures on the popish controversy in the Adam de Brome chapel of St Mary's; and it was these and his exchanges with Jager that inspired his thought 'of publishing some Lectures on Romanism' in July. With the break of a fortnight in London with Frederic Rogers in late July, the lectures preoccupied him as he wrote and rewrote them 'an incredible number of times'; – 'I write and re-write', he told Jemima in November, 'and Rogers, who is here for a week, plucks'.[2] In September, his beloved Bishop, Bagot, came to consecrate the chapel at Littlemore which Mrs Newman had not lived to see. The Vicar 'gave away buns to [the] children', and the Bishop expressed himself 'so much pleased' and 'gratified' with Newman's sermon as to ask him for a copy. 'I have always looked back on it as gauche', wrote Newman, 'that I did not *transcribe* the sermon, but sent to him the half illegible MS as it was. Rest his soul!' Bagot expressed 'sincere delight'.[3] The new chapel at Littlemore, dedicated to SS Mary and Nicholas, was served first by Isaac Williams, then from 1837 by another curate, John Rouse Bloxam, whose hero-worship of Newman was to be lifelong. The building itself, with a raised chancel, a stone altar with some handsome carved work and a central recess behind it with a cross, represented rank Popery to some. The prominence given to the altar was a very cautious step towards that radical liturgical and sacramental reordering which was to transform hitherto pulpit and preacher-dominated churches all over England.

November 1836 saw the appearance of Newman's poems in the *Lyra Apostolica*, 109 in all, most of them written on his continental journey, with another 46 poems by Keble and a scattering from Isaac Williams, Hurrell, Bowden and even one by the most unpoetical Robert Wilberforce. The verses performed their propagandist function, as Newman had described it to Rogers, of 'making an effective quasi-political engine',[4] by strongly expressing Church opinion in an easily assimilable, imaginative form. Newman got Samuel Wilberforce to review the volumes in a popular manner, but there is no contemporary evidence for Isaac Williams' story that Newman had been so 'annoyed with the reflections of the review upon himself'[5] that he never wrote verses again – until *The Dream of Gerontius*. The claim is partly contradicted by his translations from the Breviary, but the impulse in Newman to compose original verses required a striking challenge or personal crisis like the visit to the Mediterranean; and he may have known that he could never be a professional poet as he was already a master of prose.

Newman spent a fortnight in London in December 1836 with his former pupil Robert Williams, now Tory MP for Dorchester, breakfasted with and visited his University MP Sir Robert Inglis and saw a good deal of his old friend, the Devonian squire Thomas Dyke Acland, who was also staying with Robert Williams. 'I have been at the Dentist's every day', he wrote to Jemima. 'Today he has been engaged 40 minutes in burning out the nerves of a tooth – it is to be finished tomorrow.'[6] By the end of the month, he had got to his publisher the whole of the *Lectures on the Prophetical Office of the Church, viewed relatively to Romanism and Popular Protestantism*, its argument being that Anglicanism occupied the *Via Media* or middle way between them. It was to be his principal contribution to a distinctively Anglican divinity, as it sought to define the peculiar theological position of the Church of England and to provide a justification for her existence as a separate Christian Communion beside the Churches of the Reformation and Rome.

Newman's case had two parts: that Rome can be answered with an adequate theory of Tradition, but that the Church of England must receive the Anglo-Catholic theory of Tradition, and wash off the Erastian and Protestant stains upon her. It was here that Newman was alone among the new Anglo-Catholics in frankly acknowledging the difficulty in defining the excellence of Anglo-Catholicism negatively, as a mean between the two extremes of Protestantism and Popery which had not existed in Antiquity, but which in the present had the benefit of flesh and blood reality. 'Protestantism and Popery are real religions', wrote Newman; 'no one can doubt about them; they have furnished the mould in which nations have been cast; but the *Via Media* has never existed except on paper, it has never been reduced to practice; it is known, not positively, but negatively, in its differences from the rival creeds, not in its own properties; and can only be described as a third system, neither the one nor the other, partly both, cutting between them, and, as if with a critical fastidiousness, trifling with them both . . . What is this but to fancy a road over mountains and rivers, which has never been cut? When we profess our *Via Media*, as the very truth of the Apostles, we seem to be mere antiquarians or pedants, amusing ourselves with illusions or learned subtilties, and unable to grapple with things as they are.'[7] In this acknowledgement of the imperfections of Anglicanism, Newman was in no sense distinctively High Church, and his talk of 'paper theories' deeply upset more old fashioned High Churchmen like Rose. His position was perhaps unique to himself in just this, that his vision of the Church of England was one which still had to be realized, as a 'paper theory' to be made real.

Not that the theory of the *Via Media* had ever lacked defenders. Newman approached Martin Joseph Routh, the President of Magdalen, to ask permission to dedicate the work to him, for Routh, who was to live into his hundredth year, was the editor of the writings of the pre-Nicene fathers, and represented in Oxford the continuity of the older High Church tradition. Routh was a man with a wicked, even a heartless, sense of humour: when told that a Magdalen Fellow had died dead drunk in the night, he demanded the right to guess the name, to show that he knew which of his colleagues would have died drunk. Routh had advised another man who wanted to dedicate a book to him to choose a better patron, but would 'not say so to Mr Newman, as I am sure he is not looking to get on in life'.[8] The dedication cost Newman some anxiety, as he did not want to flatter Routh, who was a fanatical dry-as-dust old bibliophile and a passive rather than an active supporter of the Oxford Movement; but there is no evidence for Tom Mozley's story that the dedication rebukes Routh for neglecting the discipline of his college in devoting all his energies to living a long life, by way of the earnest prayer that what Routh had witnessed to others 'may be his own support and protection in the day of account'.[9] Yet Routh was a symbol of a particular theological viewpoint. 'I have tried', Newman told him, 'as far as may be, to follow the line of doctrine marked out by our great divines, of whom perhaps I have chiefly followed Bramhall, then Laud, Hammond, Field, Stillingfleet, Beveridge and others of the same school.'[10]

All these writers had lived, for a time at least, in the seventeenth century, the golden era of Anglican theology; but they still constituted a problem. William Beveridge had been a High Church Calvinist, while Edward Stillingfleet had been sufficient of a Latitudinarian to defend episcopacy as good but not as necessary to a Church, and to advocate union with the Presbyterians. Even the High Church tradition looked like a theological Noah's Ark containing beasts both clean and unclean: 'it still remains to be tried', wrote Newman in the *Lectures*, 'whether what is called Anglicanism, the religion of Andrews, Laud, Hammond, Butler, and Wilson is capable of being professed . . . on a large sphere of action';[11] and that required hard theological research. 'We have a vast inheritance, but no inventory of our treasures. All is given us in profusion; it remains for us to catalogue, sort, distribute, select, harmonize, and complete.'[12] The Anglican tradition needed to be put in proper order, so that the gold could be separated from the dross, the expressions of individual opinion from Catholic truth, the guesses of genius from the first principles of the faith of the Church of England.

It appeared, however, that these first principles were not exclusively popish or Protestant. Newman argued that the Anglo-Catholic agrees with the Protestant in making Scripture the ultimate appeal in matters of faith; but he agrees with the Papist in invoking the authority of Antiquity as well. The error of Protestants is that their alleged *sole* ground of faith is Scripture, on the principle that the Bible and the Bible only is the religion of Protestants, when their failure to agree among themselves shows that the Bible is not its own interpreter, and that it requires an interpretation which by itself it does not supply. The Protestant principle of an unfettered right of private judgement on Scripture had bred infidelity; in Germany, Lutheranism had declined into rationalism, in Switzerland, Calvinism into Socinianism. In any case, the various Protestant Churches represent rival traditions which go beyond Scripture, so that there is no substance to their claim to have dispensed with Tradition altogether, and it is their defect to work by traditions which on their own theory they cannot recognize for what they are.

This is only the general usage of mankind, which holds the great majority of its opinions on the basis of traditions as all-encompassing as the air, though we fail to see them. 'Murderers are hanged by *custom*', writes Newman, in his starkest illustration. 'Such as this is the Tradition of the Church.'[13] Yet such tradition is far more subtle than any law. 'It is latent, but it lives. It is silent, like the rapids of a river, before the rocks intercept it. It is the Church's unconscious habit of opinion and feeling; which she reflects upon, masters, and expresses, according to the emergency';[14] and

Roman Catholics are right to insist on Tradition as a part of that Rule of Faith which is the life blood of Christianity.

But if Protestants are wrong in principle and Papists right in invoking Tradition, yet Papists have in their 'beautiful theory' an abuse of right principle, as Rome's tradition adds to or contradicts the Catholic faith of antiquity, which by the sheer force of her infallibility, she then imposes on believers. Thus she rejects a proper right of private judgement, for that is the great privilege of the God-directed and conscience-guided Christian, to proclaim the Christian faith, even by standing like Athanasius with the whole world ranged against him. 'The humblest and meanest among Christians', Newman insisted, 'may defend the faith against the whole Church, if the need arise. He has as much stake in it and as much right to it, as Bishop or Archbishop, and has nothing to limit him but his intellectual capacity of doing so':[15] 'any one', Newman wrote to Jemima, 'layman, woman, child, has a right to hold up the standard of the faith against Bishops, Archdeacons, and Clergy'.[16] This provided the necessary balance to Newman's clericalism, and was to be reinforced in his mind by the appointment of the liberal Edward Stanley as Bishop of Norwich who had, he thought, denied the Creed: 'when a bishop is heretical, man, woman, or child has licence to oppose him'.[17]

The judgement has a relevance to more recent controversies in the Church of England. A great many heretics have been in episcopal orders. But just as there is this proper right of private judgement which is not Protestant, so there is a proper doctrine of Tradition which is not papist; and that is to be discerned by distinguishing the Episcopal Tradition in the Creeds, which all Christians must receive, from the Prophetical Tradition, which embodies the whole range of Christian theological reflection and religious thought. Thus Newman developed the distinction which he had already expounded to Jager. The Prophetical Tradition exists in the writings of the Fathers, in the decisions of General Councils, and even in the Thirty-nine Articles, though these are local enactments and will carry less weight than others for which there is a universal authority. Newman dismissed the decrees of Trent as but 'the *ruins* and *perversions* of Primitive Tradition'.[18] But if some elements in the Prophetical Tradition are less important than others, must Christians receive it as a whole, when it contains matters of debate, and error and misunderstanding and folklore and superstition? Newman's answer is that the Church is our mother, and we are her children. She does not force her teachings on us with violence as Rome does. But we ought to receive the Prophetical Tradition with love, trust and confidence, as children listening to our mother. We need not affirm everything in the Prophetical Tradition, though it will contain truths so near to the Episcopal Tradition that no faithful Christian would think of denying them. We should not hastily dispute or deny any part, for there is a middle way, between active affirmation and denial, a way of receiving the tradition as a child does his mother's teaching, in trust and confidence and love.

There is in this a profounder truth. The ordinary Christian does not encounter the Church's doctrinal teaching in the writings of theologians but in the trust and confidence and love of the Church's worship, as set forth in the Book of Common Prayer. Religion for Newman began for all believers in devotion, as it began in apostolic devotion to the person of Christ; and theology in the Prophetical and Episcopal Traditions is the rational explication of this devotion, as faith, using reason as its instrument, seeks out an understanding of itself. Thus it is the *lex orandi* or law of prayer which determines the *lex credendi* or what one must believe; or putting it more simply, the kind of God in whom the Christian believes is the God to whom he says his prayers. The Christian religion is wholly contained within the Prayer Book, as it is wholly contained in the life of prayer. For the Church, wrote Newman:

transmits the ancient Catholic Faith simply and intelligibly. Not the most unlettered of her members can miss her meaning. She speaks in her formularies and services. The Daily Prayer, the Occasional Offices, the Order of the Sacraments, the Ordination Services, presents [sic] one and the same strong, plain, edifying language to rich and poor, learned and unlearned, and that not as the invention of this Reformer or that, but as the witness of all Saints from the beginning. The very titles of the Prayers and Creeds show this; such as, the 'Apostles'' and 'the Nicene Creeds', 'the Creed of St. Athanasius', 'the Catholic Faith', 'the Catholic Religion', a 'Prayer of St. Chrysostom', and the like. It is undeniable, that a stranger taking up the Prayer-Book would feel it was no modern production; the very Latin titles to the Psalms and Hymns would prove it. It claims to be Catholic; nor is there any one of any party to deny, that on the whole it is. To follow the Church, then, in this day, is to follow the Prayer-Book, instead of following preachers, who are but individuals. Its words are not the accidental out-pouring of this or that age or country, but the joint and accordant testimony of that innumerable company of Saints, whom we are bound to follow. They are the accents of the Church Catholic and Apostolic as it manifests itself in England.[19]

It was, therefore, in the worship and devotion of the Prayer Book that the Catholic faith was to be learned and understood, not in argument or academic learning or fine preaching, but in simple humility and holiness of heart.

Yet devotion was never far from polemic, and polemic from an intellectual problem. Newman hoped and thought that the *Lectures* would prove him no Romanist to the world; but his insistence that the Church was 'indefectible' in her teaching in the detail of the Episcopal Tradition and in broad outline in the Prophetical, was difficult to distinguish from Roman infallibility, and at one point at least, Newman unguardedly spoke of the Church as infallible. The Protestants were his more immediate target. 'I say nothing, I believe', Newman wrote to Jemima, 'without the highest authority among our writers, yet it is so strong that every thing I have as yet said is milk and water to it – and this makes me anxious. It is all the difference between drifting snow and a hard snow ball. It seems to me like hitting the Peculiars etc a most uncommon blow in the face.'[20] Before publication of the *Lectures* in March 1837, he heard that he had been discussed by the Evangelical ministers gathered around the Revd Daniel Wilson, Vicar of St Mary's, Islington – 'a regular don – a conceited self sufficient man', Newman described him to Pusey, 'with 18 (?) clergymen dependent on him, and looked up to as a Bishop'.[21] Newman rallied to defend Pusey himself when the moderately Evangelical *Christian Observer* at last lost all patience with Tractarians, and assailed 'the absurdity, the irrational fanaticism, the intellectual drivelling' of Pusey's three Tracts on baptism, declaring that he 'ought to lecture at Maynooth, or at the Vatican, and not in the chair of Oxford'.[22]

The newspaper's grounds of complaint against Pusey were two: that he had declared the Old Testament saints like Abraham sanctified but not regenerate by the Spirit, because Regeneration was conferred by baptism and the Jewish saints had never been baptised; and that the Advertisement for the Tract – for which Pusey had not been responsible – declared that the Sacraments, in certain cases, may, in Newman's words, 'be of benefit to persons unconscious during their administration'.[23] Newman's replies defending Pusey appeared in the *Observer* in February and March 1837. The first point was simply the old one at issue between Evangelicals who denied and High Churchmen who asserted that Regeneration came with baptism not conversion. Newman also made his response the vehicle for a statement of the patristic doctrine of the indwelling Spirit, by which he was to attempt to undercut the differences between the Popish and Protestant theologies.

On the influence of the sacrament on an unconscious dying man, Newman was content with the lower defence, that we cannot be sure that no grace had been conveyed; but by the date of the appearance of his final contributions to the controversy, he had also to answer the *Observer*'s charges that his views were irreconcilable with the Tudor Books of Homilies, and with the Thirty-nine Articles, and especially with their teaching on the doctrine of justification. The Homilies, official Tudor sermon books whose authority was upheld by Article XXXV, taught that Rome was Antichrist: a doctrine which the *Observer* demanded to know if Newman held. He dodged the challenge, claimed to hold the general teaching of the Homilies, and demanded in *tu quoque* to know if the *Observer* could subscribe to expressions in the Homilies which implied the existence of Pope Joan and that the Apocryphal Books were part of Scripture. No one could be required to believe in every detail in large works by uninspired authors, which must contain incidental errors. As for the Thirty-nine Articles, the first five, Newman insisted, contained 'Catholic and Apostolic Truth'; the sixth to the eighteenth were true according to his own private judgement, though he demurred at some interpretations of Article XVII on Predestination. The last twenty-one Articles he received literally, but according to his own particular sense, 'because I think', he wrote, 'they *never* had any one simple meaning'.[24] This was a dangerous admission, provoking the very doubt about his tendency to Romanism which he wanted to dispel. 'It amuses me beyond measure', he wrote to Maria Giberne, 'to see how angry these people are made by their very incapacity. They put me in mind of a naughty child put atop of the bookcase, very frightened, but very furious.'[25] But Newman's own position was a vulnerable one, and his later attempt to impose a non-Protestant 'Catholic' meaning on the Articles was to bring the Oxford Movement to a crisis over its commitment to the Church of England.

Newman complained to the *Observer* that his February letters had occupied 'not so much as seven pages of your larger type . . . It has elicited from you in answer about sixty pages of your closest'.[26] This was to fight at a disadvantage. 'As to the Christian Observer', he told Bowden, 'it seems as if [the non-Juror Charles] Leslie's remark was right – viz., that one could not fight with scavengers without using the dirt from the kennel as well as they.'[27] He expected his contribution in the journal for May 'to be cut up into portions like butcher's meat like Atreus's sons and nephews';[28] but though the editor wanted a further contribution on the doctrine of justification, Newman discontinued the letters, alleging the journal's failure to furnish more definite charges against Pusey. A book of lectures on justification was now coalescing in his mind around the exchange, just as the *Prophetical Office* had taken form around the controversy with Jager.

In the midst of this anti-Protestant crusade, his apocalyptic spirit survived. He replied briefly to a curious enquiry from Henry Edward Manning about the understanding of the millennium in Justin and Jerome,[29] but to another correspondent, he declared the possible truth of the theory popular among radical Evangelicals of the premillennial Advent, the Lord's Second Coming before the millennium to a largely faithless earth.[30] It was the most otherworldly kind of consolation that he applied to Henry Manning as his wife lay dying of consumption like Froude: for, Newman wrote, 'those we love are not nearest to us when in the flesh, but they come into our very hearts as being spiritual beings, when they are removed from us . . . our treasure being removed hence, leads us to think more of Heaven and less of earth'.[31] 'The thought of the dead is more to us than the sight of the living.'[32] The strangest expression of his apocalyptic mood came in his famous letter to Samuel Wood on a patristic notion, the gloss on a strange passage in Genesis, that 'though the Devil, Satan, fell from the beginning, the *Angels* fell before the deluge falling in love with the daughters of men'. Newman linked this to the doctrine of the Book of Daniel that every nation

162

had a Guardian Angel, and wondered if 'John Bull is a spirit neither of heaven nor of hell', in an extension of the idea of *ethos*, that nations have a personality which is the earthly projection of a fallen spirit. The principle also suggested that the character of a nation or people is a neutral force which can be turned to good or evil, 'like loadestones carrying us to the right or left when one would go straight'.[33] It is, of course, the juxtaposition of the burly John Bull with the usual ethereal image of an angel – even one which has coupled with the daughters of men – that makes it sound comical: but as Newman said of the idea in the *Apologia*, recalling the young man who would dance though dancing lost him his bride, 'Hippoclides doesn't care'.[34]

Nor did Newman care when the ultra-Evangelical Peter Maurice, a chaplain of New College and All Souls, and Curate of the Oxford parish of Kennington, denounced the arrangement for worship in Littlemore in *The Popery of Oxford confronted, disavowed, and repudiated*,[35] and placarded the walls of the Colleges with an advertisement for it declaring Newman and Pusey to be Papists. 'The Kebles heard from Truro of an Oxford man who deposed he went into Littlemore Chapel, found lights burning, and was told they burned day and night', wrote Newman to Jemima. 'Daman (our fellow) was told by the clergyman at Ilfracombe (an Oxford man and pupil of mine) that I wore on my surplice a rich illuminated cross. The Coachman of the Coach which passes Littlemore at three when the bell is ringing seems regularly to give the passengers an account of us about as veracious I suppose, as those of Oxford guides generally are.'[36] Against this, Newman secured a retraction of the charges of introducing popish innovations into worship by George Townsend, the Canon of Durham who is the hero of Monsignor Knox's famous essay on the man who went to Rome to convert the Pope in 1850.[37] Again, Newman gathered many small crumbs of comfort: an extravagant encomium from Sir Francis Palgrave, the anonymous London lady who had sent him a rich chalice, the wine-merchant's clerk brought to Anglo-Catholic views by the ultra-Protestant *Record*, the formation of bodies of Anglo-Catholic opinion in the Colleges, Walter Hook's conversion of three Wesleyan Ministers who 'came to criticize and caught a Tartar'. 'The general cry seems to be, these principles are very dangerous, subtle, persuasive, and far spreading – and by all means do not *examine* into them. Again, I ask, is this language for the 19th century?'[38] Newman nicely captured the mingled horror and fascination with crypto-popery, which was foreign, exotic and dangerous, and left him open to the usual charge against innovators, of corrupting the wild or adventurous or rebellious young.

Perhaps his deepest cause for comfort was the spread of his opinions among the young men of Oxford and beyond. 'Every man of talent', wrote one such impressionable youth, 'who during the last six years has come to Oxford has joined Newman, and when he preaches at St Mary's (on every Sunday afternoon) all the men of talent in the University come to hear him, although at the loss of their dinner. His triumph over the *mental* empire of Oxford was said to be complete!'[39] This was an exaggeration, though it was gloomily underscored by the hostile Whately. The better known were those who followed him to Rome. The charming and exquisite young aesthete, Frederick William Faber, like Newman of Huguenot ancestry, came up in 1833 and quickly fell beneath the master's spell. The brilliant logician William George Ward, the sharpest philosopher whom Newman converted, with the mind of an archangel and the body of a rhinoceros, became his disciple in 1838, as he found in Newman the resolution of his own inner tension between the realism of the Benthamite Utilitarians and the moral earnestness and depth of Thomas Arnold. It was these young men who coined the motto 'Credo in Newmannum', a nice if mildly blasphemous variant on 'Credo in unum Deum'; and it was they who seized on Newman's ideas and pushed them further than he wanted or intended to go.

Yet Newman's own inner demon was hurrying him in the same direction, as he and Keble gathered Froude's papers for publication: an event which was to be a disaster for their party, but was a long and deeply meditated one. 'The age is so very sluggish', wrote Newman of one of Keble's sermons, 'that it will not hear unless you bawl – you must first tread on its toes, and then apologize.'[40] But what if no apology were to be acceptable? Keble, Pusey, Isaac Williams, Rogers and Wood were all for the immediate publication of Froude's papers; Newman alone confessed some fears. One fear was over the lack of reference to Christ in Froude's religious writings, for which Newman wrote a not wholly convincing apology. He thought, however, that Froude's letters would 'show his mind, his unaffectedness, playfulness, brilliancy . . . his utter hatred of pretence and humbug'. Froude's dislike of '*show*' in religion would moderate the charge of formalism against High Churchmen, and the correspondence would draw out the growth of his mind: 'we never', wrote Newman, quoting a friend, 'have the history of men in the most interesting period of their life, from eighteen to twenty-eight or thirty, when they are *forming*'.[41] In August 1837, Archdeacon Froude sent Newman his son's private journal of 1826–7, 'giving an account of his fastings, etc., and his minute faults and temptations at the time'.[42] As the date of publication of the first two volumes drew near, 24 February 1838, so Newman's apprehensions grew.

He had given ammunition to his enemies. Froude's self-torments over his moral peccadilloes and his amateur efforts at asceticism and fasting could only excite in stout Protestant breasts either pity or derision. But what was frightening were the asides about the Reformation. 'Odious Protestantism sticks in peoples gizzards.' 'Really I hate the Reformation and the Reformers more and more.'[43] To Newman, Froude's every word was alive with the sound of his voice and the delight of his presence, but the public merely had the bald print before them, and the 'biting epigrams caused foe to exult and friend to shrink'.[44] One old-fashioned High Churchman, Edward

Churton, Rector of Crayke in the diocese of Durham, wrote to Pusey that 'there are sentences and even pages of that book, which I could wish almost to have lost my right hand sooner than have seen published'.[45] Newman acknowledged to Manning that he was in hot water, but hoped to 'turn it into steam, and direct it aright'.[46]

In one sense, this judgement was acute: he was giving orthodoxy the notoriety and excitement of revolution and heresy, and thereby multiplying his followers. On 30 July 1838, the anti-Tractarian Lord Morpeth read extracts from the *Remains* in the Commons, and defended the official state subsidy to the Roman Catholic seminary of Maynooth in Ireland on the ground that Popery was also taught at Oxford. The young High Churchman Gladstone defended Newman by distinguishing his opinions from Froude's, but it shocked the ordinary English mind that the very University which was the guardian of the nation's youth was subverting the national religion.

Newman also had reason to fear public reaction to his *Lectures on Justification* which appeared in March. For Luther and the Reformers, the doctrine of justification by faith alone, which they derived from St Paul's Epistle to the Romans, had been the *doctrina vel stantis vel cadentis ecclesiae*, the doctrine on which the Church stands or falls, and had divided Europe into hostile armies by distinguishing Protestant Christianity as a religion of salvation through faith in Christ from the Roman Catholic religion of salvation by faith and works. Newman's book is his greatest attempt to deploy the method of the Anglican *Via Media* to a particular theological subject, and to undercut the debate between Protestant and Papist by recalling both to the faith of the Bible and Fathers of the undivided Church before the Reformation and Counter-Reformation divided it.

The key to the problem for Newman lay in the patristic doctrine of God's indwelling in the soul to give it a new quality of supernatural life. As God was made man to make men gods, as Newman's hero Athanasius had proclaimed, so God inheres within man, remoulding him in holiness and righteousness. Thus man is saved not merely by grace, but by the divine presence itself, as Newman was later to hymn it in *The Dream of Gerontius*, which describes the soul's translation after death into eternal life:

> And that a higher gift than grace
> Should flesh and blood refine,
> God's presence, and His very Self,
> And Essence all-divine.[47]

Our flesh and blood are refined in the image of God by his very presence in the soul.

This presence, is, then, also a Trinitarian one, for each of the Persons plays its part in the divine economy or plan of salvation. We are saved by nothing less than 'the *habitation* in us of God the Father and the Word

Incarnate through the Holy Ghost'.[48] The spirit of adoption whereby we cry abba, father, places the Father's presence within us as his sons; and Christ is present in us by his Spirit, which makes us temples of the Holy Ghost. Moreover, this process occurs through the power of Christ's death and Resurrection and Ascension: the last being the theme of the gloriously poetic assertion that

> His ascent bodily, is His descent spiritually; that His taking our nature up to God, is the descent of God into us; that He has truly, though in an unknown sense, taken us to God, or brought down God to us, as we view it. Thus when St. Paul says that our life is hid with Him in God, we may suppose him to intimate, that our principle of existence is no longer a mortal, earthly principle, such as Adam's after his fall, but that we are baptized and hidden anew in God's glory, in that Shekinah of light and purity which we lost when Adam fell, – that we are new-created, transformed, spiritualized, glorified in the Divine nature, – that through the participation of Christ, we receive, as through a channel, the true presence of God within and without us, imbuing us with sanctity and immortality . . . This is the one great gift of God purchased by the Atonement, which is light instead of darkness and the shadow of death, power instead of weakness, bondage and suffering, spirit instead of the flesh, which is the token of our acceptance with God, the propitiation of our sins in His sight, and the seed and element of renovation.[49]

It is Christ's rising from the dead and Ascension into heaven which transmits to us the salvation earned by his death, as in the spirit we die and rise and ascend with him, and are changed from glory into glory.

In this, Newman was exploring a richer soteriology or theology of salvation than one which spoke simply and solely of the death on the Cross, by showing the significance of the death for the other great mysteries of the Trinity, Resurrection and Ascension. The sting for Protestants lay in the implication of the argument for the doctrine of justification by faith alone. Newman agreed with the Protestant teaching that in justification, God *declares* the sinner just and righteous though he is in fact none of these things, because Christ has assumed the guilt and punishment for all his sins upon the Cross; and in this, Protestants are right to speak of justification as *pardon*, which the sinner can do nothing by his own good works and strivings to deserve. But Newman appended to the Protestant doctrine the Catholic position. Justification is not merely God's pardon, for his indwelling Word then effects what it declares. God does not merely pronounce the sinner forgiven: he also *makes* him just, as he renews or regenerates him by his own divine indwelling. Man is thereby reborn into a new quality of life, and in this second birth, God implants his own objective presence, Father, Son and Spirit in the soul, recreating it in holiness and righteousness. Justification is therefore, both God's *declaring* just, as Protestants say, in pardon; and as Catholics say, God's *making* just in regeneration or renewal.

It would seem, therefore, that Newman had merely added the Protestant position to the Papist one. In fact, he retained a Protestant element in his formula by making God's pardon of the sinner precede his regeneration where Roman Catholics inverted this, arguing that God forgives men in the degree and measure that he has first made them just and holy. But Newman's argument was nearer Rome than the Protestants, for where the latter thought of justification as the initial *act* of divine pardon, restoring the sinner to a right relationship with God, Newman had, like the Roman Catholics, come to mean by justification the whole *process* of salvation including both pardon and renewal. Protestants, on the other hand, had carefully distinguished justification as pardon from sanctification or making holy, as they generally agreed that man's good works had a part in such sanctification, but that no good work could prompt God's free and gratuitous pardon in justification by faith alone.

These differences might seem technical to the modern reader, but the Roman Catholic insistence that good works play a part in justification, and have merit in the sight of God, implied a vast system of devotion and practical piety by which such grace and merit could be secured. Of course, these works only have merit because of the salvation earned by Christ's death upon the Cross, which Catholics and Protestants agreed to call the 'meritorious' cause of justification. But they disagreed about the 'formal' and 'instrumental' causes of justification.[50] In classical Protestantism, the 'formal' cause is the *imputation* of the merits of Christ's suffering and death to man, which as a righteousness that he lacks, secures his pardon. Christ enters the dock in the sinner's place, and though innocent, incurs his guilt and punishment. The sinner remains a sinner, though justified, the only change being in the manner in which God regards him. This, thought Newman, was not a 'real' position, because God's Word had not effected what it declares, but had left the sinner in the same condition as before, ingloriously sinful, in 'an unreal righteousness and a real corruption', unable to observe the moral law. But it was the glory of the Gospel that unlike the older Judaism, it enabled man to obey the law, and for leaving man powerless, a prey to sin, the Protestant system drew from Newman a great burst of rhetorical indignation. 'I answer that the Law is past, and that I will not be brought into bondage by shadows . . . Reputed justification was the gift of the Law; but grace and truth came by Jesus Christ. Away then with this modern, this private, this arbitrary, this unscriptural system, which promising liberty conspires against it; which abolishes Sacraments to introduce barren and dead ordinances; and for the real participation of Christ, and justification through His Spirit, would, at the very marriage feast, feed us on shells and husks, who hunger and thirst after righteousness.'[51]

Against such an unreality, the Roman Catholics had a real position, that justification produces a real righteousness and not a token one, as their formal cause of justification is the divine 'infusion' of the grace won by Christ's merits to make the sinner holy. Newman thought that the danger with the view of such *infused* or 'inherent' graces was that in the popular Roman devotional system, they became the sinner's property 'as a something to bargain about, and buy, and traffic with, as if religion were, not an approach to Things above us, but a commerce with our equals concerning things we can master'.[52] Newman's *Via Media* suggested a third possibility, that the divine presence was neither *imputed* nor *infused* but *imparted*, not 'inherent' in man but *'adherent'* to him, just because it remains distinct from him; not to buy or traffic with, as if it were in any sense his possession, but as the independent transforming power of God within himself. Again, on this understanding of justification, Newman was in agreement in principle with the Roman system; yet he also declared a subtle polemical distinction from it and identified its corruption.

So also with the instrumental cause of justification, which for Protestants was faith, for Roman Catholics the sacraments and especially baptism. Newman agreed with Roman Catholics that baptism is the initial instrument of our justification as of our regeneration, and even when the believer has faith before his baptism, it is baptism which makes his faith justifying. Yet Newman was apparently bound by Article XI, which taught justification by faith alone. His solution was not an entirely happy one, to make baptism the sole *external* instrument of justification and faith the sole *internal* one. But if our justification includes our sanctification, there is a seeming casuistry in his argument that while faith justifies us hand in hand with hope and love, hope and love are not 'instruments' of justification: as if hope and love could have no place in making us just and holy. Newman clung to the formula which his argument had made meaningless. There was, however, in the seventeenth-century George Bull's *Harmonia Apostolica*, a good Anglican precedent for Newman's further seemingly popish argument that we are justified by faith *and* works, a harmony worked out to weaken the Reformation doctrine by reconciling the contradiction between the Epistles of Paul and James, who flatly said that 'by works a man is justified, and not by faith alone'. Martin Luther had called James 'a right strawy epistle': but as the Epistle to the Hebrews uses the same illustrations of faith as James of works, Newman had a basis in Scripture as well as in Anglican theology for blurring the sharp distinction between justification and sanctification in the stricter Protestant tradition.

It could, then, be said, that Newman had abandoned justification by faith alone, if we are also justified, as he argued, by works and sacraments if not by hope and love. Yet he saw some value in the Protestant formula, and that is the very opposite of the popular Evangelical view. For this seemed to say, 'Get *faith*; become spiritual . . . you must be conscious of a change wrought in you . . . '[53] In short, justification by faith could wrongly mean dwelling on faith by itself and not on Christ as its object. Or as Newman wrote to Lord Lifford in a letter acknowledging the influence upon him of Thomas Scott and Charles Simeon, 'the so-called Evangelical School makes a *certain inward experience*, a certain conscious state of feeling, the *evidence* of justification'.[54] But, 'To look at Christ is to be justified by faith; to think of being justified by faith is to look from Christ'.[55] 'True faith is what may be called colourless, like air or water; it is but the medium through which the soul sees Christ; and the soul as little really rests upon it and contemplates it, as the eye can see the air.'[56] Faith should be unconscious of itself, and conscious only of its object; and to say that we are justified by faith alone may be a useful way of saying that we are justified by Christ alone, in that total process which from beginning to end may be called justification or regeneration or sanctification, depending on how we view it, a process in which faith and works and sacraments and obedience to the moral law all play their essential parts.

Newman's remarks about Luther may understandably make Luther too much the modern Evangelical: 'He found Christians in bondage to their works and observances; . . . and he left them in bondage to their feelings'.[57] Again, Newman's reading of Luther is suspect,[58] and his understanding of the divine indwelling displays an unremarked resemblance to Calvin: they had both read Athanasius after all.[59] Yet Newman's attempt to do justice to the strengths of the Roman Catholic and Protestant positions has a modern parallel in the ARCIC statement on justification, the most recent attempt to bridge the gulf of the Reformation by Canterbury and Rome. This agreement may, however, like Newman's argument, do no more than mirror the weakening link over three centuries between the mainstream Anglican tradition and the cardinal doctrine of the Protestant Reformers, and in the current state of Anglican theology, looks like mere compromise and muddle.

Newman's book was a mass of self-contradiction and a puzzle to his sympathetic and learned Durham critic George Stanley Faber, an old-fashioned High Church Protestant, sometimes accounted an Evangelical, who unlike many Protestants revered the Fathers, and was uncle to Newman's disciple Frederick William Faber, himself the son of a secretary to the Bishop of Durham. The difference between the generations showed the wider shift away from Anglican Protestantism, and moderate as well as radical Evangelicals hastened to decry and denounce the Oxford Movement and all its works. The mass of Churchmen, however, were still sound Protestants. Henceforth they thought that in attacking Protestantism, Newman was betraying the Church, and the English state and nation and people.

Yet his anti-Romanism was still profound. His review of the French liberal Catholic Félicité de Lamennais' *Affairs of Rome* in the *British Critic* drew the conclusion that the Gallican Church and the Papacy were even more in a condition of captivity to the State and to secular politics than England. But his own revulsion from Romanism was in part political in nature, for he was in greater sympathy with the archreactionary Pope Gregory XVI than with a liberal Catholic like Lamennais, whose passion for liberty, equality and progress made him the mouthpiece of the Utilitarian philosophy of the age. 'We almost could fancy,' wrote Newman with mock incredulity, 'he held that the multitude of men were at bottom actually good Christians',[60] and with this fondness for democracy, it was 'not wonderful that . . . he cordially approves of what the Roman Church and Mr O'Connell are doing in Ireland . . . '[61] The Tory in Newman was still prominent in his judgement that Romanism showed its error in espousing rebellion, but Newman proved an accurate prophet in suggesting that the same spirit in Lamennais 'which would lead him to throw off civil authority, may urge him under disappointment to deny the authority of Religion itself'.[62] Newman could see that the nineteenth-century revolt against Christianity was in very large part political in its causes; but he refused to draw the obvious conclusion, drawn by Lamennais himself, that religion would remain strong wherever, as in Ireland or Poland, the Church was in general sympathy with the political aspirations of her people.

14

The Via Media: Indian Summer

Newman at thirty-six was 'a dark, middle-aged, middle-sized man, with lanky black hair and large spectacles, thin, very gentlemanly, and very insinuating'.[1] He was dependent on his spectacles, and had to grope blindly to find them. To James Anthony Froude, his appearance was heroic. 'His head was large, his face remarkably like that of Julius Caesar.' From his absorption in controversy he might appear obsessed. Yet 'he seemed always', wrote Froude, 'to be better informed on common topics of conversation than any one else who was present . . . He was lightness itself – the lightness of elastic strength'.[2] He was inclined 'to talk on light, amusing subjects'[3] in society, and to chat with students on any subject under the sun except Tractarian theology. Though he drank little, he was entrusted to buy the wines for high table. Samuel Wilberforce found his silence in the Oriel Common Room painful: but if the others present that evening were uncongenial, he drew in his horns.[4] In a quiet domestic circle, he was excellent company. Like many bachelors, he was accumulating godchildren, three in a year. When George Ryder asked him to be sponsor to his child, Newman complained to Henry Wilberforce, 'I wish one could sell one's compliance . . . I should have liked to [have] stopped with such as your little boy. You had claims on me which G. Ryder has not'.[5] His Bowden godson Charles and the Pusey children loved him. After dinner, wrote a visitor, one young Pusey 'climbed Newman's knee and hugged him. Newman put his spectacles on him, and next on his sister, and great was the merriment of the Puseyan progeny'.[6] He then told them the story of the old woman's magic broomstick which became two magic broomsticks when she broke it in half.

Such mild frivolity was needed in the Pusey household. Pusey's wife Maria, a learned and literary lady of considerable character and intellect, had been a prey to doubt, and only gradually came to her husband's opinions. In 1837, the couple sold their horses and carriage and Maria sold her jewels to build churches in London; but having been born a Dissenter, she then worried herself sick that she had not been validly baptized, and for three and a half months abstained from communion. Newman performed the rite conditionally in a private ceremony on Easter eve in 1838, which gave her 'unspeakable comfort', as did his sermon on a 'A Particular Provi-

171

dence', on the infinite tenderness and unrelenting justice of Christ on the sinner's death.[7] Maria was increasingly an invalid; and while Pusey was an affectionate father, he maintained his fasting regime of 'plain food', even when his nine-year old son Philip seemed to be dying of the illness which left him deaf and a life-long cripple. Pusey regarded the death of his daughter Katherine in 1832 as a punishment for his sins, and amid the encircling gloom of Pusey's home, Newman's obvious happiness shone like a light. 'It was, in a human point of view', he wrote, 'the happiest time of my life. I was truly at home . . . "Bees, by the instinct of nature, do love their hives, and birds their nests." I did not suppose that such sunshine would last, though I knew not what would be its termination. It was the time of plenty, and, during its seven years, I tried to lay up as much as I could for the dearth which was to follow it. We prospered and spread.'[8]

It was a sign of this happy state of mind that though he was overwhelmed by literary work, his appetite for it was unbounded. In January 1838, he became the editor of the *British Critic* and so gained a new platform for his views. 'I will pay you seven gold sovereigns (guineas would sound better) for every sheet', he wrote, in asking for contributions from Robert Wilson.[9] 'I shall expect your Articles with the seasons', he told Manning, 'something sharp in winter, promising in Spring, flourishing in summer, and fruitful in Autumn.'[10] He projected a house of studies in Oxford in the early summer, of young men under the superintendence of Tom Mozley's brother, the promising young theologian James, to help him with his labours of editing and translation. The availability of fellowships and the dangers of being branded Tractarian kept all but a very few of the most dedicated disciples away.

Whatever assistance Newman received, however, his printed output was astonishing. The last letters on the Church of the Fathers appeared in the *British Magazine* in 1837; but 1838 saw the appearance of the third edition of the *Lyra Apostolica*; the *Lectures on Justification*; another volume of the *Tracts for the Times* and another volume of sermons; two edited volumes of hymns from the Latin Breviary; an edition of Christopher Sutton's *Godly Meditations*; the first two volumes of the *Library of the Fathers* and four lengthy reviews in the *British Critic*, which in its hunger for copy, made large inroads on its editor's time. There was also the demand upon him from his cure of souls – not merely in conducting services and the rites of passage, but in the expansion of his public role, as in the opening of a poor school at Littlemore, which now had to be worked without female family assistance. He felt remote from his parishioners, but some at least were content to venerate him from afar. The blind daughter of the Principal of Brasenose ever after heard his voice in Isaiah, especially in the Advent readings, and a later Vicar of St Mary's, Cosmo Gordon Lang, who claimed still to feel his presence there, recalled an old lady's memory of the beauty of his enunciation: 'Mr Newman used very often to wear a rather dirty surplice, but when he read the lessons we thought he was in heaven'.[11]

Others were less warmly appreciative. On 20 May 1838, a sermon was preached against the Oxford Movement by the Lady Margaret Professor of Divinity, Godfrey Faussett, in Newman's own University Church, condemning the tendencies to Popery in both the Tracts and Froude's *Remains*. Newman's defence cited Froude's anti-Roman remarks about *'wretched Tridentines'* and calling for Rome's *'total overthrow'*. He denied, however, that papal Rome was Antichrist, replying to Faussett's assertions with a not too subtle *tu quoque*: that the very errors which Anglicans alleged against Rome were alleged by Dissenters against Anglicans. Yet Newman was incapable of avoiding deeper themes than polemic: his remarks about his own understanding of the Real Presence in the Eucharist betray a scepticism about the reliability of the information provided by our senses, and about the relativity of human conceptions of space and time:

> Presence then is a relative word, depending on the channels of communication existing between the object and the person to whom it is present. It is almost a correlative of the senses. A fly may be as near an edifice as a man: yet we do not call it present to the fly, because he cannot see it, and we do call it present to the man, because he can. . . . As sight for certain purposes annihilates space, so other unknown conditions of our being, bodily or spiritual, may practically annihilate it for other purposes. Such may be the Sacramental Presence. We kneel before the Heavenly Throne, and distance vanishes; it is as if that Throne were the Altar close to us.[12]

The reply to Faussett is more in the well-trodden way of contemporary controversy, as in the catena of passages from the Anglican Fathers to prove the importance of fasting, which reiterated Newman's old point that the Protestants of his own age were more Protestant than their forebears. Newman had no great respect for Faussett, whom he compared to 'an old piece of ordnance, which can do nothing but fire – or like an old macaw with one speech . . . He can do nothing but fire, fire'.[13] Newman was also delighted that his reply had outsold Faussett's attack, 750 to the Professor's 500: 'Who would have thought persons would buy an *answer* without the *question*.'[14] Faussett, however, had fired at Hampden, and he represented both the opinion of the senior old guard in the University and that of the conservative establishment among the clergy, whom Newman had now forever lost.

The heightening of tensions between the rival religious traditions left more moderate High Churchmen exposed to attack. 'You are, indeed, in the thickest fire of the enemy', Newman wrote to Walter Hook, beset by Evangelicals and Dissenters in Leeds; 'and I often think how easy it is for us to sit quietly here sheltered from bullets, while you often get what is meant to hit us'.[15] There were some moderate Churchmen of whom Newman was highly suspicious. Samuel Wilberforce disliked Newman's domination of his brothers Robert and Henry, and was interpreted as having attacked him in an afternoon sermon at St Mary's. Newman then declined Samuel's offer to review for the *British Critic*, declaring himself 'not confident enough in your general approval of the body of opinions which Pusey and myself hold, to consider it advisable that we should cooperate very closely'.[16]

Wilberforce had drifted into the Anglican mainstream, the abiding place of old-fashioned churchmen like Tom Keble, who was distressed by Newman's Advent Sermons on the patristic idea of Antichrist, delivered in 1835 but published as Tract 83 in 1838. Keble still thought papal Rome Antichrist, the mysterious figure in St John's Epistles whose coming is a sign of the last days; but Newman's anti-Protestantism was only implicit as he sidestepped this 'historicist' view, in describing the 'futurist' consensus of the Fathers that Antichrist would come at the end of the world as an individual, probably Jewish, who would restore the Temple rites and rule from Rome over a reinvigorated pagan Roman Empire.[17] For Rome, unlike its prototype Babylon, had not yet perished, but had been preserved by the Christian Church. The Roman Empire was dormant, not dead; and as the last of the empires which figured as the fourth Beast of Daniel and as the Beast of Revelation, its power would revive to slaughter the saints in the years before Christ's return in judgement.

The pagan, apostate character of the Roman Empire and city still bore a problematic relation to the Roman Church, so that Newman afterwards thought that Bishop Newton was still on his mind even in 1838. But Newman did not insist that these predictions were certain. Rather, he thought that in men like Julian the Apostate, they had been partly fulfilled in a foreshadowing of events still to come. The argument was, however, in its pessimism and hostility to the idea of progress, a heaven-sent weapon against political and religious liberalism, which Newman identified 'with the fair promises in which Satan is sure to hide his poison! . . . He promises you civil liberty; he promises you equality; he promises you trade and wealth . . . he promises you reform'.[18] Newman could not be sure that the current liberal Apostasy from Christianity was the final portent of the end, and cautioned that Babylon and Rome were but the prototypes of urban avarice and irreligion, of 'that arrogant, ungodly, falsely liberal, and worldly spirit, which great cities make dominant in a country'.[19] London and Paris, like Babylon, were ripe for divine judgement, and this and the hint that Antichrist's miracles might be the wonders of modern science were calculated to arouse the apprehension that these were indeed the last days. The Tract imparts the sense of insecurity and melancholy of much of Newman's Anglican preaching, and marks the wholesale transfer of the apocalyptic temper from Evangelicalism into Anglo-Catholicism, as an instrument to judge liberalism and consign it to the everlasting bonfire.

Yet if there was this Protestant brimstone element in Newman's teaching about liberalism, there was a liberal element in his anti-Protestantism, as no one has ever surpassed him in tempering the sword of dogma in the fire of doubt. The Victorian scientist T. H. Huxley coined the word 'agnostic' to define the man who alleges a lack of evidence either to affirm or deny God's existence; and Huxley, with his super-sensitivity to questions of evidence, declared that 'a Primer of Infidelity' could be compiled from Newman's writings. It is the sceptical element which is dominant in Newman's Tract 85, later republished as 'Holy Scripture in its Relation to the Catholic Creed', which argues that the Bible cannot prove the whole of Christianity by itself. Scripture nowhere expressly teaches the divinity of the Holy Ghost or Infant Baptism or the observance of Sunday instead of the Jewish sabbath or even the necessity of communal worship. Only one or two texts maintain so important a doctrine as Original Sin. Scripture contains a multitude of further elements which would seem strange or superstitious or magical outside it, from the serpent which tempted Eve to Balaam's speaking ass to St Peter's money tribute in the fish to the adoration of Christ under the image of a lamb. What would a Protestant think of a Church Father who, like St Paul, wrought miracles through his touch on an apron or, like St Peter, through the falling of his shadow? Again, the text has on its surface a mass of minor contradictions, while there is less early evidence that some parts of it should be within the Canon, than for practices like speaking of the Christian Altar, which Protestants regarded as non-Scriptural and popish. Having rehearsed the difficulties, implausibilities and problems posed by Scripture in the best modern manner through a hundred and fifty printed pages, Newman insisted that its meaning does not lie on the surface of the text, but needs to be understood by a principle which Scripture implies and requires, that of Church authority and tradition. 'Sectaries commonly give up the Church doctrines, and go by the Church's Bible; but if the doctrines cannot be proved true, neither can the Bible; they stand or fall together.' The principle which makes sense of both is Christ's abiding presence in his Church. 'I will accept her doctrines, and her rites, and her Bible, – not one, and not the other, but all . . . I love her Bible, her doctrines, her rites, and therefore I believe.'[20]

Yet as in the *Prophetical Office*, Newman was still insistent that there is much in Church tradition which need not be believed, even in the writings of the Fathers. So he argued in his introduction to *The Catechetical Lectures of S. Cyril, Archbishop of Jerusalem*, the second volume in the new Anglo-Catholic series, *A Library of Fathers of the Holy Catholic Church, anterior to the division of the East and West*. The first, also published in 1838, was Pusey's classic translation of Augustine's *Confessions*; the second was translated by Newman's new young disciple Richard Church, with Newman's assistance.

In the introduction, Newman declared that the Fathers are to be believed where they agree, as witnesses to Apostolical tradition. But they disagree, and their work contains 'individual, local, or transitory opinion'[21] as well as truth – a distinction echoing Newman's statement in the *Prophetical Office* of the need to separate the gold from the dross in the writings of the Anglican theologians. But in both the Fathers and the Anglican tradition there is a core of truth, the very heart of which is what is 'fundamental' to Christian believing. It was in this insistence on identifying what was 'fundamental' that Newman's differed from William Palmer, whose two volume *Treatise on the Church of Christ* presented the High Anglican vision of the Church as surviving in three great branches which preserved the Apostolic ministry of rule by bishops, the Roman Church, the Greek and the Anglican.[22] Palmer denied the value of distinguishing the 'fundamentals' of the faith common to all the Churches from the accidental errors in which they differed from one another. But Newman thought that Palmer's own argument presupposed just such a distinction, as on Palmer's theory, a special Roman belief, like papal infallibility, could not be a 'fundamental' of the faith, when it was rejected by the Orthodox and the Anglicans, indeed by many Roman Catholics. Rather, all three Churches held to the substance of the truth, which in its primitive essentials had survived their divisions.

Newman's theory and Palmer's had this common characteristic, that they placed an enormous emphasis on the office and authority of the bishop, as the transmitter of Apostolic teaching and ministry from generation to generation. The problem lay in fitting this theory to the contemporary Anglican episcopate. The *Library of Fathers* bore on its title page the figure of John the Baptist with his scroll, 'vox clamantis in deserto', the voice crying in the wilderness; but the series was fulsomely dedicated, in anxious supplication for official approval, to William Howley as Archbishop of Canterbury. It was, after all, important that the Primate and his bishops should believe in the Oxford Movement's theory about them. Newman's own ideal of devotion to the Bishop was founded on the principle of the Epistles of St Ignatius of Antioch, written within eighty years of the death of the Lord, expounding the ideal of episcopal monarchy, in which the visible Bishop stands in a special authoritative relation to the Bishop Invisible in God. 'My own Bishop was my Pope', Newman recalled in the *Apologia*. 'I knew no other; the successor of the Apostles, the Vicar of Christ.' His reward was his bishop, Richard Bagot, 'a man of noble mind', as Newman recalled him, 'and as kind-hearted and as considerate as he was noble . . . May his name be ever blessed!'[23] His memory to Newman remained fragrant for a quarter of a century, and Newman's loyalty was not to be tested to the limit, unlike that of the Anglo-Catholics who came after him.

But their relationship had its problems. Newman dedicated the *Lectures on Justification* to Bagot, and expected him to endorse the Tracts in his Charge to his diocese of 14 August 1838, delivered in St Mary's. Bagot acquitted the Tractarians of the charge of ritual innovations, and suggested that with one or two excesses, they were reviving a strict observance of the Prayer Book rubrics in a wholly praiseworthy manner. But the Bishop was also plagued by complaints that the Tractarians taught Popery, and in his Charge he administered a mild rebuke, 'lest in their admiration of antiquity, they revert to practices which heretofore have ended in superstition'.[24]

This was a flea-bite, but Newman was crushed. 'What he said was very slight indeed', he wrote to Bowden, 'but a Bishop's lightest word ex Cathedra is heavy . . . Well, my dear B. has not this come suddenly and taken away your breath?'[25] Bagot was, however, appalled by Newman's over-reaction, an offer, supported by Keble, and sent through the Archdeacon, to withdraw the Tracts in whole or in part. Bagot insisted in his reply that Newman 'cannot have fully or accurately heard what I did say'.[26] As Keble wrote to Newman about the Bishop, 'seeing how little most of us care for the sentiments of our Diocesans, he has naturally assumed that his words would not be taken as they were uttered, and is now startled to find that they are so'.[27] Newman had paid a Bishop the astonishing compliment, novel among Anglicans, of taking seriously what he said.

Keble also thought that good could come of the affair if it were to prevent the Bishop from 'taking counsel chiefly of the men whom mortals call High and Dry'.[28] Bagot inserted a footnote in the printed version of the Charge to soften the sharpness of the text, but given Newman's exalted conception of the episcopal office – 'His word is law. I am under his jurisdiction'[29] – he was more deeply hurt than he cared to show. He opened his heart to Pusey, declaring that Bagot 'has never been my *friend* – he has never supported me – His letting me dedicating [sic] that book to him was the only thing he have [sic] done for me, and very grateful I feel . . . Sometimes as I have stood by as he put on his robes, I felt as if it would be such a relief if I could have fallen at his feet and kissed them – . . . though from the kindness of his nature he has been ever kind to me, yet he has shewn me, *as* me, no favor – unless being made Rural Dean was such, which under the circumstances I do not think was much'.[30] Newman was reduced to tears by consolation from Keble with a line from Virgil: 'O passi graviora, dabit Deus his quoque finem'. 'No one has encouraged me but you – ', he replied to Keble. 'Pusey was so cast down when he heard it, that he himself needed comfort.'[31]

The incident illustrates Newman's over-sensitivity, but it also revealed the insufficiency of his Ignatian theory of episcopal monarchy. He had already faced the possibility of an heretical bishop, but had not thought out its implications. If the bishop is a heretic, there must be an authority to which the Christian can appeal for his correction. As the Anglo-Catholic movement took form against the background of hardening episcopal opposition, so it was forced to defy its diocesans by appealing to a wider authority

– to the Prayer Book, or the Catholic faith of the ancient Church, or even to the practice of contemporary Roman Catholicism. This wider appeal was implicit in the logic of Newman's own practice, as Keble and Pusey by remaining Anglicans were to discover. For the moment, however, Newman was left to feel his way towards a theory of the Church which was more satisfying than one which left all ultimate decisions in the local bishop's hands.

Bagot's reaction posed another question with a new seriousness: how far could the Tractarians safely go? Newman thought that people 'will always lag a little behind in order to be safe and moderate, and to have the satisfaction of abusing you':[32] advice hardly needed by its recipient, Frederick Faber, who was never to care much what people thought of him. But while Froude's *Remains* gained recruits like Ward, the half-committed and neutral were being driven away. Edward Churton told Newman of the perplexity of his followers in a letter regretting the *Remains*, which Newman described to Keble as 'half penitential, and half nouthetetic'[33] – i.e. admonitory – but he had another set-back from such faint hearts when the clergyman Sir George Prevost, with Tom Keble's connivance, wrote to deplore the project undertaken by Samuel Wood and Robert Williams to translate the Roman breviary, and offered to pay the costs of its suspension. In deference to Newman's embarrassment, the work was discontinued, and all that survives are Newman's translations of some of the breviary hymns for the daily offices, magically invoking the image of light, as in the verses for Saturday Vespers:

> The red sun is gone,
>   Thou Light of the heart,
> Blessed Three, Holy One,
> To Thy servants a sun
>   Everlasting impart.
>
> There were Lauds in the morn,
>   Here are Vespers at even;
> O may we adorn
> Thy Temple new born
>   With our voices in Heaven.
>
> To the Father be praise,
>   And praise to the Son
> And the Spirit always,
> While the infinite days
>   Of eternity run.[34]

There was refuge on these heights from the disappointments of earth: 'you know, my dear N. you are a very sensitive person',[35] wrote Keble of the failure of the breviary plan, with the air of one imparting a hidden truth. Newman ran into another storm over the further project to construct a memorial in Oxford to the Protestant Reformers Cranmer, Latimer and Ridley, burnt in the city in the reign of Mary. The scheme's proponent was Newman's former pupil Golightly, whom Newman had regarded with amused affection, for all his militant Protestantism. 'Golius would not goliare or γολίζειν, i.e. be golius, unless he acted as he did', wrote Newman to Froude in 1835. 'At present he goes about declaiming against my patronage of Clem.[ent] of Alex[andria] – my incaution – my strange sayings so very unsatisfactory . . . '[36] Newman asked him to serve as his curate at Littlemore in 1836, but Golightly had gone around denouncing Pusey's severe notions about the forgiveness of post-baptismal sin, and was understood to have preached against him. Under the circumstances, Newman was reluctant to license Golightly formally and so make him independent, so Golightly declined the curacy, to Newman's regret. A further bout of goliaring in early 1837 brought down on Golightly a severe wigging from Pusey, and he fast became a dangerous enemy. As a wealthy man, he could do as he pleased, but he was above all a militant antipapist, and in holding the meeting in his house to launch the Martyrs' Memorial, he and some of his supporters had a secondary purpose, to test the Tractarians' loyalty to the Reformation.

The last point was taken by Pusey, who told Newman that the scheme was 'spoken of as a hit against you', so that while he himself was not wholly adverse to it, and even welcomed the alternative proposed forms of the Memorial, a market cross or 'a Cathedral with shrines!', he 'would not join in any thing which did not satisfy you'.[37] Pusey, with his knowledge of German, was never as hostile to the Reformers as Newman and Keble, who urged Pusey to make his own decision without reference to what they might do. Newman's own position was that the Memorial did not touch on doctrine, but he had 'no sort of confidence' in Cranmer as a representative of Catholicism or of the English Church, and while everyone could feel pity and horror at the martyrs' cruel deaths, he thought of Cranmer, 'Men are for him now – they will be less and less so. The more he is talked of, the less he will be borne'.[38]

His refusal to subscribe, however, proved his opposition's case, which was given an airing in the *Record*'s claim that he had declared the Evangelical Bishops of Chester and Winchester unfit to occupy their sees. The prelates concerned, the Sumner brothers, agreed with Newman that the report was 'manifestly absurd' or 'worse than absurd',[39] and to George Ryder, Newman called it 'a great fat lie, a lie to the back bone, and in all its component parts, and in its soul and body, inside and out, in all sides of it, and in its very origin . . . its father and mother are lies and all its ancestry – and to complete it, it is about me'.[40] To the ordinary mind, however, his anti-Protestantism made him automatically a Papist. It was, no doubt, the constant reiteration of the charge that helped sow the first seeds of the thought that he should be one.

Any popish tendency was anathema to Hugh James Rose, to whom Newman dedicated the fourth volume of his sermons. The offer reached Rose just as he was setting off for Italy in a last effort to recover from TB. In January 1839, Newman heard that Rose had died before reaching Rome. 'Poor Rose, or happy', wrote Newman to Rogers, 'that he is taken off just as the battle begins!'[41] Few men can have had a finer epitaph by anticipation than Rose's, in Newman's sermon in the volume which bears the dedication, on 'The Invisible World'. 'Once only in the year, yet once, does the world which we see show forth its hidden powers . . . Then the leaves come out, and the blossoms on the fruit trees, and flowers . . . So it is with the coming of that Eternal Spring . . . The earth that we see does not satisfy us; it is but a beginning . . . A world of Saints and Angels, a glorious world, the palace of God, the mountain of the Lord of Hosts, the heavenly Jerusalem, the throne of God and Christ, . . . lie hid in what we see . . . Shine forth, O Lord, as when on Thy nativity Thine Angels visited the shepherds: let Thy glory blossom forth as bloom and foliage on the trees; change with Thy mighty power this visible world into that diviner world, which as yet we see not; destroy what we see, that it may pass and be transformed into what we believe.'[42]

Newman meant this volume of sermons to be his best.[43] In more philosophical vein, he pursued the themes of comparison and contrast between faith and sight in two further *University Sermons*. The first, 'Faith and Reason, contrasted as Habits of Mind', took from the Epistle to the Hebrews the text that faith is '*the evidence of things not seen*', and argued that its desire is its main evidence. Even when faith invokes the evidence of sight, what is good evidence of a religious truth to one man is not good evidence to another, because the one will be disposed by the whole direction of his personality to consider one inference from the evidence probable, while another with a different moral predisposition will take a different view of the same evidence. Though 'a given evidence does not vary in force, the antecedent probability attending it does vary without limit, according to the temper of the mind surveying it'. Christians who proved God's existence from the evidences of design in creation had no better arguments than atheists who interpreted these evidences of design in a different manner. 'It is indeed a great question', wrote Newman sceptically, 'whether Atheism is not as philosophically consistent with the phenomena of the physical world, taken by themselves, as the doctrine of a creative and governing Power.' The resort to evidence-mongering was the special weakness of the preceding century, 'a time when love was cold'. Such arguments proved nothing to men of unawakened hearts, and only carried conviction to those whose hearts were already awake. 'A mutilated and defective evidence suffices for persuasion where the heart is alive; but dead evidences, however perfect, can but create a dead faith.'[44] In this, as in the further sermon, 'The Nature of Faith in Relation to Reason', Newman argued that faith is perfectly rational, as 'the reasoning of a religious mind, or of what Scripture calls a right or renewed heart'.[45] But such reasoning does not rest on compelling evidence; rather, it is a complex and subtle effort to infer what is probably true, in the light of all the personal convictions that one holds.

'I have preached two sermons', Newman wrote wryly to Rogers, 'which have greatly enlightened me in my subject, and, I believe, perplexed all my hearers.'[46] 'The Tracts', he added to Rogers a week later, 'are selling faster than they can print them.'[47] He drew up a collection of the Tractarians' attacks on Rome to counter the still swelling chorus of accusations against them of Popery, now joined by a synod of Anglican clergy in Ireland. He also had to deal with domestic calamity: Bowden, smitten by tubercular illness like Froude and Rose, set off to Rome for a cure. 'Fac ut vivat, Misericors Deus, Johannes G. Bowden, quem olim mihi dedisti conturbernalem cùm adolescens essem', he prayed. 'Make live, O Merciful God, John G. [sic] Bowden, whom you gave me as a companion when young.'[48] Newman's consolation to Pusey on his wife Maria's death was, Pusey wrote, 'like the visit of an angel'.[49] 'It is now twenty-one years since Pusey became attached to his late wife, when he was a boy', wrote Newman to his sister. 'For ten years after he was kept in suspense, and eleven years ago he married her. Thus she has been the one object on earth in which his thoughts have centred for the greater part of his life.'[50] Her legacy to Newman was his obit book, which came into its own as friend after friend died, and was commemorated yearly in prayers and masses. Newman had to assuage Pusey's sense of guilt about Maria. She was buried with her daughter Katherine in the central aisle of the nave of Christ Church Cathedral, under a stone inscribed with a popish breviary prayer for the dead: 'Requiem aeternam dona eis, Domine, et lux perpetua luceat eis'. The widower had to traverse the gravestone daily, as he dedicated himself to mourning, keeping his eyes in public lowered and his face unsmiling. Ever after in Tom Quad he kept his gaze on the ground, in fear if he looked up of a vision of 'the shroud on his wife's coffin fluttering in the wind'.[51]

Pusey passed his remaining forty-three years a penitent, avoiding the old family drawing room in his house in Christ Church. In 1839, Newman himself embarked on a more penitential course, by increasing the severity of his observance of Lent, abstaining from sugar, pastry, fish, fowl and toast when not dining out, refusing second helpings of meat and eating nothing but the rare biscuit before 5 p.m. on Wednesdays and Fridays, with a still severer regime in Passion Week. He noted one Wednesday a guilty glass of port.[52] The regime became more savage in 1840, as he was further attracted to the ascetic and monastic ideal. The ideal was there in the Fathers; but the contemporary model was only to hand in Rome.

15

The Via Media: First Doubts

Whatever the future, Newman claimed a deeper inner peace. 'In the spring of 1839 my position in the Anglican Church was at its height', he wrote. 'I had supreme confidence in my controversial *status*, and I had a great and still growing success, in recommending it to others.'[1] In an article in the *British Critic* in April 1839, he surveyed its sources and successes, from Brighton to Elginshire. He rooted them, as he later summarized his argument, in the romantic 're-action from the dry and superficial character of the religious teaching and the literature of the last generation, or century, and as a result of the need which was felt both by the hearts and the intellects of the nation for a deeper philosophy . . . '[2] The evidence for this sense of need for a deeper philosophy lay in the writings of Scott, Coleridge, Southey and Wordsworth, as well as in influences which were more directly religious: the wonder was that such various currents had given rise to a movement so notorious and widespread. As he recalled:

> From beginnings so small, from elements of thought so fortuitous, with prospects so unpromising, the Anglo-Catholic party suddenly became a power in the National Church, and an object of alarm to her rulers and friends . . . And, in fact, they [the originators] could only say that those doctrines were in the air; that to assert was to prove, and that to explain was to persuade; . . . If we inquire what the world thought of it, we have still more to raise our wonder; for, not to mention the excitement it caused in England, the Movement and its party-names were known to the police of Italy and to the back-woodmen of America. And so it proceeded, getting stronger and stronger every year, till it came into collision with the Nation, and that Church of the Nation, which it began by professing especially to serve.[3]

This confidence in the international outreach of the Movement was one theme of Newman's essay in October 1839 on the triumphant expansion of the American Episcopal Church. He also reflected, however, on its ambiguity, expressing his irritation at the 'Protestant' in her title, and attacking the notion of 'a Protestant-Episcopal Cathedral'. 'Sooner', he wrote, 'shall we set eyes on a griffin, or a wivern, than [on] so gross a violation of all the laws of unity and entireness.'[4] But in writing the essay, he did not doubt that the American Church had the Catholic principle within her, or that Anglo-Catholicism could flourish in the New World.

What shook Newman's confidence in his position was his summer reading between mid-June and the end of August 1839, as he steadily mastered the materials of the fifth-century Monophysite controversy, in which the heretical Monophysites asserted that there was only one nature in Christ, a divine nature and not a human one. The matter was the more interesting to Newman, because the heresy was hatched in his own beloved Church of Alexandria among the disciples of Athanasius' great interpreter St Cyril; and some have seen in Newman's own Christology a Monophysite tinge, in an overstress on the divinity rather than the humanity of Christ. In assessing the parties to the controversy, Newman carefully distinguished the radical Monophysite Eutyches from both a more moderate Monophysite position and the orthodoxy of the Council of Chalcedon. He was struck, however, by a parallel which he discerned between past and present. Eutyches, like the Protestants, upheld one extreme position; the orthodox, like modern Rome, upheld another; and it was the moderate Monophysites who maintained a learned and subtle *Via Media* between the extremes, which resembled in its mediatorial tone and temper the modern Church of England. 'I saw my face in that mirror, and I was a Monophysite.' 'The shadow of the fifth century was on the sixteenth. It was like a spirit rising from the troubled waters of the old world, with the shape and lineaments of the new.'[5]

'Of all passages of history, since history has been', Newman recalled in the *Apologia*, 'who would have thought of going to the sayings and doings of old Eutyches, that *delirius senex*, as (I think) Petavius calls him, and to the enormities of the unprincipled Dioscorus, in order to be converted to Rome!'[6] The immediate impact of the Monophysite parallel on Newman is not quite clear either from his Monophysite manuscripts or from the contemporary correspondence, but derives from his afterthoughts about it. He was, however, impressed by 'the great power of the Pope (as great as he claims now almost)'[7] at the Council of Chalcedon, which defined the orthodox doctrine of two natures in Christ, the human and the divine, according to the formula of Pope Leo's Tome.

What, however, crystallized Newman's doubt was an article by Nicholas Wiseman in the *Dublin Review* in August 1839, which employed Newman's favourite device of paralleling past and present by comparing the Anglican with the Donatist schismatics in Africa in the fourth century. Newman read the article and was at first unimpressed, but Robert Williams 'pointed out the palmary words of St Augustine' cited by Wiseman, 'Securus judicat orbis terrarum', the whole world judges surely. Williams 'repeated these words again and again, and, when he was gone, they kept ringing in my ears'. 'They gave a cogency to the Article', wrote Newman, 'which had escaped me at first.'[8] He had appealed to Antiquity, but 'here then Antiquity was deciding against itself' by making as the ultimate and infallible court of appeal in a local religious dispute, not the invocation of a past authority, but the present judgement of the whole Christian world.

That judgement by the living Church on the African Donatists told equally against another local schism, the Anglican, cut off, as if by water, from the body of the Universal Church. Newman described the argument to Rogers as 'the first real hit from Romanism which has happened to me . . . it has given me a stomach-ache. You see the whole history of the Monophysites has been a sort of alterative. And now comes this dose at the end of it. It does certainly come upon one that we are not at the bottom of things. At this moment we have sprung a leak . . . '[9] On a walk with Henry Wilberforce in the New Forest, Newman borrowed a metaphor from the scenery and declared that 'a vista has been opened before me, to the end of which I do not see'.[10] Wilberforce, thunderstruck at the thought of Rome lying unseen on the far horizon, hoped that Newman might die first. Newman asked his friends to pray for this, if it was not the will of God. His recollections of the incident were still more dramatic. 'Securus judicat orbis terrarum': these 'struck me with a power which I never had felt from any words before . . . they were like the "Turn again Whittington" of the chime; . . . or, . . . the "Tolle lege, –tolle, lege", of the child, which converted St Augustine himself . . . By those great words of the ancient Father, interpreting and summing up the long and varied course of ecclesiastical history, the theory of the *Via Media* was absolutely pulverized.'[11]

By Newman's own account, the impression was not a lasting one, but his weird and masterly metaphors for the shock indicate a deeper unsettlement. 'I had seen the shadow of a hand upon the wall . . . He who has seen a ghost, cannot be as if he had never seen it. The heavens had opened and closed again. The thought for the moment had been, "The Church of Rome will be found right after all".'[12] The stomach-ache, the leak, the vista, the shadow of a hand, the ghost, the rising spirit, the opening heaven, like the Monophysite in the mirror and the incantatory power of the words themselves, convey Newman's subtle movement from a strident anti-Romanism. They led to his increasing reluctance to attack the Roman Church as a sister Church, and a desire to benefit Rome and England equally. The crowning irony of the incident was that Robert Williams should have been so disturbed by it, and that Newman feared most of all his secession to Rome. Williams remained 'an anxiously religious man, now, as then, very dear to me',[13] when Newman wrote the *Apologia* in 1864; but Williams had now taken to Evangelical prophetic literature, and reverted to a firm dogmatic Protestantism.

Newman's immediate response was an article on the Catholicity of the Anglican Church for the *British Critic*, which argued that Roman and Anglo-Catholics each had a strong point and a weak one. The Anglo-Catholic declared 'We go by Antiquity; that is, by the Apostles. Ancient consent is our standard of faith'. The Roman Catholic declared 'We go by Catholicity. Universal consent is our standard of faith'. Thus the Anglo-Catholic claimed the 'Apostolic' Note or Mark of the Church; he had preserved the faith of the Apostles while the Roman Catholic had added to it. The Roman Catholic claimed the 'Catholic' Note or Mark of the Church; he had preserved the ancient Church's claim to a universal living teaching authority, where the Anglo-Catholic had no such authority, and was 'estranged from the great body of Christians over the world'.[14] Newman thought that superficially, the imaginative advantage in the debate was Rome's. 'It is very obvious to the whole world that the English Church is separated from the rest of Christendom; it is not evident, except to a very few, that the faith of Rome is an addition to the primitive.'[15] Yet the implication of Newman's argument was that Rome and England were equally Churches, though equally defective: and that if Rome had corrupted the ancient Church, the Church of England now fell short of a full Catholicism.

Newman's answer to the difficulty as an Anglo-Catholic was not wholly convincing. He offered in explanation of the Roman Catholic additions to the faith the very idea of doctrinal development which was to justify his own Roman Catholic conversion; and while he attacked the principle of development as implying that a modern Romanist knows more of Christianity than the Apostles, he was obviously still struck by the image which he adapted from Augustine, 'that the English Church is cut off from the Catholic body, a ray from the sun, a branch from the tree, a channel from the fountain'.[16] He was also impressed by Wiseman's claim that the modern Roman Church would look more like the ancient Church to a visitor like Basil or Athanasius. In defence of the English Church's lack of Catholicity, he argued that the essence of the Church consists in the possession of the monarchial episcopal order, on the model provided by Ignatius and Cyprian, so that intercommunion in an authoritative body is the ideal perfection of ecclesiastical unity, not its essence. Moreover the Anglican Church has 'the note of life, a tough life and a vigorous';[17] and Newman's conclusion denies Romanists the further Note of the Church, of sanctity or Holiness:

Till we see in them as a Church more straightforwardness, truth, and openness, . . . less of a political, scheming, grasping spirit, less of intrigue, less that looks hollow and superficial, less accommodation to the tastes of the vulgar, less subserviency to the vices of the rich, less humouring of men's morbid and wayward imaginations, . . . less intimacy with the revolutionary spirit of the day, we will keep aloof from them as we do. . . . We see . . . its leaders in alliance with a political party notorious in the *orbis terrarum* as a sort of standard in every place for liberalism and infidelity . . . We see its agents smiling and nodding and ducking to attract attention, as gipsies make up to truant boys, holding out tales for the nursery, and pretty pictures, and gold gingerbread, and physic concealed in jam, and sugar-plums for good children.

Who can but feel shame when the religion of Ximenes, Borromeo, and Pascal is so overlaid? . . . We Englishmen like manliness, openness, consistency, truth. Rome will never gain on us till she learns these virtues . . . [18]

Here was a striking indictment of that Roman Catholic want of truth and manliness with which Kingsley would charge the Roman Catholic Newman. Yet Newman was himself more attracted than this suggests to Rome as a practical system, and as he thought of becoming a Brother of Charity in London, he wrote that the 'Capuchin in the "Promessi Sposi" [the Italian Catholic novel by Manzoni] has stuck in my heart like a dart'.[19] It was almost as if his anti-Roman polemic was an emotional defence against a reluctant sympathy.

Such a sympathy was becoming stronger among his younger followers, who were increasingly given to needless popish extravagance. John Morris of Exeter, nicknamed Simon Stylites because of his oddities, a man as 'little possessed of tact or common sense as . . . great in other departments', caused a sensation by preaching in St Mary's in Newman's absence, on the theme that the brute creation should be made to fast on fast days. 'May he (*salvis ossibus suis*)', wrote Newman in his wrath, 'have a fasting horse the next time he goes steeple-chasing.'[20] Morris' subsequent sermon on the Roman doctrine of the Mass provoked a protest from the Vice-Chancellor to the Bishop, and while Morris was episcopally admonished, the Vice-Chancellor withdrew from St Mary's with his family. There was a further embarrassment when on the advice of the Archdeacon, Newman decided to tell Bagot that his curate, Bloxam, who was hobnobbing with the Roman Catholic medievalist Goths, had been wrongly charged with bowing at the elevation of the host at Mass in the Earl of Shrewsbury's chapel at Alton Towers.[21] Bagot's response betrayed irritation that Newman should have troubled him about the matter: but the correspondence elicited the Bishop's satisfaction with the 'sound and high Church principles'[22] which Newman was spreading in the Church of England.

Newman had difficulty himself with even meeting Roman Catholics. William Palmer of Magdalen College, an enthusiastic, not to say fanatical, Tractarian, invited him to dine with the convert Catholic priest the Honourable George Spencer, the son, brother and uncle of successive Earls Spencer, and the proponent of a crusade for the conversion of England to Roman Catholicism. Newman at first refused to meet Spencer because he was '*in loco apostatae*', and when Palmer was pressing, Newman said 'I did not like to put myself out of the way – that if R. C.'s and A. C.'s met together, it should be in sackcloth, rather than at a pleasant party . . . ' Newman, however, felt it 'pompous' to decline a call from Spencer, and found him 'a gentlemanlike, mild, pleasing man, but sadly smooth';[23] he wondered if the Roman discipline and confessional practice had made him so. Spencer presented his mission as one not of controversy, but of persuading Catholics and Protestants to pray for one another. Newman wrote afterwards to apologize for not meeting Spencer at dinner, but made his apology an attack on the Roman Catholic alliance with the Whigs, radicals and Irishmen opposed to the Church Establishment: ' . . . your acts are contrary to your words', he wrote. 'You invite us to a union of hearts, at the same time that you are doing all you can . . . to destroy our Church . . . You are leagued with our enemies. "The voice is Jacob's voice, but the hands are the hands of Esau" . . . Break off, I would say, with Mr O'Connell in Ireland and the liberal party in England, or come not to us with overtures for mutual prayers and religious sympathy.'[24] If liberalism was Antichrist, as Newman now believed, and yet remained in alliance with Rome, then this could only serve to preserve such remnants of his belief in the popish Antichrist as still remained.

The mood in which Newman regarded Rome was, then, heavily coloured by his apocalyptic view of the impending onslaught on Christianity, as he expounded it to Jemima. 'Those wretched Socialists on the one hand, then Carlyle on the other – a man of first-rate ability, I suppose, and quite fascinating as a writer. His book on the "French Revolution" is most taking (to me).' But then Carlyle wanted to pick and choose what he wanted from Christianity; while Newman took as gloomy a view of the liberal Anglican school of historians of Arnold and Henry Hart Milman. 'Then you have all your political economists, who *cannot* accept (it is impossible) the Scripture rules about almsgiving, renunciation of wealth, self-denial, etc., and then your geologists, giving up parts of the Old Testament.'[25] The present was darkness indeed.

Yet Newman's own vision of the never-ending war between the Church and the world suggested another conclusion, that the losses and gains of the present were like those of the past. He offered both views, of a past as bad as and worse than the present, in an historical production, *The Church of the Fathers*, dedicated to Isaac Williams, 'the prettiest book I have done',[26] he told Bowden, containing his letters on Basil and Gregory, Ambrose and Anthony and Augustine, which had already appeared in the *British Magazine* from 1833. The work opens with a backward glance at 'the reigns of our blessed martyr St Charles, and king George the Good', but the threatened change in the relations between Church and State would now, Newman thought, turn the Church from its dependence on the great and powerful, to dependence on the multitude. He admitted his former 'great repugnance to the notion', which had been imposed upon him by the State: 'if I have . . . turned from the government to the people, it has been simply because I was forced to do so'.[27] Not that the Church derives its authority from the poor: yet the poor 'are her members . . . by a special right', and 'the Church, when purest and when most powerful, *has* depended for its influence on its consideration with the many'.[28] But Newman's reading of the early Church's history was pervaded by his sense of the present crisis of the Church, which gives the work its note of doom, as in his conclusion, the story of St Martin's glittering vision which claims to be Christ, but which disappears in a stench when challenged to show its wounds. 'I suppose it means in this day', wrote Newman,

> that Christ comes not in pride of intellect, or reputation for ability. These are the glittering robes in which Satan is now arraying. Many spirits are abroad, more are issuing from the pit: the credentials which they display, are the precious gifts of mind, beauty, richness, depth, originality. Christian, look hard at them with Martin in silence, and then ask for the print of the nails.[29]

The image suggests the mood of self-abnegation and self-effacement in which Newman returned to Littlemore in spring 1840, to do service for Bloxam who had resigned his curacy and been called away to his father's death-bed. Newman had written in 1836 to Jemima, 'God intends me to be lonely'.[30] In March 1840, he made the penultimate entry on his memories of his illness in Sicily, and he wondered 'what am I writing it for?'.

> I only have found one who even took that sort of affectionate interest in me as to be pleased with such details – and that is H. Wilberforce and what shall I ever see of him? This is the sort of interest which a wife takes and none but she – it is a woman's interest – and that interest, so be it, shall never be taken in me ... I have a repugnance to a clergyman's marrying ... whether a prejudice or not, it shocks me. And therefore I willingly give up the possession of that sympathy ... Yet, not the less do I feel the need of it ... Shall I ever have in my old age spiritual children who will take an interest such as a wife does? How time is getting on! ... What a dream is life. ... time is nothing except as the seed of eternity.[31]

His final note was about his old blue cloak which he had denied Gennaro: 'I have brought it up here to Littlemore, and on some cold nights I have had it on my bed. I have so few things to sympathize with me, that I take to clokes [sic]'.[32]

Yet he was not sorry to withdraw from his duties in Oxford and to immerse himself in his Littlemore poor school. 'I have been reforming', he told Jemima, 'or at least lecturing against uncombed hair and dirty faces and hands; but I find I am not deep in the philosophy of school-girl tidiness.'[33] His catechizing, 'very striking, done with such spirit, and the children so up to it, answering with the greatest alacrity',[34] attracted a student audience from Oxford: 'the children are improving in their singing', he informed Jemima. 'I have had the audacity to lead them and teach them some new tunes. Also I have rummaged out a violin and strung it, and on Mondays and Thursdays have begun to *lead* them with it, a party of between twenty great and little in the schoolroom . . . Lectured with unblushing effrontery on the necessity of their keeping their work clean, and set them to knit stockings.'[35]

There was also a happiness in the beauty of the chapel and its altar cloth, whose elaborateness amazed even the workwomen who had made it. 'Indeed we are all so happy that we are afraid of being too happy. We have got some roses, wall-flowers, and sweet-briar, and the Chapel smells as if to remind one of the Holy Sepulchre.'[36] This interest in church furnishing was unusual in Newman; who as an Anglican, always celebrated a north-end communion in Protestant fashion; the early promptings to a higher ritual at Littlemore were Bloxam's. In May 1840, Newman and some friends bought ten acres of land around the chapel, and he was planning cells, each one with sitting room, bedroom and cold bathroom. In June he thought of a cloister, and a central heating system of hot water pipes to save money on building fire places and chimneys. He planned the planting of larches and firs, hornbeam and elm, and talked to Jemima of building a proper monastic house. 'This may lead ultimately to my resigning my Fellowship; but these are visions as yet. The painted glass is up, and most beautiful it is. The children are improving in their singing; we hope soon to be able to chant the whole service with them. My library is in most apple-pie order.'[37] Bloxham was succeeded as curate by the equally devoted William Copeland. Newman called Littlemore his Torres Vedras. His retreat from Oxford and thus from the Oxford Movement had begun.

In October 1840, he proposed to Keble that he give up St Mary's, in part because his influence was not so much on his parishioners – 'I have no personal, no pastoral acquaintance with them', he wrote, as on the University men, so that he was 'converting a parochial charge into a sort of University office'. All his innovations – 'Saints'-days Services, daily Services, and Lectures', even the Weekly Communion, had been taken up by students and academics, not by parishioners, while the University Heads of Houses were hostile to Newman's teaching – understandably so, he thought, as it was not calculated 'to defend that system of religion which has been received for 300 years', and was, as Newman admitted to Keble, disposing the young towards Rome. The more that Newman exalted the primitive Church, the more he thought that his system led on to Rome, because Rome was 'the only representative of the Primitive Church besides ourselves', and many of the Early Church's doctrines 'have far greater, or their only scope, in the Roman system'.[38] He concluded that if English Catholics would only break with O'Connell, the rise of Anglican heresy would make conversion to Rome even more attractive to Anglicans. Keble persuaded Newman for the time to remain at St Mary's, but Newman was now discussing the likelihood of Roman conversions. The likelihood was realized in November 1840 when an English ordinand, allegedly influenced by Pusey, became a Roman Catholic in a public ceremony in Belgium.

There were difficulties about joining the Roman Communion in England. One Roman convert, the fanatical Gothic Revival architect, Augustus Pugin, one of Shrewsbury's circle, came to Oxford, and, reported Newman, 'speaks strongly against the R. C. body, and says that if 200 of the ablest and best of our men were to go over, they would be received coldly. I think our way certainly is to form alliances with *foreigners*; the jealousies (natural) with R. C.'s at home preclude any-thing good'.[39] A curious rumour began to circulate among the Anglo-Goths that Newman had seen a vision telling him to remain an Anglican in order to work for reunion between England and Rome. Pugin had his Gothic axe to grind, and was to find the Anglo-Catholics better Goths than his fellow Romans, but his point, the insular character of English Roman Catholicism, was to make 'Old Catholics' and converts odd bed-fellows. Newman, however, was now privately prepared to consider even a form of Petrine primacy. 'It is quite consistent to say', he concluded, 'that I think Rome the *centre* of unity, and yet not to say that she is infallible, when she is by herself . . . I do not fear at all any number of persons as likely to go to Rome, if I am secure about myself. If I can trust myself, I can trust others.'[40]

But the '*centre* of unity' could hardly be Antichrist, and Newman exorcised the antipapal ghost in his review of the *Prophecies relating to Antichrist in the writings of Daniel and St Paul* by James Henthorn Todd, a Trinity College, Dublin Professor who wrote to dispel the overwhelmingly popular popish Antichrist of Irish Protestants. As Todd told Newman, he was attracted to the new Oxford High Churchmanship in the ultra-Protestant environs of Trinity College, and it was on good patristic principles that he followed S. R. Maitland in making the prophecies in Daniel and Revelation 'futurist', a prediction of the Antichrist to come at the end of the world. Todd afterwards apologized to Newman for attacking the typological Antichrist set forth in Newman's Tract 83, as savouring 'more of poetry than of theology',[41] but he was critical of Newman for retaining, like the Fathers, the historicist element of the Roman Empire in his futurist scheme, when the Empire had now ceased to exist: 'my chief object', he told Newman, 'was to refute the theory of Mede . . . which is the basis of the Protestant interpretations – and to shew that the discarded system of the antient Church was more consistent with Scripture and with itself . . . '[42] On the principles of the seventeenth-century Puritan Joseph Mede, Daniel and Revelation contained a blueprint for the whole of human history, but Todd was one with the Fathers in ascribing the prophecies concerning the Antichrist not to the papal past but to an individual in the future.

Newman's interest was not in the detailed historical arguments, but in their wider significance. He disclaimed any leanings to Romanism: 'we owe her of late years nothing at all', he wrote, 'except indeed, according to the Scripture rule, love for hatred . . . '[43] The true test of her Antichristian character was holiness: could she produce saints? 'Who, indeed, but the like of ascetic Daniel, much-suffering Paul, and contemplative John, will suffice to establish the paradox that Carlo Borromeo sucked the breast of Babylon, and that Pascal died in her arms?'[44] Protestants were therefore impaled on a dilemma; they had either to deny the force of the prophecies about Antichrist, by acknowledging that the Roman saints like à Kempis were obviously saved, or to strain credulity by denying their sanctity, with the assurance that 'every one who has lived and died in that communion is utterly and irretrievably perished for ever'.[45]

It was on that score of holiness that Newman found his former millennial mentor Bishop Newton wanting, as a notorious preferment-seeker, ecclesiastical careerist and pluralist,

> so liquorish of preferment, . . . who cast a regretful look back upon his dinner when he was at supper, and anticipated his morning chocolate in his evening muffins, who will say that this is the man, not merely to unchurch, but to smite, to ban, to wither the whole of Christendom for many centuries . . . will it be pleasant to have exchanged St Chrysostom for Newton . . . ? Is this good company to live and die in? Who would not rather be found even with Whitfield [sic] and Wesley, than with ecclesiastics whose life is literary ease at the best, whose highest flights attain but to Downing Street or the levee?[46]

These were the accents of an other-worldly Evangelical, a Wesley, denouncing in Newton the corruptions of an eighteenth-century Church Establishment given over to lax worldliness.

Newman's main point, however, was less an attack on the Establishment than the *tu quoque* argument that the charge that Rome was Antichrist bore with equal weight upon the Church of England. A Sandemanian, a Ranter or a Quaker might call Rome Babylon, but this argument was not open to Anglicans. If Rome was Antichrist as an establishment, then so was Canterbury, which bore all the other marks of the Beast, an episcopal hierarchy, an Apostolic Succession, priesthood, formal worship and sacraments. '(Oh, Dr Newton!)', exclaimed Newman when he discovered that worldly prelate decrying Popery for making 'a gain of godliness, and teaching for *filthy lucre's* sake': 'we think no English divine does us a service who so vaguely delineates Antichrist that at a little distance his picture looks not very unlike ourselves'.[47] Nor did even the Kirk escape this 'frightful imputation'. 'We have', wrote Newman,

> a strange paper before us, . . . written by a late Fellow of a College in

the University of Oxford, which, after deciding that the first Beast [of Revelation] is the Papacy, the seven horns the seven sacraments, . . . goes on to say, that the second Beast is the Queen's supremacy, the two horns like a lamb, are the two Universities, Oxford and Cambridge, the image to the first Beast, the book of Common Prayer, the name of the second Beast the supreme head of the Church, and ends by warning the Kirk that the Queen's High Commissioner in the General Assembly 'sits there, as in the Temple of God, showing himself that he is God' . . .

Thus Newton's arguments 'involve the Primitive Church, our own, the Kirk – nay, all sects and denominations whatever, – in one common ruin', insofar as they all stand forth as Christ's representatives with officers who preach and administer the sacraments in his name, as Christ himself.[48]

What then of Richard Baxter's jibe that 'If the Pope was not Antichrist, he had bad luck to be so like him'?[49] It was this imaginative likeness which had so struck Newman as a young man, and from which he was still fighting to be free. Newman replied that as the Antichrist simulates Christ, it is the counterfeit, so like the real Christ, which deceives. Rome will look like Christ, as she also looks like Antichrist, just as the real coin resembles the forgery. But Anglicans cannot call Rome Antichrist if they acknowledge her ministry and sacraments, and though modern Roman Catholics are 'a low-minded, double-dealing, worldly-minded set',[50] this was not so in the glory of her saints.

Newman's true imaginative liberation came in his conclusion, a curiously literal inversion of Protestant prophecy, in finding in the medieval Church, not a realization of Antichrist, but an 'imperial Church', anticipated in the glorious prophecies concerning Israel of old. Her 'wealth and splendour, the rich embellishment of her temples, the jewelled dress of her ministers, the offerings, shrines, pageants, and processions', were not the purple and pearls of the sorceress of Revelation, but the camels and gold and incense and cedar from Midian and Ephah, Sheba and Lebanon, and the '*sapphires*' and '*agates*' of the heavenly Jerusalem.[51] Newman offered this understanding of the prophecies as an antidote to his now fading image of the papal whore. But he did not doubt their actual fulfilment: in that literalism, he remained an Evangelical, whatever else he had become.

Again, even as an opponent of a pre-critical view of prophecy, Newman's viewpoint was not that of modern criticism; indeed he assailed the first principles of such criticism in his attack on Henry Hart Milman's *History of Christianity*, in which he detected the cloven hoof of liberal Anglican divinity. Milman's work was written as a factual social and political account of the Christian past and an external study of natural events and causes, without reference to their divine inspiration and origin. But Milman could not help showing his theological petticoat. Newman argued that Milman's reduction of essential Christian doctrine to a belief in God's gift through Christ of human immortality, and his attendant inclination to rationalize miracle away, and to discard angels and demons as projections of religious experience, tended to a deeper unbelief than Milman could recognize himself. 'Principles have a life and power independent of their authors, and make their way in spite of them.'[52]

Milman was also guilty of the fallacy of supposing that an idea in Christianity is discredited if it can be shown to be of pagan origin. Newman summarized the point:

> The doctrine of the Divine Word is Platonic; the doctrine of the Incarnation is Indian; of a divine kingdom is Judaic; of Angels and demons is Magian; the connexion of sin with the body is Gnostic; celibacy is known to Bonze and Talapoin; a sacerdotal order is Egyptian; the idea of a new birth is Chinese and Eleusinian; belief in sacramental virtue is Pythagorean; and honours to the dead are a polytheism.

But where Milman argued 'These things are in heathenism, therefore they are not Christian', Newman argued that 'these things are in Christianity, therefore they are not heathen'.[53] Such truths, scattered across the world by its Moral Governor, may arise and exist in heathen systems, but they have their fulfilment in Christianity. The Church

> began in Chaldea, and then sojourned among the Canaanites, and went down into Egypt, and thence passed into Arabia, till she rested in her own land. Next she encountered the merchants of Tyre, and the wisdom of the East country, and the luxury of Sheba. Then she was carried away to Babylon, and wandered to the schools of Greece. And wherever she went, in trouble or in triumph, still she was a living spirit, the mind and voice of the Most High,[54]

gathering in truth from the falsehood around her. So Christians saw her. But what 'tenet of Christianity will escape proscription, if the principle is once admitted, that a sufficient account is given of an opinion, and a sufficient ground for making light of it, as soon as it is historically referred to some human origin?'[55] Rather, once-heathen truths should be regarded as the shadows of greater truths still to be revealed. 'We are not distressed to be told that the doctrine of the angelic host came from Babylon, while we know that they did sing at the Nativity; nor that the vision of a Mediator is in Philo, if in very deed He died for us on Calvary.'[56]

It can only have been a want of sense of irony that led the liberal Arthur Stanley to describe this exquisitely polite but devastating attack as 'more favourable than might have been expected'.[57] It turns the liberal idea on its head, and points out that the meaning of evidence depends on the principles which one applies to it. But it also questions a fundamental principle of secular modernity. Newman was too good a student of Hume not to be in one sense a modern. Yet as a critic of modernity, he points out that its own assumptions are unprovable at precisely the points where they are in conflict with Christianity; and that in this conflict, the problem of truth is not one that reason alone can resolve.

The deepest truth was to be found in prayer. Newman's Tract 88 was a translation from the Greek of part of the *Preces Privatae* of the seventeenth-century divine Lancelot Andrewes, and in Church's view, was 'one of those rare translations which make an old book new'.[58] The work is a tissue of texts from Scripture, of self-examination and entreaty and prayer for righteousness, not least in the time of trial.

> O Hope of all the ends of the earth,
> and of them that remain in the broad sea;
> O Thou on whom our fathers hoped,
> and Thou didst deliver them;
> on whom they waited,
> and were not confounded;
> O my Hope from my youth,
> from my mother's breasts;
> on whom I have been cast from the womb,
> be Thou my hope
> now and evermore,
> and my portion in the land of the living.[59]

In the coming agony of unconversion and conversion, what refuge was there but God?

16

Tract 90

Newman was now a national figure, and achieved a national audience for his antiliberalism through John Walter III, son of the proprietor of *The Times*, who to his father's grief had taken up Tractarianism. The newspaper had been scathing about the 'isolated barbarism' of the Oxford High Churchmen, who were 'fitter to sympathize with the monks of the Escurial than with a free and reflecting people'[1]: but it was increasingly worried about the implications of the alliance of Dissenters, O'Connellites and Whigs for the survival of the Church of England. This carried over into a sympathy for Newman's hostility to the Conservative Sir Robert Peel, whom Newman had not forgiven as the 'Rat' who had turned his coat on the issue of Catholic Emancipation in 1829, and had set up the Ecclesiastical Commission to reform the Church in 1835. On opening a Reading Room at Tamworth, a sort of Mechanics' Institute open to the professors of all creeds and none, Sir Robert uttered – and then published – some unguarded expressions indicating the death of the old Tory philosophy of the Anglican confessional state. At the urging of John Walter Senior, Newman saw his chance and pounced, with a series of seven letters in *The Times* in February 1841 signed 'Catholicus', later republished as 'The Tamworth Reading Room', to prove how this ostensibly Tory leader had surrendered to the secularism of the age.

Newman thought that Peel was enunciating the Utilitarian radical ideas of Bentham and his disciples, Brougham and Lushington, when in the 1820s they founded the first non-religious institute of English higher education: 'the scene [is] Gower Street', wrote Newman, 'the speaker Mr Brougham or Dr Lushington, and the occasion, the laying the first stone . . . of the then-called London University'.[2] Now the same philosophy was in the mouth of the leader of the English Tories: 'Such is the reward in 1841 for unpopularity in 1827'.[3] For Peel's principle was Bentham's, that mankind is to be saved by a non-denominational education in scientific knowledge. It is science that makes a man wiser and better, for it will enable him to calculate rightly, on Bentham's principle of what makes him happy by giving him pain or pleasure: or as Newman paraphrased this, 'the knowledge which carries virtue along with it, is the knowledge how to take care of number one'.[4]

195

But Newman argued that to know the good is not to do it. 'A labouring man knows he should not go to the ale-house, and his wife knows she should not filch when she goes out charing.'[5] Newman acknowledged a difference in this between Brougham and Peel, and Bentham, who 'had not a spark of poetry in him',[6] for what appeared in Bentham as pure rational calculation was offered by Brougham and Peel as a lofty imaginative ideal, the Stoic resort in grief and woe to the consolations of scientific knowledge or philosophy. 'Such', Newman concluded with sarcasm, 'is this new art of living, offered to the labouring classes, . . . in a severe winter, snow on the ground, glass falling, bread rising, coal at 20d the cwt., and no work.'[7] But 'Secular Knowledge [is] not a direct Means of Moral Improvement'. The achievement of virtue must be sought 'in graver and holier places than in Libraries and Reading-rooms',[8] and 'glory, science, knowledge, . . . never healed a wounded heart, nor changed a sinful one'.[9] Knowledge can refine manners. 'The poor indulge in low pleasures; they use bad language, swear loudly and recklessly, laugh at coarse jests, and are rude and boorish'; but to improve only their taste would be to exchange 'a gross fault for a more subtle one'. So, too, with University students: 'external discipline may change the fashionable excess, but cannot allay the principle of sinning. Stop cigars, they will take to drinking parties; stop drinking, they gamble; stop gambling, and a worse license follows. You do not get rid of vice by human expedients . . . '[10] Neither discipline nor knowledge by itself can change the human heart; that is the office of dogmatic religion.

Poor Peel: he had haplessly strayed into a rather simple-minded refutation of Newman's whole philosophy, in his assumption that reason or rational knowledge alone is the highway to Christian truth. Newman's refutation is one of his finest bursts of rhetoric:

This is why Science has so little of a religious tendency; deductions have no power of persuasion. The heart is commonly reached, not through the reason, but through the imagination, by means of direct impressions, by the testimony of facts and events, by history, by description. Persons influence us, voices melt us, looks subdue us, deeds inflame us. Many a man will live and die upon a dogma: no man will be a martyr for a conclusion . . . No one, I say, will die for his own calculations; he dies for realities . . . Logic makes but a sorry rhetoric with the multitude; first shoot round corners, and you may not despair of converting by a syllogism . . . To most men argument makes the point in hand only more doubtful, and considerably less impressive. After all, man is *not* a reasoning animal; he is a seeing, feeling, contemplating, acting animal . . . Life is not long enough for a religion of inferences; we shall never have done beginning, if we determine to begin with proof . . . Resolve to believe nothing, and you must prove your proofs and analyze your elements, sinking further and further, and finding 'in the lowest depth a lower deep', till you come to the broad bosom of scepticism . . . Life is for action. If we insist on proofs for everything, we shall never come to action: to act you must assume, and that assumption is faith.[11]

Newman was not in this an irrationalist; he insisted that some assumptions are more reasonable than others. But the 'realities' for which men live and die are not constructions built on reason alone. Imagination and personal influence, melting voices and flaming deeds, sight and feeling and the need to act, have a legitimate place in creating belief and unbelief. This is why Brougham, unlike Bentham, had defended his useful knowledge society by appealing to the imagination with a pantheon of heroes of every philosophy and none, and why Peel argued that the wonder aroused by science leads men to the knowledge of God. But 'wonder is not religion', wrote Newman, 'or we should be worshipping our railroads'.[12] As for Peel's rather tasteless notion of meditating on the wonders of nature on one's death-bed, 'Rather stay your hunger with corn grown in Jupiter, and warm yourself by the Moon'.[13]

The consolations of religion were quite different from those offered by philosophy, even though philosophy was, when properly employed, the useful servant of religion. Thus the religious mind found an after-confirmation for its faith in the wonder aroused by the proofs of God's existence from design. But their role was to confirm faith, not to create it. No atheist need be convinced by such proofs, which by themselves only point to the existence of a 'Divine Intelligence' or Brougham's 'great architect of nature', not to the 'Moral Governor' and 'particular Providence' of Christians.[14] It is the *already* believing mind which discerns its God in the natural world.

Brougham and Peel also offended by rejecting Newman's sort of dogmatic Christianity. Brougham put his faith in Deism, Peel in a quasi-Anglican non-denominationalism, as in his proposal that the Reading Room should exclude works of 'controversial divinity'. But 'Christianity is faith', wrote Newman, 'faith implies a doctrine; a doctrine propositions; propositions yes or no, yes or no differences. Differences, then, are the natural attendants on Christianity, and you cannot have Christianity, and not have differences. When, then, Sir Robert Peel calls such differences points of "party feeling", what is this but to insult Christianity?'[15]

This was the heart of the matter. The Church of England's loss of a monopoly of power led a realistic politician like Peel to edge towards Christian ecumenism away from Anglican confessionalism, and to abandon the old exclusive Tory commitment to the Church. To that problem, as to how the Church would reassert its authority over everyone, Newman had no practical answer. 'People say to me, that it is but a dream to suppose that Christianity should regain the organic power in human society which once it possessed. I cannot help that; I never said it could. I am not a politician . . .'[16] It is noteworthy that as a politician, Peel had not abandoned his hopes for a non-denominational Christianity as a foundation for the social order. He was, however, naive in expecting secular science to support it. Newman saw that knowledge *by itself* did not create religious and moral citizens. It has hardly required the scientific abominations of this century to prove Newman right and Peel wrong. On the other hand, Newman underestimated the powers of applied science to add to the sum of human happiness. That change has chiefly occurred in this century; but it was well and truly begun in his own.

Newman's letters aroused some wonder and indignation in the political world, which speculated about an alliance between the new High Churchmen and anti-Peelite High Toryism: but they also meant that their author had the Thunderer's sympathy in the storm of execration that followed.

Newman was often accused of guile; but only a Nathanael could have so exposed himself to his enemy. The Oxford Movement had set out to recall the Church of England to the dogmas of Catholic Christianity. But the Church also enjoyed its own unique set of formularies in the Thirty-nine Articles, modelled on the Lutheran and Calvinist confessions of the sixteenth-century, and stating, albeit with moderation and circumspection, the Church's repudiation of Roman error and its commitment to Protestant dogma. The rise of the seventeenth-century Arminian school within Anglicanism had meant the eclipse of Anglican Calvinism, and as has been suggested, modified the Church's interpretation of so central a Protestant doctrine as that of justification by faith alone; and Latitudinarians and liberals had always regarded the Articles as something of an embarrassment, as 'Articles of peace', not so much to be professed as ignored. This liberal unease was increasingly articulate after 1830, and the amendment of the Articles was among the measures of reform brought before the House of Lords by Whately in 1840. Arnold was a signatory to the petition, and opposition to the Articles was the strategy of that very liberal school which Newman feared as subversive of the Christian faith in England.

Newman's attack in the *Lectures on Justification* on the Protestant understanding on the Article on Justification had placed him in clear breach of its obvious meaning; but in this at least, he could appeal to a long line of Anglican divines before him. Some, however, of his more radical followers like Robert Williams who were attracted to Rome, insisted on the discrepancy between the Protestantism of the Articles and Anglican Catholicism. The Articles seemed opposed to the Catholic faith, and yet the Church of England still claimed to be the Catholic Church in England: it had to be shown that the contradiction was more apparent than real. It was with this end in view that Newman wrote Tract 90 to calm the more wayward of his own supporters. He wanted to prove that the Articles could be read in a Catholic sense, so that an Anglo-Catholic could remain in good conscience a member of the Church of England.

The exercise might look like squaring the circle, and Newman's introduc-

198

tion to the Tract indicates a distinct unease: 'while our Prayer Book is acknowledged on all hands to be of Catholic origin', he wrote, 'our Articles also, the offspring of an uncatholic age, are, through GOD's good providence, to say the least, not uncatholic, and may be subscribed by those who aim at being catholic in heart and doctrine'.[17] There is a half-heartedness about the 'not uncatholic' which betrayed Newman's underlying thought, that the Articles had been left deliberately unclear in order to keep within the Elizabethan Church a large quasi-Catholic population. 'The Protestant Confession', Newman concluded, 'was drawn up with the purpose of including Catholics; and Catholics now will not be excluded. What was an Economy in the Reformers, is a protection to us. What would have been a perplexity to us then, is a perplexity to Protestants now.'[18] Modern Protestants were caught in the trap laid by their Protestant forebears, who had been less than brutally anti-Catholic. Pusey and Manning wanted Newman to exclude these words, but he considered it essential to his argument that the framers of the Articles had been 'double-tongued'. These broad hints that Anglicanism had been hatched in ambiguity also surfaced in the introduction in an unfortunate reference to 'the stammering lips of ambiguous formularies',[19] which was far too frank a confession of the dogmatic defectiveness of Anglicanism, and of Newman's acute sense of the difference between the Church's faith and a full, if non-Roman, Catholicism.

Newman discussed only fourteen of the Articles, and his remarks about Justification did not add to what he had said before. He shocked his readers, however, by extracting from a number of the Articles a sense which contradicted their obvious literal meaning. Thus Article XXI declares that General Councils may err. By close legal peering at the text, Newman showed that the Article is compatible with a belief in conciliar infallibility. Article XXII denies the 'Romish Doctrine concerning Purgatory, Pardons, Worshipping and Adoration, as well of Images as of Reliques, and also invocation of Saints', as 'a fond thing vainly invented . . . but rather repugnant to the Word of God'. Newman argued that there are true doctrinal understandings of these things, Primitive and Greek and Catholic as well as Roman. He demonstrated the existence of a surprisingly Popish element in the Books of Homilies; and in the prescribed public readings of the Homilies, he pointed to the survival of patristic Catholicism in the Church of England, which in its practical teaching, had gone some way beyond an unambiguous Protestantism.

Thus there was a purgatorial doctrine which was patristic but not 'Romish'; but Newman went to the very edge of a logical precipice in declaring that by Romish 'is not meant the Tridentine doctrine, because this [Article] was drawn up before [the publication of] the decree of the Council of Trent'. In short, 'Romish' does not refer to the Roman Church's teaching at Trent; in damning what is 'Romish', the article does not damn what is 'Roman Catholic'.[20] Only Newman's disciples had the key to the distinction, Newman's preoccupation with the difference ᵤetween the Church's formal doctrinal pronouncements, on the one hand, and on the other, the unofficial speculations of theologians and the devotional practice of the faithful. In Newman's view, the Article damned the Roman schools and ill-educated superstitious Papists, not the promulgated dogmas of the Roman Church. A modern reader might be impressed by the severity of Newman's anti-Roman judgement on popular Catholic practice. Yet the contemporary Protestant was right to feel disquiet. However inexpertly, the framers of the Articles had meant to censure official Roman Catholic doctrines in censuring 'Romish' ones, so that Newman's distinction between 'Romish' and 'Roman Catholic' was open to the charge of sophistry.

On the other hand, Newman accepted that Article XXVIII condemns the Roman Church's doctrine of Transubstantiation *tout court*, and he admitted that the doctrine gave him 'great offence',[21] though it is arguable whether he had accurately understood it. He distinguished, however, between the condemnation in Article XXXI of the 'sacrifices of Masses' and the 'sacrifice of the Mass', on the ground that the Article outlawed such popular devotional abuses as private or solitary Masses, not the official doctrine that the Mass is a sacrifice. This was the one point in the Tract on which Newman as a Roman Catholic later thought that he had been wrong and his critics right: the Article on the 'sacrifices of Masses' clearly condemned the Roman doctrine that the Mass is a sacrifice. He had an easier time with Article XXXII which attacked Roman priestly celibacy by denying that the ordinance was 'commanded by God's Law'. As Newman pointed out, the Article completely missed its target, for the Roman practice rests not on divine law but on the law of the Church. Yet Newman agreed with Article XXXVII denying papal jurisdiction in England, on the ground that the 'Papacy began in the exertions and passions of man; and what man can make, man can destroy'.[22] On Transubstantiation and the Papacy, even on much Roman practice, Newman maintained his anti-Romanism. In that respect, the work was not pro-Roman, but was intended to prevent conversions to Romanism; so that Newman could not be rightly accused of holding the best living in the Church of England with the worse doctrines of the Church of Rome.

Newman did not expect Tract 90 to cause a fuss. Nor did Keble or Henry Wilberforce. He was, however, unlucky in his timing, as at the beginning of March, in a debate on the Maynooth Grant in Parliament, his old critic Lord Morpeth alleged that certain Oxford graduates had disclaimed 'the doctrines of the Protestant Church to which they belonged'.[23] Morpeth's argument was pure *tu quoque*, that there could be no objection to subsidizing the Roman seminary of Maynooth in Ireland when the same doctrines were taught in Oxford; and his charge was echoed by O'Connell. *The Times* defended the Oxford men by distinguishing Roman Popery from Oxonian Catholicism. The movement was now of political moment, and anyone with a political or religious interest in preventing the reinforcement of Toryism and Puseyism by one another had reason to want Newman disgraced.

The agent for just such an agitation was to hand in Golightly, the sort of minor passionate provincial figure with the time and talent to raise a national storm. Golightly brandished the Tract in the streets of Oxford, bought most of the available copies to send to the bishops and clergy, demanded interviews with the Heads of Houses, and though repulsed from Exeter, where the Rector was a Newmanite, won a large majority of the collegiate principals to his cause. It was Golightly, again, who put together a posse of academics to answer the Tract, an unlikely alliance of two Evangelical college tutors and two liberal ones, 'gentlemen', so Church told Rogers, 'who had scarcely the happiness of each other's acquaintance till Golly's skill harnessed them together'.[24] Only one of the four, the liberal ex-Presbyterian Scot A. C. Tait of Balliol, later Archbishop of Canterbury, was a man of real distinction: he had been shaken by the Tract which was passed to him by the gleeful W. G. Ward. The other liberal, H. B. Wilson, was in 1860 to be the storm centre of the liberal manifesto *Essays and Reviews*, and was to be tried as a liberal for denying the Articles himself. Tait drew up the letter to Newman as Editor of the Tracts which declared the Church's shame to Oxford. The letter asserted that the Tract had denied that the Articles condemned the Roman Church's errors on five points, purgatory, pardons, the worship of images and relics, the invocation of saints and the Mass.[25] The paradox was that these were precisely among the matters in which Newman was most uneasy about Roman practice, but the protesters could exploit the want of clarity about Newman's rejection of what was directly popish in Roman Catholic doctrines, even while he argued that the Articles allowed his own restricted Anglo-Catholic sense of them.

Newman acknowledged the tutors' letter on 8 March 1841. On the 9th, he wrote to Jemima that he had 'got into what may prove a serious mess here'.[26] On the 12th, he told her that 'I fear I am clean dished. The Heads of Houses are at this very moment concocting a manifesto against me. Do not think I fear for my cause. We have had too great a run of luck'.[27] Only Routh of Magdalen and Richards of Exeter refused to support a vote of censure on the Tract. Newman received encouragement from Keble and Pusey, Perceval and even Palmer of Worcester, and wrote in a day an open letter to an old but firmly neutral friend of Pusey's, Canon R. W. Jelf of Christ Church, defending the Tract. Before it could be published, the Vice-Chancellor promulgated on 16 March a resolution for the Hebdomadal Board, agreed the previous day, that the 'modes of interpretation such as are suggested in the said Tract, evading rather than explaining the sense of the Thirty-nine Articles',[28] were inconsistent with the University Statutes. Newman was hurt by the charge of evasion, and as even Hawkins felt, had not been given the opportunity to defend himself. He now had to fear censure by the University Convocation as well as the howl of disapproval from the Church at large.

In the *Letter to Jelf*, he was forced, despite his increasing unwillingness to rant at Rome, to reassert his hostility to Romanism as 'a popular system' preaching the Blessed Virgin and Saints and Purgatory rather than the Trinity and Incarnation: 'I consider its existing creed and popular worship to be as near idolatry as any portion of that Church can be'.[29] In brief, his approval of some parts of Tridentine teaching did not imply his approval of the authoritative creed of contemporary Romanism. He was pushed, however, by his own logic, to urge the liberal position that the Articles were Articles of peace, allowing beyond the Creed 'a great diversity in doctrine' and liberty of interpretation.[30] He also made explicit his viewpoint that the Articles were to be understood, 'not in the sense of their framers', but in the light of the *'belief of the Catholic Church'*.[31] This was a principle wholly subversive of the obvious meaning of the text. Protestant readers found further cause for worry in Newman's effort to place his argument in the wider perspective of the 'great progress of the religious mind of our Church to something deeper and truer than satisfied the last century'.[32] Again, Newman gave as examples Scott, Wordsworth, Coleridge, Alexander Knox and Edward Irving: but then came the sting. 'The age is moving towards something, and most unhappily the one religious communion among us which has of late years been practically in possession of this something, is the Church of Rome. She alone, amid all the errors and evils of her practical system, has given free scope to the feelings of awe, mystery, tenderness, reverence, devotedness, and other feelings which may be especially called Catholic.'[33]

Newman was, then, simply doing all he could 'to keep members of our Church from straggling in the direction of Rome',[34] but the admission was calculated to feed the popular suspicion that he was in the van with them. Nor was he likely to allay such fears by declaring that while some Anglo-Catholics denied 'that the Reformers were uncatholic', 'I consider the question quite an open one'.[35]

Protestant suspicion of Newman was voiced by the Bishop of London, Blomfield, when Walter Hook of Leeds defended him: 'It is to my mind', wrote Blomfield, 'the strongest possible evidence of the evil tendency of the Oxford Tracts that they should have made it necessary for Mr Newman to put forth such a commentary on our Articles, to prevent his disciples from becoming papists.'[36] Bagot himself mildly asked Newman not to discuss the Articles in the Tracts again; Newman's delight about the gentleness of the admonition was apparent in the warmth of his reply.[37] But then Archbishop Howley voiced his alarm to Bagot, and on 24 March Pusey was summoned to Cuddesdon to be told that the Tracts should be discontinued and that Newman should be asked to make it public that he was suppressing Tract 90 at his Bishop's bidding. Newman told Keble that as the Heads of Houses had called the Tract an 'evasion', to submit to the Bishop without question would be tantamount to admitting that the Tract had been episcopally condemned.[38] 'I cannot acquiesce or co-operate in such a proceeding', wrote Newman to Hook. '. . . I am a representative at this moment of the interests of many: I cannot betray them. . . . I shall be observing my duty to the Bishop by suppressing the Tract, and my duty to my principles by resigning my living . . . The Bishop himself is all kindness, not so the authorities in London.'[39] Hook advised Newman to insist on the Bishop's acting constitutionally through his court and proper officers. Keble told Newman to suppress Tract 90 out of obedience to Bagot, on the understanding that the Bishop left him free to hold his own opinions. If the Bishop were to allow this, then he would be allowing Newman's view of the Articles, 'which is a great point gained'.[40] But Keble also thought that if the Bishop would not permit this, then Newman should resign from St Mary's.

Newman's offer of resignation made Bagot retreat. It was decided, with Howley's approval, that Newman should declare in a public letter that he had accepted Bagot's wish to suspend the Tracts, but that the Bishop should not condemn Tract 90 or any Tract. Newman's letter to Bagot was delivered to the press page by page as it was written. In his collected works it stands as a stout little pamphlet of thirty pages.[41] He made clear his anti-Romanism by distinguishing between the Roman Church 'as a true Church' built on the Apostles and Prophets and Christ himself, and the Popish system which had corrupted her. 'I have spoken quite what I feel', Newman answered Keble, 'yet I think I have managed to wedge in a good many bits of Catholicism, which *now* come out with the Bishop's sanction. How odd it is that one should be *able* to act from the heart, yet from the head too . . . We are all in very good spirits here, and jubilant . . .'[42] Bagot wrote himself to express his 'entire satisfaction and gratification'. He continued:

> It is a comfort to me too (now that a calm has, as I hope, succeeded the threatened storm) to feel assured that, though I have, perhaps, caused pain to one in whom I feel much interest, and for whom I have a great regard, you will never regret having written that letter to me.[43]

'You may say also', wrote Newman to Jemima, 'that the hubbub required the Bishop to do *something*, but that of himself he had no wish . . . My own Bishop has been as kind as possible . . . submission is victory . . . people will see that (like the Whigs) we are ducks in a pond, knocked over but not knocked out.'[44]

In fact, Newman *was* 'knocked out' as a champion of the Church of England. He later recognized in the storm of indignation against the Tract 'much of real religious feeling, much of honest and true principle, much of straightforward ignorant common sense . . . I was actually fallen into the hands of the Philistines . . . my place in the Movement was lost; public confidence was at an end; my occupation was gone. It was simply an impossibility that I could say any thing henceforth to good effect, when I had been posted up by the marshal on the battery-hatch of every College of my University, after the manner of discommoned pastry-cooks, and when in every part of the country and every class of society, through every organ and opportunity of opinion, in newspapers, in periodicals, at meetings, in pulpits, at dinner-tables, in coffee-rooms, in railway carriages, I was denounced as a traitor who had laid his train and was detected in the very act of firing it . . . '[45] The chorus of abuse by the bishops whom Newman professed to hold in special reverence was still to come.

This was only one of the paradoxes of Tract 90. Newman was not the first Anglican to drive a coach and horses through the Thirty-nine Articles; but this had not been attempted by High Churchmen before him. They had especially prided themselves on their loyalty to the Prayer Book, against the irregularities of free-preaching Evangelicals and the liberals who wanted Christian doctrine watered down. It was the Latitudinarian rationalists of the school of Locke and Hoadly who wished to weaken the dogmatic force of the Articles, and to claim a wider freedom of opinion in the Church for all the clergy. It was Dr Hampden who had fought to abolish subscription to the Articles as a condition for entry into Oxford. Yet now Newman, the arch-foe of rationalism and liberalism, had taken this liberty still further by showing that the Articles were not even a security against Roman Catholic doctrine; and who thereby advanced the liberal principle by destroying the Articles as a defence against it. For the Articles were no protection for anything, if they did not guarantee the Protestantism of the Church of England; and the development of Anglo-Catholicism in doctrine and ritual was to depend on Anglo-Catholics taking just this kind of liberty with the Prayer Book and with the Articles which were part of it.

Newman did not want such freedom of opinion in the Church of England. He wanted a wholly Catholic – that is, Anglo-Catholic – Church. He wished to restore the authority of Bishop and priest to teach the Catholic faith, through the *Book of Common Prayer*. The ultimate effect of Tract 90, however, was to confirm the Church of England's development into a liberal institution tolerant of diversity and even heresy within itself. That quintessential liberal Anglican, Arthur Stanley, wrote to his friend Tait that 'when I read the monition of the heads I felt the halter at my own throat'.[46] It was the Hebdomadal Board which was attempting by its censures to preserve the confessional university that Newman was undermining; and by undermining academic confessionalism and the discipline of the Board, Newman was doing the liberals' work rather better than the liberals themselves.

Henceforth in order to survive, the Oxford Movement found itself in the older liberal position of opposition to authority: the authority of the Protestant Articles and of the Protestant State and of the Protestant bishops whose office the Tractarians had been exalting. The Oxford Movement began as a reassertion of the authority of the Church, but it helped to weaken that authority. Faced with Protestant authorities, the Anglo-Catholic clergy defied them with a gusto which continued almost to this day; and for all its high doctrine of the office of bishop, Anglo-Catholicism has been in practice Presbyterian, with an infallible priest-pope in every parish. The Movement survived in the end because Protestant bishops and the Protestant State found that they had no powers to put the Tractarians down, or to force them to subscribe to the Articles in a Protestant sense. The bishop was, on Tractarian theory, the successor of the Apostles. The bishop was Newman's pope. But the Movement spread and flourished because Church authority in general and episcopal authority in particular were powerless to prevent the spread of a new kind of Catholic churchmanship, the Tractarian, up and down the parishes of England – on the liberal principle, as one party in the Church.

England's difficulty, then as now, was Rome's opportunity. Nicholas Wiseman had become titular Bishop of Melipotamus, a defunct Cretan see whose pompous name caused mirth among Protestants, and among Catholics sustained his dignity as Coadjutor to the Vicar Apostolic of the Central District, Thomas Walsh. Wiseman was convinced by Tract 90 that Newman had 'no other end but *Rome*'.[47] It was, therefore, in an ostensibly eirenic spirit that he denied in a public letter Newman's distinction between the decrees of Trent and the teaching of the modern Roman Church. He recalled that Froude had called Papists 'wretched Tridentines'. 'It seems hard', Wiseman wrote, 'that now we should be deprived of even this "wretched" title, and sunk by you a step lower in the scale of degradation.'[48] Wiseman also sent to Bloxam's friend Phillipps an Italian devotional book to pass to Newman, to show him that official works of Catholic piety were not superstitious as he claimed. This was the very argument which the Roman Catholic Newman was to deploy against Pusey when the latter complained of the Mariolatrous and hagiographical corruptions of Roman Catholic devotion.

Newman himself complained to Wiseman about the Bishop's charge that in the *Letter to Jelf*, Newman had exploited anti-Roman prejudice to shield himself from attack, when he [Newman] was 'actually suffering from his own communion for his kind feelings towards the Church of Rome'.[49] Wiseman pacifically agreed to omit the charge in any subsequent editions of his letter. Newman left the task of publicly answering Wiseman to William Palmer of Worcester, 'a controversialist who was seldom embarrassed by seeing two sides to a question'.[50] Yet Wiseman was isolated in his own communion. He was supported by the medievalist circle around Phillipps and Pugin, who looked increasingly to the Oxford Movement to convert England to Roman Catholicism. But the native English Catholics were wary of the Tractarians, whom they took at their word in seeking to keep potential converts in the Church of England: 'the embrace of Mr Newman', wrote one, 'is the kiss that would betray us'.[51] These 'Old Catholics' with their centuries of circumspection and reserve were suspicious of Wiseman's zeal for converts, as of Father Spencer's crusade for the nation's conversion; and their suspicions of the Tractarians were fortified by the ex-Quaker Frederick Lucas, founding editor in 1840 of the *Tablet* weekly newspaper, who embodied a new and most un-Quaker kind of belligerent Catholicism, and whose sympathies lay not with Wiseman and aristocrats like Shrewsbury but with O'Connell and the Irish Catholics. O'Connell himself had no reason to love either Newman or other Oxonian Tories, and Wiseman's Tractarianophilia was delicately poised between English Catholic reserve towards the Oxford men, and sheer Hibernian popish aggressiveness.

It was, however, a gentle Irish Catholic, Dr Charles Russell, Professor of Ecclesiastical History at Maynooth, who on Newman's own account of it, 'had, perhaps, more to do with my conversion than any one else'. His virtues were almost negative: 'he was always gentle, mild, unobtrusive, uncontroversial. He let me alone.'[52] Russell's first letter to Newman tried to unravel an element in Tract 90 about which Newman was not quite coherent, his acceptance of Article XXVIII denouncing Transubstantiation as implying a fleshy and carnal understanding of Christ's presence in the Sacrament. Russell's political moderation was also to Newman's taste. The Irishman sent Newman seminary textbooks to try to show him that his view of Roman corruptions was a false one; and the friendship with Russell is notable as Newman's sole warm connection with a Roman Catholic before he himself became one.

'I was indeed in prudence taking steps towards eventually withdrawing from St Mary's', Newman recalled of the time of publishing Tract 90, 'and I was not confident about my permanent adhesion to the Anglican creed; but I was in no actual perplexity or trouble of mind.'[53] He spent the summer of 1841 at Littlemore, and in July, he resigned the *British Critic* to Tom Mozley, in whose indulgent hands it became the mouthpiece of the Romanizing school of Frederick Oakeley and W. G. Ward. Newman himself 'determined to put aside all controversy', as he set out to translate the anti-Arian treatises of St Athanasius for the Library of the Fathers. In September 1841, he received the first proofs and set to work on the complicated notes, working away from eight to twelve hours a day. The toil was a refuge from trouble, for 'between July and November [1841]', he was to write, 'I received three blows which broke me'.[54]

The first was the direct outcome of the work on Athanasius. 'I saw clearly, that in the history of Arianism, the pure Arians were the Protestants, the semi-Arians were the Anglicans, and that Rome now was what it was then. The truth lay, not with the *Via Media*, but with what was called "the extreme party".'[55] The second blow was a series of 'broadsides' from the bishops in episcopal charges against Tract 90 which continued into 1842. Their Evangelical Lordships of Chester and Calcutta, the Bishop of Gloucester and the Archbishop of Armagh, even the savage old High Church Henry Phillpotts of Exeter, who saw in Newmanism the *reductio ad absurdum* of his own principles – all thundered their disapproval. Sumner of Winchester refused to ordain Keble's deacon-curate Peter Young, in part on the basis of Young's refusal to repudiate Tract 90, and the century-long war began between the new High Churchmen and the very bishops whose authority these same High Churchmen had sought to uphold.

The third blow to Newman was the affair of the Jerusalem bishopric, which highlighted the piebald and particoloured ecclesial character of the Church of England. The progenitor of this scheme for a Protestant bishop in Jerusalem alternately appointed by England and Prussia was Newman's anti-Catholic critic, the Prussian diplomat Chevalier Bunsen. Bunsen's sovereign Frederick William IV wished to impose bishops on the State Church in Prussia, and to achieve the foothold in the Near East enjoyed by the French as protectors of the Latin Christians and by the Russians as protectors of the Orthodox. This *raison d'état* was reinforced in England by powerful religious considerations. To Evangelicals, the scheme meant hastening the Second Coming by creating a new Protestant mission to the Jews. The older High Churchmen like Howley and Blomfield welcomed the possible extension of episcopal order, as did Hook and Palmer of Worcester and even Pusey. The new Anglo-Prussian Bishop of Jerusalem, Michael Solomon Alexander, borne to his see in *HMS Devastation*, was a Prussian Jew converted to Christianity who had become Professor of Hebrew at King's College, London. He was to preside over a very few Protestants and even fewer converted Jews, and was forbidden by the Ottomans to proselytize among Moslems or the native Christians, so that the intrinsic importance of the incident was wholly out of proportion to the ecclesiastical disturbance which it caused.

For Newman, the offensiveness of the scheme lay in the assumption that the Church of England was Protestant like the Prussian, in the accompanying Evangelical philojudaic passion for restoring the Temple, and in the Anglo-Prussian willingness to support heretical Monophysites and Nestorians and even the Moslems, against the existing eastern Catholic Churches, Greek and Latin. Newman was especially appalled by the official English episcopal sanction for 'this atrocious Jerusalem Bishop affair'. After Howley had consecrated Alexander, Newman told Jemima that the 'Archbishop is doing all he can to unchurch us';[56] it was difficult to remember that he had once venerated Howley.

The issue could hardly have encapsulated more of Newman's dislikes: a foreign Protestant State, guilty of Erastian tyranny over its own Church; an ecclesiastical measure taken for political reasons, and supported by an odd Evangelical enthusiasm for 'a Bishop of the *circumcision*',[57] a converted Jew, as if the Old Law had never been replaced by the New. Would an unambiguously Catholic Church behave in such a manner? 'Many persons', wrote

Newman, 'are doubtful whether we have the Notes of the true Church upon us; every act of the Church, such as this of coalescing with foreign heretics, *weakens* the proof. And in some cases it may be the last straw that breaks the horse's back.'[58] In November 1841, he sent his personal protest to Howley and Bagot. 'Lutheranism and Calvinism are heresies, repugnant to Scripture, springing up three centuries since, and anathematized by East as well as West . . . I in my place, being a priest of the English Church and Vicar of St Mary the Virgin's, Oxford, by way of relieving my conscience, do hereby solemnly protest against the measure aforesaid, and disown it . . . '[59] 'I never heard of any good or harm it has ever done', Newman wrote of the measure in the *Apologia*, 'except what it has done for me . . . It brought me on to the beginning of the end.'[60] 'I was on my death-bed, as regards my membership with the Anglican Church.'[61]

17

Death-bed at Littlemore

'A death-bed has scarcely a history', wrote Newman; 'it is a tedious decline, with seasons of rallying and seasons of falling back; and since the end is foreseen, or what is called a matter of time, it has little interest for the reader, especially if he has a kind heart.'[1] His metaphor was oddly chosen, as it dwells on his rejection of one Church rather than his adoption of another, but it indicates the anguish and suffering of the process. Newman believed in a God who had revealed himself and his salvation to his people, his royal priesthood, the Church. Newman no longer believed in the *Via Media*. He was, therefore, without a theory on which to defend the Church of England as God's church, and he wanted to become a Roman Catholic. But having once been certain of his religious loyalty, he was now a prey to every shade of doubt. It took four years to move him to submit to Rome on the double certitude that Rome was exclusively the Church of Christ and that the Church of England was no part of it.

It is difficult to decide how far Newman's opinions were transformed by the Church of England's determination to prove that she was as heretical and Protestant as he feared her to be, as in Howley's warm welcome in January 1842 for a Protestant No-Popery declamation from the Evangelical capital of Cheltenham. This clamour against Newman's disloyalty would have had less effect had his secret conscience been proof against it; and controversy was a strain anyway. It was kept burning by Pusey, who converted the election by Convocation of a successor to Keble as Professor of Poetry at Oxford into an occasion for a further Protestant demonstration, by a partisan declaration in favour of Isaac Williams, against the Protestant candidate, the classicist James Garbett. Williams was notorious as the author of Tracts 80 and 87 on Reserve, but he had also written some fine religious poetry, unlike Garbett, who though a translator, was not an original poet at all. Moderate churchmen were alarmed that this referendum on Tractarian principles would only damage the Church and their own convictions, and Gladstone, with some support from the bishops, including Bagot, tried and failed to persuade both candidates to withdraw; but Williams himself gave up the contest a week before the vote, when he learned that Garbett had received 921 pledges to his own 623, proving that though the new High Churchmen and their friends were a minority, they had become a substantial one.

But they were also, increasingly, a marginal and disunited one: their inspiration had slipped into the shadows. It is hardly surprising in the light of Newman's once fierce anti-Romanism that a sympathizer with the movement like the theologically gifted George Moberly should assure Richard Church of his unrelenting opposition to the Tridentine decrees, which depressed Newman with a sense of how far even good men had to move. He himself frightened Robert Wilberforce by suggesting that 'in the controversies of the early centuries the Roman Church was ever on the right side'. 'I don't think that I ever was so shocked by any communication . . . as by your letter of this morning . . . ', replied Wilberforce. 'The more I study Scripture, the more am I impressed with the resemblance between the Romish principle in the Church and the Babylon of St John . . . '[2] In the following decade, Wilberforce was to prove to be the finest systematic theologian in the Church of England, before going to Rome himself. If this was his reaction, others would be still more disturbed. Yet more disturbed was the condition of those who had said their 'Credo in Newmannum', who had looked to Newman to renew the Church or had been merely drawn to a new religious life by the *Parochial Sermons*, and now felt themselves spiritually orphaned and uncertain as their champion stood doubtful of himself.

These doubts were doubled by Newman's absence from the fray. As he busied himself with putting up bookcases at Littlemore, his very retirement attracted suspicion. He recalled his feelings in the *Apologia*. 'I cannot walk into or out of my house, but curious eyes are upon me. Why will you not let me die in peace? Wounded brutes creep into some hole to die in, and no one grudges it them. Let me alone, I shall not trouble you long . . . One day when I entered my house, I found a flight of Under-graduates inside. Heads of Houses, as mounted patrols, walked their horses round those poor cottages. Doctors of Divinity dived into the hidden recesses of that private tenement uninvited, and drew domestic conclusions from what they saw there. I had thought that an Englishman's house was his castle; but the newspapers thought otherwise.'[3] In April 1842, Bagot himself wrote to Newman, in a tone of apology, about a journalist's report 'that a so-called Anglo-Catholic Monastery is in process of erection at Littlemore, and that the cells of dormitories, the chapel, the refectory, the cloisters all may be seen advancing to perfection, under the eye of a parish priest of the Diocese of Oxford'. Bagot knew Newman too well not to be aware that he was 'the last man living'[4] to attempt to revive Roman monasticism without telling his Bishop, but Bagot wanted Newman's authority to contradict the report. Newman replied 'that no "monastery is in process of erection", there is no "chapel", no "refectory", hardly a dining-room or parlour. The "cloisters" are my shed connecting the cottages . . . I am attempting nothing ecclesiastical, but something personal and private'. Given, however, that he had so roused public interest in himself, he had the less cause for indignation and hurt that there was such keen speculation about his 'Newmaynooth', as it was called, with reference to the controversial Catholic seminary in Ireland. 'What have I done', he asked Bagot, 'that I am to be called to account by the world for my private actions in a way in which no one else is called? Why may I not have that liberty which all others are allowed?'[5]

This denial that Littlemore was in any sense a monastery was a little disingenuous. Newman's retirement was a spiritual retreat, a withdrawal into himself to find truth through holiness; and that ideal of holiness was a monastic one. 'I am almost in despair of keeping men together. The only possible way is a monastery', he wrote in January 1842 to the Anglo-Catholic lawyer, James Robert Hope, who formed with Gladstone and Manning a triumvirate of friends to be broken by Roman conversion. 'Men want an outlet', Newman continued, 'for their devotional and penitential feelings, and if we do not grant it, to a dead certainty they will go where they can find it.'[6] He admitted to Bagot to be devoting himself to 'a life of greater religious regularity',[7] but he was reciting the hours of the Roman breviary, beginning with Matins and Lauds at five o'clock in the morning, concluding with Compline at a quarter past ten at night, and omitting only the Antiphons which invoked the Virgin Mary. To the Roman observance, he added daily Morning Prayer and Evensong in public in Littlemore Chapel.

The other element in his quasi-monasticism was the development of a community life, as younger men joined him. The first, in spring 1842, was John Dobrée Dalgairns, an unstable enthusiast who had already raised a public storm by calling in *L'Univers* for closer sympathies between Tractarians and Roman Catholics. The next, in July, was William Lockhart, from a family who wanted to keep William from Rome. Lockhart promised to stay with Newman three years; others, like Mark Pattison and Hurrell Froude's younger brother James Anthony, were occasional visitors who took part in the religious observance of the place. Newman was a great deal closer to Pattison than to Froude; but both men, fine writers and distinguished scholars, were to shake off his leadership when he became a Roman Catholic, and adopt the liberal cause. A more enduring disciple was the curate David Lewis, who was to become a Roman Catholic, marry a peer's daughter, and enrich English spirituality with translations of the Spanish Carmelite mystics. Despite the existence of a definite community, Littlemore was not a monastery in the formal sense, with vows and enclosure, or with the luxuries of Roman extra-liturgical devotion; but even as a device to prevent conversions to Rome, it was calculated to enlarge the appetite for the very sort of popish sanctity which it was intended to assuage.

Bagot's own anxiety to distinguish the Movement's mean from its extreme was the theme of his Charge in St Mary's in May 1842, which began by praising the Movement against journalistic misrepresentations, but went on

211

in muffled language to criticize Tract 90 for making the Articles mean anything. The allegation at first worried Newman; later it hurt. Bagot also severely censured the Movement's extremists, like William Palmer of Magdalen and Frederick Oakeley. His remarks about Calvinists and Puritans weighed the balance a little the other way: there was no such balance among the Heads of the Hebdomadal Board, who recommended the repeal of the statutes against Hampden. This, however, was a little too partisan for many non-Tractarians, and the proposal was thrown out by the Convocation in June, the Tractarians being joined by the mass of still anti-liberal and middling orthodox churchmen. Hampden's revenge was to require a radical young Tractarian, Richard Gell Macmullen, to defend two anti-Tractarian theses on the Eucharist and Scripture as a requirement for the award of a BD degree. The Macmullen affair dragged on for two years through the University courts, exposing the rich possibilities for academic litigation in a theological controversy which was nothing less than the destruction from within of the old Protestant High Church ideology of unreformed Oxford.

The fiercest opponents of that ideology were arguably not the liberals but the Tractarian Romanizers, especially William George Ward and Oakeley, who through the *British Critic*, upheld Rome as the standard of a true Catholicism. Newman's account is touched by his later estrangement from Ward, but his irritation arose from his perception that a movement is identified in the public mind by its extremists. 'Nothing was clearer concerning them', wrote Newman in the *Apologia*, 'than that they needed to be kept in order; and on me who had had so much to do with the making of them, that duty was as clearly incumbent; and it is equally clear . . . that I was just the person, above all others, who could not undertake it.'[8] Newman had upset some of his old friends, who had no Roman sympathies and who were best placed to oppose those who did. He had few personal friends among the Romanizers, but 'though I could not trust in their firmness of purpose, for, like a swarm of flies, they might come and go', he had 'an intense sympathy' for their Romeward tendency, which he could not honestly oppose.[9] Gladstone was astonished to learn in July 1842 from Robert Williams that Oakeley and Ward disowned no Roman doctrine and wanted corporate reunion with Rome on Rome's terms. Newman's explanation of the matter to Pusey in October 1842 made a distinction which would have appalled any honest Protestant: 'as to the matter of doctrine, I certainly do think the Pope the Head of the Church. Nay I thought all churchmen so thought; only they said that his doctrine, tyranny etc. suspended his just powers here'. 'As to my being entirely with Oakeley and Ward, I think my sympathies *are* entirely with them; but really I cannot determine whether my opinions are.'[10]

Despite Newman's insistence on distinguishing his feelings from his hard-won rational convictions, he was resistant to Ward's ruthless logical deduction of Roman Catholic conclusions from Newmanian premises. 'I had a great dislike of paper logic. For myself, it was not logic that carried me on; as well might one say that the quicksilver in the barometer changes the weather. It is the concrete being that reasons; pass a number of years, and I find my mind in a new place; how? the whole man moves; paper logic is but the record of it. All the logic in the world would not have made me move faster towards Rome than I did; as well might you say that I have arrived at the end of my journey, because I see the village church before me . . . Great acts take time.'[11]

'The whole man moves . . . Great acts take time . . . ' Newman's horarium at Littlemore allowed him nine hours of daily study, and in 1842, he conceived his new Library of British Saints, with contributions by various friends and followers. Volume six of his *Parochial Sermons*[12] appeared, and his translations of the *Select Treatises of S Athanasius, Archbishop of Alexandria, in controversy with the Arians*,[13] an exposition of the heresiology of his hero. He also published his translation of the volume of the Abbé Fleury's *Ecclesiastical History* for the late fourth century.[14] Newman's preface to this last appeared again, in 1843, as *An Essay on the Miracles recorded in the Ecclesiastical History of the Early Ages*. It has been called 'a jumble of twisted dialectic about historical evidence, which it is not too strong to describe as repellent',[15] and has always been the target of Newman's severest critics.[16] Yet his argument is the obvious one against Protestants who believe in the miracles of Scripture but deny those of church history, that 'What God did once, He *is* likely to do again'.[17] Granted the Scriptural miracles, there is an antecedent probability that some at least of the later ecclesiastical miracles had also occurred, and this prior consideration will influence the Christian's approach to the evidence that they have done so. Of course, the believer, like the sceptic, has to weigh this evidence with care, and reject those miracles for which sufficient evidence is unavailable. But Newman's essay caused scandal by his examples of miracles for which he thought the evidence sufficient, from the Thundering Legion, whose prayers brought rain to a drought-stricken Roman army, to St Helena's discovery of the True Cross, and St Gregory Thaumaturge's prayer which stopped the course of a dangerous river.

The work is as uncomfortable to believers as to sceptics, because Newman's battery of arguments against the sceptic raises as many sceptical arguments as it resolves. On the other hand, his logic is correct, that a believer in a God who can work miracles in Scripture is at least open to the evidence for a miracle reported in the course of Christian history which will look less likely or impossible to a determined unbeliever. In this, Newman remained true to his beginnings as a supernaturalist, and in terms of the old Evangelical divisions, the essay paradoxically placed him among those radical Protestants who expected God's wonders in the present as of old.

This idea of continuity between Scripture and Tradition underlies the theory which resolved Newman's difficulties with Rome, of the development of Christian doctrine. The idea owed something to the ruthless questioning of Ward, who dinned it into Newman's ears; but it is also an answer to a larger problem, as to how the Christianity of the New Testament had become the imperial religion of later Roman and medieval history.

This was the theme of a sermon which Newman took an hour and a half to deliver on the feast of the Purification of the Virgin in February 1843. His text, Luke 2.19, declares that 'Mary kept all these things, and pondered them in her heart': for what she pondered in her heart was that whole truth about her Son which was to become the Christian religion. Newman drew the contrast between her faith and the vast libraries of divinity which had arisen from it. 'And this world of thought is the expansion of a few words, uttered, as if casually, by the fishermen of Galilee . . . Stranger surely is it that St John should be a theologian, than that St Peter should be a prince.' The implication, however, is that the Christian Revelation, given to the Virgin and the Apostles, was the implicit impression on their minds and hearts of an idea which it would take long ages to define in reason. 'Even centuries might pass without the formal expression of a truth, which had been all along the secret life of millions of faithful souls.' Thus 'we form creeds as a chief mode of perpetuating the impression' which was unnecessary when the person of Christ stood before the first Christians, for the Creeds arose as a means of clarifying and preserving in reason that impression of the divine which Mary had pondered in her heart.[18]

This theory reflects Newman's understanding of mind, which may be possessed by ideas of which it is hardly conscious, even to its harm: 'how many men are burdened with an idea, which haunts them through a great part of their lives . . . ?'[19] Again, there is Newman's complicated view of Revelation, which does not consist simply in formally stated credal propositions, but is imparted in an impression at a level of knowledge deeper than the understanding. In this his account is not altogether straightforward, as he was to grant that such propositions form a part of Revelation, even though they must, like all statements in human language about God, fall short of the deity they describe. In this, Newman guarded himself against the liberal implications of his argument, that if Revelation was not given in the formal propositions of the Creeds, then the Creeds can be scrapped or redefined with advancing scientific knowledge. Rather, there may be 'a certain correspondence between the idea, though earthly, and its heavenly archetype',[20] between the human statement and the God whom it reveals. Thus the Virgin, Newman implied, could not perhaps have passed a test on the Christological decrees of the fifth-century Council of Chalcedon, but those formal definitions were the necessary explanation in reason and argument of the knowledge she had pondered in her heart. The difference between her implicit knowledge of Christianity and the more explicit knowledge of the Creeds is a consequence of the development of doctrine, both forms of understanding being attempts to grasp, albeit in a different manner, the reality of their divine incarnate Object.

This was no more than an extension of Newman's old ideas of Economy and Reserve. God accommodates his Revelation to human understanding, as a teacher to children, so that a fable may embody a higher truth. Indeed 'a lie is the nearest approach to the truth',[21] when a truth can only be imparted through a lie. In this, Newman played on the borders of scepticism: how can we know if the earth goes round the sun or the sun the earth, unless we know what motion is? Our beliefs may 'be but an accidental result of our present senses',[22] when other senses might be possible. This scepticism about the reliability of natural knowledge goes back to Locke, but for Newman, the fallibility of the human mind only enhanced his sense of the mystery of God, dimly revealed through his strange economies. One of his finer passages in the sermon concerns the knowledge of God given mysteriously in the vast outpouring of music from the seven notes of the scale. 'What science brings so much out of so little? Out of what poor elements does some great master in it create his new world!'

Can it be that those mysterious stirrings of heart, and keen emotions, and strange yearnings after we know not what, and awful impressions from we know not whence, should be wrought in us by what is unsubstantial, and comes and goes, and begins and ends in itself? It is not so; it cannot be. No; they have escaped from some higher sphere; they are the outpourings of eternal harmony in the medium of created sound; they are echoes from our Home; they are the voice of Angels, or the Magnificat of Saints, or the living laws of Divine Governance, or the Divine Attributes; something are they besides themselves, which we cannot compass, which we cannot utter, – though mortal man, and he perhaps not otherwise distinguished above his fellows, has the gift of eliciting them.[23]

The sermon on development was the last of Newman's *University Sermons*, which he published as a collection in 1843. It greatly impressed Jemima, who thought it made 'deep things so very simple', but who wondered why Newman thought that music had fourteen notes[24] – 'a gross blunder', he replied, arising from 'publishing hot bread . . . The greater part of the sermons, at least, cannot plead haste for their imperfection'.[25] He himself told Hope that they were 'the least theological' of his books,[26] and was surprised when they ran in a fortnight to a second edition, given the abstruseness of their subject. Good judges have considered them among his finest work.

The publication also heralded his departure from the Anglican ministry. There was a newspaper scandal when in January 1843, the youthful Rector of Leadenham, Bernard Smith, became a Roman Catholic, and his bishop, Kaye of Lincoln, claimed that Newman had advised Smith to retain his living as a Papist. With Pusey's help Newman had the Bishop quizzed and the story contradicted; but the fuss gave a sinister twist to his anonymous but easily identifiable retraction of his fiercer attacks on Rome, in the form of an entry in the *Conservative Journal*. Newman included in the retraction Hurrell Froude's rebuke to him for such 'cursing and swearing . . . How mistaken we may ourselves be on many points that are only gradually opening to us!'[27]

He as yet took back nothing about his anti-Roman remarks on devotion to the Virgin and Saints or the granting of indulgences. But his artless confession that his language had been due, 'in no small measure, to an impetuous temper, a hope of approving myself to persons I respect, and a wish to repel the charge of Romanism',[28] was too self-abnegatory and provoked the charge of hypocrisy. 'It is a thing which makes me every now and then feel as if I were in a dream', wrote Whately to Hawkins, 'to find people going on believing men who *proclaim* themselves liars.' Newman, Whately thought, had nothing to learn from 'the *Slanderer* himself!'[29] The charge was capped by the Revd Francis Close of Cheltenham, who declared at a public dinner in March 1843 that he would not trust Newman as the author of Tract 90 with his purse. Newman's own explanation of his retraction in the *Apologia* was that while pleading guilty to violent language, he was like the boy on the scaffold condemned for a crime, who bit off his mother's ear, because 'his mother's indulgence when he was a boy, had a good deal to do with it'. Having been misled by the Anglican divines, he was in a humour 'to bite off their ears'.[30]

This conviction of the falsehood of Anglican teaching revived his sense of his false position at St Mary's. 'What men learn from me, who learn anything', he wrote to Keble on 14 March 1843, 'is to lean towards doctrines and practices which our Church does not sanction. There was a time when I tried to balance this by strong statements against Rome . . . But now, when I feel I can do this no more, . . . I am in danger of acting as a traitor to that system, to which I must profess attachment or I should not have the opportunity of acting at all.'[31]

Poor Keble had never doubted and would never doubt the Church of England. He needed all his love of Newman to show an exquisite tact and tenderness for a tortured frame of mind for which he felt no sympathy. 'Some thoughts are like hideous dreams', Newman told him in May, 'and we wake from them, and think they will never return; and though they do return, we cannot be sure still that they are more than vague fancies; and till one is so sure they are not, . . . one does not like, or rather it is wrong, to mention them to another.'[32] 'Oh forgive me, my dear Keble, and be merciful to me in a matter, in which, if I have not your compassion, my faith is so weak and I have so little sense of my own uprightness, that I shall have no refuge in the testimony of my conscience, such as St. Paul felt, and shall be unable to appeal from you to a higher judgement seat . . . I am very far *more* sure that England is in schism, than that the Roman additions to the Primitive Creed may not be developments, arising out of a keen and vivid realizing of the Divine Depositum of faith'. Attacks came to Newman as 'witnesses to my conscience against my secret unfaithfulness to the English Church', as well as showing 'how very far she is from even aspiring to Catholicity'.[33]

Newman's opinions gave great pain to others beside Keble. They caused a decisive break with his beloved Frederic Rogers, who accused him of pretending an Anglican loyalty while leading men to Rome, and then wrote in anguish of his unworthiness of the intimacy which he was losing.[34] Rogers' suffering letter helped stiffen Newman's resolve to resign his parish, as did his Oriel colleague Charles Page Eden's hostile insistence that were he to succeed Newman as Vicar of St Mary's, 'he would not engage even to let me read daily prayers at Littlemore . . . ' Newman's 'hideous dream', he explained to Keble, was 'to suspect oneself external to the Catholic Church, having publicly, earnestly, frequently, insisted on the ordinary necessity of being within it'. 'I do not think I could take the Oath of Supremacy again . . . A detection would be far more calamitous, than a quiet withdrawal while things were so tranquil.' He would, by remaining, be encouraging younger men to 'take the validity of their interpretation of the Articles etc. from me *on faith*', which was 'a cruelty to them, as well as a treachery towards the Church'.

Newman was, however, still persevering with his idea of the previous summer to employ his young men 'who were in danger of running wild' to write a series of lives of the English or British saints, by bringing the wild men 'from doctrine to history, from speculation to fact; again, as giving them an interest in the English soil and English Church, and keeping them from seeking sympathy in Rome as she is . . . ' There was, he explained to Keble, the difficulty of causing 'much surprise and talk' by giving up the project, and while he asked whether the project was incompatible 'with my holding St. Mary's, being what I am',[35] the 'Lives' might be considered a guarantee of his remaining in Anglican communion as a Fellow of Oriel.

Keble had to weigh to a nicety all these nuanced doubts; to separate out the many fine threads of an intellect and sensibility raised to a fine pitch of morbid oversensitivity by an intolerable position. On 30 May 1843, Keble conceded the main point: 'I dare not press your retaining St Mary's: it does seem to involve such constant peril of sin . . . '[36] He encouraged Newman, however, to persevere with his plan for the library of saints. This project went forward, and in September 1843, Newman published a prospectus and drew up an elaborate calendar. The difficulty with it was, as he explained to James Hope, that 'Church History is made up of these three elements – miracles, monkery, Popery',[37] and to express any historical sympathy with one's subject was to sympathize with these.

With Newman in retirement, the Movement's chief public figure was now Pusey, and in mid May 1843, he preached a sermon in Christ Church

Cathedral upholding the Catholic doctrine of the Real Presence in the Eucharist. The sermon was promptly delated as heretical by Newman's old foe Faussett to the Vice-Chancellor, Philip Wynter, President of St John's, who was also sorely tried by the wayward Thomas Morris' public resort to Laud for his prayers. Wynter convened a court of six Doctors of Divinity, including the accuser, Faussett, to judge the sermon: by an irony Faussett stood in for Hampden, who was still under the ban for which the Tractarians had fought. They found against Pusey in his absence, and when he refused to recant, suspended him as a preacher for two years. Newman feared for his friend's health, feeling that it had been 'the excitement of an *object*', the Oxford Movement, which had 'strangely' improved Pusey's poor physical condition from a decade before.[38] In fact, Pusey was as sanguine as ever about Anglicanism, even though the suspension cost him his conservative reputation. His faith was untroubled by the disgrace, and it was as Puseyites, not Newmanites, that the Anglo-Catholics were to remain within the Church of England.

There was an odd contrast between Newman's inner disquiet and the outward turmoil of events, and the unhurried calm of the little community at Littlemore, which was joined in the summer by Ambrose St John, kinsman of Lord St John of Bletso, and former curate to Henry Wilberforce. St John was to become Newman's 'Angel Guardian', and, though Newman's intellectual inferior, came to fill the void in his heart left by Froude. 'From the first', wrote Newman, 'he loved me with an intensity of love, which was unaccountable.'[39] Forty-seven years later, their bones were to be mingled beneath the same gravestone in a common grave. St John already accepted Transubstantiation and the Invocation of the Saints, and accompanied, and in the end preceded, Newman on the last stage of the road to Rome.

Newman's only earthly needs were books and friendship; his most intimate letters of his last Anglican years were to the Vicar of Hursley. 'O my dear Keble', wrote Newman in August 1843, 'you know far better and more deeply than I, that "the time is short" – and that the highest blessings are not earthly – nay, the highest are commonly purchased by a privation of the earthly.'[40] Newman received a further spur to giving up St Mary's in August when William Lockhart broke his promise to remain at Littlemore for three years and was received into the Roman Church by a saintly Italian missioner, Luigi Gentili, of the Rosminian Order of Charity, which Lockhart proceeded to join himself. 'You may fancy', Newman told Keble, 'how sick this makes me.'[41] It was a portent of Newman's own reception by another Italian holy man, and his own departure to an order of Italian origin.

But with his own impending resignation from St Mary's, he had to cope with a distress in others similar to the distress which Lockhart had caused him. The most sympathetic of his siblings, Jemima, reported her own disquiet and that of their old aunt Elizabeth, and enclosed a long and moving letter from her sister-in-law Anne Mozley, dwelling on her spiritual and moral debt to Newman, and on the dread of losing him general among his disciples. 'These people have a claim upon him: he has witnessed to the world, and they have received his witness; he has taught and they have striven to be obedient pupils . . . He has undertaken the charge and cannot now shake them off . . . There is something sad enough and discouraging enough in being shunned and eyed with distrust by neighbours, friends, and clergy.' This could be easily borne while there was comfort from Littlemore and St Mary's 'on many a dreary day'. But 'our watchman, whose cry used to cheer us, is heard no more'.[42]

Jemima added for herself that 'whichever way you decide it will be a noble and true part, and not taken up from any impulse, or caprice, or pique, but on true and right principles that will carry a blessing with them'. Newman was sorry for the pain he was giving, but his reply dwelt on his own pain. 'Is it a light thing to give up Littlemore? Am I not providing dreariness for myself? If others, whom I am pierced to think about, because I cannot help them, suffer, shall not I suffer in my own way?'[43]

Meanwhile he was in the false position of urging restraint on others. Thus he pleaded with Faber for 'a certain term of probation . . . were I tempted to go to Rome, I should for three years pray, and get my friends to pray, that I might die rather than go, if going were wrong'.[44] In September 1843, he had to act still more urgently when his brother-in-law Tom Mozley was swept off his feet by the fervent peasant Catholicism of Normandy, left Harriett in Caen and came home to become a Roman Catholic. Newman went straight down to the vicarage at Cholderton to persuade him to post-pone the decision for two years, but the ignorant Harriett, who came back from Caen to find Tom all but a Papist, blamed her brother – and even in some degree Jemima – for the near loss of her home and means of livelihood, and never forgave him. Their relations ceased in 1843, and it was left to Jemima to bear in patience with him and to remain, with Mary dead and Charles, Francis and Harriett all estranged from him, the lone loving sibling of the family.

This general irritation is understandable: Newman's friends felt the ten-sion of his indecision about his parish. On 1 September, he wrote twice to Keble declaring himself 'ready still to keep St Mary's, if you think best',[45] but giving reasons, including Lockhart's departure, why he should resign at once. On the same day, he told James Mozley that 'I am not a good son enough of the Church of England to feel I can in conscience hold preferment under her. I love the Church of Rome too well.'[46] It was not until 7 September that he sent off his letter of resignation to Bagot on a note of complaint that 'so many Bishops have said such things of me, and no one [has] undertaken my part in respect to that interpretation of the Articles under which alone I can subscribe them'. As for the Church of England, 'I am not relaxing my zeal till it has been disowned by her rulers. I have not retired from her service till I have lost or forfeited her confidence.'[47]

The note of complaint was sustained in a far more rhetorical manner in Newman's last Anglican sermon, 'The Parting of Friends', preached at a communion service at Littlemore on Sunday 25 September. The occasion was one of special drama. The whole church, altar, windows, pew ends and Mrs Newman's tomb, sculpted by Newman's boyhood friend Westmacott, were lavishly decorated with dahlias, passion-flowers and fuschias, and the school children in the new frocks and bonnets which were Newman's parting gift chanted a psalm in procession before the packed congregation, which spilled over into the churchyard set with chairs. Edward Bellasis, who was to be one of the trio of Newman's London lawyer friends, with Hope and Edward Badeley, wrote to his wife that he would never forget the sermon or the preacher, 'the faltering voice, the long pauses, the perceptible and hardly successful efforts at restraining himself, together with the deep interest of the subject, were almost overpowering'.[48] Newman contrasted Orpah who left her mother-in-law for the world with a kiss – some saw an unkind reference here to Lockhart – with Ruth who clave to her, and the whole congregation wept, the preacher alone being dry-eyed, as he described David's departure from Jonathan at the court of Saul, and delivered his plaint at the treatment by his Church: 'O my mother! whence is this unto thee, that thou hast good things poured upon thee and canst not keep them, and bearest children, yet darest not own them? why hast thou not . . . the heart to rejoice in their love? . . . Thou makest them "stand all the day idle" . . . '[49] 'After the sermon, Newman received the Communion, but took no further part in officiating. Dr Pusey consecrated the elements in tears, and once or twice became entirely overcome and stopped altogether.'[50] The event signalled the breaking of the brotherhood. Its emotions may seem excessive, but it signalled the failure of Newman's hope for a Catholic Christian England which had begun so bravely a decade before.

Newman's sermon was published before the end of the year with others over which Keble laboured with corrections and suggestions; one, entitled 'Elijah the Prophet of the Latter Days',[51] expressed Newman's sense of self-identification with the great prophetic exile from the Temple who had not ordered the ten northern tribes of Israel in schism to return to the obedience of Jerusalem. Yet Newman still wanted to remain in the Anglican Communion, in a distinction that must have puzzled its recipient Jemima. 'I do so despair of the Church of England, and am so evidently cast off by her, and, on the other hand, I am so drawn to the Church of Rome, that I think it *safer*, as a matter of honesty, *not* to keep my living. This is a very different thing from having any *intention* of joining the Church of Rome.' Not that he could yet publicly avow this 'state of *doubt*', which people would not understand, but he could no longer be 'a *teacher* and a *champion* for our Church'.[52]

It was understandably painful to write out the long history of his doubts to men like James Mozley and Manning, to whom he also showed his bitterness about the Church of England's poor treatment of him. 'No decency has been observed in the attacks upon me from authority: no protests have appeared against them . . . the English Church is showing herself intrinsically and radically alien from Catholic principles, so do I feel the difficulties in defending her claims to be a branch of the Catholic Church.'[53] Manning passed this letter to Gladstone, who was greatly alarmed. Manning reasonably and gently chided Newman for his impatience: 'could you expect the living generation to change the opinions, prejudices, and habits of a whole life in a few years at one bidding?' Newman had achieved so much, and if Anglican Catholicity was still defective, 'is it not the condition of the Church in all ages?'[54] Newman saw that he must be more blunt: Manning's arguments were shadows. He had resigned St Mary's, he told the Archdeacon, 'because I think the Church of Rome the Catholic Church, and ours not a part of the Catholic Church, because not in communion with Rome'.[55] Manning apologized for his letter: 'ignorant of the one master key of all I was led to shallow thoughts of the matter'.[56] Again he showed Newman's letter to Gladstone, who wrote, 'My first thought is, "I stagger to and fro, like a drunken man, and am at my wits' end" '.[57] Gladstone imagined that the letter contained an admission of insincerity which would disgrace Newman and discredit his cause. Gladstone, a High Anglican loyal to his Church to his fingers' ends, would suffer no greater personal pain until Manning and Hope took the road to Rome. Again, Gladstone would experience the same sense of betrayal by Manning, who after 1847, found himself in Newman's position of doubt, but felt bound to hide these doubts from the incurably Anglican Gladstone, who would never know such an inner division against himself.

Manning also showed Newman's letters to Pusey who, ever sanguine, did not think that Newman's 'portentous expressions'[58] implied his impending defection. But it seems to have been in something like a state of shock that Manning responded by preaching a thunderous No-Popery sermon on Guy Fawkes day in Oxford, and then on 6 November walked out to Littlemore to assure Newman of his personal goodwill. Newman apparently gave James Anthony Froude, who was in the house, instructions that he would not see him. 'I went and told Manning, who was greatly distressed', recalled Froude, 'and I walked along the road some way with him, to give him what comfort I could.'[59] So distressed was Manning that he forgot his hat and walked back to Oxford bareheaded – then regarded as a major break of decorum. It was Manning's first experience of Newman's inability to separate persons and principles, and of his unforgiving strain, when as a rival cardinal, he came to embody the alternative to Manning's own unbending Ultramontanism.

Yet Newman was softened by a letter from Manning expressing his distress that the metaphor of Orpah's kiss had been intended for himself as one who 'would leave you for the world'.[60] 'Really, unless it were so sad a matter, I should smile', replied Newman; 'the thought is as far from me as

221

the Antipodes. Rather I am the person who to myself always seem, and reasonably, the criminal . . . the circumstance of such men as yourself being contented to remain is the strongest argument in favour of my own remaining. It is my constant prayer, that if others are right I may be drawn back – that nothing may part us.'[61] Gladstone was shown this letter as well, and wondered if Manning could get the Bishops to moderate their charges and so avert the 'inexpressible calamity' of Newman's secession. 'Cords of silk should one by one be thrown over him to bind him to the Church. Every manifestation of sympathy and confidence in him, as a man, must have some small effect.'[62]

Manning was less safe than he seemed. Gladstone was to be haunted by his Catholic convert sister Helen, who used Protestant works as lavatory paper. It was, however, a measure of the sensitivity and perceptiveness of two of the greatest Churchmen of their generation that they should have tried so hard to prevent Newman's loss, and saw, as the English hierarchy did not see, the symbolic and spiritual significance of such a blow to Anglican Christianity – 'a blow to the Church of England', as Gladstone's own great rival Disraeli was to describe it, with his usual imaginative insight, 'under which it still reels'.[63] They also saw accurately enough the degree of Newman's hurt and tried to salve it. A future Archbishop of Canterbury, Cosmo Gordon Lang, dreamed when young that a cloaked figure with 'a voice of singular sweetness and yet decisiveness' drew him from a first-class railway carriage: 'I think you must turn and come third-class with me'. The figure in third-class was Newman. Other Anglicans would never understand Newman's voluntary exile from that other Eden of the Establishment, from the golden world of the Anglican episcopal palace and deanery and public school. But in his entering on that exile, it was holiness not hurt that was carrying him out of the Church of England.

18

Development to Rome

The winter of 1844 was severe, and visited Newman with unaccustomed colds. His birthday, and the ailing Bowden's, fell on Ash Wednesday, and in what was to prove his last birthday letter to Bowden, he confessed his difficulty about discussing his Romeward tendency: 'I am not worthy of friends. With my opinions, to the full of which I dare not confess, I feel like a guilty person . . . I have nothing to bear but the anxiety which I feel for my friends' anxiety for me, and perplexity.'[1] His feelings were complex and various, but all ultimately depressing, and his minute analysis of them – an inheritance from his Evangelicalism – is the dissection of a sickness of the heart.

Yet his complaint about Evangelicalism had always been that it relied on subjective feeling. Keble suggested as the work of the Evil One a range of feelings distinctive to Newman himself: 'a certain restlessness, a longing after something more, something analogous to a very exquisite ear in music, which would keep you, I should think, in spite of yourself, intellectually and morally dissatisfied wherever you were'.[2] 'What I wish is,' Newman replied, 'not to go by my own judgement, but by something external, like the pillar of the cloud in the desert. Such is the united movement of *many*.'[3] This quest for God's hand in a general movement of minds and hearts to Rome was, however, less important than his own inner search for an assurance of the Divine Will. Recounting to Keble God's innumerable mercies towards him from the time of his conversion, he asked, 'Am I in a delusion, given over to believing a lie? . . . Does any subtle feeling or temptation, which I cannot detect, govern me, and bias my judgement? . . . Has He led me thus far to destroy me in the wilderness?'[4]

Keble still thought that Newman was looking for a non-existent perfection: perhaps as Newman might have himself suggested, 'the *whole* Church may be so lowered by sin, as to hinder one's finding on earth anything which *seems* really to answer to the Church of the Scriptures?' The danger of disappointment was scepticism. 'I have always fancied', Keble added, 'that perhaps you were over sanguine in making things square, and did not quite allow enough for Bishop Butler's notion of doubt and intellectual difficulty being some men's intended element and appropriate trial.'[5] Newman was all too aware himself that his failure might precipitate some of his followers into the worst of intellectual states, scepticism, as was indeed to occur, for scepticism was the obvious consequence of discovering that Anglicanism was an unsatisfactory and muddled compromise between Protestant private judgement and the authority of Rome.

As yet Newman knew next to nothing of Roman Catholics in the flesh, though he had a brief prophetic glimpse on St John the Baptist's day in 1844 of Dalgairns' friend Fr Dominic Barberi, an Italian Passionist, who as a farm lad had dreamed of England's conversion to Catholicism. Newman was also losing one of his ties to Anglicanism, his oldest Oxford friend Bowden, who was dying of tuberculosis at Roehampton. Bowden was 'most wonderfully calm and cheerful . . . ' Newman wrote to Keble. 'As I sat by him, he could not help half laughing again and again, and could only say "It is your face – it reminds me of old times".'[6] While in London in July, Newman sat for a drawing by George Richmond commissioned by Henry Wilberforce. It remains the most glamorous likeness of him, an effect partly achieved by omitting his glasses, which were inserted by Maria Giberne in her copy. The image has a smiling serenity and self-confidence that belies the sickness in the sitter's heart.

Newman did not trust his feelings; yet it would be difficult to say if his reason or his feelings told him that Rome was right and England wrong. 'I have acted like persons who pinch themselves to be sure that they are not asleep and dreaming', he wrote to Badeley. 'That I had one and one only view was certain, but then was it a delusion? Was it the accident of an excitement?' He compared his own dispirited condition to that 'of a patient in a consumption' and his friends, who deny that his symptoms are fatal, despite the physician who knows otherwise: 'we are children, of this dying or dead system in which we have lived all our days. We cannot, we will not, believe what the real state of the case is. We cannot be persuaded to open our eyes . . . Consider the shock with which child, parent, or wife hears of the inevitable blow. It is like a dream. Nothing would convince but the actual sight of the calamity which cannot be explained away'. There was 'no bier and funeral of a Church' to convince the reluctant believer that its malady was fatal.[7] Newman was, if not certain of Rome, yet sure that such certainty of Rome's rightness would come.

The attendant sense of the hopelessness of Anglicanism was reinforced by the Church of England's willingness to tolerate anything but Catholicism itself. When in 1844 W. G. Ward caused a furore by upholding Roman Catholic conceptions of sanctity and doctrine in his book *The Ideal of a Christian Church*, Newman could not think that Archbishop Howley 'will refuse to Wardism what has before now been granted in our Church to Wesleyans, Sabellians, Socinians and Swedenborgians'.[8] Ward, however, gave calculated offence, not merely to Protestants but to most loyal churchmen. He rejoiced – 'oh, most joyful, most wonderful, most unexpected sight!' – that some English churchmen were possessed by 'the whole cycle of

Roman doctrine', and boasted that 'in subscribing the articles I renounce
no one Roman doctrine'.[9] The book revived the topicality of Tract 90,
exposed Newman to further harassment, and opened the last stage of his
Oxonian war. He was, however, a reluctant warrior, a mere camp follower
in the ill-fought and unsuccessful campaign by the Tractarian skirmishers
to defeat the election of the Evangelical Benjamin Symons, 'Big Ben',
Warden of Wadham, to the position of Vice-Chancellor, as a known
opponent of the cause and as one of the doctors who had suspended Pusey.
The opening of a railway station at Oxford brought in a rush of MAs to
crush the Anglo-Catholic party in the vote on Symons, and the Hebdomadal
Board prepared for the next battle against the Anglo-Catholic enemy within.

Newman's remoteness from these events was of a piece with his slow
sundering from his beloved University. 'I go into Oxford, and find myself
out of place', he told Jemima. 'Everything seems to say to me, "This is not
your home". The college seems strange to me, and even the college servants
seem to look as if I were getting strange to them.'[10] The sense of strangeness
was enhanced by Bowden's death on 15 September. 'He was sent to call on
me the day after I came into residence – he introduced me to College and
University – he is the link between me and Oxford. I have ever known
Oxford in him. In losing him I seem to lose Oxford. We used to live in
each other's rooms as Undergraduates, and men used to mistake our names
and call us by each other's. When he married, he used to make a similar
mistake himself, and call me Elizabeth and her Newman. And now for
several years past, though loving him with all my heart, I have shrunk from
him, feeling that I had opinions that I dared not tell him . . . .'[11]

Bowden's death-bed roused a lingering spark in Newman of the reality
of Anglicanism. He wrote to Ambrose St John that 'when one sees so blessed
an end . . . of one who really fed on our ordinances and got strength from
them – and see the same continued in a whole family, the little children
finding quite a solace of their pain in the Daily Prayer, it is impossible not
to feel more at ease in our Church, as at least a sort of Zoar, a place of
refuge and temporary rest because of the steepness of the way. Only may
we be kept from unlawful security, lest we have Moab and Ammon for our
progeny, the enemies of Israel'.[12] Moab and Ammon were the Evangelicals
and liberals. Yet Newman complained to Keble of his spiritual numbness,
as Bowden lay dead in the drawing room of the house in Grosvenor Place
which Newman had known for twenty-four years. 'So many persons have I
seen there, so kind to me – they are all gone. The furniture is all the same
– the ornaments on the mantelpiece – and there lies now my oldest friend,
so dear to me – and I with so little of faith or hope, as dead as a stone, and
detesting myself.'[13]

Keble solaced Newman on his seeming hard-heartedness, commenting on
the ease of Bowden's death: 'it seems very much to realize George Herbert's
notion, of going from earth to paradise as from one room to another . . . '.[14]

'I sobbed bitterly over his coffin', Newman recalled, 'to think that he had left me still dark as to what the way of truth was, and what I ought to do in order to please God and fulfil His will.'[15] This suggests self-preoccupation. But he had much to do in consoling Elizabeth Bowden and her family. He spent Bowden's legacy of a hundred pounds on books, his only luxury. He approved of an application by Dalgairns to Dominic Barberi for hairshirts and scourges. Newman's doctor, Babington, thought him 'shrunk and debilitated' and in danger of 'premature decrepitude'.[16] Newman complained in November 1844 to Jemima's husband that she was being insufficiently sympathetic. She explained that she and aunt Elizabeth had been badly upset by a report in the *Morning Chronicle* that he had become a Papist; he called its author, Golightly, 'a man literally without bowels'.[17] Supporting others, he needed support himself.

Newman was himself assailed with letters either begging him to remain an Anglican, or like the epistles from a strong-minded young lady, Mary Holmes, agonizing in a state of indecision like his own. In autumn 1843, she was writing to him almost daily, as she exalted him into a father-figure who then disappointed her by his lack of warmth: 'you are made of marble . . . ' she wrote in 1844. 'Cruel, hard-hearted Mr Newman, you would not even deign to tell me how you are . . . You keep me in the Church by a spell I cannot comprehend or break.' Newman gently assured her that he had no authority over her, as in November 1844, she departed for Rome, from which she professed she would '*almost* be willing to be killed on the railroad' that he might follow her.[18]

This was a very up-to-date form of martyrdom. His old friend Maria Giberne, the Movement's Pallas Athene, was practising the medieval austerity of sleeping on the floor and rising to read Matins at three. To Maria, Newman insisted in November 1844 that 'I am still where I was; I am not moving. Two things, however, seem plain, that every one is prepared for such an event, next, that every one expects it of me . . . However, I do not think it either suitable or likely.'[19] He still looked to the opinions of others to guide him, and corresponded calmly with Hurrell Froude's brother, William Froude, who tended to scepticism, and with William's wife, a highly cultivated and intelligent woman with whom correspondence was easy. He did not lack for high-placed sympathizers. Judge Sir John Coleridge passed on to Keble the suggestion of a private address of sympathy; 'wherever I go, there is some one to whom you have been a channel of untold blessing', wrote Keble; ' . . . the very air of England around you would say the same, if it could be made vocal'.[20] Some were as vocal about the possibility of his secession. 'Here at home in our own communion, what confusion to our friends, what triumph to your enemies! . . . What hope, humanly speaking, can remain to our poor humbled Church, after such a blow? . . . '

Tu Patronus es, tu Parens,
Si deseris tu, periimus.

[Thou our Patron art, and Parent,
If thou dost desert, we perish.][21]

One young lady disciple, later a Dominican nun, Maria Poole, whom Newman described as 'a gifted and deeply earnest lady', was more humorously to describe him as one of the chief of a body of pilgrims seeking the king's highway across a barren common. She then saw 'the most daring of our leaders, (the same who had first forced his way through the palisade, . . .) suddenly stop short, and declare that he would go on no further. He did not, however, take the leap at once, but quietly sat down on the top of the fence with his feet hanging towards the road, as if he meant to take his time about it, and let himself down easily'. Newman described his own condition as one of 'a religious selfishness'; he had to save his own soul on the principle of 'Physician, heal thyself'.[22]

Such healing was difficult under the fire provoked by W. G. Ward. The Hebdomadal Board summoned Ward in late November 1844 to ask if he renounced six of the most sensational extracts from the *Ideal*. He declined to comment, and on 13 December, the Vice-Chancellor made public three resolutions for submission to the vote of Convocation on 13 February 1845, the first declaring the six incriminated extracts inconsistent with the Articles, the second depriving Ward of his degrees, and the third amending the University Statutes with a test requiring subscription to the Articles in the sense intended by their sixteenth-century framers. The proposal for a new test caused uproar among the liberals like Ward's friend A. C. Tait of Balliol and F. D. Maurice, who as Ward pointed out, no more received the Articles in their Tudor sense than he did.

Newman described the Test to Elizabeth Bowden as 'Golightlyism', requiring Golightly's appointment as 'the Oculus Vice Cancellarii' to find out all delinquents from the Tudor formulae.[23] Newman disagreed with Ward that the Articles did not condemn any Roman doctrine, but 'it does hurt one's sense of justice', he wrote to James Mozley, 'that, considering the atrocious heresies which have been published without censure on the other side, he must be visited so severely for being over-Catholic . . . Is it impossible to persuade men who come up against the Test also to vote for Ward?'[24] Degrading Ward also seemed unjust to Newman because '*hardly one or two persons agree with him* . . . hardly any one else is touched – no party is repressed – no principle is affirmed . . . So painful a matter as a formal punishment is not to be inflicted except of necessity . . . '[25] What need, under the circumstances, was there to censure a solitary eccentric like Ward?

The Hebdomadal Board had to abandon its proposal for a test, but that left the Articles open to the possibility of popish interpretation, and provoked a requisition to the Board signed by 474 members of Convocation calling for a censure on Tract 90. The Board now asked Convocation to implement its own condemnation of the Tract of four years before, together with the condemnation of Ward. James Mozley sent the news to Newman, who replied that 'I am . . . as though a dead man, and Hebdomadal Boards can do me neither good nor harm. What really pains me . . . is the pain which friends will feel on my account; yet this pain has a selfish compensation . . . to have friends who feel for me as you do.'[26]

The coupling of Newman with Ward was a blunder, as it enhanced Ward's position among moderate Churchmen fearful of losing Newman and determined to show their love of Newman by defending Ward. Gladstone told Pusey that the measure treated Newman 'worse than a dog',[27] and they were joined by liberals like Stanley, who distributed an elaborate comparison, entitled 'Nemesis', of the attacks on Hampden in 1836 and on Ward and Newman in 1845. 'The victors of 1836 are the victims of 1845. The victors of 1845 are the victims of 1836. The assailants are assailed, the assailed are the assailants. The condemners are condemned, the condemned are the condemners. "The wheel is come full circle".' Stanley urged that there were 'principles of justice equally applicable to opposite cases',[28] and that liberals should be consistent in defending that liberty of interpretation of religious formularies to which Ward and Newman were in principle opposed.

Just as the Proctors had stepped in to save Hampden, so the Proctors in 1845, both friends of Newman, one of them Richard Church, indicated their intention before the Convocation to veto the censure on Newman. Twelve hundred voters, noble and clerical, legal and academic, crowded the Sheldonian Theatre on the 13 February to hear Ward make a brilliant and uncompromising defence of his right to hold Roman Catholic opinions in the Church of England, on the grounds that most Anglicans subscribed to the Articles in a 'non-natural' sense and that the Anglican Church had no coherent and logical theology anyway. This should have outraged every vestige of Anglican loyalty, so the Assembly was stunned by the size of the minority of three hundred and eighty-six who dared to vote not to censure the *Ideal*. The narrow majority for stripping Ward of his degrees, a mere fifty-eight over those opposed, was a moral triumph for its victim. The Proctors then vetoed the censure on Tract 90. Ward was escorted back to Balliol by his old friend Tait, who had voted to condemn the *Ideal*, but not for Ward's degradation, and by a mob of cheering undergraduates who snowballed the Vice-Chancellor. Ward's academic status was now that of an undergraduate himself, and he celebrated the occasion with a set of verses on the theme of 'degradation', to be repeated in the varied accents of his opponents. In his cheerful innocence, he hardly needed Newman's solemn consolation: 'No decree of council or Convocation, unless a special divine power goes with it, can destroy opinion . . . – your course is only just begun . . .'[29]

But their Anglican course was nearly over. Newman's birthday letter from Keble for 1845 dwelt upon the past: 'One thing I should like to do would be to choose out some one of the old days when we most enjoyed ourselves together, either with dear Hurrell Froude or in thought and talk of him, and live over it again for an hour or two –'.[30] In March, Newman told his friends of his intention to resign his fellowship: 'what can be worse than this?' wrote Jemima. 'It is like hearing that some dear friend must die.'[31] Newman's reply declared the 'stern necessity' of his course, in spite of all his inclinations to the contrary. 'I have a good name with many; I am deliberately sacrificing it. I have a bad name with more; I am fulfilling all their worst wishes, and giving them their most coveted triumph. I am distressing all I love, unsettling all I have instructed or aided . . . Pity me, my dear Jemima . . . What hope have I but in Him?'[32]

The only light amid this encircling gloom was shed by Ward's own cheerful buffoonery. He brought public ridicule on Tractarian principles by announcing his marriage in *The Times* as a lower state than the celibacy to which he was too sensual a creature to aspire. Newman was personally more sympathetic to Frederick Oakeley, who shared Ward's opinions, but advertised them in a less flamboyant manner. Oakeley was incumbent of the London chapel of Margaret Street, and his Bishop tried to get him suspended through the ecclesiastical Court of Arches, but he was supported by his congregation which included Hope, Bellasis and Badeley. Newman, however, wrote to Hope and Bellasis urging that Oakeley resign, on the ground of the untenability of remaining a Roman Catholic within the Church of England. Oakeley's subsequent resignation did not inhibit the Bishop from securing his suspension. In July, another Bishop assured the world of Newman's impending secession, and that few would follow him. Ward was received into the Roman Church by a Jesuit in September 1845. According to a dubious but famous legend, the waiting Wiseman heard with doubt a report from the convert Bernard Smith that in June 1845 Newman had received him wearing grey trousers, a sure sign that he no longer regarded himself as a clergyman.[33] But the world wondered at his delay.

The delay was caused by Newman's anxiety to finish his essay on development first. The 'stern necessity' of conversion required a reasoned apology; and for all the temperamental and intellectual differences between Ward and Newman, it was Ward who more than any other of Newman's contemporaries supplied him with the intellectual principle of his subsequent conversion to Rome by thrusting upon him the idea of doctrinal development which Ward had imbibed from the German Catholic J. A. Möhler. Newman's work on development had a slow beginning. He felt thoroughly knocked up and promised himself six months' rest, when at the end of 1844, he finished his notes and translation of Athanasius. Even when the new project made its peremptory demands, he spent, he told Mrs William Froude, 'two months in reading and writing which came to nothing' at the beginning of 1845, and then when fairly launched in March, had to write and rewrite again. 'Perhaps one gets over-sensitive even about style, as one gets on in life . . . Besides re-writing, every part has to be worked out and defined as in moulding a statue. I get on, as a person walks with a lame ankle, who does get on, and gets to his journey's end, but not comfortably.'[34] He had written three chapters by June, and described it as 'a sort of obscure philosophical work, . . . with little to interest, and much to disappoint. But I hate making a splash'.[35]

The book on development was, however, a deeply personal one, as it was a projection of Newman's own capacity for growth in mind and soul to the whole of Christian history. Implicit rather than explicit in the work is a comparison of the institution and the individual; Christianity itself must show its capacity for growth and change, as in the mind seeking truth, and the soul seeking holiness. Newman had himself undergone a development from Evangelicalism via liberalism to a dogmatic High Churchmanship of his own defining: 'here below, to live is to change', he wrote, 'and to be perfect is to have changed often';[36] and that was to open him to the principle that Rome is the One True Church because she has within herself an inner power of development and growth, which is the only evidence of life.

The idea of development was also an answer to the stock polemical charge against Rome that Rome had corrupted early Christianity by adding to it new doctrines like those concerning the Virgin or the Papacy. But the principle of development was the resolution of another problem which was posed to Anglo-Catholicism or indeed to any form of traditional Christianity, the difference between the New Testament and the highly sophisticated Christological and Trinitarian dogmas of the Nicene and Athanasian Creeds. Anglo-Catholics appealed to the fixed standard of Antiquity, yet Antiquity showed development within itself. Indeed Protestants invoked the fixed standard of Scripture, though this also showed internal development. Newman insisted that he could not be blamed if the principle which made sense of the changes within Scripture and Tradition and which justified the Athanasian Creed, also justified the sixteenth-century Tridentine 'Creed of Pope Pius IV'. Some such theory was needed to explain the occurrence of doctrinal development in the ancient Church, and it was not his fault that the theory converted the stock objection to Rome, that Rome had changed, into a presumptive argument in her favour.

In this, Newman was also reversing his view on the seventeenth-century difference between the French Jesuit Petavius and the Anglican George Bull: Petavius had described, Bull had generally denied, a lack of doctrinal uniformity before the Council of Nicaea. Yet Roman Catholicism had been prepared to boast that it was '*semper eadem*', unchanging. It is true that some of its theologians had allowed for the deduction of new dogma from existing dogma, or the more explicit teaching of dogmas held implicitly already. Möhler added the life-giving principle of the Spirit in the Church. But though Newman mentioned Möhler in his completed work, the reference only proved that he had not read him; and the form at least of his argument for development was really all his own.

The argument, however, was couched with becoming modesty. Newman did not pretend that it had a binding certainty. He called it an hypothesis to account for a difficulty, the existence of doctrinal development in Christian history. In so far as he sought to demonstrate that there had been change, he claimed to be writing historically. In so far as he sought to interpret this change, he rested not on certainty but on Butler's probability principle. He especially relied on one antecedent probability, that if God had given his Spirit to his Church, then his Revelation, granted in Scripture and Tradition, had been accorded divine protection. The truth of those doctrinal developments which had occurred could only be guaranteed by the presumption of the Spirit's abiding presence in the Church. It is, then, the rather tentative hypothetical, historical and probabilist elements of the work which lend it charm; for it sought not to prove the truth of Roman Christianity as a logical certainty, but merely to remove a popular objection to it.

Yet the aim of the work is even narrower than this suggests. It is certainly not addressed to sceptics or unbelievers. Nor is it addressed to Protestants, whom Newman summarily dismissed with an appeal to Christian history. Christianity, as a great brute historical fact, had existed for eighteen centuries. Yet before 1520, there were no Protestants, who ever since that date, have been a minority in Christendom. Looked at impartially, classical, historical, dogmatic ecclesiastical Christianity is Catholic. To be deep in history is to cease to be Protestant, which is why Protestants make their appeal to the Bible alone. To be deep in history is to be Catholic; and here the choice really lies between England and Rome. Gladstone was to complain that Newman ignored the Eastern Orthodox; but then Newman regarded the Orthodox as witnesses for the greater part of Catholicity, and his search for a religious body which was organically and authoritatively one implied a western ecclesiology and not an eastern one. In the course of the work, Newman turned aside to refute the Protestants; but in essence, the book was addressed to his Anglo-Catholic readers and his dying Anglo-Catholic self.

Anglo-Catholics, he argued, rest their case on the so-called 'canon' defined by the fifth-century Vincent of Lerins, that the Catholic faith is what all Christians everywhere at all times believe. Thus as a matter of history, a Roman corruption like the Papacy, or the veneration of the Virgin and Saints, can be distinguished from a truly Catholic doctrine like the authority of the bishop because all Catholics everywhere have acknowledged bishops whereas not all have accepted popes. Yet when applied to church history, the canon seems to fail: for in the centuries before Nicaea, the Fathers had often erred, as in asserting the inequality and subordination of the Son to the Father. Antiquity also bore witness to different Catholic doctrines with differing degrees of evidence, but this was not wholly a testimony against Rome. Thus there was less early evidence for a belief in Original Sin than for a primitive idea of purgatory; more evidence for the need for unity than for the Apostolic Succession, for the papal primacy than for the Real Presence in the Eucharist, and for the invocation of saints than for the canon of Scripture. In short, there was more clear evidence for specifically Roman Catholic doctrines than for doctrines which England and Rome already held together; and an Anglo-Catholic who accepted one set of 'Catholic' developments had no intrinsic reason for not accepting Roman ones as well.

Any such changes must, of course, still bear testimony to a once and for all divine Revelation; and Christian history has been the stage for the unfolding of the original Christian idea. Newman refused to define too explicitly the Christian 'idea' thus divinely revealed; he described it as making an 'impression' on the mind of Christ's disciples, an impression so complex, so various, so rich in its possibilities that centuries might be employed in understanding all that it contained. Truth is the daughter of time, and an idea shows what it is in what it becomes: a principle which Newman thought justified the interpretation of the early evidence for Christianity by the abundant information about it in the fourth and fifth centuries. The content of the Christian faith had been rendered explicit as it evolved forms of worship and found expression through once-pagan philosophies and political and social systems, and as it applied its ethic to the ever-changing circumstances of a wider world.

Development had, therefore, demonstrated the infinite fecundity of Christianity, on the analogy of change in nature, and as the divine gift grew and developed with the natural and historical parts of it. Development had also occurred through the rise of heretical ideas, which had then provoked doctrinal definition to condemn them. Theological reflection was required on questions which Scripture had left open, like the baptism of infants or the state of the dead between death and Judgement Day; and Scripture – even the canon of Scripture – had demanded an interpretation which the Scriptures do not supply. Indeed the Scriptures remain an unexplored and unsubdued land, with highlands and valleys, full of concealed wonders and choice treasure; or, to change the metaphor, a treasure house from which the Church is ever bringing forth treasures old and new. There had been development within Scripture, and its metaphors of Christ's kingdom, the seed of the sower, the grain of mustard seed, suggest that principle of life and growth by which the Christian idea ever unfolds and renews itself.

But not all change is development, or Protestantism and liberalism could be defended by it. Rather, there are seven historical criteria by which developments can be known to be true and not corruptions. A true development must preserve the 'type' of early Christianity. It must show a continuity with it. It must have a power to assimilate new ideas. It must flow logically from the apostolic faith. It must be true to its original in the past, but it must also anticipate its future. A true development must display a chronic vigour – perhaps dying in one place, but gaining life in another. In the end, heresies prove themselves to be such by dying; orthodoxy always wins. In this, Newman's dominant model of the Church is an organic one, in that the note of a true development is simply life: a false development dies, like the rotten limb which falls from a tree. But he expounds a subordinate theme of development as a complex, implicit, non-deductive and non-syllogistic logical progression. His theory would be disproved if it could be shown that in essential matters, the Church had contradicted herself, so that the theory implies her infallibility. 'Indeed it is one of the popular charges against the Catholic Church at this very time, that she is "incorrigible"; – change she cannot, if we listen to St. Athanasius or St. Leo; change she never will, if we believe the controversialist or alarmist of the present day.'[37]

There is only a verbal contradiction between this claim that the Church never changes and that to be perfect is to have changed often. Development is not purposeless random change; it is logically and biologically determined by the Church's existing identity. Thus her power of development is confined by her past and present and future, and is limited by the inner logic of the Christian idea, which is always true to itself. The Church can no more permit lasting false development than the body can grow an extra limb.

In this, the *Essay on Development* is essentially conservative: it is not a defence of any sort of change, as some liberals might suggest, but of those changes which can be shown to have a biological and logical continuity from the past into the present. Yet such continuities can only be demonstrated with probability, and the greatness of the *Essay* lies not so much in its intrinsic logical force as in the power with which it evokes the imaginative resemblance in 'type' between early Christianity and modern Romanism. Not that the resemblance is a perfect mirror image, for the Church could only be one with the early Church if she had the evidence of eighteen centuries of life and growth upon her. Rather, the Catholic Church is the same in all times and places, as a grown tree is one with the acorn from which it sprang, or as a child is the man whom he becomes. The child does not exactly resemble the man, but there is an identity of type, and here, Newman reverted to Wiseman's suggestion that if Athanasius or Ambrose were to visit modern England, they would turn aside from the glorious Establishment to the humble popish mission chapel: they would recognize there the child fully grown.

Perhaps the chief of these points of imaginative resemblance is the one which spoke to Newman's Evangelical other-worldliness. One passage of rhetoric summarizes its many aspects, common to ancient and modern Catholic Christianity:

There is a religious communion claiming a divine commission, and calling all other religious bodies around it heretical or infidel; it is a well-organized, well-disciplined body; it is a sort of secret society, binding together its members by influences and by engagements which it is difficult for strangers to ascertain. It is spread over the known world; it may be weak or insignificant locally, but it is strong on the whole from its continuity; it is smaller than other religious bodies together, but larger than each separately. It is a natural enemy to governments external to itself; it is intolerant and engrossing, and tends to a new modelling of society; it breaks laws, it divides families. It is a gross superstition; it is charged with the foulest crimes; it is despised by the intellect of the day; it is frightful to the imagination of the many. And there is but one communion such.[38]

The true Church will be despised by the intellect of the day, enlightened statesmen will scorn it as the superstition of the multitude, and yet it frightens their imagination. Repulsiveness to power and authority and intellect becomes a defining note or mark of the Christian Church.

This is, on one level, a return to Newman's Evangelicalism. The true Church consists in that body of Christians called out of the wicked world. The argument was appropriate to Newman's condition of leaving a rich and powerful Establishment for an outcast despised sect. It less clearly applied to those times and places in which the Catholic Church is or had been supported by the State and was powerful herself; but then Newman was to develop the idea that such worldly prosperity for the Church might not save more souls.

In his correspondence with Gladstone, who had just resigned from the government over its increased grant to the Irish Catholic seminary of Maynooth, Newman enunciated the double principle which he thought Gladstone shared, that the State should ideally have a Christian conscience, and yet the Christian should not abandon his duty of public service to the State, under the new circumstances in which it was ceasing to have one.[39] Gladstone's protest against a government grant to the Catholic seminary had been in line with Newman's old insistence on the Anglican confessional State. Gladstone now thought the Maynooth grant a proper one, but would not remain in government to administer a policy of which he had once disapproved. It was by different theological paths that Newman and Gladstone were forced to recognize the new circumstances in which the Church could no longer expect the State to support Christian truth. The Anglo-Catholic movement had two interdependent ideals, the restoration of a traditionally Christian England and the creation of a powerful and independent English Church. By abandoning the State Church, Newman embraced a vision of the Church in which the kingdoms of this world were nothing.

Newman's argument could stress the resemblance between the ancient and modern Church, because the modern Church was returning in some degree back into the old Church of the catacombs. Yet one aspect of that resemblance might, on Protestant principles, have pointed Newman to a different conclusion. The Scots Evangelicals in 1843 showed their other-worldly horror of a Church controlled by worldly statesmen by 'disrupting' and seceding from the Presbyterian Establishment. The Calvinist secession churches elsewhere in Europe did the same; and if sheer repulsiveness to worldlings constituted true Christianity, there was much to commend the Irvingites and Plymouth Brethren. The conclusion of Newman's *Essay* again echoes the Evangelical teaching of Thomas Scott's *Force of Truth*, and reminds the reader of the Evangelical origins in Newman of his call to other-worldliness:

Such were the thoughts concerning the 'Blessed Vision of Peace', of one whose long-continued petition had been that the Most Merciful would not despise the work of His own Hands, nor leave him to himself; – while yet his eyes were dim, and his breast laden, and he could but employ Reason in the things of Faith. And now, dear Reader, time is short, eternity is long. Put not from you what you have here found; regard it not as mere matter of present controversy; set not out resolved to refute it, and looking about for the best way of doing so; seduce not yourself with the imagination that it comes of disappointment, or disgust, or restlessness, or wounded feeling, or undue sensibility, or other weakness. Wrap not yourself round in associations of years past; nor determine that to be truth which you wish to be so, nor make an idol of cherished anticipations. Time is short, eternity is long.

Nunc dimittis servum tuum, Domine,
Secundum verbum tuum in pace:
Quia viderunt oculi mei salutare tuum.[40]

It was just such a call which had made Newman an Evangelical, and now made him a Roman Catholic.

'As I advanced', he recalled of the writing of the *Essay on Development*, 'my difficulties so cleared away that I ceased to speak of "the Roman Catholics", and boldly called them Catholics. Before I got to the end, I resolved to be received, and the book remains in the state in which it was then, unfinished.'[41] He had wanted to delay till the book was actually out before submitting to Rome, but in late September 1845, a number of his younger disciples took matters into their own hands. Richard Stanton indicated that he intended becoming a Roman Catholic when he briefly left Littlemore on the 24th, Dalgairns was received into the Roman Church by Barberi at the Passionist house at Aston on 29th, and on the 30 September, Ambrose St John was received at the Catholic college of Prior Park near Bath: 'when they went', wrote Newman, 'it was as if I were losing my own bowels'.[42] On 3 October, he wrote resigning his Oriel Fellowship to Hawkins, who replied coldly hoping that even as a Roman Catholic, Newman would 'at least be saved from some of the worst errors of the Church of Rome, such as praying to human Mediators or falling down before images – because in you, with all the great advantages with which God has blessed and tried you, I must believe such errors to be most deeply sinful'.[43]

Then came the external call. Dalgairns' friend Barberi was to stay at Littlemore on his way to Belgium. He arrived on the evening of 8 October 1845, soaked from hours in the rain on top of the Birmingham coach. Newman knelt before the dripping priest beside the fire and asked for admission into 'the One Fold of the Redeemer'.[44] Two of his followers, Stanton and Frederick Bowles, were received with him next day. One genteel family at Littlemore, the Woodmasons, who had a son intending to go to Oriel, decided to become Roman Catholics as well.

Newman had written to Henry Wilberforce announcing his intention to become a Catholic on the 7th, and to dozens of friends and relations on the following days. There was a special note containing 'sweet words' for his aunt Elizabeth who, he learned from Jemima, had first reacted to the news as 'the greatest grief that has ever befallen her'.[45] 'He alone', responded Newman, 'knows how much you are in my heart, or how it pierces my heart so to distress you.'[46] John Mozley had replied with such harshness to Newman's enquiry about publishing the *Development of Doctrine* that Newman 'could have gone to bed from very grief or despair. I walked out, instead of working, sick at heart, with hands hanging down and feeble knees'. Mozley assumed the book would attack the Church of England. Jemima was the medium for the shame and complaints of the family, and wanted her brother to leave Littlemore. She still corresponded, and in 1848, Newman dined with the household on his way through Derby, and repeated the psalms with his aunt and nephew. But Jemima could or would not have her brother in her house thereafter, and he felt bitterly the loss of not knowing her growing children. He never saw Harriett again, and did not see her daughter Grace again until he was in his ninetieth year, two days before his death. Tom Mozley resolved his divisions by becoming a writer for *The Times*, and resigned his parish in 1847. James Mozley was the sharpest critic of the *Development of Doctrine*. Newman's Foudrinier cousins found it inconvenient to receive him for many years.

Some friends were more understanding than family. 'Tu autem, Domine, miserere nobis. E. B. P. Kyrie eleison Christe Eleison Kyrie Eleison',[47] wrote Pusey on the back of Newman's letter announcing his conversion; but he had already reconciled himself to the belief that his friend would be labouring elsewhere in the Lord's vineyard. Keble walked about with Newman's note all day at Hursley, 'not daring to open it, knowing intuitively what tidings it told'.[48] Characteristically, Keble accused himself of coldness. 'I keep on thinking', he wrote to Newman, ' "If I had been different perhaps N. would have been guided to see things differently, and we might have been spared so many broken hearts and bewildered spirits" . . . My dearest Newman, you have been a kind and helpful friend to me in a way in which scarce any one else could have been . . . I must cling to the belief that we are not really parted . . . God bless you and reward you a thousandfold [for] all your help in every way to me unworthy, and to so many others. May you have peace where you are gone, and help us in some way to get peace; but somehow I scarce think it will be in the way of controversy.'[49]

There was no interruption of Newman's friendship with Henry Wilberforce, and old Routh of Magdalen continued to be kind as of old. So did the Oxford astronomer Manuel Johnson, with whom he stayed on his last night in Oxford. Newman also remained on good terms with the Littlemore squire, Charles Crawley, to whom he was to arrange the sale of the 'monastery' land. His humbler parishioners remembered him kindly. Others were less kind. He did not see Rogers, Copeland, Isaac Williams and the Kebles from 1846 until the 1860s. Henry Woodgate did not speak to him for twenty years. Samuel Rickards never spoke to him again. To become a Roman Catholic was still a sort of living death, of exclusion from many public employments and of ostracism from decent society. The exclusion from Oxford was a bitter one. 'Catholics did not make us Catholics; Oxford made us Catholics', he was to write;[50] but he had left Oxford to the liberals who, he believed, had beaten him on a fair field; the secularization of the University, in part the consequence of the divisons that he had created, began five years later. To the later liberal Mark Pattison, the Movement's failure in Oxford was an escape from nightmare, and a return to proper scholarly study. Newman made of it an elegiac tragedy. 'There used to be much snapdragon growing on the walls opposite my freshman's rooms there', he was to recall of Trinity in the *Apologia*, 'and I had for years taken it as the emblem of my own perpetual residence even unto death in my University . . . I have never seen Oxford since [1846], excepting its spires, as they are seen from the railway'.[51] From a purely worldly view, he had abandoned almost everything – incumbency, fellowship, even his reading public and the profits from his writings, above all his good name and reputation. It was to take decades to recover even the last of them.

Part Three

The Holy Roman Church

19

The Roman Oratory

'I hardly ever was at a Roman service; even abroad I knew no Roman Catholics', Newman told Jemima in the year before his conversion. 'I have no sympathies with them as a party. I am giving up everything.'[1] 'I kept aloof from Catholics', he later wrote, 'from a feeling of duty.'[2] Newman did not meet until the day after his conversion the Jesuit missioner at Oxford, Robert Newsham, who had ministered in Newman's former parish of St Clement's for nearly thirty years; and his new communion was either abhorrent or unknown to him. He was entering the Church of the Irish, whose radical politics had always appalled him, and of Spain and France, England's traditional enemies. He was violating his conservative instincts as a Tory and his patriotic instincts as an Englishman. He was forty-four, and most of his life seemed to be over. He was joining a despised and outcast sect, which he had opposed and vilified, and which might expect him to begin his work and thought and career all over again. The symbol of the transition was Fr Dominic's administration of conditional baptism to the converts, to make up for any defect in the Anglican rite. Newman was confirmed at the Midland seminary of Oscott on 1 November, taking the additional name of Mary, and he noted that Rome had 'never acknowledged English Orders', so that whatever his own doubts about the matter, he was a mere 'layman in her eyes'.[3]

His intellectual position was also an awkward one. He had been converted to Roman Catholicism by his own logic, not Rome's, almost to a faith of his own defining. In the yet unpublished *Essay on the Development of Christian Doctrine*, he had seemingly rejected the normal Roman apologetic stance, that the Church's faith was true because it was always the same. Rather, he had argued that the faith was fixed in the deeper sense that it had preserved its essential identity by changing. Wiseman at first 'absolutely declined' to read the *Essay*, on the ground that while it might contain error, as Newman's 'course of reasoning', 'it was *a fact*, which all his seeing could not alter'.[4] Wiseman briefly changed his mind, but on Newman's protest, he returned the proofs of the volume unread, with a letter from the Pope to Wiseman congratulating ' "Joannem Henricum Newman Puseistarum factionis ducem" on his recovery from the heresy in which "miserrimè jacuerat" '.[5] Wiseman combined this kindness with the offer to Newman of the residence of Old Oscott College, named by Newman Maryvale, near the splendid Pugin Gothic seminary of New Oscott of which Wiseman was President, six miles from Birmingham. Old Oscott was 'dismally ugly',[6] but with room for twenty to thirty people, it would enable Newman's converts to keep together under one roof, as they prepared themselves for the Roman priesthood. Maryvale was to be to Newman a portent. Wiseman encouraged him in a 'special reverence and admiration'[7] for the founder of the Italian Oratory, St Philip Neri, the 'Apostle of Rome', who was said to have converted the sixteenth-century pagan city back to Christianity; and Maryvale in Latin was Sancta Maria in Valle, in Italian Santa Maria in Vallicella, the dedication of St Philip's Chiesa Nuova in Rome.

Wiseman's kindness did something to smooth over the strangeness to Newman of the English Roman Catholic tradition. Catholicism had survived in the sixteenth century as a radical redefinition of the unreformed medieval Catholicism which at Elizabeth's accession in 1558 had included the great mass of Englishmen. The new Protestant State and bishops thought that the old faith would die away. They were confounded by the Oxford Movement of their generation, the stream of Oxbridge graduates who left England to found and staff new continental Catholic seminaries in Douai, Lisbon, Seville and Rome. These priest-manufactures despatched a new generation of missionaries to England, bringing the good news from Trent and dying for the work of bringing it. Apart from two episcopal appointments in the 1620s, the mission Church which they founded was without even a provisional hierarchy until the Pope appointed one between 1685 and 1688. Its clergy were in disproportionate numbers regulars, mostly Jesuits or Benedictines, whose disputes with the secular priesthood were to endure for more than three centuries. Its congregations were dominated by aristocratic and gentry households in northern England, above all in Lancashire. These genteel families appointed and dismissed the clergy. They made the characteristic unit of recusant Catholicism a country estate with a chaplain and hidden chapel, and their sons and daughters financed and staffed the complex of English Catholic colleges, convents and monasteries on the continent. Despite the many Catholic martyrs and legislation designed to beggar the Catholic laity, English Catholicism survived the early modern era as the religion of the quality, and that gave English Popery a certain social chic which has lasted ever since.

By 1800, however, this rural, lay-controlled and upper-crust institution was undergoing a transformation into a wholly different kind of Church. The Evangelical Revival among Nonconformists had its Roman Catholic parallel in a new political activism and middle-class religious seriousness. The Emancipation Acts of 1778 and 1791 legalized Catholic worship. The French Revolution returned the English convents and colleges on the continent to England, and despatched seven thousand Gallic priests and religious to exile in Albion; most of them were birds of passage and pensioners on

English charity, though some did pastoral work of lasting effectiveness. The Emancipation Act of 1829 threw open public and political office to Catholics on a tide of democratic and revolutionary Catholic peasant agitation in Ireland. The immigration of rural Catholics to the towns created new urban missions beyond gentry influence, and these missions were multiplied and swollen by the ever rising pauper influx of Irish people into England who were accustomed to priestly leadership and laid the foundations for a new kind of English clericalism. Clericalism meant the creation of an effective authority in the bishop, and Rome recognized the boom in the Roman Church in England by doubling the number of its episcopal Vicars Apostolic from four to eight in 1840. New churches, convents and schools radiated an air of renaissance which was to under-emphasize the achievement of the tradition in the past, in the excitement of expansion in the present and hope for the future.

The heart of the matter was the transformation of the insular temper of English Catholic devotion. English Catholics used as their manual of prayer the eighteenth-century Bishop Richard Challoner's *Garden of the Soul*, a work which was based on a piety rooted in English medieval mysticism. This was in keeping with a reserve of feeling natural to an intensely private faith which had of necessity dispensed with the public ritual and flamboyant aids to worship of the Counter-Reformation baroque. Until the nineteenth century, the Mass itself was called 'prayers'. Priests were plain Mr, not 'Father', and had nothing distinctively priestly in their demeanour or dress.

This decorum had been reinforced by Augustan formalism, but it succumbed to the religious excitements of the new age. The Romantic mood demanded its devotional due. The Gothic Revival school around the Earl of Shrewsbury set out to reintroduce the whole paraphernalia of medieval architecture, art, music and liturgy, from pointed arches, encaustic tiles and stained glass to vestments, incense and plain chant. Wiseman spearheaded the popularization of the devotions of Counter-Reformation Rome, with a novel ardour and tenderness of sentiment towards the Virgin and Saints and the Blessed Sacrament, while Fr George Spencer preached his crusade of prayer for the conversion of England. The imported Italian orders, Rosminian and Passionist, introduced a revivalist fervour in preaching to reclaim poor Irish Catholics and to convert rich English ones. Here was a wealth of possibilities for tension and conflict, in a community comprised of aristocrats and paupers, English and Irish, radicals and Whigs and Tories, and a laity losing its authority to a clergy traditionally divided among themselves. All these were exposed to a transformation from within by a range of influences, Romantic, medievalist and Italian, and all were a prey to those ailments inseparable from new forms of energy and life.

The converts like Newman were strong-minded men and women who did nothing to discourage these controversies. Newman chose the Counter-Reformation Jesuit St Francis Borgia over the apostle to the English, St

Paulinus, as the patron for his first Communion, and in his early years as a Roman Catholic, he was to veer to Wiseman's sort of baroque Catholicism against both the medievalist Goths and the restraint of the English Roman Catholic tradition. Newman was dazzled by the devotional luxury of his new communion after the spartan diet of Anglicanism, and found in the presence of the Blessed Sacrament and in the Catholic love of the saints, so like his own love of friends, new and unspeakable comforts.

He could, however, be exquisitely sensitive towards his old friends in the Anglican communion, above all, to his master, Keble: 'May the Holy Trinity, Father, Son, and Spirit, return to you sevenfold, My dear Keble, all the good, of which you have been the instrument towards me, since I first knew you', he wrote. 'To you I owe it, humanly speaking, that I am what and where I am. Others have helped me in various ways, but no one can I name but you, among those I ever knew, except one who is gone . . . '[8] Yet their relationship ceased in 1846, when Newman did not reply to the last of Keble's letters. Pusey was hurt that the converts sought to convert others, instead of being content with labouring elsewhere in the Lord's vineyard. Newman dwelt cruelly on Pusey's lack of credentials for 'keeping souls in a system which you cannot . . . rest upon any authority besides your own'.[9] Some High Churchmen resented the converts; William Upton Richards thought that Newman had undergone 'deterioration' in 'ethos' since his conversion,[10] a charge to be reiterated when Newman was tried for libel. Others were still divided against themselves. Not all who thought of conversion followed it through, but hesitated, went half way and then turned back. William Alexander removed his name from his college books and set off for Birmingham, but changed his mind that night 'in the small attic of a cheap hotel',[11] and ended up years later as the Anglican Primate of All Ireland.

'To argue and preach out of place is just the way to disgust Englishmen with religion',[12] wrote Newman. The best argument was the convert himself. But to those whom he had real hopes of converting, Newman could be direct. 'Oh my dear B. *how long*? Is it safe?'[13] he wrote to Bloxam, while he told Henry Wilberforce that 'You must go one way or the other', and that Henry's 'fear' of his influence was 'a piece of nauseous humbug',[14] though he then apologized. Bloxam was to remain a life-long member of the Church of England, the Henry Wilberforce family was to take another four years to leave the Establishment, and the most intellectually brilliant of the family, Robert Wilberforce, took four years longer. But others in Newman's circle followed his immediate lead: his former curate David Lewis; Maria Giberne, who set herself up as a painter in Rome; Henry Bacchus, the brother of Maria's friend Selina; Manning's cousin the Marquise de Salvo, the widow of a Sicilian nobleman; and the largest single contingent, brought over by Frederick Faber, who was received with his two servants and a band of young men from his parish, whom he had been teaching a popish path to sanctity. Faber left to the affectionate applause of his villagers, who had been touched by his devotion to them, and Newman had to counsel Faber to return two boys, who fled from home to follow him, to their irate father.

Faber's disciples included Thomas Knox, the grandson of the Earls of Ranfurly and Kilmorey, and Newman's former eccentric curate, John Morris. The flow of conversions continued through 1846, with the Ryders, who to Newman's delight brought in his first Catholic godson, Lisle, and gave him another reason for gently upbraiding the father of another godson, Henry Wilberforce. Newman had more to do with the reception of Bowden's widow Elizabeth, whose father Sir John Swinburne, of the old Northumbrian family, had been baptized a Catholic in 1762, but at his majority had conformed to the Church of England. 'I will be no party to this baiting of you', Newman told Elizabeth. '. . . I am not capable of stunning you with arguments, or stifling you with folios, or subduing you by an urgent tone or a confident manner.'[15] Newman's relaxed approach had its reward. Elizabeth's younger son Charles was Newman's godson, and came over to Rome soon after, but the older boy John was at Eton, and was torn between his mother's change of religion and his uncle Henry's desire that he should remain an Anglican. Newman showed tact and wisdom in letting John choose for himself. 'Leave nature to itself',[16] he wrote, a satisfaction to be crowned when John decided to become an Oratorian priest, and when in 1852 Henry Bowden was received into the Church with his family. Newman was perhaps longest in angling for the soul of Mrs Catherine Froude, a highly intelligent woman who was mother to another of Newman's godsons, and who over the years received from Newman a complete correspondence course in the philosophical fundamentals of the faith. She became a Catholic in 1857. The *Grammar of Assent* was to be written for her unconvertible engineer-husband.

The Romeward movement was, then, sometimes of individuals, sometimes of families, sometimes of friends. George Dudley Ryder was the son of the Church's first Evangelical bishop, but was also cousin to the convert Ambrose Lisle Phillipps and brother-in-law to Manning and the Wilberforces. Elizabeth Bowden was linked to a vanishing seigneurial Catholicism, and had a convert cousin who was to become the parish priest at the church she was to build in Fulham. The converts were nearly all the refined and cultivated products of the Anglican Revival, middle-class people with gentry or noble connections, who had fallen under the spell of Anglo-Catholicism. None were members of Newman's family, and it was his friends and not his middle-class commercial family who accompanied him to Rome.

Newman's treatment by his new co-religionists was at first one of pride. To the letter of congratulation from the English curial Cardinal, Charles Acton, who was from a Shropshire county family inter-married with the German and Italian aristocracies, he described himself as 'one about whom there has been far more talk for good and bad than he deserves . . .'.[17] But he was warmly received when on 21 November 1845, he visited the new Pugin Gothic seminary of St Edmund's, Ware, and there formed a life-long friendship with Robert Whitty, 'who, though an Irishman', he wrote, 'is one of the most remarkable persons I have seen'.[18] He arrived at Oscott again on 24 November, amid the chaos and noise of a festival in honour of St Cecilia, and 'found the whole establishment tuning fiddles and making punch'. The festal punch, which Wiseman insisted was lemonade, was so strong that Newman 'was obliged to dilute it to twice or thrice its quantity with water'. The Cecilia concert was splendid, though he could not rid his mind of the tune of the concluding comic song Mynheer Vandunck, and sat writing in the Stranger's Room, 'the chimney almost vibrating – my ankles fanned with a continuous stream of air – and the shrieking and screaming of the keyhole and casements making me shiver'. 'I think they fancy I never eat', he complained. ' . . . I literally have had to pick up a crust from the floor left at breakfast . . . '[19]

From the uncomfortable glory of Oscott's Pugin Gothic, Newman took his disciple Robert Coffin to be received into the Church amid the neo-classical splendour of the school at Prior Park, the megalomaniac creation of the late Benedictine Bishop Peter Augustine Baines, who in setting up the institution, which boasted a quarter of a mile of facade, had tried to wreck Downside and Ampleforth Abbeys. Newman set out on St Stephen's day in 1845 to make a further tour from Littlemore of Catholic establishments, St Edmund's, Oscott, the Passionists at Aston and Rosminians at Ratcliffe, the Cistercians at Mount St Bernard, the Mary Ward Sisters at York and the great northern seminary of Ushaw, where he was 'especially pleased' and found its President Charles Newsham, brother of the Oxford missioner, 'a very taking man'.[20] He went on to the Jesuits at Stonyhurst, which he reached after a ten-mile walk, met Catholic bishops at York, Durham and Liverpool, and returned via Oscott and London to Littlemore. 'This is being a pilgrim', he told Miss Giberne, 'though I had no peas in my shoes.'[21]

On 22 February 1846, he left Littlemore, and 'could not help kissing my bed, and mantelpiece [sic], and other parts of the house',[22] for memory of his happy quiet time there. On the fifth anniversary of the attack on Tract 90 by the Heads of Houses, he heard that the Pope was sending him a silver crucifix with a piece of the true cross; and in April, he learned that he was to go to Rome in June to be prepared for the priesthood at the College of the Sacred Propaganda, the great international missionary College of the Roman Catholic Church. 'I shall be like a child going to a new school',[23] he wrote to Mrs Bowden. 'Only fancy', he added to George Ryder, whom he congratulated on his conversion, 'my return to school at my age.'[24] The movement meant leaving for a time his community at Maryvale, but he was glad to escape the ferment of Oscott under Wiseman. 'The place has no bottom . . . ', he wrote to Dalgairns. 'Oscott is a place of dissipation. Tribes of women, and hosts of visitors.' Remarkably, Newman still thought Wiseman 'a punctual precise man',[25] but his natural element was creative chaos, as Newman was to discover.

There is little contemporary evidence for Newman's later thoughts in dejection of the discomfort of his time at Maryvale, when he 'was the gaze of so many eyes at Oscott, as if some wild incomprehensible beast, caught by the hunter, and a spectacle for Dr. Wiseman to exhibit to strangers, as himself being the hunter who captured it!' He felt afterwards that he had been urged to conform to 'ways, habits, religious observances . . . , without any delicacy towards my feelings', and that he was lectured by old Catholics and converts: by Wiseman through John Morris, whose sojourn at Maryvale was a failure, as he expected others to wait upon him; by Canon Lorain of Langres through his protégé Dalgairns; by the Maryvale chaplain Dr Louis Acquerone through Newman's Littlemore disciple John Walker, nicknamed 'dismal Johnny'; even by the able ex-Anglican cleric John Moore Capes, at the bidding of Dr Baggs of Prior Park. In June 1846, Newman 'was made an humiliation at my minor orders & at the examination for them; and I had to stand at Dr. Wiseman's door waiting for Confession amid the Oscott boys. I did not realize these as indignities at the time', but 'felt their dreariness'.[26]

There was also the problem of what he and his disciples should become, Vincentians or Dominicans or Jesuits or even a Congregation of the Holy Trinity to adore and defend 'the *Mysteries* of Faith'[27] under the patronage of St Mary. He was awkward in clerical dress: on a visit to Mrs Bowden in London in July 1846 for her reception into the Church, he felt odd in the streets in his new rigout: 'fancy *me*, who have never been in costume, wearing a straight cut collar to my coat, and having a long skirt to it. I know I look like a fool . . . '[28]

In the event, he did not set out for Rome until after he had seen on 1 September 1846 the consecration of Pugin's showpiece church at Cheadle, at the invitation of its benefactor the Earl of Shrewsbury: 'the most splendid building I ever saw', he wrote in July in the first flush of his enthusiasm over the sumptuous colouring. 'The Chapel of the Blessed Sacrament is, on entering, a blaze of light – and I could not help saying to myself "Porta Coeli".'[29] The journey to Rome with St John meant being lionized by the clergy along the way, and included a tour of the Catholic institutions of Paris, and a visit to the new shrine of Our Lady of Victories, but at Langres – 'Do not tell it beyond Maryvale', he wrote home – the state breakfasts and dinners every day of dishes dressed in oil, 'the wines and mode of living', took their toll. Robert 'Coffin and St John began having a sort of cholera – I was inconvenienced in another way by the eggs, and when I attempted to take medicine had a sort of cholera too'. There was also the trial of responding to the French style of formal clerical bowing: 'for me, who hardly ever made a formal bow in my life, I can hardly keep my countenance, as I put my elbows to my hips and make a segment of a circle, the lower vertebrae being the centre and my head the circumference'.[30] At Milan, he was enchanted with the 'brightness, grace, and simplicity of the classical style': it seemed more appropriate to 'St Mary or St Gabriel than any thing in Gothic'.[31] Here, as the memory of Cheadle faded, Newman recalled that he had 'loved Trinity Chapel at Oxford more than any other building'.[32] These were the seeds of what for Pugin would be an apostasy from Gothic to Baroque.

Newman was not enchanted with every Italian habit. 'They spit everywhere – they spit on the kneeling boards – they encourage it, and as if for amusement go on every ten seconds.'[33] But it was now the marble Gothic of the Duomo at Milan that was 'the most beautiful building I ever saw', with its pinnacles 'like bright snow against the blue sky'. Here he heard that at Florence the Dominicans were 'manufacturers of scented water, etc. and had very choice wines in their cellar', which helped to sink the idea of becoming Dominicans.[34] At Milan he also befriended Count Giacomo Mellerio, the patron of the philosopher Rosmini and of every Catholic good work, and from Milan visited the treasures of Monza. On 28 October 1846, Newman and St John reached Rome, stayed at a hotel frequented by other English Catholics, and then were given fine rooms in Propaganda formed by uniting two bedrooms with a glazed partition at the end of the corridor, the space between them acting as a passage and reception room. 'All the furniture is quite new . . . We begged off carpets, and they have painted the brick.'[35] 'We have worked muslin curtains', Newman protested, 'and curtains to our beds. It is really quite absurd, considering our habits', meaning those of the last Spartan years at Littlemore. Their hosts made both men eat meat on Friday for their health. 'Indeed they seem to treat us like wax dolls or mantle piece [sic] ornaments',[36] with an unfailing over-attention and kindness.

There was, however, some anxiety in official quarters about a virulent attack on the *Essay on Development* by an American journalist, Orestes Brownson, a Boston Catholic convert of only two years' standing: as an ex-Unitarian minister, Brownson felt that Newman's remarks about the formal unorthodoxy of the pre-Nicene Fathers gave ammunition to his former fellow-Unitarians. The sharpest of the Roman theologians, Giovanni Perrone, had interpreted a passage in the *Lectures on the Prophetical Office* as declaring the Roman Pontiff the Devil, and Newman complained to the Collegio Romano of reports that its professors had been refuting the *Essay on Development* in their lectures. He could only try to frighten them with the argument that such disapproval would hurt the Catholic cause in England. He received bland words of reassurance but still feared that the volume might be put on the Index. Dalgairns, now the Abbé Dalgairns, was translating bits of the *University Sermons* into French, and the journalist Jules Gondon was translating the *Essay*. Newman was particularly anxious to remove the possible prejudice against his statement that God's existence could not be proven with certainty. His own view, he told another convert-follower, William Penny, was 'that antecedent probability is the great instrument of conviction in religious (nay in all) matters'.[37] We judge of evidence in the light of our own first principles.

Newman and St John were summoned at half-an-hour's notice to call on the Pope, after a heavy rain which had turned the superabundant dung in the streets to slush, and left their mantellas with 'a *very deep* fringe of the nastiest stuff I ever saw'. They dipped them in water 'to hide the colour of the dirt' from the eyes of His Holiness, who told them a pleasant story about a convert cleric and gave Newman an oil painting of the Mater Dolorosa and St John a coronation medal.[38] 'When I knelt down to kiss his foot on entrance', wrote Newman to Dalgairns, 'I knocked my head against his knee – A friend of mine, Miss Giberne, on being presented, took up his foot in her hands; it is a wonder she did not throw him over.'[39]

Newman and St John also accompanied the Old Catholic Lord Clifford on a visit to the exiled Abbess Macrina, a refugee from Russian persecution who had taken an interest in the English converts. The Englishmen were happy enough in Propaganda, where the Rector Antonio Bresciani was 'a man of real delicacy as well as kindness',[40] and the students were youngsters from all the corners of the earth with thirty-two languages among them. The Pax, wrote Newman to Henry Wilberforce, was 'like Pentecost come again'.[41] The food was ample, coffee and milk, 'or on fast days coffee and chocolate' were available for breakfast with 'burnt bread too, as much as we want – and the Rector insisted we should, à l'Anglaise, have butter – but we have gradually dispensed with that'. Dinner at twelve o'clock was 'a large plate of broth or soup, either macaroni, or plain bread, or barley, or indian corn, or pease, or cabbage, bouilli follows . . . then roast veal or a made dish – on holidays another dish, pudding or the like follows – and two apples or chestnuts . . . Wine ad libitum'.[42] The costume of cassock and mantella, the latter of cassock length, were impossible to preserve from the dirt in the streets, but the cassock could be protected instead with a 'fareola', 'a very very full large handsome cloke, reaching down to the feet, – also the gift of Propaganda, – with a velvet collar, and frogs at the neck. Above all, a stupendous triangular hat – so contrived as to be susceptible of every puff of wind, but cocked so high in front as to afford the face no protection against the sun.'[43]

What with morning lectures in Latin on morals and dogmatics, in which Newman was not unknown to fall asleep, and a full range of services, he seldom got down until four in the afternoon to his own principal Roman study, the writing of four Latin treatises on St Athanasius, constructed from his notes to his Anglican translations, dedicated to Bresciani, and intended to prove to the Romans that he 'had bonâ fide given attention to the *documents* of ancient theology'.[44] Later there would be interruptions from a young

Italian missionary learning English and from English visitors, before St John called him between six and seven for tea. Their worst privation was the cold of the dreadful Roman winter of 1846–7, with torrential rain and ice and snow, and to his Maryvale correspondents Newman pictured the falling coals in their hearth, as he wrote from the brick-floored room of an unheated building.

Newman was no Italian. The Earl of Shrewsbury's son-in-law, Prince Borghese, asked him at a few hours' notice to preach at the funeral of a complete stranger, the Earl's Irish niece; the sermon, in the Irish Franciscan church of Sant' Isidoro, displeased the Catholics by its lack of Latin fluency, while the Protestants 'who came for the music or from respect to the family . . . did not relish receiving a lecture', and one said that Newman 'ought to be thrown into the Tyber'.[45] The Pope was said to be displeased at the discourse, which should have been 'Miele' not 'Aceto'. Newman's future enemy George Talbot also expressed a feline displeasure, and Newman stored the incident in memory as a failure. 'O, I was a sort of sucking child, just as much knowing what I should say, what I should not say, and saying nothing right, not from want of tact so much as from sheer ignorance.'[46]

Nor did Newman like the people of Rome, and was struck 'with their horrible cruelty to animals – also with their dishonesty, lying and stealing apparently without any conscience – and thirdly with their extreme dirt'.[47] Leo XII's attempt at reforming the state of the streets had merely provoked mockery at his funeral; there was a need for a new St Philip Neri. It was the figure of St Philip who turned Newman's mind back to Wiseman's suggestion that he become an Oratorian. Philip, he told Jemima, 'reminds me in so many ways of Keble, that I can fancy what Keble would have been, if God's will had been he should have been born in another place and age; he was formed on the same type of extreme hatred of humbug, playfulness, nay oddity, tender love for others, and severity . . . '[48] On 17 January 1847, Newman wrote to Wiseman that 'we come round to your Lordship's original idea, and feel we cannot do better than be Oratorians'.[49] Newman's aim was 'a body of priests labouring in the conversion of great towns', perhaps among the youths with a little education and no religion attracted to mechanics institutes and clubs. But the Rule of the Oratory did not at first seem appropriate to 'a country of heretics and Saxons. E.g. four sermons running every day, disciplining before or with a congregation, going in a troop from Church to Church, sitting down on grass and singing . . . '[50]

The Pope had, moreover, forbidden changes to the Rule. But Newman befriended the great Oratorian historian Father Augustine Theiner, at the lovely Oratorian house by the Chiesa Nuova, and on 28 January 1847, he discussed his plan for the Oratory with the friendly Secretary of Propaganda, Giovanni Brunelli. On 14 February, Newman submitted a formal letter on the subject to the Cardinal Prefect Giacomo Fransoni; Brunelli declared of the proposal 'Mi piace immensamente'.[51] The Oratorian use of music in religion – their sacred concerts had given rise to the Oratorio – was an attraction to Newman, as was the 'time for reading and writing',[52] and an elasticity enabling the congregation to attempt as much or as little pastoral work as it wanted. In high good humour, Newman wrote of seeking the services of a man like 'Fat Marshall', Henry Marshall, a convert with an 'immense rotundity' and abundance of humour 'to please boys and young men, and keep them together', and he wanted 'a regular good mimic' to 'take off' the great guns of Exeter Hall. St John wanted Irish wits, but Fr Dominic thought them slovenly. 'If we have not spirit, it will be like bottled beer with the cork out',[53] wrote Newman, who made an enemy when he gently rebuffed Talbot's application to join the new order, by repeating Brunelli's insistence that no one should join him in Rome 'but the party who lived together in England'.[54]

His preparation for ordination was a nine day retreat with the Jesuits at S Eusebio, where his Latin notes of his rigorous self-examination complained of 'a wound or cancer' in his mind that prevented him from becoming a good Oratorian: an inability to rise above prescribed duty, a dislike of 'poverty, troubles, restrictions, inconveniences', a fear of bad health, an Epicurean love of 'tranquility, security, a life among friends, and among books', and a sense of embarrassment at his involvement in the difficult minutiae of some of the extra-liturgical aspects of the cult: Exposition, Benediction, indulgences and Novenas. 'I am querulous, timid, lazy, suspicious', he wrote; 'I crawl along the ground; feeble, downcast and despondent'. He lacked a 'practical, lively and present faith' against 'the evil spirit in my heart'. Without suffering any diminution in his faith, he had lost his 'simple confidence in the word of God', and 'fallen into a kind of despair and a gloomy state of mind'. 'And I feel acutely that I am no longer young, but that my best years are spent, and I am sad at the thought of the years that have gone by; and I see myself to be fit for nothing, a useless log.'[55]

This was not the mood in which he emerged to the delight of the brilliant light and crystal air of the Roman Spring and to excursions to Tivoli and Monte Cavo, the Alban Mount, with its views recalling Taormina. 'You see Terracina in one direction – Corsica (on a clear day) in another – on one side the lakes of Albano and Nemi, the country of the Volsci and Corioli, Cicero's Tusculum etc etc, and the whole territory which is the subject of Virgil's last books and Livy's first – and on the other side, volcanic hills close at hand, then the range of Sabine hills, and then the snowy Appenines.'[56] Newman's future Oratorian companions gathered round him from France and England, Dalgairns, Stanton, Bowles, William Penny and Robert Coffin, who were lodged with the Passionists. Newman tried to entice Bloxam to pope with the assurance that in Rome, the Oratorians were 'the ritualists of the place': 'you have nothing to do, but to put your rooms in order, get into a Mediterranean steamer as if for a summer trip, and be received quietly at Malta . . . '[57] The plan to send Newman's party to the empty Oratory at Malta was Theiner's, but this meant placing themselves under Cardinal Pietro Ostini, who talked of a scheme of the Pope's for dividing the community in two, some to train in Malta and some in Rome. Newman wrote to the Pope asking that they all remain together, to which Pius replied, ' "Siete tranquilli" . . . he would do everything – he would keep us together – and we should be kept at Rome'.[58] It was decided that Newman and his friends should receive their formation at the Cistercian Bernardine convent of Santa Croce in Gerusalemme, one of the seven pilgrimage churches of the city, founded by St Helena on soil from Calvary; 'if there be a centre of the Church', wrote Newman, 'we shall be there, when we are on earth from Jerusalem in the midst of Rome . . . The Pope . . . says, "Stiano tranquilli –" *I* will do all'.[59]

Newman was ordained deacon with Ambrose St John in St John Lateran on 29 May 1847 and priest in the chapel of Propaganda by Cardinal Fransoni the next day. He said his first Mass, on Corpus Christi, in the Jesuit Chapel of the College, his server on the occasion being the preacher at his funeral, William Clifford. He then accompanied the Rector in his *carrozza* to St Peter's for the procession of the feast. The following day, he said the community Mass at Propaganda, and the students all kissed his hand. On 28 June, he joined his little community at Santa Croce, after saying Mass at Sant' Andrea for the repose of the soul of Daniel O'Connell whom he had once loathed. The party kept 'calling Rome "Oxford" and talk of "walking into Oxford" ',[60] because Rome was as far from Santa Croce as Oxford from Littlemore.

The training of the fledgling Oratorians, by Fr Carlo Rossi, which Newman was to find 'dreary', included 'room-sweeping, slop-emptying, dinner-serving, bed making, shoe blacking';[61] but the routine also permitted more Catholic tourism, to visit the Oratory in Naples, and to make expeditions from Naples to Pozzuoli and Baiae, to Nocera where Newman said Mass over the body of St Alfonso di Liguori, to Pompeii and Vesuvius, and to the Benedictines at Monte Cassino where he opened a visitor's book with an inscription recalling the debt owed to the Abbey by Christianity in England. He was taken with the special class of Neapolitan miracles, with the liquefaction of the blood of Santa Patrizia on her feast day, and he took down the story of San Pantaleon's blood near Amalfi which liquified in the presence of a relic of the Cross. He could not linger to see the most famous of liquefactions, of San Gennaro, but was impressed by the undoubted faith of the Italian clergy in this class of miracles. In his enthusiasm for all things Catholic, he was determined to go the whole Neapolitan hog. He would later have his reservations.

On his return to Rome, Newman saw his new friend Monsignor Giovanni Palma, the kindly if hideous Propaganda Secretary without nose or teeth, whom Newman was later to call his 'only friend' in Rome.[62] Palma read him the Brief for the English Oratory, which was not to be approved until November. To one aspirant to join the Oratory, Thomas Knox, who hoped for the strict Sulpician ideal of sacerdotal training, Newman invoked Thucydides' comparison of Spartans and Athenians. 'We are Athenians, the Jesuits Spartans. Ours is in one respect more anxious and difficult – we have no vows, we have fewer rules – yet we must keep together – we require a knowledge of each other, which the Jesuits do not require. A Jesuit is like a soldier in the phalanx – an Oratorian like a legionary – he fights by himself – he guides himself by "carità" – which means by tact, self-knowledge, knowledge of others . . . it requires training *with* those with whom he is to live.'[63] Newman wished to rule by love and not command; an ideal fraught with endless emotional difficulties, and exhausting in its demands on sensitivity, tact and time.

This ideal was in no way to the detriment of the Jesuits: 'I have no where seen such holiness and selfdevotion',[64] he told Jemima, recalling the kindness of their house in Naples. But as a race apart from the people around them, they were hated as reactionaries, like the Tories in 1832. On 10 October 1847, Newman reported to Wiseman that the Pope had made him Superior of the English Oratory, 'with power to choose the four Deputies'[65] who would comprise the governing body of his house, and that the statutes of the Order were going to press. On 3 December, Newman and St John presented the Brief establishing the new community at the Vatican, but decided not to wait around to act as bearers of the Bull to re-establish the English Catholic hierarchy. To escape the closure of the Alps by snow, and to be in England for Christmas, they rushed the journey home with only two notable pauses, to say Mass in the Holy House at Loreto on the feast of its miraculous translation to its site, and in the Chapel Royal at Munich, where Newman met the greatest of German Catholic church historians, Ignaz von Döllinger. Their luggage included the *corpo santo* of St Valentine from the catacombs, secured by St John with Palma's assistance in the teeth of opposition from the sacristan of St Peter's. At Verona, the party had to 'pay duty on it as a mummy!'[66] Its feast at the Birmingham Oratory is now kept on Newman's birthday.

Newman arrived in England on Christmas Eve, and said his first Mass on English soil at Christmas in Mrs Bowden's private chapel at Chelsea, with his godson Charles Bowden as his server. At a Christmas lunch with Wiseman, now appointed pro-Vicar Apostolic of the London District, he was told of Faber's offer to join the Oratory with his Brothers of the Will of God. Newman noted the difficulties: that Faber's ideal was more '*poetical*' and ascetic than the Oratory, which would have to take in his lay brothers and reconcile 'his *country* sphere' at St Wilfrid's at Cotton Hall in Staffordshire with Newman's city one.[67] The new community was established on 1 February 1848 at Maryvale, with six priests, Newman, St John, Dalgairns, Penny, Stanton and Coffin, and with Thomas Knox as a novice, and three lay brothers, two from St Wilfrid's. Of this original brotherhood, only St John was to persevere with Newman to the end. The rest of Faber's community, two priests, three intending priests and eleven lay brothers, were admitted on the 14th. The beginning was troubled by Wiseman's losing for two months a box belonging to Newman containing a £1500 railway bond, and by the cost of St Wilfrid's. The mission had received a massive injection of funds from Faber's rich disciple William Antony Hutchison, was too expensive to maintain and was in a country area outside Newman's Brief, but could only be abandoned at the displeasure of its patron Lord Shrewsbury. Just as unsatisfactory was a series of Lenten sermons in the London Catholic chapels that Newman agreed to preach at Wiseman's invitation. Newman later called it 'a blunder & failure, which even now I cannot think of without a raw sensitiveness'.[68]

Newman's quality as a preacher, of strength and sweetness in great restraint and seeming feebleness of voice and manner, was noted in February 1848 by the eighteen-year-old Edward White Benson, later Archbishop of Canterbury, writing to the future Bishop J. B. Lightfoot of Durham; but Benson's worship of Newman was mingled with horror:

> But oh, Lightfoot, never you turn Romanist if you are to have a face like that – it was awful – the terrible lines deeply ploughed all over his face, and the craft that sat upon his retreating forehead and sunken eyes . . . Then if you had seen how his eye glistened and his whole face glowed, as he turned round to the Altar, lifting his Priest's cap, and bowing low, while he pronounced His name, and with such a voice – you could not but have felt your heart yearn towards him, and when you observed what a thrill ran through the congregation, you must have said, 'Surely if there be a man whom God has raised up in this generation with more than common powers to glorify His name, this man is he' – but how was it spoiled when he linked in 'the Name of the Holy Mother of God'; when he joined together 'Jesu! Maria!' How painful was it to think that he had been once an English Churchman; . . .

Benson was moved to quote Pusey's opinion which he had once laughed at, that Newman had been 'removed from us for that we valued him not as we should have done, and were unworthy of him'. Yet Benson also conceived that Newman had 'sinned the sin of those who have left their first love. *Ora pro Jacobo* [sic] *Henrico Newman*'.[69] It was with the same fascinated horror, at Mrs George Ryder's death-bed in 1850, that Samuel Wilberforce wrote to his brother Robert that he had heard Newman's voice, 'a volcano's roar, tamed into the softness of the flute-stop', and turned his face away from the 'serpentine form' of the 'Father Superior'.[70] So alien had Newman now become to his non-Catholic fellow country men.

This sense of his unconventionality was reinforced by the appearance in

1848 of his novel *Loss and Gain*, a fictional account of an Oxford conversion that he had written for his own entertainment while in Rome. It was conceived in part to compensate the publisher James Burns on the loss of his Anglican clientele on his conversion to Catholicism, but it also attempts an analysis of the muddle and incoherence of Newman's journey towards the Church, and its 'over-sensitive and melancholy' hero, Charles Reding, is a portrait of its author. What impressed readers, however, was the wicked sense of fun in the satiric portraits of High, Low and Liberal Churchmen, of the over-earnest and humourless Evangelical, the frivolous Anglo-Catholic dandy-aesthete and the astute Latitudinarian who knows how little he can safely believe. *Fraser's Magazine* remarked that 'a book of this kind, a book of jokes and gossip, of eating and drinking, of smartnesses, levities and most probable personalities – appears as a somewhat undignified vehicle for the opinions of one who has long been revered as a prophet and a saint'.[71] In the conversation pieces, like the tea-table gossip of Evangelicals pondering a report of the dying Pope Sixtus XVI's conversion to Protestantism by a Mr O'Niggins of the Roman Priest Conversion Branch Tract Society, Newman set out to capture the shop-talk of the subcultures of the Church of England, and artfully wove them into a devastating exposure of the inconsistencies, insincerities and occasional silliness of the rival schools of Anglican theology.

There were, however, rival subcultures within the dogmatic unity of Rome, and Newman had to mediate in a semi-comic exchange of mutual cursing between Ambrose Lisle Phillipps and Faber, who declared war over their rival preferences for Gothic and Baroque. Newman loyally supported his subordinate. He preached in May 1848 at the opening of Mrs Bowden's Pugin-designed church in Fulham, and told Maria Giberne that in details, 'Pugin is perfect but his altars are so small that you can't have a Pontifical High Mass at them, his tabernacles so low that you can scarce have exposition, his East windows so large that every thing else is hidden in the glare, and his skreens so heavy that you might as well have the function in [the] Sacristy, for the seeing it by the Congregation'.[72] Mrs Bowden had countermanded the screen which she found Pugin building though she had forbidden it. 'He is intolerant, and . . . a bigot', declared Newman of Pugin to Phillipps. The 'living ritual of the 19th century' needed 'the living architecture of the 19th century'. 'Gothic is now like an old dress, which fitted a man well twenty years back but must be altered to fit him now.' Newman had never been interested in Anglican ritualism, and as he now recalled to Phillipps, 'there seemed to me something excessive and unreal in it'.[73] Newman's was the case for modern baroque; more usually he was prepared to regard art and architecture as matters concerned with inessentials, though he had his own sober Roman preference.

Newman's community was finding it difficult to establish its permanent base. At first he accepted a £9000 church in Bayswater, but Faber did not like to leave him for a daughter house, the neighbourhood was neither rich nor poor, and their Brief intended the Oratory, understandably, given the origins of its members, in a phrase inserted by the Pope himself, for the 'splendidioris, doctioris, et honestioris ordinis hominum coetus'; or, as Newman translated this, *'The Pope has not sent us to the poor, but to the rich'*.[74] The new Vicar Apostolic of the Central District, William Bernard Ullathorne, wanted an Oratory in Birmingham, and Newman decided against Bayswater because the offer did not include a community house, which he thought more important than a church, as the house 'will build a Church, but a Church will not build a house'.[75] Moreover Ullathorne's invitation to Birmingham enabled the Oratory at Michaelmas 1848 to give up Maryvale without infringing the Papal Brief, which referred to a Birmingham Oratory. For the moment, the community moved to Cotton to plan the new house in the city for the New Year, when Faber as novice master would remain with a number of the younger brethren at St Wilfrid's.

All this negotiation to secure a future meant a mass of administration and financial business that tried Newman severely. 'My head is so stupid today that I take up my pen, as the only thing I can do, even if that', wrote Newman to Ambrose St John, complaining of a cold and poor health. ' . . . At times the sense of weight (of responsibility) and of desolateness has come on me so strongly, that I could fancy it might grow equal to any pain . . . ' Some of the 'giovani' had 'shown so little kindness when I have done things for them, treated me with so little confidence, as to throw me back upon myself . . . one is tempted to say, "How much happier for me . . . to be a single unfettered convert – " but if this had been so, I should not have known you, Carissime – so good and evil go together'.[76]

Newman's sense of a lack of support from below was complicated by a tiff with his diocesan. Ullathorne was the Yorkshire quintessence of the restraint, solidity and sobriety of the English Catholic tradition, and he was not pleased by Faber's series of modern saints' lives, begun in 1847 before Faber had become an Oratorian, and continued on his own account thereafter. The works were intended, as translations from French, Spanish and Italian, to raise the spiritual temperature of English Catholicism, by giving prominence to those revivalist, ascetic and contemplative emphases in the religious life in which the converts and Italians held the native tradition to be deficient. This naturally inspired Old Catholic resentment, and the clergyman-editor of *Dolman's Magazine*, Edward Price, though himself a convert from Presbyterianism, vigorously attacked the first volume in the series, on St Rose of Lima, which contained both a passage implying an idolatrous devotion to a statue, and the charnel-house horrors of Rose's extreme mortifications.

Like his fellow bishop Wareing, Ullathorne disliked the frank descriptions in the series of ecclesiastical abuses, and Newman reluctantly suspended the 'Lives': 'these old priests will be satisfied with nothing – they have pursued us with criticisms ever since we were Catholics',[77] he wrote to John Moore Capes, who defended him in the columns of his new Catholic periodical, the *Rambler*.[78] Frederick Lucas, as integrally Ultramontane as ever, was equally vociferous in his support for the series in the *Tablet*. But Ullathorne's censure of Price was half-hearted, to Newman's disgust, and it was Wiseman who forced Price to make the fulsome retraction that enabled Faber to resume publication of the 'Lives' in January 1849, the Oratory assuming from August full corporate editorial responsibility for the series as a whole. Newman thought that in the controversy, Ullathorne had ignored his status as Superior, and the Bishop had accused him of 'acute sensitiveness' and 'intellectual pride'.[79] The two men would have time to learn to like and respect one another. The Oratory moved to Alcester Street in Birmingham on 26 January 1849, and the Superior and his Bishop would both live in the city for the remaining forty years of their long and busy lives.

20

The Birmingham Oratory

Newman's new chapel was a former gin distillery, which he opened on the Feast of the Purification, an anniversary sacred to him through its association with his former *alma mater* of Oriel. 'We began with forgetting to light the Altar Candles', he wrote to Faber, 'and ended by having to hunt for a corporal for the Tabernacle.'[1] The chapel was near the Irish slums of Birmingham, and the Oratory's first experience in the city was of the immigrant Irish. Newman's congregations on the Sunday following the opening were packed, with a sea of five to six hundred heads at evening Benediction, and in the following week he had forty-six boys turn up for catechizing, exclusive of girls and young men:[2] 'boys and girls flow in for instructions', he wrote, 'as herrings in the season. But it is not enough to catch your fish; you must throw the bad away'.[3] The congregation had to ask for police protection from disrupters, perhaps inspired by the Wesleyans. Newman had, in effect, opened a mission to the poor. Unlike Faber, he could redefine the 'honestioris' of his Brief as sharp-witted Brummagems, but while he never lacked wealthy disciples, Birmingham would never be fashionable London.

Much of the rest of Newman's life was concerned with the emotional and administrative difficulties of realizing the Oratorian ideal of a free and voluntary brotherhood, bound by mutual affection rather than by a rigid monastic Rule or permanent religious vows. The community at St Wilfrid's wanted a decision about their future, and through Faber, they complained to Newman that he was too dependent in his 'particular friendship' with the unpopular Ambrose St John, while the Gordon brothers declared that Newman showed them a want of affection. Philip Gordon was at St Wilfrid's, and Newman's 'note about nothing' repaired the imagined breach:

Many is the time I have stood over the fire at breakfast or looked at you at Recreation, hunting for something to talk about. The song says that 'Love cannot live on flowers;' not so; yet it requires material, if not for sustenance, at least for display. And I have fancied too that younger and lighter minds perhaps could not, if they would, care much for one who has had so much to wear him down.[4]

'And now what can I say in return', wrote Newman to Joseph Gordon, 'but that with all my heart I love you? as you would see, if you could look into it; – but such is our condition in this world, that persons who love each other, cannot, from their respective peculiarities, at once enter into the enjoyment of the mutual consciousness of that love.'[5]

But Newman wanted to be saved from the 'affection and devotion' of Thomas Knox,[6] 'Francis' in religion, who having vowed special obedience to his superior, could not endure the thought of coming to Birmingham. 'It grows on me for many reasons', wrote Newman to Faber, 'that separation is the only cure of our difficulties',[7] by creating another Oratory in London. This would solve the problem of numbers. 'The Oratory is a family – 6 children form a fair fire side – I would allow 11 including novices – which makes 12 with the Padre. More than that is, I think, simple evil . . .'[8] Faber, however, was reluctant to leave Newman, and Newman was determined not to leave Birmingham: in part because the Pope had named him Superior of the Birmingham Oratory, in part because he was convinced that London would leave him no time for literary effort, what with missionary work, 'measures for the good of Catholicism, projects for bills in Parliament . . . Golden Square soirees, Committees, preaching for public objects, speeches at meetings'.[9] He thought briefly in March 1849 that his London residence might be necessary, and 'said if I went I would leave my Library behind, for that it was impossible to read and write in London'.[10] The difficulty lay in cutting the community in two on the basis of two distinct criteria, those who wanted to go to London or Birmingham, and those who would follow him or Faber.

This was the sticking point for the Oratory's new novice Robert Whitty, who only joined Christmas 1848, having declared his intention to do so years before. Whitty was anathema to Faber: 'Never take another Irishman, Padre mio',[11] wrote Faber to Newman; but Whitty had his heart set on an Oratory to evangelize the hundred thousand Irish poor in London. Another intending Irish novice, James McQuoin, had the same idea, and Newman's solution was that they could establish a second London Oratory if Faber's did not suit them. In the event, Whitty and McQuoin could stomach neither Faber nor Birmingham, and Whitty was quickly snatched up as Wiseman's Vicar General and Provost of the Chapter of Westminster. In his after career as a Jesuit, he was English Provincial and Assistant to the General. With him, as with Robert Coffin, Faber's antipathy may have prevented a larger development of the Oratory than it was destined to achieve.

The community divided in mid April, when Faber and his party set off for London, where three wealthy friends, the Earl of Arundel, David Lewis and the former guardsman Alexander Fullerton, husband of the Catholic novelist Lady Georgiana, found them an Oratory in a former gin shop in King William Street near the Strand. Newman was sorriest to lose the flighty Dalgairns, the first of his disciples to last the course at Littlemore, and reflected that seven years was 'the term of *contubernium* [tent companionship] with my friends',[12] as with Froude and Rogers before him. Dalgairns avoided a formal leave taking, but wrote afterwards to know the reason for Newman's displeasure with him, and received a rocket for letting his youthful penitents run riot through the house. 'I found them strumming on the Piano, they ate the sugar and the jam and stole the candles; you laughed when it was complained of . . . They flung about the ink in the guest room, broke the chairs, squandered coal and gas, broke into the closet, took out the Crucifix, and put it back head downwards . . . You gave them the lay brothers' books, and they made away with them . . . They took to playing tricks with the gas. I say nothing of their rudeness to me personally . . . They have ended, since you went, with stealing a book from F. William and a silver Cross from Br Charles . . . you must beware of "having your leg over the harrows –" your safety, Carissime, lies in subjection; do not set up for yourself, wherever you are.' Newman claimed to lack the self-confidence and self-possession for exciting confidence in others and setting Dalgairns right. 'I am old; and you have the fits of reliance on me, and fits of mistrust and suspicion.'[13]

Towards the end of April 1849, the Birmingham house was a ferment of departures and arrivals: 'every one', wrote Newman to Capes, 'taking his place, as one used in a stage coach, accommodating legs and stowing parcels. You know what a scene there is on deck when a vessel is just under weigh – packages, boxes, mackintoshes, live fowls, and quamish women strewed about in all directions'.[14] Newman nonetheless began to feel the security of being at home, after ten years of wandering. But his means were straitened, as most of the richer Fathers departed with Faber, and Newman had to dip into what was left of his private capital: 'the offertory is increasing, though not steadily –', he wrote to Antony Hutchison, who had followed his master Faber to London, '½crowns and shillings sometimes are discovered amid the halfpence. O for a private California'.[15]

His chief practical problem over the next two years was to get rid of the encumbrance of St Wilfrid's, which brought him into conflict with both Ullathorne and Shrewsbury. When he indicated to Ullathorne his wish to abandon the mission to an Irish priest, the Bishop accused him of exercising the patron's right of presentation, and pointed out the interdict that could follow from shutting down a church. Faber in correspondence with Ullathorne and Shrewsbury, treated St Wilfrid's as the Oratorians' private property, to be disposed of as they pleased, and Newman had to side with the Bishop against him. 'I identified myself wholly with you last Autumn', wrote Newman, recalling the Lives of the Saints ' – and now you seem to wish to show the world that after all there is something unmanageable in you, that you can't be relied on, that you are fickle, take up schemes, give them up, insult benefactors, are heartless and wilful . . . All this will get to

Rome . . . your letter can be made a handle against you, and against the Oratory.'[16]

Faber did withdraw his letter to Ullathorne. Newman thought that St Wilfrid's might become a school, 'the Eton of the Oratory – a place where Fathers would turn with warm associations of boyhood or at least youth – a place where they were to be buried'.[17] The community had a few boys to teach, including Newman's godson George Lisle Ryder, who brought not only his fishing rod but a small and needed income; his pranks were treated gently, like showering the saintly lay brother Aloysius Boland with flour. All Newman's schemes for St Wilfrid's, however, foundered on the lack of interest in the matter in London. In July 1849, the Oratory's ablest new recruit, John Stanislas Flanagan, was as yet unordained, and Newman had only five priests to help him in Birmingham, as Coffin and Penny were still at St Wilfrid's. 'We want to form a little school of possible Oratorians there', he told Miss Giberne, 'but can't find the boys. Our married friends will not turn Catholic.'[18]

While Birmingham stagnated, London prospered. 'They are taken up most warmly by the high people, Lord Arundel, Mr Fullerton, etc.', wrote Newman, 'and have presents of monstrances, chalices, hardware, Bass's pale ale, painted walls etc. etc. without end.'[19] Though the Strand chapel was stunk out by the Irish poor, this was no worse than Birmingham, where Newman concluded 'that poverty is not what makes the Irish such beasts', as he noted that at midnight, the Oratory passage 'smelt like one of the "for Gentlemen" on the railroad station', the Irish having been there eight hours before. 'F. Ambrose has caught two bugs, one on his face, in the confessional, and now I recognize the smell of bugs in certain penitents strong . . . a sort of turpentine smell.'[20] Newman went with Ambrose to Bilston to minister to the victims of cholera – 'every one crying as if we were going to be killed'[21] – but found the scourge nearly over and nothing to do. During the pestilence, 'Multitudes crowded for reception into the Church, and, alas, could not be received for want of instructors and confessors'.[22] Faber was on a similar errand of mercy to the cholera-stricken Irish hop-pickers in Henry Wilberforce's parish of East Farleigh in Kent, and noted that Henry would 'hardly let me out of his sight, for fear he should catch it, and want to make his confession.'[23] Newman was as hard on Henry as ever: 'I can't understand at all how you dare to keep your living – you have no right to it at all',[24] but it was the prayers of the poor which were held to have converted the Wilberforce family to Catholicism in the following year. The first '*grazia*' achieved by the application of St Philip's relics in Birmingham was the recovery from near death of a convert factory girl, and it was the poor who crammed the church: 'the congregation forcibly pushes back the Church doors', wrote Newman, 'the porch is crowded, and we give Benediction right into the street, people kneeling on the opposite pavement'.[25]

In this, Newman was not doing 'any thing with the thinking classes; and, as life is short, this is somewhat painful to me'.[26] He felt intellectually unemployed. He was in Birmingham essentially because Wiseman had put him there, during the brief decade when the Central District had been the centre of the Catholic Revival; and his chief publication of 1849, his *Discourses addressed to Mixed Congregations*, dedicated to Wiseman, was a collection of addresses and sermons, though one of these, 'Neglect of Divine Calls and Warnings', on the danger of damnation by living no worse than a life of average selfishness, is still calculated to make the reader tremble, for its subtle analysis of a very ordinary human state and its everlasting punishment. His correspondence with enquirers, which lasted the rest of his life, was one sort of apostolate; but his desire for a school was in opposition to the Oratorian Rule, and was torpedoed by a Rescript from Propaganda, accidentally prompted by Ullathorne through Dr Thomas Grant, Rector of the English College in Rome, insisting on the surrender of St Wilfrid's and on keeping to the Rule '*exactissime*'.[27]

Here was a puzzle; Rome thought that Newman wanted to establish a dependent Oratory at St Wilfrid's, and insisted that the place should go, the Bishop and patron that it should remain. It reminded Newman of 'the man who bought an Elephant, and was too poor to keep [it], and too merciful to kill it, and was unable to persuade anyone to accept of it'.[28] Newman broached the idea of a college at St Wilfrid's for older students intending for the Church. The Rescript also forbade the Oratory to conduct an ordinary mission. Newman dreamt of employing as a curate 'some young Irishman who loves work, would say Mass late, would whip up the people in the alleys, and would be satisfied with such marks of courtesy as a magnificent Society might show to a small person'.[29] His difficulty was that of finding a role for the Oratory distinct from the roles of the run of secular and regular clergy.

The largest cloud to disappear was that of worry over money. Edward Caswall, a former Anglican clergyman and a gifted minor poet, whose translations of the breviary hymns are still in common use, decided after his wife's death to join the Oratory, and endowed it with £9000 and a further £1000 for Masses in his wife's memory.[30] The bequest, together with £300 to Newman from his Milanese acquaintance, Count Mellerio, enabled him to plan the construction of a community house. The site of the present Oratory in Edgbaston was bought in May 1850, and subscriptions for the church were invited in July. The architect of the house was an Irish civil engineer, Terence Flanagan, brother to John Stanislas Flanagan, and employed 1,700,000 ugly red bricks in a building which is substantial rather than beautiful. Only the crumbling stone dressings to the windows look as if they were not meant to last forever.

The move to Edgbaston was to mean leaving the Alcester Street mission to a secular priest; and as Newman found his feet in Birmingham, so he resumed his intellectual labours, writing his *Lectures on Certain Difficulties felt by Anglicans in submitting to the Catholic Church*, which were delivered in the London Oratory between 9 May and 5 July 1850 at the general rate of two a week. The first seven lectures were a polemic against his old Anglo-Catholic self, and argued that the Oxford Movement's only end was Rome; the second lot of five were an astonishingly frank portrayal of the abuses of religion characteristic of Catholic countries, which the author made as vivid as possible to argue that the worst of these were not an objection to Catholicism. The most colourful of these were to be exploited by Charles Kingsley in his attack on Newman in 1864, but their publication was followed by the award of a papal doctorate of divinity. Newman was henceforth to be called 'Dr Newman' for nearly thirty years, until he was made a Cardinal.

Newman was also still Superior of the Oratory in London, and had to deal with complaints about Faber's eccentricities as Rector, his extravagance, his headaches which prevented him from working and his intermittent quarrelsomeness. Yet Faber was 'working more like a steamengine than a man',[31] and it was this that helped push him to the point of breakdown. The London Oratory went back on their engagement to help sustain St Wilfrid's, and in September 1850, Newman in conversation with Shrewsbury, 'charged in column, broke his line, and threw him into confusion'[32] by telling him that the Oratory could not maintain a community there. There was a prospect of passing the mission to the Redemptorists, but Faber did not help much to solve the problem. 'In nothing has the London House supported me',[33] Newman wrote to Dalgairns, and the closure of St Wilfrid's raised the further difficulty of assigning a role to its Rector, Robert Coffin. On 9 October 1850, Newman issued a decree releasing the London Oratorians from their allegiance to the Birmingham house, including Coffin, and Faber was elected the London Superior.[34] The London house took charge of the disposal of St Wilfrid's, which was sold to the Passionists, and Coffin, who had been over-influenced by an eccentric resident artist at St Wilfrid's, the Baron Gottlieb von Schroeter, quickly abandoned a plan to spend some years in learning the spirit of the institute in the Oratory in Florence, and left the congregation to become a Redemptorist. Newman told von Schroeter that he had done his 'utmost to ruin the Institution of St Philip',[35] but Coffin's subsequent career as Provincial of his order and then Bishop of Southwark suggests that as with Whitty, his was a serious loss, and that his antipathy to Faber cost the Oratory a gifted pioneer.

Faber's own health broke down in 1851, and he went abroad, at first intending to visit the Holy Land; but he turned back in Malta and visited Oratories in Sicily and Italy before reaching London in December. Though he spent some time recuperating at a retreat in the country, neither Hutchison nor Dalgairns was pleased at his early return. Newman had to reconcile Dalgairns to Faber's continuing as Superior, and after the death of Joseph

Gordon, which left the Birmingham Oratory much weakened, to secure Dalgairns' return to Birmingham. Thus the London Oratory continued to bedevil Newman with its practical problems. It made an abortive attempt to purchase Lord Aberdeen's Argyll House in 1852, and it was only in 1853 that it acquired a permanent home in the new and fashionable suburb of Brompton.

These domestic events were overshadowed by national and international ones. The Gorham Judgement by the Privy Council in 1850 declared legal the Evangelical doctrine of Baptismal Regeneration, and showed up the Church of England both as an heretical and a parliamentary Church in the eyes of the many Anglo-Catholics who now turned to Rome. It was ironical that the Archbishop of Canterbury who concurred in the judgement was the very John Bird Sumner whose work had helped convert Newman to a belief in Baptismal Regeneration and placed his feet on the path to Anglo-Catholicism. On 29 September 1850, Pius IX, lately returned to Rome from his exile in Gaeta, re-established the Catholic hierarchy in England, with twelve diocesan bishops under Wiseman as Cardinal Archbishop of Westminster, and with Ullathorne as the first Bishop of Birmingham. *The Times* took the lead in whipping up a great national No-Popery excitement over the pompous empurpled pastoral letter, 'Given out of the Flaminian Gate' by Wiseman, implying to anyone unversed in ecclesiastical hyperbole his own government of the country and anticipating England's return to the Roman obedience. 'I wish he could be kept from England for a while', wrote Newman in irritation, 'and the hierarchy set on foot sub silentio.'[36] As Wiseman's acting Vicar General, Robert Whitty, and Wiseman's convert lawyer, George Bowyer, asked Newman for advice on how to meet the furore, a minority of Old Catholics like the Duke of Norfolk and Lord Beaumont took the anti-Catholic side. Newman now thought that Wiseman should face and disarm his critics, the course which in the event the Cardinal followed, but it was Newman himself, with his Oratorian costume and prominent hooked nose, who figured as 'Mr Newboy' to Wiseman's 'Mr Wiseboy' in those cartoons in *Punch* which did so much to turn that journal, then only ten years old, into a national institution. 'Caswall's brother', wrote Newman, 'was followed by the rabble the other day in London, having on a long cloke which they took for an Oratorian. He faced round, pulled aside the cloke, and showed his trousers – When they saw him all sound below, they gave him a cheer and left him.'[37] The London Oratorians were burnt in effigy, and the excitement was exploited by the Prime Minister, Lord John Russell, in a letter denouncing the 'Papal Aggression' to his old tutor the Bishop of Durham. Russell proposed an Ecclesiastical Titles Bill to deny the new Catholic Bishops their claim to use the names of their sees, in an apparent reversal of the long Whig and liberal tradition of support for Roman Catholic freedoms.

Newman claimed to hate rows, but was not sorry to see the humbug exposed 'that John Bull had become instinct with a diviner spirit, that liberals were Catholics, and the race of squires and parsons was extinct . . . '[38] Any anti-Catholic measures would alienate the Catholics from the Whigs. 'I hope', he wrote, invoking the shade of Hurrell Froude, 'we are rid of them for ever.' No-Popery would also 'consolidate the Catholic interest all over the Empire',[39] and would disgust the liberals of Russell's own party. The prospect even had its comic possibilities. If the new hier-archy were proven to be against the Common Law, then 'our Bishops go to prison – there the Cardinal will change his Cardinalitian Basilica – and for St Pudentiana will take S Niccolò in carcere. If the Government can be kept from laying its paws on our property, it will be most edifying and consolatory, and do much good to religion. Then the Holy Father will write a letter to his venerable Brother Nicholas or William Bernard on his sufferings, and they will be shipped off to join Smith O'Brien',[40] the trans-ported Young Irelander. It was premature to make jokes about imprison-ment, as events were to prove. There was a riot in November outside the Birmingham Oratory at the evening service at the lying-in-state of a young Oratorian dead of consumption, John Cooke, and Newman had to send for the police, but the conflict was for all its excitement in one sense a sham one, as he came quickly to see: it was difficult to take effective legislative measures against Catholics in the heyday of liberal England in the mid century.

Yet the agitation touched private and personal relations, as families were divided and individuals were rabbled and assaulted and Catholic servants and employees dismissed, or simply suffering ostracism or denunciation or abuse. Newman preached a sermon at Ullathorne's installation as Bishop, 'Christ upon the Waters', described by *The Times* as 'a mixture of blasphemy and absurdity' and a 'frightful perversion'[41] of language, for comparing the Catholic Revival with the Resurrection. Newman's former disciple John Walter III, now the newspaper's proprietor, declared in a speech that Newman's like might be 'kicked out' of England, and Newman returned him his gift of a Madonna del Gran Duca with a gentle note of reproach nicely calculated to bring its recipient to heel:

Once on a time a young man made his Senior a present . . . It was a Madonna, and that Senior put her over his bed-head, and . . . used to say 'John Walter gave me that picture,' and he never said so without thinking kindly of him.

 . . . at length there was a day when the young man made a speech before a whole county; and . . . wished that all who were such as that elderly man was, were kicked out of the kingdom.

What then could that elderly man do, before he was kicked out, but send back to that young man, who once had an innocent conscience and a gentle heart, that same sweet Madonna . . . [42]

This heaping of coals had the desired result in a letter of apology; 'they may insult us in parliament', Newman concluded, 'but I don't see how any act they pass can hurt us'.[43] The Ecclesiastical Titles Act, the illiberal measure of liberals, was ultimately calculated only to delight bigoted Protestant Tories; it was a dead letter from the first and was to be repealed in 1871 by Gladstone. The limits of the agitation were made clear in Birmingham itself, where the radicals effectively dissuaded a No-Popery meeting from urging any new State measure against the Roman Catholic Church.

There was worse abuse of Faber, whom the Irvingite MP Henry Drummond improbably described as going 'about the country seducing young women'.[44] Drummond was being fed stories by Pierce Connelly, an American Episcopalian clergyman who had separated from his wife Cornelia and their children to become a Catholic priest and chaplain to Shrewsbury. He then returned to the Church of England and failed in legal moves to command the restoration of conjugal relations with Cornelia, who had founded a successful teaching order. The slur on Faber, never a lady's man, had its comic side. Five of the London Oratory's lay fratelli were taking the discipline with the community. 'Are you not afraid', Newman asked Faber, 'of this getting into Punch, with a picture of F. Faber in the act?'[45] There was also a grim note of humour when Henry Wilberforce's uncle Richard Spooner, MP for North Warwickshire, claimed that the Edgbaston 'convent' was being fitted with 'underground cells'. 'They run under the kitchen and its neighbourhood', wrote Newman to the Editor of the *Morning Chronicle*. 'One is to be a larder, another is to be a coal-hole; beer, perhaps wine, may occupy a third. As to the rest, Mr Spooner ought to know that we have had ideas of baking and brewing . . . '[46] Newman was defended by his own MP, and there was a solemn inspection of the 'cells' by the Mayor of Birmingham. But the irony of Newman's letter was lost on Spooner, who read it to the Commons as proof of his fears; and when a member of the community fell ill, Newman thought that 'we shall be said to have poisoned him, and Mr Spooner will demand an inquest'.[47]

The worst, however, that Newman had to fear for the moment was the rumour that he might be made Bishop of Nottingham; he protested against the possibility to George Talbot, now a Papal Chamberlain with daily access to the Pope. 'My *line* is different', Newman told him: ' – it is to oppose the infidels of the day . . . *My writings would be at an end*, were I a Bishop. I might publish a sermon or two, but the work of a *life* would be lost.'[48] Newman thought the Church not ripe for the hierarchy. 'Now they have one, they can't fill up the sees, positively can't.' He encouraged Capes' metropolitan lectures in defence of the faith by laymen, against Ullathorne who, Newman thought, 'has a horror of laymen, and I am sure they may be made in this day the strength of the Church'.[49]

Ullathorne rejected lay discussion of the Faith as an encouragement to the Irish to brawl in pubs. Yet the demand for educated Catholic laymen was outrun by the supply, as the Gorham Judgement and the Papal Aggression brought in their wake a new wave of graduate converts. Newman himself received a number of clergy and laymen from Pusey's own foundation of St Saviour's, Leeds, with its plate in memory of Pusey's daughter Lucy. The Leeds converts planned to establish another Oratory, and while this came to nothing, one of their party, William Paine Neville, joined the Birmingham Oratory and in later life became Newman's secretary and nurse. Newman's great lawyer friend Edward Bellasis was received in December 1850. The most distinguished of the converts were Manning and his lawyer friend James Hope, received on 6 April 1851 in London.

It was, then, just as the Catholic ranks were swollen with ex-Anglican talent that the new Archbishop of Armagh, Paul Cullen, wrote at Robert Whitty's suggestion to ask Newman's advice about the appointment of a superior and professors for the new Catholic University of Ireland. Cullen had known Newman when Rector of the Irish College in Rome as censor of Newman's treatises on Athanasius, and the new institution was intended to provide a tertiary education for the Irish laity, in opposition to the 'Godless' non-denominational Queen's Colleges established in Ireland in the 1840s by Newman's old antagonist Sir Robert Peel. Cullen also asked Newman to lecture, but had no conception of the range and depth of Newman's thought about the parlous contemporary condition of Catholic lay and theological education, the consequence in Newman's view of the French Revolution, which had closed Catholic Universities throughout Europe. 'At this moment', wrote Newman to John Moore Capes, 'where are our schools of theology? a scattered and persecuted Jesuit School – one at Louvain – some ghosts of a short lived birth at Munich – hardly a theologian at Rome.'[50] Again, Newman's vision for Dublin, in part suggested by Cullen, was already of a university far grander than one for Catholic Ireland. 'It will be the Catholic University of the English tongue for the whole world',[51] he wrote to the newly converted Thomas William Allies, suggesting that he take a chair. Allies' loss of a rich living had plunged his family into poverty, and Newman pressed among others on Cullen the cause of Henry Wilberforce, David Lewis, Spencer Northcote, Edward Walford, Edward Thompson and Robert Ornsby, whose wife had 'cast him off and returned to her parents',[52] as it was these married converts who tended to stand most in need of support, and yet who were excluded as laymen from the service of the Church.

At dinner with Newman in Birmingham on 18 July 1851, Cullen first proposed that he be the President or Rector of the University, and though Newman agreed only to be Prefect of Studies, he was urged to the higher office by his fellow-Oratorians, on the ground as he told Cullen, that he ought not to have a subordinate place elsewhere'.[53] With the cleric Patrick Leahy and a gallant landowner Myles O'Reilly, who was to defend Spoleto for the Pope, Newman was one of a subcommittee of three which met in

Birmingham in August 1851 to send out a questionnaire to experts on the organization of the University, and at the end of September, he travelled with Allies as secretary to Thurles in Tipperary to draw up a report on the University and to consult with Cullen. The report was agreed and Newman was appointed Rector on 12 November.

It was to Cullen that Newman dedicated the work ultimately entitled *Lectures on the Present Position of Catholics in England*, delivered in the Corn Exchange between 30 June and 1 September 1851 and printed and published at once in weekly numbers. Newman's initial audience included Henry Wilberforce and Wilberforce's newly converted and promptly priested brother-in-law Henry Edward Manning. The lectures made wicked satirical use of the polemic thrown up by the Papal Aggression, and opened with a brilliant comparison between English No-Popery and an imaginary anti-English indignation meeting in Moscow, in which the speaker rouses his audience to a frenzy with an inspired declamation against the legal maxims of Blackstone that '*The King can do no wrong*' and that 'THE KING NEVER DIES'.[54] 'Alexander Pope, too, calls Queen Anne a goddess',[55] adds the impassioned Muscovite speaker, heaping together whole hecatombs of texts and events grotesquely misunderstood, 'and Addison, with a servility only equalled by his profaneness, cries out, "Thee, goddess, thee Britannia's isle adores".'[56] Victoria, he continues, was eighteen when she came to the throne in 1837; the multiple of eighteen and thirty-seven is 666, the number of the Beast.[57] In this, Newman satirized anti-Catholicism as an odd compound of ignorance and prejudice, yet as an all-powerful tradition, 'the tradition of the Court, and of the Law, and of Society, and of Literature, strong in themselves, and acting on each other'.[58] It was this effortless assumption of superiority and impregnability that had bred the assured Anglican fulminations against Rome of the previous year, which Newman compared to a clamour of bells:

> Not by an act of volition, but by a sort of mechanical impulse, bishop and dean, archdeacon and canon, rector and curate, one after another, each on his high tower, off they set, swinging and booming, tolling and chiming, with nervous intenseness, and thickening emotion, and deepening volume, the old dingdong . . . jingling and clamouring and ringing the changes on their poor half-dozen notes, all about 'the Popish aggression,' 'insolent and insidious,' 'insidious and insolent,' 'insolent and atrocious,' 'atrocious and insolent,' 'atrocious, insolent, and ungrateful,' 'ungrateful, insolent, and atrocious,' 'foul and offensive,' 'pestilent and horrid,' 'subtle and unholy,' 'audacious and revolting,' 'contemptible and shameless,' 'malignant,' 'frightful,' 'mad,' 'meretricious,' . . . bobs, and bobs-royal, and triple-bob-majors, and grandsires, – to the extent of their compass and the full ring of their metal, in honour of Queen Bess, and to the confusion of the Holy Father and the Princes of the Church.[59]

Newman also made play of Spooner's accusation against him: a 'gentle-man of blameless character, a county member', a relation of one of his dearest friends, Henry Wilberforce, had charged him 'with delighting in blood, with enjoying the shrieks and groans of agony and despair, with presiding at a banquet of dislocated limbs, quivering muscles, and wild countenances'.[60] Perhaps in half a century these rumours in the 'Edgbaston Tradition' of the underground torture-chambers of the Oratory might rouse a mob to rescue from Newman's 'cells' or cellars 'certain legs of mutton and pats of butter from imprisonment, and to hold an inquest over a dozen packing-cases, some old hampers, a knife board, and a range of empty blacking bottles'.[61] Among the new Protestant prophets bearing false witness and preaching slander was the ex-Dominican Giovanni Giacinto Achilli, a rising star of the No-Popery lecture circuit, who had come to Birmingham to expose the Inquisition which, he claimed, had imprisoned him; and with Achilli, Newman had fun indeed:

Ah! Dr. Achilli, . . . He has a something to tell, it is true; he *has* a scandal to reveal, he *has* an argument to exhibit . . . It is indeed our great con-fusion, that our Holy Mother could have had a priest like him . . . 'Mothers of families,' he seems to say 'gentle maidens, innocent children, look at me . . . Can any church live over the imputation of such a production as I am? . . . I am that Father Achilli, who, as early as 1826, was deprived of my faculty to lecture, for an offence which my superiors did their best to conceal . . . I am that Achilli, who in the diocese of Viterbo in February, 1831, robbed of her honour a young woman of eighteen; who in September, 1833, was found guilty of a second such crime, in the case of a person of twenty-eight; and who perpetrated a third in July, 1834, in the case of another aged twenty-four . . . I am that son of St. Dominic who is known to have repeated the offence at Capua, in 1834 or 1835; and at Naples again, in 1840, in the case of a child of fifteen. I am he who chose the sacristy of the church for one of these crimes, and Good Friday for another . . . I am the Cavaliere Achilli, who then went to Corfu, made the wife of a tailor faithless to her husband, and lived publicly and travelled about with the wife of a chorus-singer. I am that Professor in the Protestant College at Malta, who with two others was dismissed from my post for offences which the authorities cannot get themselves to describe . . .' Yes, you are an incontrovertible proof, that priests may fall and friars break their vows. You are your own witness; but while you *need* not go out of yourself for your argument, neither are you *able* . . . the beginning and the ending you are both.[62]

These charges had already been aired by Wiseman in the *Dublin Review* for July 1850, and Newman took care to find out from James Hope and David Lewis whether he could be charged with libel. Hope advised him that there was no great danger of prosecution if the charges were true and had not been answered when they had appeared in print before.

Newman was, none the less, 'in a great stew',[63] as he told Lewis, in making the charges, but his worst fears were realized at the end of August 1851 when he heard that Achilli's friends in the Evangelical Alliance intended to prosecute him. Ullathorne presided at a Catholic rally to support him in the Corn Exchange in October, and Fathers Joseph Gordon and Nicholas Darnell were sent to Italy to gather evidence. The legal notice of the prosecution was served on Newman on 27 October, but Wiseman did nothing to find the papers proving Achilli's immoralities which might have stopped the case from going to trial. The Cardinal only produced the papers when it was too late, in the very hour when the rule for the trial was made absolute, nor did he give Darnell introductions strong enough to compel the production of evidence by the Neapolitan police.

His errors were compounded by others. Newman's counsel, the Attorney General, Sir Alexander Cockburn, thought wrongly that Edward Badeley's affidavit would postpone a decision for a trial until Easter, and when that was rejected, would not consider a stronger form. The judge set to try the case, John Campbell, a militant Protestant, the son of a Presbyterian minister, and later Lord Chancellor, was hostile to Newman from the first, and the very Birmingham urchins cried after him 'Six months in quad'.[64] 'I am sorting my papers, and making up my affairs, just as if I were going to die',[65] wrote Newman. He despatched a lawyer to Rome to collect affidavits from Achilli's victims. Stanislas Flanagan scoured England for the Italian Passionist Vincent Grotti, to get him to go to Italy for evidence, and Maria Giberne was deputed 'to pounce on one woman at Naples, another at Viterbo, and forthwith to return with one in each hand'. Achilli had even made advances to his servant in England, Harriett Harris, and there would be no want of witnesses to appear for Newman at his trial.

Evidence, however, had to overcome prejudice, and Richard Stanton reported to Faber on 4 December that Newman was now '*not less* restless and excited than when in London, and I fear more so'.[66] In Newman's uncertainty, he welcomed the cross as a compensation for years of prosperity and happiness, and drew up a Litany invoking the ten St Johns who had known some kind of confinement, together with the patrons of Naples, Capua, Corfu, Malta, Viterbo and London where Achilli had committed his enormities. Meanwhile Newman relied on a crusade of prayer for him, as the Poor Clares increased their austerities in his favour, and Ushaw College laid on a Novena, and the Dominican foundress, Mother Margaret Mary Hallahan, formerly Ullathorne's housekeeper, a great admirer of Newman and advocate for him with the Bishop, had her favourite image of the Virgin carried in procession on three successive days, and gently upbraided Newman's lack of faith in her heavenly patroness: 'I wish you could have heard twenty Nuns scalding you', she wrote, 'for wanting confidence in my own Beloved Mother'.[67]

These prayers were answered in January 1852, when Newman heard from Joseph Gordon that Rosa di Alessandris, one of Achilli's victims at Viterbo, had made a sworn statement, and that another, Elena (Gippina) Giustini, would come to England to give evidence, as would Sophia Maria Balisano, brought from Naples by Father Grotti. They were placed under the care of Maria Giberne in Paris, and Newman exhorted her to allow Gippina's spiritless husband an unlimited supply of cigars and public entertainment: 'is there no equestrial exhibition? no harmless play? no giant or dwarf? no panorama, cosmorama, diorama, dissolving views, steam incubation of chickens, or *menagerie* (the jardin des plants!) which he would like to see'. This harmless fun indicated relief. 'It amuses me', Newman told Maria, 'that you should be thought capable of such a tail.'[68] From February 1852, he had the distraction of moving his books and papers to the new Oratorian house in Edgbaston, his final home, but his worry was still intense. He thought that his counsel Cockburn, though a hater of Evangelicals, had so far ruined his cause, and was insufficiently committed to attacking Achilli, being 'a man of profligate life himself'.[69] Achilli's lawyers tried delay when confronted with witnesses, whose upkeep began costing Newman forty pounds a week. The Cardinal himself presided over a meeting in London in March 1852 of wealthy and influential Catholic supporters of the 'Newman Defence Fund' for Newman's cause: they included a number of new converts, like Hope, Bellasis and one of Newman's most faithful new disciples, the convert Irish MP William Monsell. It is not surprising that under the strain, he found the composition of his first lectures for the Irish University agonizing, and only felt that he had got through the task with the special help of the Virgin Mary. In May, he reported a further postponement through Cockburn's 'treachery',[70] but he failed in his attempt to get rid of the lawyer, on the eve of his departure for Ireland.

The Irish lectures were published as *Discourses on University Education*, and revised afterwards as part of *The Idea of a University*. Newman boarded at a former mansion converted into a luxurious school at 6 Harcourt Street, and he had an ideal room in which to speak and perfect acoustics for his voice, and was amazed at the Irish cleverness, the very attendants offering analyses of the lectures which were attended by the best Catholic intellects in Dublin. The achievement was the more astonishing, as he steeled himself for his trial, which took place in the fourth week of June 1852. He seemed calm and unmoved as he prayed in the tribune of the London Oratory, and at the end of June, he could only be grateful to Cockburn for the 'power and effect' of his defence, in 'the cause of a person of another religion, and of habits of thought and place in society altogether different from their own'.[71] But Campbell summed up against him, and the jury found for Achilli. 'We consider', wrote the hitherto hostile *Times*, 'that a great blow has been given to the administration of justice in this country, and Roman Catholics will have henceforth only too good reason for asserting, that there is no justice for them in cases tending to arouse the Protestant feelings of judges and juries.'[72] Newman heard of the conviction by a telegram from his newly converted Catholic lawyer-friend Edward Badeley which arrived at 11 p.m. He felt that he had gained the moral victory: '*you must none of you be doleful*', he told Faber. 'We are floored, if we think ourselves floored . . . We must have no indignation against Judge and Jury, or any thing else – they act according to their nature . . . Poor shadows, what are they to us!'[73] He now had six months to wait for his sentence.

Meanwhile he had to be in Dublin on 29 June for Cullen's installation as Archbishop; their first practical disagreement was to be in March 1853 over Cullen's unilateral attempt to appoint Dr James Taylor university Vice-President. Wiseman had no sooner heard of the verdict over Achilli than he invited Newman to preach in July 1852 at the First Provincial Synod of the new hierarchy at Oscott, and the occasion, with the thirteen new bishops and all the senior clergy in attendance, called forth one of Newman's most famous productions, 'The Second Spring', with its haunting opening on the blight and decay of youthful promise, and its peroration on the eternal springtime of the Church:

> The world grows old, but the Church is ever young . . . 'Arise, make haste, my love, my dove, my beautiful one, and come. For the winter is now past . . . ' Arise, Mary, and go forth in thy strength into that north country, which once was thine own . . . A second temple rises on the ruins of the old. Canterbury has gone its way, and York is gone, and Durham is gone, and Winchester is gone . . . but the Church in England has died, and the Church lives again. Westminster and Nottingham, Beverley and Hexham, Northampton and Shrewsbury, if the world lasts, shall be names as musical to the ear, as stirring to the heart, as the glories we have lost; and Saints shall rise out of them, if God so will, and Doctors once again shall give the law to Israel, and Preachers call to penance and to justice, as at the beginning.[74]

The sermon is the bane of English Catholic historiography in its dim and dismal view of the vigorous if hidden Catholic life in England in the previous three centuries as 'a set of poor Irishmen, coming and going at harvest time, . . . an elderly person, . . . grave and solitary, and strange, though noble in bearing, and said to be of good family . . . An old-fashioned house of gloomy appearance, closed in with high walls, with an iron gate, and yews . . . '[75] Yet in Newman's evocation of the hopes of the present, he perfectly captured the mood of the moment among the Oscott Fathers:

> The bishops and clergy were nearly all in tears. And when the preacher

came out from the Synod, they crowded upon him, giving full flow to the ardent outpourings of their gratitude. It was an indescribable scene; a scene so overpowering to the gentle preacher, that Dr Manning rescued him from it, and quietly accompanied him to his room.[76]

The Cardinal himself was enjoying one of his own greatest successes as the author of the decrees by which the Synod gave form and order to the renascent Church. During the sermon, he 'fairly gave up the effort at dignity and self-control, and sobbed like a child'.

There is no reference to this triumph in Newman's correspondence; he was overwhelmed by the death of Harriett in July and by the need to keep up a head of steam in turning out his *University Discourses*, which gave him more trouble in the writing than anything else he ever wrote. He also had to acknowledge and encourage the flow of money towards the expenses of his trial, now mounting to a massive £6000. His subsequent tour of Ireland was a nightmare. He was 'killed with kindness' with 'the exuberant hearty affection' of the Irish priesthood and people. He could not endure the soft featherbeds, or take pleasure 'in large *legs* of coarse veal, boiled mutton as red as in the shambles, and blood shot kidneys'.[77] Harriett's death was followed in August by that of his beloved aunt Elizabeth. His legal bills were massive, but so were the subscriptions to honour them. France had raised £1000 by August, while one Irish parish and two priests in Limerick each subscribed £40, to make the English contributions seem small. 'I feel it at once most cruel, yet a great honour', wrote Newman to the two priests of the diocese of Limerick who had sent him the diocesan offering of £312, 'that I should call forth such lavish offerings from so impoverished a people . . . '[78]

There were offerings from both the Oratory and soldiery of Malta, and from the assembled American hierarchy under Francis Kenrick as Archbishop of Baltimore. But Newman was, as he confessed, a most reluctant martyr. One specialist declared that 'unless I got out of anxiety and let my nerves rest, I should die Swift's death',[79] and medical affidavits were ready to plead his ill-health against imprisonment, but when called to judgement at last on 22 November, he reluctantly followed the advice of his five lawyers and demanded a retrial. Cockburn then subjected Campbell to a two to three hour harangue, 'a most masterly exposure', as Newman called it, 'of Judge and Jury'.[80] He was supported by a host of genteel friends, the Earl of Arundel, Bowyer, Monsell and John Ball among MPs, Bellasis, Henry Bowden and Alexander Fullerton, while the doyen of the Old Catholic gentry Charles Langdale and a number of metropolitan priests looked on from the gallery.[81]

For all the trauma of the proceedings, this was martyrdom in style. James Hope had married Sir Walter Scott's granddaughter, and invited Newman to spend Christmas 1852 recuperating at Scott's mansion at Abbotsford with the Arundels, a prospect made the more delightful by Newman's veneration for Scott, and by the household's dedicated round of religious observance. The holiday was troubled by Newman's inadequate attempt to deal at long distance with Fr Nicholas Darnell's bungled dismissal of a lay brother for a greatly magnified offence, his 'spiritual love' for Newman's friend Frances Wootten, which Newman considered 'not any open scandal, or extraordinary depravity, but . . . a gross very gross case of self-deception. Such a case is afflicting, but not horrible . . . '[82] He was still at Abbotsford on 20 January 1853, as his counsel argued for a new trial in London; Campbell refused it, and on 31 January Newman was called into court to be sentenced, supported by a cohort of his faithful attendants, including Bellasis, Bowyer, Monsell and Henry Bowden. Newman was prepared to plead that imprisonment would be his death. His lawyer insisted that Newman's charges against Achilli still stood. By a misunderstanding with the Judge, Newman did not make his prepared speech, which effectively repeated his charges against Achilli: 'I accused him of having broken oaths; he convicts me by taking his oath he has not broken them . . . There is a God above us. He has never failed me; He does not fail me now'.[83]

In passing sentence, Sir John Coleridge, his erstwhile Tractarian admirer, pronounced Newman's moral deterioration while a convert, as evidenced by the bitterness of his attack on Achilli: 'Surely, if you had felt yourself called upon to act as the judge, and as the executioner', declaimed Coleridge, 'of a man so foul and so wretched as you described Dr Achilli to be, you should have approached that task with feelings of sorrow and sadness . . . '[84] 'Oh! What a sweet musical, almost unearthly voice it was, so unlike any other we had heard', wrote Coleridge of Newman in his diary, wondering if it had been 'out of place' to lecture him, and yet assuring himself that Newman was *'over-praised'*.[85] But his sentence – £100 fine, and imprisonment until it was paid – was greeted with a burst of laughter, and was tantamount to acquittal; and, wrote Newman, 'we walked off in triumph amid the hurrahs of 200 paddies'.[86]

Newman wrote of 'poor Coleridge's prose' that 'mere habit, as in the case of the skinned eels, would keep me from being annoyed. I have not been the but [sic] of slander and scorn for 20 years for nothing'.[87] In later editions of the work, the specific charges against Achilli were omitted and asterisks and a Latin sentence inserted: 'DE ILLIS QUAE SEQUEBANTUR POSTERORUM IUDICIUM SIT. In fest. Nativ. S. Joan. Bapt. 1852'. 'About the things that followed let posterity be judge.'[88] To respectable society, however, Newman had, whether right or wrong, been mixed up in something disgraceful, both popish and sexually sordid. The strain had, moreover, lasted sixteen months, leaving him exhausted, and as he mourned the death of his Oratorian friend Father Joseph Gordon, he told Henry Wilberforce that 'I think I have now passed into my Autumn'.[89]

21

The Catholic University

'They who play at bowls, must expect rubbers',[1] wrote Newman of the sufferings of his trial. The success of the appeal for his expenses encouraged the creditors of the bankrupt Monmouthshire and Glamorganshire Banking Company to 'put the skrew on Catholics' by pressing Ullathorne as a shareholder for a further payment on the Company's debts of £250,000. Ullathorne and John Moore, the President of Oscott, were sent to the Bennett's Hill prison, whence Ullathorne, formerly a chaplain to convicts in Australia, cheerfully reported to Newman that they had said Mass 'much in the style of [the imprisoned] Pius VII and Cardinal Pacca, a style not new, of course, to me . . . Even our old Governor, a great character, once a Bow Street officer, and now as peremptory as fate, and as short as crumpets, says with the rest of the world that it is our duty to resist and not to pay'.[2] 'He has already given them £1000 – if he bribes them again', wrote Newman of Ullathorne, 'he will in due time be arrested again, and so they will go on squeezing him.'[3] Ullathorne and Moore were released after ten days. Newman's own legal expenses came to over £9000, and the collections for him among Catholics to nearly £13,000. He was to spend £2600 of it on a new church for his Catholic University in Dublin. He sent £400 to the French nuns of the Society of the Faithful Virgin at Norwood who had been acquitted of cruelty to one of their charges but left to pay their legal costs. He authorized the diversion of a Dutch subscription to his costs to the persecuted Archbishop of Freiburg-im-Breisgau, and later used some of the money from America to buy the cemetery for the Oratory at Rednal, where he was to build a house as a rural retreat. The appeal had, however, been an international one: so his primary charities were to France at Norwood, to Freiburg in Germany and to Dublin in Ireland.

Meanwhile, he did not understand why he was waiting to be called to the Catholic University: two years had passed since the invitation to be President, and Cullen would not reply to his letters of enquiry. Newman later decided that Cullen had learned from Rome 'the virtue of delay; he simply left questions to settle themselves'.[4] The difficulty also lay in the divisions among the Irish bishops: Cullen wanted a safely Catholic and denominational university; his archenemy in the hierarchy, John MacHale, Archbishop of Tuam, a militant patriot christened by O'Connell the 'Lion of the Fold of Judah', wanted a solely Irish university; and there were still bishops who looked wistfully to the non-denominational ideal of the state-funded Queen's Colleges. As Apostolic Delegate to the Irish Church, Cullen held an unprecedented authority in Ireland which caused jealousy of him among the bishops, who had other reasons for suspecting an elite institution modelled on Oxford, a mere five years after the Famine. The danger flag was hoisted in September 1853 by Monsignor Talbot in Rome, who asked Miss Giberne if Newman was 'capable of taking the management of the Irish University where he will have to battle continually with all the Paddies'. Maria loyally blasted him with the assurance that Newman 'could move mountains'[5]; but it was to become increasingly clear to him that he was an instrument in Cullen's hands for fighting a war against other Irishmen.

The call to Ireland, 'in a day or two!'[6] only came in October 1853. Newman had to fit his visit to Dublin on 4 November into the delivery in Liverpool of his *Lectures on the History of the Turks in its Relation to Christianity*, a theme in part suggested by the crisis which led to the Crimean War in 1854. The Lectures are an extraordinary production, with the old Evangelical apocalyptic overtones in their picture of the empire of the Ottoman Antichrist, which still had its 'brute clutch' on 'the Danube, the Euphrates, and the Nile; which embraces the Pindus, the Taurus, the Caucasus, Mount Sinai, the Libyan mountains, and the Atlas . . . and which, having no history itself, is heir to the historical names of Constantinople and Nicaea, Nicomedia and Caesarea, Jerusalem and Damascus, Nineveh and Babylon, Mecca and Bagdad, Antioch and Alexandria, ignorantly holding in possession one-half of the history of the whole world. There it lies and will not die'.[7]

There is a gross one-sidedness to a view of the Turks as a people who created nothing of themselves but who as warriors, exploited or slaughtered the nations under their rule. Yet the author's invocation of the ancient war between Christendom and Islam from the time of the Crusades and of the centuries of struggle to free Eastern Europe from Turkish rule, has an imaginative grandeur that won it a public hearing, and may have influenced that section of opinion which regretted the alliance with the Turkish power in the following year.

Newman's own reaction to the war was one of total horror. 'I have no mercy on Turkey', he told Jemima, 'and . . . should imitate the man in the story, who, when another cried out "Stop thief, he has got my hat, and I am too drunk to run after him", said "Well, if you are quite sure you can't, I will make bold to take your wig" . . . The Turks *must* go . . . '[8] 'I have hated the war heartily from the first, thought it unnecessary, and considered Whig pride to have been the moving principle of it.'[9] 'And, whereas Turkey lies below water mark, and that water is the great ravening empire of Russia, we have attempted, not like Mrs Partington with a broom, but by mounds and dykes, to keep the ocean out. Turkey must go; yet we have attempted to set Humpty Dumpty on the wall again – and have enveloped ourselves in illusions and shams . . . Three years before we had undertaken the Pope, whose arms are spiritual – we go on to the Czar, whose arms are fleshly – Perhaps the second blunder is the punishment of the first.'[10]

Newman's visits to Liverpool to lecture, to Dublin on university business, and to Clifton, left him with a three week cold from mid November 1853, though he had to rise to preach at the formal opening of his new Edgbaston church. 'I cannot bear this gadding to and fro',[11] he told Mrs Bowden, as he fended off preaching invitations which would have had him rushing all over the country. His principal worry was the unsatisfactory condition of the Irish University. The invitation of October had come from only two of the bishops on the University Committee, one being the other Primate, Dixon, who, Newman thought, 'was in fact in this matter nothing more than the proxy of Dr Cullen',[12] though Dixon himself was never to show Newman anything but kindness. Cullen's sole acknowledgement of Newman as Rector had been his presence at the lectures on university education. With this lack of firm authorization from above, Newman felt his exposed position as a mere convert 'acting on my own hook . . . an Englishman, taking upon himself to teach the Paddies what education was . . . a propagandist, . . . without means, looking out for a situation, and finding and feathering a nest from the pockets of the Irish . . . That I intended to make a good thing of it, was actually said'.[13]

Seeking a proper authority for himself, he wrote to Cullen on 24 December 1853 asking to 'be publicly admitted or recognized as Rector of the University'.[14] The reply through Fr James Taylor, the secretary of the University Committee, declined the proposal on the ground that the University did not yet possess its principal building, a Georgian mansion on St Stephen's Green, and that a majority of the bishops had yet to support it. James Hope, now called Hope-Scott in honour of his wife's grandfather, advised Newman not to resign, and he tried again with a letter to Cullen on 30 December; the Archbishop wrote a vaguely reassuring reply, indicating that he thought of recognition of Newman's position as Rector as a document rather than what Newman had requested, a formal ceremony. Newman turned to Cardinal Wiseman in Rome: 'I ask nothing else but a fair stage, nothing but a locus standi, if it be but an inch of Irish ground . . .'[15] Newman later considered that Wiseman remembered his conviction over Achilli, 'and wished to make up to me what perhaps he was conscious had come by his own slovenly ways of going on'.[16] The Cardinal translated Newman's letter for the Pope, and at a private audience with Pius IX in January 1854, he urged that Newman be made a bishop; the proposal, he said, had received Cullen's 'hearty concurrence'[17] at their meeting at Amiens in October. Wiseman promptly wrote to Newman that the Pope had even mentioned in passing a possible episcopal title *in partibus infidelium*, Porfirio. Wiseman had already written to Cullen suggesting that the Pope was well disposed to a formal university foundation, and that 'a preliminary Brief might be issued, . . . confirming Dr Newman as Rector . . . If your Grace thinks so too, the thing is done'.[18]

Taylor passed this last suggestion to Newman, but Newman himself feared that 'the Cardinal will do too much, and that we shall have a University set up before we know where we are'. He thought of going to Rome himself, and returning 'with a prestige, as if I had a blunderbuss in my pocket'.[19] On 31 January 1854, he heard from Wiseman about the proposed bishopric. Cullen, however, gently poured cold water on the scheme. He warned Propaganda that given Ireland's bad treatment 'by not only Protestant but also Catholic England', Newman should not be made a bishop at the wish of an English cardinal. The jealousy between the nations 'would spoil everything, no matter how good it was in itself'. Rather, the proposal should come from Propaganda itself: but that, he implied, would be a mistake for which Rome would then bear responsibility. The University would be 'supported by the contributions of the poor', who would resent an ostentatious or prominent or expensive President. It would be the better for the moment to delay, as Wiseman's 'grandiose ideas'[20] were conceived in ignorance of Ireland.

These arguments killed off Newman's bishopric, by pointing up the political delicacy of the situation, in which Cullen himself was exposed to the charge that he was an enemy of all things Irish by some of the leading Irish Nationalist priests and politicians as well as by his archiepiscopal opponent MacHale. Under the circumstances, Paul the Prudent chose the safest course. It was for this very prudence that Rome valued his counsel: but the ecclesiastical virtue did not involve frankness.

Newman's embarrassment at the failure of the honour to materialize was the greater as his impending consecration was public knowledge. He told only Ullathorne, but the Bishop himself had already eulogized him as 'Right Reverend' at a public dinner. The appointment was announced in the *Tablet*. Richard Stanton exhorted Newman to wear violet stockings and a black 'berretta and zucchetto', and not the 'French abomination' in violet, and the London Oratory bought him three mitres.[21] William Monsell gave him a pectoral cross, the Earl of Arundel a massive gold chain, Mrs Bowden a Maltese filigree cross and chain, and Hope-Scott a ring and a 'morse' or cope-clasp ornamented with his dead wife's jewels. Ullathorne was still wondering about the delay in the consecration as late as June. On 29 April, however, Newman received a hint that the proposal had fallen through from Cullen, who pointed to the description of him, in the papal brief of 20 March establishing the University, as 'egregiis animi dotibus ornatus'[22] – adorned with outstanding gifts of soul; *this*, the Archbishop intimated to him, was the distinction promised him from Rome. Newman never asked why the bishopric was not confirmed, but neither Cullen, nor Wiseman nor Ullathorne ever told him that it would not be: 'nor', wrote Newman, 'did they make any chance remark by which I have been able to form any idea why that elevation which was thought by Pope, Cardinal, and Archbishop so expedient for the University, or at least so settled a point, which was so publicly announced, was suddenly and silently reversed'. 'Miss Giberne, to my great vexation', he concluded, at a papal audience said, ' "Holy Father, why don't you make Fr Newman a Bishop?" She reported that he looked much confused and took a great deal of snuff.'[23]

Before this reverse, in early 1854, Newman set off to drum up support for the Catholic University in Ireland. He refused to envision a hodman's death at Kilkenny, which he kept distinct in his mind from Killarney by remembering the cats, when the Bishop took him over the perilous scaffolding of the cathedral. He also trembled at the mutton on the Bishop's table, 'and how it blushed on the first cut, but his Lordship was merciful, and let me dine in the brown'.[24] At a gathering of priests at Carlow he went to sleep after dinner, to be awoken by the announcement that he would explain the University. At Kilkenny, 'the merry conceit of the Paddy'[25] left him at the house of the Protestant Bishop, an old enemy in controversy; while at Waterford, he told Austin Mills, he had to make an impromptu speech to seventy be-medalled blue-clad schoolgirls, and wrote

how, when it was ended, the Mother Schoolmistress did not know he had made it, or even begun it, and still asked for his speech. And how . . . to make it up, he asked for a holiday for the girls, and how the Mother Schoolmistress flatly refused him, by reason (as he verily believes) because she would not recognize and accept his speech, and wanted another, and thought she had dressed up her girls for nothing – and how he nevertheless drank her raspberry's vinegar, which much resembles a nun's anger, being a sweet acid, and how he thought to himself, it being his birthday, that he was full old to be forgiven if he would not at a moment act the spiritual jack pudding to a girl's school.[26]

Yet everywhere, he was welcomed with open arms, and all were 'on one point it seems quite agreed, to be kind to me'.[27] Not that this kindness meant active support. The Bishop of Limerick lent his name, but refused money, and 'should not be supposed to prophesy anything but failure'.[28] Newman drew up a Memorandum on 29 April 1854 on the objects of the University for a meeting of the bishops, which confirmed its Fundamental Constitution in May. Newman asked Cullen for the dignity of a Vicar Generalship like Louvain's or some similar position, to signify episcopal approval for his office. 'Of course nothing came of this appeal!'[29] he noted, though Cullen had originally suggested it. On 4 June, however, Cullen installed him as Rector at a High Mass on Whit Sunday in the pro-Cathedral in Dublin, and he launched his *University Gazette* containing the first section of what was to become *The Office and Work of Universities*. He learned that the medical school in Cecilia Street in Dublin was up for sale and acquired it for the University: as the first Catholic Medical school in Dublin, in a city in which the profession was still overwhelmingly Protestant, it was to prove a lasting success from its opening in 1855. Newman also planned an Observatory, and begged his old friend the Oxford astronomer Manuel Johnson for a notable 'Observer'. 'If he nourished his beard, smoked, and talked broken English, so much the better, if he was a clever fellow and a good (respectable) Catholic . . . with the kind of testimonials which a friend of mine [Johnson himself] once showed to Sir Robert Peel.'[30]

The first University term began without pomp on 3 November 1854. By the end of term there were twenty-seven students, which had increased to sixty-four by spring, and through the session Newman and his Professors delivered their inaugural lectures. The closest of the staff to Newman was Dalgairns' brother-in-law Robert Ornsby, the Professor of Greek and Latin Literature. At the semi-collegiate St Mary's, at 16 Harcourt Street, Newman himself presided over a houseful of students – 'two English, two French, two Irish, and two Scotch – and among these, Lady Lothian's son, Lord H. Kerr's son, the Countess de la Pasture's son, the Vicomte de Vaulchier, and Sir Regd Barnewall'.[31] This gathering was the product of his own personal influence, which continued in a quiet manner, quite unlike the clamour of Faber's celebrated successes, to bear fruit in the conversion of old friends, Robert Wilberforce and the Earl of Dunraven, while he also guided into the Church his old opponent's son, Thomas Arnold the second, who had gone to be an Inspector of Schools in Tasmania.

This was the beginning of the gentle Arnold's religious adventures; his termagent wife, outraged at her husband's loss of his post, was said by Newman to have put a stone through the Catholic chapel window. Against Arnold's gain to the Church and to Newman's circle of friends was the collapse in summer 1855 of his friendship with George Ryder, who withdrew his two sons Henry and Lisle from Newman's tutelage in Dublin, under the impression that Newman was deliberately alienating their affections. Within months, Henry had decided to join the Oratory, where as Fr Ignatius Ryder he was to succeed Newman as its second Superior. Though Newman never cared for Henry personally, there was something in George Ryder's suspicion that he had been displaced as a natural father by a spiritual one.

Newman's problems with the University stemmed from Cullen's caution and clericalism. Cullen said that Newman could only appoint professors with the approval of the four Irish Archbishops. MacHale, however, regarded Newman as Cullen's creature and intimated that in the matters of University appointments and the Medical School, Newman had exceeded his authority. 'The Lion, solus, has roared at me', wrote Newman to St John, '– and I have roared again – and the two roarings are done up in a letter and sent to Dr Cullen at Rome.'[32] The embarrassment of being shown up as less of a Nationalist than MacHale, as well as his own anti-Englishness, may have made Cullen suspicious of Newman's English appointments, but then Cullen was suspicious of laymen altogether. Newman considered the University 'mainly for the sake of the laity', and wanted 'to fill the Professorial Chairs with laymen, except those which are more or less theological',[33] but the University's financial committee never met, and Cullen would not respond to Newman's request for a lay financial committee to give the better-off laity a say in the institution and so encourage them to send their sons. Instead, Newman recalled, the laity 'were treated like good little boys – were told to shut their eyes and open their mouths, and take what we give to them'.[34]

Still worse than Newman's English appointments in Cullen's eyes were some of his Irish ones. The Archbishop insisted on regarding the 1848 rebels of the Young Ireland movement as anticlericals like their contemporaries in Young Italy; but they had talent and learning, and Newman naturally turned to them. They had been 'quasi rebels', he thought, who had mainly 'cooled down'. 'I did not care much for their political opinions', he recalled, but they were 'the ablest men who had belonged to the University'. He could 'never be sorry for asking their assistance – not to take them would have been preposterous'.[35] He made Eugene O'Curry, the greatest Irish scholar of his generation, 'anima candidissima',[36] whitest of souls, as Newman called him, Professor of Irish History and Archaeology; Newman attended all his lectures and secured their publication as *Lectures on the Manuscript Materials of Ancient Irish History* and a specially ordered fount of Irish type. Newman appointed another ex-Young Irelander, John O'Hagan, Lecturer in Political Economy, while yet another, William Sullivan, who as Newman wrote, was 'a rough man, but clever and, to me, engaging, from his honesty and sharpness',[37] became Professor of Chemistry.

Newman was suspect to Cullen for his friendship with these men, and with his sometime enemy Frederick Lucas, as in Cullen's eyes, Lucas and his Tenant League were besmirched by their association with the former Young Irelanders. The Archbishop's attempts to disassociate the priesthood from the politics of the Tenant League and from Lucas were, moreover, inextricably bound up with his feud with Lucas' friend MacHale. Cullen, Lucas and MacHale all carried their causes to Rome in December 1854, during the celebrations of the papal definition of the Immaculate Conception. MacHale was furious to learn that Propaganda had placed the University under the four Irish Archbishops, in effect under Cullen, and Cullen wrote from Rome to Newman that his enemies like Lucas wished the world to believe that he, Cullen, wanted 'to sell the Irish Church [to the Whig administration], and the price is to be a charter for the University . . . your authority is quoted to prove that I am really become a slave of the government . . . '[38]

Newman could only write to Cullen an amazed denial that he had said anything of the kind. As to Lucas, Newman replied, 'I know him and respect him highly – but I think he is simply mazed and wild, when he speaks of

your Grace having done this or that, *if* (as people say) he says it'.[39] There
is no evidence that Lucas tried, as Cullen thought, to involve Newman in
his war against Cullen, but Newman's own personal regard for Lucas, one
of his advisors on Ireland with Ornsby and Henry Wilberforce, did not
allow him to break their friendship, which continued to feed Cullen's suspicions. Lucas' premature death in 1855 robbed Newman and the University
of a friend who might have interceded on their behalf with MacHale. The
irony of Newman's position was that as a sometime Anglican enemy of
Daniel O'Connell – and of Lucas – he should be under a cloud with an
Irish Archbishop for patronizing and employing Irish rebels; even while his
own Englishness and his connection with Cullen laid him open to the
hostility of Irish Nationalists like MacHale.

Yet Cullen himself did not scruple to complain about Newman to Rome:
that he was inefficient and inattentive to detail, especially to discipline, that
he allowed the students to smoke and be out at all hours, and tried to serve
two masters, the University and the Oratory: 'He cannot spend a great part
of the year in England and govern a university here'. The Archbishop
hoped that Rome would not make Newman a bishop 'until he has properly
arranged all the affairs of the university'.[40] Newman's attitude to discipline
was looser than Cullen's; the one was based on Oxford, the other on an
Irish seminary. Not that Newman was especially liberal: he had tried to
impose a stricter discipline in Oriel, and even the billiard table in the Dublin
house was introduced with a ban on betting, to keep the young men out of
temptation's way. As to the charge of his absence, he wrote in September
1855, 'I was in Ireland 46 weeks running; except 6 Sundays',[41] and had
faithfully discharged all the duties of correspondence with the University
secretary, Thomas Stratton, and produced a proper annual report.

This was not an obvious time to produce a piece of light literature. In
the spring of 1848, Newman began a novel, *Callista*, about the Church in
North Africa, during the Decian persecution of the third century; but he
finished little more than three chapters, and laid it aside, only resuming
and completing it in the summer of 1855. The work followed on Charles
Kingsley's erotic onslaught on Newman's beloved Church of Alexandria, in
Hypatia, published in 1852–3, and on Wiseman's novel, *Fabiola*, about the
Christianity of the Roman Catacombs, which appeared in 1854. Newman
had glimpsed the coast of North Africa on his Mediterranean journey in
1832, and the land inflamed the imagination of a number of nineteenth-
century writers, like Flaubert in *Salammbo*. Even Newman's work has its
share of horrors, notably a passage describing the witch Gurta's crucifixion
of a child and the torture and martyrdom of the heroine Callista. Only a
little less gruesome are the masterly account of a plague of locusts, the
diabolical possession and reduction to idiocy of the wild and wayward semi-
Christian Juba – the idiocy being a mechanism that wins him salvation –
and an anti-Christian riot and its attendant killings, with the horrified and

brutal reaction to this lower-class violence of the 'respectable' priesthoods and citizens and of the Roman soldiery.

The last incident recalled the anti-Catholic riots of Newman's own time, and other references are also contemporary. The religion of Agellius' uncle Jucundus, a selfish but amiable old buffer, is pure Establishmentarianism; its content is pagan and Roman but its form anticipates Erastian Anglicanism. 'We own it jars on our patriotism', declared one reviewer, 'to see . . . a Briton born satirise England as heathen Rome, and not very obscurely prophesy for her the same doom',[42] but then Newman had declared the British Empire under divine judgement while still an Anglican. The philosopher Polemo is a kind of cossetted modern liberal. There are unwitting anachronisms that Newman had feared to commit: he purged from later editions a reference to the South American passion flower, but retained the equally South American tomatoes. The psychological interest of the work lies in the conflicting ideas and passions in the mind of the hero Agellius, a wholly believable amalgam of love and religion, and in the elements in Callista's conversion, into which Newman projected his own early fascination with and repulsion from Roman Catholicism. Callista herself is a spirited creation, the very embodiment of Greek pagan virtue, her nature needing completion by grace, her native refinement by Christianity. She embodies Newman's conception of Christian humanism, that tempering of Hellenism by the Gospel which was his own personal and educational ideal.

The volume illustrates Newman's facility for turning his pen to anything, as does a series of letters signed 'Catholicus' which he wrote in March–April 1855 for Henry Wilberforce's *Weekly Register* on the crisis in the Crimea. Newman argued that the freedoms of the British Constitution were unsuitable for fighting a war. The decentralization of power in Britain was a blessing compared with Russian autocracy or American democracy: 'I have no liking', he wrote, 'for the tyranny whether of autocrat or mob; no taste for being whirled off to Siberia, or tarred and feathered in the far West . . .'[43] The outcome of freedom was the individual enterprise of the imperial Briton. 'He is on the top of the Andes, or in a diving-bell in the Pacific, or taking notes at Timbuctoo, or grubbing at the Pyramids, or scouring over the Pampas, or acting as prime minister to the king of Dahomey, or smoking the pipe of friendship with the Red Indians, or hutting at the Pole.'[44]

But the price of the Constitutional State that nurtured free men was a weak government which 'cannot conduct a war'. 'England, surely, is the paradise of little men, and the purgatory of great ones',[45] because the little men were jealous of their freedoms and suspicious of great men and great power. England lacked great men as soldiers or saints, as little men showed the same jealousy of the soldier as of the parson, and towards each had adopted, through the devices of 'a National Church, and a Constitutional Army', 'precautions borrowed from the necessary treatment of wild animals, – (1) to tie him up, (2) to pare his claws, and (3) to keep him low'.[46]

Church and Army were therefore hamstrung by a staff of gentlemen without professional training; and 'the ignorant, intemperate public, who clamour for an unwise war, and then . . . proceed to beat their zealous servants in the midst of the fight', were ignoring 'difficulties which lie in the very nature of things'.[47]

·*Callista* and 'Catholicus' were minor recreations from the affairs of the University; what knocked Newman off course was trouble with the London Oratory, which appealed to Propaganda in August 1855 to suspend the clause of the English Oratorian rule that forbade the hearing of nuns' confessions. The London House said nothing of the matter to Newman, though it was accustomed to defer to his judgement in fine detail. The only hint of what was afoot came from Stanton, who in describing the London Oratory's doings in September said that the community had asked for instructions about whether to continue confessing nuns. He gave no indication of where the instructions were being sought: Newman imagined the Roman Oratory. But on 16 October 1855, Dalgairns, who disliked the order that he should cease hearing the confessions of nuns in Birmingham, showed Newman a copy of Faber's application on the point to Propaganda. Ullathorne called at the Oratory next day to tell Newman that Rome had consulted him about the London Oratory's appeal, that he had written to support it – he wanted Dalgairns to continue as confessor – and that Rome had issued a Rescript with the requested dispensation. Newman at once, on 18 October, drew up a solemn protest to Cardinal Fransoni. While he was opposed to Oratorians acting as conventional confessors, he was much more disturbed that the London House should have unilaterally tried to alter their common Rule; 'as *I* brought the Rule of the English Oratory from Rome in my hand', he wrote to Ambrose St John, 'and gave it myself to the Brompton Fathers, and admitted them upon it, there was a congruity, decency, consideration, in their not trying to meddle with it, without a reference to me'.[48]

To protect his own community from London, he wanted recognition from Propaganda that London and Birmingham were wholly independent of each other, like the Oratories in Italy. Faber only wanted the dispensation for London, and the document applied to both houses because Propaganda did not imagine that Faber was acting by himself. Fransoni's reply to Newman of 10 December indicated that the dispensation was permissive, and Birmingham could ignore it as it chose. Why, then, the fuss? Newman's feelings were partly personal: Faber had deceived him, and Dalgairns was his accomplice. His point of principle was that the Rule was the foundation of the Oratory, the more so because its members did not take monastic vows. To Cullen, he wrote of the danger of becoming like the French Oratory by submerging the independence of the English houses, and declared his intention to go immediately to Rome: 'unless we look sharp', he told Hope-Scott, 'the energy of the London House will disturb the orbit and motion of the

Bm House, as some whacking planet may put out Ceres or Pomona. Out of sight, out [of] mind, so I am going to Rome'.[49]

Newman also asked Wiseman for his opinion of the two resolutions that he wanted to lay before Propaganda: that any decision by Propaganda for one House should apply to that one only; and that any request for an interpretation of the Rule in Rome should be submitted to other Houses for their opinion. Wiseman passed the letter on to Faber, to whom he also sent Newman's announcement of his Roman journey. 'I have communicated to you all that I have received from Dr N.', wrote Wiseman to Faber, 'and have not shown him anything I have received from you.'[50]

Faber interpreted Newman's resolutions as a claim to exercise a '*generalate*' over the whole Congregation, and said so in a submission to Propaganda and in a circular letter which he sent to thirteen Italian Oratories. Newman and St John set out on St Stephen's Day 1855, and called at the Oratories at Turin, and at Brescia and at Verona, where unknown to the travellers, the Superior had received Faber's letter and showed a suspicious familiarity with the object of Newman's journey. Newman's questions to his hosts about the Rule were stated abstractly: he discovered that nearly all were opposed to confessing nuns, but he did not mention the quarrel with the London House. The puzzled Provost of the Florence Oratory replied to Faber of Newman's visit that the two Englishmen were in perfect agreement: 'We were at once surprised and consoled when we heard from the mouth of F. Newman that the purpose of his journey was to prevent the introduction of a Generalate!'[51] In Rome, St John saw the circular letter from Faber with the supporting documentation for Propaganda on the table of the Superior of the Chiesa Nuova, and Newman himself saw the Propaganda submission addressed in Stanton's hand on the desk of the Pope, who received them kindly, granted their request for a 'female oratory' for nurses and indulgences for their other works. The Propaganda Secretary Barnabò advised Newman not to present his 'Supplica', 'asking that nothing done by the Holy See by one Oratory might affect another', on the ground that, wrote Newman, it 'would *diminish* my power, inasmuch as I was *Deputato Apostolico* for setting up the Oratory in any part of England'[52] – indeed in Ireland also. Newman's strategy had been to restrict the influence of Brompton by a declaration of independence that restricted his own influence as well. That effectively refuted Faber's charge, of which Newman was ignorant, that he wanted power over the London house. Rome, however, confirmed his own pre-eminence in England, and had no intention of compelling the Birmingham Oratory to confess nuns.

The mission was, then, partly a success; but it was also partly a failure. Newman thought that as the Roman officials did not like additional work, 'there is a primâ facie prejudice against any one who comes to Rome to oppose, or protest, or interfere, or explain', particularly if this involved 'scrupulousness' or a lack of trust.[53] The London Oratory's complaints left a nasty taste in Roman mouths, especially Barnabò's, and predisposed him to listen when Newman was delated to Rome in 1859.

Newman's return to London was a lightning four days by train: it had not been so in 1833. Stanton wrote from London that his conduct towards Brompton and its Superior had been 'very severe and even harsh', and hoped that their old friendship had not 'ended so unpleasantly, in a manner so painful'.[54] Newman thought the letter 'most affectionate', and sent Antony Hutchison a subscription to his poor schools, but he still returned Brompton their mitres. Hutchison complained that his community found itself 'cut off and in a manner excommunicated by you, without really knowing what fault it has committed'.[55] Newman replied that he refused to read Hutchison's letter, and would only discuss the matter it contained if formally approached by Stanton as Secretary to the London Congregation, though he wrote six days later offering a weekly Mass for Hutchison's return to health. Faber complained that Newman had addressed him formally as Father Faber and returned the mitres: 'to you simply I shall owe my salvation, if I am saved, nor can I forget that I have once loved you as I never loved a friend before. You have cast me from you, perhaps justly . . . Oh that St Philip's Day might see his English children at one again'.[56]

Newman's reply was cool: 'almost every word of it', replied Faber, 'seems full of alienation'.[57] Newman still refused to discuss the cause of the dissension, except formally through Stanton as Secretary. 'When I get to Rome', Newman protested to him in a passage cancelled from the letter sent, 'I find Propaganda, Chiesa Nuova, and the Holy Father himself pre-occupied against me by letters from your Congregation, which I see on Fr Concha's table and in the Holy Father's hand: letters the contents of which I never wish to know.'[58]

The clumsy Wiseman ladled fat on the fire by asking Newman his permission to dedicate to Newman and Faber jointly a panegyric on St Philip Neri. Newman asked as a condition, that the Birmingham Fathers be included in the dedication; Wiseman sent Newman's letter to the London Oratory and, as Newman later told his wealthy Scottish convert Robert Monteith, Wiseman proceeded, through Fr Faber, 'freely to show my private letter to various persons, without my leave or knowledge, and to comment on it through Fr Faber behind my back in most disrespectful terms'.[59] This might have served to justify his own developing conviction about Wiseman. 'The Cardinal', he told Henry Wilberforce, 'has a thousand good points, but you must never *trust* him.'[60] Newman followed through his letter to Wiseman with another, containing two sets of proposals of 1850, the first from Faber, giving him a pre-eminence in the Oratory's affairs. Newman sent a copy to Faber, who pointed out to Wiseman that on Newman's own account, these resolutions were only to last three years; the London Oratory had begged forgiveness and could now 'only hope that time may bring about some softening of his feelings towards us'.[61]

To his own Fathers in Birmingham, Newman described the incident as 'a conspiracy to force the Birmingham Oratory, by means of Propaganda; into a line of missionary work which it held to be unoratorian'.[62] He softened the charge by calling the 'conspiracy' unintentional, and omitted the word altogether in the copy of the letter sent to London; but this did not mitigate his pain. 'I saw papers in the Pope's hand, injurious to one who had done them no harm, who had not even mentioned their name, whose blessing they now ask.'[63] The Brompton Fathers in response now frankly referred to Newman's 'unkind and disrespectful' treatment of them throughout the affair: 'We did our best for peace according to our light: and we have failed. The ties of confidence and affection are broken. Alienation and coldness are henceforth to take the place of devotion and love. The memories of the past, dear still as memories, are not to live over again in the present. Such was not our choice or our wish. It is your act. We are simply passive in the matter'.[64] Newman concluded about Brompton that 'it is a great relief not to have a secret enemy – and that I think we had till now'.[65] He thought that the London Oratorians had decided that his own 'unconstitutional authority' as Founder would be 'exerted *against* us, for he will never trust us or love us again'.[66] 'Again, any one who defends himself, puts himself in the wrong. Si on s'excuse, on s'accuse . . . This is why they make a fuss at Brompton, they are afraid of me.'[67] Faber's protestations of affection arose from 'extreme irritation and restlessness': they would prove sincere only if they '*continue*', 'for he is too clever not to understand perfectly well that he never can replace himself in my confidence, do what he will . . . prudence and dignity require us to be silent. Aren't there quarrels enough among Catholics, without our having one of our own?'[68] When Hutchison and Stanton went to Rome in 1856 to ask for a separate Brief for the London House, the Pope insisted that Newman be consulted, but as Barnabò, now Cardinal Prefect of Propaganda, told Stanton and Hutchison, Newman had himself suggested that the Houses should have separate Briefs, and he now wrote to Rome to support Brompton's application. He remained their Founder – or as the Cardinal put it, 'else you would be bastardi';[69] and as such, it is Newman's statue, not Faber's, that now stands outside the Brompton Oratory.

The principal immediate casualty of the affair was the erratic Dalgairns, who was confronted with the rest of the community by Newman's request for a vote of support for his conception of the spirit of the Oratory. Dalgairns had been advised by his French friend Canon Lorain to return to London; he asked for a discussion with Newman before the vote was taken. Dalgairns' restless spirit wanted a more 'spiritual' Oratory in the French rather than in the Italian style of Oratory, and he convinced Newman of the genuineness of his own 'intellectual conviction' that the idea of the London House was 'more like the historical Philippine idea than was that of the Birmingham house'. 'I cannot tell you how kind he was', wrote Dalgairns to Faber about

Newman. 'Do you remember an expression in Callista about "eyes blue as the sapphires of the Eternal City". His eyes looked then just like a Saint's and he spoke and acted like one, so disinterestedly, so gently. He said how much he loved me; he then said that he felt quite sure he had no resentful feeling against the London house . . . How very small I feel beside him; if I were not such a restless selfish blackguard I could live with him.'[70]

Yet Dalgairns was convinced that 'the original sin of all my restlessness at Birmingham lay in my departure from London', which welcomed his return to Brompton. It was, perhaps, his emotional sensitivity that made him a good confessor for nuns. The anger generated by the incident on both sides, and the feline element in Brompton's response – following a joke by Barnabò, they took to calling Newman 'il Babbo', 'daddy' – suggest wounded love as much as wounded pride. Brompton was in the wrong, and its protestations of bewildered affection hardly concealed a refusal to apologize. But Newman cannot be acquitted of 'resentful feeling' either. His elaborate memoranda about the quarrel glow with indignation and with a sense that Faber had been a burden from the first, seizing on the *éclat* of the Oratorian name and depriving him of some of his best recruits. When in 1857, Faber praised Ambrose St John's translation of the *Raccolta*, the Roman collection of indulgenced prayers, and his friend John Morris criticized Newman's translation of the 'Anima Christi' within it, Newman told his friend that Faber 'is getting over you . . . He is the fox, complimenting you on your beauty, and hoping to get hold of the cheese, which is myself . . . I was fuming at the impertinence of the writer praising "the Birmingham Oratory" and now I find it is Fr Faber! He wishes to sooth [sic] us like children who are teething. "Pretty Dear".'[71]

Brompton also drove Newman back upon himself. It was in the fashion. 'All the world goes to London –', Newman wrote, 'to know people up and down the world, is to know people in London. That is Fr Faber's position – and he is, as they say, master of the situation.'[72] Brompton had the ear of the Cardinal and of some of the leading Catholic laity, and to Newman's mind alienated or threatened to alienate his friends like Henry Wilberforce, Elizabeth Bowden and the Duke of Norfolk. To one who valued friendship as much as Newman, this hurt him personally, and injured the reputation and prospects of his own Oratory.

Against London, Birmingham looked more and more like a backwater. Brompton, through Faber's sometimes florid and impassioned books of piety, articulated the content of the neo-Ultramontane Devotional Revolution within English Catholicism. Newman disassociated himself from Faber's books – he denied that he had read any save part of one, *The Blessed Sacrament*, which was dedicated to him. But he recognized that Faber and not he was forming the mind of the younger generation. Indeed Newman was increasingly remote from the Ultramontane mainstream and suspect to it. Thus the antagonism between the two houses was one cause of his isolation and propagated the rumour which was to become a point of faith with old friends like W. G. Ward, that he was less than wholeheartedly and integrally Catholic.

'All that sad quarrel with the London House was owing to Fr Dalgairns thinking he might do what he pleased in my absence' [in Dublin], wrote Newman, somewhat sweepingly. Cullen wanted him in Dublin, the health of his house required him in Birmingham, and the Pope wanted him in both places at once. Newman felt that his real vocation was overlooked by authority. 'The thing that riles me most', he wrote to Monsell, 'is the deference and admiration expressed for *me* (e.g. by H. Wilberforce) *while they ignore my Oratory*.'[73]

Both Cullen and Newman hoped for an Oratory in Dublin, a natural connection for the University, and it was with this in mind that Newman built the University Church, and acquired the summer retreat of Mount Salus at Dalkey, which Cullen allegedly described to Newman as 'a more desirable home than a back street in Birmingham'.[74] But the transfer of the Oratory to Dublin was never a practical possibility, and when the difficulty with Faber arose, Cullen thought that Newman had run away to Rome. When in 1856, Newman asked the Archbishop to open the University Church, Cullen enquired worriedly about the long-term arrangements for preserving it as a religious building, which Newman thought might have been asked before. 'I am very glad to have elicited your Grace's questions', he replied coldly. 'I should have been still more gratified to have elicited them some time ago.'[75] Cullen, thought Newman, was quite 'dragged down with anxiety'; 'he makes no one his friend, because he will confide in no body, and be considerate to no body. Every one feels he is emphatically *close* – and, while this repels friends, it fills enemies with nameless suspicions of horrible conspiracies against Bishops and Priests and the rights of St Patrick. I wonder how his health will stand it – he is as vehement against the young Irelanders as against the McHalites – against the McHalites as against the English'.[76] 'I wonder', Newman later wrote of Cullen, 'he does not cook his own dinners.'[77]

Everything in Ireland depended on Cullen; and Newman felt that Cullen distrusted him, because he trusted no one. In June 1856, the Irish hierarchy left unheeded Newman's request for a lay committee representing the Archbishop to supervize his University expenditure. The Irish clergy, Newman thought, wanted 'a population of peasants ruled over by a patriotic priesthood patriarchally'. His closest Irish episcopal friend, Bishop David Moriarty, wanted a university for poor scholars, while for the mass of priests, a 'gentleman is an evil', and they considered that the 'University is for gentlemen'. Newman thought that this must be true to a degree, 'unless the age of poor scholars revived, which, I assume, is not to be'.[78]

His theoretical doubts were sharpened by practical ones. Cullen at first opposed Tom Arnold's appointment as Professor of English. Newman was

£2000 in debt over the University Church, built in Byzantine basilica style, 'to my taste', he told his architect and Professor of Fine Arts, the universally gifted convert-cleric John Hungerford Pollen, '. . . the most beautiful one in the three Kingdoms';[79] and he was owed £300 towards the expenses of his houses in Dublin. The Irish bishops expected him to found an Irish Oratory, and were reluctant to remit the debt on the church which they wanted him to discharge himself from presents and collections. Cullen offered to let him borrow £800 rather than the whole £2000 from the University Fund, 'which', wrote Newman, 'does not save me the trouble of going elsewhere'.[80] 'My letters are a daily burden', he complained to Henry Wilberforce, 'and, did I not answer them by return of post, they would soon get my head under water and drown me. Every hour or half hour of the day I have people calling on me. I have to entertain strangers at dinner, I have to attend inaugural Lectures – four last week, I have to stop Professors resigning, and Houses revolting. I have to keep accounts and find money, when I have none.'[81]

His own university house received the young Princes de Ligne and the Polish Count Stephen Zamoyski, who was rumoured to be dissolute – 'so', wrote Newman gaily, 'I suppose we shall soon be as lax and disreputable as Ch[rist] Ch[urch]';[82] but the aristocratic complexion of his house, and its easy discipline, did not do anything to endear the University to the bishops. The MacHaleite Bishop Cantwell of Meath complained of the want of archiepiscopal supervision of expenditure, and Newman reminded him of the lack of a lay committee to exercise the regular supervision which would be impossible to the four archbishops. Cantwell wrote to MacHale that 'Rome should be informed of such monstrous expenditure by an institution conferring such little benefit'.[83] Yet Newman suffered far more from 'the narrowness and party-spirit of Dr Cullen . . . if I have any personal annoyance, it is in his treatment of me'.[84] Cullen himself told Barnabò in 1858 that Newman allowed his young men to go dancing and keep horses, an embarrassment to an institution funded by the pennies of the poor.

In April 1857, in letters to all the Irish bishops, Newman signified his intention to resign on the following 14 November. The shortest and curtest letter was to MacHale. Three of the four archbishops, MacHale excepted, wrote to the Birmingham Oratory, pleading for Newman's retention. Newman himself drafted the elaborate and courteous letter of 6 August 1857 from his own House declining: 'the absence of a head, (Bishops must know as well as any one,)' he told Hope-Scott, 'is almost ruin to a body of labourers'.[85] Two of his community had died, two, Darnell and St John, had been ill, Dalgairns had departed. From February 1858, he declined his Irish Rectorial salary of £500 a year.

Yet though not in residence, 1858 still saw Newman nearly as busy as ever for Dublin, and publishing the University periodical *Atlantis*,[86] largely edited for him by Sullivan, though he himself wrote three articles for it on the history of the Benedictine order. He was more than ever dissatisfied with his position. Not that he laid the whole blame on the Irish, who had 'gone out of their way to appoint an English Rector – the English have done nothing to support him'. The English had failed to rise to his vision of a University for the English-speaking world; but then the University was 'abused in Ireland for being English, and neglected in England for being Irish'.[87] He tested this lack of support for the University in England by writing as 'Q in the Corner' a series of anonymous attacks upon it in Henry Wilberforce's *Weekly Register*. The apathy in England in response confirmed him in his view that he was throwing himself out of his proper sphere of action: 'what special claim had a University exclusively Irish upon my time?'[88]

Cullen did not bother to inform him of the application to the government for a university charter, and worried about a similar petition drawn up by Newman and signed by the professors. The last straws in 1858 were the failure to heed his request for a Vice-Rector, a demand from the archbishops that Newman should reside longer in Dublin, and their appointment of a new Dean in St Patrick's House which was clearly Newman's right and responsibility. Cullen, wrote Newman to Ornsby, his closest ally among the staff, 'has treated me from the first like a scrub . . . I have wished to organise a method of collection by which we should have money enough – he never has done any thing but take my letters, crumple them up, put them in the fire, and write me no answer. And so with every thing else. The Archbishops *formally promised* to buy my Church, as soon as the papers could be made out, last August year, thanking me for the liberality of my terms; now they refuse, under pretence of Dr McHale not coming in to it. So Dr McHale is to be brought in as a bugbear, when it suits them. Dr Cullen rides over the Episcopal Decrees, and puts in a Dean in St Patrick's without saying a word to me'.[89] '*He* has been, and is, ruining us', Newman wrote to William Monsell about Cullen. 'He will do nothing, let us do nothing; he will give no answers to questions, or imply he grants and then pull you up when you have acted. He is perfectly impracticable.'[90] The University Trustees had agreed to buy Newman's Dublin church in 1857, but he had to borrow from the Oratory and to pay the interest on the £2500 which he owed for building it, above his own contribution, until the purchase was concluded in 1863–4. Though nineteen professors, two demonstrators and three Deans of Houses petitioned him to remain as Rector, he formally resigned on 12 November 1858.

It was to Ambrose St John that he discharged his disappointments. 'I am most sad', he wrote in 1856, 'I have a load of care on me, and no one to take pity on me.'

I go to Rome to be snubbed. I come to Dublin to be repelled by Dr McHale and worn away by Dr Cullen. The Cardinal taunts me with his

Dedications, and Fr Faber insults me with his letters . . . I cannot explain any thing to friend or foe intelligibly. Ryder strikes me, for I can call it nothing else . . . I can only think of my own lines, tho' Christians are worse to bear than heathens, 'Sit in the gate and be the heathen's jest – silent and self possessed.' What enormous irritation Job must have felt, when his friends came and prosed to him. And then there is old Talbot with his platitudes, and Fr Dalgairns scouting my distinct request, and going on corresponding with our Fathers. What is to be the end of it? Dr Whitty talks of my being sent to Rome to advise them about the University. Catch me going except under a sacratissimum praeceptum. Cardinal Bo would like all the gossip I could give him – for every word of mine *would* be gossip, not advice or counsel.[91]

This disgust with authority in the Church had still to reach its full fine flowering in 1859, but it had already left its mark on Newman's preaching. 'When we say that Christ loves His Church, we mean that He loves, nothing of earthly nature, but the fruit of His own grace.'[92] In its earthly dimension, the Church offered nothing at all. Both Hope-Scott and St John were driven to complain of his 'croaking',[93] which in 1858 Newman justified to St John: 'To let out one's feeling is a great relief, and I don't think an unlawful one'. His three confidants in the Oratory were Henry Bittleston, the Irish Stanislas Flanagan and St John himself. 'Job too', Newman told St John, 'had three friends – and he let out to them – yet he was "the most patient of men".'[94] The difficulty of balance for the biographer is that all this grumbling is recorded on paper: it would be simply lost to the air – or the telephone – in this century.

Yet for all its pain, the University was the occasion of a series of Newman's major works. Between June and October 1854 he published in the *Catholic University Gazette* a series of articles on University history which he dedicated to Hope-Scott as *The Office and Work of Universities* in 1856; it later figured among his *Historical Sketches*, and contains the celebrated judgement on the Church's contribution to European culture popularized by Chesterton: 'Not a man in Europe now, who talks bravely against the Church, but owes it to the Church, that he can talk at all'.[95]

In 1859, Newman dedicated his eight sermons to the Catholic University to Manning, who was now Provost of Westminster, special assistant to Wiseman and founder of a controversial community, the Oblates of St Charles Borromeo, at Bayswater. The most important of these university productions were his *Lectures and Essays on University Subjects*, nearly all of which had appeared in the *Catholic University Gazette*, and which were separately published with a dedication to the faithful Monsell in 1859. In 1873, Newman combined his *Discourses on University Education* of 1852 with the *Lectures* to make his classic *The Idea of a University*: which, according to G. M. Young, is one of the two works (with Aristotle's *Ethics*) which should be preserved on education, while 'the rest might, with no loss to humanity and possibly some advantage, be pulped'.[96]

The *Idea* is in fact the classic answer to the age-old question, 'What has Athens to do with Jerusalem?' The tension within the Western inheritance between Hellenism and Judaeo-Christianity, reason and faith, knowledge and religion, was one in which Newman was, of course, on the side of Christian Revelation. But the Greek intellectual inheritance, chastened and subdued to a Christian purpose, and embodied in the idea of a University, was not, therefore, one to be despised. Newman in the *Idea* called the University 'a place of *teaching* universal *knowledge*',[97] and he defended the right of Theology to be taught in the University on the ground that it is also a science among the sciences, and that all the sciences must be taught there.

But the aim of the University is not so much even to teach the particular sciences, though of course it does so, but to impart to its students a 'real cultivation of mind'.[98] This is ultimately rooted in a general knowledge of all the sciences, yet goes beyond it, for there is a 'true enlargement of mind which is the power of viewing many things at once as one whole, of referring them severally to their true place in the universal system, of understanding their respective values, and determining their mutual dependence'.[99] No man can know everything; but an educated man has not merely the general information to put the specialism in its place, but an ability to judge wisely out of synoptic imaginative vision of knowledge as a whole.

Such a power of judging in the mind is, therefore, much more than the possession of knowledge, which it transcends. But it is also to be distinguished from the mere 'viewiness' of holding a great number of integrated opinions, which is the 'unreal' condition of the informed but uncultivated men who remain boys all their lives. 'Viewiness' was, in Newman's view, embodied in 'Universal-Knowledge' men like Brougham, and was the particular bane of the nineteenth century.

The opposite of 'viewiness' was in a good sense 'liberal'. It was that Oxonian ideal of a 'Liberal Education', which in 1808–10, had been assailed by the supporters of the Scottish universities for its '*inutility*' and then by radicals for its '*religious exclusiveness*'.[100] This Oxford training, however, was an education in how to think on the basis of a precise knowledge of things, rather than the inculcation, as in Newman's old bug-bear, the University of London, of a collection of obviously 'useful' specialisms. Again, Oxford imparted its vision of the world as much through the influence of a community of young men on one another as through a system of lectures and examinations. Students learn most from one another, and Newman thought that a university with residence but no exams more valuable than one with exams but no residence.

The danger of a mere examination drilling in specialisms, which are perfectly proper in themselves, is their improper influence outside their proper province. Political Economy, which is rightly concerned with the creation of wealth, has no right to dictate itself as an ultimate good to ethics, which lies beyond its bounds. Rather, the cultivated or liberal mind will take a wider view than that of the specialism itself. There is, then, an ultimate value in the liberal training of the mind, which is demonstrable quite independently of the teaching of Catholic theology, even though it is in harmony with it. Cultivation is an end in itself, without reference to its obvious extra-academic technical or commercial usefulness, or even its value to religion.

Newman thought, however, that such a 'general culture of mind is the best aid to professional and scientific study, and educated men can do what illiterate cannot';[101] in that sense, cultivation has an end outside itself. He was in agreement with his age in placing the humanities, the Greek and Latin classics especially, at the heart of cultivation, with theology and ethics, which do range into other disciplines. Yet he did not despise the natural sciences or a more specialist or vocational training; he merely insisted that these can benefit from this quality of 'cultivation' as well.

What is the possessor of such a culture, the product of a 'Liberal Education', to be called? In the decade after the Famine, in a University funded by the pennies of the poor, Newman anticipated the criticism of an Irish audience of the term 'gentleman' as an 'antiquated variety of human nature and remnant of feudalism'.[102] He could not avoid the term altogether, but gave it his own special sense. The educated man was the man of 'philosophic habit', who unites the three elements of universal and particular knowledge and a coherent vision infusing them. But this ideal had produced what was virtually a new religious type in the 'gentleman', 'the creation, not of Christianity, but of civilization', a moral ideal of refinement and gentility that was a power in the land. Thus it had abolished duelling, which Christianity had been powerless to do; and Newman offered his famous account of its strengths:

Hence it is that it is almost a definition of a gentleman to say he is one who never inflicts pain . . . He is mainly occupied in merely removing the obstacles which hinder the free and unembarrassed action of those about him; and he concurs with their movements rather than takes the initiative himself . . . The true gentleman in like manner carefully avoids whatever may cause a jar or a jolt in the minds of those with whom he is cast; – all clashing of opinion, or collision of feeling, all restraint, or suspicion, or gloom, or resentment; his great concern being to make every one at their ease and at home. He has his eyes on all his company; he is tender towards the bashful, gentle towards the distant, and merciful towards the absurd; he can recollect to whom he is speaking; he guards against unseasonable allusions, or topics which may irritate; he is seldom prominent in conversation, and never wearisome . . . From a long-sighted prudence, he observes the maxim of the ancient sage, that we should ever conduct ourselves towards our enemy as if he were one day to be our friend. He has too much good sense to be affronted at insults, he is too well employed to remember injuries, and too indolent to bear malice. He is patient, forbearing, and resigned, on philosophical principles; he submits to pain, because it is inevitable, to bereavement, because it is irreparable, and to death, because it is his destiny . . . If he be an unbeliever, he will be too profound and large-minded to ridicule religion or to act against it; he is too wise to be a dogmatist or fanatic in his infidelity. He respects piety and devotion; he even supports institutions as venerable, beautiful, or useful, to which he does not assent; he honours the ministers of religion, and it contents him to decline its mysteries without assailing or denouncing them.[103]

But such an ideal type is a better judge of manners than morality. Far from simply admiring this paragon, as is sometimes assumed, Newman regarded it as wholly insufficient without the Gospel. The filthiest and most uncultivated Catholic peasant infused with the grace of the sacraments has a prospect of heaven denied to the man who had all these natural virtues and nothing more. Most saints are not gentlemen, and most gentlemen are not saints.

Yet Newman would not abandon the ideal altogether, for while it had no necessary connection with Christianity, it existed inside the Church as well as outside it. His own dear friends, Keble and Pusey, had been modelled upon it, and his taste in saints was in St Philip Neri and St Francis de Sales, Christian gentlemen of good birth and education who had known both Athens and Jerusalem. The balance and tension between the two ideals, of cultivation and Christianity, has been summed up by G. M. Young, who wrote that Newman

employs all his magic to enlarge and refine and exalt this conception of intellectual cultivation as a good in itself, worth while for itself, to be prized and esteemed for itself beyond all knowledge and all professional skill; while, all the time, so earnestly does he affirm its inadequacy, its shortcomings on the moral side, its need to be steadied and purified by religion, that at the end we feel that what we have heard is the final utterance, never to be repeated or needing to be supplemented, of Christian Humanism: as if the spirit evoked by Erasmus had found its voice at last.[104]

Newman was therefore defending the University both as a great good in itself and as a good needing supplementation by a greater. He withdrew from the finished version of the work Discourse V, in which he argued that, regardless of religion, the end of a university was not faith or belief but knowledge; a viewpoint which he considered to be in conflict with the University's Papal Brief of 1854. This was not because he thought his position false; but at the time he held the University to be under the special providence of the Holy See, uniting England and Ireland as of old. He was still imaginatively a strong Ultramontane. A great rhetorical passage in the *Idea* summarizes his sanguine view of Rome: the Catholic University, he wrote

is the decision of the Holy See; St. Peter has spoken, it is he who has enjoined that which seems to us so unpromising. He has spoken, and has a claim on us to trust him. He is no recluse, no solitary student, no dreamer about the past, no doter upon the dead and gone, no projector of the visionary. He for eighteen hundred years has lived in the world; he has seen all fortunes, he has encountered all adversaries, he has shaped himself for all emergencies . . . He came first upon an age of refinement and luxury like our own, and, in spite of the persecutor, fertile in the resources of his cruelty, he soon gathered, out of all classes of society, the slave, the soldier, the high-born lady, and the sophist, materials enough to form a people to his Master's honour. The savage hordes come down in torrents from the north, and Peter went out to meet them, and by his very eye he sobered them, and backed them in their full career. They turned aside and flooded the whole earth, but only to be more surely civilized by him, and to be made ten times more his children even than the older populations which they had overwhelmed. Lawless kings arose, sagacious as the Roman, passionate as the Hun, yet in him they found their match, and were shattered, and he lived on. The gates of the earth were opened to the east and west, and men poured out to take possession; but he went with them by his missionaries, to China, to Mexico, carried along by zeal and charity, as far as those children of men were led by enterprise, covetousness, or ambition. Has he failed in his successes up to this hour? Did he, in our fathers' day, fail in his struggle with Joseph of Germany and his confederates, with Napoleon, a greater name, and his dependent kings, that, though in another kind of fight, he should fail in ours? What grey hairs are on the head of Judah, whose youth is renewed like the eagle's, whose feet are like the feet of harts, and underneath the Everlasting arms?[105]

Newman's private notion that a particular providence attached to papal acts did not last; and it was the failure of Rome to support him over the University that all but killed it. As he recorded:

a sentiment which history has impressed upon me, and impresses still, has been very considerably weakened as far as the present Pope is concerned . . . I cannot help thinking in particular, that, if he had known more of the state of things in Ireland . . . then at least he would have abstained from decreeing a Catholic University. I was a poor innocent as regards the actual state of things in Ireland when I went there, and did not care to think about it, for I relied on the word of the Pope, but from the event I am led to think it not rash to say that I knew as much about Ireland as he did.[106]

Newman never lost his affection for Pio Nono, but his reservations about the Papacy's this-worldly wisdom dramatically altered his view of Rome's place within the Holy Catholic Church.

Liberal Catholicism: I

'One by one, like the sparks upon burnt paper, my earlier recollections are going out', wrote Newman to Manuel Johnson in 1857.[1] Johnson himself died suddenly in 1859, not only confirming Newman's worries about his own ill-health but sharpening his concern about how to use the time left for his life work, not knowing if he would have a long life or a short one. He wrote a dozen sets of notes in 1857 on philosophical subjects, including his remarks on John Stuart Mill's *Logic*[2] and an 'Opus magnum' which he sketched in outline to deal with the intellectual challenge to the Church in the nineteenth century.[3] Then in August 1857, Wiseman asked him to implement the ninth decree of the Second Provincial Synod of Westminster of 1855 by editing a new translation of Holy Scripture. Newman accepted the commission on 14 September. He fitted up a room in the Oratory as a Scriptorium, sent Wiseman elaborate calculations of his future costs, and after a delay, got no very satisfactory answer. The Cardinal, an initiator rather than an administrator, wanted to leave everything to Newman, and indeed the hierarchy assigned him the copyright in 1858, but the three Bishops appointed to arrange this, Wiseman, Ullathorne and Thomas Grant of Southwark, never did so. Nor did Wiseman respond to a proposal from the American hierarchy, communicated to Newman by Bishop Patrick Lynch of Charleston, that he should co-operate with Archbishop Francis Kenrick of Baltimore who had already translated the Vulgate New Testament. In his reply to Lynch, Newman expressed himself willing 'to concur in any measure on which the bishops of England shall determine': but in Newman's own words, written in 1864, Wiseman

> gave *me* to manage the *American* difficulty – not that he said so, but he sent me the American Bishops' letters, wished me to answer them, and did not answer them himself. If I am right, he did not send me a single line with the American letters, but simply the letters. I foresaw clearly that I should have endless trouble with publishers, American hierarchy, Propaganda etc. etc. if I took this upon me. So I waited *till* I heard something more about it, but I have never heard till this day any thing.[4]

Newman did not blame Kenrick, whose translation was far advanced, or the Americans, who sought to include him in their project and naturally wanted to avoid the financial loss and embarrassment of a competing translation. Wiseman could not be faulted for his goodness of intention or kindness of heart. His inefficiency was exacerbated by ill-health: yet he cannot be wholly acquitted of Newman's charge of 'washing his hands of the whole affair'.[5]

A more lasting venture was the Oratory school, set up at the suggestion of Edward Bellasis and a circle of Newman's London friends. Newman's ambition was to provide an education that would be no less English for being Catholic. The Oratory already had the care of the Birmingham workhouse served by Fr Flanagan, and Caswall had begun a poor mission at Smethwick. It had tried in 1856 to establish a hospital which foundered on the early deaths of the gentlewomen who came to it as nurses, and had established in 1857 an orphanage through the agency of Newman's penitent, Catherine Anne Bathurst, which was continued by Austin Mills. This, however, was all work among the poor. What was now envisioned was a public school for the 'splendidioris' of the papal brief, and Newman's own reference to Bellasis about the need to exclude 'Undesirable boys'[6] – boys who were not quite gentlemen – clearly reflected the class-bound character of the institution. 'The one object of the school,' Newman wrote, 'is . . . the education of the sons of gentlemen'.[7] He saw himself as raising up an educated elite, who would be the Catholic leadership of the coming generation.

Wiseman sent Bellasis an enormous questionnaire about the school,[8] but then decided that he had no right to do so. Newman feared that the Cardinal had been 'put up to it by others'[9] – at the Brompton Oratory. Wiseman also advised Ullathorne that the Bishop would bear responsibility for the project, and without giving clear reasons, Ullathorne told Newman that the school was 'sure to be a failure'.[10] Brompton took the view that a school was un-Oratorian, in a nice reiteration of Newman's objection to hearing nuns' confessions; but this at least inhibited Faber from setting up another school in competition. Newman secured the support of two score eminent Catholic laymen, with the Duke of Norfolk at their head, and the Oratory took the formal decision to establish the institution on 21 April 1858. The work required building and fund-raising among the patrons of the school, whose eminence, Newman told Bellasis, was the more necessary in that 'we are sure of having to encounter much prejudice, opposition, criticism, adverse whispering, and ready belief of tales told to our disadvantage'.[11] Newman later heard that under Faber's influence, the Duke of Norfolk had declared 'that the Birmingham Oratory was not the place for a school':[12] a remark of which Newman himself implicitly admitted the justice in thinking that while the Oratory had to be in a town, a public school should ideally be in the country. In fact, Faber told Sir John Acton 'that he would not only tolerate but assist the school. The promise of course is worthless',[13]

Acton continued to Newman's headmaster Nicholas Darnell, an old Wyke-hamist, suggesting its publication to guard against the danger of betrayal, but Faber did nothing to spoil the venture even with the Howards, and after the Duke's premature death in 1860, the advent of his juvenile heir at the Oratory was to show this. The school was launched with seven boys in May 1859. In March 1861, the community decided to erect a new building, and by 1862 there were seventy boys. The institution very quickly became a modest educational success, despite the fact that it could not attract a large enough number of boys to make it pay.

The school was one labour for an educated laity; but the English Catholic talent for internal squabbling was to precipitate disaster for Newman, when the swashbuckling young intellectual John Acton drew him into the crusade for the theological regeneration of English Catholicism. Acton had all the confidence of a Catholic cosmopolitan. Though descended from a line of Shropshire baronets, his Acton grandfather had been Prime Minister of Naples. His uncle was the cardinal who had welcomed Newman into the Church; while on his mother's side, he had a great great-uncle who had been the last Archbishop of Mainz and a grandfather who was the German Duke of Dalberg. By his mother's second marriage to Earl Granville, he had an intimate knowledge of the sceptical English Whig aristocracy. He had been to school under the great Dupanloup, later Bishop of Orleans, and at Oscott under Wiseman. His mind had been formed at Munich by the greatest of modern Catholic Church historians, Ignaz von Döllinger; and he combined an intellectual restlessness with deep devotion, and a massive scholarship with an utter irreverence for those in authority.

Acton's instrument was the *Rambler*. John Moore Capes, who was already in ill-odour with church authority, ceased to be its editor-proprietor in 1857, his chief reward being a warm tribute from Newman, who had then to cope with Capes' developing doubts about Roman Catholicism. Capes was succeeded as editor in February 1858 by a still more waspish convert, his helper Richard Simpson, with Acton as his principal assistant: and they promptly fell foul of Wiseman, by publishing a letter from the Catholic historian John Lingard's biographer Canon Mark Tierney, attacking Wiseman's assertion in his *Recollections of the Last Four Popes* that it was Lamennais and not Lingard whom Pope Leo XII had made a cardinal *in petto*. The question was unresolvable, as the secret had died with the Pope; but Wiseman was especially sensitive to any insult from the Old Catholic party, as he was in bitter conflict with his Old Catholic Coadjutor-Archbishop George Errington and the members of the Westminster Cathedral Chapter, in part over his favour to converts. Acton exacerbated the *Rambler*'s first offence by describing St Augustine as the 'father of Jansenism' in the issue for August 1858. While Acton regarded the matter as purely one of historical scholarship, the judgement also made the greatest of the Latin Fathers responsible for the most notorious of modern popish heresies. Acton got Döllinger to

300

contribute a whole letter-article to the *Rambler* on the point, but it was denounced by Professor John Gillow of Ushaw, and with Faber's support, Wiseman decided to delate Döllinger's letter to Rome. On 30 December 1858, Acton called at the Oratory to give Newman an account of the affair: he wrote a report of the meeting to Richard Simpson:

I had a 3 hours' talk with the venerable Noggs who came out at last with his real sentiments to an extent which startled me, with respect both to things and persons, as H. E. [Wiseman], Ward, Dalgairns, etc., etc., natural inclination of men in power to tyrannise, ignorance and presumption of our would-be theologians, in short what you and I would comfortably say over a glass of whiskey. I did not think he could ever cast aside his diplomacy and buttonment so entirely, and was quite surprised at the intense interest he betrayed in the Rambler. He was quite miserable when I told him the news and moaned for a long time, rocking himself backwards and forward over the fire, like an old woman with the toothache. He thinks the move provoked both by the hope of breaking down the R. and by jealousy of Döllinger. He asked whether we suspected any one, and at last inclined to the notion that the source is in Brompton. He has no present advice, being ignorant of the course of such affairs in Rome, except that we should declare, if you can make up your mind to do so, that we do not treat theology in our pages.[14]

The 'venerable Noggs'' formal response to the encounter, written to Acton on the following day, was to sympathize with Döllinger and make light of his offence, 'for what kind of offence is it, to take a certain historical view of the person of heretics, while condemning their writings? Mayn't I say that Luther was a loving and amiable papa, and yet abominate him?' But Newman thought 'it was a mistake to treat of Theology proper at all; and a double mistake to treat it in a Magazine fashion. And a third mistake, for laymen to do so'.[15] He wanted the *Rambler* to resume its course as a *literary* journal, adopting 'the policy of Wellington in the lines of Torres Vedras, who kept within shelter, while the enemy scoured the plain, but kept a sharp eye on him, and took him at disadvantage, whenever it was possible'. By being 'instructive, clever and amusing', the *Rambler* could disarm its critics, and 'affect public opinion without offending piety or good sense'.[16] Newman valued the *Rambler* as a means of raising the intellectual understanding of the educated laity; but this could be done without raising difficult issues in theology. Acton and Simpson agreed to avoid theology, but rightly thought that their history or politics had theological implications and might cause equal offence. Acton also disagreed with Newman fundamentally over the respect due to ecclesiastical authority even when that authority was wrong. Newman considered that it was generally due outward obedience even when it was not due internal assent; Acton increasingly wanted to defy it.

Acton proved a true prophet in predicting the hierarchy's sensitivity on matters other than pure theology. In the issue of the *Rambler* for January 1859, the Catholic school inspector, Scott Nasmyth Stokes, outraged the Catholic bishops by urging Catholics to co-operate with the Duke of Newcastle's Royal Commission on Education. Their refusal to do so was the result of the Catholic Poor School Committee's own bungling; it had failed to nominate a Catholic representative to the Commission, and then had taken offence at the lack of one. But the bishops misunderstood the Commission as a plot to impose a Protestant inspectorate on Catholic schools, and decided to exclude its inspectors. Stokes' subsequent defence of his first article in the *Rambler*, in February 1859, moved Wiseman, Errington and Grant to get Ullathorne to ask Newman on 16 February to take over the editorship himself, on the principle, as Ullathorne wrote to Newman, 'that every thing was always safe with you'.[17]

On 18 or 19 February in Birmingham, Simpson agreed to Newman's request that he resign under pressure from the bishops, who threatened to denounce him in their Pastorals: 'I yield to their threats',[18] wrote Simpson to Newman. But Simpson wanted freedom to make the whole affair public were the magazine to cease publication, and reimbursement of his expenses from the bishops for the suppression of the March issue, which had already been set up in print. Newman found Ullathorne open to these conditions; but Wiseman declined them, fearing that Simpson and Stokes would vindicate themselves in the journal, even under another editor. The bishops' pastorals would still have to address the educational issue, wrote Wiseman to Ullathorne; 'Mr Simpson's retirement will be worth nothing, without some guarantee against the repetition of the same faults'.[19] On 25 February 1859, Ullathorne read Newman the Cardinal's letter. 'Therefore', wrote Newman to Simpson, 'the whole negotiation or arrangement is at an end.'[20] But the next day Ullathorne showed Newman a further letter from Wiseman, indicating his deeper objection, to Acton succeeding Simpson as editor, which forced Newman to take up the paper to save it because no one else was able to do so. 'I found myself between two fires', he wrote to Robert Ornsby; ' – I could find no one (even had any one been willing) to become Editor, who would not either offend the Bishops or the last Editor and his friends.'[21]

'I have the extreme mortification of being Editor of the Rambler', wrote Newman to Henry Wilberforce. 'I have never had in my life (in its time) so great a one. It is like a bad dream . . . ' 'My own object', he later wrote, 'was to save Simpson etc. and to cover up differences.'[22] His advertisement of Lady Day 1859 tried to square the circle: 'to combine devotion to the Church with discrimination and candour in the treatment of her opponents; to reconcile freedom of thought with implicit faith; . . . to encourage a manly

investigation of subjects of public interest under a deep sense of the prerogatives of ecclesiastical authority'.[23] To Manning, Newman compared himself
to Brunel's steamship, the Great Eastern, which had stuck fast at her
launching: 'I too was striving to steer an unmanageable vessel through the
shallows and narrows of the Thames . . . '.[24] His own uncontroversial offerings to the magazine for May and July included 'The Mission of the Isles
of the North', later republished as 'The Northmen and Normans in England
and Ireland', about the Papacy's providential use of them.[25] Just as safe
was the opening tribute in the first article to Wiseman on his wildly successful tour of Ireland, and Newman's famous tribute to the qualities of the
Irish people, and his regret for their understandable hatred of England.

Yet Newman stuck fast in the mud in his very first issue for May, offending
Wiseman by defending Stokes, and offering in support of the rights of lay
opinion the argument that 'even in the preparation of a dogmatic definition
the faithful are consulted, as lately in the instance of the Immaculate
Conception . . . '.[26] The passage alerted the hostility of the vigilant John
Gillow in Ushaw, to whom Newman replied that he spoke only of consul-
tation in the passive sense, as in 'consulting a barometer about the weather'.[27] Newman quoted Perrone's work on the Immaculate Conception in
his favour, but he had little sympathy from Ullathorne, who thought the
argument as earlier stated by the French theologian Petavius 'as a whole
ridiculous', as Petavius rejected 'all proof of the doctrine as derived from
the Church teaching, and accepts it exclusively from the Church taught'.[28]
For Ullathorne as for Gillow, 'the Church teaching', the *ecclesia docens*, meant
the clergy; and this *ecclesia docens* was infallible, not the laity, who were
merely the passive *ecclesia docta*, the Church taught. When on 22 May,
Ullathorne met Newman, the latter said that 'he saw one side, I another –
. . . He said something like, "Who are the Laity?" I answered that the
Church would look foolish without them – *not* those words'.[29] Ullathorne
did not support him, and advised him to resign as editor of the *Rambler* after
the issue for July, which Newman agreed to do. Gillow was pacified for the
moment by Newman's explanation of 'consult', and must be excused for
not understanding Newman's use of the word in other than its primary
meaning, of asking for active advice or counsel. There was, however, also
criticism of the *Rambler* by Frederick Oakeley in the *Tablet*, and Newman
saw the incident in the light of the ecclesiastical politics of Wiseman's
conflict with the Coadjutor-Archbishop Errington. 'The same influence', he
wrote, 'which is intriguing to get Dr Errington away from England and is
stopping the Rambler, will, if there is an opening by my death, attempt to
get power over the Bm Oratory.'[30]

Newman's final issue of July as editor only compounded his offence, as
he chose to expand and justify his assertions of May, in an essay entitled
'On Consulting the Faithful in Matters of Doctrine'. He insisted that the
'*consensus fidelium*', the united testimony of the faithful, laity as well as clergy,

was an evidence of the content of Catholic doctrine which was treated with every consideration by the Papacy. Father Perrone had suggested this as a partial resolution of Newman's difficulties over doctrinal development, drawing attention to the witness to the Church's teachings in her 'public acts, liturgies, feasts, prayers', which united pastors and people. Thus the people are 'a *mirror*, in which the Bishops see themselves. Well, I suppose', added Newman, 'a person may *consult* his glass, and in that way may know things about himself which he can learn in no other way.'[31] The reference to prayer as a witness to the content of the Church's faith recalled Newman's argument in his *Lectures on the Prophetical Office*. His appeal in the *University Sermons* to a level of believing deeper than reason was echoed in his definition of the *consensus fidelium* as a sort of instinct or phronema, a collective power to judge truth and heresy 'deep in the bosom of the mystical body of Christ'.[32] And in the same vein, of looking to a popular religious instinct, he quoted in the third person his own *Lectures on Anglican Difficulties*:

> Drive a stake into a river's bed, and you will at once ascertain which way it is running, and at what speed; throw up even a straw upon the air, and you will see which way the wind blows; submit your heretical and Catholic principle to the action of the multitude, and you will be able to pronounce at once whether it is imbued with Catholic truth or with heretical falsehood.[33]

It was, however, in the Church of the Fathers that he always felt most at home; and that was his undoing, for he went far beyond any of his previous utterances to argue that in the Arian controversy of the fourth century, 'the divine tradition committed to the infallible Church was proclaimed and maintained far more by the faithful than by the Episcopate . . . in that time of immense confusion the divine dogma of our Lord's divinity was proclaimed, enforced, maintained, and (humanly speaking) preserved, far more by the "Ecclesia docta" than by the "Ecclesia docens" . . . '[34] The 'Nicene dogma was maintained during the greater part of the 4th century',

1. not by the unswerving firmness of the Holy See, Councils, or Bishops, but
2. by the 'consensus fidelium'.
I. On the one hand, then, I say, that there was a temporary suspense of the functions of the 'Ecclesia docens'. The body of Bishops failed in their confession of the faith.[35]

Newman followed this up with ten pages of evidence on the apostasy of the bishops, and sixteen on the laity's fidelity. He admitted, of course, that this stage of things did not, happily, exist in the present. 'Never was the

Episcopate of Christendom so devoted to the Holy See, so religious, so earnest . . . Though the laity be but the reflection or echo of the clergy in matters of faith, yet there is something in the "pastorum et fidelium *conspiratio*," which is not in the pastors alone'.[36] Newman softened his conclusion with a pious rhapsody from Dalgairns' work on the Sacred Heart about the popular victory of the doctrine of the Virgin's Motherhood of God over Nestorius at the Council of Ephesus; but his final paragraph tartly drew his moral for the Church in his own day:

> the Ecclesia docens is more happy when she has such enthusiastic partisans . . . than when she cuts off the faithful from the study of her divine doctrines . . . and requires from them a *fides implicita* in her word, which in the educated classes will terminate in indifference, and in the poorer in superstition.[37]

The concluding sentence was a brutal hit at the actual state of the Church in Latin countries for combining aristocratic indifference with popular superstition. Having been the champion of the revival of church authority, Newman sought to blunt the edge of Ultramontane hyper-clericalism, and as in the Church of England, he was to find himself the victim of the very authority which he had been exalting.

This was to end with a bang, not a whimper. His defence of 'consult' failed to convince Ullathorne, and the conclusion to the essay incensed Gillow. 'All would have been well', Newman afterwards thought, 'but for the unlucky paragraph . . . on the Arianizing Hierarchy',[38] with its argument that the Church's infallible authority had suffered a 'temporary suspense'. He continued to correspond with Acton and Simpson as they resumed the *Rambler*, and to contribute to it: he surprised Acton with his amoral attitudes to authority, by publishing a letter called 'Napoleonism not impious', and compared Napoleon III with Constantine as a benefactor of the Church, suggesting to Acton to his distress, that if Constantine's immorality was no objection to his claims upon the Church's gratitude, nor was Napoleon's. Newman made no formal announcement that he had ceased to be editor, but his involvement with the journal was less than the public was aware. Gillow sent Newman his protest about the essay 'On Consulting the Faithful' in August 1859. 'I fear', he wrote, 'that the tendency of this Article may be to induce speculative minds to think disparagingly of the infallibility of the Church . . . '[39] There was no apology for Newman's essay in the *Rambler* for September, and in October, Bishop Brown of Newport complained to the Secretary of Propaganda Gaetano Bedini that at the Third Provincial Synod of Westminster in July, Wiseman, Manning and Ullathorne had 'agreed in lamenting that Newman should have so expressed himself, and Dr Manning went [to the Oratory] to expostulate with him, but obtained no other result except the assurance of Newman that he did not *mean* to say, the Church had fallen into error'.[40] Cardinal Barnabò, when told of Newman's offence, remembered Faber's accusations of 1855 and declared that he was not surprised.[41]

Yet Newman was still trying to help the *Rambler* on its proper course. He found on the back page of his proofs of an article on St John Chrysostom, which he was contributing to the issue for November 1859, the first page of an essay by Richard Simpson on 'Toleration', attacking Pope Gregory XVI and violating the understanding to keep clear of theology without a ruling from a censor. Newman refused to allow publication of his own article unless Simpson revised his: Simpson's article was cancelled, leaving Simpson distressed. Newman himself thought that Simpson's essay 'would have simply dished us'.[42] In response to a letter in the *Tablet* which assumed that Newman was still the editor of the journal, Newman made it public that he was not, in sweeping terms which wrongly implied that he had no connection with the periodical at all. Its circulation fell by 40%. His exaggeration was the consequence of his difficult position. There was no easy reconciliation between the gadfly spirit of Simpson and the prickly authority of Wiseman, between stimulating the Catholic intellect and appeasing Westminster and Rome.

Newman was caught between two forces. He had offended the school of Simpson without appeasing the school of Wiseman. In November 1859, he heard at Oscott of Bishop Brown's delation to Rome of his article on the faithful, and drafted a request to Brown for an explanation of the condemnation which he did not send. Meanwhile Barnabò also indicated to Ullathorne in Rome that he wanted an explanation of the article from Newman, as '*Le Pape est beaucoup peignée*' [sic].[43] Ullathorne also had to defend Newman to Wiseman, then in residence at the English College, and reminded the Cardinal that Wiseman had shown others Newman's confidential letter about the disputed dedication of his Neri lecture to Manning and Faber, and spoke of the débâcle over the translation of Scripture. 'At last', recalled Ullathorne, 'the Cardinal burst into tears, and said – "Tell Newman I will do any thing I can for him".'[44] Wiseman was himself in a difficult position. He was identified with Ultramontane converts like Manning and Faber in his conflict with allegedly Gallican Old Catholics like Errington; but here were Old Catholics like Brown and Gillow denouncing the converts like Newman and Simpson for heresy.

On his return to Birmingham, Ullathorne got word to Newman of the message from Propaganda. Newman left his sick-bed to come to Ullathorne by cab, and wrote off to Wiseman in Rome, offering Propaganda a full explanation of the *Rambler* article, and requesting Propaganda's translations of the controversial passages. But while Wiseman passed this letter to Propaganda, he did not make its content clear, nor did he send the list of passages, drawn up by Propaganda as requiring an explanation, to Newman himself. In March 1860, Manning joined the Cardinal in order to prosecute the

Errington affair; and on 29 April, Manning wrote to Newman offering him any help in his power, and declaring that Wiseman would bring the matter of the *Rambler* to an acceptable conclusion on his return to England. Wiseman's negligence can be explained by his illness, the onset of diabetes, and by his preoccupation with the Errington affair, as well as by his legendary inefficiency. Nor, as was later stated, can Manning be accused of deliberately withholding from Propaganda Newman's offer of an explanation. On the other hand, Manning knew that Newman was under suspicion at headquarters, and is open to the charge of finding it convenient to leave him there. Barnabò was to be thunderstruck when, seven years later, Ambrose St John produced a copy of Newman's letter to Wiseman. ' "Why", he said, "Cardinal Wiseman was at Propaganda, and we never heard of this".'[45] The matter was then cleared up; but for the next seven years, Newman's name would be mud in Rome.

Worse still, he had failed in his aspiration to build a bridge between his conservative co-religionists and the liberal Catholic school around Acton, or to take the lead in raising the intellectual level of English Catholicism. Oddly, it was Manning who had seen the value of Newman's role: there were, he wrote, 'men who deserve a good and fair treatment', who 'cannot be put down or checked like boys'. Manning feared the emergence of 'a kind of De Lamennais School among some who, like him were intellectual champions of the Church, and nothing will produce this so surely as snubbing'. These liberals needed a leader like Newman to direct them, as 'he grapples with their intellectual difficulties'.[46] Instead, he 'entered the front lines of the battle with his *Essay on Consulting the Faithful* and when it backfired retreated to the rear as one of the first casualties'.[47] Newman was not a 'liberal Catholic'; but his attempt to guide the 'liberal Catholics' was quickly over.

23

Liberal Catholicism: II

After his retirement from the *Rambler*, Newman expressed mingled relief and regret. 'I feel like a person who has been long out in the dust and rain, and whose hat, coat and shoes show it.'[1] He wanted time to nurse his ailing congregation and to put his papers in order. 'Last year I proposed to myself a fallow year in 1859', he wrote in September, declining to promise articles for the *Rambler*. 'What a fallow year it has been and is likely to be!'[2] He recalled that he had failed his Schools in 1820, and been forced out of his Oriel tutorship in 1830. 'Then again I set to work and by 1840 had become somebody once more, when on Febry 27, 1841, Number 90 was attacked, and down I fell again.' He had recovered to become a Roman DD in 1850, but in 1851 had fallen foul of the law over Achilli, and had predicted to Ward that 'in another ten years, I shall be had up before Rome'.[3] Now he was old:

The greater part of our devotion in youth, our faith, hope, cheerfulness, perseverence is natural . . . Old men are in soul as stiff, as lean, as blood-less as their bodies, except so far as grace penetrates and softens them . . . I more and more wonder at *old* saints. St Aloysius or St Francis Xavier or St Carlo, are nothing to St Philip. O Philip gain me some little portion of thy fervour. I live more and more in the past, and in hopes that the past may revive in the future. My God, when shall I learn that I have so parted with the world, that, though I may wish to make friends with it, it will not make friends with me?

When I was young, I thought that with all my heart I gave up the world for Thee . . . I prayed earnestly that I might not rise to any ecclesi-astical dignity. When I was going up for my B.A. examination, I prayed fervently & again & again that I might not gain honours, if they would do me spiritual harm . . . And that, I repeat, because I think, as death comes on, his cold breath is felt on soul as on body, and that, viewed naturally, my soul is half dead now, whereas then it was in the freshness and fervour of youth . . . O my God, not as a matter of sentiment, not as a matter of literary exhibition, do I put this down. O rid me of this frightful *cowardice*, for this is at the bottom of all my ills. When I was young, I was bold, because I was ignorant – now I have lost my boldness, because I have had [sic] advanced in experience. I am able to count the cost, better than I did, of being brave for Thy sake, and therefore I shrink from sacrifices. Here is a second reason, over and above the deadness of my soul, why I have so little faith or love in me.[4]

The outcome, described by Wilfrid Ward as 'Sad Days',[5] was another retirement not unlike Littlemore. Yet the sadness was relieved by humour. 'I liken myself to Tithonous in the last Cornhill Magazine fading out from the world', wrote Newman to Miss Holmes, 'and having nothing to do with its interests or its affairs. I have fallen off in flesh and shrunk up during the past year, and am like a grey grasshopper or the evaporating mist of the morning.'[6] The death of friends stimulated hypochondria and wonder about his own longevity. 'There is Robert Wilberforce dies at 54 – there is Lord Lyndhurst making speeches at 88.'[7] Newman retained his lively interest in the Catholic University, through his eventual successor as Rector, Bartholomew Woodlock, and in the possibilities of a Catholic college in Oxford, and maintained an enormous apologetic correspondence with men and women troubled in their religion, and with his circle of eight devout lady friends, to whom he could freely unburden his soul.

This correspondence, with its lightness of touch, does not sound like someone sunk in continuous depression. But when Acton saw Newman in February 1860, he was struck by Newman's 'bitterness' of spirit, and the similarity of his language – though 'more vehement' – to Döllinger's.[8] Acton considered Newman's continuing services essential to the *Rambler*, and in June, pleaded his own exposed position 'in the midst of a hostile and illiterate episcopate, an ignorant clergy, a prejudiced and divided laity, with the cliques at Brompton, York Place, Ushaw always on the watch, . . . with no auxiliary or adviser but Simpson'.[9]

This could have described Newman's own sense of isolation, which was increased by an odd exchange with another convert, Henry Oxenham, who had written in the *Rambler* for July 1860 an anonymous attack on the 'principle of police'[10] in too narrow a seminary education. As Oxenham cited Newman's *University Lectures* in his own favour, Newman replied to defend Catholic seminary training, from the decrees of the Council of Trent and from his own writings. Newman accidentally assumed – for he did not know his opponent's identity – the initials 'H.O.', possibly as Henry of the Oratory. Oxenham naturally thought this a hit against his anonymity, and his angry rejoinder again cited Newman's writings against 'H.O.', so that he was crushed on discovering that his antagonist was Newman and that he was claiming to understand the Master better than he did himself. Oxenham also invoked the argument of Newman's article 'On consulting the faithful'. Like other liberal Catholics, he looked to Newman as *their* authority, and having been refused ordination by Wiseman, and believing in the validity of his Anglican orders, was for a time to be a master at the

Oratory school. On the Ultramontane side, W. G. Ward told Newman of his delight on discovering that Newman was 'H.O.', but Ward could not help continuing to suspect Newman of being of unsound opinions which were far less Ultramontane than his own.

But as Newman noted, Rome itself had as yet taken no public action against the *Rambler*. It only did so when the journal became embroiled in papal politics. Newman's sympathies with the Liberal Catholics were reflected in his unwillingness to join wholeheartedly in Manning's Ultramontane crusade in support of the Temporal Power of the Pope as an Italian prince, which was under increasing pressure from the partisans of a united Italy. 'It is the Pope's vocation to be in hot water, – it is his element –' wrote Newman. ' . . . No one can touch his real power; and, . . . if his temporal power is curtailed, there is some providential purpose in it.'[11] Acton defended the Temporal Power in the *Rambler* in January 1860, but like Newman, he did not do so on purely religious grounds, and declared it 'not absolutely essential to the nature and ends of the Church'.[12] Acton's assistant Thomas Wetherell actually supported Italian nationalism. Newman sent a letter of general sympathy for the Papacy to a public meeting in Birmingham presided over by Ullathorne in February 1860. 'The Bishop', he noted wryly, ' "consulted the faithful" for two hours and a half',[13] but Newman would not attend the gathering himself because 'its *real* object' was to insist on the 'necessity' of the Temporal Power, when that point was not an article of faith but of political expedience. 'The Pontifical States find, admit, of *no employment whatever* for the young men, who are in consequence forced to go into mischief, if they go into any thing', wrote Newman to Miss Holmes. 'Fancy the state of Birmingham, if the rising generation had nothing to do but to lounge in the streets and throng the theatre.'[14] In similar vein was his argument to Thomas Allies that medieval Christendom was not of necessity the *supremum bonum* of religion: were more souls saved 'under the Christian Theocracy than under the Roman Emperors, or under the English Georges?'[15] So too, he sympathized with his Liberal Irish MP friend William Monsell, in Monsell's outright opposition to the Temporal Power. Clement XIV, though a sovereign, wrote Newman, had suppressed the Jesuits. Pius VII, though a prisoner, had resisted Napoleon. 'Contrast the act of Clement with the act of Pius. The subject-Pontiff has it.'[16]

The Cardinal Secretary of State, the brave and astute though personally corrupt Antonelli, noted this unwillingness to support the Temporal Power among the Irish Catholic MPs, and wrote to Wiseman blaming the *Rambler*. Acton complained about the rumoured attack to Newman, who utterly failed to give him satisfaction, by refusing to make his reservations about the Temporal Power public. When Faber had complained to Rome in 1855, Newman now wrote to Acton, 'who saved us . . . ? It was the Pope himself, and the Pope only. I am bound in gratitude to him'.[17] Newman also objected to Simpson's indirect assault in the *Rambler* on Rome, in his life of the sixteenth-century martyr Edmund Campion; Simpson condemned Pope St Pius V's deposition of Elizabeth as a heretic and usurper, a sensitive matter as this papal claim to the right to depose kings was an aspect of the Temporal Power. Newman slammed Simpson to Acton: 'It was an abrupt, unmeasured attack upon a Saint . . . I don't wonder at a saying which I hear reported of a Dominican, that he would like to have the burning of the Author.'[18] The comment was written in humour, but it pierced Acton's heart. So, too, did Newman's view of the normal duty of outward deference to authority even when wrong. For Acton, Newman's refusal to run counter to constituted superiors was to make him the lost leader, who saw the right but failed to do it, and sacrificed liberty to tyranny.

Newman, however, did make a private protest. He wrote to Manning declaring that he would not fancy 'that I am capable of writing any thing in the shape of a threat', but he insisted that he would resign from the new Catholic Academia should Wiseman in his Inaugural Address at its opening session 'put out any matter, bearing on the same question in the same way' in favour of the Temporal Power.[19] This was the beginning of the famous rift between Newman and Manning, but they were not yet self-consciously estranged; indeed Manning dedicated to Newman an extraordinary series of lectures applying prophecy to the Papacy in the best Evangelical manner, and causing heartache in the Vatican by predicting that Rome would apostatize from the faith.[20] Newman defended the lectures to Acton, and yet more loudly (if humorously) damned Acton's colleague.

I DESPAIR of Simpson being other than he is – he will always be clever, amusing, brilliant, and *suggestive*. He will always be flicking his whip at Bishops, cutting them in tender places, throwing stones at sacred Congregations, and, as he rides along the high road, discharging pea shooters at Cardinals who happen by bad luck to look out of [a] window. I fear I must say I despair of any periodical in which he has a part.[21]

'We don't write books *in order* to attack Saints', Newman told Acton. 'If the necessity of criticism lies plump in our way, and cannot be turned, then we do it, but not with glee.'[22] Acton was to develop an exactly contrary opinion of the historian as a hanging judge for bad behaviour, especially the behaviour of bad Catholics, and most especially when this bad behaviour had cramped or confined human freedom. But Newman was simply battle-weary, tired of this unceasing tug of war. 'The truth is, I have been in constant hot water . . . for full thirty years –', he wrote to Acton, 'and it has at length boiled me – I wish it may serve in part for a purgatory.'[23] To Maria Giberne, now trying on direct instructions from the Virgin her vocation with the Visitation order in France, yet anxious to sally forth to defend the Pope in person, Newman wrote that his 'writing days are for the present over', overborne by the 'long cares I have had, the disappointments of religious hopes, and the sense of cruelty in word and in deed on the part of those from whom I deserved other things . . . '[24] Even his community was a disappointment. He was deeply hurt when in 1859, its ex-Episcopalian American member Robert Tillotson abruptly decided on a visit to New York to enter Fr Isaac Hecker's new Paulist order. 'Fr Ryder told you truly that I am in perfect charity with you', wrote Newman to Tillotson two years after his defection. 'I do not say more, for I could not say what I think about you without offending you. I pray God to forgive you.'[25] The letter recalls Newman's favourite quotation about Rowena in Scott's *Ivanhoe*, who forgave as a Christian – that is, not at all. The melancholy Frederick Bowles, brother to one of Newman's closest friends, Emily Bowles, left the Oratory in 1860. The really able and active Irishman, John Stanislas Flanagan, who was for a time Newman's closest confidant next to Ambrose St John, had to recuperate from an infected lung in Italy, and though he retained Newman's friendship, he never became a settled member of the community again.

Flanagan's departure had to do with his dislike of the Oratory school, which posed its own domestic problems. In September 1860, Mrs F. R. Ward and Lord Charles Thynne, who both had sons in the school, warned Newman that rumours that he was a Garibaldian and in his dotage were being spread by the wife of Robert Moody, an ex-Anglican curate who taught in the school. Newman catechized the Moodys, and suspected them of authoring a batch of malicious valentines to the Oratorian Fathers on St Valentine's Day in 1861.

The one addressed to Newman showed a feline musical wit:

> Ca Ca Caliban
> Get us a master get Dr Newman
> Sang the priests of San
> Phillipo Neri.

> Ca Ca Caliban
> We are heartily tired of our Dr Newman
> Sang the priests of San
> Phillippo Neri

> Ca- Ca- Caliban
> Oh! who will relieve us of Dr Newman
> and his wretched Development Theory

> Ca- Ca- Caliban
> We wish that the Pope would Dr Newman
> Send back to his post at Dunleary.[26]

Also possibly involved was the Moodys' intimate, Fr Nicholas Darnell. Darnell, the son of the fabulously rich Rector of Stanhope in County Durham, was the able and enthusiastic headmaster of the school, and dreamed of turning it into a Catholic Eton. He was a strict disciplinarian whom Newman thought too fond of floggings, if indulgent of smoking; but Darnell was developing the school as an institution independent of the Oratory, to the extent of looking for another site for it. The crisis came early in December 1861, when some older pupils, the Duke of Norfolk and his friends, met the Matron, Mrs Wootten, at the Birmingham Dog Show, in company with a delicate pupil. Darnell issued an edict forbidding her to take boys on the sick list outside the house or to allow any boy not on the sick list to enter her room without a master's permission.

Frances Wootten was not intimidated. She mothered the younger boys and was popular with their mothers; she was a doctor's widow, of independent means, a convert from Oxford and Newman's devoted disciple. She offered her resignation, which Newman rejected as 'calamitous', from the school. To Darnell, he insisted that 'without my name the School would not be'.[27] Darnell accused him of making over his charge 'to an insolent perverse, and blindly frantic woman'.[28] Darnell thought that Newman's offer, in Darnell's words, was of 'a Coordinate Jurisdiction – Mrs Wootten supreme in the house, myself in the School . . . '[29] Newman proposed another division of influence – an upper school for Darnell, a lower school under another master in Mrs Wootten's care. Edward Bellasis, who had boys in the school, passed on Hope-Scott's advice that Newman must assert his authority. Darnell would not remain with Mrs Wootten at any price, and the other four masters threatened to resign with Darnell. They all offered to remain until Easter if Mrs Wootten were kept away. Newman answered that 'I would rather do it all myself till I dropped, than avail myself of such assistance'.[30] 'Need I say', wrote Darnell in parting, 'that in spite of your infatuation, and my own coldness and pride, I love you from my heart and shall always love you, better if possible, than my own Father.'[31]

The situation was quickly retrieved. Two of the masters, James Marshall and the Abbé Rougemont, apologized and were re-employed. Newman pleaded with Darnell to return. 'You have a place in our hearts', he wrote, 'and are rooted both in the Oratory and among our people. Why will you destroy the work of so many years, and leave all our affections lacerated and bleeding?'[32] The Moodys and the fourth master, Henry Oxenham, departed, St John took over as headmaster, and Newman secured replacements, one of them Thomas Arnold. Darnell went on to become a schoolmaster and mission priest in Northumberland. Flanagan, who had supported him, resided from 1863 in the Oratory's poor mission in Smethwick, and in 1865 returned to Ireland, though his friendship with Newman remained warm. Within a year, Rougemont had turned out to be a rogue: he ran away with a boy's watch, leaving behind false moustaches, brightly coloured neckties, compromising letters and disease-stained linen, and was gaoled for stealing jewellery, plate and clothing from his Irish employer. The school itself reassembled and lost no pupils by the scandal of the resignations. 'We have met', Newman reported triumphantly to John Hungerford Pollen, 'without the loss of a single boy.'[33] He declared to Mother Margaret Mary Hallahan that he 'never was in sharper distress and never was in shorter'.[34] But though William Neville was ordained in 1861, and Henry Ryder in 1862, the Oratory had no more than seven priest-members in 1864, and many of the house and school duties, in examining and letter-writing to anxious parents, fell on Newman himself.

It was the school that he gave as his final reason to William Neville's friend James Laird Patterson for his continuing failure to write books:

1. Because, in matters of controversy, I am a miles emeritus, rude donatus.
2. Because no one serves on Parliamentary Committees after he is 60.
3. Because Rigaud's steam engine which was hard to start, was hard to stop.
4. Because Hannibal's elephants never could learn the goose step.
5. Because Garibaldi's chaplains in ordinary never do write.
6. Because books that do not sell do not pay the printing.
7. Because just now I am teaching little boys nonsense verses . . . [35]

Perhaps the deepest reason, however, was number 5: his humorous public aside in 1860, when asking for prayers for the Sicilian Oratory, about 'an able general' who had conquered Sicily, produced the rumour that he was himself a Garibaldian, which the Oratory's ex-organist spread obligingly to London and Rome.[36]

The rumours about Newman among Catholics suspicious of his loyalty to Rome, like W. G. Ward, were only less fantastic than their Anglican reflection, that he was returning to the Church of England or even becoming an unbeliever, which Newman had to deny when they reached the newspapers. Thus G. Noel Hoare, an ultra-Protestant country gentleman of Blatherwycke Park, Lincolnshire, asserted, in Newman's paraphrase, that 'I am "living *in Paris* the *unhappy* life of a *hopeless sceptic* and a *notorious* scoffer at the Catholic Religion". I can only repeat, What shocking untruths! . . . Who is this Mr G. Noel Hoare? In an age of light, where in the world has the unfortunate man been living? Of what select circle is he the oracle? What bad luck has seduced him into print?'.[37] In the vehemence of Newman's reaction to these reports as they spread like an infection from one newspaper to another, he insisted

that Protestantism is the dreariest of possible religions; that the thought of the Anglican service makes me shiver, and the thought of the Thirty-nine Articles makes me shudder. Return to the Church of England! no; 'the net is broken, and we are delivered'. I should be a consummate fool (to use a mild term) if in my old age I left 'the land flowing with milk and honey' for the city of confusion and the house of bondage.[38]

This fierceness naturally gave offence to an old Anglican friend like Charles Crawley of Littlemore, and seemed to contradict Newman's own view of Anglicanism as 'a breakwater against infidelity',[39] and his warm memories of his worship as an Anglican; but his feelings were mixed, and drew on recollections of early desolate services at St Mary's, and on his revulsion from the Anglican system as such:

> 'Twas a palace of ice,
>   hard and cold as were they,
> And when summer came,
>   it all melted away.[40]

The same verses recalled the eyes of the Madonna, like 'the deep glowing blue of Italy's skies'. He had, in his own view, changed his religion from one of ice to one of warmth and flesh and blood.

Yet humanly speaking, Newman told Manning in August 1862 that he found his new Church 'very little but desert and desolateness' and 'that all my human affections were with those whom I had left'; this, he noted, was one of the last occasions when Manning, that 'great pumper', 'wormed' anything out of him.[41] On 21 January 1863, he resorted to his Journal: 'as a Protestant, I felt my religion dreary, but not my life – but, as a Catholic, my life dreary, not my religion'.[42] In this mood he looked to his old Anglican friends for consolation. In May 1860, he resumed contact with his former curate Isaac Williams. A chance meeting in London in 1862 renewed his connection with another ex-curate William Copeland, whom he at once invited to the Oratory. 'I am tempted to preach to you', Newman wrote to Copeland, telling him to keep a kindly Lent, 'and beg you to be very gentle with yourself – for I want you to live many years, and never, never again to be so cruel to me as you were for near 17 long years . . . you all have so simply treated me as *dead*.'[43]

Keble wrote in August 1863 after a silence which had lasted since 1846, with news of himself and his wife and nephew Tom, and about the profits of the *Lyra Apostolica*, which Newman had given him. 'Did you ever read Mrs Sheridan's Tale of Nourjahad! . . .', wrote Newman by return post. 'I am like one of the seven sleepers awakened . . . I cannot think of little Tom but as of the boy I carried pick a back, when he was tired in getting from the steep valley to the table land of Bisley . . . there is nothing I love better than you, and Isaac, and Copeland and many others I could name, except Him whom I ought to love best of all and supremely . . . none *but* He, *can* make up for the losses of those old familiar faces which haunt me continually.'[44]

Still more affecting was his first meeting in more than twenty years with Frederic Rogers at the Oratory later in the month: 'he burst into tears', wrote Newman, 'and would not let go my hands – then his first words were "How altered you are – " ' The lapse of so long a time brings itself out in no other way so vividly. In memory, actions and doings of years ago appear like yesterday – and indeed in the course of the day, he was led to cry out "Oh how like *you*!" ' Newman was delighted to discover Rogers not a sceptic, and they chatted about the failed Bible translation, the Catholic University, 'Birmingham habits, Birmingham villas, architecture': 'I saw', wrote Rogers to his wife about the occasion, ' . . . that a joke at Ward's expense was not unacceptable'. Rogers caught Newman's 'kind of impatient and half mournful "Ah, tzt" . . . which seemed to say, "Why is he not with me . . . ?" ' Rogers sensed that Newman's isolation among Catholics had turned him back on his old Anglican friends and memories, 'almost alone in a large house with none of his old friends about him, overworked, and that in a way which is not his own . . . thrown away by the communion to which he has devoted himself, and evidently sensible that he is so thrown away'.[45]

Newman had few holidays. He went to Ventnor on the Isle of Wight in 1861, where he had been with Bowden in 1825, and where he thought the undercliff 'the most beautiful sea place I know in England'.[46] In November he visited friends in London, Pollens, Bowdens and Wilberforces; William Wilberforce Junior, the oldest brother, who had lost his father's fortune, became a Catholic in 1863, leaving only Bishop Samuel of Oxford outside the Roman Church. Newman was also photographed for the first time. There was further relief from the Oratory at the end of September 1862, when money from a friend enabled Newman to take a five week holiday in Deal and Ramsgate. 'This is not the most ornate place in the world – ', he wrote to Bloxam, 'but the Deal boatman and the pipe-loving sailor are more welcome objects to me in the landscape, than fine gentlemen wateringplace cockneys, crinolines, porkpie hats, and little dogs with blue-ribbons on. If this fails, I shall get into some lighthouse, or martello tower, and there be with the pelican and owl. I am bathing, that, like Medea's cauldron, it may make me young ago [again].' His peace was disturbed by a report of Edward Bellasis' quarrel on a railway journey with Bishop James Brown of Shrewsbury about the orthodoxy of the Oratory School. 'One ought to be a Warrior or Black Prince to sustain such shot', wrote Newman to Bellasis with reference to the new ironclad warships which bore these names. He was worried about such careless denigration of the school. 'I suppose', he added icily to Bittleston, 'Bishops are above the 10 commandments.'[47]

Any reflections on Newman's orthodoxy also reflected on the school. When in 1862, Wiseman attacked the *Home and Foreign Review*, Acton's successor to the *Rambler*, Newman praised Acton's reply, and Acton felt that 'for the first time Newman declared himself completely on my side'.[48] Newman was, however, annoyed with an article in the issue for October

1862 by Simpson, quite gratuitously arguing the scientific unreliability of Genesis in a review of a book by Döllinger. 'I should call it', wrote Newman to Thomas Arnold of the review, 'a speculation edged with an insinuation.'[49] Newman then wholeheartedly approved a letter of condemnation of the *Rambler* and *Home and Foreign Review* by Ullathorne, because, as Newman told Acton, it declared specific passages 'to contain certain doctrines which have been condemned at Rome'.[50] Acton thought this 'singularly absurd'.[51] Ullathorne passed a copy of Newman's letter to Wiseman as proof of Newman's good predilections, and the Cardinal rejoiced, as did Ward and Manning, and Talbot in Rome.

Newman, however, did not agree with Ullathorne. He was simply declaring his duty to submit outwardly to an episcopal argument which was clearly stated and defined. He was also not willing to support the *Home and Foreign* in a false position: if Acton 'had given up Simpson, and gone frankly to our Bishop and said so', he wrote afterwards, 'the latter never would have taken part against him'.[52] Simpson 'ruins and will ruin every thing that he has to do with. *I wash my hands* of every thing that he has to do with . . . as the Old Duke said that a great country cannot have a little war, so it is true that a man who has been mixed up with men as different from each other as Simpson and Ward, and that on large and delicate subjects, cannot have a little explanation; and if I attempted one, I might be making a dozen fresh holes while I darned one'.[53]

There was, however, the further complexity that Newman thought that Simpson had substantially answered Ullathorne's condemnation in his reply, and Newman 'listened unsympathetically'[54] when the Bishop called to explain his views on 26 December 1862. Newman now feared that Ullathorne had mistaken his submission to Ullathorne's ruling for agreement, and he submitted to W. G. Ward a draft letter for the Bishop making their actual disagreement plain. Ward urged him in honesty to be still more explicit. 'I cannot deny', wrote Newman to Ullathorne, 'that a certain sympathy with his [Simpson's] intentions has been at the root of my pain at his performances.'[55] Just as he had offered to burn his *Essay on the Development of Christian Doctrine* if authority had required it when he became a Catholic, so now he told Ullathorne that his letter of October about Simpson had been 'an act of *obedience*', not of approval of the Bishop's views. 'I felt', he later wrote, 'I should only put the Bishop's back up, had I not rounded my angles.'[56] In fact, Ullathorne claimed in reply that he had not misunderstood Newman's reluctance to condemn Simpson, and while the Bishop returned to the attack on the *Rambler* and *Home and Foreign* in a further letter, his relations with Newman remained friendly. Ullathorne was always in spirit an Old Catholic; he was not of the neo-Ultramontane party of Ward and Manning. He had his Old Catholic reservations about converts, and told Manning that he was preaching with a mitre on his head when

Manning was still a heretic, but he no longer regarded Newman with deep suspicion.

Yet Newman's position was now an intolerable one: he was perfectly placed between warring armies. 'A man who has been mixed up with two such different people as Ward and Simpson', he said, 'cannot explain himself without writing a volume.'[57] He was neither a neo-Ultramontane like Ward nor a Liberal Catholic like Simpson. He wanted a proper liberty for scholars which was less than Simpson's, and a proper authority that was less than Ward's. He wanted a new sort of *via media* between Actonian anarchy and Roman tyranny, a middle way which was wholly acceptable to no one but himself.

Indeed Newman had wholly alienated Acton, though in his letters to intimates like William Monsell and Emily Bowles, his view of the wisdom of authority was hardly less savage than Acton's own. His most passionate outburst was to Emily:

This country is under Propaganda, and Propaganda is too shallow to have the wish to use such as me. It is rather afraid of such. If I know myself, no one can have been more loyal to the Holy See than I am. I love the Pope personally into the bargain. But Propaganda is a quasi-military power, extraordinary, for missionary countries, rough and ready. It does not understand an intellectual movement. It likes quick results – scalps from beaten foes by the hundred. Our Bishop once on his return from Rome, said pointedly to me what I am sure came as a quasi message from Propaganda, that at Rome 'they liked good news' . . .

This age of the Church is peculiar – in former times, primitive and medieval, there was not the extreme centralization which now is in use. If a private theologian said any thing free, another answered him. If the controversy grew, then it went to a Bishop, a theological faculty, or to some foreign University. The Holy See was but the court of ultimate appeal. *Now*, if I, as a private priest, put any thing into print, *Propaganda* answers me at once. How can I fight with such a chain on my arm? It is like the Persians driven on to fight *under the lash*. There was true private judgment in the primitive and medieval schools – there are no schools now, no private judgment (in the *religious* sense of the phrase,) no freedom, that is, of opinion. That is, no exercise of the intellect. No, the system goes on by the tradition of the intellect of former times . . .

There was some talk, when the Bishop put in his plea against me, of calling me to Rome. Call me to Rome! What does that mean? It means to sever an old man from his Home, to subject him to intercourse with persons whose languages are strange to him: it means to bring him to a climate, which is unhealthy to him – to food, and to floors, which are almost starvation on one hand, and involve restless days and nights on the other – it means to oblige him to dance attendance on Propaganda week after week and month after month – it means his death. (It was the punishment on Dr Baines in 1840–1 to keep him at the door of Propaganda for a year.) . . .

Others have been killed there before me. Lucas went of his own accord indeed – but when he got there, oh how much did he, as loyal a son of the Church and Holy See as ever was, what did he suffer because Dr Cullen was against him! He wandered, (as Dr Cullen *said* in a letter he published in a sort of triumph,) he wandered from Church to Church without a friend, and hardly got an audience from the Pope. And I too should go from St Philip to our Lady, and to St Peter and St Paul, and to St Laurence and to St Cecilia, and, if it happened to me, as to Lucas, should come back to die.[58]

He consoled himself that the saints had suffered from Rome like him before him; but these outbursts showed a mind at the peak of its powers, pent up by years of silence and disappointment, dwelling on past pains and pleasures, old loves and hates, and prepared in full autobiographical mode to pour itself out before the world.

Newman's sense of hurt found expression in a sometimes macabre sense of humour. 'Fr Faber', he wrote in 1861, 'having been in his own belief given over, and in immediate prospect of death, suddenly got up, shaved himself, and announces his intention of coming to town next Monday. John Bowden gave us a sort of hagiographical account of it . . . and gave the Brompton judgment that it was a grazia.'[59] Newman was unmoved by a letter from Faber craving forgiveness. 'It was good fun sailing on with the stream, speaking against the Brummagem Oratory, and criticizing me as slow. It was good fun playing against us in 1855, 1856', wrote Newman with satisfaction. 'But now anxious times are coming on *him*.'[60] In May 1862, Dalgairns wrote that Faber was ill with Bright's disease; in June, the unfeeling Newman asked 'How many times has Fr Faber been a-dying?'[61] In July 1863, Faber's closest friend Antony Hutchison died, worn out with his labours among the poor, and on 20 July, Newman spent a quarter of an hour with Faber, now swollen with dropsy, *en route* to a holiday in France and Germany. 'He said he had loved me the best of any one in the world, next to the late Duke of Norfolk. He said a sermon of mine at St Mary's had been the turning point of his life – for it gave him the first notion he had of supernatural grace.' He also claimed to have been in 'a minority of one' in his community in wanting to consult Newman before appealing to Rome. The memorandum about Faber which Newman drew up at Ostend was not forgiving.[62] It was his first continental holiday since 1833, with a visit to the Wilberforces at Saint-Germains and his first journey down the Moselle to Coblenz and down the Rhine to Bonn, and to Aix-la-Chapelle where he fell down a flight of hotel stairs without injury. Faber died in September. 'They absolutely and *intentionally* threw me off eight years ago just', wrote Newman to Maria Giberne about the London Oratory, the day before he went down to Brompton for Faber's requiem. He added that it was 'touching, both pleasant and sad', that as Faber and Hutchison 'had been undivided in their lives, they should be undivided in their deaths'.[63] Newman always acknowledged Faber's virtues, but he did not easily forgive a breach of trust, and as his later remarks show, Faber was not forgiven.

Yet one old friend turned foe was forgiven. Mutual pride and suspicion prevented any meeting between Newman and Whately when they lived and worked cheek by jowl on St Stephen's Green in Dublin; but when the Archbishop died in October 1863, Newman wrote for the *Weekly Register* the noblest of tributes to his spirit: that what Whately had done

> was to break to pieces the idols which blocked out the light, and to clear a space for undertakings which he did not himself attempt. It was his to preach the simple but momentous principles, that religion need not be afraid of argument, that faith can fearlessly appeal to right reason, that inquiry does but strengthen the foundations of revelation, and that the Church is founded in the truth, and truth alone.[64]

But did the Roman Church care for truth? Old loves were near allied to new hurts, when in December 1863 Newman received from an unknown admirer, William Pope, a copy of the January 1864 issue of *Macmillan's Magazine*, containing a review with a libel upon him:

> Truth, for its own sake, had never been a virtue with the Roman clergy. Father Newman informs us that it need not, and on the whole ought not to be; that cunning is the weapon which Heaven has given to the saints wherewith to withstand the brute male force of the wicked world which marries and is given in marriage. Whether his notion be doctrinally correct or not, it is at least historically so.[65]

The attack cried out for an answer. The die was cast and the floodgates were open.

24

Apologia

'Now you have begun what will last to Eternity – one day, which has no ending',[1] wrote Newman in January 1864 to Maria Giberne, who after failing her novitiate at Paray-le-Monial had at last been professed a religious as Sister Maria Pia of the Visitation convent at Autun. The year was also to recover for Newman the national stature that he was never afterwards to lose, as a figure of whom, in spite of religious differences, the ordinary Englishman would feel proud. The revolution in Newman's fortunes was due to Charles Kingsley as the author of the libel in *Macmillan's*, and to Kingsley's extraordinary compounding of his original offence. He wrote on 6 January to Newman declaring his authorship, and referring to Newman's works in general and to his Anglican sermon on 'Wisdom and Innocence' for proof of the assertion that the Roman clergy did not care for truth for its own sake. 'It was in consequence of that sermon', wrote Kingsley, 'that I finally shook off the strong influence which your writings exerted on me . . . I am most happy to hear from you that I mistook . . . your meaning; and I shall be most happy, on your showing me that I have wronged you, to retract my accusation as publicly as I have made it.'[2]

This was not an adequate apology. As Newman pointed out in his reply, the sermon on 'Wisdom and Innocence' had been written before he was a Roman Catholic; it was seventeen pages, in which Kingsley had stigmatized no one passage for censure, though this was less vague than Kingsley's appeal to the 'many passages' in Newman's writings which he also alleged sustained the charge. Newman could not know that Kingsley's memory was at fault: he had flung off Newman's influence long before the sermon in 1844. 'When I received your letter, taking upon yourself the authorship, I was amazed',[3] concluded Newman; a statement which has been questioned because the cover of the magazine bore Kingsley's name. Alexander Macmillan wrote to Newman in a more accommodating vein, recalling his own delight and his brother's in Newman's sermons, and admitting the 'injustice' of Kingsley's charges against Newman personally. But Macmillan declared that he had not considered unjust the charge against the Roman clergy.[4] Newman's response expressed astonishment at the last: 'Most wonderful phenomenon! An educated man, breathing English air, and walking in the light of the nineteenth century, thinks that neither I nor any members of my communion feel any difficulty in allowing that "Truth for its own sake need not and on the whole ought not to be, a virtue with the Roman clergy" '.[5] Newman added that he regarded Kingsley's letter as public property; Kingsley conceded this.

Kingsley agreed to publish an amende in *Macmillan's Magazine* so little to Newman's satisfaction that he placed the paragraphs of the apology against his own '*Unjust, but too probable, popular rendering*' of them:

2. Dr. Newman has, by letter, expressed in the strongest terms his denial of the meaning which I have put upon his words.	2. I have set before Dr. Newman, as he challenged me to do, extracts from his writings, and he has affixed to them what he conceives to be their legitimate sense, to the denial of that in which I understood them.
3. No man knows the use of words better than Dr Newman; no man, therefore, has a better right to define what he does, or does not, mean by them.	3. He has done this with the skill of a great master of verbal fence, who knows, as well as any man living, how to insinuate a doctrine without committing himself to it.
4. It only remains, therefore, for me to express my hearty regret at having so seriously mistaken him, and my hearty pleasure at finding him on the side of truth, in this or any other matter.	4. However, while I heartily regret that I have so seriously mistaken the sense which he assures me his words were meant to bear, I cannot but feel a hearty pleasure also, at having brought him, for once in a way, to confess that after all truth is a Christian virtue.[6]

Newman's lawyer friend Edward Badeley confirmed this view of Kingsley's letter: it did not quote any passage from Newman's writings in evidence, wrote Badeley, and it was 'only by your declaring that you did not mean what you really and in effect said, that he finds that he made a false charge. And so far from making any proper apology, he concludes with a most offensive and insolent sneer – Such an apology, I think, would not be deemed sufficient in any Court of Justice, or in any society of Gentlemen, and I have no hesitation in declaring that I consider it a disgrace to the writer'.[7]

Kingsley assured Newman that he did 'think it probable that the good sense and honesty of the British Public will misinterpret my apology'. But he agreed to omit the offending passages in his published statement of redress, which simply declared that 'Dr. Newman has by letter expressed, in the strongest terms, his denial of the meaning which I have put upon his words. It only remains, therefore, for me to express my hearty regret at having so seriously mistaken him'. 'Having done this', wrote Kingsley, 'and having frankly accepted your assertion that I was mistaken, I have done as much as an English gentleman can expect from another.'[8]

Newman again pointed out to Macmillan that this was unsatisfactory, quoting Badeley's opinion with his own. He then decided to publish the whole correspondence. 'Had Mr Kingsley shown a particle of the frankness which your own letter displayed, my trouble would have been spared', he told Macmillan. 'All of us are liable to error . . . had he [Kingsley], in his justification, been able . . . to produce any passage from any work of mine, of an ambiguous character, I should have felt obliged to him for giving me the opportunity of explaining it . . . '[9] The pamphlet containing the correspondence was published by Longman, and was a runaway bestseller, not least for the concluding 'Reflections' by Newman, a page of brilliant sarcasm more likely to amuse than to win him friends.

Mr. Kingsley begins then by exclaiming, – 'O the chicanery, the wholesale fraud, the vile hypocrisy, the conscience-killing tyranny of Rome! We have not far to seek for an evidence of it. There's Father Newman to wit: one living specimen is worth a hundred dead ones. He, a Priest writing of Priests, tells us that lying is never any harm.'

I interpose: 'You are taking a most extraordinary liberty with my name. If I have said this, tell me when and where.'

Mr. Kingsley replies: 'You said it, Reverend Sir, in a Sermon which you preached, when a Protestant, as Vicar of St Mary's, and published in 1844; and I could read you a very salutary lecture on the effects which that Sermon had at the time on my own opinion of you.'

I make answer: 'Oh . . . *Not*, it seems, as a Priest speaking of Priests; – but let us have the passage.'

Mr. Kingsley relaxes: 'Do you know, I like your *tone*. From your *tone* I rejoice, greatly rejoice, to be able to believe that you did not mean what you said.'

I rejoin: '*Mean* it! I maintain I never said it, whether as a Protestant or as a Catholic.'

Mr. Kingsley replies: 'I waive that point'.

I object: 'Is it possible! What? Waive the main question! I either said it or I didn't. You have made a monstrous charge against me; direct, distinct, public. You are bound to prove it as directly, as distinctly, as publicly; – or to own you can't.'

'Well', says Mr. Kingsley, 'if you are quite sure you did not say it, I'll take your word for it; I really will.'

My *word*! I am dumb. Somehow I thought it was my *word* that happened to be on trial. The *word* of a Professor of lying, that he does not lie!

But Mr. Kingsley re-assures me: 'We are both gentlemen', he says: 'I have done as much as one English gentleman can expect from another.'

I begin to see: he thought me a gentleman at the very time that he said I taught lying on system. After all, it is not I, but it is Mr. Kingsley who did not mean what he said. 'Habemus confitentem reum.'

So we have confessedly come round to this, preaching without practising; the common theme of satirists from Juvenal to Walter Scott! 'I left Baby Charles and Steenie laying his duty before him', says King James of the reprobate Dalgarno: 'O Geordie, jingling Geordie, it was grand to hear Baby Charles laying down the guilt of dissimulation, and Steenie lecturing on the turpitude of incontinence.'[10]

Had the matter rested there, the honours might have been even. The public knew that Kingsley had apologized, and without looking too closely into the matter might have taken Newman's logical and rhetorical victory with a pinch of salt. There had been no discussion of the general point at issue, the truthfulness of the Roman clergy. The *Saturday Review* depicted Newman as a 'lithe and supple' serpent, 'erect, defiant, and pitiless', and even the sympathetic Richard Holt Hutton, editor of the *Spectator*, saw Kingsley as possibly 'too helpless a victim'. Hutton admired both Newman and Kingsley, and while acknowledging 'Kingsley's high feeling and generous courage', thought that the subtitle of one of his books, 'Loose Thoughts for Loose Thinkers', represented 'too closely the character of his rough but manly intellect, so that a more opportune Protestant ram for Father Newman's sacrificial knife could scarcely have been found'. Hutton, a brusque and eccentric but kindly man, owed a great debt to Newman, having been brought from Unitarianism to the Church of England by Newman's writings. Yet he also thought Newman showed 'that peculiar hardness tending to cruelty which most easily allies itself with a keen intellectual sense of the supernatural . . .'[11] Newman was deeply appreciative of Hutton's praise, though it was a two-edged compliment, tending towards Kingsley's insinuation that Newman was too clever by half. But Hutton's love of Newman and his eminence as an arbiter of the literary world won Newman a public hearing which was to make all the difference in what followed.

Kingsley's decision to reply was a terrible blunder, but he was as Newman said 'a furious foolish fellow',[12] acting under an inner compulsion, 'a score of more than twenty years to pay',[13] he called it, which was the consequence of his own curious psychosexual history. As an insecure and emotional young man, he had been attracted to Newman's ideal of monastic purity, but had violently reacted against it when delivered from it, as he saw it himself, by an ecstatically happy marriage. His feelings found expression in his erotic drawings of himself and his bride naked upon a cross, and in his sado-masochistic celebration in verse of the martyrdoms of SS Timothy and Maura; and he had come to understand the Reformation as a sexual revolution in which the primitive manly Teutonic family virtues had been rescued from the false asceticism of Mediterranean monasticism and from the priestly effeminacy of Latin Christianity.[14]

Kingsley's cult of English Christian manliness involved a contempt for those peoples, Celtic and Latin, enslaved to a feminine Catholicism, and embodied the fear and loathing of the Victorian Protestant paterfamilias for the priest who intruded his authority into the family. This widespread sentiment was inflamed by offspring who became Catholics, and who thereby invested their rebellion against their sires with the ultimate sanction of an exotic and alien religion. Behind Kingsley's ire lay the experience of his own loved ones. Mrs Kingsley in her youth had thought of becoming a Catholic; her sister, later married to James Anthony Froude, had actually become one. Catholicism for Kingsley spoke to the weaker, feminine part of human nature, and offered the false authorities of priestcraft and conventualism in place of the one authority which a good woman needed, the love of a good man. Male celibates and women who chose to be nuns were rebelling against nature: one of the ugliest forms of Victorian anti-Catholicism was the Protestant pornography about convents, depicting helpless women who were mercilessly manipulated by perverted men. Kingsley's own cult of muscular Christianity and his relentless athleticism were part of his deliberate rejection of the feminine in himself: truth and manliness were kindred virtues, and Catholicism had neither. To this he added the prejudices of the Victorian sanitary reformer and progressive. In the manner of Max Weber's famous association of Protestantism and capitalism, Kingsley connected Catholicism and monasticism with the ignorance, backwardness, fecklessness and dirt of the Celts and Latins, and extolled industry and cleanliness as Anglo-Saxon and Teutonic, Protestant and manly. Kingsley had thereby fused into an imaginatively coherent whole a range of classic Victorian attitudes, against which Newman stood for a false sacerdotal authority in its most insidiously attractive form. Kingsley was fierce precisely because he had felt and resisted the power of the magician's spell. It was too easy to let his feelings rip, knowing that he was voicing the general opinions of his Protestant fellow countrymen.

Kingsley's rhetorical advantage was, therefore, that he was asserting no more than a truism, the intrinsic absurdity of Roman Catholicism; but he overplayed his hand by vulgar abuse and innuendo, which was, in Newman's famous phrase, '*poisoning the wells*'[15] of criticism. In Kingsley's pamphlet 'What, then, does Dr. Newman mean?' he claimed that Newman's show of courtesy and dignity had suddenly changed to one which proved 'how the atmosphere of the Romish priesthood has degraded his notions of what is due to himself'. He added that as he had granted Newman's honesty, it depended 'entirely on Dr. Newman whether he shall sustain the reputation which he has so recently acquired'.[16] Some of Kingsley's charges were based on slipshod paraphrases of Newman's words. Because Newman asserted that humble and holy monks and nuns were 'Christians after the very pattern given us in Scripture', Kingsley thought that Newman was declaring them 'the only perfect Christians'.[17] Newman allowed to Christians the arts of 'defencelessness' as employed by 'ill-used and oppressed children', in order to defend themselves with the wisdom of the serpent; Kingsley therefore accused him of bidding Christians imitate 'the "arts" of the basest of animals and of men',[18] as practised by the priestcraft of the medieval Church, and this in a sermon 'delivered before fanatic and hot-headed young men, who hung over his every word'.[19] But was this not the product of deliberate art? Newman had been suspected 'of writing a whole sermon . . . for the sake of one single passing hint – one phrase, one epithet, one little barbed arrow which, as he swept magnificently past on the stream of his calm eloquence, seemingly unconscious of all presences, save those unseen, he delivered unheeded, as with his fingertip, to the very heart of an uninitiated hearer, never to be withdrawn again'.[20] Newman had thereby sown the seed of that popish double-dealing which had injured 'the straightforwardness and truthfulness' of the young men who had absorbed it, and so 'spread misery and shame into many an English home'.[21]

Kingsley saw the same influence in Newman's Anglo-Catholic series of medieval saints' lives. He acknowledged that some of these, like his brother-in-law J. A. Froude's *Life of St Neot*, frankly bore the mark of their legendary character upon them; but he thought that others had sapped 'the very foundation of historic truth', as when St Peter's visit to England, admitted to be a pious legend, was declared to have its 'effect upon devout minds'[22] in spite of the utter want of evidence for it. In the same series, Kingsley mocked the miracles of St Walburga and of the oil which flowed from her bones, and the story in her life of St Sturme's preternatural discernment of the evil in a bathing party of unbaptized Germans by their stench. A Catholic monk might have thought it a miracle to be 'shocked at his fellow-creatures' evil smell; but in Oxford gentlemen, accustomed to the use of soap and water, it is too bad'.[23] Kingsley also ridiculed Newman's apology for certain contemporary Catholic miracles and relics in his *Lectures on the Present Position of Catholics in England*. Newman had written that if the Tower of London was not shut against sightseers, 'because the coats of mail or pikes there may have half legendary tales connected with them', why should not 'the country people come up in joyous companies, singing and piping, to see the holy coat [of Christ] at Treves?' Even more damaging was Newman's acknowledgement of the authenticity of the relics at Rome, of 'the liquefaction of the blood of St. Januarius, at Naples', and 'the motion of the eyes of the pictures of the Madonna in the Roman States'. 'How art thou fallen from heaven', exploded Kingsley, 'O Lucifer, son of the Morning!'[24]

Kingsley himself thought that the issue here was not so much Newman's honesty as his credulity. It was almost too honest of Newman to paint the popish objects of Protestant hostility in the most lurid terms, the better to provide a defence of them. For Kingsley, this was 'a perverse pleasure in saying something shocking to plain English notions'; but then Newman himself discerned a gulf between 'plain English notions'[25] and truth. Kingsley cited two such passages from the *Lectures on Certain Difficulties felt by Anglicans*, one of them, paradoxically, on the wickedness of the slightest lie. Kingsley quoted a statement embodying the severest moral indifference to worldly happiness: that the Catholic Church

> holds it better for sun and moon to drop from heaven, for the earth to fail, and for all the many millions on it to die of starvation in extremest agony, so far as temporal affliction goes, than that one soul, I will not say should be lost, but should commit one single venial sin, should tell one wilful untruth, or should steal one poor farthing without excuse.[26]

The second passage seems to contradict this:

> Take a mere beggar woman, lazy, ragged, and filthy, and not over-scrupulous of truth . . . but if she is chaste, sober, and cheerful, and goes to her religious duties . . . she will, in the eyes of the Church, have a prospect of heaven, quite closed and refused to the State's pattern-man, the just, the upright, the generous, the honourable, the conscientious, if he be all this, not from a supernatural power . . . but from mere natural virtue.[27]

This sharp dissociation of religion from respectability was quite beyond Kingsley, who wrote that it practically taught 'the whole Celtic Irish population, that as long as they are chaste (which they cannot well help being, being married almost before they are men and women) and sober (which they cannot well help being, being too poor to get enough whisky to make them drunk), and "go to their religious duties" – an expression on which I make no comment – they may look down upon the Protestant gentry . . . '[28] His following rhapsody on the superior generosity, virtue, truthfulness and civilization of these gentry belonged to the realm of English Celtophobia and invoked a class prejudice as well as a racial one.

Newman's list of the sins of Latin Catholic culture had also partially exculpated the 'feeble old woman, who first genuflects before the Blessed Sacrament, and then steals her neighbour's handkerchief or prayer-book': 'she worships, and she sins; she kneels because she believes . . . She may be out of God's grace; she is not altogether out of His sight'.[29] Kingsley also held up for execration Newman's honest depiction of miracle plays and relic-selling at a popular fair, by which he had tried to show how in Latin countries religion permeates the whole of life in a manner 'profane to a population [as in Britain] which only half believes; not profane to those who believe wholly, who one and all have a vision within which corresponds with what they see . . . '[30] But these apologies for Celtic rags and Mediterranean superstition appalled Kingsley less than a further passage in which Newman had described, in the intensity of worship of a closed religious order, in 'a realized heaven upon earth', 'a weak sister', a hysteric, who had faked the stigmata. Dr Newman, retorted Kingsley, 'will remain upon his trial as long as Englishmen know how to guard the women whom God has committed to their charge. If the British public shall ever need informing that Dr Newman wrote that passage, I trust there will be always one man left in England to inform them of the fact, for the sake of the ladies of this land'.[31]

Kingsley also put his finger crudely but effectively on the sceptical element in Newman's mind which was so suspect to thinkers less subtle than himself. Newman had argued that the ultimate truth of whether the earth goes round the sun or the sun around the earth depends on the character of motion which is a mystery. If motion were but an accident of sense experience, then either proposition could be true in different scientific systems. Such philosophical sophistication was beyond the blunt-minded Kingsley, with his direct and simple view of truth. Newman's sceptical tendency appeared even more sinister when placed beside the old charges against the Oxford Movement of practising 'reserve' and 'economy' in imparting Christian doctrine: 'Yes, Dr. Newman', wrote Kingsley, 'is a very economical person', teaching – in the words of St Clement – 'that, in certain cases, a lie is the nearest approach to the truth'.[32] Newman also stood accused of professing the popular teaching of the eighteenth-century casuist St Alfonso di Liguori that there were circumstances in which a lie was lawful: how could Kingsley not know that in debate with Newman, he was 'the dupe of some cunning equivocation, of one of the three kinds laid down as permissible'[33] by St Alfonso. Not that these sins could be laid at the door of all Catholics; Kingsley complimented the honesty of the old English Catholic gentry at the expense of 'the majority of the Romish priesthood' and of 'those hapless Irish Celts over whom they rule'. Kingsley concluded that if Newman continued 'to "economize" and "divide" the words of his adversaries as he has done mine, he will run great danger of forfeiting once more his reputation for honesty'.[34]

Newman had 'prepared myself from the first'[35] to defend himself from his life and writings, though he complained that he had only arranged his papers to 1836. Nor was he alone. In March 1864, he received a supportive address from the clergy of the Archdiocese of Westminster,[36] and had to thank 'with all my heart' an equally helpful notice by Hutton in the *Spectator*, directed against Kingsley's reply.[37] Newman had, however, the disadvantage of not wholly believing in his cause, in so far as he agreed with Kingsley that many of the Roman clergy did not care for truth: he was to write to his Jesuit friend Fr Henry Coleridge of a proposal for an historical review, 'who would bear it? Unless one doctored all one's facts, one should be

thought a bad Catholic'.[38] So too, he dreaded not the letter but the application of the 'Munich Brief' published in March 1864, directed by the Pope
against Döllinger and his school, and according to Acton condemning the
Home and Foreign Review, which then ceased publication. Newman himself
regarded the Brief as 'a providential intimation . . . to be silent'[39] on questions of Science and Scripture. Acton congratulated Newman on his reply
to Kingsley for not trying to vindicate the Roman clergy's truthfulness.[40]
Newman was doing exactly what the *Apologia* was to imply that he was not,
going into battle like the Persians under the lash.

Newman's reply to Kingsley in weekly parts was published by Longman.
He began writing in late March, and his seven pamphlets appeared on
Thursdays between 21 April and 2 June. He wrote standing at his desk and
often weeping, working one shift of sixteen hours and another of twenty-
two. From Copeland, Keble and Rogers, he gathered letters and opinions
and corrections on his proofs. When Keble and Copeland both objected to
his claim that most of the then English bishops could not hold a candle to
Bagot, Newman put the candle out; but as he wrote to Copeland, the
Northampton vicar to whom they equally objected, who had wondered if
the Tracts were Whately's work, 'was no friend of yours, and is dead; so
he lives'.[41] It was also now that Newman resumed his broken intimacy with
the once devoted Richard Church. 'Excuse my penmanship', he wrote to
Church, 'my fingers have been *walking* nearly 20 miles a day.'[42] 'Longman
would not let me delay – but I can't be sorry', he told Rogers, 'for I really
do not think I could possibly have got myself to write a line except under
strict compulsion. I have now been for five weeks at it, from morning to
night, and I shall have three weeks more.'[43] Hope-Scott also sent a line of
encouragement. 'I never have been in such a stress of brain, and such pain
of heart', replied Newman, ' . . . constantly in tears, and constantly crying
out with distress – I am sure I never could say what I am saying in cool
blood –.'[44] 'I am sorry to say I am getting knocked up', he wrote to his
printer Rivington late in May, 'and am unable to tell whether I shall not
have to stop.'[45] He had sometimes to discard much of what he had written,
and still satisfy the printers. At times the writing was like 'ploughing in
very stiff clay'.[46] The priests of the Birmingham diocese presented him on
1 June with an address of congratulation on the work at their Synod; his
reply moved them to tears. On the same day, he wrote a letter of condolence
to William Froude on the death of his daughter, the only child to remain a
Protestant. On 12 June, he noted, 'sent back my LAST proof to the
Printer'.[47] The masterpiece – as it was generally declared to be – was
complete.

The *Apologia* spoke to very different parts of human nature. The two
opening tracts, 'Mr. Kingsley's Method of Disputation' and 'True Mode of
Meeting Mr. Kingsley', were polemical, but they swept the author into the
confidence of his readers by opening his heart. They would not, he hoped, be

ungenerous or harsh with a man . . . whose natural impulse it has ever been to speak out; who has ever spoken too much rather than too little; who would have saved himself many a scrape, if he had been wise enough to hold his tongue; . . . who has never shrunk from confessing a fault when he felt that he had committed one; who has ever consulted for others more than for himself; who has given up much that he loved and prized and could have retained, but that he loved honesty better than name, and Truth better than dear friends.

And now I am in a train of thought higher and more serene than any which slanders can disturb. Away with you, Mr. Kingsley, and fly into space . . . '[48]

The reader, caught by the wit of Newman's response to the charges against him, was then to be moved to sympathy by his apology for his life. 'I must, I said, give the true key to my whole life; I must show what I am . . . that the phantom may be extinguished which gibbers instead of me. I wish to be known as a living man, and not as a scarecrow which is dressed up in my clothes . . . I will vanquish, not my Accuser, but my judges.'[49]

Given the circumstances of its composition, the central portion of the *Apologia*, issued as parts III–VI and known as the *History of My Religious Opinions*, is hardly critical autobiography. Rather, it is the spiritual romance of a soul in its love and hates, and though the facts as Newman reported them were coloured and occasionally distorted by his imagination, the work convinced not so much by its truthfulness as by its obvious allegiance to the spirit of truth, a burning sincerity.

Newman carried his narrative to 1845 when he had become a Catholic; from that time, he wrote, 'I have no further history of my religious opinions to narrate . . . it was like coming into port after a rough sea . . . '[50] He offered in part VII a general justification of the reasonableness of his religious position, which bristles with aphorisms: 'Ten thousand difficulties do not make one doubt'.[51] On Transubstantiation, he restated his metaphysical agnosticism. 'What do I know of substance or matter? just as much as the greatest philosophers, and that is nothing at all.'[52] What but the Catholic Church could 'withstand and baffle the fierce energy of passion and the all-corroding, all-dissolving scepticism of the intellect in religious inquiries?'[53] This scepticism about the unaided powers of the mind to reach right religious conclusions gave no pleasure to the Aristotelian neo-scholastics in Newman's own communion. Nor did they like Newman's kindred assertion that the tendency of reason by itself 'is towards a simple unbelief in matters of religion'.[54] He was uncompromising in his rejection of Protestant *sola scriptura*. No book, not even Bible, could 'make a stand against the wild living intellect of man'.[55] The Church rescues human nature from its misery, 'not simply by restoring it on its own level, but by lifting it up to a higher level than its own',[56] while 'the initial error of what afterwards became heresy was the urging forward some truth against the prohibition of authority at an unseasonable time'.[57] 'I trust that all European races will ever have a place in the Church, and . . . the loss of the English, not to say the German element, in its composition has been a most serious misfortune.'[58] This defence of English reserve in devotion against Italianate extravagance declared what was suitable for one culture and not another. And in two great passages of prose poetry, Newman expressed the Augustinian sense of the distance between a fallen creation and its Creator.

Starting then with the being of a God, (which, as I have said, is as certain to me as the certainty of my own existence, though when I try to put the grounds of that certainty into logical shape I find a difficulty in doing so in mood and figure to my satisfaction,) I look out of myself into the world of men, and there I see a sight which fills me with unspeakable distress. The world seems simply to give the lie to that great truth, of which my whole being is so full; and the effect upon me is, in consequence, as a matter of necessity, as confusing as if it denied that I am in existence myself. If I looked into a mirror, and did not see my face, I should have the sort of feeling which actually comes upon me, when I look into this living busy world, and see no reflexion of its Creator. This is, to me, one of those great difficulties of this absolute primary truth, to which I referred just now. Were it not for this voice, speaking so clearly in my conscience and my heart, I should be an atheist, or a pantheist, or a polytheist when I looked into the world. I am speaking for myself only; and I am far from denying the real force of the arguments in proof of a God, drawn from the general facts of human society and the course of history, but these do not warm me or enlighten me; they do not take away the winter of my desolation, or make the buds unfold and the leaves grow within me, and my moral being rejoice. The sight of the world is nothing else than the prophet's scroll, full of 'lamentations, and mourning, and woe'.

To consider the world in its length and breadth, its various history, the many races of man, their starts, their fortunes, their mutual alienation, their conflicts; and then their ways, habits, governments, forms of worship; their enterprises, their aimless courses, their random achievements and acquirements, the impotent conclusion of long-standing facts, the tokens so faint and broken of superintending design, the blind evolution of what turn out to be great powers or truths, the progress of things, as if from unreasoning elements, not towards final causes, the greatness and little-ness of man, his far-reaching aims, his short duration, the curtain hung over his futurity, the disappointments of life, the defeat of good, the success of evil, physical pain, mental anguish, the prevalence and intensity of sin, the pervading idolatries, the corruptions, the dreary hopeless irre-ligion, that condition of the whole race, so fearfully yet exactly described in the Apostle's words, 'having no hope and without God in the world',

– all this is a vision to dizzy and appal; and inflicts upon the mind the sense of a profound mystery, which is absolutely beyond human solution.[59]

More characteristically Victorian, but still haunting, is the subsequent comparison of the human condition with the mystery of 'a boy of good make and mind', without history or ancestry, of whom one could only conclude that his parents had reason to be ashamed. The concluding section of part VII, on the Christian and Oratorian ideal of brotherhood, is a piece of rhetoric almost as great.

I have closed this history of myself with St. Philip's name upon St. Philip's feast-day; and, having done so, to whom can I more suitably offer it, as a memorial of affection and gratitude, than to St. Philip's sons, my dearest brothers of this House, the Priests of the Birmingham Oratory, AMBROSE ST. JOHN, HENRY AUSTIN MILLS, HENRY BITTLE-STON, EDWARD CASWALL, WILLIAM PAINE NEVILLE, and HENRY IGNATIUS DUDLEY RYDER? who have been so faithful to me; who have been so sensitive of my needs; who have been so indulgent to my failings; who have carried me through so many trials; who have grudged no sacrifice, if I asked for it; who have been so cheerful under discouragements of my causing; who have done so many good works, and let me have the credit of them; – with whom I have lived so long, with whom I hope to die.

And to you especially, dear AMBROSE ST. JOHN; whom God gave me, when He took every one else away; who are the link between my old life and my new; who have now for twenty-one years been so devoted to me, so patient, so zealous, so tender; who have let me lean so hard upon you; who have watched me so narrowly; who have never thought of yourself, if I was in question.

And in you I gather up and bear in memory those familiar affectionate companions and counsellors, who in Oxford were given to me, one after another, to be my daily solace and relief; and all those others, of great name and high example, who were my thorough friends, and showed me true attachment in times long past; and also those many younger men, whether I knew them or not, who have never been disloyal to me by word or deed; and of all these, thus various in their relations to me, those more especially who have since joined the Catholic Church.

And I earnestly pray for this whole company, with a hope against hope, that all of us, who once were so united, and so happy in our union, may even now be brought at length, by the Power of the Divine Will, into One Fold and under One Shepherd.[60]

It was not Newman's intention to make himself the hero of the Oxford Movement, but the vividness of his own recollections of it gave his judgement an authority which a century of scholarship has hardly shaken and which has cast its other participants into the shade. The Movement attracted fine scholars and theologians like Pusey and Richard Church, but Newman was its only original genius. It is, no doubt, unfair that through the quality of his mind and the magic of his words, his viewpoint should prevail over every other, and that the *Apologia* should shape the later influential history of the Oxford Movement written by Richard Church under its shadow. Newman had made himself both the Virgil and Aeneas of the drama, its epic poet and its hero.

Part VII of the *Apologia* also replied to Kingsley's accusations against Alphonsus Liguori, in part by showing that Protestant casuists had argued that there were circumstances under which a man could rightly lie. An appendix, an Answer in Detail to Mr. Kingsley's Accusations', echoed the Thirty-nine Articles in its list of thirty-nine 'blots' or factual errors. The second edition of the following year, published under the title of *History of My Religious Opinions*, omitted the controversial matter in parts I and II and all the personal references in the 'Answer in Detail' to Kingsley, who became a 'popular writer' and 'my Accuser'. This detached the main body of the book from the controversy which had produced it, and made the appeal to the reader wholly one of sympathy, as if in recognition that the brilliant sarcasm of the assault on Kingsley was more likely to amuse than win support: 'Your history', as it was said to Newman, 'is more to your purpose than all your arguments'.[61]

There is much that could be said on Kingsley's behalf. Newman had implied, as Kingsley said, that monks and nuns were the only Bible Christians. Newman should not have called his sermon on 'Wisdom and Innocence' 'Protestant': it was properly Anglo-Catholic. Kingsley was right, and Newman was wrong, about the marvels in Walburga's life, which unlike those in Neot's had been presented as sober history. Newman misread Sturme's horror of the dirty Germans as a miracle. His dissent from Liguori's moral opinions about the lawfulness of lying did not represent the mind of his own Church; the theologians he cited on the other side did not have Liguori's authority. Nor were the Anglican authorities he quoted as permitting lying in agreement with Liguori on the lawfulness of equivocation by using words in a double sense. Newman's own utterances were sometimes equivocal, and his was an equivocal position in defending the intellectual honesty of his Church, when he doubted it himself.[62]

Yet Newman's assumptions deserved a criticism more refined than Kingsley's, and he was lucky in the feverish state of mental health of his opponent; Mrs Kingsley inhibited her husband from reading the work until it was all published, and while he planned 'such a revanche' on Newman as would make him wince, he told Macmillan that Newman's position was too intrinsically absurd for reply. 'Deliberately, after 20 years of thought, I struck as hard as I could. Deliberately I shall strike again, if it so pleases me, though not one literary man in England approved . . . If I am to bandy words, it must be with sane persons.' Kingsley did not want 'to put myself a second time, by any fresh act of courtesy, into the power of one who, like a treacherous ape, lifts to you meek and suppliant eyes, till he thinks he has you within his reach, and then springs, gibbering and biting, at your face'.[63]

This crude rhetoric was a private confirmation of George Eliot's judgement on Kingsley's pamphlet as 'thoroughly vicious', a 'mixture of arrogance, coarse impertinence and unscrupulousness with real intellectual incompetence'.[64] Kingsley also ignored Newman's strength, that the heart of the author spoke directly to the reader's heart. Thus to Eliot, the *Apologia* was 'the revelation of a life – how different in form from one's own, yet with how close a fellowship in its needs and burthens'.[65] The hostile critics were those least susceptible to Newman's appeal to human sympathy, the Catholic and the anti-Christian rationalists at opposite ends of the religious spectrum. The atheist James Fitzjames Stephen, of the once-Evangelical family, thought that Newman was honest but that he used sceptical arguments to establish 'superstition by sophistry';[66] while apart from Ward, who remained Newman's philosophical disciple, the radical Ultramontanes like Manning disliked Newman's disparagement of the power of unaided reason to establish religious truth. The *Apologia* was in itself an argument for a personal logic of believing rather than an abstract paper one, but thereby disgusted another young Ultramontane, Herbert Vaughan, by its 'egotism'. Manning called the work 'a voice from the dead'.[67] Ward was not mentioned in the work, but also disliked its anti-Ultramontanism, and forced the resignation of his assistants on the *Dublin Review*, Henry Coleridge and Edward Healy Thompson, rather than allow it to be praised. Years later, Ward dreamed that he was talking at dinner to a veiled lady whose conversation was more fascinating than any one's since John Henry Newman's. 'I am John Henry Newman', said the lady, throwing back her veil. The *Apologia* spoke to Ward in siren voices. It was an unwelcome reminder of a power in the Church not his own, now emerging from the grave into life.

Oxford Again

'I hear murmurs about my book, which may give me trouble', wrote Newman to the Irish poet Aubrey de Vere. ' . . . I think it very hard that I may not write under the antecedent concession that I am a fallible mortal, but that every turn of expression is to be turned into a dogmatic enunciation.'[1] Yet Newman did not show tact after Monsignor George Talbot turned up at the Oratory in his absence to invite him to preach a course of Lenten sermons in his church in Rome: where, Talbot added in a letter written the day after, Newman 'would have a more educated Audience of Protestants than could ever be the case in England'.[2] Newman cited this offensive sentence in his reply. 'However, Birmingham people have souls', he added, 'and I have neither taste nor talent for the sort of work, which you cut out for me: and I beg to decline your offer.'[3]

The whole affair must have looked to Talbot like a calculated insult. The Fathers stayed in their rooms during his visit, apart from the gentle Austin Mills, who chatted to him evasively in the boys' refectory. When Talbot asked whether Newman read, Mills, 'determined not to give anything away, made the perfectly safe reply that he did not know, he saw Newman take out books from the library'.[4] Talbot's sudden friendliness after Newman's years of obscurity reminded Newman of the two actors catapulted to sudden fame who had declined the Countess of Buckingham's invitation because one was playing the clown at Sadler's Wells and the other the yellow dwarf in the pantomime. 'What is Brummagen [sic] to Mgr Talbot but a region of snobs', Newman added to St John. 'Yet souls are souls, your Rt reverence.'[5] Talbot had the ear of both Manning and the Pope: his invitation was foolishly and egotistically expressed, but it could have been refused with less savagery.

This lack of diplomacy did not stand Newman well when he re-entered ecclesiastical politics. In August 1864, he was offered for £8000 the five-acre site of the Oxford workhouse behind St Giles'. Later in the month, Ullathorne offered the Oxford mission to the Oratory, and Newman set about raising the money for the land from his own resources and wealthy friends. There was a party of English Catholics who wanted their sons to go to Oxford and regarded a Catholic hall under Newman's superintendence as a guarantee that the University would not injure their Catholic faith or morals. The plan was compromised by some of its supporters, like the ruthlessly intellectual Edmund Ffoulkes, an Anglican convert and a leader of the Association for the Promotion of the Unity of Christendom, an ecumenical prayer society of Anglicans and Catholics condemned by Rome in 1864. Ffoulkes was later to return to the Church of England and become Vicar of St Mary's, Oxford. Newman was kind to the Association's organizers like Ambrose Phillipps and F. G. Lee, and was sympathetic to the idea of a Catholic hall at Oxford, though he soon changed his mind about this, and though he did not intend to reside in Oxford himself.

He was, moreover, aware of enormous practical difficulties. An Oratory would only have a role at Oxford if there were Catholic undergraduates. Otherwise, wrote Newman, we 'should bother ourselves for 100 Catholics – and these in alliance with men like Sadler the pastry cook. We should be in the false position of being supported by radical dissenters who were envious of the University, and should be expected by Catholics to earn their applause by kidnapping Undergraduates'.[6] Even now, Newman was tender to the Anglican Tory tradition of old Oxford. Yet in July 1863 and January 1864, Cardinal Barnabò, primed by Manning, had written to Ullathorne opposing Catholics and Catholic halls at the Protestant universities. The subsequent resolutions to discourage Catholics at Oxford passed by the English hierarchy in Low Week 1864 were not enforced, and in September Newman accepted the Oxford mission merely in the hopes of building a church as a memorial to the Tractarian converts and of founding an Oratory in the future. Such an Oratory was, however, still dependent, if not on a Catholic hall, on Catholics attending the University, and that the Church was obviously reluctant to allow.

Newman's negotiations for a portion of the Oxford land were brought to a crisis in October by the sudden death of the vendor, and he had to buy the whole site from the heirs. The money, £8400, had to be raised by Christmas. 'Am I, after all', wrote Newman to Hope-Scott, 'to end my days in prison?'[7] He disturbed the dinner hour of Wiseman, who was dying by inches. 'He listened to the Oxford plan, half querulously', wrote Newman, ' – and said that he thought the collection for [Talbot's church of] St Thomas at Rome would interfere with getting money from the Continent.'[8]

It was said that the Cardinal had afterwards written to Rome about Newman's 'insolence'. Newman's strongest opponent, however, was Manning, who told Propaganda that Wiseman was 'entirely opposed to any contact between the faithful in England and the heretical intellectual culture of the country'. Manning was careful in his official communications in expressing criticism of individuals: but he also reported that 'it is being said on all sides' that the purpose of Newman's Oxford mission 'is to set up a college later on'.[9] This was not true of Newman, but it was true of his supporters, who wanted the advantage of an Oxford education for their sons. Moreover the idea of Newman's return had a still wider appeal: the

Dean of Christ Church would have welcomed it, and Newman's Anglican godson at Christ Church assured him that the town would escort him back in procession.

Thus the Oxford church would be inescapably a university church, and in his circular of October–November 1864 appealing for money to build it, Newman had to refer to its role of pastoral care of Catholic students in the University. Ullathorne naturally interpreted this 'as favourable to the education of Catholics at Oxford',[10] and Newman agreed not to issue the circular until after an episcopal meeting which would consider the University question in December. 'The same dreadful jealousy of the laity, which has ruined things in Dublin', he wrote to Thomas Allies, 'is now at the bottom of this unwillingness to let our youths go to Oxford . . . Propaganda and our leading Bishops fear the natural influence of the laity: which would be their greatest, or (humanly speaking) is rather their only, defence against the world.'[11] A few days before the bishops' meeting, Newman heard from his convert friends Lord Charles Thynne and Thomas Gaisford of a list of questions drawn up by Wiseman and distributed to many of the university converts but not to Newman, asking about the desirability of Catholics attending Oxford. Newman thought the questions 'deplorable – deplorable because they are not questions, but arguments – worse than "leading questions" – They might as well have been summed up in one, viz. "Are you or are you not one of those wicked men who advocate Oxford Education?" '[12] The bishops' meeting agreed that there should be no Catholic hall at Oxford, and that Catholics should be warned against going there; but the irritable Wiseman, whose diabetes was a torment, could not persuade them to an outright prohibition. The matter now went to Propaganda, reviving Newman's old fears of Barnabò: 'How could I tell', Newman wrote, 'that, when I had half built the Church, there would not be a fresh interference?'[13] 'We are certainly under a tyranny', he told William Monsell; 'one or two persons, such as Manning seem to do everything.'[14]

It was not quite fair to put down everything, as Newman did to Acton on the closure of the *Home and Foreign Review*, to 'the dull tyranny of Manning and Ward'.[15] The bishops were already opposed to a Catholic hall at Oxford as a danger to Catholic youth. Moreover, as Newman recognized, they had before them an impressive body of testimony in response to the questionnaire from Oxford converts like Newman's former disciple Robert Coffin and his former curate David Lewis, expressing strong opposition to Catholics at Oxford.[16] Newman was not simply opposed to 'a small active clique',[17] but to the defensive Catholic mentality of his day. Confronted with this testimony, Propaganda, which was happiest when agreeing to local opinion, acted on 16 January 1865 to confirm the bishops' judgement, and ignored a long memorial from supporters of the scheme drawn up by Edward Bellasis and Thomas Wetherell. In the same month Newman heard from Pusey that the University would buy his whole Oxford site for £9000, which would cover his purchase price and costs. After a protest from his original vendor, Newman gave him his £100 of profit. 'The land being sold', he wrote to Ullathorne on 10 February 1865, 'I believe your Lordship considers the arrangement for the Oratory to take the Oxford Mission as at an end. I certainly so consider [it] myself.'[18]

Five days later Wiseman died, and astonishingly the whole of London seemed to turn out to mourn him. 'Alas!' wrote Newman to Ffoulkes, 'that his last act has been to extinguish a hope of a great future . . . '[19] Newman was similarly critical of the savagely anti-liberal papal encyclical *Quanta Cura* and the accompanying Syllabus of Errors, condemning eighty errors of the age, including 'progress, liberalism and modern civilization'. Yet for Newman this was less sweeping a condemnation than its partisans and perhaps the Pope himself wanted it to be. Newman insisted that the meaning of the condemnations lay in the context of the papal documents from which they were originally taken: 'though drawn up with far more care and skill than the Act of Parliament through which O'Connell was to drive his coach and four', he wrote, 'yet it cannot . . . say all that an Ultra party would wish it to say'.[20] This was a 'minimalist' interpretation of the Syllabus, like Bishop Dupanloup's in France, and it anticipated the restricted view that Newman was to take of the definition of papal infallibility in 1870.

Such minimism, however, confirmed Newman's estrangement from contemporary Roman opinion. The bishops meeting under Ullathorne on 23 March 1865 declared their public opposition to a Catholic college at Oxford or Cambridge, and Newman subsequently saw the circular from Propaganda which convinced him 'that the extinguisher on Oxford was the Pope's *own* act . . . If so, we may at once reconcile ourselves to it. Another Pontiff, in another generation, may reverse it'.[21] This is difficult, however, to reconcile with Newman's underlying view that Manning manipulated Wiseman who manipulated the English bishops and Rome. It would be truer to say that there was a general ecclesiastical policy opposed to mixed education on principle for both rich and poor. This was clouded by personalities, but was a matter on which the greater part of the Church was agreed. Newman was its victim, but in taking the matter so personally, he was doubly so.

The policy in its extreme form seemed to triumph with the astonishing election of Manning as Archbishop of Westminster, the Pope's own choice over the favourite, Ullathorne. It was in its way, as Newman recognized, a stunning compliment to the converts: from Archdeacon to Archbishop in fourteen years. Manning 'has a great power of winning men, when he chooses',[22] Newman told Miss Bowles. But to Allies he wrote that 'if you write to inspire me with confidence in the Archbishop, laterem lavas' – 'you are washing a brick',[23] a Latin metaphor from *Phormio* for vain labour. Newman added to Monsell that Manning 'is so mysterious, that I don't know how one can ever have confidence in him'.[24] Manning's early policy in his archiepiscopate was, however, to be straightforward enough, that of making the English Catholic Church more Roman than Rome.

Manning invited Newman to his consecration as 'among the first'[25] of his old friends, but Newman's reaction was suspicious. He had heard that Manning wanted him made 'a Bishop in partibus' a year or two before – to muzzle him by making him a lord: he told Manning that he would only attend the consecration as a friend, and if this proposal were to be abandoned.[26] With seeming reluctance, Manning accepted Newman's wishes in the matter, and when Newman knelt to receive his blessing in the sacristy after the ceremony, raised him up to embrace him. Newman may have partly shared the 'secret satisfaction' which he described among Oxford Anglicans 'that one, taken from the gremium Universitatis, should be the winning horse at Rome'.[27]

The delight of the visit to London for the consecration was the two days spent with two Oxford Anglicans, Rogers and Church; they afterwards bought Newman a violin, which he had taken up 'after 16 years of utter and absolute separation from it'; 'like Orpheus, I shall make the Rednal wilderness resound with some solitary strains'.[28] There was an even more affecting reunion with Keble and Pusey at Hursley Vicarage on 12 September 1865. Newman and Keble did not recognize each other, while Newman was shocked by Pusey's enlarged head and facial features and paunch. Newman's own sensations were painful. 'There were three old men, who had worked together vigorously in their prime. This is what they have come to – poor human nature – after 20 years they meet together round a table, but without a common cause, or free outspoken thoughts – . . . and all of them with broken prospects.' But Pusey was 'full of polemics and of hope', and Keble 'as delightful as ever – and, it *seemed* to me as if he felt a sympathy and intimacy with me which he did not find with Pusey'.[29] To Church, Newman spoke of Keble's 'sweet pleading earnestness'.[30] Keble died in the following year.

Pusey's latest polemic was his *Eirenicon*, so called for its enthusiasm for reunion with Rome, but the enthusiasm was tempered by its onslaught on Roman Catholicism for teaching the Ultramontane extravagances of Manning and Ward and the Marian excesses of Faber: 'as an Irenicum, it can only raise a smile', wrote Newman to Keble, ' – and I wish that were all it would raise'.[31] Newman's own published reply to Pusey appeared in January 1866, and trod a careful path between what Newman rejected as hyper-Catholic and what he held to be proper Roman doctrine. Newman rejoiced at Pusey's proposals for reconciliation: he said that no one else influenced 'so large a circle of men, so virtuous, so able, so learned, so zealous'.[32] But, he wrote to Pusey, 'you discharge your olive-branch as if from a catapult',[33] by attacking Rome and its corruptions together. Newman derived the proper basis of Marian devotion from a catena of passages extolling Mary as the Second Eve and as the Mother of God, in the writings of the Fathers in whom Pusey claimed to believe: 'did not', Newman wrote, 'the all-Wise know the human heart when He took to Himself a Mother?'[34] Newman adroitly refused to make any defence of Manning, 'because of his office',[35] but he would not allow that the other two Papists whom Pusey had assailed, Ward and Faber, were in any sense 'spokesmen for English Catholics'.[36] Indeed, wrote Newman, some of Pusey's foreign examples of super-Marian pietism 'affected me with grief and almost anger'.[37] 'They seem to me like a bad dream . . . There is nothing of them in the Missal, in the Roman Catechism, in the Roman *Raccolta*, in the Imitation of Christ, in Gother, Challoner, Milner or Wiseman . . . '[38] Newman thereby invoked the sober restraint of the English Catholic tradition, recalling that when he had become a Roman Catholic, Thomas Griffiths as Vicar Apostolic of the London District 'warned me against books of devotion of the Italian school . . . I took him to caution me against a character and tone of religion, excellent in its place, not suited for England';[39] indeed, Newman added on his own account, at its worst, 'calculated to prejudice inquirers, to frighten the unlearned, to unsettle consciences, to provoke blasphemy, and to work the loss of souls'.[40]

The *Letter* brought some golden compliments from influential clergy; from Ullathorne, who replied at length to an article on Newman by the *Tablet*'s hostile Roman correspondent, E. R. Martin; from the aristocratic Bishop Clifford who was to preach at Newman's funeral; even from Bishop Thomas Brown of Newport, who had delated him to Rome. This support proved to be utterly necessary. Newman trod carefully. He did not risk attack from Ward by following through his intention of replying to Pusey's strictures on the neo-Ultramontane idolatry of Rome, and kept private his preference for trusting more 'in the future contrition of the Romans, than in the present patronage of Gallic or Austrian or Spanish bayonets'.[41] He contemplated, but did not pursue, a public denial of Ward's claim that the Syllabus was infallible, fearing 'some blow on the Oratory',[42] but equally fearing that without a public contradiction of such an extravagant opinion more converts would, like Thomas Arnold, lapse from Catholicism. On papal infallibility itself, he paced the same middle way: 'I have ever thought it likely to be true', he told Ward, 'never thought it certain. I think too, its definition inexpedient and unlikely'.[43] Ward decided to attack Newman's slur on foreign Catholic devotion in an article in the *Dublin Review*, but Ullathorne and Clifford both refused to act as censor for Ward's essay, on the ground that they agreed with Newman themselves. Ward's warmest supporters were his sons and daughters, one of them Newman's future biographer Wilfrid, and they recorded their indignation in their children's newspaper: 'Why the opinion of a private priest like Dr Newman concerning who are and who are not exponents of Catholicism should go for more than the Archbishop's known convictions, is hard to say . . . '[44]

Manning's view of Newman's *Letter* was not public, but Talbot set out to stiffen it: 'every Englishman is naturally anti-Roman', wrote the Papal Chamberlain to the Archbishop. 'To be Roman is to an Englishman an effort. Dr Newman is more English than the English. His spirit must be crushed.'[45] Manning replied that Newman

> has become the centre of those who hold low views about the Holy See, are anti-Roman, cold and silent, to say no more, about the Temporal Power, national, English, critical of Catholic devotions, and always on the lower side. I see no danger of a Cisalpine Club rising again, but I see much danger of an English Catholicism of which Newman is the highest type. It is the old Anglican, patristic, literary, Oxford tone transplanted into the Church. It takes the line of deprecating exaggerations, foreign devotions, Ultramontanism, anti-national sympathies. In one word, it is worldly Catholicism, and it will have the worldly on its side, and will deceive many.[46]

The outcome of this polarization was that Newman became a hero to the very Old Catholics who had distrusted him; indeed a hero to all of those, from Sir George Bowyer to the Jesuits, whom the strong-handed Manning had in some way offended. One of Newman's strongest supporters now was the very Bishop Brown who had delated him. Brown was softened to tears with his audience, the Benedictine nuns of Colwich, on reading to them Newman's longest poem, *The Dream of Gerontius*, which appeared in Miss Fanny Taylor's new periodical *The Month* in May and June 1865, and was separately published with a dedication to Fr John Joseph Gordon, the first of Newman's Oratorians close to him to have died. The words are now inseparable from the music of Elgar, and two of the rhyming passages, 'Firmly I believe and truly' and 'Praise to the Holiest in the height', are among the best-known hymns in English. The frank Christian eschatology of the poem in its form as an oratorio must sound even more odd than most sacred music to secular sensibilities: one modern conductor, Simon Rattle, has called Newman's ideas 'repulsive'. Yet despite the chorus of demons,

> Chuck'd down,
> By the sheer might,
> Of a despot's will,[47]

as they complain, the poem considerably mitigates even the terrors of purgatory, depicted as water, after the purifying fire.

> Softly and gently, dearly-ransom'd soul,
> In my most loving arms I now enfold thee,
> And, o'er the penal waters, as they roll,
> I poise thee, and I lower thee, and hold thee.[48]

This is mild even by comparison with Faber's 'Holy souls' in Purgatory, who in his hymn still burnt this hour amid the cleansing flames. Elgar's music might be called strangulated Wagner in an English chapel; the poem leaves the soul in purgatory, as the music never reaches God. Yet at times, as in the great 'Proficiscere, anima Christiana', with its tremendous supporting choir of the whole host of heaven, the melody seizes on the inner triumph of the words, from the office for the dead:

> Go, in the name
> Of Angels and Archangels; in the name
> Of Thrones and Dominations; in the name
> Of Princedoms and of Powers; and in the name
> Of Cherubim and Seraphim, go forth![49]

Even Kingsley privately expressed his 'awe and admiration', though disliking the soul's popish 'entourage' of saints and angels.[50] In the conclusion it is as if the composer had fused the inner music of Newman's own soul and of the spheres together, and had heard those spirits 'singing aye in air' whose robes are the air and whose faces look on God.

These satisfactions were not wholly ethereal. 'I always sleep better after music', wrote Newman to Church. 'There must be some electric current passing from the strings through the fingers into the brain and down the spinal marrow. Perhaps thought is music.'[51] He sometimes set his own words to music, though he denied his compositions the dignity of the name. In April 1865, he reported excellent health, due also 'to great care, a shower bath, cold [cod] liver oil, and a respirator'.[52] At the end of the year, he fell seriously ill, for the first time since 1833, and could only rejoice that this had not happened during the heat of composing his exchanges with Kingsley and Pusey. One small token of his recovery of his reputation was Jemima's invitation to him in October 1865 to stay at Derby 'after 18 years excommunicating me': 'you have let all your family grow up and I not know them', he complained to her, with a further complaint that the message had not come from her husband: 'for who ever heard of an invitation except from the master of the House?'[53]

The ultimate rehabilitation would have been a return to Oxford, in spite of Newman's reiterated determination not to go there: even seeing the place would, he wrote, 'be a cruel thing – it is like the dead coming to the dead. O dear, dear, how I dread it . . . '[54] Ullathorne again offered him the Oxford mission in August 1865, when Newman had again 'bought some land, but for the chances of the future, not as connected with myself'.[55] 'I had no wish', he wrote in a draft letter to Robert Whitty not sent, 'to disturb my quiet by bootless labours, by controversy with great men, by correspondence with Propaganda, by journeys to Rome, by anxieties, suspenses, disappointments, and scandals.'[56] Ullathorne disliked Newman's new site, opposite

Christ Church, as too blatantly near the University, but he once again offered Newman the mission in March 1866. Newman once again propounded his difficulties. He did not mind 'that Catholics should be discouraged going to Oxford without being forbidden';[57] but he wanted Barnabò to assure him that he would not again cause him trouble and expense by choking off the project in mid-career, perhaps with a church half-built. Nor did he want to face in Birmingham the active preaching against any connection with the University enjoined by Manning on the clergy through the Synod of Westminster. Newman accepted the mission on 8 June. On 11 June, Ullathorne petitioned Propaganda for approval of an Oxford Oratory to be placed under Birmingham, and Manning warned Talbot of the new challenge: 'I think Propaganda can hardly know the effects of Dr Newman's going to Oxford', wrote the Archbishop. 'The English national spirit is spreading among Catholics, and we shall have dangers'.[58]

Manning was right about the fact: in June 1866, Newman went to London to sit for his bust by Thomas Woolner, to breakfast with Gladstone and to meet a bevy of rich English, Scottish and Irish Catholics with an interest in the University. 'So you see', he wrote to St John, 'in my old age I am learning to be a man of fashion.'[59] In July, however, Cardinal Karl August von Reisach, Prefect of the Congregation of Studies, visited England, and was escorted about by his friend the ex-Oratorian Robert Coffin, a strong opponent of Newman's Oxford project, who among other places of Catholic interest showed the Cardinal the site of Newman's proposed Oxford church. Reisach was not a very acute observer; he drew the conclusion from the English cricketer's obedience to the umpire 'that Englishmen must naturally be submissive to authority'.[60] There is some doubt as to whether the purpose of his visit was, as has been generally assumed, to look into the Oxford matter at first hand – Reisach did not even discuss the matter with Ullathorne – and whether Newman was deliberately left out of the Cardinal's itinerary.[61] It seems that Manning suggested a meeting, and that Ullathorne replied that Newman was away from home. But Reisach came as near to Edgbaston as Oscott, and when Newman heard afterwards of the visit from Emily Bowles, he naturally thought that he had been snubbed. Certainly the Cardinal spent his time in England exclusively with those opposed to the Oxford scheme, like W. G. Ward, of whom Newman wrote that 'it is a one sided way of getting at the true state of things to be content with the information of a violent partizan'.[62]

Meanwhile Barnabò replied to Ullathorne's petition by asking why and whether the fears that an Oratory would attract Catholics to Oxford had disappeared. The Bishop in his reply admitted that while Newman's name would attract funds for the church, it 'will also exercise an indirect attraction for those parents who are disposed to send their sons to the University. But Fr Newman does not intend to change his residence from Birmingham, but to place at Oxford some of the Fathers of the Oratory, and to make visits there from time to time'.[63] Ullathorne, however, also indicated to Barnabò that he had counteracted the intention expressed by Newman in his circular, on the Oxford Oratory in 1864, to take part in the mixed education of Catholic youths in Oxford. The Bishop sent a copy of his letter to Barnabò to Newman who was holidaying in Switzerland in August with Ambrose St John. Newman at once replied that he had never approved of mixed education in Oxford, but that Barnabò should be given to understand more clearly that he had 'no calling whatever to go to Oxford, except it be in order to take care of Catholic undergraduates or to convert graduates'.[64] This exposed the weakness in his own position; though he was also insisting that Oxford Catholics needed pastoral care if their parents intended to send them there anyway. Newman now believed that Ullathorne wanted him to use his name to build the church at Oxford, and nothing more. The Bishop advised Newman in September that it would be best not to seem anxious by writing at once to Barnabò to correct his letter. Newman drew up a scathing memorandum, to which he later added that Ullathorne had smiled as if to say, 'So you felt I had kicked your shins in my letter to his Eminence, – well you may have borne it pretty well'. 'I think', Newman concluded, 'Bishops fancy that, as justice does not exist between the Creator and His creatures, between man and the brute creation, so there is none between themselves and their subjects . . . The Bishop's manner was, as if he was *testing* my spirit.'[65]

In October, Newman received into the Church one of the most remarkable of the Oxford converts of the century, the poet Gerard Manley Hopkins. An Oxford presence would be a sort of apostolate to such intellectuals. Ultramontane attitudes to the intellect, however, were a refusal of the opportunities of the age. Again, Newman's frankest expression of opinion was to Emily Bowles:

At present things are in appearence as effete, though in a different way, (thank God) as they were in the tenth century. We are sinking into a sort of Novationism [sic], the heresy which the early Popes so strenuously resisted. Instead of aiming at being a world-wide power, we are shrinking into ourselves, narrowing the lines of communion, trembling at freedom of thought, and using the language of dismay and despair at the prospect before us, instead of, with the high spirit of the warrior, going out conquering and to conquer.[66]

Yet all seemed clear when on Christmas Day 1866 Ullathorne sent Newman a copy of a further letter from Barnabò apparently granting permission for an Oxford Oratory, to be subject to Birmingham during Newman's lifetime, on the proviso that this did not attract Catholics to Oxford. The decision was a clever Roman compromise, between Ullathorne's desire for an Oxford Oratory and Manning's opposition to Catholics at Oxford.

Ullathorne felt bound, however, to spare Newman's feelings by withholding a sentence in Barnabò's letter which declared that should Newman seek to reside at Oxford he should be 'blande suaviterique'[67] – blandly and suavely – dissuaded from doing so, a reasonable decision on the principle that Newman's presence in Oxford would make a nonsense of Rome's opposition to Catholics going there. But Ullathorne made matters worse by withholding out of mistaken kindness the instruction from Newman, intending to seek to secure its remission when he went to Rome himself in 1867.

Unfortunately the secret prohibition was an opportunity too good to be missed to discredit Newman's orthodoxy. The first issue of the *Westminster Gazette*, a newspaper started at Manning's behest by the journalist Edmund Sheridan Purcell, declared that 'The *on dit* at Oxford is, that Dr Newman has abandoned his plan of going to Oxford, in deference to the opinion of a most eminent prelate in Rome'.[68] 'And what is the dodge', wrote Newman, 'of this new paper saying so, and fathering it as a coward on *Oxford?*'[69] Ullathorne, however, promised amendment for the letter by writing to Barnabò, convincing Newman that he 'really *is* hand and glove [sic] with us'.[70] As for Manning, wrote Newman, he 'wanted to gain me over; now, he will break me, if he can'.[71] On 24 January 1867, Newman sent out a circular appealing for funds for the Oxford Oratory as approved by Ullathorne and Rome, with a list of subscriptions already received of over £3500. He planned to take the mission over in April. The matter was complicated by Fr William Neville's commitment to buy another Oxford site as well, involving him in an enormous financial liability; the circular itself appealed for £8000 to £10,000.

Newman's intimation of fresh trouble came in a letter of 11 March from Barnabò, indicating that the Pope himself had been 'deeply saddened' by the 'recent unhappy perversion of a number of Catholic youths' at Oxford, and that Propaganda had heard that Newman himself was 'actively engaged in preparing' a number of entrants to the University. He was asked 'to abstain altogether from any activity or deed which may have the appearance of directly or indirectly favouring the entry of Catholic youths into the said University'.[72] Newman sharply replied that he had not heard of any direct prohibition; that he had two pupils preparing for Oxford, one a New Zealander committed to his charge by the lad's bishop; that he had never heard of any Catholic losing his faith at Oxford; and that he was doing no more for men going there than Oscott or Stonyhurst. 'For the rest', he concluded, 'I will not conceal my surprise, most Eminent Father, that after my twenty years of most faithful service, your Eminence reposes so little confidence in me in the matter: – but God will see to it (*sed viderit Deus*). With the deepest respect, and kissing the Sacred Purple . . . '[73] This icy leave-taking reinforced the insult. To Sir Justin Sheil, whose sons were at the Oratory School, Newman argued that if Oxford was dangerous, it was no more so 'than Woolwich, than the army, than London – . . . you cannot keep young men under glass cases'.[74] Meanwhile Ullathorne passed on to Newman information he had received from Frederick Neve, an old Oriel man and Rector of the English College, that Bishop Grant of Southwark, Manning and his henchman Dr Herbert Vaughan had all complained about the Oxford Oratory to Rome, and that Vaughan and the Irish Benedictine Bernard Smith had told Barnabò that Newman was preparing youths for Oxford.

Newman decided that Ambrose St John would have to go to Rome to clear his reputation and save the school. Ullathorne showed him a letter of support from his sometime delator Bishop Thomas Brown, who had zealously defended Newman in person to Talbot, but Talbot had 'stuck to his disproved conclusion', wrote Brown to Ullathorne, 'as a parrot does to its empty words'.[75] To another of his supporters, Bishop David Moriarty of Kerry, Newman denounced 'a knot of men, who wish me kept from the place at any price'.[76] This was not too harsh: E. R. Martin in the *Weekly Register* declared that Newman 'has no longer, in Roman opinion, the high place he once held . . . having allowed his great name to be linked with that of one of the bitterest haters of the Church of Rome', as the dedicatee of Henry Oxenham's translation of an anti-papal work by Döllinger. 'Good soldier of the faith as Dr Newman has been, and devoted Catholic as he still doubtless is', wrote Martin, 'a mission of so delicate a nature . . . could not safely be entrusted to one who had compromised himself . . . Only an Ultramontane without a taint in his fidelity could enter such an arena as that of Oxford life' to Rome's advantage. Martin hit at Newman's new Anglican public by denouncing by anticipation what the 'Anglican papers of the mosquito or flea tribe' would make of this, 'for Anglicans of the advanced school love slander as Mrs Gamp loves her bottle . . . ' Martin asserted that Newman had also, in the *Apologia*, said what heretics had said everywhere, 'that they appeal from Rome drunk to Rome sober'.[77]

When Ullathorne saw the *Register* he realized that the Roman opposition to Newman's return to Oxford was now public, and at once wrote to Newman about the reserved clause 'blandè suaviterque' in Barnabò's letter. Newman took the slighting of the project badly. As William Neville recalled,

Newman, sunshine on his face, talked of the prospect. 'Earlier failures do not matter now,' said he; 'I see that I have been reserved by God for this. There are signs of a religious reaction in Oxford against the liberalism and indifferentism of ten years ago . . . Such men as Mark Pattison may conceivably be won over. Although I am not young, I feel as full of life and thought as ever I did. It may prove to be the inauguration of a second Oxford Movement'.

Newman and Neville discussed who his student hearers in church would be, and where they would sit, so that he could address them naturally:

Thus happily they returned to the Oratory. The servant, who opened the door to admit them, at once gave Newman a long blue envelope, and said: 'Canon Estcourt has called from the Bishop's house and asked to be sure to give you this immediately on your return.' Newman opened and read the letter, and turned to Neville: 'All is over, I am not allowed to go.' No word more was spoken. The Father covered his face with his hands, and left his friend, who went to his room and unpacked his portmanteau.[78]

Newman replied to Ullathorne that he could not accept the mission on Rome's condition. 'If I am missioner at Oxford, I claim to be there, as much or as little as I please.'[79] There was the further difficulty of knowing for how much of the year his residence in Oxford was prohibited. He stopped St John and his companion Fr Henry Bittleston who had now reached Hope-Scott's villa at Hyères from proceeding further to Rome. 'How too can you trust people', he rhetorically asked St John, 'even though they are "blandi and suaves", when this secret instruction to the Bishop shows that such blandness and sweetness are hollow?'[80] Newman thought that he was feared 'as a vicious animal – they address me blandè suaviterique lest I should kick out, or jump at their throat . . . ' Ullathorne had no doubt 'got immense credit at Propaganda for years, for his wonderful skill in keeping a wild beast like me in order – his blanditiae et suavitates must have told much in his favour, when the Archiepiscopal see was vacant, and explains Propaganda's desire to have him to fill it'.[81] A few days later Newman decided that it would not do to make an enemy of Ullathorne. 'He is nearly our only friend', though 'badgered on all sides'.[82] 'No sort of blame attaches to our Bishop who is my good friend', he told Henry Wilberforce: ' – he hoped to have made these crooked ways straight, which he could not prevent existing, for they were not his ways . . . '[83]

Newman had also to admit that the Martin's Roman letter had proved a blessing in disguise. 'It let the cat out of the bag', he wrote to St John. 'It obliged the Bishop at once to relieve himself of his secret instruction',[84] and it forced Ullathorne to draw up an elaborate documentary account of the history of the Oxford mission exculpating Newman himself. But its startling effect was on his friends, won and kept by long years of publication, letter-writing, school-mastering and spiritual advice and counsel. The *Weekly Register* was in the hands of William Wilberforce junior, whose father was himself one of Newman's friends; the father wrote to apologize for the lapse in publishing Martin's letter as the result of a hiatus between editors, while the *Register* declared that 'our Roman Correspondent has scandalised Catholic England . . . '[85] Meanwhile William Monsell through the aristocratic Stafford Club got up an Address signed by the hundred most prestigious Catholic lay names in the country, beginning with the Duke of Norfolk's guardian Lord Edward Fitzalan Howard, the Deputy Earl Marshal, and followed by five earls and scores of MPs, judges and landed gentlemen. This roll-call of honour was appended to a triumphant vindication:

> We, the undersigned, have been deeply pained at some anonymous attacks which have been made upon you. . . we feel that every blow that touches you inflicts a wound upon the Catholic Church in this country. We hope, therefore, that you will not think it presumptuous in us to express our gratitude for all we owe you, and to assure you how heartily we appreciate the services which, under God, you have been the means of rendering to our Holy Religion.[86]

This was a little like reading one's own funeral panegyric: for all his trials, Newman was never wholly without honour in his own country.

To Manning, the Address showed 'the absence of Catholic instinct', and was *'directed and sustained by those who wish young Catholics to go to Oxford'*.[87] To Talbot, it was 'the most offensive production that has appeared in England since the times of Dr Milner', and was a new challenge by the laity to the power of the clergy of the Roman Church. 'What is the province of the laity?' asked Talbot. 'To hunt, to shoot, to entertain? These matters they understand, but to meddle with ecclesiastical matters they have no right at all, and this affair of Newman is a matter purely ecclesiastical.' Only Ward was 'an exception to all rule, because he is really a theologian . . . Dr Newman is the most dangerous man in England, and you will see that he will make use of the laity against your Grace'. Talbot warned Manning that if he did 'not fight the battle of the Holy See against the detestable spirit growing up in England, he [the Pope] will begin to regret Cardinal Wiseman, who knew how to keep the laity in order'. Talbot warned Manning of whisperings in Rome against him, and of Barnabò, 'how ready he is to throw the blame of everything on others'. Ullathorne was also guilty of not telling Newman of the prohibition on his going to Oxford, and the bishops were to be condemned for their fear of the laity.[88] Talbot's letter is one of the more famous productions of ecclesiastical intrigue, and should be treated with caution as an enunciation of Ultramontane attitudes, as its author was under heavy pressure and was only two years away from confinement to a lunatic asylum. Still, the importance of the epistle lies in its vivid statement of the overly clerical spirit that Newman was combatting. There was an element of truth in Manning's charge that the supporters of the Oxford project only wanted 'to have latch-keys to Grosvenor Square',[89] that they were simply snobs greedy for social status for their children. Newman looked increasingly like the figurehead of an aristocratic conspiracy, opposed to ecclesiastics some of whom, like Manning, had a far profounder social conscience than himself. But Newman equally stood for a principle, an openness to the doubts and difficulties of the Victorian mind. The irony was that the Oxonian clerical and anti-liberal should have become the opponent of clericalism and anti-liberalism himself.

It should also be said for Manning that he was not opposing the Oxford Oratory in principle to Rome, but defending Rome's own opposition to mixed education. However, Newman distrusted Rome as much as he distrusted Manning. 'I have not had an atom of confidence in Propaganda', he told Hope-Scott; '. . . my whole ecclesiastical life, since Mgr Palma's death in 1847 [in fact in 1848], has been one long time of neglect and unkind usage.'[90] Barnabò's secret instruction 'pace Eminentissimi Cardinalis, is as imbecile as it is crooked and cruel'.[91] St John was now sent on to Rome, with Ignatius Ryder's adjuration ringing in his ears that as every man has his price, so the price of a cardinal or monsignor was English snuff: 'I am serious', wrote Newman; ' – could you not borrow a quantity from Hope-Scott, and on leaving Cardinal Barnabo, slip the fragrant douceur into his hand as you kiss it'.[92] Newman defined St John's mission to Ullathorne as that of simply answering the slanders on his character and conduct rife at Rome. He did not seriously think that Rome would now give permission for his residence in Oxford. He thought that Manning, Ward and Talbot considered themselves to be the Church, like the 'three tailors of Tooley St' in Southwark who had petitioned Parliament as 'We the people of England': 'such tyranny and terrorism as they exercise, please God, shall have no power over me', declared Newman, 'nor will I think myself disobedient to the Church because I utterly ignore them – '.[93]

It is in this context that Newman first referred to the ecclesiastical *cause célèbre* of the decade, with the Pope's announcement in 1867 of the First Vatican Council. 'There is a great attempt', Newman wrote to Hope-Scott, 'by W. G. Ward, Dr Murray of Maynooth, and Fr Schrader the Jesuit of Rome and Vienna, to bring in a new theory of Papal Infallibility, which would make it a mortal sin, to be visited by damnation, not to hold the Temporal Power necessary to the Papacy.'[94] When Newman's fellow Oratorian Ignatius Ryder replied to Ward's view of Roman infallibility, Ward declared that he and Newman were of 'different religions', and must publicly and officially regard each other with 'the greatest aversion'. This was in spite of Ward's lingering affection for his old master, who wondered if Ward was as mad as his wife, an Ultramontane so fierce that she had arranged a sculptor to shave the beard of St Thomas' statue at St Edmund's, Ware. 'Ward says that he loves me so', wrote Newman, 'that he should like to pass an eternity with me, but that whenever he sees Manning he makes him creep . . . yet that Manning has the truth and I have not'.[95] Newman's reply to Ward echoed his letter to Emily Bowles:

Pardon me if I say that you are making a Church within a Church, as the Novatians of old did within the Catholic pale, and as, outside the Catholic pale, the Evangelicals of the Establishment. As they talk of 'vital religion' and 'vital doctrines', and will not allow that their brethren 'know the Gospel' or are 'Gospel preachers' unless they profess the small shibboleths of their own sect, so you are doing your best to make a party in the Catholic Church, and in St Paul's words are *'dividing Christ'* by exalting your opinions into dogmas . . . I protest then again, not against your tenets, but against what I must call your schismatical spirit.[96]

But Rome at its narrowest was never as narrow as Ward. St John reported to Newman that 'the Italians think us all; Manning, Talbot, you, Ward etc a lot of queer quarrelsome Inglesi . . . '[97] Barnabò told St John and Bittleston that on Oxford, Rome had a consistent policy. 'The Holy See', the Cardinal declared, 'would never sanction mixed education',[98] and could not encourage it by allowing Newman in Oxford. Barnabò also blamed Ullathorne for not making clear the papal instruction. The Oratorians had a more amusing meeting with Talbot, who brought up the scapegrace young Charles Weld-Blundell, who had left Christ Church '£7,000 in debt and gone off with an actress', as an example of a Catholic ruined by Oxford. Another, Christopher Redington, had mocked Rome's claim to possess the bones of the Apostles. 'Is he not following his [liberal] Father in this?' asked St John. Talbot replied, 'and his Mother too who is as bad as himself.' 'Then', rejoined St John, 'it is rather hard to lay it all to Oxford.'[99]

Talbot's principal complaint, like Barnabò's, was that Bishop Brown had delated Newman to Rome for heresy in the *Rambler*, and though the matter was not raised at St John's audience with the Pope, Pius described Acton and the liberal Catholics as 'not Catholics di cuore', of the heart. Newman had, however, agreed to give Barnabò a full explanation of his *Rambler* article in a letter to Wiseman in 1860, and he now sent a copy of this letter to St John and Bittleston, who reported that Barnabò, when shown it, was 'quite thunder-struck'. 'Why, he said, Cardinal Wiseman was in Propaganda and we never heard of this. He said, it quite cleared you (morally I suppose).'[100] In fact, the substance of Newman's letter in 1860 had reached Barnabò who had not taken it in, while Newman had relied on Manning's slipshod assurance that all would be well in Rome. 'Barnabò', reported St John of a second audience, 'was very warm [and] downright hearty, [and] said he loved you.' He called Newman 'un sant' uomo' persecuted like the saints before him. 'Poor old man', wrote St John of the Cardinal. 'He is really a very good hearted man. He said to me " . . . I know Manning best, but I love Newman . . . " '[101] There was to be no change of policy, which Newman thought was dictated by the desire to keep Catholics 'a distinct caste' at the price of their 'inferiority in mind'[102] to their Protestant neighbours. But the Pope asked kindly about the number and age of the Oratorian community, teased the fat and ageing St John that he was a 'vecchione'[103] who had lost his freshness, blessed Bittleston's work for the prisoners in

Birmingham gaol and a dying penitent of St John's, and showed no reserve or lack of friendliness.

St John had to dispel the belief that he had come to Rome as the champion of mixed education; Newman also owed something to his old critic Cullen, who declared it 'inexpedient'[104] to subject to examination by the Holy Office Newman's published sermon on 'The Pope and the Revolution' which, while defending the Temporal Power, listed the objections to it and said that the Papacy would survive its loss.[105] Newman now felt his reputation cleared, when in August 1867 a Rescript came from Propaganda to the bishops, declaring that Oxford and Cambridge would expose a youth to 'a proximate occasion of mortal sin',[106] and that the bishops should issue pastoral letters making this clear. On Hope-Scott's advice, Newman issued a circular dated the Feast of the Assumption making it clear that Rome's sole reason for refusing to allow him in Oxford was the fear that his name would attract Catholic youths there. The circular offered the subscribers to the Oxford Oratory the return of their money, with the option of leaving it with him in case the project revived.[107] In the outcome he was left with all but £150, and with more than £2000 for a purpose of his personal choice. On 18 August 1867, he finally relinquished the Oxford mission to Ullathorne, who declared in reply that 'you have been shamefully misrepresented at Rome, and that by countrymen of our own'.[108] The chief of these traducers was the Primate of England. 'I never shall trust him', Newman had written to Ullathorne, 'till he has gone through purgatory and has no infirmities upon him';[109] and not until Newman was a cardinal did he forget and forgive him.

26

The Grammar

Manning's butler was called Newman. ' "Sorry to disturb, you, sir" ', he said to a late departing guest, J. E. C. Bodley, ' "but you see the Cardinal doesn't jump straight into bed like you and me: he has his little readings to do".' 'This', Bodley added, 'was Newman's "Apologia".'[1] The Victorians linked their great men in antithetical doublets – Gladstone and Disraeli, Dickens and Thackeray, Browning and Tennyson, Freeman and Froude; and Newman and Manning remain inseparably connected by their bonds of likeness and unlikeness. Though Manning was a brilliant speaker and Newman highly practical, with an extraordinary speed in mentally reckoning up his accounts, they appear before the modern reader as the Martha and Mary of the Victorian Catholic Church, or to change the metaphor, as Lytton Strachey's eagle and dove, the unyielding autocrat and the gentle dreamer.[2] Strachey himself came to acknowledge the inadequacy of the comparison – Newman was more like a hawk than a dove – and because the modern world had sided with Newman, it needs to remember that there is a case for Manning. Their differences came to a head in August 1867, when Manning initiated a correspondence with a view to restoring an old friendship, but Newman told the Archbishop of his own 'distressing mistrust' of him, and even with the good offices of a mutual friend, Frederick Oakeley, the exchange degenerated into politely expressed accusations and counter-accusations, which Newman wrote 'as a protest, and an appeal to posterity'.[3]

Manning was wrong to identify Newman lock, stock and barrel with the *Rambler* and the liberal Catholics, but he was not wrong to interpret Newman's attitude to him as hostile, and to suspect Newman of hostility to his own kind of defence of the Temporal Power. But the differences went deeper, into different habits of mind. Manning was a politician with all a politician's ruthlessness: in 1867, he and Talbot forced Frederick Neve, a convert of 1845 actively sympathetic to Newman, to resign the rectorship of the English College. But Manning saw no reason why intellectual and practical differences should cloud a personal friendship, even though in pursuit of a policy he would use a friendship to his own end. On the other hand, Newman gave unflinching loyalty to those who returned it, and where there had been a violation of that loyalty, no future friendship was possible. Manning called Newman a 'great hater'.[4] His offer of seven Masses for Manning's intention was repaid by Manning with unctuous interest, but Manning did want a reconciliation. 'I do not know', Newman wrote to him in 1869, 'whether I am on my head or my heels, when I have active relations with you'.[5]

Manning had other virtues to which Newman did not aspire. In 1867, the Archbishop began to win that national reputation as a crusader on social issues on which his reputation for greatness depends. Francis Newman, since 1846 a distinguished Professor of Latin at the 'Godless' University College, London, and the butt of a famous essay by Matthew Arnold as a translator of Homer, was on the platform with Manning in Manchester when the Archbishop denounced the drink trade, and Francis wrote to his brother to share what he felt would now be an *'interest in common'*. Francis was horrified by Newman's polite rebuff, a withering expression of uninterested aloofness: 'As to what you tell me of Archbishop Manning, I have heard that some also of our Irish bishops think that too many drink-shops are licensed. As for me, I do not know whether we have too many or too few'.[6]

This social indifferentism was in spite of Newman's growing liberalism on some wider political issues, stimulated by his distrust of the Temporal Power. 'Every thing I have heard of the regime of the Bourbons makes me rejoice in their overthrow, and I trust they will never be restored.'[7] Even open infidelity in Italy was better than covert. 'Is it not shocking that, Irish people being what they are, we should have burned into them such a hatred of us?' wrote Newman to Mrs Froude. ' . . . Whatever bitterness there is in them, we are the cause of it . . . '[8] To Keble's biographer, Sir John Coleridge, his judge in the Achilli trial, Newman wrote that at his last meeting with Keble, he (Newman) had said that he would have had to oppose Gladstone at Oxford, because Gladstone wanted to disestablish the Protestant Church of Ireland. But Keble had said, 'And is not that just?'[9] Newman's position was now a revolutionary one, at least when compared with his youth. He saw that the old political order in Europe was in ruins, which he urged should be swept away. In correspondence with Matthew Arnold, he wondered if the democratic Lamennais 'will be a true prophet after all', and whether, as he had said himself of the Church of the Fathers, the Catholic Church of the future might again become 'a popular power'.[10]

It was, however, Manning who set out to make the Church a popular power by speaking to the social conscience of England; but Manning's answers to intellectual doubt were simply the closely reasoned evidences of Christianity of the textbooks of his youth supplemented by the doctrine of papal infallibility, and it was Newman who spoke to the mood of high Victorian doubt, as he took up the threads of his old friendships among Anglicans. The publication in early 1868 of his *Verses on Various Occasions*, dedicated to Edward Badeley, assembled between two covers his Anglican and Catholic poetry and *The Dream of Gerontius*; it won the plaudits of Gladstone and was the subject of Oxford lecture by Sir Francis Doyle. 'I have been so little used to praise in my life', Newman wrote to Fr Henry

Coleridge, 'that I feel like the good woman in the song, "O, cried the little woman, Sure it is not I!" '[11]

In June 1868, Newman went with St John on a day trip by rail to Littlemore, where the Vicar of the parish found him weeping helplessly in the churchyard and took him the rounds of old parishioners who recalled him kindly. Through William Copeland, he republished his Anglican sermons, and nearly twenty thousand volumes were sold in a year, winning him the goodwill of multitudes of Nonconformists as well as of Anglicans. To the admiring editor of the Dissenting *British Quarterly*, he spoke of 'our controversy with the spirit of infidelity', under the dominical rule, 'He that is not against us is for us'.[12] Certain aspects of that challenge caused him no problems whatsoever. 'Mr Darwin's theory *need* not then be atheistical, be it true or not', he wrote to his assiduous and garrulous correspondent Canon John Walker, the parish priest of Scarborough; 'it may simply be suggesting a larger idea of Divine Prescience and Skill.'[13] 'Darwin does not *profess* to oppose Religion', he told Pusey. 'I think he deserves an honorary degree as much as many others, who have had one.'[14] To correspondents worried about hell, he denied that damnation need mean endless suffering, as the other-worldly state has no consciousness of time; and he insisted on how little about hell had been officially determined or defined. Beyond his passionate attachment to the Holy Roman Church, he had become one of the great intellectual Victorian witnesses to the reality of the unseen world, in a world in which faith was increasingly assailed.

The Oratory itself was a major undertaking, which in the classic Victorian manner accumulated good works. 'We are very few Fathers, and each has his work', Newman wrote to Henry Wilberforce: 'one has the jail – another the Orphanage – two have the School – another has the Parish – another the Poor Schools.' The growth of the fifty-strong orphanage, a product of the poor school, entailed further school work, and left Newman with most of the 'great *domestic* works, the care of the Library, the Sacristy, the Accounts . . .'[15] He produced the Oratory school's Latin play, Terence's *Phormio*, in May 1865, and partly in the interests of morality, published expurgated school editions of *Phormio* in 1864, of *Eunuchus* in 1865 and of *Andria* in 1870. Much of his correspondence lay in helping likely converts like the Honourable Colin Lindsay, the founding President of the High Church English Church Union, whom he received into the Church in 1868. Lindsay's successor as President was Newman's admirer Lord Halifax, nephew of his dead friend Samuel Wood.

But other Catholics felt mounting doubts about papal infallibility. To Dalgairns' old friend the convert Orientalist Peter le Page Renouf, who had written a pamphlet attacking the doctrine by arguing that the seventh-century Pope Honorius had approved the Monothelite heresy, Newman objected that any definition of infallibility must be hedged round with conditions, which Honorius must have failed to observe. Newman had judged the matter as early as 1851;[16] it was only now becoming topical. 'I hold the Pope's Infallibility, not as a dogma', he wrote, 'but as a theological opinion; that is, not as a certainty, but as a probability.' In this, he was treading again a middle path. He could not disagree with the dogma itself, if moderately defined; but he disapproved of Ward's pistol-wielding approach, 'Your money or your life', which made the doctrine binding on Catholics and was thereby 'occasioning the loss of souls'.[17]

It was, however, difficult to publish this position. In December 1867, Newman received the singular honour of an invitation via Monsell from the greatest of nineteenth-century French bishops, Dupanloup, to go to the Council as his theologian. Newman replied that he was *'too old'*,[18] but Cardinal Prospero Caterini subsequently wrote to Ullathorne to ask Newman to be a theological consultor to one of the conciliar commissions. He refused: the project would break the thread of his present work, which might not be finished in old age; it would involve him with 'strange persons',[19] uncongenial superiors and committees and lose him his independence. He warmly thanked Bishop William Clifford for proposing him as a consultor, but told Monsell that apart from Clifford, most of the English hierarchy were only 'echoes of the Archbishop', and that while Goss of Liverpool and Brown of Newport would *'fret'*, the infallibilists might talk them over. Newman expected nothing even from Ullathorne, who 'has no spirit, when it comes to the point', out of a habit of monastic obedience.[20] Brown wrote four times begging Newman to go to Rome as a theologian. Newman choked him off in his own third reply, by rudely quoting Matthew 18.15, advising one brother to tell another of his fault, and reminding Brown that he had delated Newman to Rome, instead of quietly setting him right. It was a prejudice that he feared he would renew, 'selling out my newly acquired stock of credit in these Catholic Circles',[21] were he to reply to Renouf's pamphlet honestly and openly.

This was also his fear as in 1868 he took up the thread of a work on which he had made half a dozen beginnings, on the character of religious certitude: 'whenever I attempted, the sight I saw vanished, plunged into a thicket, curled itself up like a hedgehog, or changed colours like a chameleon'. It was on holiday at Glion in Switzerland in 1866 that he found the 'Open Sesame' to the problem in the idea that certitude is a form of assent, and 'pursued it about the Lake of Lucerne'.[22] To disarm the suspiciousness of his fellow Papists, he subjected his text as he wrote it to the gentlest and acutest of critics, Charles Meynell, Professor of Philosophy at Oscott. An essential part of the *Grammar* was Newman's favourite proof, going back to the 1820s, of God's existence from conscience. 'Now, if this is a wasp-nest, tell me', wrote Newman. 'If the Church has said otherwise, I give it all up – but somehow it is so mixed up with my whole book, that, if it is not safe, I shall not go on.'[23] Meynell was reassuring, in fear and trembling lest some unguarded word might abort a masterpiece. 'I say the

Church is a good Mother and will condemn no man for his Logic.'[24] This was not what Newman thought himself. 'Our theological philosophers', he told Henry Wilberforce, 'are like the old nurses who wrap the unhappy infant in swaddling bands or boards . . . What influence should I have with Protestants and Infidels, if a pack of Catholic critics opened at my back fiercely, saying that this remark was illogical, that unheard of, a third realistic, a fourth, idealistic, a fifth sceptical, and a sixth temerarious, or shocking to pious ears? . . . I cannot make a table stand on two or three legs . . . what an irritabile genus Catholic philosophers are . . . they think they do the free Church of God service, by subjecting her to an etiquette as grievous as that which led to the King of Spain being burned to cinders.'[25]

The *Grammar* is on one level an argument against Victorian doubt, as Newman encountered it in his old doubting friend William Froude. The long-suffering Froude had seen almost his whole family turn papist under Newman's patient tutelage. But Froude was an engineer and a disciple of Isambard Kingdom Brunel, and was an inventor of the technique of testing warships through models in a bath; he therefore required perfect proofs of his conclusions, or his ships would have sunk and his bridges fallen down. Such activity made a virtue of doubt: why, then, was doubt not a virtue in religion, and how could Christianity claim to be certain when it lacked the perfect formal demonstration required to satisfy an engineer? Newman had a partial answer from Aristotle, that moral argument does not have the certainty of mathematical, and from Bishop Butler, that religious argument does not rest on formal proof but on accumulated probabilities. Moreover, he had already indicated in his *University Sermons* that religion does not depend on reason alone. Just as empirical science requires the evidence provided by sense-experience for its materials, so it is conscience that imprints the image of God upon our minds, and without that image no true argument in religion is possible.

Newman was drawing on John Locke's principle that we perceive an object through the complex of images of sight, touch and scent which the object impresses on our minds. Such sense-experience gives us an image of the object; Newman thought of experience as an experience of individual objects, and it is only our experience of such real individual objects that is real, not the abstractions that we derive from them. This made him, in the long Western tradition, a 'nominalist' who thinks of classes of objects as a mere man-made convention for labelling and grouping individuals, against the 'realist' who asserts that such general classes of things have a real independent existence as ideas. We have a real 'apprehension' of individuals, and a notional apprehension of the general notions that we abstract from them. If I see a rose and touch it and enjoy its scent I am 'really' apprehending it. But if I have only heard of roses, through a general account of them, then my understanding of roses as a class is purely 'notional', and has none of the inner resonance, depth and reality which the sight, touch and scent of the rose convey.

Newman thought it possible to have a 'real apprehension' of a rose though none was present, through the power of memory. It was equally possible to apprehend 'really' past emotional states or an imaginary object like a dragon, through the impression of the separate real images of a serpent and of fire. Again, because reality consists in what the individual finds real, it is possible to apprehend 'really' objects which are in themselves abstractions, like a beloved nation or institution or ideal, which conveys a 'real' image of itself. The two different kinds of apprehension, however, divide the world of experience into two, between matters of which we have a real inner knowledge, from a first-hand encounter with unique and particular individual objects, whether these are physical or not, and those which we only know at second hand through the general notions that we imbibe from reading or other people.

This means, therefore, that different individuals will find differing kinds of meaning in the same propositions. Thus 'Dulce et decorum est pro patria mori' might have been a mere abstraction to its author, the poet Horace, who ran away from the battlefield of Philippi; 'whereas it would be the record of experiences, a sovereign dogma, a grand aspiration, inflaming the imagination, piercing the heart, of a Wallace or a Tell'.[26] Newman's own rhetoric soars to make clear the distinction:

Let us consider, too, how differently young and old are affected by the words of some classic author, such as Homer or Horace. Passages, which to a boy are but rhetorical commonplaces, neither better nor worse than a hundred others which any clever writer might supply, which he gets by heart and thinks very fine, and imitates, as he thinks, successfully, in his own flowing versification, at length come home to him, when long years have passed, and he has had experience of life, and pierce him, as if he had never before known them, with their sad earnestness and vivid exactness. Then he comes to understand how it is that lines, the birth of some chance morning or evening at an Ionian festival, or among the Sabine hills, have lasted generation after generation, for thousands of years, with a power over the mind, and a charm, which the current literature of his own day, with all its obvious advantages, is utterly unable to rival. Perhaps this is the reason of the medieval opinion about Virgil, as if a prophet or magician; his single words and phrases, his pathetic half lines, giving utterance, as the voice of Nature himself, to that pain and weariness, yet hope of better things, which is the experience of her children in every time.[27]

So too with the Athanasian Creed, 'the war-song of faith, with which we warn first ourselves, then each other, and then all those who are within its hearing, and the hearing of the Truth, who our God is, and how we must worship Him, and how vast our responsibility will be, if we know what to believe, and yet believe not . . . For myself, I have ever felt it as the most simple and sublime, the most devotional formulary to which Christianity has given birth . . . '[28] As for the Trinity, a formal theological deduction from the revealed truths that God is Father, Son and Spirit, Newman argued that the believer grasps the Trinity not so much through the doctrine in itself but indirectly through the propositions which make the doctrine up, and through the Church which teaches it; just as a white light is glorious when broken into colour. Though Newman's argument is very different in form, there is an odd reminiscence here of Hampden's notion that a doctrine like the Trinity is only true in so far as it is true to the scriptural facts from which it is deduced.

But very different to Hampden is Newman's declaration that there is a sense in which the believer does apprehend the Trinity, as in the Athanasian Creed. Chanted as a war-song, it speaks to the imagination, it demands a response that is real not notional, and that comes from the whole person and not just the reason on its own.

The distinction between the real and the notional also recalls Newman's remarks about 'viewiness' in the *Idea of a University*, the light-headed holding and voicing of opinions which do not rest on long experience and settled conviction. So it is also with argument, which comes in two types: we can argue about matters which we have really apprehended in imagination in their individual and concrete particulars, or we can argue from the abstractions that lie at least at one remove from real experience itself.

Arguments, however, are comprised of statements or propositions; and Newman opens his book with a dry-as-dust analysis of the forms of verbal propositions, into questions, conclusions and assertions. He suggests that this ordering of three sorts of proposition represents a progression through three acts or states of mind. The doubting mind questions; the arguing or inferring mind concludes; and if we then unconditionally assert that conclusion, without reference to the arguments that support it, then we are making an assent. This conception of unconditional assent is perhaps the central idea of the *Grammar*. But the quality of our argument depends upon our experience of its terms: so that we make real inferences and assents to propositions about objects of which we have real experience; and we draw notional inferences from and make notional assents to propositions about objects of which we have only an abstract or notional idea.

Newman was, then, distinguishing between two 'habits of mind', between two kinds of rationality and 'modes of thought', one personal, concrete and particular, the other abstract, formal and universal.[29] But this is not simply a distinction between religious argument and formal logic. Rather it is the difference between our arguments about personal relations or politics or ethics or aesthetics as well as theology, the activities which arise from our real experience of concrete particularities, and the abstract proofs of mathematics and syllogistic logic. No such binding proof is available in moral matters, so that a concrete image of a particularly barbaric duel was needed to bring home to the English public the truth of the abstract principle that duelling was barbarous. Not that assent produces moral action by itself; 'but the images in which it lives, representing as they do the concrete, have the power of the concrete upon the affections and passions, and by means of these indirectly become operative',[30] and so create the real mainsprings of collective behaviour as well as of individual. These images

form the mind out of which they grow, and impart to it a seriousness and manliness which inspires in other minds a confidence in its views, and is one secret of persuasiveness and influence in the public stage of the world. They create, as the case may be, heroes and saints, great leaders, statesmen, preachers, and reformers, the pioneers of discovery in science, visionaries, fanatics, knight-errants, demagogues, and adventurers. They have given to the world men of one idea, of immense energy, of adamantine will, of revolutionary power. They kindle sympathies between man and man, and knit together the innumerable units which constitute a race and a nation. They become the principle of its political existence; they impart to it homogeneity of thought and fellowship of purpose. They have given form to the medieval theocracy and to the Mahometan superstition; they are now the life both of 'Holy Russia', and of that freedom of speech and action which is the special boast of Englishmen.[31]

Such assents can be a matter of general agreement, but as they lead to the formation of character, so they are intimately connected with what is individual and personal. 'They depend on personal experience; and the experience of one man is not the experience of another.' One man's religion or politics is not another's, because what is real in concrete particulars arises from what is real in individual experience. 'Real assent, then, as the experience which it presupposes, is proper to the individual, and, as such, thwarts rather than promotes the intercourse of man with man. It shuts itself up, as it were, in its own home . . .'[32] Men differ politically or ethically or religiously because their different arguments go back to different choices in what they are as persons. This is, in a sense, Newman alone with his Creator. The mind has a privileged position in relation to the world around it, in finding reality in one set of images and not in another, and in assenting to propositions which embody whatever it discovers to be real.

As individuals come to their convictions through different sorts of personal experience, so they will obviously argue until the cows come home. But they also possess a stock of notions in common which enables them to argue until the cows come home. Language promotes the intercourse of man and man through its abstractions; and the most abstract form of argument, mathematics, is also the most binding on everyone, making possible an agreed public exactitude and precision. But the notional abstractions of language are a kind of second-best medium which can never exhaust the meanings of the private self, while mathematics is concerned with universal truths which are true regardless of the objects to which they refer: four and three are seven, for any objects under the sun. When it comes to arguing from individual experience, the logic of 'formal inference' from abstractions simply leaves a host of particularities of interest, importance and relevance to the matter in hand out of the account; and in religion as in life, as in all kinds of personal knowledge, 'formal inference' and the notional assent that arises from it are an attenuation, a simplification and an impoverishment of the concreteness, complexity and richness of experience itself.

There is nothing wrong with 'formal inference' in its place. But it does not genuinely inform, as it merely states the formal logical relations between propositions, telling us the meaning of the information we already have. We can obviously trust formal inference, because it gives us certainties; but why should we trust informal? On Locke's view, we can only hold a truth with the degree of assurance that we have evidence for it, yet Newman was impressed by the prevalence of a mass of absolute assents, e.g. to the proposition that Great Britain is an island, which do not, as Locke had implied, become more certain if one adduces additional evidence for them. Keble held that there must be doubt in religion as it rests on probable arguments which fall short of certainty. But Newman thought that by accepting the mind's habitual operations, certitude is attainable as a mental state, though it only rests on accumulated probabilities in strict logic. Certainty, then, is a property of propositions, but it is distinct from certitude as a state of mind, and the mind is in practice quite content with certitudes which it would be absurd to doubt, even though the supporting arguments for them are in logic merely probable.

Most such reasoning is never subjected to formal analysis, and is 'implicit' rather than explicit, as it arises from the innate power of the judging mind to reach reliable conclusions from the evidence before it by processes of which it is barely conscious. This power to pass straight from facts to conclusions is what Newman calls the 'Illative Sense', 'a grand word for a common thing',[33] as he described it to Meynell. In a Newton or Napoleon, the Illative Sense amounts to genius, but it is a special gift with a weather-wise peasant and mere common sense in the multitude. Thus Newton could assert the rule for ascertaining the imaginary roots of equations without offering formal proof of it – in this, even mathematics may dispense with formal argument, – while Napoleon could read directly from the battlefield the size and disposition of an opposing army. The peasant can read the clouds, and the multitude can judge all sorts of practical issues with complete assurance. The mind in these matters has passed from fact to conclusion without notional, propositional or linguistic intermediaries. The Illative

Sense recalls Aristotle's 'phronesis',[34] and Newman urges us simply to accept it: 'instead of devising, what cannot be, some sufficient science of reasoning which may compel certitude in concrete conclusions, [we ought] to confess that there is no ultimate test of truth besides the testimony born to truth by the mind itself'.[35] There is no formal proof of the reliability of the Illative Sense, a point which Newman recognized as the weakness in his argument. The Illative Sense is an habitual mental operation, a power to judge in which the mind out of its own resources brings to its materials for argument something over and above the materials themselves.

Newman distinguished simple assents, which are held without self-conscious examination, from complex assents which have been verified by conscious argument and reflection. He restricted his use of certitude to holding propositions which the holder could never doubt. Newman declares that this puzzling notion admits of exceptions, but his deeper thought is that certitudes are usually 'indefectible' because they are integral to personality: the holder cannot doubt them without ceasing to be what he is. Newman nullified the counter-instance of St Paul because his conversion had been miraculous. Thus a certitude may turn out to be a mere conviction, if the holder comes to abandon it. A change in opinion shows what we really believe, in the depths of what we are. A Protestant might become a Catholic or Unitarian or atheist; but if he became a Catholic, then this would show that he held one Protestant conviction more deeply than the others, the divinity of Christ. The Unitarian would develop his Unitarianism from the Protestant principle of *sola scriptura*, the atheist his atheism from a conviction of the Protestant right of private judgement. Newman's argument arose out of his belief that certain fixed convictions underlay all his own changes in religion. His conception of certitude was the product of his consciousness of the unity and continuity of his own religious history, in which the dogmas of the faith had been essential to the coherence and development of his personality, as he became ever more completely himself.

Newman asserted in this the primacy of action over thought: probability is the very guide of life and is sufficient for certitude because we have to act without waiting for certain proofs, time being short and eternity long. Thus the appropriation of certitude from mere probabilities is part of Newman's conception of a personal truth personally worked out in practical activity and through spiritual growth. Newman also anticipated the now fashionable philosophical notion that rationality is not restricted to the binding forms of formal or syllogistic or mathematical argument, but that other types of human discourse, from politics to theology, have their underlying grammars and are reasonable, not in the sense that they can be abstractly proven, but because they are self-coherent and make sense of both our practical activity and the external world.[36] Some modern philosophers like Wittgenstein argue the absurdity of doubting obvious certainties for which there is no compelling proof, though they defend this from a theory of language which is the opposite of Newman's, that speech is no mere abstraction from reality but is itself a reality, a form of life or a game with rules, so that to deny that Great Britain is an island is to repudiate an essential rule in the game and so reduce the game itself to nonsense. This in turn implies that the objective criterion of certainty is the language of the public community which uses it, but Newman acknowledged no such community in religion except the Catholic Church, which in turn depended on God, 'a Power, greater than human teaching and human argument, to make our beliefs true and our minds one'.[37]

God, then, supplies the defects of our reasoning powers in religion, for just as we are called to believe what we cannot prove with certainty, so he is a mystery beyond our reason and experience, and we are therefore called to believe what we cannot wholly understand. Whately's Aristotelian *Logic* had expelled the complex psychology of what goes on in the mind from the paper logic of formal binding proof. Newman substituted a personal and psychological logic for an abstract formal one, and stressed the non-rational origin of those first principles from which our remaining beliefs will follow. The latter part of the *Grammar* is a passionate plea for the intrinsic reasonableness of Catholicism as the proper embodiment of a revelation given by God, not discovered by human reason, a revelation with divine authority. The whole of Newman's thought lies between the poles of two God-given popes, the private peremptory if fallible pope of conscience, the witness to the God within, creating that hunger for God which is satisfied and fulfilled by the public pope of the external revelation of God in Scripture and Tradition, as upheld in the witness of the infallible Church. Newman never doubted the infallibility of the Church, which sustained him in the battle over papal infallibility. His own anxieties had that other consolation, the certitude that growth into truth is a personal growth through present suffering. When Gerard Manley Hopkins joined the Society of Jesus, Newman solaced him in his doubts. 'Don't call "the Jesuit discipline hard" ', he wrote: 'it will bring you to heaven.'[38]

The Vatican Council

'The *one* question which is occupying people's minds is "Will the Pope's infallibility be determined"?' wrote Newman to Pusey of the forthcoming Vatican Council. '*All* questions sink before that.'[1] Pusey, working on yet another Eirenicon, is an insular figure against the backdrop of the international drama unfolding beneath the dome of Peter. On 8 December 1869, the feast of the Immaculate Conception, some six hundred bishops, the great majority of them belonging to the Latin rite and clad in silver copes and tall linen mitres, processed to their seats in the north transept of the basilica, singing the *Veni Creator*. 'Outside was the dense mass of the faithful', wrote Bishop Ullathorne, 'and the sound of their voices and feet was as the sound of many murmuring waters on a seashore.'[2]

The bishops and the fifty thousand packed in and round St Peter's represented a Church which had undergone a transformation in Newman's lifetime. It was not a Roman Catholic, but a sometime Clapham Evangelical, Thomas Babington Macaulay, who had written in 1840 the most powerful of all panegyrics to her recovered glory:

The Papacy remains, not in decay, not a mere antique, but full of life and youthful vigour. The Catholic Church is still sending forth to the furthest ends of the world missionaries as zealous as those who landed in Kent with Augustine, and still confronting hostile kings with the same spirit with which she confronted Attila. The number of her children is greater than in any former age . . . She saw the commencement of all the governments and of all the ecclesiastical establishments that now exist in the world; and we feel no assurance that she is not destined to see the end of them all. She was great and respected before the Saxon had set foot on Britain, before the Frank had passed the Rhine, when Grecian eloquence still flourished at Antioch, when idols were still worshipped in the temple of Mecca. And she may still exist in undiminished vigour when some traveller from New Zealand shall, in the midst of a vast solitude, take his stand on a broken arch of London Bridge to sketch the ruins of St Paul's.[3]

Macaulay was a man to admire the big battalions, and thirty years after his description, Protestants were more than ever aware of the triumphs and tribulations of the renascent but embattled Roman Church. The Irish diaspora alone had created new Catholic hierarchies across the British Empire and North America, while French missionary enterprise had spread the faith through China, the Far East and Africa. In much of Latin Europe and Latin America, the conflict between clerical conservatives and anticlerical liberals meant both a decline in religious influence and practice in some places and a faith reaffirmed by the challenge in others. Nowhere was this more so than in France, where more new active orders of religious women were established than in any other century of Christian history, and where an expiatory popular fervour, often highly counter-revolutionary in character, found an outlet in mass pilgrimages to the sites of the new apparitions of the Virgin. Marian pietism was heavily Ultramontane: the Virgin at Lourdes in 1858 confirmed the doctrine of the Immaculate Conception defined by Pope Pius in 1854: the Pope called Mary immaculate, and his Church called him infallible. The Syllabus of Errors rallied conservatives everywhere to his cause, but in countries where the mass of Catholics were both radical and devout, as in Ireland or Poland, his anathematization of heresy became part of their hate of their oppressors.

Love and hate went together. As a pope whose years were to exceed the years of Peter, sweet-tempered, kindly, witty and forgiving to his enemies, Pius enjoyed a cult of personality like no pope before him, a cult which grew and swelled as Catholics deplored his loss of the Papal States to the Italian revolutionaries. To missionary clergy and nuns and seminarians, his charm was irresistible, and the modern industrial means of mass communication and manufacture carried his speeches into the new Catholic popular press and his picture into every Catholic home. The huge new missionary territories and their bishops were immediately under the authority of the Sacred Propaganda, and better communications made Roman authority more effective than at any time in Christian history, as the Papacy, unhindered for the first time in its career by the civil power, gathered all this huge new jurisdiction to itself. Rome itself became the centre for the great episcopal gatherings for the canonization of the Japanese martyrs in 1862 and for the eighteen hundredth anniversary of the martyrdoms of St Peter and St Paul in 1867. These gave a focus to Ultramontanism both as the trades unionism of the clergy and as the patriotism of Catholics proud of their fortress Church in her defiance of her enemies. The spokesman of the international Catholic mood at its fiercest was the peasant journalist Louis Veuillot, and in the columns of his newspaper *L'Univers*, the *Daily Mail* of the French priesthood, Pius was the embodied Holy Ghost and his every word was an oracle of God.

But Ultramontanism was by no means acceptable to all. Veuillot's extremism repelled French liberal Catholics like Dupanloup and Montalembert, as well as old-fashioned Gallicans for whom the only infallible authority

364

in the Church was a universal council. In Austria, Hungary and Germany, the aristocratic prelates of proud and ancient sees regarded the Pope as no more than *primus inter pares*, and had no wish to outrage the secular power by exalting the Papacy at its expense. The great Bishop Strossmayer, founder of South Slav nationalism, feared the effect of defining infallibility on relations with the Eastern Orthodox; many American bishops feared its effect on relations with Protestants. The accidents of history left much of liberal or Gallican northern and central Europe under-represented at the Council, as there the dioceses were huge, having often begun as chaplaincies to princes: while the Roman civic tradition in Italy meant that its hierarchy was over-represented, with more than two hundred sees. Most of the Italians were papal partisans: many, being poor, were housed at the Pope's expense, prompting his famous untranslatable pun, 'Non so se il Papa uscirà di questo Concilio fallibile od infallibile; ma questo è certo che sarà fallito'.[4]

All Catholics, however, believed in the infallibility of the Church and of its general councils, and most of the opponents of defining papal infallibility claimed to be 'inopportunist', opposed not in principle to the definition but to the desirability of defining it just now. The heart of the opposition was, however, opposed to the definition altogether, and this was the liberal Catholic circle stirred up and stimulated by Döllinger and Acton. Acton wanted his High Church friend Gladstone, as Prime Minister, to get Britain to intervene against the Council. Döllinger hoped the same of Bavaria, and through his publications under the names of 'Janus' and 'Quirinus', gave the world a view of the Papacy and of the proceedings of the Council which made them stink in liberal nostrils for half a century. Much of this misinformation was spread in Britain by *The Times* correspondent, Newman's brother-in-law Tom Mozley. Mozley knew no French or Italian, but he had a lively pen, and his Borgiaesque accounts, a distillation of local English gossip, fed the Protestant and liberal prejudices of the nation's breakfast tables, even while they caused bewildered hilarity among the English-speaking prelates in Rome.

By a singular irony, it was Manning whose astute committee skills, not too scrupulously exercised, made him the 'whip' of the infallibilist majority. Newman, on the other hand, had the pastoral care of a large clientele of ecclesiastical gypsies of no fixed abode, anxious souls troubled to know if infallibility were true, wanting to become or remain Roman Catholics but battered by the past and present papal scandals bandied about by the press. 'To begin with [the] doctrine of the Pope is to begin to build St Peter's from the cross and ball',[5] wrote Newman, who thought a definition would impede the conversion of High Anglicans and cripple the Church's mission to well-disposed Protestants and liberals. Hyacinth Loyson, a famous French Carmelite preacher, visited Newman in 1868 as a fellow opponent of the definition, though they made little of each other's native language.[6] A year later Loyson denounced papal infallibility in unmeasured terms, as Newman warned him of giving ammunition to Protestants 'who are nothing less than infidels – They will use you, and secretly smile at you; or if not they, then the Author of Evil . . . '[7] Loyson subsequently left his order and the Church for a rich American widow. Newman found himself again in a *via media*, condemning the tyranny of authority on the one hand, and fearing the sensitivity, ignorance and irresponsibility of its critics on the other.

Yet Newman had no doubt that Providence would ensure a proper outcome to the Council, the Spirit overriding the follies of men. He thought that Manning himself had 'thrown himself upon or into this middle party, joining them and raising the terms of the compromise',[8] but in that very act had fallen short of the extreme definition that he wanted himself. The Church could not err, so all would be well; but there was still no pressing need for the definition in the present. 'What have we done', asked Newman, 'that we can't be left alone?' It was proposed to carry the matter by acclamation. 'Have the men who entertain such a project', wrote Newman to Bishop Moriarty of Kerry, 'any regard at all for the souls of their brethren? The frogs [in Aesop] said to the boys who threw stones at them "It is fun to you, but death to us".'[9] To Ullathorne in Rome, Newman finally exploded in a burst of righteous wrath, in what he afterwards called 'one of the most confidential letters that I ever wrote in my life':[10]

When we are all at rest, and have no doubts, and at least practically, not to say doctrinally, hold the Holy Father to be infallible, suddenly there is thunder in the clear sky, and we are told to prepare for something we know not what to try our faith we know not how. No impending danger is to be averted, but a great difficulty is to be created. Is this the proper work for an Ecumenical Council? As to myself personally, please God, I do not expect any trial at all; but I cannot help suffering with the various souls which are suffering, and I look with anxiety at the prospect of having to defend decisions, which may be not difficult to my private judgement, but may be most difficult to maintain logically in the face of historical facts. What have we done to be treated, as the faithful never were treated before? When has definition of doctrine de fide been a luxury of devotion, and not a stern painful necessity? Why should an aggressive insolent faction be allowed to 'make the heart of the just to mourn, whom the Lord hath not made sorrowful?' Why can't we be let alone, when we have pursued peace, and thought no evil? I assure you, my dear Lord, some of the truest minds are driven one way and another, and do not know where to rest their feet; one day determining to give up all theology as a bad job, and recklessly to believe henceforth almost that the Pope is impeccable; at another tempted to believe all the worst which a book like Janus says; others doubting about the capacity possessed by Bishops, drawn from all corners of the earth, to judge what is fitting for European society, and then again angry with the Holy See for listening to the flattery of a clique of Jesuits, Redemptorists, and converts.

Then again, think of the store of Pontifical scandals in the history of 18 centuries, which have partly been poured out and partly are still to come. What Murphy[11] inflicted upon us in one way, M Veuillot indirectly is bringing on us in another.

And then again, the blight which is falling upon the multitude of Anglican ritualists etc who themselves perhaps, at least their leaders, may never become Catholics, but who are leavening the various English denominations and parties (far beyond their own range) with principles and sentiments tending toward their ultimate absorption in the Catholic Church.

With these thoughts before me, I am continually asking myself whether I ought not to make my feelings public; but all I do is to pray those great early Doctors of the Church, whose intercession would decide the matter, Augustine and the rest, to avert so great a calamity. If it is God's will that the Pope's infallibility should be defined, then it is His blessed Will to throw back 'the times and the moments' of that triumph which He has destined for His Kingdom; and I shall feel I have but to bow my head to His adorable, inscrutable Providence . . . [12]

Ullathorne replied reasuringly: 'If you could but see, as I see, Schemata brought in, only to be pulled to pieces, and sent out again, bleeding in every limb, to be reconstructed by the special committees . . . '[13] But Newman's letter was too good as ammunition to the inopportunists to remain private, as Acton and Döllinger spread about their antipapal scandal and as even the devout and dying Montalembert thundered against 'the idol . . . in the Vatican'.[14] Ullathorne showed Newman's letter to Clifford, who made a copy which was copied by Errington, though when Moriarty and Errington wanted it translated for Cardinal Barili, Ullathorne discouraged them. But Ullathorne also showed a copy to Archbishop Connolly of Halifax, and through one of these channels, it got back to England. The *Standard* newspaper published the words 'aggressive insolent faction'. Newman looked at his heavily scored draft, and wrote to deny that he had used the phrase. He did, however, admit its justice. 'That I deeply deplore the policy, the spirit, the measures of various persons, lay and ecclesiastical, who are urging the definition of that theological opinion', he added, 'I have neither intention nor wish to deny.'[15] But Sir John Simeon, a convert liberal Catholic, promptly wrote from the House of Commons to Newman that the phrase was in copies of the letter circulating in London. Newman looked again at his draft, found the words there, and hastened to apologize to the *Standard* for his error. 'Don't mind for me, my dear Lord – ', he wrote to Ullathorne. 'I have had too many knocks to care for this.'[16]

'I have got into a great scrape,'[17] he told Monsell, asking if he should publish the whole letter on his own account. Monsell advised against, pointing out the offensiveness of another of Newman's phrases, 'a clique of Jesuits, Redemptorists, and converts'. Newman was referring to the Roman Jesuits of the *Civiltà Cattolica*, and would have to apologize to the English Jesuits, who included some of his warmest supporters like Henry Coleridge. He decided, however, that only full publication of the letter would enable him to explain it. Meanwhile, warm congratulations on the document began to arrive, from Ambrose de Lisle, Brown of Newport and the ailing Anglo-Gallican Bishop Goss of Liverpool, who had decided *en route* to miss the Council and winter at Cannes. Newman learned via Miss Bowles that the letter had given Montalembert '*his last sensation of joy upon earth*'.[18] Döllinger also wrote to thank him, but Newman's reply stressed the limits of their agreement, and pointed to the defect, as he saw it, in Döllinger's historical method. A Catholic who could accept as God-given the decisions of past councils in spite of the irregularities attending them should have no ultimate difficulty with the present one. 'I suppose', Newman told Döllinger, 'in all Councils there has been intrigue, violence, management, because the truth is held in earthen vessels. But God over rules. I do not see that the Vatican Council or the Council of Florence, is worse than the 2nd General Council in this respect, or than the 3rd.'[19] Döllinger advised Acton that Newman would submit to the conciliar decision when it came. To both he was once more the lost leader, who would fight a skirmish and run away.

Newman was then again the piggy in the middle, as he was attacked for the letter to Ullathorne by his sometime disciple Dalgairns, and less politely in *L'Univers* by Veuillot, whom Newman had criticized personally, and who wrongly accused him of not thanking the journal for the money it had raised for the Achilli trial.[20] In the event, the definition of infallibility was carried at the last public session of the Council on 18 July 1870, and Tom Mozley excelled himself in describing the drama of the thunderstorm that attended it:

> The storm, which had been threatening all the morning, burst now with the utmost violence, and to many a superstitious mind might have conveyed the idea that it was an expression of divine wrath, as 'no doubt it will be interpreted by numbers', said one officer of the Palatine Guard. And so the 'placets' of the Fathers struggled through the storm, while the thunder pealed above and the lightning flashed in at every window and down through the dome and every smaller cupola, dividing if not absorbing the attention of the crowd. 'Placet', shouted his Eminence or his Grace, and a loud clap of thunder followed in response, and then the lightning darted about the baldacchino and every part of the church and the conciliar hall, as if announcing the response.
>
> . . . The storm was at its height when the result of the voting was taken up to the Pope, and the darkness was so thick that a huge taper was

necessarily brought and placed by his side as he read the words 'Nosque, sacro approbante Concilio, illa, ut lecta sunt, definimus et apostolica auctoritate confirmamus.' And again the lightning flickered around the hall, and the thunder pealed. The 'Te Deum' and the Benediction followed; the entire crowd fell on their knees, and the Pope blessed them in those clear sweet tones distinguishable among a thousand.[21]

Newman expressed himself to de Lisle as 'pleased'[22] with the moderation of the definition. Unlike Trent, however, Vatican I was not unanimous, and while only two bishops remained at the final session in July to vote against the decree, one from a Neapolitan hill-town and the other from Little Rock, Arkansas, more than eighty had already departed after a compromise was refused by the Pope himself. 'I think the promoters of the dogma have behaved very cruelly, tyrannically, and deceitfully . . . ', Newman wrote. But he doubted that 'God would allow 530 bishops to go wrong . . . Perhaps the definition will *limit* the Pope's power'.[23] The acid test would be his maxim of old, 'Securus judicat orbis terrarum',[24] of whether the whole Catholic world received it. He heard of an Ultra who thought that Catholics should pray only to the Virgin: 'God preserve us, if we have such madmen among us', he wrote, 'with their lighted brands'.[25] 'I doubt', he wrote on 21 August 1870, 'whether it is yet an article of faith.'[26] But 'the Ultra party are much disappointed',[27] as the definition restricted infallibility to faith and morals, and could not even be held to infallibilize the Syllabus of Errors. 'They have only got *authoritatively* pronounced *that* which Fr Ryder maintained against Mr Ward.'[28] To one anxious correspondent, Newman quoted William Cowper:

> Beware of desperate steps – the darkest day
> Live till to-morrow, will have passed away.[29]

Newman also felt that the definition had brought its own punishment. It was immediately followed by the outbreak of the Franco-Prussian War, the withdrawal of French troops from Rome and the surrender of the city to an Italian army. The Pope had been declared infallible, but had lost the temporal power which had been his for a thousand years. 'We have come to a climax of tyranny', Newman wrote to Lady Simeon. 'It is not good for a Pope to live 20 years. It is [an] anomaly and bears no good fruit; he becomes a god, has no one to contradict him . . . and does cruel things without meaning it.'[30] Newman wondered to Monsell if it was 'in the disposition of Providence that the same man should be both infallible in spirituals and absolute in temporals. The definition of July involved the dethronement of September'.[31] 'I cannot think thunder and lightning a mark of approbation', he concluded, ' . . . and the sudden destruction of the Pope's temporal power does not seem a sign of approval either.'[32] It was for God to put matters right in the future. A future council would no doubt 'trim the boat' and make good any want of balance in the definition. Providence might have punished the Papacy, but it had also taken care of the Church.

Any lingering doubt was resolved in Newman's mind by the submission of the *orbis terrarum* to the infallibility decree, as even the gallant Gallicans of France and the proud prince prelates of Austria and Hungary surrendered one by one, like slowly drowning whales. The only prominent figures to stand out against the definition were the German university professors, who led a middle-class minority of 'Old Catholics' into formal schism from the Church. Newman continued to think Döllinger 'treated very cruelly',[33] but also thought he lacked 'imagination, considerateness, charity'[34] in his rigid historical literalism about past papal errors, and tied 'you down like Shylock to the letter of the bond'.[35] Newman maintained an enormous correspondence of reassurance to liberal or lapsed or lapsing Catholics, but he only entered public controversy when no Catholic cleric came forward to answer the denunciation of infallibility by *The Times*, by way of its attack on papal approval of the St Bartholomew's Day massacre, on the three hundredth anniversary of the atrocity in 1872. 'No Pope', wrote Newman to the editor, 'can make evil good . . . If any Pope has, with his eyes open, approved of treachery or cruelty, let those defend that Pope, who can . . . Craft and cruelty, and whatever is base and wicked have a sure *nemesis*, and eventually strike the heads of those who are guilty of them . . . Infallibility is not impeccability.'[36] Newman otherwise declined suggestions that he publish on the subject, but he had endlessly rehearsed his argument about infallibility in his letters, on the true and restricted meaning of the definition, before he was moved to go public in 1875.

'I seem to have done nothing and to have frittered away all my time and labour upon dreams',[37] Newman told Lady Simeon. The dreams had at last the solidity of a long line of thick volumes in hard covers, and acquired a new audience as Newman began to republish with Basil Pickering more of his old Anglican writings, beginning with his essays on ecclesiastical miracles. By December 1871, Newman had republished or was republishing most of his Anglican works with Rivingtons, Lumley and Pickering and most of his Catholic ones with Pickering and Burns and Oates, including the bulk of his reviews for the *British Critic*. The project enabled him to provide notes and afterthoughts and corrections to his old opinions, to tinker endlessly with his prose, and to produce definitive texts of all his major works. The appearance of *Loss and Gain* under his own name – its original publication had been anonymous – enabled him to repay another old debt by dedicating the work to his gentle Maynooth mentor Charles Russell. There was a much more recondite air to the volume of *Tracts Theological and Ecclesiastical*, which contained his Roman dissertations in Latin on Athanasius an ingenious essay written for *The Atlantis* on the relations between the dates of the Christian and calendar years, and some minor learned works on the Fathers, including his notes on the text of the seven epistles of St Ignatius, begun in 1828 and brought up to date with more recent scholarship in 1870. The essay on the 'Causes of the Rise and Successes of Arianism' in the same volume received its final form in 1872. In 1874 he wrote an 'Autobiographical Memoir' for St John, written formally in the third person, and it was St John whom he intended to edit his Remains. In a decade of hard practical activity – he wrote more than sixty notes to Pickering in 1870–1 alone – he edited and presided over the appearance of his own *opera omnia*. He also systematically transcribed, arranged and destroyed old letters. It was the achievement of a tidy mind, which was its own satisfaction, putting its house in perfect order while daily awaiting its call to God.

Newman outlived a host of younger friends. Serjeant Bellasis died early in 1873, recalling on his death-bed the dedication of the *Grammar* as the greatest gratification of his life.[38] Newman paid a last visit to Hope-Scott at Abbotsford in July 1872, and to Henry Wilberforce in April 1873; both died later that year. Of the former Newman wrote, 'I lose one of those whom I love most in the world, one who has gone out of his way to know me, who has ever been faithful to me, who stood by me in great difficulties, who has aided me in great needs, and who is one of the sweetest-tempered, gentlest, most religious-minded men I ever knew'.[39] Newman preached at the Farm Street requiem for Hope-Scott, and at Wilberforce's requiem, and wrote a brief but charming memoir of Wilberforce as an introduction to his historical essays from the *Dublin Review*.[40] Henry's brother Sam had never been Newman's intimate, but his death on a fall from his horse recalled to Newman 'the vision of his coming up to residence at Oriel in 1823, leaning on Robert's arm. Ah me, what an age ago! It is a new world; yet to the great Creator of worlds it is but yesterday'.[41] Henry Woodgate, who was incumbent of a parish near Birmingham, died in 1874, having enjoyed nine years of an ancient Oxford friendship which Newman resumed after his oblique reference to it in the *Apologia* us lost.

Two other old friends, the Anglican English Rogers and the Catholic Irish Monsell, both Liberals, were raised to the peerage as Lords Blachford and Emly by Gladstone in 1871 and 1874. Newman had new friendships with some younger people – with William Froude's daughter Isy, who married the Cambridge geologist Baron Anatole von Hügel, with Anatole's brother Baron Friedrich von Hügel, and Hope-Scott's daughter Mary Monica (Mamo), in whom the line of Walter Scott alone survived. Mamo wrote to Newman in 1874 to announce her engagement and her 'sad pleasure' in revisiting her father's old haunts in Hyères. 'How sorrow and joy go together in this life, a joy in our deepest sorrow, a sorrow in our most abounding joy!' wrote Newman. 'But both joy and sorrow are well, if they lead us on towards heaven.'[42] He declined her wedding invitation, being 'too old and dull to present myself on so bright an occasion'.[43] He sat for a portrait commissioned by local notables by W. T. Roden, who depicted him as lugubrious, even despairing, and also sat for a drawing by Lady Coleridge, whose husband, an admirer of Newman, was the brother to his Jesuit friend Henry, both sons of the judge who had lectured him in 1853. The Evangelical Edward Bickersteth sent him a copy of his poem on the Last Things, *Yesterday, To-day, and For Ever*. 'I can but bow before the great mystery', wrote Newman in thanks, 'that those are divided here and look for the means of grace and glory in such different directions, who have so much in common in faith and hope.'[44]

This eirenic mood was overshadowed in the aftermath of the Council by the persecution of the Church in the new kingdom of Italy and in the new German Empire, where Church and State each seemed to claim an absolute loyalty, making it appear to Liberals and Protestants that Italians and Germans could not be both good Catholics and good citizens. Anticlerical Italian administrations and the Falk laws of Bismarck's Kulturkampf alike defined Catholicism as the enemy of modern nationalism, and opposed the Catholic Church to the modern nation State as a state within a state, as an *imperium in imperio*, as a supranational state and an omnipresent foreign power. The medieval conflict between Empire and Papacy and Guelf and Ghibbeline gave the argument a great historic resonance in Germany and Italy; but Henry VIII's repudiation of Rome, Mary's burnings and St Pius V's deposition of Elizabeth as a heretic and usurper also lent it plausibility in England. Moreover just as German Catholics were the least loyal subjects of the German Empire, so Irish Catholics were the least loyal subjects of the British Empire, and the apparent absoluteness of the claim to infallibility aroused the old fear that Romanism meant rebellion.

British Catholics had always expected opposition from Orange Tory Protestants, champions, as Newman had once been, of the union of Church and State. But most Catholics had been as much hurt as surprised by the hostility of the British Liberals, as in 1850, when a Whig Prime Minister had turned on his former Catholic friends. It was, however, almost an accident that the Roman Church was assailed in October 1874 by the Liberal leader Gladstone, who had suffered electoral defeat earlier in the year and so had more leisure for those theological pursuits which were the main interest of his life. Gladstone's administration was fatally weakened in 1873 by the Irish Catholic Church's rejection of his University Bill, which he blamed on the Vatican decrees. But his anti-Romanism was of an unusual English type, being a kind of liberal Catholicism: in September 1874, he visited his friend Döllinger in Munich. As a devout High Churchman, he had often been accused of Popery himself. Now he denounced Rome as substituting

> for the proud boast of *semper eadem* a policy of violence and change in faith; when she had refurbished and paraded anew every rusty tool she

was fondly thought to have disused; when no one can become her convert, without renouncing his moral and mental freedom, and placing his civil loyalty and duty at the mercy of another; and when she has equally repudiated modern thought and ancient history.[45]

The 'policy of violence and change in faith' was the view of the Council propagated by Döllinger; the 'modern thought' was the whole body of liberal opinion anathematized in the Syllabus; the 'ancient history' was the proof that past popes had erred. Gladstone's remarks were directed against the Ultramontanes; but the notion that Catholic converts had to renounce their 'moral and mental freedom' and were wanting in 'civil loyalty' was especially offensive to the Papists in Gladstone's own Liberal entourage, like Newman's disciple the Marquis of Ripon, himself the son of a Prime Minister, who had resigned the Grand Mastership of the English Freemasons to become a Catholic even while Gladstone was writing. Another Catholic and Liberal ex-Minister, Emly, urged Newman to reply. Newman began in early October 1874 to write with difficulty, but on the 27th gave it up. Meanwhile, in early November Gladstone expanded his paragraph into a pamphlet, *The Vatican Decrees in their Bearing on Civil Allegiance: a Political Expostulation*, declaring in the most lurid language that the 'myrmidons of the apostolic chamber' had mounted in the Syllabus of Errors and the Vatican Decrees 'so daring a raid upon the civil sphere', in order to restore the temporal power even 'on the ashes of the city, and amidst the whitening bones of the people'.[46]

The Ariadne's thread through the picturesque and tangled mazes of Gladstone's prose was the idea that the Vatican Council had made Catholics the political slaves of the Pope, so that in secular matters they owed obedience to the Pope and not the Queen. Englishmen could only read his words as those of an ex-Prime Minister, the leader of that Liberal Party which was the champion of the freedom of Catholics, now declaring that their religious faith was incompatible with civil liberty.

Ambrose de Lisle failed to impress Gladstone with Newman's argument that papal infallibility was limited to the enunciation of general principles, and so was no sanction for particular papal political acts. Newman was also in contact with Gladstone through Acton, and took the point made by Acton in a public letter which gave great offence to Catholics, that they could not be held party to past papal atrocities like Pius V's attempt to kill Elizabeth I. But as Newman told Emly, Gladstone's pamphlet was one which he felt he could answer. He had, however, terrible difficulty in following Gladstone's 'rambling and slovenly' logic, so that he was 'plucking every morning what I had done the day before',[47] until on 23 November 1874 the tract began to write itself. He was doubtful about publication, despite the importunities of a large number of distinguished Catholics, including the Duke of Norfolk, de Lisle, Lady Fullerton and Bishop Thomas Brown, and as late as 8

December, when Newman was sending parts of his text to Pickering for printing, he was still declining requests that he should write. Despite a sprained thumb, he finished the work on 21 December 1874 in the form of a public letter, having persuaded the reluctant and bashful Duke of Norfolk to be the addressee. That fact was an argument in itself; there was a sort of absurdity in alleging that the Earl Marshal of England was disloyal as a slave of Rome.

In fact, Gladstone's dilemma was an unreal one. It carried force only as an illiberal appeal to the English folk memory of past Catholic cruelties, but it did not deal with Catholics as they were. It was true that Irish Catholics were increasingly rebellious, but that had nothing to do with political incitement by the Pope; English administrations like Gladstone's were, if anything, accustomed to begging him to exercise his assumed political power to curb his Irish flock's excesses, an area where he was all but powerless. There was a similar absurdity to Gladstone's argument that Catholics had been granted emancipation at a time when they were Gallicans, as if their Gallicanism had been a condition of their political freedom. As Newman pointed out, the papal claims had been precisely in 1829 what they were in 1874. Nor did Newman think that Gladstone had any cause to blame on the Vatican decrees the defeat of his Irish University Bill: the Pope and the bulk of the Irish Church had been consistent for a generation in their opposition to mixed education, and Irish Catholics had the same constitutional right to act as an interest group in Parliament as the Nonconformists or the brewers. In any case, Gladstone had no intention of following his argument through to its logical conclusion, by denying Ultramontane Catholics their political freedom as men hostile to liberty itself. Newman had an easy case to argue: he was technically correct in denying that *Quanta Cura* or the Syllabus or the Vatican decrees had made papal political decisions infallible and so binding on Catholics, and Gladstone was wrong.

Newman's central aim was, however, not to attack Gladstone, but to distinguish his own precise views of the Vatican Decrees and the limits of papal power from the wilder claims of the neo-Ultramontanes. For this, Gladstone had provided no more than a pretext: 'Catholics may in good measure thank themselves, and no one else', wrote Newman in the opening pages of the *Letter*,

for having alienated from them so religious a mind. There are those among us, as it must be confessed, who for years past have conducted themselves as if no responsibility attached to wild words and overbearing deeds; who have stated truths in the most paradoxical form, and stretched principles till they were close upon snapping; and who at length, having done their best to set the house on fire, leave to others the task of putting out the flame. The English people are sufficiently sensitive of the claims

374

of the Pope, without having them, as if in defiance, flourished in their faces.[48]

If Gladstone had misunderstood Rome, Rome's neo-Ultramontane partisans had given him excuse; and with this flourish, Newman defied Manning and Ward and all their works.

The Ultramontane movement had, however, become a reassertion of the freedom of the Church against the all-embracing modern liberal State. On that essential principle, Newman agreed with the neo-Ultramontanes, as he named the Pope 'the one faithful representative'[49] of the ancient Church in her resistance to the civil power. Christ had left his people a kingdom, but 'where is it? If all that can be found of it is what can be discerned at Constantinople or Canterbury, I say, it has disappeared'.[50] 'As to the Oriental Churches, every one knows in what bondage they lie, whether they are under the rule of the Czar or of the Sultan.'[51] Not so modern Rome, or the Church of the Fathers. The Oxford Movement had been an attempt to reclaim their spirit, against Caesarism and Erastianism: Hurrell Froude had described the Church as ' "united" to the State as Israel to Egypt', while Keble had called any alliance on these terms *'not only fatal, but monstrous!'*[52] If the Pope now claimed the title of Vicar of Christ or of Pope itself, it was because he now alone guaranteed that full measure of ecclesiastical independence once asserted by all the bishops of the ancient ecumenical world.

What infallibility did not mean, however, was what Gladstone seemed to think it meant, an infallibility in the realm of morals which made any single papal directive absolutely binding on Catholics. Any Catholic textbook on morality would show how small a place papal decisions take up there, these being confined to condemnations of general principles where some difficulty or doubt had arisen. The greater part of the moral law was perfectly clear, and rested not on the Pope but on the internal authority of conscience: so 'that there are extreme cases in which Conscience may come into collision with the word of a Pope, and is to be followed in spite of that word'.[53] This was the doctrine of conscience which Catholics shared with 'Anglicans, Wesleyans, the various Presbyterian sects in Scotland',[54] 'the internal witness of both the existence and the law of God', which took as its rule and measure of duty 'not utility, nor expedience, nor the happiness of the greatest number'.[55] On general moral issues, mankind has no extraordinary need of the Pope, because it has a private pope within:

Conscience is the aboriginal Vicar of Christ, a prophet in its informations, a monarch in its peremptoriness, a priest in its blessings and anathemas, and, even though the eternal priesthood throughout the Church could cease to be, in it the sacerdotal principle would remain and would have a sway.[56]

In this, conscience was the voice of God, our inner pope: and it was that understanding of conscience which stood in contrast to the 'so-called liberty of conscience' condemned by Pope Gregory XVI and by Pius IX in *Quanta Cura*, the right of any man to think and to act for himself without reference to the God within. But as one can only accept papal authority conscientiously, so any pope who spoke against conscience in the true sense 'would commit a suicidal act . . . The Pope, who comes of Revelation, has no jurisdiction over Nature . . . ' Indeed when 'the Papal chair was filled by men, who gave themselves up to luxury, security, and a Pagan kind of Christianity . . . the Church lost, thereby, and has lost to this day, one-half of Europe . . . '[57] But such behaviour had nothing to do with infallibility, and nor did the papal powers of excommunication and interdict:

Was St. Peter infallible on that occasion at Antioch when St. Paul withstood him? was St. Victor infallible when he separated from his communion the Asiatic Churches? or Liberius when in like manner he excommunicated Athanasius? And, to come to later times, was Gregory XIII., when he had a medal struck in honour of the Bartholomew massacre? Or Paul IV in his conduct towards Elizabeth? or Sextus V. when he blessed the Armada? or Urban VIII. when he persecuted Galileo? No Catholic ever pretends that these Popes were infallible in these acts.[58]

Infallibility could not be extended to particular acts from the general moral truths which the Pope was bound to uphold. 'Certainly, if I am obliged to bring religion into after-dinner toasts, (which indeed does not seem quite the thing)', wrote Newman, 'I shall drink, – to the Pope, if you please, – still, to Conscience first, and to the Pope afterwards.'[59] Conscience, then, takes priority over papal authority, should there be conflict between them: 'were I actually a soldier or sailor in her Majesty's service, and sent to take part in a war which I could not in my conscience see to be unjust, and should the Pope suddenly bid all Catholic soldiers and sailors to retire from the service, . . . I should not obey him'.[60]

Gladstone agreed with Newman that the encyclical *Quanta Cura* and the accompanying Syllabus of Errors did not claim to be infallible; but Gladstone thought that this made them no less binding on Catholics. Newman's reply was a subtle restatement of that principle of the confessional State, the State which upheld the one true religion, to which he and Gladstone had devoted their young lives. Now, men 'born in the new civilization, are shocked to witness in the abiding Papal system the words, ways, and works of their grandfathers. In my own lifetime has that old world been alive, and has gone its way'.[61] The Pope was merely expounding the Church of Englandism of Newman's youth, the ancient principle of European civilization which had survived the Reformation. 'We were faithful to the tradition of fifteen hundred years. All this was called Toryism, and men gloried in the name; now it is called Popery and reviled. When I was young the State had a conscience, and the Chief Justice of the day pronounced . . . that Christianity was the law of the land.'[62] All that was then changed by recent historical circumstance, and Newman took a shuddering glance back over the death of the old world for which he had fought:

the whole theory of Toryism, hitherto acted on, came to pieces and went the way of all flesh . . . Not a hundred Popes could have hindered it . . . The Pope has denounced the sentiment that he ought to come to terms with 'progress, liberalism, and the new civilization'. I have no thought at all of disputing his words. I leave the great problem to the future. God will guide other Popes to act when Pius goes, as He has guided him. No one can dislike the democratic principle more than I do. No one mourns, for instance, more than I, over the state of Oxford, given up, alas! to 'liberalism and progress', to the forfeiture of her great medieval motto, 'Dominus illuminatio mea', and with a consequent call on her to go to Parliament or the Heralds College for a new one; but what can we do? All I know is, that Toryism, that is, loyalty to persons, 'springs immortal in the human breast;' that Religion is a spiritual loyalty; and that Catholicity is the only divine form of Religion.[63]

Newman might have much more brutally detailed Gladstone's own inconsistencies in abandoning his youthful Toryism. His target, again, was really elsewhere, among the neo-Ultramontanes, as he denied that the Syllabus had any direct dogmatic authority and argued that its condemnations had to be understood in the context of the original documents from which they were cited, and by way of a professional theological exegesis of the technical language contained in them. It was, however, Newman's conclusion that gave greatest offence in Rome:

Now, the Rock of St. Peter on its summit enjoys a pure and serene atmosphere, but there is a great deal of Roman *malaria* at the foot of it. While the Holy Father was in great earnestness and charity addressing the Catholic world by his Cardinal Minister, there were circles of light-minded men in his city who were laying bets with each other whether the Syllabus would 'make a row in Europe' or not. . . . it was very easy to kindle a flame in the mass of English and other visitors at Rome which with a very little nursing was soon strong enough to take care of itself.[64]

The passage has a decided ambiguity. On its surface, the 'light-minded men' were simply the Roman gambling fraternity; but a wider reference for the meaning of 'Roman *malaria*' was possible to Newman's readers, and to Rome itself.

It remained for Newman to explain the sense in which he received infallibility, as a self-confessed 'minimizer' of the meaning of the doctrine. In this, he was greatly assisted by the work *True and False Infallibility* by the Secretary General of the Council, Bishop Joseph Fessler, himself an Ultramontane, translated from the German by Ambrose St John. As Newman summarized the matter, the Pope only

> speaks *ex cathedrâ*, or infallibly, when he speaks, first, as the Universal Teacher; secondly, in the name and with the authority of the Apostles; thirdly, on a point of faith or morals; fourthly, with the purpose of binding every member of the Church to accept and believe his decision.
>
> These conditions of course contract the range of his infallibility most materially. Hence [the eighteenth-century Dominican theologian Charles-René] Billuart speaking of the Pope, says, 'Neither in conversation, nor in discussion, nor in interpreting Scripture or the Fathers, nor in consulting, nor in giving his reasons for the point which he has defined, nor in answering letters, nor in private deliberations, supposing he is setting forth his own opinion, is the Pope infallible,' t. ii., p. 110. And for this simple reason, because, on these various occasions of speaking his mind, he is not in the chair of the universal doctor.[65]

Nor is the Pope infallible, any more than a council is infallible, in matters of physical science unrelated to the dogma defined, in the prefaces or introductions to definitions, in his supporting reasons or arguments, or even in his occasional or incidental teachings in matters of faith or morals in papal encyclicals. To teach infallibly, the Pope must also intend to be teaching a doctrine necessary to salvation, and therefore binding on all Christians; and in such teaching, he is merely divinely assisted, not directly inspired. In the strict sense he does not define new doctrine; his authority only extends to the enunciation of truths already within the deposit of doctrine taught by the Apostles, or within the universal natural or moral law.

This 'wise and gentle *minimism*',[66] as Newman called it, has a further paradoxical safeguard, that what is infallible in papal utterances is a matter of expert interpretation by the *Schola Theologorum*, the collective judgement of the body of theologians, which is not itself infallible. Indeed, it was Newman's understanding of the Vatican decrees which in the years after his death was tacitly received by the Church; and it is generally accepted now that papal infallibility has been unambiguously exercised only twice in the modern period, in defining the Marian doctrines of the Immaculate Conception in 1854 and of the Assumption in 1950.

'I am like a man who has gone up in a balloon, and has a chance of all sorts of adventures, from gas escapes, from currents of air, from intanglements in forests, from the wide sea, and does not feel himself safe till he gets back to his fireside',[67] wrote Newman to Charles Russell of Maynooth, in the aftermath of the pamphlet's appearance. At first, it seemed that he need hardly worry. Gladstone appreciated Newman's 'genial and gentle' handling of him, declaring that Newman had invested 'even these painful subjects with something of a golden glow'.[68] Newman's reply to Gladstone had a touch of the self-consciousness of one Eminent Victorian writing to another: 'from the time that you were launched into public life', Newman wrote, 'you have retained a hold on my thoughts and on my gratitude . . . What a fate it is, that, now when so memorable a career has reached its formal termination, I should be the man, on the very day on which it is closed, to present to you . . . a controversial pamphlet as my offering . . . I do not think I ever can be sorry for what I have done, but I never can cease to be sorry for the necessity of doing it'.[69] Gladstone replied that his attack had not been on Roman Catholics but on 'Vaticanismus'. What Newman thought was the end of Gladstone's career, his withdrawal from the Liberal leadership, was a new beginning.

Other High Church readers like Pusey's biographer Henry Liddon were also appreciative of Newman's essay, but his dearest reward was the almost uniform applause of his fellow Catholics. There was approval from Archbishop Errington and Bishops Ullathorne, Clifford and William Vaughan, from the Fullertons, de Lisle and Thomas Allies, from George Bowyer and John Pope Hennessy, and most glowingly, in a pastoral from Cardinal Cullen, read in all the Dublin churches, describing Newman as 'the great and pious and learned rector of the Catholic University, whom Ireland will ever revere'.[70] This was the first that Newman had heard from Cullen since 1862, and he was overwhelmed; he replied to the Cardinal that no commendation of the pamphlet had 'given me such heartfelt pleasure as your Eminence's notice of me'.[71] Cullen was reputed a stiff Ultramontane, but even Herbert Vaughan approved, while Newman's letter to W. G. Ward, which was at least appreciative of Ward's straightforwardness, received a sad reply, declaring that the breach between them had left Ward 'a kind of intellectual orphan'.[72] Ward's essay in the *Dublin Review* dissented from the tone of two or three of Newman's passages, but unsaid his old assertion that Catholics had to believe the Syllabus was infallible.[73] Later Ward would change his mind again, and in the *Dublin*, complain of 'the language of extraordinary severity'[74] with which the *Letter* had attacked the neo-Ultramontanes. An Italian Jesuit, Paul Bottalla, also assailed Newman in the *Liverpool Times*; but after a life of controversy, it seemed strange to Newman to enjoy so much unstinted praise.

Clifford and Errington warned Newman that there might be trouble in Rome over his assertion that the Pope had inherited the prerogatives of the bishops of the ancient Church, as if he had not always possessed them. On the 3 February 1875, Cardinal Franchi, who had followed Barnabò as Prefect of Propaganda, wrote to Manning that while the first part of the *Letter to Norfolk* was triumphant ('trionfante'), the second part contained propositions calculated to do great harm to the minds of the faithful ('a far molto male nelle menti dei fedeli').[75] Franchi also wrote in stronger terms to Ullathorne. Manning was always the statesman, and was not one to let personal pique ruin Newman's Roman triumph. His reply to Franchi begged that 'no *public* action' to be taken over Newman.

1. The heart of the revered Fr Newman is as right and as Catholic as it is possible to be.
2. His pamphlet exercises a most powerful influence upon the non-Catholics of this country.
3. In like manner, the effect of it on Catholics of an intractable disposition and incorrect ideas is a wholesome one.
4. The said Father has never hitherto so openly defended the prerogatives and infallible magisterium of the Roman Pontiff, although he has always believed and proclaimed these truths . . .

Any censure would only revive the blaze of domestic controversy, 'now by the grace of God extinguished'.[76] Ullathorne wrote in similar vein: Newman might have written 'incautiously and imprudently' about the sins of past popes, but 'this arises from his method of argument *ex abundantia concessionis*. His method wins the minds of Protestants'.[77] These letters did not pacify Rome. The Pope himself indicated to Manning's agent that while he did not intend condemning Newman, 'he would wish that some friend might let Newman know that there were some objectionable passages in his pamphlet. He had heard, he said, that good had been effected by it, and that the notion of Newman's opposition to the Pope was completely dispelled'.[78]

This mixed blame and praise bore fruit on 22 October 1875 when Franchi sent a list of eleven censurable propositions in the *Letter* to Ullathorne, asking the Bishop to point out to Newman 'how pernicious they may be to others'.[79] The Roman censor declared heretical two of Newman's letters written shortly after the Council and cited by Newman in the work to show his changing mind, while his attacks on the popes in the *Letter* were 'false and contrary to genuine history', and the remark about 'Roman *malaria*' was stigmatized, with unconscious humour, as 'troppo irreverente' to the Curia Romana.[80] Ullathorne sensibly replied on 2 December that a year had elapsed without controversy in England; that if he carried the censures to Newman, he would see that they were Roman; that Newman 'has often complained that the authorities at Rome do not deal with him directly and openly, but by intermediaries and secretly';[81] and that if Rome wanted action it should act itself.

In Newman's previous scrapes with Rome, the attacks had come from England, and Rome had displayed a puzzled inactivity. In his last scrape, Rome itself had taken the initiative and Newman's national standing in England had united the English Catholics round him.

The chief casualty of the affair was Ambrose St John, who though overburdened with duties in the church and in the school had sat up all night translating Fessler's book on infallibility from German. After thirty years' hard work for Newman and the Oratory, he collapsed, apparently with heat stroke, after walking on a hot day, 28 April 1875, from the opening of a Passionist chapel at Harborne. He spent four weeks after in a state of intermittent excitement or delirium. On his last evening, wrote Newman, he 'hugged me close to him, so close that I laughed and said "he will give me a stiff neck." I did not understand he was taking leave of me'. He clung to Newman even while he ate some bread and butter – the doctor had recommended generous feeding – and when Newman at last freed himself 'took my hand, and clasped it so tight as to frighten me . . . I called to those about him to loosen his hand, little thinking that it was to be his last sign of love'.[82]

The mocking weather was glorious: 'I never recollect such a May',[83] wrote Newman. St John seemed to be recovering, then died on the night of the 24th. After his death, Newman said the office for the dead and then the dawn Mass at 2 a.m. on the 25th, St Philip's Eve, for the repose of his closest friend's soul. 'At Rome 28 years ago he was always so working for and relieving me of all trouble', wrote Newman to Blachford, 'that being young and Saxon looking, the Romans called him my Angel Guardian. As far as this world was concerned I was his first and last.'[84] 'I am under the greatest affliction which has ever befallen me',[85] he told the Oratory's former schoolteacher Robert Moody, asking for his prayers. 'It is an open wound', he wrote to Miss Holmes, 'which in old men cannot be healed.'[86] There is no evidence for the story that Newman spent the night of St John's death lying by the corpse; but their names are joined in the simplest of crosses which stands above their common grave.

28

The Via Media Revisited

One pleasure of Newman's old age was the affection of Richard Church's children, Helen, Mary and Edith, who presented him in 1870 with a copy of *Alice in Wonderland* and an explanation – it seems strange that he needed it – of its famous parodies. Church himself had achieved some literary eminence, but he became a national figure in 1871 when, much against his own wishes, Gladstone plucked him from the obscurity of his Somersetshire parish to make him Dean of the long-neglected cathedral of St Paul's. In 1876, his daughters sent Newman *The Hunting of the Snark*, with its dedicatory poem 'in memory of golden summer hours and whispers of a summer sea'. As Newman wrote to Helen, it reawakened his own earliest memory:

> The little book is not all of it nonsense, though amusing nonsense; it has two pleasant prefixes of another sort. One of them is the 'Inscription to a dear child'; the style of which, in words and manner, is so entirely of the school of Keble, that it could not have been written had the Christian Year never made its appearance.
>
> The other, 'the Easter greeting to every child etc' is likely to touch the hearts of old men more than of those for whom it is intended. I recollect well my own thoughts and feelings, such as the author describes, as I lay in my crib in the early spring, with outdoor scents, sounds and sights wakening me up, and especially the cheerful ring of the mower's scythe on the lawn, which Milton long before me had noted; – and how in coming down stairs slowly, for I brought down both feet on each step, I said to myself 'This is June!' though what my particular experience of June was, and how it was broad enough to be of matter of reflection, I really cannot tell.
>
> Can't you, Mary, and Edith recollect something of the same kind? though you may not think so much of it as I do now?
>
> May the day come for all of us, of which Easter is the promise, when that first spring, may return to us, and a sweetness which cannot die may gladden our garden.[1]

The letter was passed to Carroll, who was touched by the remarks about the 'Easter greeting'. Newman was also now closer to Jemima's grown-up children, who had been cut off from him in their childhood by his conversion; he settled £20 of his annuity on his neice Jane Mozley and enjoyed a long correspondence with his nephew the mathematician John Rickards Mozley, while he developed a warm respect and affection for his former disciple, Jemima's sister-in-law Anne Mozley. Newman also had the devotion of the fifty-seven year old Emily Bowles, who when Frances Wootten died full of good works in 1876 gallantly succeeded her as matron of the school. Miss Bowles was touched to find Newman waiting for her in person at New Street station. There was only the occasional distinguished visitor at the Oratory, exclusive of the parents of the boys at the school. The Baron von Hügel recalled Newman's ecstasies in the Botanical Gardens over the blooming rhododendrons and azaleas, 'as evidence of the work of Mind'.[2] This, how-ever, was von Hügel's only visit to Newman; as the greatest Roman Catholic theologian of the next generation, the Baron would be more critical of Newman's person – he thought that Newman was a puritan depressive who lacked the joy of the Roman saints[3] – but he always worshipped his mind. Much of Newman's old-age melancholy was simply the result of the death of friends, or their unconscionable time in dying, as with the faithful Edward Caswall. 'I always say', wrote Newman to Monsell ' "No one has ever had such friends as I have had!" . . . And now pray for me, for these strokes, the penance for living long, are very trying.'[4]

Newman made his last main entries in his journal in 1874 and 1876, and juxtaposed the love of friends with his many disappointments.

I have been startled on considering, that in the last 15 years I have only written two books, the Apologia and the Essay on Assent – of which the former was almost extempore. What have I been doing with my time. . .

Another reason, closely connected with this, was my habit, or even nature, of not writing & publishing without a *call* . . .

I have before now said in writing to Cardinals Wiseman & Barnabò, when I considered myself treated with slight and unfairness, 'So this is the return made to me for working for the Catholic cause for so many years', i.e. to that effect. –

I feel it still, and ever shall – but it was not a disappointed ambition which I was then expressing in words, but a scorn and wonder at the *injustice* shown me, and at the demand of toadyism on my part, if I was to get their favour, & the favour of Rome.

I knew perfectly well, when I so wrote, that such language would look like disappointment at having received no promotion, and moreover was the worst way of getting it . . .

As to my freedom from ambitious views, I don't know that I need defend myself from the imputation of them. Qui s'excuse, s'accuse. But in fact I have from the first presaged that I should get no thanks for what I was doing . . .

In 1850 in a Sermon at St Chad's, 'As to ourselves, the world has long ago done its worst against us. . . . We know our place and our fortunes &c'. . .

I am dissatisfied with the whole of this book. It is more or less a complaint from one end to the other. But it represents what has been the real state of my mind, and what my Cross has been.

O how light a Cross – think what the Crosses of others are! And think of the compensation, compensation in even this world – I have touched on it in a parenthesis in the foregoing page. I have had, it is true, no recognition in high quarters – but what warm kind letters in private have I had! and how many! and what public acknowledgements! How ungrateful I am, or should I be, if such letters and such notices failed to content me.[5]

These consolations included the continuing regard of Gladstone, who unsuccessfully invited Newman to Hawarden to meet Tennyson. Gladstone had been tempted to write to Newman about his *Lectures on the Turks*, in order to draw him into the controversy over Gladstone's own denunciation of the Turkish atrocities in Bulgaria. Newman declined to be party to the agitation: given the atheists and anti-Catholics in Gladstone's list of supporters, he could only have subscribed to it on political grounds, and thought priests best kept out of politics.[6] In June 1877, Gladstone visited the modern municipal wonder of Joseph Chamberlain's Birmingham and, when Chamberlain asked him what he wished to see, asked to see Newman. 'The wonderful pair were nervous and constrained, and each seemed a little relieved when, after twenty minutes of commonplace conversation, they rose to part.'[7]

The encounter suggests the exchange of formal courtesies between two stately galleons, each sufficient to itself. Gladstone was a distant disciple; for others, Newman's allure was bound up with the allure of Rome. He was the principal third player in the continuing tragicomedy of Thomas Arnold, who at the maximum of inconvenience to his family and himself asked Newman to receive him back into the Roman Catholic Church, thereby losing the chance of the Oxford chair of Anglo-Saxon. The enraged Mrs Arnold thundered her loathing at Newman, who had for the second time brought her husband into the Roman Church, to the destruction of his worldly prospects; 'and', she wrote, 'from the bottom of my heart I curse you for it. You know well how very weak and unstable he is, and you also know that he has a wife and eight children . . . for the second time you counselled him to ignore every social duty and become a pervert. He has brought utter ruin upon us all, but what is that to you?' Newman could not help being amused that 'so sweet and amiable a fellow as Arnold should have such a yoke fellow – but, except as an aesthetic contrast, it is marvellous that such a pair should be'.[8]

One at least of Newman's achievements now seemed to have a future. By August 1877, the Oratory itself was in a healthier condition, with four novices and the prospect of more. There had been few new members in the 1860s. The Lancastrian John Norris entered in 1865, and Thomas Alder Pope, after the deaths of his wife and children, in 1867. Both were ordained in 1869. As Pio Nono noticed at St John's audience in 1867, the community was an ageing one. But two of the sons of Newman's beloved Serjeant Bellasis decided to become Oratorians, Richard in 1875 and Henry in 1877; the convert clergyman Arthur Hutton entered in 1876; and other recruits included a fine Oxford scholar, Thomas Eaglesim, in 1878, and in 1877 J. R. R. Tolkien's warm and boisterous future guardian Francis Morgan, who had a private income from Spanish sherry and was to make the Oratory the young Tolkien's second home. These gains were balanced by the loss of Henry Bittleston through a financial peccadillo in 1879. After failing a vocation with the Carthusians, he became a mission-priest under a great north London evangelist, George Bampfield. The joker in the new intake was the brilliant but erratic Hutton. Newman wrote a preface to Hutton's refutation of Anglican Orders, published in 1879, but took exception to the 'unkindness and uppishness' of some of his remarks about reunion with the Anglicans, though he looked to Hutton to become 'one of the lights and supports' of his Oratory.[9] He was to be sadly disabused.

The Oratory and his writings were Newman's two life works. He embarked on his last major publication requiring extensive new writing in December 1876, a two-volume collection of his chief Anglican polemical works entitled *The Via Media*.[10] The first volume was the third edition of the *Lectures on the Prophetical Office of the Church*. The second volume was an assemblage of eleven more occasional pieces, spanning his tract on the Church Missionary Society of 1830 to his retraction of his anti-Catholic statements in 1841, and including a good deal of the documentation of Tract 90. For the first volume, the *Lectures on the Prophetical Office*, Newman wrote a new preface which serves as a restatement of his position towards the Anglican *Via Media* as a whole. As his final exposition of his theory of the Church, and his theory of religion, it remains one of his important intellectual legacies.

One intention of the preface was simply to restate his answer as a Roman Catholic to his former criticisms of Rome. There was no point in changing the text of his writings as an Anglican to exclude old error. '*Litera scripta manet*':[11] the written word remains. But lest others after his death should republish the poison, he was also supplying the antidote. His *Lectures on the Prophetical Office* had, Newman thought, too simply ascribed Roman error to Roman theology, whereas elsewhere, as in Tract 90, he had deployed his favourite distinctions between an intellectual theology and popular devotion, to distinguish the Roman Church's official theological teaching from the superstitious abuses rife among ordinary Roman Catholics. There was yet a further distinction between Catholicism as an intellectual and a popular system, and its political and institutional form, which in the Roman Papacy looked to otherwise sympathetic non-Catholics like tyranny.

'It is so ordered on high', wrote Newman in one of his frankest admissions, 'that in our day Holy Church should present just that aspect to my country-men which is most consonant with their ingrained prejudices against her,'[12] as a popular superstition and as a political tyranny. Newman's resolution of the problem ultimately derived from Calvin's distinctions between Christ's offices as Prophet, Priest and King which Newman asserted are, in so far as men on earth are equal to the task, discharged on earth by 'Holy Church, His mystical Body and Bride, a Divine Institution, and the shrine and organ of the Paraclete, who speaks through her till the end comes':

He is Prophet, Priest, and King; and after His pattern, and in human measure, Holy Church has a triple office too: not the Prophetical alone and in isolation, as these Lectures virtually teach, but three offices, which are indivisible, though diverse, viz. teaching, rule, and sacred ministry . . .

Christianity, then, is at once a philosophy, a political power, and a religious rite: as a religion, it is Holy; as a philosophy, it is Apostolic; as a political power, it is imperial, that is, One and Catholic. As a religion, its special centre of action is pastor and flock; as a philosophy, the Schools; as a rule, the Papacy and its Curia.[13]

Thus the prophetical office embraces all the philosophical, intellectual and theological aspects of faith; the regal, its administration and government; the priestly, worship, prayer, spirituality and every aspect of the devotional life. The first is primarily exercised by the theologians, the third by the clergy and laity, the second by the Pope and Curia; and this remains true, even though there is an overlap in these functions, in so far as the bishop both rules and teaches, and the Pope exercises these offices as well. What impressed Newman, however, was the difficulty of holding these elements together, for they use different instruments and serve different ends. Devotion serves worship; theology serves truth; and rule serves order or expedience: goals which tend to be incompatible with one another in everyday life, as well as in matters of religion. ' "Who", in St Paul's words, "is sufficient for these things?" Who, even with divine aid, shall successfully administer offices so independent of each other, so divergent, and so con-flicting? What line of conduct, except on the long, the very long run, is at once edifying, expedient, and true?'[14] The Church is promised a formal theological infallibility. But only impeccability would have kept her from corruption, and each of these offices has its own tendency to run to excess: devotion tends to become superstition, theology to become rationalism and rule to become tyranny.

It is, however, in the nature of these instruments to prevent the excesses of the others. But 'ambition, craft, cruelty, and superstition are not commonly the characteristic of theologians'. Theology tends to control these ills; 'nor is religion ever in greater danger than when, in consequence of national or international troubles, the Schools of theology have . . . ceased to be'.[15] Newman thereby voiced in a veiled fashion the complaint that in his own century the decay of the theological schools and the growth of papal power had meant that the theologians in the Church had too little influence, and the regal office of Rome had too much.

Newman therefore had a very large conception of the function of the theologian and theology:

Theology is the fundamental and regulating principle of the whole Church system. It is commensurate with Revelation, and Revelation is the initial and essential idea of Christianity. It is the subject-matter, the formal cause, the expression, of the Prophetical Office, and, as being such, has created both the Regal Office and the Sacerdotal. And it has in a certain sense a power of jurisdiction over those offices, as being its own creations, theologians being ever in request and in employment in keeping within bounds both the political and popular elements in the Church's constitution, – elements which are far more congenial than itself to the human mind, are far more liable to excess and corruption, and are ever struggling to liberate themselves from those restraints which are in truth necessary for their well-being.[16]

There is, then, a sense in which the theologian has created the worshipping office of the priesthood and people and the regal office of the Pope, and has a kind of logical primacy over them; and as mankind is more likely to be superstitious or tyrannical than rationalist, so the theological office ideally acts as a curb or check on popular superstition and on papal actions taken out of expedience or tyranny.

This does not mean, however, that it is the theologian's role to rule. That is, by definition, the task of the regal office. Moreover, as Newman had written elsewhere, the original life of religion lies in devotion, which is required to supply the reason with its raw materials, so that the priestly office has a kind of chronological primacy over the prophetical. In any case mankind needs order and love as well as truth: 'theology cannot always have its own way; it is too hard, too intellectual, too exact, to be always equitable, or to be always compassionate; and it sometimes has a conflict or overthrow, or has to consent to a truce or a compromise, in consequence of the rival force of religious sentiment or ecclesiastical interests; and that, sometimes in great matters, sometimes in unimportant'.[17] Thus the Church will sometimes permit a bogus relic to sustain a popular devotion or one which errs by excess of love. There is a time when the whole truth must be told, but at others there is a positive duty of concealment, in religion as in society at large:

> Veracity, like other virtues, lies in a mean. Truth indeed, but not necessarily the whole truth, is the rule of Society. Every class and profession has its secrets; the family lawyer, the medical adviser, the politician, as well as the priest. The physician often dares not tell the whole truth to his patient about his case, knowing that to do so would destroy his chance of recovery. Statesmen in Parliament, I suppose, fight each other with second-best arguments, the real reasons for the policy which they are respectively advocating being, as each is conscious to each, not these, but reasons of state, secrets whether of her Majesty's Privy Council or of diplomacy. As to the polite world, which, to be sure, is in itself not much of an authority, I think an authoress of the last century illustrates in a tale how it would not hold together, if every one told the whole truth to every one, as to what he thought of him. From the time that the Creator clothed Adam, concealment is in some sense the necessity of our fall.[18]

This might sound like an apology for lying, but is another illustration of a strand of argument in the *Grammar*, that religious debate and religious conviction parallel those in other forms of life. Thus if there is a conflict between truth and authority, or truth and devotion, it is the particular circumstances of the case which decide which good should prevail. The Church had silenced Galileo, because he was in conflict with the then popular understanding of Scripture, and it was charity to delay the reception of the new interpretation until it could be harmonized with the imagination of the Catholic world. But then God himself had told his chosen people only such truth as they could bear. In his divine economy, he had disclosed his revelation gradually and partially; under the old dispensation, he had permitted divorce, cruelty and even occasionally the idolatry which it had been the Old Law's special mission to destroy. As St Paul declared, God had 'winked' at the heathens' ignorance.[19] That time had passed with the coming of Christ; but even Our Lord had found acceptable the woman's 'fetish reverence to the hem of His garment'. So too,

> the poor Neapolitan crone, who chatters to the crucifix, refers that crucifix in her deep mental consciousness to an original who once hung upon a cross in flesh and blood; but if, nevertheless she is puzzle-headed enough to assign virtue to it in itself, she does no more than the woman in the Gospel . . . Yet He praised her before the multitude, praised her for what might, not without reason, be called an idolatrous act; for in His new law He was opening the meaning of the word 'idolatry,' and applying it to various sins, to the adoration paid to rich men, to the thirst after gain, to ambition, and the pride of life, idolatries worse in His judgment than

the idolatry of ignorance, but not commonly startling or shocking to educated minds.[20]

In its accommodation to ordinary understanding, the Church had to make do with human nature as it was. Even St Paul had become ' "to the Jews as a Jew, that he might gain the Jews, and to them that were without the law, as if he were without the law, and became all things to all men that he might save all" '.[21] So too, St John might be said 'to have used the language of heathen classics with the purpose of interesting and gaining the Platonizing Jews',[22] just as the Jesuits tried to convert the eastern heathen by imitating their customs. Of course, 'tolerance may sometimes lead to pious frauds, which are simply wicked',[23] but the presentation of a truth may come in peculiar forms, and the scientific reason of the theologian must sometimes defer to the language of love.

The argument does not attract the modern mind which considers the ruthless pursuit of truth for its own sake the highest of virtues, and has hardly questioned whether the human appetite for truth, in such matters as nuclear research or genetic engineering, needs the restraint of either authority or popular opinion. Newman's examples of the influence of one office upon another also sound odd to the modern ear; as when he uses in illustration of the regal on the priestly the Labarum of Constantine. 'The sacred symbol of unresisting suffering, of self-sacrificing love, of life-giving grace, of celestial peace, became in the hands of the first Christian Emperor, with the sanction of the Church, his banner in fierce battle and the pledge of victory for his sword.'[24] As the implication of Newman's argument is that now one office rules, and now another, he does not hesitate to suggest that certain doctrinal issues like the validity of simoniacal or heretical or schismatic ordinations should be decided on the basis of what was practically or politically expedient; as, at least on the gravest occasions, 'no act could be theologically an error, which was absolutely and undeniably necessary for the unity, sanctity, and peace of the Church'.[25]

Newman's ultimate view of the Church is, then, one in which neither the priestly nor the prophetical nor the regal offices unduly predominate. Rather, they ideally stand in a judicious constitutional relationship to one another, respecting their separate provinces and maintaining an orderly balance and tension in which the one completes and supplies what the others lack. There is an implication that competition and conflict among them may be fruitful, as in the self-regulating systems of classical political economy or the Darwinian struggle of the fittest for survival – a strange innovation on traditional Christian ecclesiology, in which conflict had usually been regarded as sin. A friendly Anglican correspondent, Canon Robert Jenkins, thought that the 'evil of Roman divinity is the resolute determination to destroy all passing discords by false concords – and even to force every note into unison with the great keynote of the Pope . . . '[26] Newman retorted to this '*musical* theory of divinity' that 'the Pope is the key note, the Bishops the third, the Priests the 5th, the people the octave and the Protestants the flat 7th which needs resolving'.[27]

The chief importance of the preface, however, is that it contains a complete theory of religion: that any faith worth its salt will contain these three indispensable elements, a body of devotion and worship, an intellectual system and an institutional form and authority. Newman's conception was given a heavier statement in glutinous Germanic English in the famous second chapter of von Hügel's *Mystical Element of Religion*,[28] with the accompanying argument that in most religious traditions one or other aspect of the three tends to predominate, as in the famous story of the appearance of the Holy Family to three religious: the mystical Franciscan falls to his knees in ecstasy, the intellectual Dominican asks the Virgin her opinion of the doctrine of the Immaculate Conception, the institutional Benedictine suggests that St Joseph might consider sending his little boy to Downside Abbey school. Newman's idea thereby pinpoints the three great dangers to any religion, of superstition, rationalism and institutionalism, each the abuse of devotion, reason and order, which are essential goods in themselves.

In June 1877, Newman turned to a recasting of his *Essay on Development*, leaving him only his translations of Athanasius to republish, after which he felt that he could sing his '*Nunc dimittis*'. The publication of a Catholic selection of his Anglican sermons left him with the difficulty of purging them of non-Catholic doctrine and vocabulary. It was to be a difficulty renewed in the 1880s, when he refused to take part in a presentation of his complete works to the Holy Father, on the ground that so much Anglican error was mixed up in them.

That old error was bound up with his first great loyalty to Oxford, and Newman's reconsideration of his Oxford teaching was crowned in December 1877 by an invitation from the President of Trinity, Samuel William Wayte, to become the college's first Honorary Fellow. Newman wanted to accept with warmth, recalling his undergraduate days, and 'those good friends, nearly all now gone, whom I loved so much during them';[29] but he asked if he needed to put his name back on the university books, and declared that he must get the permission of his fellow Oratorians and of Ullathorne, and that he must not be understood to be implying approval of non-religious education. He was also anxious not to incur any new duties beyond his strength. He described the honour to Ullathorne as 'a very great compliment, perhaps the greatest I ever received . . . Trinity College has been the one and only seat of my affections at Oxford, and to see once more, before I am taken away, what I never thought I should see again, the place where I began the battle of life, with my good angel by my side, is a prospect almost too much for me to bear'.[30]

Despite his recent pastoral thundering against mixed education, Ullathorne replied that only good could come from the honour. Newman accepted it on 20 December, declaring it 'a most strange good fortune, after a long sixty years and more, to become again a freshman of my first and dear College'.[31] 'What a trial it will be!' he wrote to Maria Giberne, who was pining in exile for England: 'so many, not to say, nearly all I knew dead, and the place so altered.'[32] On 2 January 1878, the faithful Caswall died at last: the January calendar was now thick with anniversaries for Newman's Masses. 'So now', wrote Newman to Emily Bowles, recalling Fathers Joseph Gordon and Ambrose St John, 'the three most energetic and influential of the first Fathers of our Oratory lie together; and the three who from the first threw in their lot with me, from the moment they could do so . . . St Philip must see to their reward . . .'[33] 'And then it is so strange that I am going into the world again, and the Oxford world . . . it is strangely out of keeping with my morning and evening, with the mementos of the departed in my Mass, with my bed at night which is hung around with dear faces . . .'[34]

Having recast his *Essay on Development* for its third edition, he asked Wayte through Dean Church to accept the dedication of the work, with some trepidation about its polemical content: but, as he put it, he gave it 'because I have nothing else but it to offer . . .'[35] The return to Oxford with Neville, on 26 February 1878, was a minor triumph: he saw his old tutor Thomas Short, who was nearly ninety, called on Pusey, and saw Keble's memorial college. Newman's former rooms at Trinity had been decorated by their undergraduate occupant with pictures of actors and actresses. The historian James Bryce wrote that Newman's speech at dinner, with its reference to Thomas Short's famous lamb chops, mingled sadness and pleasure in a manner 'tenderly pathetic to us younger people . . . the voice so often heard in St Mary's retaining, faint though it had grown, the sweet modulations Oxford knew so well, and the aged face worn deep with the lines of thought, struggle and sorrow'.[36] To Maria Giberne, who demanded a full account of the occasion, Newman wrote with a 'sigh and smile' that 'I can only say with the "Needy knife grinder", "Story? heaven bless you, I have none to tell you – " . . . I know it was a trial to me and a pleasure – but I could not say more, if you put me on the rack – '.[37] Wayte was surprised to note that by leaving behind his master's gown and collecting his visiting cards, Newman intended to return to Trinity, so that Newman wondered if he was expected back, and feared 'lest they should find me too much of a good thing'.[38] One consequence of the visit was that James Bryce, as a Fellow of Oriel, encouraged the college to commission one of two portraits of Newman from the artist Walter William Ouless. After half a lifetime of exile from Oxford, Newman was once more an acknowledged prophet in his own country. A still more startling rehabilitation was to follow.

29

'And now a Cardinal'

It is always pleasant when a pupil rewards a teacher. Henry Fitzalan Howard, fifteenth Duke of Norfolk, was an industrious, conscientious, conservative, dignified, sometimes pompous young man who, abandoning the liberal Whig traditions of his own family, had become a Tory. He was very much aware, in the high Victorian manner, of his position and responsibilities as the titular lay leader of the English Catholic community, and was an active politician and a great philanthropist and paternalist, with a profound sense of his duty to his dependants and inferiors. He was acutely conscious both of Newman's spiritual stature in the echelons of upper-class religious England, and of the excuse which the doubts cast by other Catholics on Newman's Roman orthodoxy gave to Newman's non-Catholic admirers for despising and avoiding the Roman Catholic Church. The Duke saw in the grant of a cardinalate to Newman a means of demonstrating Newman's utter orthodoxy, of rewarding his converts, of removing an obstacle to the submission to Rome of non-Catholics under Newman's influence, and of increasing the popularity and prestige of both the Papacy and the English Catholic community in the eyes of educated Englishmen.

Leo XIII's anxiety to repair the breaches between Rome and the ruling powers of Europe enhanced the influence of a great English peer like Norfolk, who had a special claim on the Church's gratitude. His ecclesiastical charities were to be enormous – they were to include the massive new churches in Arundel and Norwich – and his linguist-cousin Edward Henry Howard had become a curial cardinal in 1877. Thus the Duke had the influence to push the proposal to make Newman a cardinal, and with the convert Marquis of Ripon and the Old Catholic Lord Petre he asked Manning to lay the matter before the Holy See. Manning's draft of a letter to the Cardinal Secretary of State Lorenzo Nina asking for the honour was everything that could be desired. Manning paid tribute to 'the singular and unequalled services rendered by Dr Newman to the Catholic faith . . . His submission to the Church has alone done more to awaken the mind of Englishmen to the Catholic religion . . . The veneration for his powers, his learning, and his life of singular piety and integrity is almost as deeply felt by the non Catholic population of this country as by the members of the Catholic Church . . . Nevertheless he has continued for thirty years without any token or mark of the confidence of the Holy See . . . It is obviously not only most desirable that this should be corrected: but obviously right that Dr Newman should be cleared of any unjust suspicion'. Manning recalled Rome's failure to follow through its original resolve to make Newman a bishop, and his own subsequent rejection of the proposal when it was renewed. 'There remains therefore only one mark of confidence of the Holy See to so distinguished a Priest. And no greater gratification to the Catholics of England could be given than by the elevation of Dr Newman into the Sacred College.'[1]

The letter was Manning at his best, statesmanlike and disregarding his private opinions in the interests of both justice and the Church. But it hardly reflected his private opinions as he afterwards retailed them to the intimate of his old age, the young J. E. C. Bodley. Manning's remarks were without personal bitterness, but 'the conversation moved to theological ground, and Manning's tone changed':

'From an observation you made,' he said, 'I gather that you are under the impression that Doctor Newman is a good Catholic.' I replied that such was my vague belief. He retorted: 'Either you are ignorant of the Catholic doctrine, or of the works of Doctor Newman' – he always said 'Doctor Newman' in Oxford fashion, and never gave him the title of Cardinal. After asking me which of Newman's books I had read, he proceeded to tick off on his tapering fingers, in his usual way, ten distinct heresies to be found in the most widely-read works of Dr Newman. This seemed to me, at the time, on a par with Voltaire's discovery of a series of heresies in the Lord's Prayer.[2]

The passage has its comic side, but Manning's private conviction that Newman was a heretic may explain the Cardinal's seeming failure in duty and charity in what followed.

The Duke approved Manning's letter to Nina, which with a few changes, kind to Manning, suggested by the Ultramontane Petre, was passed to Howard for delivery to Rome, but Howard delayed in England, so that the letter did not reach its destination in time for the Duke's audience with the Pope in December 1878. The Duke wrote to Manning from Paris asking him to write again to Rome, and reported to Ripon that, as the Pope had no prejudice against Newman, he had high hopes that the mission would succeed.[3] On 29 January 1879, Manning sent Nina's favourable reply to Ullathorne, and asked the Bishop to approach Newman to find out if he would accept the honour if it were to be offered. Newman was too unwell to visit Ullathorne at Oscott, but the Bishop requested that an Oratorian priest be sent for to take Newman the message, and supported this with a letter setting out seven reasons why Newman should accept. Ullathorne placed fifth in his list of arguments that Newman's elevation 'would bring for ever to an end those idle and mischievous rumours . . . that you have not the complete confidence of the Holy See'. 'The Pope', Ullathorne added, 'would scarcely I think, require you to live in Rome, unless it were your desire',[4] even though Roman residence was generally required of members of the Sacred College who were not themselves pastoral bishops of a see.

Newman replied to Ullathorne that he was not wanting in 'a sense of gratitude or the splendour of dignity' of an honour so far above him, 'the great honour which the Holy Father proposes with wonderful kindness to confer on one so insignificant, an honour quite transcendent and unparalleled, than which his Holiness has none greater to bestow'. He continued:

> For I am, indeed, old and distrustful of myself; I have lived now thirty years 'in my little nest' in my much loved Oratory, sheltered and happy, and would therefore entreat his Holiness not to take me from St Philip, my Father and Patron.
>
> By the love and reverence with which a long succession of Popes have regarded and trusted my St Philip, I pray and entreat his Holiness in compassion of my diffidence of mind, in consideration of my feeble health, my nearly eighty years, the retired course of my life from my youth, my ignorance of foreign languages, and my lack of experience in business, to let me die where I have so long lived. Since I know now and henceforth that his Holiness thinks kindly of me, what more can I desire?[5]

The letter did not directly accept or decline the cardinalate, but after Newman had seen Ullathorne at Oscott on 3 February 1879 the Bishop wrote again to Manning, enclosing a Latin copy of Newman's letter for Nina, but placing Newman's own interpretation on it:

> Dr Newman has far too humble and delicate a mind to dream of thinking or saying anything which could look like hinting at any kind of terms with the Sovereign Pontiff . . . nothing stands in the way of his most grateful acceptance except what he tells me greatly distresses him, namely the having to leave the Oratory at a critical period of its existence . . . [6]

'Your letter reached me safely', replied Manning to Ullathorne, 'and I will forward the enclosure [Newman's letter] to Cardinal Nina.'[7] In Dom Cuthbert Butler's judgement, this aroused Ullathorne's suspicion that Manning intended to send Newman's letter to Nina without Ullathorne's gloss upon it.[8] To make doubly sure that all was well, Ullathorne wrote again to Manning to drive the point home: Newman, he wrote

> is very much aged and softened with age and the trials he has had especially by the loss of his two brethren St John and Caswall, he can never refer to these losses without weeping and becoming speechless for the time . . . If the Holy Father thinks well to confer on him the dignity,

leaving him where he is, I know how immensely he would be gratified . . . '9

On 4 February 1879, Manning sent Newman the original of his own submission in support of the cardinalate, and Newman's acknowledgement was a little ambiguous: 'I could not be so ungracious whether to the Holy Father or to the friends at home who have interested themselves in this matter, as to decline what was so kindly proposed, provided that it did not involve unfaithfulness to St Philip'.[10]

With this letter and Ullathorne's before him, however, it is impossible that Manning could have misunderstood Newman's meaning, and the Cardinal set out for Rome with Ullathorne's letter in his bag. From Paris, however, he wrote baldly to Norfolk that 'Dr Newman declined the offer for many reasons of age, health, habits, etc etc, and wrote a letter fully detailing his reasons to the Bishop: to be sent to Rome: which has been done'.[11] Norfolk passed on the news to Ripon, and rumours that Newman had refused the honour began to circulate in London. Ullathorne was now thoroughly alarmed, and on 11 February wrote to Nina explaining Newman's difficulty: 'And thus he said to me: "How can I possibly intimate, or in any way suggest conditions – it would be altogether unbecoming." I answered: "Write your letter, and leave it to me to give the needful explanations". . . . But', added Ullathorne to Nina,

when the most eminent Cardinal [Manning], in acknowledging the receipt of the letters, said that he would forward Fr Newman's to your Eminence, without a word about mine, and when I found it reported and believed in London, that Fr Newman had shrunk from and declined that very great honour I began to fear that my explanatory letter had not been sent on to Rome.[12]

Ullathorne gave copies of these letters to Thomas Pope for Newman, who received letters from Emily Bowles and Fr Coleridge based on London gossip, asking if he had refused the hat. Coleridge had his information from Manning's Vicar General Daniel Gilbert and from Manning's letter to Norfolk. Then on 18 February 1879 there appeared a paragraph in *The Times*:

We are informed that Pope Leo XIII has intimated his desire to raise Dr. Newman to the rank of Cardinal, and that, with expressions of deep respect for the Holy See, Dr. Newman has excused himself from accepting the Sacred Purple. It is understood that some years ago the late Pope offered the Prelacy to Dr. Newman, who declined it in the same spirit which has caused him now to shrink from the higher dignity.[13]

Newman was naturally angry, and wrote a memorandum:

> Were such an offer made to me as the Papers state my answer would be intended for the Pope. With him lies the interpretation of it, but for any one to take upon himself to intercept it half way, and to give his own interpretation to the world is to say the least a great impertinence.[14]

The announcement caused an explosion of comment in the non-Catholic press. Norfolk heard that Herbert Vaughan had ordered the insertion of a notice in the *Tablet* that Newman had declined the cardinalate, and Norfolk and Ripon decided at the half-yearly meeting of the aristocratic Catholic Union on 20 February to abandon confidentiality and to move and second resolutions, expressing gratitude to the Pope for the offer and congratulating Newman on the honour of receiving it. On the same day, Newman wrote to Norfolk to thank him for his 'affectionate interest . . . in the application to Rome about me', and to point the finger of suspicion at Manning:

> As to the statement of my refusing a Cardinal's hat, which is in the Papers, you must not believe it, for this reason
>
> Of course it implies that an offer has been made me, and I have sent my answer to it. Now I have ever understood that it is a point of propriety and honour to consider such communications *sacred*. The statement therefore cannot come from me. Nor could it come from Rome, for it was made public before my answer got to Rome – It could only come then from some one who, not only read my letter, but, instead of leaving the *Pope* to interpret it, took upon himself to put an interpretation upon it, and published that interpretation to the world. A private letter, addressed to Roman authorities, is *intercepted* on its way and *published* in the English Papers. How is it possible than [that] any one can have done this?
>
> And besides, I am quite sure that, if so high a honour was offered me, I should not answer it by a blunt refusal.[15]

'How is it possible that any one can have done this?' Newman was blunter still in his reply to another convert, the Marquis of Bute, who figures as Manning's dupe in Disraeli's novel *Lothair*.[16] 'One cannot have half of a dignity . . . ', Newman wrote to Ripon. 'But am I to leave my "nido" . . . ? Was it not Caligula who made his horse a Consul, and would not the Pope be reviving by his proceeding the memory of that extravagance?'[17] Newman assumed that Ullathorne's letters interpreting his own had gone to Rome. Ripon sent Newman's letter on to Norfolk. The Duke had no idea of the existence of Ullathorne's explanation of Newman's 'refusal', but he could now clearly see where the land lay and on 22 February wrote to Manning with a copy of Newman's letter to him of the 20th, expressing the hope that Manning would draw Newman's letter to the Pope's attention. 'I gather from it', Norfolk told Manning, 'that Father Newman did not mean the Pope to interpret his letter in the way in which it has been interpreted by the papers ... the Pope ought to know that Father Newman did not mean in his letter what the papers say he did.'[18] 'Who, I wonder, told you that Father Newman had declined', wrote Norfolk to Manning in a further, apparently guileless letter of 23 February. 'The public report may have come from the same source.'[19]

On 25 February Manning received in Rome Norfolk's first letter, of 22 February, together with his abrasive enclosure from Newman. Manning promptly went to the Pope and got his permission for Newman to remain as a cardinal in Birmingham. Manning also replied at once to Norfolk:

> This is the first moment that I have doubted the plain meaning of Dr Newman's letter to Cardinal Nina ...
>
> I understood this note as saying that he had declined it ...
>
> A fatality seems to hang over us.
>
> I sent the draft of my letter which you, Lord Ripon, and Lord Petre had to Dr Newman that he might see what I had written and done. I will not deny that his letter has given me much pain.
>
> This is the second time that I have acted as a true and old friend of Dr Newman's, and in both instances it has ended in misunderstanding – and 'the rent is made worse' ... [20]

Manning's insistence that until 25 February he had misunderstood Newman's original letter to Nina is wholly incompatible with Ullathorne's careful explanation of Newman's meaning, yet had Manning been really so Machiavellian? He had hardly behaved in such a way as to bring what he wished to pass. By publicizing Newman's seeming refusal, he had given Newman the opportunity to make his meaning perfectly clear. As it is, Manning stands convicted of an extraordinarily clumsy misreading or suppression and publicization of confidential documents in order to deprive Newman of his honour. But the opportunity would not have arisen had Newman been direct and not delicate, and had simply accepted the honour while giving perfectly good reasons why he could not reside in Rome.

Perhaps Manning had a right to be aggrieved. The offer gave great delight to his Catholic enemies like Archbishop Errington, George Bowyer and the Jesuits, to Bishop Thomas Brown and Ambrose de Lisle, who were all fulsome in their congratulations. The Archbishop's critics in the non-Catholic world seized the story of Newman's refusal to make an odious comparison. Thus *Punch* declaimed

CORONATUS, NON PILEATUS

A Cardinal's Hat! Fancy Newman in *that*,
For the crown o'er his grey temples spread!

'Tis the good and great head would honour the hat,
Not the hat that would honour the head.

There's many a priest craves it: no wonder *he* waives it,
Or that we, the soiled head-cover scanning,
Exclaim with one breath, *sans* distinction of faith,
Would they wish Newman ranked with old Manning?[21]

Manning's policy, then, best suited anti-Catholics. '*Persevere in your refusal of the Cardinalate*', Frank Newman urged, on the ground that otherwise Newman would lose his 'post of deep moral value' to non-Catholics. Newman replied that 'this must be viewed relatively to Unitarians Theists and Sceptics on the one side, and Catholics and Anglicans on the other. I wish to be of religious service, such as I can, to both parties – but, if I must choose between Theists and Catholics, "blood is thicker than water" '.[22] Anti-Catholics like Frank were hostile to Newman's acceptance of the hat for the very reason that Norfolk and Newman himself desired it, to demonstrate that his teaching was Catholic and that his books were trustworthy, as generally approved by Rome. There was a touch about Francis of the tailless fox; he wanted his brother to be a heretic like himself.

On 1 March, Ullathorne passed to Newman a letter from Manning indicating that all obstacles to Newman's cardinalate were now removed. 'You may fancy how I am overcome by the Pope's goodness', he replied.[23] Ullathorne reported to Manning that Newman had declared to his fellow Oratorians, 'The cloud is lifted from me forever'.[24]

On 4 March, Newman acknowledged to Manning the Pope's 'condescending goodness' in allowing him to remain in Birmingham. On the same day, Newman received a letter from Lady Herbert of Lea, imploring him not to persist in his refusal of the honour.[25] As Lady Herbert stood in a special relationship as penitent and friend to both Manning and the equally Ultramontane Herbert Vaughan, Newman wrote further letters of acceptance to Howard and Manning on 5 March, 'thinking that the impression which existed some fortnight since, that I had declined it, may still prevail'.[26] Newman sent a copy of Lady Herbert's letter to Norfolk: 'Does it not seem to show that some one is still spreading the report that I have declined the dignity, and am stiff? What has been done once may be done twice . . . I cannot but feel that I have some reason for what I say, Excuse me if it is a fidget'.[27] Newman's suspicions were not allayed by Manning's own reply to him, written on 8 March from Rome, offering Newman an explanation of his misunderstanding of the affair in his characteristic one-line paragraphs.

I fully believed that, for the reasons given in your letter, you declined what might be offered.

But the Bishop expressed his hope that you might under a change of conditions accept it.

This confirmed my belief that as it stood you declined it.

And your letter to me of a day or two later still further confirmed my belief.

I started for Rome taking with me the Bishop's letter: not knowing what might be done here.

Manning added that the letter from Norfolk had at once corrected his misunderstanding. 'I write this', he concluded, 'because if I misunderstood your intention it was by an error which I repaired the instant I knew it.'[28] This adroit performance can only remind one of the boy caught with his hand in the jam jar, who can still make the most plausible excuses.

It was the hour of triumph, the sweeter for its long delay, and Newman, labouring to answer a flood of congratulatory mail, must be forgiven a little gentle crowing. As he told Mother Mary Imelda Poole of the Dominican convent at Stone, 'it is a wonderful Providence, that even before my death that acquittal of me comes, which I knew would come some day or other, though not in my life time'.[29] 'Haec mutatio dexterae Excelsi!' he wrote to Church: 'all the stories which have gone about of my being a half Catholic, a liberal Catholic, under a cloud, not to be trusted, are now at an end. Poor Ward can no longer call me a heretic . . .'[30] To David Lewis, he could only marvel. 'What a change from being a Scholar of Trinity to being a member of the Sacred College.'[31] Norfolk wrote that the Catholic aristocracy had opened a subscription fund as a mark of affection and respect. 'I have said all my life, and I repeat to myself now "Never had a man such good friends".' Newman added that Manning had written a full explanation of what had happened, 'and you will be glad to hear me say that I wish it all swept out of everyone's mind and my own – and shall be sorry if it is not so'.[32] Norfolk himself expressed to Manning 'great pain' that Newman 'should have written to me in the terms he did if he meant those terms to apply in any way to you'. Yet Norfolk also confessed that he would not have understood Newman's original letter to Manning 'as implying an unconditional refusal' – rather, he would have interpreted it as meaning that Manning 'should be able to inform the authorities, that his only real reason for declining was one they could easily remove . . .'[33] Manning still affected innocence: he told Norfolk that because he had no belief that the Holy See 'dispenses with residence except in the case of Bishops holding Sees, it seemed to me a refusal'.[34] As Norfolk did not know of Ullathorne's explanation to Manning of Newman's original letter, he did not know that Manning had no excuse.

Manning sent to Newman Nina's formal offer of the hat on 15 March. Nina's letter is notable for its typically Roman geographical vagueness, as Newman was addressed as a 'Priest of the Oratory of London': a still sensitive matter, given the bad blood between Brompton and Birmingham.[35] Manning's covering letter with Nina's was warm: Newman wrote a coldly formal reply. Newman was still responding to the notes of congratulation from the surviving friends and acquaintances of a long lifetime, many of whom, like William Lockhart and George Ryder, had at some time crossed him but still held him in honour. Bishops, Jesuits, Benedictines, Cathedral Chapters sent in formal addresses: they included Manning's own foundation, the Oblates of St Charles Borromeo. 'I am overwhelmed and wearied out with answering letters', wrote Newman to Blachford, 'yet letters so joyful and affectionate that I should be as hard as a stone, and as cruel as an hyena, and as ungrateful as a wild cat, if I did not welcome them . . . '[36] To Ullathorne, Newman worried about whether he could place the altar of his cardinalitial chapel in his own house beneath a room containing beds, while Manning helpfully advised him of the £700 due in fees to Rome, and about the making of his red and purple vestments. Manning also assured him that he would not have to risk his health in the night air to attend a papal audience. Because his 'medical advisers won't hear of my being in Rome in May',[37] he advised Manning that he would go there for the last week in April. He was the more apprehensive in that the Roman winter had not spared another old friend, William Palmer of Magdalen, who had remembered him in his will; his seeming over-caution was to be justified by events.

On 4 April, Newman went up to London to receive an address from the Irish Catholic MPs. It was his first public reply to the many such presentations which he was to receive, and he was horribly nervous, and had to speak *extempore*. His diffidence, however, disappeared, as he recalled the Irish subscriptions to the Achilli fund and his work for the Catholic University. After years of semi-seclusion, he was once again a public figure with a vengeance.

The snows of spring were thawing on 16 April, when Newman set off to Rome, accompanied by the inseparable William Neville, and armed with a statement of the religious beliefs of the ailing unconvertible William Froude, written by Froude on board ship off South Africa. In London, Newman visited two dying friends, William Wilberforce and his wife Mary, and from another old friend, the ecumenist Frederick George Lee, Vicar of All Saints' Lambeth, collected a copy of his parents' certificate of marriage in 1799 in Old Lambeth Parish Church. Newman had left behind his coat-of-arms; he did not remember the source, which he had himself once quoted from St Francis de Sales, of his cardinalitial motto, 'cor ad cor loquitur', 'heart speaks to heart'.[38]

Newman fell ill of a cold at Pisa, delayed two days, and did not reach the Hotel Bristol in Rome until 24 April. 'We have not settled where to pitch our tent', he wrote to Arthur Hutton. 'I make a bad hand at Italian, the easiest of languages.'[39] The weather was still poor, and Newman ventured out only for an audience on 27 April with the Pope, who had to stop him crying when he referred to his losses at the Oratory. Newman noted that Leo had 'a clear white complexion his eyes somewhat bloodshot – but this might have been the accident of the day'.[40] His present to His Holiness, not inaptly for so elegant a Latinist, was a copy of his own Latin dissertations on Athanasius. On 29 April, Newman began an immense reply on the foundations of belief to William Froude, who died in the following week and so never saw the letter. Newman himself was confined to his room in the Via Sistina with a worsening cold, in weather which he called 'cold, wet, and dangerous . . . They call it "English weather" – *I* call it Roman'.[41] 'Only fancy my having been a fortnight and more in Rome, and having only said *one* Mass, and been into *one* Church, St Peter's! . . . ', he wrote to John Norris. 'The first week in May I have always thought a golden time; and to be in Rome, and to have nothing of its blessings!'[42]

On Monday 12 May, at Cardinal Howard's home in the Palazzo della Pigna, Nina gave Newman the 'biglietto' which signified that Leo at the morning's secret consistory had made him a cardinal – still describing him by error as 'e Congregatione Londinensi'. Newman broke the seal on the document and passed it to Bishop Clifford of Clifton, who read it to the gathering of 'English and American Catholics, ecclesiastics and laymen, as well as many members of the Roman nobility and dignitaries of the Church'.[43] Newman began his 'biglietto' speech of reply in Italian, but continued in English. It was a last tilt at his oldest enemy, liberalism:

For thirty, forty, fifty years I have resisted to the best of my powers the spirit of liberalism in religion. Never did Holy Church need champions against it more sorely than now, when, alas! it is an error overspreading, as a snare, the whole earth; and on this great occasion, when it is natural for one who is in my place to look out upon the world, and upon Holy Church as in it, and upon her future, it will not, I hope, be considered out of place, if I renew the protest against it which I have made so often.

Liberalism in religion is the doctrine that there is no positive truth in religion, but that one creed is as good as another, and this is the teaching which is gaining substance and force daily. It is inconsistent with any recognition of any religion, as *true*. It teaches that all are to be tolerated, for all are matters of opinion. Revealed religion is not a truth, but a sentiment and a taste; not an objective fact, not miraculous; and it is the right of each individual to make it say just what strikes his fancy. Devotion is not necessarily founded on faith. Men may go to Protestant Churches and to Catholic, may get good from both and belong to neither. They may fraternise together in spiritual thoughts and feelings, without having any views at all of doctrine in common, or seeing the need of them. Since, then, religion is so personal a peculiarity and so private a possession, we must of necessity ignore it in the intercourse of man with man. If a man puts on a new religion every morning what is that to you? It is as impertinent to think about a man's religion as about his sources of income or his management of his family. Religion is in no sense the bond of society.

'Hitherto', Newman continued, 'the civil power has been Christian . . . Now, everywhere that goodly framework of society, which is the creation of Christianity, is throwing off Christianity', which was being replaced by 'the broad fundamental ethical truths, of justice, benevolence, veracity, and the like; proved experience; and those natural laws which exist . . . in government, trade, finance, sanitary experiments, and the intercourse of nations. As to Religion, it is a private luxury . . . The general character of this great *apostasia* is one and the same everywhere'. In Britain, Newman said that the liberal movement was borne forward by the Dissenting objections to a State religion in principle, by the need to involve men of all religions in any public enterprise, and by what was 'good and true' in liberal theory, 'the precepts of justice, truthfulness, sobriety, self-command, benevolence . . . There never was a device of the Enemy so cleverly framed and with such promise of success'. Yet it could not seriously do harm 'to the Word of God, to Holy Church, to our Almighty King, the Lion of the tribe of Judah, Faithful and True, or to His Vicar on earth. Christianity has been too often in what seemed deadly peril, that we should fear for it any new trial now . . . Providence rescues and saves His elect inheritance'.[44] The speech might have been made by the young other-worldly Evangelical. In the apostasy of the nations, God and his Word would survive the wreck, as he turned the folly of men to his own account, saving some but not all.

Newman's voice was strong, and his frailty and illness were not too apparent to the applauding Italian ladies – 'che bel vecchio! che figura', if 'pallido si, ma bellissimo'.[45] On the Tuesday morning, 13 May, Leo presented him with his biretta. On the Wednesday morning, he was laughing and talking at the English College, where the English-speaking Catholics in Rome gave him with a complete set of vestments, 'a cloth-of-silver cope and jewelled mitre, a Canon of the Mass book, a pectoral cross and chain, and a silver-gilt altar candlestick . . . together with a richly illuminated address'.[46] On Thursday morning, he received the hat at the Public Consistory with nine other members of the Sacred College, including Leo's brother. Newman's rank was that of Cardinal Deacon. It seems that the Pope intended to make him a Cardinal Presbyter but at the last moment, the vacancy was claimed by the King of Portugal. The Pope also intended to assign Newman as his cardinalitial church San Nicolò in Carcere, which had been lavishly restored by Pius IX and was in a poor area where Newman hoped that he might be of some use to local people: the church was, however, claimed by another cardinal. Newman was offered instead Sant' Adriano in Foro Romano, but the British in Rome secured for him another ancient church, San Giorgio in Velabro, as belonging to the patron saint of England.

Newman never entered San Giorgio, though he met its Rector, whose canons worked a night school, but were restricted by the government to two Masses a year. His cold turned to pneumonia, making havoc of his plans to befriend other members of the Sacred College, and to attend a celebration of his cardinalate at the Chiesa Nuova, where the Oratorians had lost most of their great house through the anticlerical government's measures of sequestration. 'I have only said mass once since I have been in Rome; have been in hardly half a dozen Churches',[47] Newman wrote to Emily Bowles. He had to decline invitations to visit the Archbishop of Turin and the English Catholic Blount family in Paris, and even to consider giving up a call on Maria Giberne at Autun. His hopes of reconciling Döllinger were dashed by a public letter in which the German historian declared 'That he [the Pope] makes Newman a Cardinal, a man so infinitely above the Romish *vulgus praelaticum*, is only conceivable when the true views of the man are unknown in Rome. If Newman had written in French, Italian, or Latin, his books would long since have been on the Index'. Newman considered that Döllinger's declaration displayed 'an irritability and want of benevolence towards me which I did not expect from him. It is ridiculous to suppose that the Romans, of all people in the world, would be wanting in acuteness. . . . '[48] He later decided that 'As to Dollinger's saying that the Pope did not know what he was doing, it is a good joke'.[49] Newman did not know that the Roman authorities could hardly have been ignorant of their own censures on the *Letter to Norfolk* in 1875.

At his final audience with Leo on 2 June, Newman asked that the Birmingham house be henceforth called the 'Oratorio del Cardinale', which would stop Rome from calling it 'di Londra'. The last request of his petition to Leo was for his ailing penitent Eleanor Watt, whom he had confessed since her girlhood, for the privilege of receiving communion once monthly without fasting. He set out from Rome on 4 June, but only reached Leghorn where he had a serious relapse and had to pass a week at the Anglo-American Hotel, where his attendants thought him dying. Neville thought that by commanding the administration of a massive dose of quinine, Newman had, under Providence, saved himself. For a second time, Italy had almost been his death.

On 5 June, he wrote a positively friendly letter to Manning thanking him and the English bishops for their congratulations.[50] On 20 June, he left Leghorn for Genoa. A planned dash from Mâcon to Maria at Autun was prevented by heavy rain. He crossed from Boulogne to Folkestone on 27 June, and at Brighton called on the ailing Mrs William Wilberforce, whose husband had died while Newman was in Rome. From Brighton, he paid a visit to the faithful Bloxam, who since 1862 had been Rector of Upper Beeding, Sussex. Finding the London hotels packed for the Agricultural

Show, he went on to Rugby, which he left early in the morning to reach the crowds packed in and round the Oratory by eleven. 'To come home again! In that word "home" how much is included', he told his congregation. There was a more heroic life than 'home life', that of Our Lord and the Apostles. But the Oratory of St Philip was 'the realisation of the family in its perfection'. He spoke of the Pope, 'the grace which shone from his face and spoke in his voice', and of his own near fatal sickness and sadness of his journey.

> And now I will ask you, my dear friends, to pray for me, that I may be as the presence of the Holy Father amongst you, and that the Holy Spirit of God may be upon this Church, upon this great city, upon its bishop, upon all its priests, upon all its inhabitants, men, women and children, and as a pledge and beginning of it I give you my benediction.

'The *Te Deum* was then sung, and thus the service ended.'[51]

Newman told Tom Arnold that he had heard in Rome 'that the Pope had been deluged with letters from England by Protestants, stating their satisfaction at his having promoted me'.[52] His chief occupation for the rest of the year was that of responding to more and more addresses and congratulations: on 20 July he 'assisted at the High Mass in *cappa magna*', and later 'gave Benediction, using mitre and crozier for the first time',[53] before hearing addresses from the Oratory School Society and the boys' mothers. On the school speech day, he received addresses from the masters and boys, the Salford Chapter and the Manchester Catholic Club, and saw the school act two scenes from his version of Terence's *Phormio*. More addresses arrived from the Lancashire clergy, the Catholic Young Men's Societies and the Total Abstinence League of the Cross. There was another such round on the Assumption, from Norfolk on behalf of the Catholics of England, Ireland and Scotland, from Ripon and Allies on behalf of the Catholic Poor School Committee, from Frederick Lucas' brother and biographer Edward on behalf of the Catholic Academia, from Norfolk on behalf of the St George's Club and from Ripon on behalf of the Teachers' Training College at Liverpool. On 4 September, the children of the Oratory's mission schools sang him in Italian 'Salve gran' Cardinale': he explained to them that Leo meant lion, but that God allowed himself to be compared to a dove and a lamb, and that from the dove and the lamb the Pope derived all his power. On 18 September, he received the address and offering from the Earl of Denbigh of the diocese of Birmingham. On 5 October, Oscott College sang High Mass *coram Cardinali*, and he preached to the students on the mystery of the Rosary. On 28 October, he received an address from his successor as Rector of the Catholic University of Ireland, Bartholomew Woodlock, now Bishop of Ardagh. There were five further Irish meetings and addresses, the two major ones being in Limerick and Dublin.[54]

Each one of Newman's replies is a small rhetorical miniature. But too much sweetness sickens, and it is difficult to feel wholly comfortable with Newman's tribute to the late Cardinal Cullen in his response to Woodlock, 'that his countenance had a light upon it which made me feel as if, during his many years at Rome, all the saints of the Holy City had been looking into it and he into theirs'.[55] Newman was thinking of Cullen's intervention on his behalf with Rome in 1867, but it was only in public that the old bitterness was wholly displaced. There were still some doubts about Newman in Ireland, and some jealousy of his honour. The Irish Archbishop of Toronto, John Joseph Lynch, reported to Newman 'a good deal of grumbling amongst the Irish at home and abroad, that England has three cardinals and poor but faithful Ireland has not one'.[56] Lynch wanted the Irish Primate to be made a cardinal. Newman delicately refused to become involved in a public agitation for the honour, which it was the Pope's sole prerogative to give. The sentiment was not to deter the presentation of a golden salver subscribed by the Catholic population of Australia, which was overwhelmingly Irish in origin.

On 3 November, Newman paid another visit to Oxford, primarily to present Keble's letters to the Warden of Keble College, E. S. Talbot. His only mark of his new dignity was 'a red skull cap under his shovel hat'.[57] An ascetic and modest bourgeois all his life, he had complained of spending £200 in Rome on clothes he would never wear, and of having to find cupboard space for them. He also had to set up a private chapel, which he dedicated to his favourite St Francis de Sales, and decorated with pictures of the saint's life by Maria Giberne. Four Anglican friends, Lords Blachford and Coleridge, and Church and Copeland, subscribed to buy him a private brougham, which they had 'quietly blazoned' with his arms, taken from an old bookplate, with the cardinal's hat and its tassels superimposed. 'I was amused', Newman wrote to Coleridge, 'at my (acting) coachman praising it for being so quiet and in good taste. Would you have expected this in this Beotian air?'[58] 'I cannot walk much', he told Blachford in 1881, 'and thus I am able to accept Sir Garnet W[olseley]'s dictum that mounted infantry are the military arm of the future – for my carriage takes me out a mile or two and sets me down to walk . . . '[59] On 25 November 1879, he sent out according to the forms prescribed from Rome, letters in Italian to his brethren in the Sacred College and to his new cousins, the Catholic kings and queens and the Emperor and Empress of Brazil. He had enjoyed a kind of apotheosis into an international *Almanach de Gotha*, and the sort of adulation more usually reserved for obituaries. The last and fondest of his sisters, Jemima, died on Christmas Day 1879, and he upset the Mozleys by a seeming coldness in his grief, and by telling them that he would say Mass for her soul. As a cardinal he did not wear mourning, and he had long been ready to sing his own 'Nunc dimittis', having pondered death over a long lifetime. It was more than thirty years since he had preached his finest words on the end of life: 'May He support us all the day long, till the shades lengthen, and the evening comes, and the busy world is hushed, and the fever of life is over, and our work is done! Then in his mercy may He give us a safe lodging, and a holy rest, and peace at the last!'[60]

30

Last Things

Newman saw his final work as one of offering a proper theological defence of Christianity in a world in which it was increasingly assailed. He was vastly encouraged by the seeming intellectual openness of the new pontificate, and wrote warmly to Leo on his encyclical encouraging a revived study of the philosophy of Aquinas.[1] Leo spoke equally warmly about him to two Birmingham Oratorians at a public audience in 1880. 'Ah mes fils il faut le conserver – le garder – le conserver.' 'But', replied John Norris, 'Holy Father he is eighty years old.' 'A look of sadness came over his [the Pope's] face and he was silent for a minute and then he brightened up and said smiling "il faut le conserver jusqu'il a quatre-vingt-dix." '[2] This last decade of life was granted to Newman, taking him into his ninetieth year. As a cardinal, with second rank in the Roman Church in England, and with precedence over all the bishops but Manning, he lived in his fellow country-men's imagination in a remote blaze of sacred purple glory, and as a gilded joss-stick in the exotic temple of late Victorian Catholicism.

By inclination and by a sense of work undone, as well as through failing health, his last years were even more than their predecessors, a period of retirement. In January 1880, he fell and broke a rib; in February, he fell out of bed and broke two. He had, however, one set of major engagements to fulfil. Between 8 and 15 May, he stayed at Norfolk House in St James's Square in London, and on 9 May attended Vespers and gave Benediction at Brompton and addressed the lay brothers of the Little Oratory, whose Prefect was Ornsby's Dublin pupil Henry Bowden. James Anthony Froude recalled that a sermon of Newman's thirty-eight years before, commending the point of Hume's argument on miracles, had 'cut at the root of all my old beliefs'. Froude was present for the sermon at Brompton, wondering if the 'same Voice which administered the poison may possibly administer the antidote'.[3] On 12 May, Newman addressed the Catholic Union of Great Britain on the conversion of England, recommending the slow work of winning friends and converts and removing prejudice, rather than living in expectation of extraordinary miracles. Norfolk as the President of the Union presented him with the golden salver from Australia. Newman also called on Dr John Ogle, a connection of his old Oxford mathematics tutor and guardian of his failing eyesight, and lunched with Elizabeth Bowden. He received a host of callers at Norfolk House, including the Fullertons and the Cecils, and farewelled the Marquis of Ripon on his leave-taking for India as Viceroy. Newman received two hundred of the clergy at the Oratory on the 13 May, and several hundred of the great and good at Norfolk House on the 14th and 15th. Manning was diplomatically absent in Rome.

Between 22 and 25 May 1880, Newman returned to Trinity in Oxford a conqueror. 'The lime walk was illuminated with limelight, and the hall was turned into a drawing-room and decorated with flowers.'[4] Newman preached twice on Trinity Sunday at the Jesuit Church of St Aloysius, and spent the Sunday evening with the occupant of his old Trinity rooms, the college scholar Douglas Sladen. 'The Cardinal, a wan little old man with a shrivelled face and a large nose, and one of the most beautiful expressions which ever appeared on a human being, talked to me for a couple of hours, prostrating me with his exquisite modesty', recalled Sladen, later a distinguished historian, ' . . . I don't think I have ever felt any honour of the kind so much. And when he differed from me on any point he would say: "Of course you have better opportunities of knowing than I have, but I should have thought so".'[5] On Monday, Newman breakfasted with the Fellows of Oriel, and delivered while seated at the Trinity Gaudy an informal speech, 'a model of perfect tact and grace'.[6] It was, as it proved, his valedictory, as he never visited Trinity again.

Newman's public engagements outside the Oratory were henceforth of the slightest. He preached at the Birmingham diocesan seminary at Olton on 21 June 1880, but otherwise tended to decline all invitations, pleading his age. He celebrated his only Pontifical High Mass on his birthday in 1881. The congregation of the Oratory presented him with W. W. Ouless' portrait on 19 June 1881, and a week later he preached at the Brompton Oratory, and sat for a further portrait by J. E. Millais. 'I put your questions to Mr Millais', he reported to Miss Giberne, 'but he was too busy to answer them'[7] – though the artist recognized Maria's Neapolitan yellow and was using her favourite ivory black. Newman inscribed a set of his works to the London Oratorians, who may have assumed that this patched up the old quarrel. Newman called on Manning, who astonished him by kissing him on his departure. Unrepentant, Manning told Wilfrid Ward that one thing 'and one thing only' had ruined 'that man's career': 'Temper! – temper!! – TEMPER!!!'[8]

The lightening of his engagements meant a return to work. Throughout the long haul over the cardinalate, Newman fretted over the delay in revising his yet unrepublished work, his *Select Treatises of St Athanasius*. He resumed it in autumn 1880, assisted by Thomas Eaglesim: it appeared in 1881. He declined invitations to write prefaces to the works of his friends, but in 1882 he edited William Palmer of Magdalen's *Notes of a Visit to the Russian Church*, from which he drew the moral that the Russian Orthodox did not recognize the Church of England. His correspondence was considerable, and was not just with old friends like Maria Giberne, herself nearly eighty, whom he consoled on her sense of spiritual desolation. 'Think of St Mary Magdalen de' Pazzi; of St Elizabeth (was it not?) with a very hard Confessor, of St Jane Francis, of St Benedict with monks who tried to poison him . . . I should never be surprised if your trial was long, but it would be, long or short, a sign of God's special love towards you.'[9] Maria was precious as one who still remembered Newman's beloved Mary. 'This is the anniversary of my dear Mary's death in 1828, an age ago', wrote Newman to Maria in January 1882; 'but she is as fresh in my memory and as dear to my heart, as if it were yesterday; and often I cannot mention her name without tears coming into my eyes.'[10]

Newman had the curious literary satisfaction of proving his remarks to Gladstone on the limitations on papal power. The indestructible Gladstone, now again Prime Minister, was in the usual position of those Victorian British statesmen who had denounced papal power and also tried to use it in Ireland. He sent Newman a batch of treasonous utterances by Irish priests, asking him to try to get the Pope to condemn them. Newman recognized the burden of Irish grievances and thought it unjust that Ireland had not been treated like Scotland. He wrote to the President of Maynooth, William Walsh, asking if it were 'a probable opinion . . . that the Irish people has never recognized . . . the sovereignty of England, and . . . therefore it is no sin to be what would be commonly called a rebel'.[11] Walsh's answer has not survived, and Newman answered Gladstone by reiterating one line of argument against him from the *Letter to the Duke of Norfolk*. 'I think you overrate the Pope's power in political and social matters. It is absolute in questions of theology, but not so in practical matters.' The Pope could declare 'Rebellion' or 'Robbery' a sin, but his action against a political party accused of them was another thing altogether. 'Again, local power and influence is often more than a match for Roman right', and intemperate priests or curates 'belong to their respective Bishops, and scarcely require the intervention of the Supreme Authority'.[12]

Newman might have instanced the revolutionary Irish priest Patrick Lavelle, who had survived the thunders of the Vatican and Cullen because he was protected by his own diocesan John MacHale. Newman may have passed on Gladstone's letter to his friend Lord O'Hagan, who had carried the British government's case against the Irish nationalist clergy to Rome. When in 1887 Gerard Manley Hopkins went to the Catholic University as Professor, Newman replied to his 'appalling' picture of the state of Ireland with a consideration he had left out of his account. 'The Irish Patriots hold that they never have yielded themselves to the sway of England and therefore . . . never have been rebels . . . If I were an Irishman, I should be (in heart) a rebel.'[13] Nor would he be drawn into a lay English Catholic attempt to get the Pope to condemn the Irish archbishops and bishops who supported the nationalist 'Plan of Campaign' against the landlords.

'How the old generation is fading away, out of sight!' Newman wrote to Emily Bowles. 'What a mystery is life! and how it comes home to such as me to think of old Nestor's melancholy lines, "as the outburst and fall of leaves, such [is] the generation of men". How inwardly miserable must the life of man be, without the Gospel! and now men are doing their utmost to destroy our sole solace.'[14] A reconciled Edward Hawkins and the greatest surviving champion of the Anglo-Catholic faith, Pusey, died in 1882. On the day that Pusey was brought to Oxford for burial, Newman set out to exorcise another ghost from his past in the sea-side resort of Tenby in Wales, where his forgotten brother Charles lay ill in a floodswept cottage by a salt marsh, having spent a quarter of a century as a recluse in the town, a pensioner on Frank's charity. Charles is said to have turned John Henry away, but lingered on until 1884. None of the new generation of Oratorians had heard of him, but Newman's eminence gave Charles publicity value, and Newman had to endure publication of a report that Charles had been dismissed as usher from a school for biting a boy, and pay £15 for a batch of compromising letters. Newman feared that more such letters might yet remain. 'He must have had some curious natural gifts', he wrote of Charles to Jemima's sister-in-law Anne Mozley, to whom he was becoming close, 'for eccentric, violent and self-willed as he was, he attached to him the mother and daughter with whom he lodged, and, the mother having died, the daughter has refused a nurse and has nursed him day and night through his last illness.'[15] The vagrant Charles might be considered the proverbial Victorian black sheep, but with his socialism, atheism and immoralism, he seems a curiously modern figure, more Genet than Victorian. Newman had him buried under a stone with the text from Psalm 137 which asks God not to despise the work of his hands.

This was Newman's last close family death, as his remaining sibling, his cantankerous and eccentric brother Frank, now a passionate vegetarian, anti-vivisectionist and supporter of women's suffrage, survived him, to broadcast his faults to the world. In December 1883, Newman heard that his old disciple Mark Pattison was dangerously ill. 'How is it', wrote Newman to Pattison, 'that I, who am so old am carried on in years beyond my juniors?' Pattison, who had become a notorious liberal, if not a covert unbeliever, was overwhelmed.

> When your letter, my dear Master was brought to my bedside this morning, and I saw your well-known handwriting, my eyes filled so with tears that I could not at first see to read what you had said.[16]

Newman still thought that infidelity was rooted in an impaired moral sense, and in his heart of hearts did not imagine that a good man could die unbelieving. He offered to visit Pattison but was gently repelled. 'Is it possible that you at eighty three can be proposing to make the journey to

410

Oxford and back only for the sake of visiting me? . . . You cannot tell what it costs me to be declining such an offer from you, an offer which thousands would esteem the highest honour that could be done them', wrote Pattison, who disliked the agitation it would cause him. 'Believe me, my dear Master, that I do not esteem it less, but it is too overwhelming and I shrink from it in terror.'[17] It was almost as if Pattison feared that Newman would restore to him the faith that he had lost. Newman took matters into his own hands, and announced his advent by a note which came to Pattison only hours before his arrival. 'I felt that it was not all personal regard which had brought him', wrote Pattison afterwards, 'but the hope, however slight, that I might still be got over in my last moments.'[18] Pattison did not like to make it clear to Newman that he looked back on his Anglo-Catholic convictions 'as the ideas of childish ignorance', having travelled a whole world from his position in 1845; in his *Memoirs* he roundly declared of Newman that 'All the grand developments of human reason, from Aristotle down to Hegel, was a sealed book to him'.[19] This is not quite incompatible with his tribute to Newman's influence; he chiefly meant to condemn Newman for his ignorance of German. At the meeting, Newman dwelt on the consolations of Catholicism and reiterated what Pattison called 'the old argument of the Apologia . . . ' 'I said in answer', Pattison continued, 'three hypotheses each less probable than the one before it.'[20] Newman did not choose to notice Pattison's infidelity, and they passed on to a harmless discussion of old Oriel. Pattison died in 1884, in the bitterness of his agnosticism.

Newman had additional proof of the new power of religious doubt in the sudden apostasy in November 1883 of Arthur Hutton, who told his fellow Oratorians in tears that he had lost belief 'even in the existence of a personal God'. 'I little thought', wrote Newman to Ignatius Ryder, 'that the pestilence, which threatened the next generation, was to show itself now in St Philip's household . . . ' Newman was appalled by Hutton's systematic unbelief, and wrote of Hutton that 'in the depth of his heart, to use his own phrase, he has been without faith all his life. I fear his remaining here, as I should fear a patient in an Epidemic'.[21] Emily Bowles thought that St Philip's picture had prophetically fallen during Hutton's first Mass, and the renegade was followed by one of the schoolteachers, who married him in 1884. He later recovered a faith sufficient to return to the Anglican ministry, though his wife is said to have refused his request for a Catholic priest on his death-bed. His memories of the Oratory published after Newman's death were unkindly, alleging Newman's favouritism with some of his fellow Oratorians and his neglect of others. He also wrote a laudatory study of Manning.

Newman's anxiety to combat the new infidelity did not mean defending untenable positions: unlike Manning, he would not oppose the Affirmation Bill in 1883 allowing the atheist Charles Bradlaugh into Parliament. So he also published a radical essay 'On the Inspiration of Scripture' in the

Nineteenth Century in February 1884,[22] drawing on notebooks which went back 1861 and to his first reactions to *Essays and Reviews*. His concern was to limit the range of Inspiration, and he defined biblical literalism as 'cloak Christianity': did one's faith depend on whether St Paul was right in thinking that he had left his cloak in Troas and not somewhere else? This agnosticism was mild enough, and passed the censures of Bishops Clifford and John Hedley, but caused a fluttering in the dovecotes of Maynooth where Professor John Healy argued that, while not *de fide*, the denial of an incidental biblical fact, like the aside that '*Nebuchodonosor*' was king of Nineveh, was inconsistent with accepting Scripture as the Word of God.[23] Newman's privately printed reply to Healy was fierce, but the matter was happily resolved with his present to Healy of a Canon of the Mass on the latter's elevation to the episcopate. Newman clearly saw that such literalism must go, and he encouraged the more adventurous of Catholic biblical scholars like William Barry and von Hügel.

In his openness to new interpretations of Scripture, Newman was true to his own beginnings. He was less agreeably self-consistent in refusing to let his old enmity with the Brompton Oratory die. The Superior, Fr William Philip Gordon, and the community's great lay pillar, the Duke of Norfolk, were both anxious that Newman should attend the opening of the Oratory's vast new baroque church, designed by the convert Herbert Gribble. Newman refused. His ground was that he would be attending as founder, but that the London Oratorians had cut off their ties with Birmingham in 1855–6 by libelling him all over Italy with the allegation that he wanted authority over them. Without making any apology or redress for an old injustice, they expected Newman to act as if nothing had happened, when his presence as their founder among them might seem to justify their old charge against him. No doubt, thought Newman, the break had been in St Philip's providence; but now, he wrote to Fr Gordon, 'I am appealed to in the name of St Philip to renew a tie which he broke thirty years ago; and am asked to take part in an act, which concerns intimately and solely the London Oratory. Thus we shall end with a recognized disruption'.[24] Norfolk had been approached by Gordon to offer Newman the hospitality of Norfolk House if he preferred it to the Oratory, but Newman cancelled from his draft of the letter a full explanation of his refusal to the Duke. Norfolk, who was wholly in the dark about the quarrel, which had happened in his early childhood, wondered to Gordon if Newman resented the loss of two of his Birmingham schoolboys as novices to London, or if 'the glory and glamour of the new church may have had something to do with "drawing the young hearts from him"' . . . It is very sad. What can one do with such an extraordinary mind'.[25] Newman's action was justified by a close and careful argument. But the only London Oratorian still alive to have taken a leading role in the events of 1855 was Richard Stanton, and it would have done Newman more credit to have come among his former brethren with a wholly gratuitous pardon. In the event, three Fathers headed by John Norris, who also knew little of the events of 1855, attended the ceremony as Newman's representatives. The Cardinal presented the church with a new chalice, which remains as another memento of a wound which never healed.

Newman's other weakness was a concern for his own reputation, as the gossip-mongers and would-be biographers seized upon him. The first, in 1881, was Edmund Sheridan Purcell, once Manning's partisan as editor of the *Westminster Gazette*, now anxious after its failure to revenge himself on his old patron by praising his enemy. Purcell sent Newman a copy of an article that he had written about him for *Celebrities of the Day*. 'My own feeling about the past is "Let bygones by bygones" ', Newman wrote to him. ' . . . I am pained to find the name of Kingsley recalled, who by his passionate attack on me became one of my best friends . . . Much less can I reconcile myself to your references to Catholic opponents as "fanatical" etc and their influence at Rome, and their "suppleness".'[26] 'I found it not only inaccurate and fulsome in its praise –', wrote Newman to Thomas Pope, 'but reviving old stories of the opposition made to me by Catholics.'[27] Purcell omitted the contentious passages, and took his revenge on Manning after his death with a not too subtly libellous biography.

Newman also reprimanded the publishers of the wholly laudatory life of him by the journalist Henry Jennings, for claiming to have secured his approval for the work. This was nothing, however, to Newman's horror at his brother-in-law Tom Mozley's *Reminiscences*. Mozley could convey the feeling and colour of events, and was worshipping of Newman's person; but he was nearly blind, and was hopelessly inaccurate, as he wrote without checking from a lifetime's store of self-improved after-dinner anecdotes. Newman read only as far as Chapter 2, and could not go a line further, though he sent Mozley a list of five errors in the chapter, which included a false account of the 'failure' of Newman senior's bank and the claim that Mrs Newman had reared her children on the writing of the English Calvinists. 'I could notice other mistakes –', wrote Newman to Mozley, 'but all that you have said is so uncalled for, that I am almost stupefied.'[28] Mozley made the corrections that Newman sent to him, but Newman never recovered from the blow. 'I don't mean to utter a word in consequence', he wrote to his brother Frank, 'for he is a wild beast who rends one's hand when put up to defend one's face.'[29] He also disliked Mozley's reproduction, apparently in a periodical, of Maria Giberne's picture of the Newmans in 1829, in which, the Cardinal wrote, 'Harriett is represented so unlike the rest that strangers must think that she is a young lady I am sweet upon'.[30] Less disagreeable, but also inaccurate, was Dean Burgon's *Twelve Good Men*, written to canonize those men in the Movement who had in Burgon's own eyes remained moderate members of the Church of England.

These unwanted attentions were the price of fame. Newman experienced more undesirable publicity over his encouragement to a Clifton teenager,

Emily Fortey, who wanted to become a Catholic against her father's wishes. Newman told her to see the local Jesuits, but his letter was copied in 1883 and published in *The Times* by the elderly clerical relation of one of Miss Fortey's friends, to her own distress and the disgust of her own father, who eventually allowed her to be received into the Roman Catholic Church. Mr Fortey, however, would not permit the appearance of his letter of complaint about the publication above his own signature, so that Newman was without redress.[31] On another occasion, he had a full vindication: in 1884 the former Foreign Secretary and Lord Privy Seal, the Earl of Malmesbury, in his *Memoirs* charged him with cowardice as an Oriel tutor, in 1826–7, in suffering his students to advance a table on him in his lectures until he was jammed into a corner, and in passively enduring a shouted rebuke from Copleston for mutilating at table a fine haunch of venison. The story of the mobile table passed into the national and Catholic newspapers, and at Newman's instigation Lord Blachford came forward to assign the tale to another Oriel Tutor, William James. But as Newman wrote in a fine snub to Malmesbury, who redoubled his offence with a half-hearted apology to a 'too indulgent and patient tutor', 'what we are told of two we may assume belongs to neither'.[32]

Another such annoyance was the publication by the publisher C. Kegan Paul of the story that in 1843 Newman had been 'not at home' at Littlemore to Manning, who after the latter's anti-Catholic Gunpower Day sermon was turned from the door by J. A. Froude. Newman doubted the tale, but it was confirmed by Froude. More agreeably, Newman assisted Richard Church with the compilation of the character sketches for what became Church's work on *The Oxford Movement*, the most influential historiographical account of the Movement, the *Apologia* alone excepted.

Newman had difficulty deciding his own biography. His *beau idéal* of such a work was Stanley's idealizing life of Thomas Arnold, which had beatified its subject while appearing to let Arnold's letters tell the story. Newman had something even more tactful in mind when he nominated his friend Robert Ornsby to write the life of Hope-Scott, which Gladstone said was 'a good piece of carpentering, but not a living biography' of the 'most winning charming man' he had ever known.[33] Newman, however, admired it. He was also greatly impressed by Anne Mozley's tact and discretion in the editing of the letters of her brother James Mozley. Like Manning, Newman wanted an Anglican to deal with his Anglican life, and invited her to edit his Anglican correspondence in January 1882. The ultimate product, which appeared after Newman's death, is also tactful but rather colourless. Newman did not relish the notion of a critical memoir of even his Anglican period, one written from a view point not his own.

His Catholic life, was, however, another matter: he did not want one written, because it would be a history of still living controversy. 'I am as if my skin was torn off (metaphorically) by the number of Memoirs written of me (written in kindness)',[34] he wrote in 1885 of one such production by Wilfrid Meynell; he exploded to Meynell about 'the very offensive caricature which disgraces his pages of my mother and her children.'[35], Maria Giberne's portrait of the Newman family, which Meynell has produced in his journal *Merry England*. The collections of material that Newman himself made for a biography were only to be used 'in defence – i.e. if enemies make misstatements or impute motives, these collections are authorities to refer to'.[36]

These would require the most sensitive handling; but a gifted and sensitive young would-be biographer was taking shape in Wilfrid Ward, the son of Newman's old antagonist, W. G. Ward. Wilfrid spent much of the eighties and early nineties writing a long and critical biography of his father, and in the course of his labours achieved a close acquaintance with the old surviving members of W. G. Ward's generation, so much so that, as G. K. Chesterton said of him, Wilfrid seemed like a member of that generation himself. Ward had, moreover, found an escape from his father's extreme Ultramontanism by adopting Newman's moderating position, and by a close and early study of Newman's philosophy was to become the acutest exponent of Newman's philosophical apologetic for Catholicism and Christianity in the generation after the Cardinal's death. Ward's attempts to become official biographer were to be complicated by Newman's exclusion of Henry Ignatius Dudley Ryder from the executorship granted to Fr William Neville, and then by the modernist crisis, when Newman's executors reacted with terror to the proofs of Ward's text, fearing that they would tar Newman's reputation with the modernist brush. There is a slightly comic aspect to Ward's worshipping cultivation of Newman in his old age, and he himself annoyed the Cardinal by allowing the publication without explicit permission of a letter in which Newman had warmly commended the argument of Ward's *The Clothes of Religion*. Like Ward's earlier work *The Wish to Believe*, the volume was a development of certain of Newman's philosophical ideas; but Newman's law against the use of his name to puff the work of others was absolute.

Newman also encouraged the early writing of Wilfrid's future wife the novelist Josephine Hope, the daughter of Newman's old friend Hope-Scott and the niece of the fifteenth Duke of Norfolk. He congratulated her on her first story *In the Way*, but thought that there was 'perhaps too much *direct* teaching and preaching in the Tale'. His conclusion showed him at his best:

Now my dear Child, I hope this criticism will not frighten you. If I was not pleased with your work, if I did not think [it] as likely to do glory to God, if I did not love you and take an interest in you, I should not have written. You must not be startled at my abruptness, that arises from the effort and trouble with which I write.[37]

Josephine was another worshipper at the Edgbaston shrine, and Newman was the mildly incongruous background presence to their courtship and marriage. In 1889 he was to send his blessing to the Wards' daughter Maisie, who seemed to be dying in her first week of life, but survived to become the best of his twentieth-century biographers, excepting only her father.

Wilfrid Ward's life-work was a continuation of Newman's crusade against unbelief. The Cardinal's final controversy was, however, about the manner in which Christianity should be defended, with the Congregationalist Andrew Martin Fairbairn, a brilliant philosopher and prose stylist who in 1886 became Principal of Mansfield College, Oxford. Fairbairn's criticism of Newman echoed that of the anti-religious James Fitzjames Stephen, who interpreted Newman as a sceptic for whom there was no alternative between atheism and Catholicism. 'It is no good our disputing', Newman wrote, 'it is like a battle between a dog and a fish –':[38] in Newman's own view, he and Stephen could not find a common ground for argument, because their differences went back to different moral choices in what they were as persons. Fairbairn's attack on Newman in the *Contemporary Review* for May 1885 was in the same rationalist mode. Newman had embraced Catholicism, he thought, because in religious matters, reason is 'corrosive, dissolving, sceptical. Hence while the conscience creates religion, the reason tends to create unbelief; the one is on the one side of God, the other against Him'.[39] Of the *Grammar of Assent*, Fairbairn wrote that the 'whole book is pervaded by the intensest philosophical scepticism', a scepticism built on 'the most empirical individualism'.[40] 'Conscience demands God, but reason will not allow the faith in Him to live; and so an infallible church is called in to . . . support the conscience, and "preserve religion in the world" by so restraining "the freedom of thought" as "to rescue it from its own suicidal excesses".'[41]

There was an element of truth in this, which is not conceded in Newman's reply in the *Contemporary* in October, in a work which shows no diminishment of his intellectual powers. Newman was stung by the charge that he was a sceptic, and spoke from the lofty heights of his great old age: 'I can, in my place and in my measure', he wrote, 'adopt the words of St Polycarp before his martyrdom: "For fourscore years and six I have served my Lord, and He never did me harm, but much good; and can I leave Him now?" '[42] Newman patiently restated his own philosophy that reason was perfectly reliable in its own sphere, as the power, in Johnson's definition, 'by which man deduces one proposition from another'.[43] But reason does not supply its own materials for argument, so that if these materials are wrong, the conclusions derived from them will be wrong, however faultless the reasoning upon them. Such a wrong use of reason was what Newman had described as ' "Reason actually and historically," "Reason in fact and concretely in fallen man," "Reason in the educated intellect of England, France, and Germany," Reason in "every Government and every civilisation through the world which is under the influence of the European mind," Reason in the "wild living intellect of man" '. This was reason in St Paul's sense of the wisdom of the world, 'as wielded by the Living World, against the teaching of the Infallible Church'.[44]

Fairbairn in his reply in the *Contemporary* for December denied that he had accused Newman of personal scepticism: 'it would require an energy and irony of invective equal to the Cardinal's own, to describe the fatuous folly of the man who would venture to make any such charge . . . What he was charged with . . . was "metaphysical" or "philosophical" scepticism',[45] a matter not of faith but of intellect. The essence of the difference between them was that, as Newman saw, without fully appreciating its import, he and Fairbairn were employing 'Reason' in quite different senses. Fairbairn's 'constitutive and interpretative Reason' was an 'architectonic faculty', conceived in a German neo-Hegelian manner as possessing the power to appropriate metaphysical truth. The English idealists of the school had developed a new confidence in the capacities of this sort of reason to forge a natural philosophy which was highly congenial to Christianity. Their idealism contributed to the Christian recovery of intellectual nerve in the late Victorian and Edwardian eras, a recovery of nerve founded in the sense that religion was in underlying harmony with the deepest philosophical insights of the age. As Fairbairn pointed out, Newman's views were rooted in Hume's scepticism about the limitations of reason in religious enquiry, and these views were, of course, utterly innocent of neo Hegelian metaphysics. But, as Newman said, he [Newman] was no metaphysician, and Fairbairn's self-confidence about reason as a highway to religious truth has suffered the eclipse of the neo-idealism which sustained it. The return of Hume to intellectual respectability has made Newman seem more modern, because he saw so clearly that there must be more to religion than reason acting on its own.

Newman was defended by the brilliant young scholar and novelist Fr William Barry, but he agonized with Blachford over whether he should reply to Fairbairn's rejoinder: 'it would', Newman wrote to Blachford, 'require a very brilliant knock down answer to Dr F. to justify my giving up my place "as an emeritus miles" and going down into the arena with a younger man. The only shade of reason for my publishing it is that I wished to say in print that in past years I had spoken too strongly once or twice against the argument [for God's existence] from final causes'.[46] In the end, he decided to print for private circulation, but not to publish, his rejoinder with a revised version of his *Contemporary* article. He made it clearer in his additional remarks that the 'moral sense' was just the religious aspect of the 'noetic faculty', as Aristotle called it, and it was this rather than reason which supplied the mind with its first principles. Religious truth was to be discovered when reason was employed on the first principles given by the moral sense. 'Dr Fairbairn, I must insist, ungraciously refuses to see a harmony

417

in such an association of two great faculties, and makes them enemies and rivals, as if I inordinately exalted the moral sense and crushed the reason.'[47]

Newman's last point was an attempt to state more clearly his acceptance of God's existence from the evidence of design in creation, in the sense of an order which was the work of a mind. He distinguished this from what was, more strictly speaking, the argument for God's existence from 'final causes' – the adaptation of means to ends in nature, for which Darwin had assigned a natural explanation. Fairbairn thanked Newman kindly for the further reply, which he was to think 'written in better temper and in a more reasonable vein'[48] than Newman's *Contemporary* article. But though he promised 'to weigh carefully its varied criticisms and elucidations',[49] it is a kind of evidence of Newman's theory of belief that as Fairbairn's views began from different first principles, so Newman's argument against them did nothing to change them, and Fairbairn published them unaltered fourteen years after.

Newman seems to have enjoyed much of his last decade, and there is a charming account of Anatole and Isy von Hügel prattling merrily to him in 1885, in 'the most talking gay party I have had for many years',[50] while his Foudrinier cousin Emmeline Deane drew his likeness. This was 'autotyped' and carried off to Eton to show the boys by his nephew, house master Harry Mozley. He seems not to have noticed the birth in 1881 of another Foudrinier-Deane connection, P. G. Wodehouse.

But old age is sad, and Newman's thoughts of mortality were fed by the steady stream of deaths of old acquaintances and friends. To the Redemptorist Thomas Bridgett, he recalled the late Robert Coffin's expression in youth as 'very sweet and modest . . . combined with a playfulness and an evident sense of humour when he conversed'.[51] Like many an English patriot, Newman was moved by the death of General Gordon at Khartoum; he was correspondingly indignant at Gladstone's failure to rescue him, and subscribed to Gordon's memorial fund. But he was overcome when lent a copy of *The Dream of Gerontius*, with Gordon's pencil markings, which the General in Khartoum had then given to *The Times*' correspondent who had also died. Gordon's faith had been deepened by reading the poem after his father's death. 'What struck me so much in his use of "The Dream etc" was that in St Paul's words he "died daily" ', wrote Newman to Blachford, ' – he was always on his death bed, fulfilling the common advice that we should ever pass the day, as if it was to be our last.'[52]

A number of old Oratory boys were in the abortive expedition to rescue Gordon, and one of these at least, a young de Lisle, had died as well. In 1886, Wilfrid Ward told Newman that another casualty of Empire, Lionel Tennyson, had his last hours on the boat back from India solaced by his reading of 'Lead, kindly light', and had repeated thrice the phrase, 'far from home.'[53] The hymn was a favourite at funerals; there were five translations into Welsh in Newman's lifetime. He could not be sorry at another death,

Miss Giberne's, in December 1885: 'She had had for near 30 years a life of penance',[54] he wrote, as he sent his news around to her few old friends still living. She had given him a lifetime's worship, not unmixed with occasional outbursts of temper. Copeland also died in 1885; his turkeys no longer supplied Newman's table, though Blachford still sent game. Newman's longest journey in 1886 was to attend another funeral, the dowager Duchess of Norfolk's Requiem at the Brompton Oratory, where he met Manning for the last time. He made the occasion an outing, spending a few days with Church at the deanery of St Paul's. It was almost his last extended departure from his 'nest' at Edgbaston.

There was an affecting meeting at the Birmingham Oratory with Ulla-thorne, last of the old Vicars Apostolic, who was recovering from a stroke, had resigned his see, and was soon to be made a titular archbishop. Newman bent his old grey head and begged his bishop's blessing. 'What could I do with him before me in such a posture?' wrote Ullathorne. 'I could not refuse without giving him great embarrassment':

> So I laid my hand on his head and said: 'My dear Lord Cardinal, notwithstanding all laws to the contrary, I pray God to bless you, and that His Holy Spirit may be full in your heart.' As I walked to the door, refusing to put on his biretta as he went with me, he said: 'I have been indoors all my life, whilst you have battled for the Church in the world'. I felt annihilated in his presence: there is a Saint in that man![55]

Newman here was not quite fair to himself. He had founded a university and schools, and churches and missions in Oxford, Birmingham and Dublin. This was not quite a life indoors.

The saint in Edgbaston was softened, but he was still capable of fierceness. He excluded from any benefit from his writings the Oratory grammar school set up without his permission by Richard Bellasis and Paul (Thomas) Eaglesim.[56] He left a careful memorandum on his expenditure on the Oratory since he had become a cardinal, to be discharged from his copyrights. Bodily he felt no pain but increasing weakness in the slow closing-down of the senses. In 1883, he found that he could no longer keep time for his fiddle playing, and offered the instrument to Richard Church's daughter Mary.[57] By 1884 he was having increasing difficulty in using his fingers to write: 'I cannot form my letters without pain and slowly'.[58] 'My pace in writing', he wrote in 1885, 'is that of a child beginning the alphabet.'[59] He was much weaker after an illness in September 1886, and was increasingly dependent on the devoted nursing of Fr William Neville. In August 1887 he consulted an oculist and Ogle about the spots before his eyes; increasingly he could only say Mass in sunlight. He managed to preach at the Oratory in honour of Leo XIII's Golden Jubilee of priesting in January 1888 and, in June, to visit London to sign his will and to pay a last visit to the melancholy ex-Oratorian, Frederick Bowles. In March Emmeline Deane painted his portrait, now in the National Portrait Gallery, and in May he took an active interest in his cousin Louisa Deane's scenery for the school Latin play, evoking a magical memory of his own young manhood, Pompeii and the background of 'foliage and rocks rising up towards Vesuvius'.[60] In July 1888, on his way to a brief holiday in Wales, he called on the Dominican nuns at Stone, and spoke of the sight of London as 'like a glimpse of the great Babylon . . . It made me think of the words, "Love not the world nor the things of the world". "Perhaps, however, I am too severe" ', he added with a touch of his old self-deprecation "and only think in that way because I am an old man" '.[61] Ullathorne had to assist him to sip his tea. The Archbishop was also frail, and died in March 1889.

Newman had a fall in October 1888, and was too ill to receive a visit from Gladstone in early November. 'I have known and admired you so long', replied Newman. 'But I can't write nor talk nor walk and hope you will take my blessing which I give from my heart.'[62] His exquisite courtesy survived his failing senses, but his apologies for his poor handwriting gave way to a lithographed line: 'I regret to say I am too old to attempt to answer letters.' 'I am too old to write; I cannot hold the pen'.[63] After Ullathorne's funeral, Herbert Vaughan described Newman to Manning as being 'doubled up like a shrimp and walking with a stick longer than his doubled body. His mind very much impaired and his memory for names curiously gone'.[64] This was an exaggeration. He was well enough to preside in the church at his birthday in 1889 and in September he congratulated Manning on his settlement of the dock strike. He himself went out into the November snow to negotiate with the Quaker George Cadbury the separate provision of a prayer room for the firm's Catholic women employees, on the unpopular ground that Catholics believed in the whole creed and that heresy consisted in affirming only part of it. The closest of his surviving Oxford friends Lord Blachford, the dearest to his heart with Froude, St John and Bowden, died a week later. He said his last Mass on Christmas Day 1889.

Yet Newman never quite gave up work. In his last year he revised his articles on biblical inspiration and on Fairbairn's attack on him for a last privately printed collection of *Stray Essays*. He appeared more decrepit in body than in mind. Wilfrid Ward, in a letter to his young wife, described him in April 1890 as 'a very sad sight, and he looked like a corpse!' Ward continued:

'The years of men are three score and ten, and after that it is labour and sorrow'. He had four score of real vigour, but it is labour and sorrow now. Fr. Neville let out that the Cardinal gets very depressed at being shut up in his room all day unable to do anything . . . Neville wants me to let him know of things which should be read to him. He evidently has a feeling of being dead practically, before he really is dead.[65]

On Ward's own account, Newman retained the liveliest interest in current affairs. He had mixed hopes of the Anglo-Catholic party, and was especially charmed with Charles Gore, to whom he had sent his picture of Keble, framed in oak allegedly from the tree on which St Edmund had been martyred. Gore's liberal Catholic manifesto *Lux Mundi* both fascinated and repelled him. To Ward he hoped for a reconciliation of orthodoxy with modern biblical criticism, but thought Gore's volume 'in substance the old story of Private Judgment'. To Neville, he said, 'It is the end of Tractarianism. They are giving up everything'.[66]

This was his old anti-liberalism, but Newman in his old age had an ecumenical strand. In his last year of life, he had Neville transcribe for an Evangelical friend George Edwards 'My Creed', his translation of 1854 of the 'Anima Christi', ascribed to Ignatius Loyola:

> Soul of Christ, be my sanctification;
> Body of Christ, be my salvation;
> Blood of Christ, fill all my veins;
> Water of Christ's side, wash out my stains;
> Passion of Christ, my comfort be;
> O good Jesus, listen to me;
> In thy wounds I fain would hide,
> Ne'er to be parted from Thy side;
> Guard me should the foe assail me;
> Call me when my life shall fail me;
> Bid me come to Thee above,
> With Thy saints to sing Thy love,
> World without end. Amen.[67]

He died as he had lived, a Catholic but an Evangelical as well, firm in 'those great and burning truths, which I learned when a boy'.[68]

On 9 August 1890, Newman received his niece Grace Langford, Tom and Harriett Mozley's only child, whom he had not seen since his estrangement from his sister in 1843. Grace had married and gone to Australia. She had also once been nursed by Maria Giberne in Rome. She spoke of Maria, the Cardinal held her hand, and recalled her as a three-year old at Manuel Johnson's Oxford Observatory.[69] The following day he fell ill with pneumonia, and died on the evening of Monday 11 August 1890. His last discernible words were to Neville: 'William, William'.[70] He was in his nineti-eth year.

So died John Henry Newman, Cardinal Deacon of the Holy Roman Church. His love and loyalty to his friends and followers, his dislike of Faber and Manning, his incomparable gifts for metaphor and irony and for touching the chords of memory in lovely prose, his deep loyalty to Oxford and distrust of Rome, his hatred of liberalism and his faith in God, had gone to dust and to eternity. The world which he had rejected honoured his passing. A vast crowd packed the Hagley Road at his Requiem, the way to Rednal was lined with mourners gentle and simple, while at the Requiem at the Brompton Oratory, which he had avoided as much as possible in life, William Neville's friend Bishop Patterson was nearly knocked off his fald-stool by the Cardinal Archbishop's diplomatic tribute to 'my brother and friend of more than sixty years'.[71] A few close friends of long standing, Lord Emly, Mrs Bowden and Emily Bowles, survived him, with Bloxam, who lowered to half mast the flag of St George on the tower of Upper Beeding church. But most of Newman's mourners were younger by more than half a lifetime, like his convert Emily Fortey, who sent flowers to lay at his feet. Within the year, his intellectual legacy was provoking controversy, as it came under attack from the liberal Edwin Abbott and was defended by Wilfrid Ward and R. H. Hutton; and liberals ever since have vacillated between assailing him and claiming him as their own. The *Via Media*, the development of doctrine, the primacy of conscience, the Illative Sense, the rights of theologians and of the laity to a place in the ecclesiastical sun, remain living theological ideas; though their author would doubtless think that the Roman Church has not yet quite found the balance between authority and liberty, and that the Church of England has as he predicted followed the primrose path down into liberalism, and has become all licence and no authority at all.

The questions that dominated his life remain unresolved, and even as an individual there can be no final judgement upon him. To some he remains 'the most attractive and most colossal egotist that ever lived',[72] a rhetorician who in Acton's words, was a 'sophist, the manipulator, and not the servant, of truth',[73] who effortlessly coloured the world to suit himself and, as a patron of right thinking in the Church, found a needless cure for his own incurably subjective cast of mind and sceptical distrust of reason in the fortress of nineteenth-century Roman Catholicism. Much in his thought might be discounted as no more than a product of its age, and of the certainties of a genteel Victorian English gentleman. The indictment, however, not only neglects Newman's earthier side – a keen nose and a sharp eye, a mordant irony, the withering force of his wit – but his lifelong quest for 'realities'. He thought it less damning to call a thing untrue than 'unreal'. It is Newman's greatness that in his sense of what is 'real', in what is individual and concrete, and flesh and blood, he can survive all criticism, and remain the greatest of modern English theologians and of modern English apologists for the universal claims of Roman Catholicism.

There was no 'mystery' or 'secret' of Newman, except in so far as any man or woman is a mystery, understood in the depths of their being by God alone. Newman believed in God and in himself; and underlying his immense intellectual sophistication was the soul of a simple Christian believer, for whom this world, for all its glories, is but the intimation of another. Yet his intellectual legacy is immense, and to Christians outside the Roman Catholic Church he stands as a sign of hope that there can be an answer to religious scepticism at the point of meeting between criticism and orthodoxy and ancient and modern; so that there is no ultimate contradiction between new truth and the truth once delivered to the saints. That truth, he thought, is to be found through that growth in holiness which is the only evidence of life, when heart speaks to heart; and it is from the shadows and images of this world that mind and heart pass into truth.

Notes

Newman's habit of rewriting his works means that they differ in both minor and major ways from edition to edition. With some works (*Prophetical Office, Justification, Development*) I have used early editions; in others, as with his poetry, I have admitted his changes from later editions. In the chapter on the *Apologia*, I have kept as elsewhere to the standard Oxford edition even where it differs from the first edition published in parts in 1864. Wilfrid Ward's Oxford edition of the two versions of 1864 and 1865 makes clear the variants between them.

For reasons of space, I have tried to limit references as much as possible to the identification of quotations, and to give the most accessible source.

ABBREVIATIONS

The large Roman numerals in the notes without other information are the volume numbers of *The Letters and Diaries of John Henry Newman*, vols XI–XXXI, eds. Charles Stephen Dessain, Edward E. Kelly, Thomas Gornall (London, 1961–72; Oxford, 1973–7); vols I–VI, eds. Ian Ker, Thomas Gornall, Gerard Tracey (Oxford, 1978–84). My work obviously owes a great deal to the scholarship supporting the *Letters and Diaries*.

Unless otherwise indicated, the works below are by Newman.

A	Martin J. Svaglic (ed.), *Apologia pro Vita Sua: Being a History of His Religious Opinions by John Henry Cardinal Newman* (Oxford, 1967).
AM	Anne Mozley (ed.), *Letters and Correspondence of John Henry Newman during his life in the English Church with a brief Autobiography*, 2 vols (London, 1891).
AW	Henry Tristram (ed.), *John Henry Newman: Autobiographical Writings* (New York, 1957).
B	[Joseph Bacchus ed.], *Correspondence of John Henry Newman with John Keble and Others 1839–1845* (London, 1917).
BC	*British Critic.*
Butler, *Ullathorne*	Dom Cuthbert Butler, *The Life & Times of Bishop Ullathorne 1806–1889*, 2 vols (London, 1926).
Butler, *Vatican Council*	Dom Cuthbert Butler, *The Vatican Council: The story told from inside in Bishop Ullathorne's Letters*, 2 vols (London, 1930).
CD	*Certain Difficulties felt by Anglicans in Catholic Teaching Considered:*

	I In Twelve Lectures addressed in 1850 to the Party of the Religious Movement of 1833; II In a Letter Addressed to the Rev. E. B. Pusey, D. D., . . . *And in a Letter addressed to the Duke of Norfolk* . . . , 2 vols (first published in this form in 1876; edition of London, 1901).
Chádwick	Owen Chadwick, *The Victorian Church*, 2 parts (edition of London, 1971 and 1970).
DA	*Discussions and Arguments on Various Subjects* (first published in this form, 1872; edition of London, 1911).
Ess	*Essays Critical and Historical*, 2 vols (London, 1871).
FN	F. W. Newman, *Contributions chiefly to the Early History of the Late Cardinal Newman* (London, 1891).
HS	*Historical Sketches*, 3 vols (first published in this form 1872–3; edition of London, 1897).
Liddon	Henry Parry Liddon, *Life of Edward Bouverie Pusey* (J. O. Johnston and R. J. Wilson eds.), 4 vols (London, 1893–5).
McGrath	Fergal McGrath, sj, *Newman's University: Idea and Reality* (London, 1951).
Mozley	Rev. T. Mozley, *Reminiscences chiefly of Oriel and the Oxford Movement*, 2 vols (2nd edition, London, 1882).
Murray	Placid Murray, osb, *Newman the Oratorian: His unpublished Oratory Papers* (Hereford, 1980).
MT, I	Meriol Trevor, *The Pillar of the Cloud* (London, 1962).
MT, II	Meriol Trevor, *Light in Winter* (London, 1962).
MW	Maisie Ward, *Young Mr Newman* (London, 1948).
O'F	Sean O'Faolain, *Newman's Way* (London, 1952).
OS	*Sermons preached on Various Occasions* (first published in this form in 1857; edition of London, 1900).
PS	*Parochial Sermons*, 6 vols (London, 1835–42).
Purcell	Edmund Sheridan Purcell, *Life of Cardinal Manning Archbishop of Westminster*, 2 vols (London, 1896).
US	*Fifteen sermons preached before the University of Oxford between A.D. 1826 and 1843* (London, 1871; republished with introductory essays by D. M. MacKinnon and J. D. Holmes, London, 1970).
VM	*The Via Media of the Anglican Church*, 2 vols (first published in this form in 1877; edition of London, 1891)
VV	*Verses on Various Occasions* (London, 1868).
Ward	W. R. Ward, *Victorian Oxford* (London, 1965).
Ward, *Newman*	Wilfrid Ward, *The Life of John Henry Cardinal Newman*, 2 vols (first published 1912; London, 1913).
Ward, *Wiseman*	Wilfrid Ward, *The Life and Times of Cardinal Wiseman*, 2 vols (London, 1897).

PREFACE

1 XIII, 419.

'AN AUTOBIOGRAPHY IN MINIATURE'

1 *AW*, 5.

INTRODUCTION

1 Fr Henry Tristram in *AW*, 22.
2 'Memorandum about the Cholera', III, 76.
3 Henri Bremond, *Newman: Essai de biographie psychologique* (Paris, 1906), xvi; cited Tristram, *AW*, 143.
4 XX, 443; cf. XI, xxii.
5 XXII, 211; cf. *AW*, 21.
6 I have taken a few pages of background from my following articles: in Chapter 7, from 'John Keble and the Victorian Churching of Romanticism', in J. R. Watson (ed.), *An Infinite Complexity: Essays in Romanticism* (Edinburgh, 1983), 226–39; in Chapter 8, from 'Nationality and liberty, protestant and catholic: Robert Southey's *Book of the Church*', in Stuart Mews (ed.), *Religion and National Identity: Studies in Church History*, XVIII (Oxford, 1982), 409–32; in Chapter 10, from ' "No Bishop, no Church!" The Tractarian Impact on Anglicanism', written with Stephen Sykes, in Geoffrey Rowell (ed.), *Tradition Renewed: The Oxford Movement Conference Papers* (London, 1986), 120–39; and in Chapter 15, from 'Newman and Prophecy, Evangelical and Catholic', in *The Journal of the United Reformed Church History Society*, III (March 1985), 160–88.

CHAPTER 1   BEGINNINGS

1 J. H. Mozley, 'Cardinal Newman and his Forebears', *Notes and Queries*, 189 (3 November 1945), 190–1; A. K., 'Cardinal Newman and his Forebears', *Notes and Queries*, 196 (14 April 1951, 26 May 1951), 164–9, 230–3.
2 O'F, 10.
3 *Ibid.*, 12.
4 XV, 396.
5 *Ibid.*, 400–1.
6 I, 4; XX, 23.
7 *Ibid.*
8 III, 172; cf. XXVI, 56, on Wordsworth's 'Ode on Immortality'.
9 *A*, 15–16.
10 Alan Smith, *The Established Church and Popular Religion 1750–1850* (London, 1971), 116.
11 XI, xvii.
12 *VV*, 134.
13 O'F, 30.
14 MW, 12.

15 *Ibid.*, 13.
16 *Ibid.*, 14.
17 AM, I, 17.
18 O'F, 22.
19 *A*, 16.
20 FN, 3; XXV, 88.
21 *AW*, 29.
22 I, 22.
23 *AW*, 5.
24 XII, 108.
25 I, 7, 9, 10.
26 FN, 3.
27 I, 7.
28 *Ibid.*, 8.
29 *A*, 16.
30 A. Dwight Culler, *The Imperial Intellect: A Study of Newman's Educational Ideal* (New Haven, 1955), 3; cf. XXV, 129.
31 *AW*, 29.
32 I, 10.
33 FN, 5.
34 AM, I, 18; XXV, 329.
35 XIII, 449.
36 *A*, 17.
37 O'F, 45–6.
38 I, 19.
39 *Ibid.*, 26.
40 IV, 331–2.
41 *Ibid.*, 332.
42 *AW*, 119, 268.

CHAPTER 2   CONVERSION

1 Ford K. Brown, *Fathers of The Victorians: the Age of Wilberforce* (Cambridge, 1961).
2 Michael Hennell, 'Evangelicalism and Worldliness 1770–1870', in G. J. Cumming and Derek Baker (eds.), *Popular Belief and Practice*, VIII, *Studies in Church History* (Cambridge, 1972), 317–60.
3 'Ten Thousand Compassions and Charities', Brown, 317–60.
4 *A*, 17.
5 *Ibid.*
6 *AW*, 181.
7 *A*, 18.
8 *Ibid.*, 17–18.
9 *Ibid.*, 19.
10 *Ibid.*, 20.
11 I, 27.
12 Newman MSS, The Oratory, Birmingham.
13 *A*, 20.
14 Aubrey de Vere, *Recollections* (London, 1897), 256.

15 Geoffrey Faber, *Oxford Apostles: A Character Study of the Oxford Movement* (London, 1934), 232.
16 *A*, 18.
17 *AW*, 166.
18 *Ibid.*, 172.
19 *Ibid.*, 79.
20 M. J. Svaglic in *A*, 478; *AW*, 80.
21 *AW*, 250; cf. XXXI, 31: 'I should say that it is difficult to realize or imagine the identity of the boy before and after 1816 . . . '
22 *AW*, 151.
23 *A*, 18–19.
24 *AW*, 151.
25 *A*, 19.
26 Louis Bouyer, *Newman. His Life and Spirituality* (London, 1958), 22–3; cited David Newsome, 'The evangelical sources of Newman's power', in John Coulson and A. M. Allchin, *The Rediscovery of Newman: An Oxford Symposium* (London, 1967), 20.
27 G. W. E. Russell, *A Short History of the Evangelical Movement* (London, 1915), 144.

CHAPTER 3   TRINITY: TRIUMPH AND FAILURE

1 FN, 6.
2 *AW*, 30.
3 *Ibid.*
4 Culler, *The Imperial Intellect*, 5.
5 *AW*, 30.
6 Matthew Arnold, 'Thyrsis', *Poems*, 2 vols (London, 1869), I, 260.
7 William Tuckwell, *Reminiscences of Oxford* (London, 1900), 3; cited Culler, 1.
8 Matthew Arnold, 'Emerson', republished in R. H. Super (ed.), *Philistinism in England and America* (Ann Arbor, 1974), 166.
9 John Murray (ed.), *The Autobiographies of Edward Gibbon* (London, 1897), 76, 81.
10 L. S. Sutherland and L. G. Mitchell (eds.), *The History of the University of Oxford*, V, *The Eighteenth Century* (Oxford, 1986).
11 David Newsome, *The Parting of Friends: A Study of the Wilberforces and Henry Manning* (London, 1966), 62.
12 I, 35.
13 *Ibid.*, 36.
14 *Ibid.*
15 *Ibid.*, 37.
16 *Ibid.*, 41.
17 *AW*, 33.
18 *Ibid.*, 156–7.
19 I, 42.
20 *Ibid.*, 48.
21 *Ibid.*, 46.
22 *Ibid.*, 48.
23 *Ibid.*, 44–5.
24 *Ibid.*, 46–7.

25 *Ibid.*, 49.
26 *Ibid.*, 50.
27 *AW*, 157–8.
28 I, 52–3.
29 *Ibid.*, 53.
30 *Ibid.*
31 *AW*, 158.
32 Culler, 11–12.
33 IV, 331.
34 I, 54–6.
35 O'F, 51.
36 Cited Culler, 12.
37 I, 58–9.
38 *St Bartholomew's Eve: A Tale of the Sixteenth Century*, in Two Cantos (Oxford, 1818–19). Newman has marked on the Bodleian Library copy which parts are by him and which are by Bowden. Also XXIV, 155.
39 *AW*, 42.
40 *St Bartholomew's Eve*, 8–9.
41 *Ibid.*, 34.
42 *The Undergraduate*, no. 3, 22.2.1819, 21–3; Culler, 13.
43 I, 62.
44 *Ibid.*, 63–4.
45 *AW*, 160–1.
46 I, 66.
47 *AW*, 37.
48 I, 67.
49 *Ibid.*, 72.
50 *Ibid.*
51 *AW*, 45.
52 I, 73–5.
53 *Ibid.*, 77–8.
54 O'F, 59.
55 I, 166.
56 *Ibid.*, 77.
57 *AW*, 45–6.
58 Culler, 18.
59 I, 83.
60 FN, 9.
61 I, 84–5.
62 *Ibid.*, 85.
63 *Ibid.*, 87.
64 *Ibid.*
65 *AW*, 47.
66 I, 95.
67 *Ibid.*, 96.

CHAPTER 4   ORIEL: TRIUMPH AND TRIBULATION

1 I, 97.
2 *Ibid.*, 101.
3 *Ibid.*, 109; XVIII, 326.
4 XIV, 127.
5 I, 111.
6 *AW*, 174.
7 *Ibid.*, 175.
8 *Ibid.*, 176.
9 I, 113.
10 *Ibid.*, 115–16.
11 *AW*, 49–50.
12 *Ibid.*, 180.
13 *Ibid.*, 179, 82.
14 O'F, 68.
15 XXV, 352.
16 I, 123.
17 Culler, 26.
18 *Ibid.*
19 I, 123.
20 *Ibid.*
21 *Ibid.*, 124.
22 *Ibid.*, 136.
23 *AW*, 185.
24 I, 133, 131.
25 *AW*, 185–6.
26 *Ibid.*, 62.
27 I, 139.
28 *Ibid.*, 131.
29 *Ibid.*, 134.
30 *Ibid.*, 139.
31 *Ibid.*, 131.
32 *AW*, 63; A, 213.
33 *AW*, 64.
34 Culler, 36.
35 *AW*, 37.
36 Culler, 38.
37 *AW*, 65.
38 XIX, 318–19.
39 *AW*, 66.
40 E. Jane Whately, *Life and Correspondence of Richard Whately, D.D. Late Archbishop of Dublin* (London, 1868), 438.
41 Culler, 38.
42 *AW*, 66–7.
43 *Ibid.*; XV, 176.
44 *AW*, 68.

45 I, 143.
46 *AW,* 187.
47 I, 154.
48 *Ibid.,* 155.
49 *Ibid.,* 156.
50 FN, 42.
51 *AW,* 189.
52 I, 162.
53 *AW,* 191.
54 *Ibid.,* 196.
55 I, 157.
56 *AW,* 74.
57 *Ibid.,* 191.
58 *Ibid.,* 193.
59 I, 170.
60 *A,* 27.
61 *AW,* 196.

CHAPTER 5   THE CRISIS OF EVANGELICALISM

1 David Newsome, *The Parting of Friends,* 1–19. Also Boyd Hilton, *The Age of Atonement: The Influence of Evangelicalism on Social and Economic Thought, 1795–1865* (Oxford, 1988), 10–19.
2 D. W. Bebbington, *Evangelicalism in Modern Britain: A History from the 1730s to the 1980s* (London, 1989), 96.
3 *AW,* 71.
4 *Ibid.*
5 *Ibid.*
6 *Ibid.,* 199.
7 *Ibid.,* 200.
8 *Ibid.,* 76.
9 *Ibid.,* 77.
10 *A,* 21.
11 *AW,* 77.
12 I, 177.
13 *AW,* 79.
14 Thomas L. Sheridan, *Newman on Justification* (Staten Island, New York, 1967), 23.
15 I, 32–3.
16 Sheridan, 82–6
17 *AW,* 202.
18 *Ibid.,* 203.
19 *Ibid.,* 77.
20 *Ibid.,* 206.
21 *A,* 22.
22 *Ibid.*

CHAPTER 6   EVANGELICAL TO LIBERAL

1 *AW*, 202–3.
2 *Ibid.*, 208.
3 I, 203.
4 *Ibid.*, 199.
5 *Ibid.*, 184.
6 *Ibid.*, 308.
7 *AW*, 205.
8 I, 212.
9 *Ibid.*, 214, 219.
10 *Ibid.*, 226, 228, 226.
11 II, 101.
12 I, 182.
13 *Ibid.*
14 On other aspects of Butler's influence on Newman, see H. F. G. Swanston, *Ideas of Order: The mid-nineteenth century renewal of Anglican Theological Method* (Assen, The Netherlands, 1974).
15 *A*, 31.
16 I, 254.
17 *A*, 25–6; I, 216, 274.
18 *AW*, 83.
19 Cited *A*, 25.
20 *Letters on the Church. By an Episcopalian* (London, 1826), 191.
21 *AW*, 69.
22 I, 277.
23 *Ibid.*, 281.
24 *Ibid.*, 282.
25 *A*, 33.
26 *Ibid.*, 34. Also Piers Brendon, *Hurrell Froude and the Oxford Movement* (London, 1974), 60–74.
27 FN, 18; Newman also suggested 1826, when Francis took his degree: I, 291.
28 I, 290–1.
29 *VV*, 4–5, 7.
30 II, 5.
31 *AW*, 89.
32 Culler, 54–5.
33 *AW*, 90.
34 Culler, 57; XXX, 419.
35 *A*, 26.

CHAPTER 7   LIBERAL TO HIGH CHURCHMAN

1 II, 10.
2 *Ibid.*, 15–16; *A*, 25.
3 *AW*, 211.

4 Peter Nockles, *Continuity and change in Anglican High Churchmanship in Britain 1792–1850*, 2 vols (Oxford D. Phil. 1982).
5 *The Journal of the Rev John Wesley*, 8 vols (London, 1909–16), II, 257.
6 'Ode to Liberty', *The Complete Poetical Works of Percy Bysshe Shelley* (Oxford, 1945), 604.
7 *A*, 29.
8 II, 20.
9 Culler, 59.
10 Cited II, 21.
11 *Ibid.*, 25; XXIII, 38.
12 II, 28.
13 *VV*, 13, 15.
14 *AW*, 212.
15 MW, 150.
16 II, 58.
17 *Ibid.*, 69.
18 *Ibid.*, 108.
19 *VV*, 20.
20 II, 44; XXII, 209.
21 II, 45; XXX, 107.
22 *AW*, 91.
23 *A*, 29.
24 II, 60.
25 Chadwick, I, 68.
26 *A*, 27.
27 II, 74.
28 *Ibid.*, 30.
29 *A*, 35.
30 II, 88.
31 *Ibid.*, 109.
32 *Ibid.*, 117–18.
33 *AW*, 96–7.
34 II, 118–19.
35 *Ibid.*, 118.
36 *Ibid.*, 120.
37 *Ibid.*, 121.
38 *Ibid.*, 125.
39 *Ibid.*, 127.
40 *A*, 26.
41 *AW*, 98.
42 *Ibid.*, 103.
43 *Ibid.*
44 II, 202.
45 *Ibid.*, 150.
46 *Ibid.*, 185.
47 *Ibid.*, 133.
48 *Ibid.*, 263.
49 *Ibid.*, 264–5.

50 Ward, 76.
51 II, 198.
52 T. C. F. Stunt, 'John Henry Newman and the Evangelicals', *The Journal of Ecclesiastical History*, XXI (1970).
53 II, 228.
54 *Ibid.*, 308.
55 Sermons 274 and 273, 19 and 12 December 1830, MSS, The Oratory, Birmingham.
56 O'F, 130–1.
57 *Ibid.*, 136, 161.
58 IV, 329–30.

CHAPTER 8   THE CRISIS OF THE CHURCH

1 J. C. D. Clark, *English Society 1688 to 1832: Ideology, Social Structure and Political Practice during the Ancien Regime* (Cambridge, 1985).
2 Peter Nockles, 'Pusey and the Question of Church and State', in Perry Butler (ed.), *Pusey Rediscovered* (London, 1983), 259–60.
3 G. W. E. Russell, *Collections and Recollections* (London, 1904), 69. For a precise statement of the inequalities of the Georgian Church see Peter Virgin, *The Church in an Age of Negligence: Ecclesiastical Structure and Problems of Church Reform 1700–1840* (Cambridge, 1989).
4 II, 130.
5 *Ibid.*, 130–1.
6 *Ess*, I, 21–3.
7 *US*, 18–19.
8 *Ibid.*, 21, 33.
9 *Ibid.*, 21, 23.
10 *Ibid.*, 29.
11 *Ibid.*, 27, 22.
12 *Ibid.*, 73.
13 *Ibid.*, 62–3.
14 *Ibid.*, 19.
15 *A*, 257.
16 II, 317.
17 *Ibid.*, 342–3.
18 *Ibid.*, 365.
19 *Ibid.*, 367.
20 *Ibid.*, 369.
21 *Ibid.*, 371.
22 *Ibid.*, 372.
23 III, 4.
24 *Ibid.*, 31.
25 *Ibid.*, 105, 113.
26 *A*, 36–7.
27 V, 399.
28 *The Arians of the Fourth Century* (London, 1890), 47, 50, 71–2.

29 *Ibid.*, 9.
30 Jean Guitton, *La Philosophie de Newman Essai sur l'idée du développement* (Paris, 1933), 3; cited MW, 345–6.
31 *Arians*, 35, 28.
32 *Ibid.*, 33–4.
33 *Ibid.*, 361.
34 *Ibid.*, 106.
35 *A*, 40.
36 *Arians*, 394.
37 III, 114.
38 *Ibid.*, 43.
39 *VV*, 105–6.
40 III, 93.
41 *Ibid.*, 130–1.
42 MT, I, 113; cf. XXI, 69.
43 G. B. Tennyson, *Victorian Devotional Poetry: The Tractarian Mode* (Cambridge, Mass., 1981), 131–2.
44 *A*, 41.
45 *VV*, 58.
46 *Ibid.*, 60–1.
47 III, 138.
48 *Ibid.*, 139; cf. *VV*, 63–4.

CHAPTER 9   SIREN LANDS

1 Jean Smith, 'Newman and Sicily', *The Downside Review*, CXVII (July 1989), 158.
2 *VV*, 70–1.
3 *A*, 42.
4 III, 162, 165.
5 *VV*, 79–80.
6 III, 170, 167.
7 *Ibid.*, 170; cf. *VV*, 83–4.
8 III, 171.
9 *Ibid.*, 176.
10 *Ibid.*, 181.
11 *Ibid.*, 206.
12 *Ibid.*, 223.
13 *Ibid.*, 211.
14 *Ibid.*, 253.
15 *Ibid.*, 227.
16 *Ibid.*, 230.
17 *Ibid.*, 232.
18 *Ibid.*, 248–9.
19 *Ibid.*, 268.
20 *Ibid.*, 260.
21 *Ibid.*, 277.
22 *Ibid.*, 232.

23 *Ibid.*, 280.
24 *Ibid.*, 297.
25 *Ibid.*, 276.
26 *A*, 43.
27 III, 186.
28 *Ibid.*, 224.
29 *A*, 42.
30 *Ibid.*
31 *A*, 42; III, 298.
32 IV, 108.
33 III, 297–8.
34 *AW*, 111.
35 III, 310.
36 *AW*, 138.
37 *Ibid.*, 111.
38 III, 302.
39 *Ibid.*, 303–5.
40 *Ibid.*, 307, 309.
41 *Ibid.*, 313–14.
42 *Ibid.*, 310.
43 *AW*, 123.
44 *Ibid.*, 124.
45 *Ibid.*, 125–6.
46 *Ibid.*, 126–7.
47 *Ibid.*, 127–9.
48 *Ibid.*, 130.
49 *Ibid.*, 131.
50 *Ibid.*, 131–3.
51 *Ibid.*, 134–5.
52 *Ibid.*, 135–6.
53 IV, 58.
54 *AW*, 133, 136.
55 *A*, 43.
56 *Ibid.*
57 *VV*, 131–2.
58 III, 316.
59 *Ibid.*, 312.
60 *AW*, 138.
61 H. B. Salvin, 'Newman's Illness in Sicily: A Review and an Interpretation', *The Dublin Review*, 238 (1964–5), 35–64.
62 *AW*, 132.
63 IV, 7–9.
64 *AW*, 122–3.
65 *Ibid.*, 138.
66 *A*, 43.
67 *VV*, 133–4.

CHAPTER 10   THE OXFORD MOVEMENT

1 IV, 3.
2 *A*, 42.
3 *Ibid.*, 43.
4 F. L. Cross, 'The Myth of July 14th, 1833', in *John Henry Newman* (London, 1933), 162–3.
5 John Keble, *National Apostasy* (republished Abingdon, 1983), 18–19.
6 *Ibid.*, 26.
7 *Ibid.*, 11–12.
8 *AW*, 119.
9 *US*, 97–8.
10 *A*, 47.
11 *Ibid.*
12 IV, 13.
13 *Ibid.*, 28.
14 *Ibid.*, 29.
15 *Ibid.*, 42.
16 Richard Hooker, *Of the Laws of Ecclesiastical Polity*, Book III, (1594), i, 3–6.
17 *Ibid.*, Book VII, xi, 8.
18 N. Sykes, *Old Priest and New Presbyter* (Cambridge, 1956).
19 Charles Daubeny, *A Guide to the Church* (London, 1798), 34–5.
20 Tract 1, 1–2.
21 *Ibid.*, 2.
22 *Ibid.*, 4.
23 Tract 2, 1, 3.
24 Tract 3, 1, 3.
25 *The Oxford Dictionary of Quotations* (Oxford, 1966), 335.
26 Tract 3, 3.
27 *Ibid.*, 5.
28 *A*, 53.
29 IV, 48.
30 *Ibid.*, 52.
31 *Ibid.*, 61.
32 *Ibid.*, 70, 69.
33 *Ibid.*, 79.
34 *Ibid.*, 78–9.
35 *Ibid.*, 69.
36 *Ibid.*, 91.
37 *Ibid.*, 93.
38 *Ibid.*, 100.
39 *Ibid.*, 98.
40 Tract 4, 5.
41 IV, 143.
42 *Ibid.*, 112.
43 *Ibid.*, 113.
44 *Ibid.*, 116–17.

45 *Ibid.*, 121.
46 *Ibid.*, 141.
47 *Ibid.*, 160.
48 *Ibid.*, 165.
49 III, 70.
50 IV, 127.
51 *Ibid.*, 169–70.
52 *Ibid.*, 170–1.
53 *Ibid.*, 176.
54 *VV*, 180.
55 IV, 184–5.
56 *Ibid.*, 189.
57 *Ibid.*, 183.
58 *Ibid.*, 203.
59 *Ibid.*, 201; original Greek in text translated.
60 *Ibid.*
61 David Newsome, 'Justification and Sanctification: Newman and the Evangelicals', *The Journal of Theological Studies*, New Series, XV (April 1964), 53.
62 *PS*, I, 359, 361, 365, 370–1, 372–3.
63 IV, 320.

CHAPTER 11   THE VIA MEDIA: AN UNCERTAIN SPRING

1 Sir Mountstuart E. Grant Duff, *Notes from a Diary, 1873–81*, 2 vols (London, 1898), II, 121.
2 IV, 56, 98.
3 William Lockhart in B, 390.
4 VI, 57.
5 J. A. Froude, *Short Studies on Great Subjects*, 4 vols (London, 1893), IV, 286.
6 M. Arnold, *Philistinism in England and America*, 165.
7 *Ibid.*
8 IV, 200.
9 *Ibid.*, 219.
10 *Ibid.*, 218.
11 *Ibid.*, 221–2.
12 *Ibid.*, 206.
13 *Ibid.*, 225.
14 *Ibid.*, 230.
15 *Ibid.*, 237.
16 *Ibid.*, 239.
17 *Ibid.*, 243.
18 *Ibid.*, 245.
19 *Ibid.*, 249–50.
20 *Ibid.*, 261.
21 Ward, 86.
22 IV, 268.
23 Ward, 86–7.

24 IV, 289.

25 *Ibid.*

26 MT, I, 169–70.

27 IV, 311.

28 *Ibid.*, 291.

29 *Ibid.*, 302.

30 *Ibid.*, 322.

31 *Ibid.*, 312.

32 *Ibid.*, 311.

33 *Ibid.*, 313.

34 *Ibid.*, 279.

35 Tract 41, 12.

36 Y. Brilioth, *The Anglican Revival Studies in the Oxford Movement* (London, 1933), 53–4.

37 Tract 38, 10.

38 IV, 323.

39 *Ibid.*, 348.

40 *Ibid.*, 348–9.

41 *Ibid.*, 357.

42 *Ibid.*, 359.

43 *Ibid.*, 315.

44 Brilioth, 54.

45 IV, 350.

46 Louis Allen, *John Henry Newman and the Abbé Jager: A Controversy on Scripture and Tradition (1834–1836)* (London, 1975), 36.

47 IV, 353; Ward, 95.

48 *Ibid.*, 354.

49 *Ibid.*, 371.

50 *Ibid.*

51 V, 19.

52 *Ibid.*, 7–8.

53 *Ibid.*, 20.

54 *Ibid.*, 25.

55 Allen, 59.

56 V, 100.

57 *Ibid.*, 21.

58 *Ibid.*, 22.

59 *Ibid.*, 39–40.

60 J. H. Thom (ed.), *The Life of the Rev Joseph Blanco White, written by himself*, 3 vols (London, 1845), II, 117.

61 V, 53; *VM*, II, 92.

62 Ward, 95–7.

63 V, 70.

64 Ward, 99.

65 V, 83.

66 *Ibid.*, 86.

67 *Ibid.*, 64.

68 *Ibid.*, 110.

69 *Ibid.*, 106.
70 *Ibid.*, 102–4.
71 Allen, 94–5.
72 *Ibid.*, 74–5.
73 *Ibid.*, 93.
74 *Ibid.*, 96–7.
75 V, 128.
76 *Ibid.*, 185.

CHAPTER 12   THE VIA MEDIA: EARLY SUMMER

1 Mozley, I, 395–6.
2 V, 124.
3 *Ibid.*, 119.
4 *A*, 15.
5 V, 178.
6 *Ibid.*, 136.
7 *Ibid.*, 151, 150.
8 *VM*, II, 95–6.
9 *Ibid.*, 99, 131.
10 *Ibid.*, 137.
11 *Ibid.*, 159.
12 *Ibid.*, 154; original Greek in text translated.
13 *Ibid.*, 199.
14 *Ibid.*, 166.
15 *Ibid.*, 164.
16 *Ibid.*, 195.
17 *Ibid.*, 154.
18 *Ibid.*, 175.
19 *Ess*, I, 57.
20 *Ibid.*, 40.
21 *Ibid.*, 42.
22 V, 116.
23 Mozley, I, 380.
24 V, 189.
25 *Ibid.*, 210; original Greek in text translated.
26 *Ibid.*, 214–15; original Greek in text translated.
27 *Ibid.*, 217.
28 Cited Ward, 99.
29 V, 235.
30 Richard Church, *The Oxford Movement: Twelve Years 1833–1845* (1890; edition of London, 1909), 166.
31 Chadwick, I, 116–17.
32 Cited 'Hampden, Renn Dickson', S. L. Ollard, Gordon Crosse and Maurice Bond (eds.), *A Dictionary of English Church History* (London, 1948), 265.
33 V, 237.
34 *Ibid.*
35 Ward, 100–1.

36 V, 243–4.
37 *Ibid.*, 249.
38 Church, *Oxford Movement*, 161.
39 V, 264–5.
40 *Ibid.*, 260.
41 Chadwick, I, 119.
42 Ward, 101.
43 V, 251.
44 Thomas Arnold, 'The Oxford Malignants and Dr Hampden', *The Edinburgh Review*, LXIII (April 1836), 237–9.
45 Chadwick, I, 120.
46 V, 252.
47 *Ibid.*, 260.
48 *Ibid.*, 263.
49 *Ibid.*, 270.
50 *Ibid.*, 273.
51 *PS*, III, vii–viii.
52 *DA*, 2–3.
53 *Ibid.*, 10, 15.
54 *Ibid.*, 17–19.
55 *Ibid.*, 22–3.
56 *Ibid.*, 24.
57 *Ibid.*, 33.
58 *Ibid.*, 34.
59 *Ibid.*, 41.
60 V, 301–3.
61 *Ibid.*, 314.
62 *Ibid.*, 299.
63 *Ibid.*
64 AM, II, 196.
65 VI, 83.
66 V, 345.
67 VI, 18.
68 *Ibid.*, 71.
69 V, 317.

CHAPTER 13   THE VIA MEDIA: HIGH SUMMER

1 VI, 47.
2 V, 328, 383.
3 *Ibid.*, 358–9.
4 III, 121.
5 Sir George Prevost (ed.), *The Autobiography of Isaac Williams* (London, 1892), 40.
6 V, 390.
7 *Lectures on the Prophetical Office of the Church, viewed relatively to Romanism and Popular Protestantism* (London, 1837), 20–1.
8 VI, 7.

9 Mozley, I, 320.
10 VI, 7.
11 *Lectures on the Prophetical Office*, 21.
12 *Ibid.*, 30.
13 *Ibid.*, 39.
14 *Ibid.*, 41.
15 *Ibid.*, 285.
16 VI, 127.
17 *Ibid.*, 174.
18 *Lectures on the Prophetical Office*, 301.
19 *Ibid.*, 313–14.
20 VI, 6.
21 *Ibid.*, 10.
22 Cited in Tract 82, *VM*, II, 150.
23 *Ibid.*, 170.
24 *Ibid.*, 191.
25 VI, 13.
26 *VM*, II, 169.
27 VI, 52.
28 *Ibid.*, 60; original Greek in text translated.
29 *Ibid.*, 33–4.
30 *Ibid.*, 36.
31 *Ibid.*, 95.
32 *Ibid.*, 102.
33 *Ibid.*, 112.
34 *A*, 39.
35 (London, 1837).
36 VI, 149.
37 R. A. Knox, 'The man who tried to convert the Pope', *Literary Distractions* (London, 1958), 114–34.
38 VI, 151.
39 *Ibid.*, 104.
40 *Ibid.*, 74.
41 *Ibid.*, 88–9.
42 *Ibid.*, 120.
43 Cited Chadwick, I, 175.
44 *Ibid.*
45 VI, 222.
46 *Ibid.*, 224.
47 *VV*, 334.
48 *Lectures on Justification* (2nd edition, London, 1840), 160.
49 *Ibid.*, 248–9.
50 Peter Toon, *Evangelical Theology 1833–1856: A Response to Tractarianism* (London, 1979), 140–70.
51 *Lectures on Justification*, 63.
52 *Ibid.*, 214.
53 *Ibid.*, 381.
54 VI, 131.

55 *Lectures on Justification*, 385.
56 *Ibid.*, 382.
57 *Ibid.*, 387.
58 Alister E. McGrath, *Justitia Dei: A History of the Christian Doctrine of Justification*, 2 vols (Cambridge, 1986), II, 126–7.
59 *Ibid.*, 130.
60 *Ess.*, I, 122.
61 *Ibid.*, 124.
62 *Ibid.*, 136.

CHAPTER 14   THE VIA MEDIA: INDIAN SUMMER

 1 VI, 164.
 2 J. A. Froude, *Short Studies on Great Subjects*, 4 vols (London, 1893), 273, 282–3.
 3 VI, 165.
 4 David Newsome, *The Parting of Friends*, 169.
 5 VI, 185.
 6 *Ibid.*, 164.
 7 Liddon, II, 91.
 8 *A*, 76–7.
 9 VI, 197.
10 *Ibid.*, 194.
11 R. D. Middleton, *Newman & Bloxam: An Oxford Friendship* (Oxford, 1947), 12–13.
12 *A letter to the Rev Godfrey Faussett, D.D., Margaret Professor of Divinity* . . . (Oxford, 1838); republished *VM*, II, 235–6.
13 VI, 254.
14 *Ibid.*, 276.
15 *Ibid.*, 207.
16 *Ibid.*, 268.
17 Sheridan Gilley, 'Newman and Prophecy, Evangelical and Catholic', *The Journal of the United Reformed Church History Society*, III (March 1985), 160–88.
18 'The Patristical Idea of Antichrist', *DA*, 60.
19 *Ibid.*, 91.
20 *DA*, 252–3.
21 'Preface', *The Catechetical Lectures of S. Cyril, Archbishop of Jerusalem* (Oxford, 1845), xx.
22 Republished as 'Palmer's View of Faith and Unity' (from the *BC*), *Ess*, I, 143–79.
23 *A*, 56.
24 VI, 286.
25 *Ibid.*, 291–2.
26 *Ibid.*, 295.
27 *Ibid.*, 302.
28 *Ibid.*
29 *Ibid.*, 305.
30 *Ibid.*, 307.
31 *Ibid.*, 309.
32 *Ibid.*, 320.

33 *Ibid.*, 323.
34 *VV*, 234.
35 VI, 348.
36 V, 185.
37 VI, 332.
38 *Ibid.*, 364.
39 *Ibid.*, 352.
40 *Ibid.*
41 AM, II, 279.
42 *PS*, IV, 238–9.
43 AM, II, 278.
44 *US*, 193, 194, 197, 200.
45 *Ibid.*, 203.
46 AM, II, 278.
47 *Ibid.*, 279.
48 *AW*, 215.
49 Liddon, II, 101.
50 AM, II, 282.
51 Liddon, II, 103.
52 *AW*, 216.

CHAPTER 15   THE VIA MEDIA: FIRST DOUBTS

1 *A*, 91.
2 *Ibid.*, 93; summarizing 'Prospects of the Anglican Church' (from the *BC*), *Ess*, I, 262–306.
3 *A*, 77; cf. *CD*, I, 96–7.
4 'The Anglo-American Church' (from the *BC*), *Ess*, I, 374.
5 *A*, 108–9.
6 *Ibid.*, 108.
7 AM, II, 294.
8 *A*, 110.
9 AM, II, 286.
10 *Ibid.*, 287.
11 *A*, 110–11.
12 *Ibid.*, 111.
13 *Ibid.*, 110.
14 'Catholicity of the Anglican Church' (from the *BC*), *Ess*, II, 6.
15 *Ibid.*, 11.
16 *Ibid.*, 38–9.
17 *Ibid.*, 59.
18 *Ibid.*, 70–2.
19 AM, II, 285.
20 *Ibid.*, 291.
21 B, 42.
22 *Ibid.*, 45.
23 AM, II, 295.

24 *A*, 118.
25 AM, II, 300.
26 *Ibid.*, 299.
27 *The Church of the Fathers* (London, 1840), 3.
28 *Ibid.*, 4.
29 *Ibid.*, 414.
30 V, 313.
31 *AW*, 137–8.
32 *Ibid.*, 138.
33 AM, II, 301.
34 *Ibid.*, 302.
35 *Ibid.*, 303.
36 *Ibid.*, 304.
37 *Ibid.*, 305.
38 *A*, 124–5.
39 AM, II, 318.
40 *Ibid.*, 319.
41 Todd to Newman, 18.6.1840, Newman MSS, The Oratory, Birmingham.
42 Todd to Newman, 13.6.1840, *ibid.*
43 'The Protestant Idea of Antichrist' (from the *BC*), *Ess*, II, 114.
44 *Ibid.*, 134.
45 Newman citing Todd, *ibid.*, 150.
46 *Ibid.*, 138–40.
47 *Ibid.*, 166–7.
48 *Ibid.*, 168–70.
49 *Ibid.*, 173.
50 *Ibid.*, 180.
51 *Ibid.*, 184–5. See 'The Imperial Image of the Church', in Paul Misner, *Papacy and Development: Newman and the Primacy of the Pope* (London, 1976), 50–7.
52 'Milman's View of Christianity' (from the *BC*), *Ess*, II, 229.
53 *Ibid.*, 231.
54 *Ibid.*, 232.
55 *Ibid.*, 241.
56 *Ibid.*, 233.
57 A. Milman, *Henry Hart Milman D.D. Dean of St. Paul's: A Biographical Sketch* (London, 1900), 144–5.
58 Cited Hugh Martin (ed.), *The Private Prayers of Lancelot Andrewes* (London, 1957), 11.
59 Tract 88, 'The Greek Devotions of Bishop Andrews, Translated and Arranged', 24.

CHAPTER 16   TRACT 90

1 *The Times*, 16 6.1834; cited *The History of the Times*, I, 'The Thunderer' in the Making, *1785–1841* (London, 1935), 405.
2 'The Tamworth Reading Room', *DA*, 255.
3 *Ibid.*, 260.

4 *Ibid.*, 262.
5 *Ibid.*
6 *Ibid.*, 263.
7 *Ibid.*, 268.
8 *Ibid.*
9 *Ibid.*, 270.
10 *Ibid.*, 273.
11 *Ibid.*, 293–5.
12 *Ibid.*, 302.
13 *Ibid.*, 304.
14 *Ibid.*, 302–3.
15 *Ibid.*, 284.
16 *Ibid.*, 292.
17 'Remarks on Certain Passages of the Thirty-Nine Articles', *VM*, II, 271–2.
18 *Ibid.*, 347–8.
19 *Ibid.*, 271.
20 *Ibid.*, 295.
21 *Ibid.*, 318.
22 *Ibid.*, 341.
23 *The History of the Times*, I, 407–8.
24 AM, II, 330.
25 *VM*, II, 359–60.
26 AM, II, 326.
27 *Ibid.*
28 *VM*, II, 362.
29 *A Letter addressed to the Rev R. W. Jelf, D.D., Canon of Christ Church, in explanation of the Ninetieth Tract . . .* , *VM*, II, 371.
30 *Ibid.*, 380.
31 *Ibid.*, 385.
32 *Ibid.*, 386.
33 *Ibid.*
34 *Ibid.*, 387.
35 'Postscript' (added after publication), *ibid.*, 391.
36 B, 91.
37 *Ibid.*, 89; AM, II, 337.
38 AM, II, 338.
39 B, 99.
40 *Ibid.*, 101.
41 *A Letter addressed to the Right Reverend Father in God, Richard, Lord Bishop of Oxford, on occasion of the Ninetieth Tract . . .* (Oxford, 1841), *VM*, II, 395–424.
42 AM, II, 341 (final words added from *ms.*)
43 *Ibid.*, 342–3.
44 *Ibid.*, 343–4.
45 A, 87–8.
46 Cited Chadwick, I, 186.
47 R. J. Schiefen, *Nicholas Wiseman and the Transformation of English Catholicism* (Shepherdstown, 1984), 118.
48 Ward, *Wiseman*, I, 376.

49 B, 130.
50 Ward, *Wiseman*, I, 377.
51 Schiefen, 122.
52 *A*, 176.
53 *Ibid.*, 128.
54 *Ibid.*, 130.
55 *Ibid.*
56 AM, II, 352.
57 *Ibid.*, 353.
58 *Ibid.*, 354.
59 *A*, 135.
60 *Ibid.*, 136.
61 *Ibid.*, 137.

CHAPTER 17   DEATH-BED AT LITTLEMORE

1 *A*, 137.
2 *Ibid.*, 150.
3 *Ibid.*, 158.
4 AM, II, 391–2.
5 *Ibid.*, 393–4.
6 B, 172.
7 AM, II, 393.
8 *A*, 151.
9 *Ibid.*, 152.
10 B, 198–9.
11 *A*, 155–6.
12 (London, 1842).
13 (Oxford, 1842).
14 (Oxford, 1842). Newman published two further volumes taking the text from AD 400 to AD 456, in 1843 and 1844.
15 Owen Chadwick, *The Mind of the Oxford Movement* (London, 1963), 42.
16 See Edwin A. Abbott, *Philomythus: An Antidote against Credulity: A Discussion of Cardinal Newman's Essay on Ecclesiastical Miracles* (London, 1891).
17 *Lectures on the Present Position of Catholics in England* (Dublin, 1857), 277; cited *A*, 432. Cf. Newman's controversy with Bishop Samuel Hinds of Norwich, XIV, 387.
18 US, 317, 323, 333.
19 *Ibid.*, 324.
20 *Ibid.*, 340.
21 *Ibid.*, 341.
22 *Ibid.*, 348.
23 *Ibid.*, 346–7.
24 AM, II, 411.
25 *Ibid.*, 411–2.
26 B, 205.
27 *VM*, II, 431.

28 *Ibid.*, 433.
29 MT, I, 287.
30 *A*, 184.
31 B, 210–11.
32 *Ibid.*, 218.
33 *Ibid.*, 219–20.
34 *Ibid.*, 221.
35 *Ibid.*, 226–9.
36 *Ibid.*, 231.
37 *Ibid.*, 282.
38 *Ibid.*, 238.
39 XXVII, 305.
40 B, 244.
41 *Ibid.*, 248.
42 AM, II, 420–1.
43 *Ibid.*, 419, 422.
44 B, 253–4.
45 *Ibid.*, 250.
46 AM, II, 423.
47 B, 262–3.
48 Edward Bellasis, *Memorials of Mr Serjeant Bellasis 1800–73* (London, 1893), 53.
49 *Sermons bearing on Subjects of the Day* (London, 1871), 407–8.
50 Bellasis, 54.
51 *Sermons on Subjects*, 376–81.
52 AM, II, 425–6.
53 B, 272–3.
54 *Ibid.*, 274–5.
55 *Ibid.*, 276.
56 *Ibid.*, 279.
57 *Ibid.*, 278.
58 *Ibid.*, 279.
59 *Ibid.*, 280.
60 *Ibid.*, 291.
61 *Ibid.*, 292–3.
62 *Ibid.*, 293.
63 W. F. Monypenny and G. E. Buckle, *The Life of Benjamin Disraeli Earl of Beaconsfield*, 6 vols (London, 1910–20), IV, 350–1.

CHAPTER 18   DEVELOPMENT TO ROME

1 AM, II, 431.
2 B, 297.
3 *Ibid.*, 300.
4 *Ibid.*, 318.
5 *Ibid.*, 320.
6 *Ibid.*, 322.
7 *Ibid.*, 329.

8 *Ibid.*, 325.
9 Cited Chadwick, I, 208.
10 AM, II, 435.
11 B, 333.
12 *Ibid.*, 334.
13 *Ibid.*, 335.
14 *Ibid.*, 336.
15 AM, II, 438.
16 *Ibid.*, 439.
17 AM, II, 444.
18 MT, I, 318–19.
19 *A*, 207.
20 B, 349.
21 *Ibid.*, 354–5.
22 *A*, 198.
23 MT, I, 345.
24 AM, II, 453.
25 B, 369.
26 AM, II, 454.
27 Liddon, II, 430.
28 W. Ward, *William George Ward and the Oxford Movement* (London, 1889), 335.
29 *Ibid.*, 345.
30 AM, II, 456.
31 *Ibid.*, 458.
32 *Ibid.*, 459, 461.
33 Ward, *Newman*, I, 83.
34 B, 381–2.
35 *Ibid.*, 379.
36 *An Essay on the Development of Christian Doctrine* (London, 1845), 39.
37 *Ibid.*, 452–3.
38 *Ibid.*, 204–5.
39 B, 375–7.
40 *Essay on Development*, 453.
41 *A*, 211.
42 XI, 3.
43 B, 388.
44 XI, 9.
45 *Ibid.*, 13.
46 AM, II, 492.
47 XI, 9.
48 *Ibid.*
49 B, 386.
50 XIX, xv.
51 *A*, 213.

CHAPTER 19   THE ROMAN ORATORY

1 AM, II, 445.
2 XI, 146.
3 *Ibid.*, 15.
4 *Ibid.*, 23.
5 *Ibid.*, 39.
6 *Ibid.*, 29.
7 *Ibid.*, 105.
8 *Ibid.*, 34.
9 *Ibid.*, 128.
10 *Ibid.*, 124.
11 *Ibid.*, 91.
12 *Ibid.*, 224.
13 *Ibid.*, 112.
14 *Ibid.*, 175, 215.
15 *Ibid.*, 186–7.
16 *Ibid.*, 206.
17 *Ibid.*, 42.
18 *Ibid.*, 39.
19 *Ibid.*, 59, 43, 45, 43.
20 *Ibid.*, 102–3, 104.
21 *Ibid.*, 96.
22 *Ibid.*, 132.
23 *Ibid.*, 151.
24 *Ibid.*, 165.
25 *Ibid.*, 195.
26 *AW*, 255.
27 XI, 196; cf. Murray, 434–5.
28 *Ibid.*, 194.
29 *Ibid.*, 210.
30 *Ibid.*, 245–6.
31 *Ibid.*, 249.
32 *Ibid.*, 252.
33 *Ibid.*, 259.
34 *Ibid.*, 260, 263.
35 *Ibid.*, 269.
36 *Ibid.*, 273.
37 *Ibid.*, 293.
38 *Ibid.*, 285–6.
39 XII, 9.
40 XI, 294.
41 *Ibid.*, 296.
42 *Ibid.*, 298–9.
43 *Ibid.*, 301.
44 XII, 60, republished in *Tracts Theological and Ecclesiastical* (London, 1902), 7–91.
45 *Ibid.*, 13.

46 *AW*, 256.
47 XII, 24.
48 *Ibid.*, 25.
49 *Ibid.*, 19–20.
50 *Ibid.*, 22.
51 *Ibid.*, 49.
52 *Ibid.*, 45.
53 *Ibid.*, 54–5.
54 *Ibid.*, 56.
55 *AW*, 245–8.
56 XII, 73.
57 *Ibid.*, 69–70.
58 *Ibid.*, 72; Murray, 439.
59 XII, 79.
60 *Ibid.*, 100.
61 *Ibid.*, 97.
62 *Ibid.*, 436.
63 *Ibid.*, 113.
64 *Ibid.*, 117.
65 *Ibid.*, 127.
66 *Ibid.*, 135.
67 *Ibid.*, 137.
68 *AW*, 256.
69 David Newsome, *Godliness & Good Learning: Four Studies on a Victorian Ideal* (London, 1961), 116–17.
70 Cited XIII, 451.
71 Margaret Maison, *Search your Soul, Eustace: A Survey of the Religious Novel in the Victorian Age* (London, 1961), 143–4.
72 XII, 215.
73 *Ibid.*, 220–2.
74 *Ibid.*, 239.
75 *Ibid.*, 281.
76 *Ibid.*, 243.
77 *Ibid.*, 340.
78 See 'The Rambler, 1848–1862', in W. E. Houghton (ed.), *The Wellesley Index to Victorian Periodicals 1824–1900*, 4 vols (Toronto, 1966–1987), II, 732–84.
79 XII, 352–3.

CHAPTER 20   THE BIRMINGHAM ORATORY

1 XIII, 24.
2 *Ibid.*, 33.
3 *Ibid.*, 47.
4 *Ibid.*, 32.
5 *Ibid.*
6 *Ibid.*, 41.
7 *Ibid.*, 38.

8 *Ibid.*, 56.
9 *Ibid.*, 94.
10 *Ibid.*, 102.
11 *Ibid.*, 104.
12 *Ibid.*, 120.
13 *Ibid.*, 130–1.
14 *Ibid.*, 127–8.
15 *Ibid.*, 135.
16 *Ibid.*, 160–1.
17 *Ibid.*, 143.
18 *Ibid.*, 238.
19 *Ibid.*
20 *Ibid.*, 254.
21 *Ibid.*, 261.
22 *Ibid.*, 378.
23 *Ibid.*, 263.
24 *Ibid.*, 270.
25 *Ibid.*, 269.
26 *Ibid.*, 286.
27 *Ibid.*, 312.
28 *Ibid.*, 342.
29 *Ibid.*, 321.
30 *Ibid.*, 432.
31 *Ibid.*, 431.
32 XIV, 62.
33 *Ibid.*, 85.
34 *Ibid.*, 97–8.
35 *Ibid.*, 147.
36 *Ibid.*, 109.
37 *Ibid.*, 117–18.
38 *Ibid.*, 154.
39 *Ibid.*, 154–5.
40 *Ibid.*, 122.
41 *Ibid.*, 141.
42 *Ibid.*, 159.
43 *Ibid.*, 161.
44 *Ibid.*, 210.
45 *Ibid.*, 211.
46 *Ibid.*, 283.
47 *Ibid.*, 288.
48 *Ibid.*, 206.
49 *Ibid.*, 213, 252.
50 *Ibid.*, 261.
51 *Ibid.*, 262.
52 *Ibid.*, 267–9.
53 *Ibid.*, 315.
54 *Lectures on the Present Position of Catholics in England* (3rd edition, Dublin, 1857), 27, 36.

55 *Ibid.*, 31–2.
56 *Ibid.*, 32.
57 *Ibid.*
58 *Ibid.*, 67.
59 *Ibid.*, 70–1.
60 *Ibid.*, 112.
61 *Ibid.*, 114.
62 XIV, 501–2.
63 *Ibid.*, 318.
64 *Ibid.*, 446.
65 *Ibid.*, 451, 450.
66 *Ibid.*, 450.
67 XV, 21.
68 *Ibid.*, 24.
69 *Ibid.*, 14.
70 *Ibid.*, 80.
71 *Ibid.*, 106.
72 *Ibid.*, 108.
73 *Ibid.*, 107.
74 *OS*, 176–7.
75 *Ibid.*, 171–2.
76 Butler, *Ullathorne*, I, 197.
77 XV, 140–1.
78 *Ibid.*, 193.
79 *Ibid.*, 200.
80 *Ibid.*, 201.
81 *Ibid.*, 202.
82 *Ibid.*, 259.
83 *Ibid.*, 526.
84 *Ibid.*, 279.
85 *Ibid.*, 284.
86 *Ibid.*, 278.
87 *Ibid.*, 285.
88 *Lectures on the Present Position of Catholics*, 191.
89 XV, 309.

CHAPTER 21   THE CATHOLIC UNIVERSITY

1 XV, 318.
2 Butler, *Ullathorne*, I, 174.
3 XV, 355.
4 XVI, 538; cf. McGrath, 179–80.
5 XV, 425.
6 *Ibid.*, 470.
7 *HS*, I, 220.
8 XVI, 322.
9 *Ibid.*, 340.

10 *Ibid.*, 341.
11 XV, 494.
12 *AW*, 304.
13 *Ibid.*, 304–5.
14 XV, 507.
15 XVI, 5.
16 *AW*, 229.
17 E. Larkin, *The Making of the Roman Catholic Church in Ireland, 1850–1860* (Chapel Hill, 1980), 235.
18 *AW*, 313.
19 *Ibid.*, 313–14.
20 Larkin, 236; cf. McGrath, 245.
21 XVI, 45, 116.
22 *Ibid.*, 121.
23 *AW*, 319; McGrath, 238–50.
24 XVI, 50.
25 *Ibid.*, 52.
26 *Ibid.*, 53.
27 *Ibid.*, 76.
28 *Ibid.*, 64.
29 *Ibid.*, 127.
30 *Ibid.*, 156.
31 *Ibid.*, 345.
32 *Ibid.*, 275; cf. McGrath, 199–201.
33 XVI, 129.
34 *AW*, 328.
35 *Ibid.*
36 XVI, 620; McGrath, 321.
37 XVI, 625; McGrath, 329.
38 XVI, 359.
39 *Ibid.*
40 *Ibid.*, 552.
41 *Ibid.*, 554.
42 A. L. Sanders, *The Victorian Historical Novel 1840–1880* (London, 1978), 140.
43 *DA*, 307.
44 *Ibid.*, 338.
45 *Ibid.*, 343.
46 *Ibid.*, 357.
47 *Ibid.*, 362.
48 XVII, 43.
49 *Ibid.*, 101.
50 *Ibid.*, 103.
51 *Ibid.*, 121.
52 *Ibid.*, 138.
53 *Ibid.*, 151.
54 *Ibid.*, 159–60.
55 *Ibid.*, 173.
56 *Ibid.*, 234–5.

57 *Ibid.*, 239.
58 *Ibid.*, 249–50.
59 *Ibid.*, 255; XIX, 101.
60 XVIII, 49.
61 XVII, 262.
62 *Ibid.*, 267.
63 *Ibid.*, 269.
64 *Ibid.*, 307.
65 *Ibid.*, 312.
66 *Ibid.*, 314.
67 *Ibid.*, 317.
68 *Ibid.*, 318–9.
69 *Ibid.*, 348.
70 *Ibid.*, 351; see Murray, 350–9.
71 XVIII, 175–6.
72 *Ibid.*, 93.
73 XVII, 502.
74 *AW*, 305; XVII, 324.
75 XVII, 212.
76 *Ibid.*, 220.
77 XIX, 379.
78 XVII, 385–6; McGrath, 388–401.
79 XVII, 440; McGrath, 357–60, 402–8.
80 XVII, 458.
81 *Ibid.*, 444.
82 *Ibid.*, 453.
83 *Ibid.*, 525.
84 *Ibid.*, 514.
85 XVIII, 111.
86 'The Atlantis, 1858–1860, 1862–1863, 1870', in W. E. Houghton (ed.), *The Wellesley Index to Victorian Periodicals 1824–1900*, 4 vols (Toronto, 1966–87), III, 53–61.
87 XVII, 513; XVIII, 228.
88 *AW*, 330; he also wrote the editorial replies: XVIII, 565–83.
89 XVIII, 487.
90 *Ibid.*, 490.
91 XVII, 426–7.
92 *OS*, 57.
93 XVIII, 218.
94 *Ibid.*, 376–7.
95 *The Office and Work of Universities* (London, 1856), 165.
96 G. M. Young, 'Newman Again', *Last Essays* (London, 1950), 165.
97 Ian Ker (ed.), *The Idea of a University* (Oxford, 1976), 5.
98 *Ibid.*, 10.
99 *Ibid.*, 122–3.
100 *Ibid.*, 20.
101 *Ibid.*, 145.
102 *Ibid.*, 5.

103 *Ibid.*, 174, 179–80.
104 Young, 100.
105 *Idea*, 28–9.
106 *AW*, 320.

CHAPTER 22   LIBERAL CATHOLICISM: I

1 XVIII, 131.
2 H. M. de Achaval and J. D. Holmes, *The Theological Papers of John Henry Newman on Faith and Certainty* (Oxford, 1976), xii–xiii, 39–50.
3 Ward, *Newman*, I, 423–5.
4 XVIII, 534; XXI, 201.
5 *Ibid.*
6 XVIII, 244.
7 XIX, 464.
8 XVIII, 284–7.
9 *Ibid.*, 310.
10 *Ibid.*, 312.
11 *Ibid.*, 331.
12 *Ibid.*, 550.
13 *Ibid.*, 554.
14 *Ibid.*, 559.
15 *Ibid.*, 560.
16 *Ibid.*, 562.
17 XIX, 42.
18 *Ibid.*, 46.
19 *Ibid.*, 55.
20 *Ibid.*, 53.
21 *Ibid.*, 90.
22 *Ibid.*, 96.
23 *Ibid.*, 88.
24 *Ibid.*, 89.
25 *HS*, III, 253–312.
26 *The Rambler*, I, new series (May 1859), 122.
27 XIX, 135.
28 *Ibid.*, 136–7.
29 *Ibid.*, 141.
30 *Ibid.*
31 John Coulson (ed.), *On Consulting the Faithful in Matters of Doctrine* (London, 1961), 72.
32 *Ibid.*, 73.
33 *Ibid.*, 75.
34 *Ibid.*, 75–6.
35 *Ibid.*, 77.
36 *Ibid.*, 103–4.
37 *Ibid.*, 106.
38 XIX, 151.

39 *Ibid.*, 205.
40 *Ibid.*, 175.
41 *Ibid.*, 241.
42 *Ibid.*, 228.
43 *Ibid.*, 276.
44 *Ibid.*, 277.
45 *Ibid.*, 290.
46 J. L. Altholz, *The Liberal Catholic Movement in England: The "Rambler" and its Contributors 1848–1864* (London, 1962), 111.
47 T. S. Bokenkotter, *Cardinal Newman as an Historian* (Louvain, 1959), 138; cited Altholz, 111.

CHAPTER 23   LIBERAL CATHOLICISM: II

1 XIX, 182.
2 *Ibid.*, 211.
3 'Memorandum. The Delation to Rome', *ibid.*, 282–3.
4 *AW*, 249–51.
5 Ward, *Newman*, I, 568–614.
6 XIX, 311.
7 *Ibid.*, 331.
8 Altholz, 127.
9 XIX, 376.
10 *Ibid.*, 553.
11 *Ibid.*, 299–300.
12 Altholz, 125.
13 XIX, 308.
14 *Ibid.*, 415.
15 *Ibid.*, 422.
16 *Ibid.*, 485.
17 *Ibid.*, 509.
18 *Ibid.*, 506.
19 *Ibid.*, 519.
20 *The Present Crisis of the Holy See tested by Prophecy* (London, 1861).
21 XX, 4–5.
22 *Ibid.*, 13.
23 *Ibid.*, 35–6.
24 *Ibid.*, 38.
25 XIX, 495.
26 MT, II, 233.
27 XX, 82.
28 *Ibid.*, 82.
29 *Ibid.*, 83.
30 *Ibid.*, 93.
31 *Ibid.*
32 *Ibid.*, 119.
33 *Ibid.*, 141.
34 *Ibid.*, 145.

35 *Ibid.*, 178.
36 XIX, 359.
37 XX, 209.
38 *Ibid.*, 216.
39 XX, 221.
40 *VV*, 256; cf. XX, 236.
41 XX, 254.
42 *AW*, 254.
43 XX, 399–400.
44 *Ibid.*, 502–3.
45 *Ibid.*, 513.
46 *Ibid.*, 56.
47 *Ibid.*, 277, 314.
48 Altholz, 194.
49 XX, 294–5.
50 *Ibid.*, 333.
51 Altholz, 195.
52 XX, 348.
53 *Ibid.*, 353.
54 *Ibid.*, 375.
55 *Ibid.*, 378.
56 *Ibid.*, 379.
57 Altholz, 196.
58 XX, 446–8.
59 *Ibid.*, 75.
60 *Ibid.*, 248.
61 *Ibid.*, 468.
62 XVII, 559.
63 XX, 530.
64 *AW*, 85.
65 *A*, 341.

CHAPTER 24   APOLOGIA

1 XXI, 31.
2 *Ibid.*, 10.
3 *Ibid.*, 11.
4 *Ibid.*, 12.
5 *Ibid.*, 13.
6 *Ibid.*, 20–1.
7 *Ibid.*, 34–5.
8 *A*, 351, 349.
9 XXI, 47.
10 *A*, 352–3.
11 *Ibid.*, xxii; XXI, 61.
12 *Ibid.*, 100.
13 *A*, xxiv.

14 Susan Chitty, *The Beast and the Monk: A Life of Charles Kingsley* (London, 1974).
15 *A*, 395.
16 *Ibid.*, 357–8.
17 *Ibid.*, 358–9.
18 *Ibid.*, 359, 362.
19 *Ibid.*, 363.
20 *Ibid.*, 362.
21 *Ibid.*, 363.
22 *Ibid.*, 366–7; *Lectures on the Present Position of Catholics*, 284.
23 *A*, 371.
24 *Ibid.*, 369.
25 *Ibid.*, 372.
26 *Ibid.*; cf. *CD*, I, 240.
27 *A*, 373; cf. *CD*, I, 249–50.
28 *A*, 373.
29 *Ibid.*, 375; cf. *CD*, I, 285–6.
30 *A*, 376; cf. *CD*, I, 287.
31 *A*, 376–7; cf. *CD*, I, 288.
32 *Ibid.*, 381, 379.
33 *Ibid.*, 381–2.
34 *Ibid.*, 384.
35 XXI, 73.
36 *Ibid.*, 79.
37 *Ibid.*, 89.
38 *Ibid.*, 160.
39 Ward, *Newman*, I, 642.
40 XXI, 94.
41 *Ibid.*, 118.
42 *Ibid.*, 105.
43 *Ibid.*
44 *Ibid.*, 107.
45 *Ibid.*, 111.
46 *Ibid.*, 132.
47 *Ibid.*, 112.
48 *A*, 396.
49 *Ibid.*, 12.
50 *Ibid.*, 214.
51 *Ibid.*
52 *Ibid.*, 215.
53 *Ibid.*, 218.
54 *Ibid.*
55 *Ibid.*, 219.
56 *Ibid.*, 222.
57 *Ibid.*, 232.
58 *Ibid.*, 240.
59 *Ibid.*, 216–18.
60 *Ibid.*, 252–3.
61 XXI, 185.

62 G. Egner, *Apologia pro Charles Kingsley* (London, 1969).
63 XXI, 120.
64 *A*, xxv.
65 *Ibid.*, lviii.
66 *Ibid.*, xliv.
67 *Ibid.*, xlviii.

CHAPTER 25   OXFORD AGAIN

1 XXI, 145.
2 *Ibid.*, 166.
3 *Ibid.*, 167.
4 Henry Tristram, *Newman and his Friends* (London, 1933), 233.
5 XXI, 166.
6 *Ibid.*, 232.
7 *Ibid.*, 273.
8 *Ibid.*, 286.
9 *Ibid.*, 308–9.
10 *Ibid.*, 320.
11 *Ibid.*, 327.
12 *Ibid.*, 343.
13 *Ibid.*, 347–8.
14 *Ibid.*, 383.
15 *Ibid.*, 84; cf. V. A. McClelland, *English Roman Catholics and Higher Education 1830–1903* (Oxford, 1973), 175 ff.
16 *Ibid.*, 208 ff.
17 XXI, 309.
18 *Ibid.*, 412–13.
19 *Ibid.*, 424.
20 *Ibid.*, 436.
21 *Ibid.*, 448–9.
22 *Ibid.*, 466.
23 *Ibid.*, 475.
24 *Ibid.*, 477.
25 *Ibid.*, 478.
26 *Ibid.*
27 XXII, 16.
28 XXI, 455, 503.
29 XXII, 52.
30 Ward, *Newman*, II, 96.
31 XXII, 69.
32 *A Letter to the Rev E. B. Pusey, D.D., on his recent Eirenicon* (London, 1866); *CD*, II, 2–3.
33 *Ibid.*, 7.
34 *Ibid.*, 86.
35 *Ibid.*, 22.
36 *Ibid.*, 23.

37 *Ibid.*, 103.
38 *Ibid.*, 114.
39 *Ibid.*, 21.
40 *Ibid.*, 115.
41 XXII, 16–17.
42 *Ibid.*, 19.
43 *Ibid.*, 157.
44 M. Ward, *The Wilfrid Wards and the Transition, I, The Nineteenth Century* (London, 1934), 32.
45 Purcell, II, 323.
46 *Ibid.*, 322–3.
47 *VV*, 314.
48 *Ibid.*, 339.
49 *Ibid.*, 301.
50 G. Egner, 165.
51 XXII, 9.
52 XXI, 455.
53 XXII, 143, 88.
54 *Ibid.*, 241.
55 *Ibid.*, 37.
56 *Ibid.*, 62.
57 *Ibid.*, 224.
58 Butler, *Ullathorne*, II, 14.
59 XXII, 252–3.
60 McClelland, 220.
61 *Ibid.*, 220–1.
62 XXII, 314.
63 Butler, *Ullathorne*, II, 15–16.
64 XXII, 277.
65 *Ibid.*, 293.
66 *Ibid.*, 314–15.
67 *Ibid.*, 331.
68 Butler, *Ullathorne*, II, 17.
69 XXIII, 3.
70 *Ibid.*, 4.
71 *Ibid.*, 10.
72 *Ibid.*, 91.
73 *Ibid.*, 94; Latin on 92.
74 *Ibid.*, 101.
75 *Ibid.*, 122.
76 *Ibid.*, 125.
77 *Ibid.*, 127.
78 Butler, *Ullathorne*, II, 21.
79 XXIII, 131.
80 *Ibid.*, 130.
81 *Ibid.*, 135–6.
82 *Ibid.*, 148.
83 *Ibid.*, 164–5.

84 *Ibid.*, 134.
85 *Ibid.*, 137.
86 *Ibid.*, 139.
87 Purcell, II, 316.
88 *Ibid.*, 318.
89 Butler, *Ullathorne*, II, 39.
90 XXIII, 151.
91 *Ibid.*, 157.
92 *Ibid.*, 177.
93 *Ibid.*, 190.
94 *Ibid.*, 143.
95 *Ibid.*, 202–3.
96 *Ibid.*, 217.
97 *Ibid.*, 209.
98 *Ibid.*, 207.
99 *Ibid.*, 219.
100 *Ibid.*, 226.
101 *Ibid.*
102 *Ibid.*, 230.
103 *Ibid.*, 220.
104 *Ibid.*, 251.
105 *OS*, 281–316.
106 XXIII, 297
107 *Ibid.*, 298–9.
108 *Ibid.*, 312.
109 *Ibid.*, 17.

CHAPTER 26   THE GRAMMAR

1 J. E. C. Bodley, *Cardinal Manning. The Decay of Idealism in France. The Institute of France* (London, 1912), 11.
2 Lytton Strachey, *Eminent Victorians: Cardinal Manning – Florence Nightingale – Dr Arnold – General Gordon* (London, 1922), 74.
3 XXIII, 290, 329.
4 Strachey, 106.
5 XXIV, 362–3.
6 XXIII, 363; FN, 110.
7 XXIV, 101.
8 *Ibid.*, 127:
9 *Ibid.*, 143.
10 XXV, 442.
11 XXIV, 29.
12 *Ibid.*, 22.
13 *Ibid.*, 77.
14 XXV, 138.
15 XXIV, 121.
16 XIV, 371.

17 XXIV, 92, 91.
18 XXIII, 396.
19 XXIV, 162.
20 *Ibid.*, 326.
21 *AW*, 267.
22 XXV, 199.
23 XXIV, 294.
24 *Ibid.*, 295.
25 *Ibid.*, 316–17.
26 *An Essay in Aid of a Grammar of Assent*: with an Introduction by Nicholas Lash (Notre Dame and London, 1979), 30. Ian Ker's edition (Oxford, 1985) contains both a summary of the critical literature and a defence of the work against its critics. On the context, see G. D. McCarthy, *The Ethics of Belief Debate* (Atlanta, Georgia, 1986).
27 Lash, *Grammar*, 78–9.
28 *Ibid,.* 117–18.
29 *Ibid.*, 46.
30 *Ibid.*, 86–7.
31 *Ibid.*, 86.
32 *Ibid.*, 82.
33 XXIV, 375.
34 *Grammar*, 277.
35 *Ibid.*, 275.
36 See Lash, Introduction, *Grammar*, 20–1.
37 *Grammar*, 293.
38 XXIV, 73.

CHAPTER 27   THE VATICAN COUNCIL

1 XXIV, 332.
2 Butler, *The Vatican Council*, I, 163.
3 T. B. Macaulay, *Critical and Historical Essays*, 2 vols (London, 1946), II, 39.
4 E. E. Y. Hales, *Pio Nono* (London, 1954), 298.
5 XXIV, 391.
6 *Ibid.*, 140.
7 *Ibid.*, 344.
8 XXV, 9.
9 *Ibid.*, 17.
10 *Ibid.*, 81.
11 The Irish No-Popery lecturer William Murphy who caused riots in Birmingham in 1867.
12 XXV, 18–19.
13 *Ibid.*, 27.
14 *Ibid.*, 48.
15 *Ibid.*, 55.
16 *Ibid.*, 63.
17 *Ibid.*, 65.

18 *Ibid.*, 123.
19 *Ibid.*, 85.
20 *Ibid.*, 124.
21 Butler, *The Vatican Council*, II, 163.
22 XXV, 164.
23 *Ibid.*, 169–70.
24 *Ibid.*, 165.
25 *Ibid.*, 177.
26 *Ibid.*, 189.
27 *Ibid.*, 220.
28 *Ibid.*, 224.
29 *Ibid.*, 220.
30 *Ibid.*, 231.
31 *Ibid.*, 245.
32 *Ibid.*, 262.
33 *Ibid.*, 430.
34 XXVI, 117.
35 *Ibid.*, 120.
36 *Ibid.*, 163–4.
37 *Ibid.*, 7.
38 *Ibid.*, 244.
39 *Ibid.*, 192–3.
40 'In the world, but not of the world', *OS*, 263–80; 'Memoir', in H. W. Wilberforce, *The Church and the Empires Historical Periods* (London, 1874), 1–16.
41 XXVI, 341–2.
42 XXVII, 75.
43 *Ibid.*, 90.
44 *Ibid.*, 89.
45 John Morley, *The Life of William Ewart Gladstone*, 3 vols (London, 1904), II, 514–15.
46 In *Rome and the Newest Fashions in Religion* (London, 1875), lix, lxi.
47 XXVII, 159.
48 *A Letter addressed to His Grace the Duke of Norfolk on occasion of Mr Gladstone's recent Expostulation* (London, 1875), 4.
49 *Ibid.*, 20.
50 *Ibid.*, 27.
51 *Ibid.*, 20.
52 *Ibid.*, 21.
53 *Ibid.*, 55.
54 *Ibid.*, 56.
55 *Ibid.*, 57.
56 *Ibid.*
57 *Ibid.*, 60–1.
58 *Ibid.*, 63.
59 *Ibid.*, 66.
60 *Ibid.*, 52.
61 *Ibid,.* 67.
62 *Ibid.*, 68.

63 *Ibid.*, 71–2.
64 *Ibid.*, 94.
65 *Ibid.*, 115.
66 *Ibid.*, 125.
67 XXVII, 198.
68 *Ibid.*, 192.
69 *Ibid.*, 193.
70 *Ibid.*, 220.
71 *Ibid.*
72 W. Ward, *William George Ward and the Catholic Revival* (London, 1893), 274.
73 XXVII, 273.
74 *Ibid.*, 376.
75 *Ibid.*, 401.
76 Butler, *Ullathorne*, II, 101–2; Italian draft, XXVII, 401–2.
77 Butler, *Ullathorne*, II, 103; Latin draft, XXVII, 404–6.
78 Butler, *Ullathorne*, II, 102–3.
79 *Ibid.*, 104.
80 *Ibid.*, 104–5.
81 *Ibid.*, 105.
82 XXVII, 420.
83 *Ibid.*, 291.
84 *Ibid.*, 305.
85 *Ibid.*, 312.
86 *Ibid.*, 352.

CHAPTER 28   THE VIA MEDIA REVISITED

1 XXVIII, 52–3.
2 *Ibid.*, 77.
3 Michael de la Bedoyere, *The Life of Baron von Hügel* (London, 1951), 32, 43.
4 XXVIII, 151.
5 *AW*, 271–5.
6 XXVIII, 142–3.
7 Morley, *Gladstone*, II, 570.
8 XXVIII, 158, 157.
9 XXIX, 188. Also Meriol Trevor, *The Arnolds: Thomas Arnold and His Family* (London, 1973), 176–9.
10 'Preface to the Third Edition' of the *Lectures on the Prophetical Office of the Church: The Via Media of the Anglican Church*, 2 vols (London, 1877).
11 *Ibid.*, I, v.
12 *Ibid.*, xxxvii.
13 *Ibid.*, xxxix–xl.
14 *Ibid.*, xlii.
15 *Ibid.*, xlvii.
16 *Ibid.*, xlvii–xlviii.
17 *Ibid.*, xlviii–xlix.
18 *Ibid.*, lix.

19 *Ibid.*, lxii.
20 *Ibid.*, lxviii.
21 *Ibid.*, lxxvi.
22 *Ibid.*, lxxvii.
23 *Ibid.*, lxvi.
24 *Ibid.*, xciv.
25 *Ibid.*, lxxxiii.
26 XXVIII, 189.
27 *Ibid.*
28 Friedrich von Hügel, 'The Three Elements of Religion', Ch. 2, *The Mystical Element of Religion as studied in St Catherine of Genoa and her Friends*, 2 vols (London, 1923), I, 50–82, especially note on 53.
29 XXVIII, 279.
30 *Ibid.*, 283–4.
31 *Ibid.*, 285.
32 *Ibid.*, 287.
33 *Ibid.*, 300.
34 *Ibid.*, 303.
35 *Ibid.*, 306.
36 Ward, *Newman*, II, 430.
37 XXVIII, 330.
38 *Ibid.*, 323.

CHAPTER 29   'AND NOW A CARDINAL'

1 XXIX, 423–4.
2 Bodley, 16–17.
3 XXIX, 424–5.
4 *Ibid.*, 17.
5 *Ibid.*, 19.
6 *Ibid.*, 20.
7 Ibid.
8 Butler, *Ullathorne*, II, 114.
9 XXIX, 20.
10 *Ibid.*, 22.
11 *Ibid.*, 23.
12 *Ibid.*, 25.
13 *Ibid.*, 29.
14 *Ibid.*
15 *Ibid.*, 31–2.
16 *Ibid.*, 33.
17 *Ibid.*, 34.
18 *Ibid.*, 47.
19 *Ibid.*
20 *Ibid.*, 48.
21 Butler, *Ullathorne*, II, 118.
22 XXIX, 44.

23 *Ibid.*, 51.
24 *Ibid.*, 58.
25 *Ibid.*
26 *Ibid.*, 60.
27 *Ibid.*, 61.
28 *Ibid.*
29 *Ibid.*, 63.
30 *Ibid.*, 72.
31 *Ibid.*, 76.
32 *Ibid.*, 77.
33 *Ibid.*, 77–8.
34 *Ibid.*, 78.
35 *Ibid.*, 84.
36 *Ibid.*, 91.
37 *Ibid.*, 100.
38 *Ibid.*, 108.
39 *Ibid.*, 107.
40 *Ibid.*, 121.
41 *Ibid.*, 123.
42 *Ibid.*, 124–5.
43 W. P. Neville (ed.), *Addresses to Cardinal Newman with his Replies etc. 1879–81* (London, 1905), 61.
44 *Ibid.*, 64–9.
45 Ward, *Newman*, II, 463.
46 Neville, *Addresses*, 71–2.
47 XXIX, 129.
48 *Ibid.*, 132–3.
49 *Ibid.*, 161.
50 *Ibid.*, 137.
51 Neville, *Addresses*, 103–6.
52 XXIX, 156.
53 *Ibid.*, 158.
54 Neville, *Addresses*, 118–208, 224–35, 244–55.
55 *Ibid.*, 233–4.
56 XXIX, 192.
57 *Ibid.*, 193.
58 *Ibid.*, 213.
59 *Ibid.*, 346.
60 'Wisdom and Innocence', *Sermons bearing on Subjects of the Day* (London, 1871), 307.

CHAPTER 30   LAST THINGS

1 XXIX, 212.
2 *Ibid.*, 228.
3 *Ibid.*, 429; cf. *ibid.*, 351.
4 *Ibid.*, 430.

5 *Ibid.*
6 Ward, *Newman*, II, 473.
7 XXIX, 398.
8 M. Ward, *The Wilfrid Wards*, 227.
9 XXIX, 324.
10 XXX, 48.
11 *Ibid.*, 32–3.
12 *Ibid.*, 37.
13 XXXI, 195.
14 XXX, 194.
15 *Ibid.*, 335.
16 *Ibid.*, 283–4.
17 *Ibid.*, 290.
18 *Ibid.*, 292–3.
19 Mark Pattison, *Memoirs* (London, 1885), 210.
20 XXX, 293.
21 *Ibid.*, 271–2.
22 Reprinted in J. Derek Holmes and Robert Murray sj (eds.), *On the Inspiration of Scripture* (London, 1967), 101–31. See also J. T. Burtchaell, *Catholic Theories of Biblical Inspiration since 1810: A Review and Critique* (Cambridge, 1969), 76–80.
23 XXX, 327.
24 *Ibid.*, 329–30.
25 *Ibid.*, 337.
26 XXIX, 388.
27 XXX, 4.
28 *Ibid.*, 94.
29 *Ibid.*, 99.
30 *Ibid.*, 402.
31 *Ibid.*, 182–3, 186.
32 *Ibid.*, 427, 431.
33 M. Ward, *The Wilfrid Wards*, 133.
34 XXXI, 83; cf. *ibid.*, 14.
35 *Ibid.*, 91.
36 XXVI, 201.
37 XXXI, 215.
38 XXIX, 337.
39 Republished in A. M. Fairbairn, *Catholicism: Roman and Anglican* (London, 1899), 125.
40 *Ibid.*, 126.
41 *Ibid.*, 140.
42 Republished in de Achaval and Holmes, [with minor revisions from *Stray Essays* (London, 1890)], 140.
43 *Ibid.*, 141.
44 *Ibid.*, 143.
45 Fairbairn, 205–6.
46 XXXI, 113.
47 Achaval and Holmes, 153.
48 Fairbairn, 205.

49 XXXI, 125.
50 *Ibid.*, 79.
51 *Ibid.*, 56.
52 *Ibid.*, 67.
53 *Ibid.*, 151.
54 *Ibid.*, 99.
55 Butler, *Ullathorne*, II, 283–4.
56 XXXI, 229.
57 XXX, 197–8.
58 *Ibid.*, 400.
59 XXXI, 40.
60 *Ibid.*, 257.
61 Butler, *Ullathorne*, II, 228.
62 XXXI, 266.
63 *Ibid.*, 273, 275.
64 MT, II, 639.
65 M. Ward, *The Wilfrid Wards*, 191.
66 XXXI, 294.
67 *Ibid.*, 282.
68 *Ibid.*, 189.
69 *Ibid.*, 299.
70 XXI, 557.
71 Purcell, II, 749.
72 Bodley, *Cardinal Manning*, 22.
73 Herbert Paul (ed.), *Letters of Lord Acton to Mary, daughter of the Right Hon. W. E. Gladstone* (London, 1904), lx.

Index